Forests

SOURCEBOOK

AGRICULTURE AND RURAL DEVELOPMENT

Seventy-five percent of the world's poor live in rural areas and most are involved in farming. In the 21st century, agriculture remains fundamental to economic growth, poverty alleviation, and environmental sustainability. The World Bank's Agriculture and Rural Development publication series presents recent analyses of issues that affect agriculture's role as a source of economic development, rural livelihoods, and environmental services. The series is intended for practical application, and we hope that it will serve to inform public discussion, policy formulation, and development planning.

Other titles in this series:

Changing the Face of the Waters: The Promise and Challenge of Sustainable Aquaculture

Enhancing Agricultural Innovation: How to Go Beyond the Strengthening of Research Systems

Reforming Agricultural Trade for Developing Countries, Volume 1: Key Issues for a Pro-Development Outcome of the Doha Round

Reforming Agricultural Trade for Developing Countries, Volume 2: Quantifying the Impact of Multilateral Trade Reform

Sustainable Land Management: Challenges, Opportunities, and Trade-Offs

Shaping the Future of Water for Agriculture: A Sourcebook for Investment in Agricultural Water Management

Agriculture Investment Sourcebook

Sustaining Forests: A Development Strategy

Forests
Sourcebook

PRACTICAL GUIDANCE FOR SUSTAINING FORESTS IN DEVELOPMENT COOPERATION

Collaborative Partnership on Forests

PROFOR

**World Bank–WWF Alliance for Forest
Conservation and Sustainable Use**

ISBN: 978-0-8213-7163-3
e-ISBN 13: 978-0-8213-7164-0
DOI: 10.1596/978-0-8213-7163-3

Library of Congress Cataloging-in-Publication Data

Forests sourcebook : practical guidance for sustaining forests in development cooperation / World Bank.
     p. cm. — (Agriculture and rural development)
   ISBN 978-0-8213-7163-3 — ISBN 978-0-8213-7164-0 (electronic)
     1. Forestry projects—Handbooks, manuals, etc. 2. Sustainable forestry—Handbooks, manuals, etc. 3. Forest management—Handbooks, manuals, etc. 4. Forest policy—Handbooks, manuals, etc. I. World Bank. II. Title: Practical guidance for sustaining forests in development cooperation. III. Series: Agriculture and rural development series.

SD387.P74F67 2008
333.75--dc22
2008001296

CONTENTS

FIGURES

TABLES

ACKNOWLEDGMENTS

The preparation of the *Forests Sourcebook* involved many people from within and outside the World Bank working on forests issues.

Many individuals made written contributions and/or provided material for use in the *Forests Sourcebook*. Contributors of material for chapters and notes from within the Bank included Kulsum Ahmed (ENV), Mario Boccucci (EASRE), Diji Chandrasekharan Behr (ARD), Robert R. Davis (LCSAR), Gerhard Dieterle (ARD), Erick Fernandes (ARD), Melissa Fossberg (EXTCN), Laura A. Ivers (CGIAR), Peter Jipp (EASRE), Emile Jurgens (EASRE), Richard Kaguamba (IFC), Robert Kirmse (ECSSD), Nalin M. Kishor (ARD), George Ledec (LCSEN), Fernando Loayza (ENV), Muthukumara S. Mani (ENV), Grant Milne (SASDA), Jessica Mott (ECSSD), Christian A. Peter (AFTEN), Stefano Pagiola (ENV), Klas Sander (ENV), and John Spears (ARD).

Contributors of material for chapters and notes from outside the Bank included Jon Anderson (MCC), Jill Blockhur (TNC, formerly ARD, World Bank), H. Carolyn Brown (University of Guelph), David Cassells (TNC, formerly ENV, World Bank), Mike Chaveas (US Forest Service International Programs), Arnoldo Contreras-Hermosilla (Consultant), Jim Douglas (Consultant), Kailash Govil (FAO), Marilyn Hoskins (Consultant), Viju Ipe (Consultant), Dirk Jäger (University of New Brunswick), Svend E. Jensby (Consultant), David Kaimowitz (Ford Foundation, formerly CIFOR), Arvind Khare (Rights and Resources Initiative), Duncan Macqueen (IIED), Augusta Molnar (Rights and Resources Initiative), Uwe Muuss (Center for Tropical and Subtropical Agriculture and Forestry, University Goettingen), Ruth Nogueron (WRI), Ruth Nussbaum (ProForest), Tapani Oksanen (Indufor, formerly ARD, World Bank), Esa Puustjarvi (Indufor), Ted Robak (University of New Brunswick), Kenneth L. Rosen-baum (Sylvan Environmental Consultants), Jade Saunders (European Forest Institute), Jeff Sayers (WWF), Cornelia Sepp (Eco-Consult), Caroline Stem (Foundations of Success), Fred Stolle (WRI), Sonja Vermeulen (IIED), Horst Wagner (Consultant), Martin Walter (University of Applied Sciences Weihenstephan), and Adrian Whiteman (FAO).

Technical editing, final editing, and assistance with developing the online version was done by Iskandarsyah A. Bakri (SDNIS), Dora N. Cudjoe (ENV), Elizabeth Cushion (ARD), Anne M. Davis Gillet (ARD), Reem Hajjar (IISD), Marketa Jonasova (ARD), Gunnar Larson (ARD), Elizabeth B. Rice (Consultant), Paul R. Turner (Consultant), and Peter Wood (IISD).

The day-to-day coordination of the *Forests Sourcebook* was carried out by Diji Chandrasekharan Behr (ARD). Editorial production of the book was handled by Mark Ingebretsen (EXTOP). Input from FAO was coordinated by Michael Martin. The overall task was managed by Gerhard Dieterle (Forests Advisor, ARD) and Diji Chandrasekharan Behr (Natural Resource Economist, ARD), who collectively assume responsibility for remaining errors and omissions.

We are also grateful for comments received on the various chapters and drafts from our colleagues, including Paola Agostini (AFTEN), Peter Dewees (ECSSD), Erick Fernandes (ARD), Robert Kirmse (ECSSD), Nalin M. Kishor (ARD), Andrey Kushlin (ECSSD), Peter Neame (IFC), Tapani Oksanen (Indufor, formerly ARD, World Bank), Klas Sander (ENV), Gerardo Segura (LCSAR), John Spears (ARD), Hosny El Lakany, David Kaimowitz (Ford Foundation, formerly CIFOR), Markku Simula, Peter Neame (IFC), Charles Di Leva (LEGEN), Harvey Himberg (QPCQC), Alexandra Bezeredi (QPCQC), Louise Buck (Cornell University and Ecoagriculture Partners), Grant Milne (SASDA), and Mohammed Bakarr (ICRAF).

ABBREVIATIONS

5MHRP	Five Million Hectares Reforestation
AAA	Analytical and Advisory Services
ADB	Asian Development Bank
AFH	Honduran Forest Agenda
AFR	Sub-Saharan Africa Region
AOP	annual operating plan
ASB	Partnership for the Tropical Forest Margins
AVHRR	Advance Very High Resolution Radiometer
AWF	African Wildlife Foundation
AZE	Alliance for Zero Extinction
BCPCPS	Beneficiary-Centered Problem Census Problem Solving
BiCF	BioCarbon Fund
BIMS	Business Information Management System
BP	Bank Policy
CAPE	Cape Action Plan for the Environment
CARPE	Central African Regional Program for the Environment
CAS	Country Assistance Strategies
CATIE	Tropical Agricultural Research and Higher Education Center, Costa Rica
CBD	Convention on Biological Diversity
CBERS	China Brazil Earth Resources Satellite
CBFM	Community-based Forest Management
CBNRM	Community Based Natural Resource Management
CCD	UN Convention to Combat Desertification
CD	compact disc
CDM	Clean Development Mechanism
CEA	country environmental analysis
CENESTA	Centre for Sustainable Development & Environment
CFCs	Community Forest Committees
CFE	Community Forest Enterprises
CFMCs	Cantonal Forest Management Companies
CI	Conservation International
CIFOR	Centre for International Forestry Research

CIPAMEX	Sección Mexicana del Consejo Internacional para la Preservación de las Aves
CIRAD	Centre International de Recherche Agronomique pour le Développement
CITES	Convention on International Trade in Endangered Species of Wild Fauna and Flora
CMP	Conservation Measures Partnership
CMS	Convention on the Conservation of Migratory Species of Wild Animals
CNONGD	Conseil National des ONG de Développement du Congo
COFO	Committee on Forestry
CRC	Citizen Report Card
CSD	United Nations Commission on Sustainable Development
DPL	Development Policy Lending
DPLs	Development Policy Loans
EAP	East Asia and Pacific
EASRD	Rural Development and Natural Resources Sector Unit, East Asia and Pacific Region, the World Bank
ECA	Europe and Central Asia
EFTRN	European Tropical Forest Research Network
EIA	environmental impact assessment
EITI	Extractive Industries Transparency Initiative
EMF	Environmental Management Framework
EMP	Environmental Management Plan
ENA	Europe and North Asia
ENVSAL	Environmental Structural Adjustment Loan
ERS-1	European Remote Sensing Satellite
ERZ	Extractive Resource
ESMF	Environmental and Social Management Framework
EU	European Union
EXTCN	External Affairs and Communication Network (World Bank)
FAO	Food and Agriculture Organization
FBD	Forest and Bee Keeping Department
FCAG	Forest Certification Assessment Guide
FCPF	Forest Carbon Partnership Facility
FDA	Forest Development Authority
FDCP	Forest Development and Conservation Project
FEMA/MT	The State Environment Foundation of Mato Grosso (Brazil)
FESP	Forest & Environment Sector Program
FLEG	Forest Law Enforcement and Governance
FLEGT	Forest Law Enforcement, Governance and Trade
FMIS	Forest Management Information System
FMIS-WG	Forest Management Information System Working Group
FMU	forest management unit
FOMAS	Forest Sector Monitoring and Assessment Process
FRA	Forest Resources Assessment
FRSCS	Forestry Sector Coordination Secretariat
FSC	Forest Stewardship Council
FSI	Forest Survey of India
FSSP	Forest Sector Support Program
FUG	Forest User Group
FUNAI	National Indian Foundation (Brazil)
GAB	good average bad
GDP	gross domestic product

GEF	Global Environment Fund
GEF	Global Environment Facility
GEMA	Grupo Economia do Meio Ambiente e Desenvolvimento Sustentável
GFC	Guyana Forestry Commission
GFTN	Global Forest and Trade Network
GIS	Geographic Information System
GNIFC	Guyana National Initiative for Forest Certification
GP	Good Practices
GPRS	Growth and Poverty Reduction Strategy
GPRS II	Ghana Growth and Poverty Reduction Strategy
GPS	Global Positioning System
GTA	Amazon Working Group
GTF	Groupe de Travail Forêts
ha	hectares
HCV	High Conservation Value
HCVFs	High Conservation Value Forests
IAF	International Accreditation Forum
IBA	Important Bird Areas
IBRD	International Bank for Reconstruction and Development
ICRAF	World Agroforestry Centre
ICSID	International Centre for Settlement of Investment Disputes
IDA	International Development Association
IEC	International Electrotechnical Commission
IEG	Independent Evaluation Group
IFC	International Finance Corporation
IFF	Intergovernmental Forum on Forests
IFRI	International Forest Resources and Institutions
IGBP	International Geosphere-Biosphere Program
IIED	International Institute for Environment and Development
ILO	International Labour Organization
IMF	International Monetary Fund
INR	Institute of Natural Resources
IPAM	Instituto de Pesquisa Ambiental da Amazônia
IPCC	Intergovernmental Panel on Climate Change
IPF/IFF	Intergovernmental Panel on Forests and Intergovernmental Forum on Forests
IPFP	Indigenous Peoples Planning Framework
IPP	Indigenous Peoples Plan
IRR	internal rates of return
ISDS	Integrated Safeguards Data Sheet
ISEAL	International Social and Environmental Accreditation and Integrated Safeguards Data Sheet Labelling
ISO	International Organization for Standardization
IT	information technology
ITTA	International Tropical Timber Agreement
ITTO	International Tropical Timber Organization
IUCN	International Union for Conservation of Nature a.k.a. World Conservation Union
IUFRO	International Union of Forest Research Organizations
IWGIA	International Working Group for Indigenous Affairs
JFM	Joint Forest Management
KABP	knowledge, attitudes, beliefs, and practices

KAPSLM	Kenya Agricultural Productivity and Sustainable Land Management
LAC	Latin America and the Caribbean
LAO PDR	Lao Peoples Democratic Republic
LATIN	Lembaga Alam Tropika Indonesia
LFI	Liberia Forest Initiative
LINAPYCO	Ligue Nationale des Pygmées du Congo
LSMS	Living Standards Measurement Surveys
LULUCF	land-use and land-use change and forestry
M&E	monitoring and evaluation
MA&D	Market Analysis & Development
MC	Micro-catchment
MCFPE	Ministerial Conference on the Protection of Forests in Europe
MDGs	Millennium Development Goals
MENA	Middle East and North Africa
MIGA	Multilateral Investment Guarantee Agency
MINEF	Ministry of the Environment and Forests (Cameroon)
MM	means of measure
MOF	Ministry of Forestry of Indonesia
MWLE	Ministry of Water, Lands & Environment
NDVI	Normalized Difference Vegetation Index
NFIs	national forest inventories
NFO	National Forest Program
NFP	National Forests Policy
NGO	nongovernmental organization
NOAA	National Oceanic and Atmospheric Agency
NRM	natural resource management
NTFP	Nontimber Forest Products
OD	Operational Directive
OD	Operational Directive
ODI	Overseas Development Institute
OECD	Organisation for Economic Co-operation and Development
OECS	Organization of Eastern Caribbean States
OED	Operations Evaluation Department
OP	Operational Policy
OPCS	Operations Policy and Country
PA	Protected Area
PEFC	Operations Policy and Country Services
PES	Payments for Environmental Services
PF	Process Framework
PIU	project implementation unit
PNG	Papua New Guinea
POVCAL	Poverty Calculator
PPPs	plans, policies, and programs
PROCYMAF	Project for Conservation and Sustainable Management of Forest Resources
PRODES	Brazilian Space Agency project
PROFOR	Program on Forests
PRS	Poverty Reduction Strategy
PRSC	poverty reduction support credit
PRSL	Policy Reform Support Loans

PRSP	Poverty Reduction Strategy Paper
PSA	Pago por Servicios Ambientales
PSAH	Pago por Servicios Ambientales Hidrológicos
PSIA	poverty and social impact analysis
RCEA	rapid CEA
RCEEE	Research Center of Ecological and Environmental Economics
REDD	Reduced Emissions from Deforestation and Degradation
REPEC	Réseau des Partenaires pour l'Environnement au Congo
RS/GIS	Remote Sensing/Geographic Information System
RSPO	Round Table on Sustainable Palm Oil
SA	Social Assessment
SAR	South Asia Region
SEA	strategic environmental assessments
SFM	Sustainable forest management
SFR	State of Forest Report
SIL	Sector Investment Loan
SIPAM	Amazon Protection System
SIVAM-SIPAM	Amazon Surveillance System
SME	small and medium enterprise
SMFE	small and medium forest enterprise
SNV	Netherlands Development Organization
SPOT	Satellite Pour l'Observation de la Terre
TEV	total economic valuation
TFAP	Tropical Forestry Action Plan
TFD	The Forests Dialogue
TM	Thematic Mapper
TOR	terms of reference
TREES	Tropical Ecosystem Environment Observation by Satellite
TRF	timber right fees
TTL	task team leader
TUC	Timber Utilization Contracts
UMD	University of Maryland
UN	United Nations
UN-CSD	United Nations Commission on Sustainable Development
UNCED	United Nations Conference on Environment and Development
UNDP	United Nations Development Programme
UNECE	Economic Commission for Europe
UNEP	United Nations Environment Programme
UNFCCC	UN Framework Convention on Climate Change
UNFF	UN Forum on Forests
USAID	U.S. Agency for International Development
USDA	United States Department of Agriculture
USFS	United States Department of Agriculture Forest Service
VPA	Voluntary Partnership Agreement
WATCH	Women Acting Together for Chang
WBCFU	World Bank Carbon Finance Unit
WBCSD	World Business Council for Sustainable Development
WBI	World Bank Institute
WBSCD	World Business Council for Sustainable Development

WCS	Wildlife Conservation Society
WHC	World Heritage Convention
WHRC	Woods Hole Research Center
WII	Winrock International India
World Bank-WWF	World Bank-World Wildlife Fund
WRI	World Resources Institute
WWF	World Wide Fund for Nature (known in the U.S. as World Wildlife Fund)

In using the chapters and notes in the *Forests Sourcebook,* the reader should keep in mind that the basic country context and conditions must be taken into account and that close coordination with government and other key stakeholders is essential before any approach is implemented.

The *Forests Sourcebook* is divided into two parts. The first contains an introduction to the book plus seven chapters covering topics associated with enhancing the contribution of forests to poverty reduction, engaging the private sector, meeting the growing demand for forest products, optimizing forest functions at the landscape level, improving forest governance, mainstreaming forest considerations into macropolicy dialogue, and monitoring forest sector activities.

Each chapter provides relevant background and context with a general overview of the fundamental issues, constraints, policies, and institutional requirements that need to be considered for specific topics. Each also provides the rationale for engagement and a brief discussion of past World Bank activities in the particular area. Most important, chapters specify future priorities and areas for scaling up activities. Each chapter also provides a list of key readings or sources of information. Often the topics presented in a chapter are closely related to issues presented in other chapters and notes. Cross-references are provided.

Associated with each chapter is a series of notes that discuss various tools or approaches for tackling specific issues highlighted in the chapter. The notes provide an overview and considerations of interest regarding a specific issue, discuss operational aspects, have recommendations for practitioners that include lessons learned, and list selected reading. Some notes have boxes that contain innovative activity profiles and good practices. Where relevant, a note has annexes that contain checklists or content for terms of reference for specific activities or relevant frameworks and definitions. Like the chapter, information presented in notes is often closely related to issues presented in other chapters and notes. Again, cross-references are provided.

The second part provides guidance for implementing the World Bank's safeguard on forests. This section of the *Forests Sourcebook* has five chapters. Chapter 8 provides a brief introduction to the World Bank's Forests Policy (OP 4.36). Chapter 9 is on applying OP 4.36. This chapter includes a discussion of the main requirements of OP 4.36, guidelines for implementation (including preparation, appraisal, and supervision requirements), definitions, and guidance on identifying critical forests and critical natural habitats through environmental assessment, which includes a discussion on protecting forests through conservation offsets. Chapter 10 is on consultation and communication in forest projects. Chapters 11 and 12 discuss the Forest Certification Assessment Guide and the World Bank's Indigenous Peoples policy, respectively.

It should be noted that the guidance on applying the World Bank's OP 4.36 pertains only to World Bank investment projects. Development Policy Loans must abide by the requirements of OP 8.60 (discussed in chapter 6, Mainstreaming Forests into Development Policy and Planning: Assessing Cross-Sectoral Impacts).

WHAT IS NOT COVERED BY THE FORESTS SOURCEBOOK

The *Forests Sourcebook* draws on bodies of completed and ongoing work that provide innovative and operationally relevant tools for implementing the World Bank's Forests Strategy. These tools often require an understanding of several other key processes and programs, some of which are not covered by the *Forests Sourcebook,* including the following:

POVERTY REDUCTION STRATEGY PAPER AND COUNTRY ASSISTANCE STRATEGY PREPARATION PROCESSES. Poverty Reduction Strategy Papers (PRSP) (see http://go.world bank.org/FXXJK3VEW0) describe a country's macroeconomic, structural, and social policies and programs to promote growth and reduce poverty, as well as associated external financing needs. PRSPs are prepared by governments through a participatory process involving civil society and development partners, including the World Bank and the International Monetary Fund (IMF). Country Assistance Strategies (CAS) (see http://go.worldbank.org/4M75 BI76J0) are business plans prepared by the World Bank for active borrowers from the International Development Association (IDA) and the International Bank for Reconstruction and Development (IBRD). The CAS takes as its starting point the country's own vision for its development, as defined in a PRSP or other country-owned process.

OTHER WORLD BANK OPERATIONAL POLICIES. This book focuses on Operational Policies on Forests (OP 4.36) and Indigenous Peoples (OP 4.10) and refers to others. All World Bank investment operations are governed by the Bank's Operational Policies, which are designed to ensure that all projects and activities are economically, financially, socially and environmentally sound. The World Bank's Operational Manual spells out the policies and provides procedures and other forms of guidance on how to comply with the policies. See http://go.worldbank.org/2G5SSZAET0.

DETAILED DISCUSSION ON DUE DILIGENCE AS PER OP 8.60. The key issues surrounding forest due diligence as per OP 8.60 are covered in chapter 6. Additional information relevant to environment, forests, and natural resources is available at http://siteresources.worldbank.org/PROJECTS/Resources/GPNChapter4Environment.pdf.

IFC ENVIRONMENTAL AND SOCIAL STANDARDS. The International Finance Corporation (IFC), a member of the World Bank Group, has its own set of environmental and social standards, including Performance Standards and Environmental, Health, and Safety Guidelines, that are applicable to all projects the IFC finances. Available at http://www.ifc.org/ifcext/enviro.nsf/Content/EnvSocStandards.

THE QUICK REFERENCE MATRIX

The matrix on the following page shows how the contents of the book is organized in terms of priority themes, the tools and approaches used to address those themes, and how themes, tools, and approaches relate to the three overarching objectives of the World Bank's Forests Strategy.

Forests Sourcebook: **Quick Reference and Guide to Contents**

World Bank Forests Strategy: Three Overarching Objectives		
Harnessing forests for poverty alleviation		
Integrating forests into sustainable economic development		
Protecting vital local and global environmental services		
Forests Sourcebook		

PART I: PRIORITY THEMES AND OPERATIONAL ASPECTS		**PART II: GUIDANCE ON IMPLEMENTING FORESTS POLICY OP 4.36**
Priority Themes	**Tools and approaches**	
INTRODUCTION	Opportunities and Challenges in the Forest Sector	
CHAPTER 1 Forests for Poverty Reduction	Note 1.1: Mainstreaming the Role of Forests in Poverty Alleviation Note 1.2: Community-Based Forest Management. Note 1.3: Indigenous Peoples and Forests Note 1.4: Property and Access Rights Note 1.5: Making Markets Work for the Forest-Dependent Poor	CHAPTER 8: Introduction to World Bank Forests Policy
CHAPTER 2 Engaging the Private Sector in Forest Sector Development	Note 2.1 Company-Community Partnerships Note 2.2 Small and Medium Enterprises Note 2.3 Innovative Marketing Arrangements: Payments for Environmental Services	CHAPTER 9: Applying Forests Policy OP 4.36
CHAPTER 3 Meeting the Growing Demand for Forest Products	Note 3.1: Mainstreaming Conservation Considerations into Productive Landscapes Note 3.2: Forest Certification Systems Note 3.3: Forest Plantations in World Bank Operations	CHAPTER 10: Consultation and Communication in Forest Sector Activities
CHAPTER 4 Optimizing Forest Functions in a Landscape	Note 4.1: Integrated Forest Landscape Land Use Planning Note 4.2: Assessing Outcomes of Landscape Interventions Note 4.3: Using Adaptive Management to Improve Project Implementation	CHAPTER 11: Forest Certification Assessment Guide: Summary on Use
CHAPTER 5 Improving Forest Governance	Note 5.1: Decentralized Forest Management Note 5.2: Reforming Forest Institutions Note 5.3: Strengthening Legal Frameworks in the Forest Sector Note 5.4: Strengthening Fiscal Systems in the Forest Sector Note 5.5: Addressing Illegal Logging and Other Forest Crime	CHAPTER 12: Applying OP 4.10 on Indigenous Peoples
CHAPTER 6 Mainstreaming Forests into Development Policy and Planning	Note 6.1: Using National Forest Programs to Mainstream Forest Issues Note 6.2: Prospects for Using Policy Lending to Proactively Enable Forest Sector Reforms Note 6.3: Identifying the Need for Analysis on Forests in Development Policy Reforms Note 6.4: Assessing Cross- Sector Impacts: Use of CEAs and SEAs	
CHAPTER 7 Monitoring and Information Systems for Forest Management	Note 7.1: National Forest Inventories Note 7.2: Establishing Forest Management Information Management Systems Note 7.3: Spatial Monitoring of Forests	

OPPORTUNITIES AND CHALLENGES IN THE FOREST SECTOR

Forests contribute to the livelihoods of more than 1.6 billion people. Forests and the forest products industry are a source of economic growth and employment, with the value of global forest products traded internationally reaching US$270 billion, of which developing countries account for more than 20 percent. Worldwide, forest industries provide employment (both formal and informal) for approximately 50 million people.

Forests are home to at least 80 percent of the world's remaining terrestrial biodiversity and are a major carbon sink regulating global climate. Forests also help to maintain the fertility of the soil, protect watersheds, and reduce the risk of natural disasters, such as floods and landslides. Global deforestation and degradation threaten biodiversity, forest-related ecological services, and rural livelihoods.

Covering 26 percent of the Earth's land surface, forests play a significant role in realizing the Millennium Development Goal (MDG) of halving the number of people living in absolute poverty by 2015. Unfortunately, rural development strategies often neglect forests because forests have been mistakenly viewed as being outside the mainstream of agricultural development. In addition to the lumber and wood products industry, the gathering and marketing of hundreds of forest products, such as forest fruits, fuelwood, and medicinal products, constitute an economic activity of enormous scale.

As human populations grow and countries around the world become more affluent, the demand for wood products, both solid wood and pulp and paper, will increase, too.

In 2005, removals of roundwood were valued at about US$64 billion, an increase of about 11 percent over removals in 1990. The demand for nonwood forest products has also increased since 1990, with removals estimated at US$4.7 billion in 2005.

The contribution of forests to the maintenance of vital ecosystem functions and societal well-being is increasingly a matter of public concern. People are realizing that water supply and quality, flood protection, soil conservation, local climate, and conservation of biodiversity all rely on the existence of functioning forest ecosystems. Most developed-country governments have now committed to increased funding for carbon sequestration and effective protection of forest biodiversity, and these commitments are likely to be extended to reducing emissions from forest land conversion.

WHY THE POTENTIAL OF FORESTS HAS NOT BEEN FULLY HARNESSED

Forests house global public goods, which, to be maintained, must be both protected and managed sustainably. At present, however, less than 5 percent of tropical forests are being managed sustainably. Despite their great economic value, forests are one of developing countries' most mismanaged resources. Many countries with substantial forest resources have been subject to corruption and serious inadequacies in forest allocation, administration, and monitoring. Illegal logging and associated trade and corruption at high levels flourish because timber rights can be extremely valuable.

Besides channeling potential timber revenue away from national development efforts—particularly from the people living in and near the forests—the low prices at which these concessions are often granted encourage waste, unsustainable management, plundering for short-term gain, and replacement by less valuable and less sustainable activities. Strengthening of governance usually touches upon sensitive local and national interests, which are benefiting from the status quo.

Furthermore, growing populations lead to an increase in the conversion of forests for other land uses (for example, clearing of forests for agriculture; see figure 1). The Food and Agriculture Organization (FAO) estimates that each year 13 million hectares of forest are permanently converted to agriculture, mostly in the tropics. Spillovers from poor policies in other sectors can also contribute to rapid rates of deforestation. This has been particularly evident in recent decades, for example, in the conversion of forest areas to oil palm plantations in Indonesia.

Although some forest products, primarily lumber and fuelwood, are delivered through markets, the economic value of many of the other forests goods and services (for example, environmental services, biodiversity, and carbon sequestration) go unrecognized by the market. Creative new mechanisms are needed to compensate those preserving environmental services and to provide incentives through market-based methods to reduce loss of forests' environmental services.

Safeguarding global public goods is not a national priority in countries struggling with problems of poverty reduction. As a result, forests' potential is unexploited in developing countries because the forest sector has to compete for development investment and governments have limited interest in investing in the sector through loans when the benefits are often global rather than national or local. These investments must compete for resources against such high priority sectors as health, education, and infrastructure. Weak governance in the forest sector is pervasive and leads to ineffective use of funds. Forest authorities often lack the capacity to implement policy reforms and programs effectively and have limited capacity to access, and make use of, extra-budgetary financing. Furthermore, incentives for the private sector to implement sustainable forest management are either absent or limited.

The forest sector represents one of the most challenging areas in the development of community and global public policy. Despite significant resource flows, international concern, and political pressure, a combination of market and institutional failures has led to forests failing to realize their potential to reduce poverty, promote economic growth, and be valued for their contributions to the local and global environment.

UNLOCKING FORESTS' POTENTIAL

The problem of sustainable forest management (SFM) is highly complex and can only be addressed by a range of actions targeted at (i) the policy framework, (ii) strengthening of governance, (iii) removal of market distortions and engaging market actors, (iv) full valuation and sharing of forest benefits through market and other mechanisms, (v) capacity building, and (vi) mobilization of adequate financial resources.

Countering the drivers of deforestation and forest degradation to enable sustainable forest management will require, among other factors, greater innovation and better coordination in global forestry dialogue, national sectoral planning, and technical analysis that addresses these forces and factors. Capturing the potential of forests to advance poverty reduction, support economic growth, and deliver local and global environmental services will require donors to work in close coordination with governments, the private sector, and other key stakeholders in the forest sector, and to link forest sector activities with national strategies. This can involve working with emerging external constraints and opportunities.

Figure 1   Main Causes of Deforestation, by World Region, 1990–2000

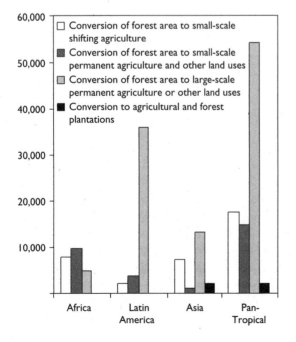

FOREST LAW ENFORCEMENT AND GOVERNANCE. Loss and degradation resulting from weak forest law enforcement and governance have occurred at the expense not only of national economies, but also of the rural people who depend on forest resources for their livelihoods. This mismanagement translates into enormous national costs. For example, failure to collect appropriate royalties and taxes from legal forest operations has a global cost to governments of about US$5 billion annually. Illegal logging results in additional losses of forest resources from public lands of at least US$10 billion to US$15 billion a year. Improvements in forest law enforcement and governance are critical to capturing the full economic potential of forests in a sustainable manner. In response, a stronger global focus has been placed on forest sector governance, accountability, and transparency (see chapter 5, Improving Forest Governance).

PRIVATE SECTOR ENGAGEMENT. Because of forests' significant commercial value, the private sector is the principal source of finance in forest production in most countries. Indeed, the level of activity and influence of the private sector in forests dwarfs that of the international community—and sometimes of the national government. Private investment in the forestry sector in developing countries and countries in transition is close to US$15 billion per year, or up to nine times more than the current official development assistance flows.[1] Official development assistance accounted for only a fraction of the funds available for forestry in the mid-1990s, and has declined sharply since then.

Private sector investment—from both domestic and foreign sources—has been on the upswing. Given this trend of increased private engagement in forest production and processing, legal and regulatory frameworks that support sustainable forest practices must be developed to promote responsible private sector investment and corporate social responsibility as well as to eliminate corruption. To enhance the role of private sector investment in poverty alleviation, effective and efficient community-company partnerships and greater support to small and medium forest enterprises will be critical.

INCREASED COMMUNITY ENGAGEMENT IN FOREST MANAGEMENT. Local communities, including indigenous and traditional groups, play an increasingly important role in forest management. Studies of the ownership and administration of forests anticipate that forest areas under recognized community ownership and reserved for community administration will nearly double between 2001 and 2015 (figure 2). Community participation in decision

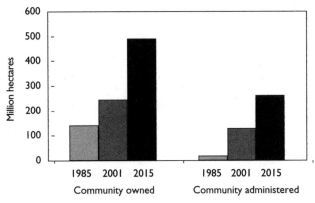

Figure 2   Community Ownership and Administration of Forests

Source: White and Martin 2002.

making and implementation is considered essential for good governance, equitable distribution of benefits, and sustainable resource management. Additionally, it is important for creating accountability and transparency.

Using forests for poverty reduction requires a strong institutional framework and an effective legal and regulatory environment, in which the rights of specific groups among the poor are recognized and protected (see note 1.3, Indigenous Peoples and Forests, and note 1.4, Property and Access Rights). Additionally, opportunities to develop sustainable forest businesses must be provided to the forest-dependent poor and other groups (see note 2.2, Small and Medium Enterprises). Therefore, development organizations, in collaboration with government and other relevant stakeholders, need an approach that focuses on participation and conflict resolution, and not just on the technical and economic aspects of forestry.

COEXISTENCE OF CONSERVATION AND PRODUCTION. Conservation and production must coexist for the full potential of forests for poverty reduction to be realized. Although large areas of the world's forests must be preserved intact for their ecological and cultural values, much of what remains will inevitably be used for productive purposes. Consequently, a dual approach covering both protection and productive use is needed.

Greater investment in the development of plantations contributes to economic growth and poverty reduction while reducing pressure on natural forests and protecting some ecosystem services. Integration of forest conservation into productive landscapes can help achieve conservation objectives, enhance the benefits of conservation, and broaden the ownership of conservation initiatives (see note

3.1, Mainstreaming Conservation Considerations into Productive Landscapes). Plantations, when coupled with promotion of environmentally and socially responsible trade in timber and forest products, have the potential to meet the rapidly growing demand of countries like China and India without sacrificing protected forest areas.

IMPROVED FOREST MANAGEMENT PRACTICES. Although biodiversity and key environmental services have traditionally been sustained through the establishment of protected areas, the wide range of competing uses for forests by diverse groups imposes constraints on how much can be achieved by protection alone. Improving forest management practices in production forests (forests where productive use is permitted) is an essential component of any strategy to protect vital local environmental services, in addition to efforts aimed at bolstering the effectiveness of management within protected areas.

INNOVATIVE FINANCING. It is highly unlikely that governments will be able to significantly scale down lumber extraction to preserve forests for their environmental services unless the costs of forgone revenue can be offset in some way. Moreover, very few countries would be prepared to borrow funds—from the World Bank or other sources—to finance forest protection as a substitute for forest production. Innovative financing options and markets for forests' environmental services, such as ecotourism, carbon offsets, reduced emissions from deforestation and degradation (REDD), and watershed management, will all have important roles to play. As carbon credits grow in value under emerging global carbon trading systems, incentives to invest in the establishment of new forested areas for their carbon benefits, and in reduced deforestation for reduced carbon emissions, will increase.

AVOIDED DEFORESTATION. Though the Kyoto Protocol has no mechanism for providing compensation for reduced deforestation, the Stern Review highlights "avoided deforestation" as a cost-effective mechanism to limit greenhouse gas emissions (Stern 2007). Present concerns about climate change have opened a window of opportunity for the framework of avoided deforestation. The Forest Carbon Partnership Facility of the World Bank is developing a financing mechanism for avoided deforestation and preparing countries to participate in this scheme. Preparations include, among other things, developing technical tools for monitoring and measuring avoided deforestation, assessing opportunity costs, and making the necessary financial transfers. Beyond the technical aspects of operationalizing this concept, an enabling environment must be created to facilitate this approach.

CROSS-SECTORAL IMPACT. Deforestation is a complex phenomenon: While there is general agreement that it is strongly influenced by economic change arising from outside the forest sector itself, its specific causes (and, equally important, its economic and social effects) vary widely between—and even within—countries. Large-scale economic change in any country, whether induced in specific reform programs or inflicted through exogenous forces beyond the control of that country, has the potential to bring about major changes in the condition of natural resources and the environment, especially in developing countries, where natural capital plays a significant role in economic growth and development and is crucial to the sustainability of these processes.

Pressures on forests from poorly aligned strategies in agriculture, transportation, energy, and industry, as well as from unsound macroeconomic policies, are major causes of forest loss and degradation. Cross-sectoral cooperation to coordinate policies is essential to avoid forest degradation, to ensure that forests are managed in a sustainable manner, and to harness opportunities created by ever-rising fossil fuel prices and improved biofuel technologies.

THE WORLD BANK'S APPROACH TO THE FOREST SECTOR

Forests are important to the World Bank's mission because of their contribution to the livelihoods of the poor, the potential they offer for sustainable economic development, and the essential global environmental services they provide.

The World Bank's 2002 Forests Strategy and Operational Policy

In 2002 the World Bank adopted a revised Forests Strategy (World Bank 2004) and Operational Policy on Forests (OP 4.36) that allow the World Bank to engage more proactively in the forest sector to help attain the goal of poverty reduction without jeopardizing forests environmental and economic values intrinsic to sustainability. The strategy was founded on three equally important and interrelated pillars:

- Harnessing the potential of forests to reduce poverty in a sustainable manner
- Integrating forests more effectively into sustainable development

- Protecting vital local and global environmental services and values

Addressing these three pillars together makes the Forests Strategy complex and multifaceted. It not only concerns growing or protecting trees but also involves a complex interaction of policy, institutions, and incentives. The strategy embodies a multisectoral approach that addresses cross-sectoral issues and takes into account the impacts of activities, policies, and practices outside the sector on forests and people who depend on forests for their livelihoods.

The 2002 Forests Strategy and operational policy marked a shift from outright prohibition of World Bank financing of commercial logging operations in primary tropical moist forests to an approach of improved forest management with targeted conservation of critical natural habitats in all types of forests. The new approach embodies explicit safeguards that require World Bank–financed investment operations to comply with independent certification standards acceptable to the World Bank.

HARNESSING THE POTENTIAL OF FORESTS TO REDUCE POVERTY. Forest outcomes are crucial for poverty reduction in many of the World Bank's client countries. For both countries with large forest endowments, and for others with limited forests, if forest issues are not fully incorporated into broad national government and assistance strategies, the overarching goals of poverty reduction will not be met.

To harness the potential of forests to reduce poverty, conditions must be created to ensure that the rural poor are able to manage their natural resources, especially the forests, for their own benefit. Capacity must be built to support and regulate community use of forests and plantations. Forest assets under various forms of community management, possibly supported by the private sector, could become major sources for global environmental services, such as biodiversity and carbon sequestration.

INTEGRATING FORESTS INTO SUSTAINABLE ECONOMIC DEVELOPMENT. Forests are one of the most mismanaged resources in many countries. Forests are seriously undervalued, many of their environmental benefits do not enter markets, and poor governance has fueled illegal activities. The rapid rates of deforestation in the last decades are largely a result of the spillover from poor policies in other sectors and lack of governance in the forest sector itself.

A main task, therefore, is to help governments improve policy, economic management, and governance in the forest sector, including forest concessions policies and allocations.

Efforts to bring about credible systems for socially, ecologically, and economically sound management of production forests should, however, also be coupled with systems for independent certification and monitoring. Identification and promotion of local, regional, and global markets for forest products is a matching priority.

PROTECTING GLOBAL FOREST VALUES. More than 600 million hectares of protected areas have been established in developing countries. While many of these areas are economically inaccessible, other areas are under increasing pressure from development and illegal activities, including logging and poaching. Many governments do not have the resources to effectively administer and protect these areas. In addition, other forests, ecologically sensitive and rich in biodiversity but outside protected areas, are under increasing threat.

Invasive pressures are likely to worsen unless significant additional funds can be made available from multiple sources, at highly concessional or grant terms, for protection, or unless effective markets for the ecosystem values of forests can be developed. The creation of new markets for the environmental services of forests, such as biodiversity, carbon sequestration, and watershed protection, are essential.

The Forests Strategy course for implementation

The World Bank's Forests Strategy charts a course for implementation based on engaging in key countries, creating partnerships, increasing analytical work, and improving coordination across the World Bank Group.[2] In line with this, the World Bank is pursuing the following:

- Selectively engaging with forest priority countries.
- Developing partnerships, such as the Global Forest Partnership, that bring together existing and emerging partnership arrangements—such as the World Bank-World Wildlife Fund (WWF) Alliance, the Program on Forests (PROFOR), and Forest Law Enforcement and Governance (FLEG) initiatives—and that enhance coordination among client countries, donors, international nongovernmental organizations, research institutions, and civil society to achieve the goals of the Forests Strategy. In the future, the strategy will continue to rely on successful efforts and enter into new partnerships as dictated by the strategy and the changing development context.
- Focusing on emerging opportunities for innovative financing of forest sector activities and continuing to facilitate concessional financing by blending Interna-

tional Bank for Reconstruction and Development (IBRD) and International Development Association (IDA) loans with grants.

■ Building a solid analytical foundation to support and facilitate engagement in the forest sector.

■ Coordinating across the World Bank Group, with a particular emphasis on the International Finance Corporation (IFC), whose operations in the sector are significant in many forest-important countries.

Operational policies for World Bank–supported investment projects

The World Bank's suite of operational policies ensures that Bank operations with potential impact on forests take forest outcomes into consideration. In line with the current Forests Strategy, OP 4.36 is proactive both in identifying and protecting critical forest conservation areas and in supporting improved forest management in production forests outside these areas. OP 4.36 applies to all World Bank investment operations that potentially affect forests, regardless of whether they are specific forest sector investments. It also encourages the incorporation of forest issues in Country Assistance Strategies (CAS) and addresses cross-sectoral impacts on forests. OP 4.36 provides for conservation of critical natural habitats and prohibits World Bank financing of any commercial harvesting or plantation development in critical natural habitats. It also allows for proactive investment support to improve forest management outside critical forest areas, with explicit safeguards to ensure that such World Bank–financed operations comply with independent certification standards acceptable to the World Bank, or operations with an agreed upon, time-bound action plan to establish compliance with these standards.

Beyond OP 4.36, relevant operational policies comprise the provisions for environmental assessment embodied in OP 4.01, which require that impacts of any proposed activity on the natural environment, human health and safety, and social aspects be taken into account under OPs 4.10 (Indigenous Peoples), 4.11 (Physical Cultural Resources), 4.12 (Involuntary Resettlement), and 4.04 (Natural Habitats). OP 4.04 in particular requires that the World Bank not support projects that, in its opinion, involve the significant conversion or degradation of critical natural habitats, and OP 4.10 requires that the World Bank only support projects in which affected Indigenous Peoples provide broad community support to the project based on prior, free, and informed consultations.

Broadly based development policy lending, by its nature, is not dealt with under safeguard policies of the type the World Bank applies to its investment lending. Development policy loans (DPLs) were originally designed to provide support for macroeconomic policy reforms, such as in trade policy and agriculture. Over time, DPLs have evolved to focus more on structural, financial sector, and social policy reforms, and on improving public sector resource management. Development policy operations now generally aim to promote competitive market structures, correct distortions in incentive regimes, establish appropriate financial monitoring and safeguards, create an environment conducive to private sector investment, encourage private sector activity, promote good governance, and mitigate short-term adverse effects of development policy. While the sorts of activities, institutional changes, and policy developments that result can certainly have impacts on forests, it is no simple task to assess what these effects will be in any given situation, as the connections with outcomes at the field level are diffuse and indirect—and thus quite inaccessible to the precise and specific requirements of the safeguard policies that apply to investment lending. The World Bank recognized this difficulty, and until recently did not subject its structural adjustment lending to compliance with the safeguard policies. An operational directive (OD 8.60) provided some guidance on environmental issues for this form of lending until it was replaced by a more detailed operational policy on DPLs (OP 8.60).[3] This policy makes explicit mention of forests and is highly relevant to the forest sector because it guides the due diligence needed to ensure that the potential for this form of lending to cause damage to natural resources, forests, and the environment is minimized in the design and approach used. Such operations are of special concern where large numbers of poor people rely on forests to some extent for their livelihoods. Where rapid economic change is occurring, perverse incentives and misallocation of resources leading to forest removal or changes in the status of use and ownership of forests will be risk factors to poverty alleviation.

THE WORLD BANK'S LENDING TO THE SECTOR

The portfolio of the World Bank's investments in forests indicates an upward trend, after having fallen in the early 2000s to historically low levels.[4] The total commitment in 2001 was US$141 million, reflecting lending from the World Bank, the Global Environment Facility (GEF), and the IFC (figure 3). Lending has remained relatively steady in fiscal 2007 (July 1, 2006 to June 30, 2007).[5] Between October 2002 and June 2007, the World Bank approved 12 stand-alone forestry projects, as well as 39 others that include forestry components. There are 13 more forestry-related projects in

Figure 3 Commitment from the World Bank, GEF, and the IFC for Forests, FY01 to FY07

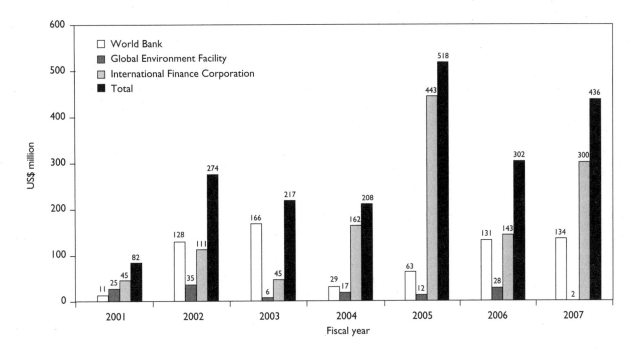

the pipeline, four of which are stand-alone forestry projects. A more proactive approach to World Bank engagement in forests, which is embodied in the Forests Strategy, and strong support for this approach from the Board of Executive Directors and senior management have been significant factors in creating the increase in activities.

Overall lending profile

The volume of lending for the five years preceding the Forests Strategy is nearly equivalent to the five years after introduction of the Forests Strategy: US$568 million between fiscal 1997 and fiscal 2001, compared with US$517 million from fiscal 2002 through fiscal 2006. After adoption of the Forests Strategy, lending slowed and has only recently regained the levels preceding the adoption. When forestry investments in projects associated with other sectors are included (that is, World Bank projects that do not have a forest sector coding), aggregate IBRD and IDA investment in the forest sector is much larger (figure 4). By this measure, total investment in forests by the World Bank was US$770 million after adoption (fiscal 2002 to fiscal 2006). Though lending in the forestry sector has not expanded since approval of the Forests Strategy in 2002, forest lending has been integrated into natural resource management, agriculture, environment, and rural development projects. Furthermore, World Bank lending has expanded to include

all types of forests, not just tropical forests: Nearly 40 percent of lending between fiscal 02 and fiscal 06 (US$204 million) has been in nontropical countries, predominantly in Eastern Europe and the Mediterranean.

Regional lending profile

The regional profile of lending has changed since 2001 (figure 5). The inclusion of temperate forests in the Forests Strategy has increased lending in the Europe and Central Asia region. In the region, the World Bank has been concentrating on an increasing demand for policy dialogue and advisory technical assistance. Projects in Armenia, Bosnia and Herzegovina, Georgia, Kazakhstan, Romania, and the Russian Federation are working to strengthen fire management, reforestation, and development of protected areas. Focus within the projects has been on training, institutional reforms, forest information, the role of the private sector, and devolution of management to local and subnational levels.

In the Sub-Saharan Africa region (AFR) since the new strategy there have been three active projects with a focus on governance in the Congo Basin (Cameroon, Democratic Republic of Congo, and Gabon). It is anticipated that over the next few years, forest activities will focus on governance-related issues, sector reform, and institution strengthening.

In general, the World Bank has had limited forestry engagement in the Middle East and North Africa region

Figure 4   IBRD/IDA and GEF Forestry-Related Lending, Including Forest Components in Nonforest Projects, 1997–2006

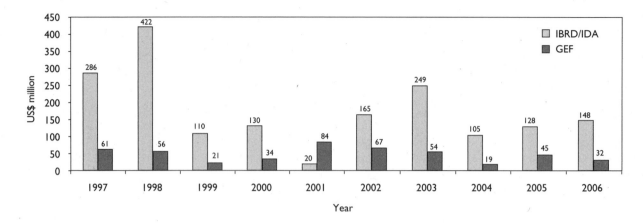

(MENA) because of its low forest cover. In Morocco, a nation with relatively extensive forests, the World Bank is involved in preparing an Integrated Forest Development Project. In the Islamic Republic of Iran, a land and water management project has a community-based forest management component.

In the East Asia and the Pacific region (EAP), the World Bank's lending has focused on plantation development in countries, such as China, that are major consumers of forest raw materials.[6] Additional focus has been on policy dialogue for development of certification schemes. Also, successful projects in Vietnam and the Lao People's Democratic

Republic are working to address governance and policy reforms.

In the South Asia region (SAR), India accounts for the bulk of lending. Lending commitments have been declining since 2003 as one generation of projects has ended (figure 5). Since then, lending awaits the results of an Analytical and Advisory Services (AAA) initiative designed to guide future lending and to reengage dialogue with the government about policy.[7]

In the Latin America and the Caribbean region (LAC), projects have concentrated on community forestry, reforestation, forest land restoration, forest certification, forest concessions, policy, and legal reforms.[8] Additional projects

Figure 5   Amount of IBRD/IDA Forestry Lending by Region, FY01–FY05

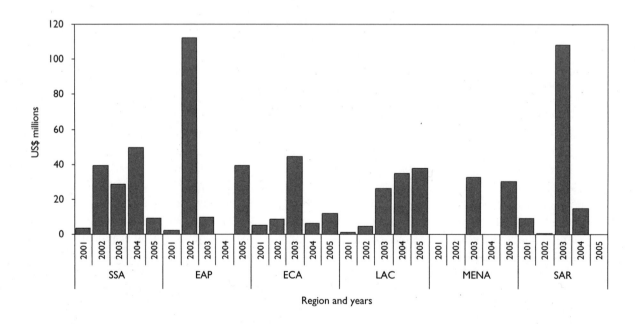

INTRODUCTION: OPPORTUNITIES AND CHALLENGES IN THE FOREST SECTOR

Figure 6   Regional Distribution of IBRD/IDA Lending,
             2001–05

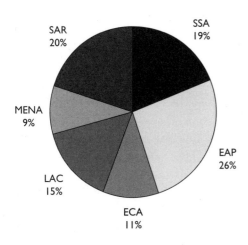

in Belize, Brazil, Colombia, Costa Rica, Ecuador, El Salvador, Honduras, Nicaragua, and Peru concern the creation and management of protected areas with an emphasis on indigenous and local community participation and forest management.

See figure 6 for a regional breakdown of lending over 2001–05.

PROGRESS TO DATE

In 2006 the World Bank commissioned an independent midterm review of the Forests Strategy implementation (Contreras-Hermosilla and Simula 2007). The review found that the World Bank has made substantial progress on all fronts outlined in the strategy. Yet the strategy has been only partially implemented in the four years since its adoption. Some of its main achievements follow.

MAINSTREAMING OF THE STRATEGY. The World Bank has sought to manage the effects of macroeconomic policy and sector programs on forest resources. Some countries have incorporated forest sector reforms into their Poverty Reduction Strategy Papers (PRSP). The Bank has supported these within the framework of CAS in countries like Cameroon, and through forest investment projects in such countries as Albania, Croatia, Romania, and Russia. The World Bank has also supported policy changes through DPLs, again for example, in Cameroon. In many other countries, however, forests have not been properly considered in the CAS or DPL, even in cases where doing so was clearly warranted by the size of the sector or its potential to alleviate

poverty, contribute to economic development, and preserve environmental values. Governments do not always make forestry a policy priority or seek Bank support, and in some instances analytical work that might have provided a framework for integrating forest issues into planning and policy making has been lacking or insufficient. The related analytical work has been highly variable and offers opportunity for improvement.

SUCCESSFUL EXTENSION TO NONTROPICAL FORESTS has extended its engagement to nontropical forests, including those in China, Georgia, Romania, the Russian Federation, and Turkey. It has also supported timber production activities in tropical moist forests in countries such as Cambodia, Cameroon, and Mexico. The integration of forest components into natural-resource and rural development programs has intensified in countries like Albania, Gabon, and Guatemala. The World Bank has also broadened its focus on forestry with new instruments, such as independent certification. It has also expanded the scope of its interventions to account for the impacts on forests of policies in other sectors, such as trade.

Despite these accomplishments, the World Bank's overall level of engagement has thus far remained insufficient for achieving the targets set in the Forests Strategy. IBRD and IDA lending volumes increased only slowly, regaining and then stabilizing at levels comparable to volumes before the adoption of the strategy. Overall World Bank involvement in natural tropical forests operations remains modest and is often surrounded by intense controversy. In many cases the relative dearth of self-standing forest projects reflects the lack of priority that clients assign to investing in forests or to introducing forest sector reforms.

POVERTY REDUCTION. Poverty reduction objectives, a pillar of the strategy as well as fundamental to the World Bank's overall mission, have been appropriately included in forest investments in a number of countries, including Albania, Gabon, and Nicaragua. In many other countries, however, poverty and the effects of forest interventions on forest-dependent people have not received adequate attention, either in the World Bank's analytical work or in its lending program.

OTHER KEY ACHIEVEMENTS include the following:

- *Strengthening forest sector governance and transparency.* World Bank activities have created a political climate for high-level regional discussions on improvement in governance and increased transparency and accountability in the sector. They have also made improving forest sector governance and institutional reform a central focus in many countries, including Cambodia, Cameroon, Democratic Republic of Congo, Gabon, Honduras, Indonesia, and Russia, and initiated the process of sector reform in some of these countries (Democratic Republic of Congo, Gabon, and Tanzania).

- *Conserving local and global ecosystem services.* The World Bank has supported and spearheaded the development of conservation through payments for environmental services schemes and improved management of protected areas through Bank projects. The World Bank also recently launched the Forest Carbon Partnership Facility (FCPF) to enable payments for REDD.
- *Facilitating responsible private investment.* Most World Bank client country governments are working to attract responsible domestic and foreign private sector investments to achieve effective conservation and sustainable management of forest resources.
- *Building strategic partnerships.* Through strategic partnerships and programs, such as the World Bank–WWF Alliance, PROFOR, and FLEG initiatives, the World Bank has been leveraging resources, aligning stakeholder interests, enabling innovation, improving outreach, and scaling up impacts. The World Bank has been actively supporting strategic partnerships at regional (for example, Congo Basin Forest Partnership) and national levels. The World Bank is currently facilitating the development of a Global Forest Partnership to galvanize synergies among forest partnerships and programs and to scale up the availability of grants for the development of the sector.

THE CHALLENGE AHEAD

The 2002 Forests Strategy emphasized a path of "cautious reengagement." Since fiscal 2002, this has included the World Bank selectively reengaging in key countries, building a solid analytical foundation for World Bank lending and grants, using partnerships to initiate and implement national and international processes for strengthening governance, enhancing poverty considerations in forest activities, and advancing forest conservation and sustainable forest management. Progress made in these areas since the start of the new strategy is described above. Still, significant gaps and challenges remain, not only across countries and regions, but also in implementation of the World Bank's priority areas. These challenges are as follows.

Key global challenges

ADDRESS POVERTY AND FOREST GOVERNANCE BY PROMOTING FOREST OWNERSHIP AND ACCESS RIGHTS. Promote greater recognition of the rights of local and indigenous groups and give greater attention to land tenure, ownership, and rights-to-resource and access issues. Emphasize and enable stakeholder participation in the formulation and implementation of policies, strategies, and programs to foster ownership and long-term sustainability of the resource.

ENHANCE THE ROLE OF FORESTS AS AN ENGINE OF ECONOMIC GROWTH AND DEVELOPMENT. Increase investments in plantations (especially in tropical countries), expand forest certification and overall forest management, and encourage responsible private sector investments, including for community-company partnerships for on-site forest enterprise development, and for market access.

PROTECT VITAL LOCAL AND GLOBAL ENVIRONMENTAL SERVICES AND VALUES. Create markets for local ecosystem services, such as water and soil erosion. Seize the potentially enormous financing opportunities emerging in the context of global climate change to increase investments for carbon sequestration and avoided deforestation to reduce emissions from deforestation and forest degradation.

ASSIST COUNTRIES TO INTEGRATE THE GLOBAL FOREST AGENDA INTO THEIR OWN NATIONAL STRATEGIES AND POLICIES AND TO HARNESS THE DEVELOPMENT OPPORTUNITIES AVAILABLE. Use the World Bank's leadership position in the global forest dialogue and take advantage of emerging economic and environmental opportunities (such as the attractiveness of biofuels, for example) to foster sustainable forest management. Integrate forest interdependencies into the design of agriculture, rural development, and natural resource management projects to ensure sustainable economic growth and rural poverty alleviation.

Key regional challenges

SUB-SAHARAN AFRICA. Continue promoting fundamental sector reforms and capacity building around the challenges of governance, environmental protection, and forest livelihoods. Expand market mechanisms to secure environmental services, and improve dry forests management.

EAST ASIA AND THE PACIFIC. Invest in plantation area expansion, expand instruments for natural forest management and biodiversity conservation, provide support to forest law enforcement and governance initiatives, and maintain well-managed environmental and social safeguard reviews.

EUROPE AND CENTRAL ASIA. Support transformation of forest management organizations into efficient service delivery institutions capable of meeting the challenges of multifunctional, landscape-level forest management; support decentralization of management to subnational entities through adequate public financing mechanisms and increased responsibilities for the private sector and local communities.

LATIN AMERICA AND THE CARIBBEAN. Support improved forest governance and institutions, sustainable harvesting and forest management, forest landscape restoration, and development of industrial plantations.

MIDDLE EAST AND NORTH AFRICA. Enhance policy and institutional reforms to position forests in a wider context of sustainable natural resource management.

SOUTH ASIA. Support the rural poor through greater access to forest resources and stronger property rights, and foster greater participation of the private sector in productive enterprises in rural areas, for local value addition and employment.

Key challenges for the World Bank

MAINSTREAM FORESTS. Strengthen forests' role in the World Bank's agenda through greater inclusion of forest sector issues in PRSPs and CASs and better alignment of Poverty Reduction Support Credits and GEF and IFC resources with the overall lending program to address poverty and livelihood issues.

IMPLEMENT SAFEGUARDS AND DUE DILIGENCE. Ensure efficacious application of the World Bank's safeguards policies (especially on the social side) in traditional forest lending projects, and strengthening due diligence for forest concerns in DPL, through increased participation, better knowledge management and communication, and focused staff training.

STRENGTHEN FOREST GOVERNANCE. Integrate forest governance into World Bank policy dialogue and projects to achieve concrete outcomes in client countries.

PURPOSE OF THE FORESTS SOURCEBOOK

The purpose of the *Forests Sourcebook* is to be a resource for World Bank clients, task managers, and other stakeholders in the design and implementation of projects in line with the Forests Strategy as they tackle the challenges ahead. The sourcebook draws on experiences from within and outside the World Bank in implementing innovative approaches for integrating the three pillars of the strategy. The sourcebook distills key points from frontier guidance material supported or published in specific subject areas, either by the World Bank or other partner organizations.

The sourcebook offers guidance to program and project managers by (i) highlighting the key issues in each chapter, (ii) suggesting approaches for implementing projects and analytical work in line with the strategy, (iii) providing links to more in-depth sources of information, and, where possible and relevant, (iv) describing tools for addressing these issues.

NOTES

1. In 2002, the World Bank estimated that total forest sector private investment in developing countries and countries in transition was in the range of US$8 billion to US$10 billion per year. In the opinion of the review team for the World Bank's independent midterm review of the Forests Strategy implementation, the 2007 figure is substantially higher (Contreras-Hermosilla and Simula (2007)). According to the FAO (2006), the plantation area in developing countries is increasing at about 1.8 million hectares per year. This represents investments of US$3 billion to US$4 billion per year. Improvements in existing forest management should be added to this, but reliable estimates do not exist. In plantation-based projects, industrial investments represent 80–90 percent of the total. Applying this coefficient—with plantation investments being 20 percent of the total—total forest investment in developing countries should be at least US$15 billion.

2. Successful implementation requires (i) being selective in World Bank activities in forests with country ownership and commitment, as broad criteria for engagement; (ii) developing partnerships (with other donors, nongovernmental organizations, and the private sector) to enable the World Bank to address forest issues through a broad spectrum of policies and in collaboration with national governments; (iii) financing the strategy by encouraging blended financing arrangements through multiple sources, including the development of markets and financial payments for environmental services from forests; (iv) increasing economic and sector work to initiate the process of building analysis, awareness, and then demand for forest investments (and for incorporation of forestry issues) into CASs and PRSPs; and

(v) coordinating across the Bank, including with International Finance Corporation (IFC), Multilateral Investment Guarantee Agency (MIGA), and World Bank Institute (WBI) for better implementation of a unified strategy.

3. This policy was approved by the World Bank's Board of Executive Directors in 2003.

4. The World Bank Group includes the International Development Association (IDA), International Bank for Reconstruction and Development (IBRD), International Centre for Settlement of Investment Disputes (ICSID), IFC, and MIGA. Aggregate investment in the forest sector tends to fluctuate from year to year because it can be heavily skewed by one or two large projects. Such fluctuations would be less if aggregate disbursements were tracked.

5. This sourcebook does not go into details, but the Global Environment Facility (GEF) is an important partner in the implementation of the Forests Strategy. In 2003–05, the GEF provided US$186.1 million for 38 forest-related projects implemented by the World Bank. The total value of these projects was US$951.8 million. The number of World Bank–implemented GEF projects has averaged 13 per year since 2000. The average size of these projects has doubled during the same period, from US$16.1 million to US$34.4 million.

6. For more details, please see the regional strategy (World Bank 2007).

7. See *Unlocking Opportunities for Forest-Dependent People* (World Bank 2006). It includes a policy report, policy dialogue, and comprehensive dissemination that will guide future World Bank lending in forestry. It is the basis for discussions with the government of India on possible reforms at the national and state levels. Important outcomes have been the formation of a forestry donor's forum, and high-level policy meetings with the Prime Minister's Office and the National Planning Commission.

8. These subjects have been the focus of Bank projects in Bolivia, Colombia, Guatemala, Honduras, Mexico, Nicaragua, Paraguay, and Peru.

REFERENCES CITED

Contreras-Hermosilla, A., and M. Simula. 2007. "The World Bank Forest Strategy: Review of Implementation." World Bank, Washington, DC.

FAO. 2006. *Global Forest Resources Assessment 2005.* Rome: FAO.

Stern, N. 2007. *The Economics of Climate Change: The Stern Review.* Cambridge: Cambridge University Press.

White, A., and A. Martin. 2002. *Who Owns the World's Forests? Forest Tenure and Public Forests in Transition.* Washington, DC: Forest Trends.

World Bank. 2004. *Sustaining Forests: A Development Strategy.* Washington, DC: World Bank.

———. 2006. *Unlocking Opportunities for Forest-Dependent People—India.* Delhi, India: Oxford University Press.

———. 2007. East Asia Region Forestry Strategy. EASRD (Rural Development and Natural Resources. East Asia & Pacific Region), World Bank, Washington, DC.

Priority Themes and Operational Aspects

CHAPTER 1

Forests for Poverty Reduction

The majority of the world's poor are concentrated in rural areas and, consequently, depend on natural resources, over which they exercise little control, for their livelihoods. It is estimated that 60 million Indigenous Peoples are totally dependent on forests, 350 million people are highly forest dependent, and 1.2 billion are dependent on agroforestry. The scale and significance of poverty issues on forest lands demand that poverty alleviation efforts give special attention to forest areas and the people living in them.

Poor rural families depend heavily on "wild" resources; in both forest-poor and forest-rich contexts, forest products are used for fuel, food, medicines, construction materials, fertilizers, and cash. Reliance on these resources often increases in times of personal, family, or social hardship, with these wild resources being especially important for women, children, and ethnic minorities. In many cases, as people get richer, they use and sell fewer of the forest products that are considered inferior goods. However, most people in Sub-Saharan Africa have not gotten richer, resulting in growing markets for all forest products as populations and urbanization increase. A similar situation is found in the poorer regions of Asia. (See box 1.1.)

Smallholders living in forest margins in diverse parts of the world earn 10–25 percent of their household incomes from nontimber forest products, many of which are either undervalued or omitted completely from conventional economic income statistics (see Note 1.1, Mainstreaming the Role of Forests in Poverty Alleviation; Ndoye, Ruiz Pérez,

and Eyebe 1999). Studies of income from indigenous natural resource management and small-scale local forest enterprises in a number of countries in Africa, and joint forest management in Madhya Pradesh state in India, are but a few of the studies showing the significant impacts of these activities on the income of poor people (see Monela et al. 2004;

Box 1.1   What Do We Mean by Poverty?

Poverty is a multidimensional concept, the measurement of which continues to be debated. A detailed overview of poverty concepts is provided in the World Bank's World Development Report on Attacking Poverty (World Bank 2001). This report states that poverty is not solely about material deprivation, but is also related to broader notions of risk, vulnerability, social inclusion, and opportunities. Poverty encompasses all forms of deprivation that prevent a person from achieving his or her aspirations.

This broader definition of poverty has policy implications because it underscores the positive interactions of interventions in a broad set of welfare dimensions. In practice, it implies that the nature of the problem must influence selection of the appropriate welfare measure.

Source: Authors' compilation from World Bank 2001.

Angelsen and Wunder 2003; and Mallik 2000 as cited in Scherr, White, and Kaimowitz 2004). A meta-review of 54 case studies that examined income from forest products in rural areas of developing countries found that forest income (ranging from US$0 to US$3,458 and averaging US$678 per year, once adjusted for purchasing power parity) made up one-fifth of household income of the population sampled for the report (Vedeld and others 2004). Wild food, fodder for animals, and fuelwood were the most important products and accounted for approximately 70 percent of forest income. Household forest income increased with increased distance from markets, suggesting that forests are important for communities with limited alternative income opportunities. In some cases, forest environmental income had a strong and significant equalizing effect on local income distribution (Vedeld and others 2004).

It is also estimated that globally 17.4 million people (full-time equivalents) earn their livings from formal sector forest-based employment (that is, enterprises with more than 20 employees) in forestry, wood industries, furniture, and pulp and paper (Poschen and Lougren 2001, as cited in Scherr, White, and Kaimowitz 2004). Poschen and Lougren estimate that an additional 30–35 million are employed—most of them in Brazil, China, India, Indonesia, and Malaysia—in the informal and subsistence forest-based sectors.

TYPES OF RELIANCE ON FORESTS. Forest uses by local populations change through the transition from hunting and gathering to sedentary agriculture, and vary with households' socioeconomic levels. Across this spectrum, forests tend to become less dense and forest cover decreases in association with growing population densities and higher market demands, and in association with changing types of forest use. There are, of course, exceptions to this trend.

Often, the proportion of overall household income from certain forest products tends to decline as households move from hunting and gathering to sedentary cultivation. This is a reflection of more than just increased income opportunities in agriculture and other domains; it is also indicative of the decreased availability of types of forest resources that were previously abundant. In other cases, the proportion of a household's income from the forest can continue to be substantial when combined with agricultural activities, even despite a decrease in high-value timber stocks in the region: a seven-year study in the Brazilian state of Amapá showed that when sawtimber, poles, and firewood are produced in a management system that combines forestry and agriculture, they can provide significant additional income for Amazonian smallholders (Pinedo-Vasquez et al. 2001).

The growing importance of nonfarm rural activities as a source of rural household income, and the significant share of the nonfarm total accounted for by forest product activities, make this one of the most important vehicles through which the forest sector can contribute to poverty alleviation. As sources of income, commercial forest product activities have, in principle, the potential to help households move out of poverty. However, as labor costs increase, many of these low-value, labor-intensive activities are abandoned. Other commercial products cease to be used as incomes increase because they are "inferior goods" for which there are ready substitutes, lowering their overall marketability. This generally shifts forest use to more valuable forest products and activities that gradually require more and more skill and capital inputs. Thus, dependence on different forest products will likely vary with socioeconomic levels: a dependence on low-valued activities will decrease as poverty is lessened and households move out of poverty, in favor of higher-valued activities with greater returns.

FORESTS IN RURAL POOR'S ASSET PORTFOLIO. Natural assets, such as forests, are of particular importance to the poor, partly because of their lack of access to financial and physical capital and formal forms of human capital, such as education. As portfolio managers, the poor draw down some forms of capital to convert to other forms; commonly, for example, the poor temporarily draw down stocks of natural capital (for example, harvesting fuelwood for sale) to invest in their portfolio, recognizing the fungibility of assets. Insistence on an unchanging "steady state" forest reserve underplays forest dynamics and can limit the options open to the poor. A flexible, comprehensive, and dynamic view of natural assets and the whole portfolio is needed. Forest products and outputs fulfill different functions for people at different socioeconomic levels, and multiple goals and strategies may be needed to reach different groups, even those depending on the same forest.

LINKAGES BETWEEN FOREST-BASED POVERTY ALLEVIATION AND RURAL LIVELIHOODS. Forest-based poverty alleviation cannot be isolated from other aspects of livelihoods. The majority of those who can benefit from forest products live outside forests; they live in predominantly agricultural landscapes, and for many of them the forest products they use come as much from the farm as the forest. Reflecting this, forest-based poverty alleviation has to be linked to other land uses, such as agriculture, grazing, and agroforestry systems. On-farm tree-growing schemes have had limited success so far; thus, new strategies of integrating multiple land uses must be explored.

A summary of the salient features of linkages between forests and livelihoods and how they have been changing are provided in table 1.1.

Forests provide a tremendous source of natural capital that can be used to alleviate poverty in two ways. The first is poverty avoidance or mitigation, in which forest resources serve as a safety net or fill gaps by providing a source of petty cash. For example, the Tawahka of Krausirpi in Honduras cope with short-term and personal shocks (for example, a poor bean harvest or a sick child) through the sale of forest products. The same community uses forest product sales (for example, bushmeat) to cope with covariate shocks, such as the rapid decline in cocoa markets following a drop in cocoa prices. The use of forests as natural insurance is important for forest dwellers because their livelihoods are characterized by unusually high levels of environmental, agricultural, epidemiological, and market uncertainty. Moreover, the remote location of most forest dwellers implies limited access to more conventional forms of insurance, including formal credit and insurance programs.

The second is poverty elimination, in which forest resources help to lift the household out of poverty by functioning as a source of savings, investment, accumulation, asset building, and permanent increases in income and welfare. As a source of income, forests can provide a decent living when markets are accessible, especially if a household is involved in the planting, harvesting, processing, transporting, and trading of forest products. These households are usually involved in varying degrees of forest management because such income from forests is seldom obtained by

Table 1.1 Changing Linkages between Forests and Poverty	
Characteristics of livelihood inputs from forests	**Impacts of change on forest livelihood inputs**
Subsistence and cultural importance Forests form an integral part of the social and cultural framework for forest dwellers.	Likely to weaken, but persists widely in some aspects (e.g., medicinal).
Forest products supplement and complement inputs of fuel, food, medicinal plant products, etc., from the farm system; often important in filling seasonal and other food gaps, particularly in hard times; forest foods enhance palatability of staple diets and provide vitamins and proteins.	Can become more important where farm output and/or nonfarm income declines. Likely to decline in importance as government relief programs or new agricultural crops make it less necessary to fall back on forest resources, as incomes rise and supplies come increasingly from purchased inputs, or as increasing labor shortages or labor costs militate against gathering activities or divert subsistence supplies to income-generating outlets.
Agricultural inputs Forests provide a starting point for rotational agriculture and protection; on-farm trees also provide shade, windbreaks, and contour vegetation; trees and forests also provide low-cost soil nutrient recycling and mulch. Arboreal forests provide arboreal fodder and forage, and fiber baskets for storing agricultural products, and wooden plows and other farm implements.	Trees can become increasingly important as a low-capital means of combating declining site productivity and a low-labor means of keeping land in productive use (e.g., home gardens). But increased capital availability, and access to purchased products, is likely to lead to substitution by other materials (e.g., by pasture crops, fertilizer, or plastic packaging).
Commercial outputs Forests help diversify the farm household economy, provide counter-seasonal sources of income, and are a source of income in hard times.	With increasing commercialization of rural use patterns, some low-input, low-return activities can grow; however, most are inferior goods and decline. Some are displaced by factory-made alternatives, and others become unprofitable and are abandoned as labor costs rise. Gathered industrial raw materials tend to be displaced by domesticated supplies or synthetic substituted.
Many products are characterized by easy or open access to the resource, and by low capital and skill entry thresholds; overwhelmingly small, usually household-based, activities; mainly low-return, producing for local markets, engaged in part-time by rural households, often to fill particular income gaps or needs; limited growth potential, but very important in coping strategies of the poor. Forest products are often particularly important for women (as entrepreneurs as well as employees).	Higher-return activities serving growing, specialized demand are more likely to prosper, particularly those serving urban as well as rural markets; an increasing proportion of the processing and trading activity is likely to become centered in small rural centers and urban locations.
Some forest products provide the basis for full-time and high-return activities; usually associated with high skill and capital entry thresholds and urban as well as rural markets.	

Source: Arnold 2001.

harvesting forest products that are open access or common property resources from unmanaged natural forests.

Another rationale for prioritizing poverty reduction through forests is the Millennium Development Goals (MDGs). Countries that have adopted these goals have set a target of halving global poverty by 2015, and for institutions such as the World Bank, reducing global poverty is the main challenge. While economic growth appears to be the means to lift the poor out of extreme poverty in the developing world, the capacity of the poor to participate in economic growth must be enhanced if they are to share in its benefits.

PAST ACTIVITIES

Between 2002 and 2005, 28 World Bank forestry projects had components focused on poverty reduction. Poverty alleviation activities included in the project portfolio varied from strengthening of land tenure rights, reform of policies and discrimination against the poor and Indigenous Peoples, development of community fuelwood plantations, increased productivity of pastures and forest lands, erosion control, and training in ecotourism, to promotion of fuel-efficient technologies for households. Investments in these projects were approximately US$130 million. See boxes 1.2 and 1.3 for successful examples.

The design of poverty reduction activities in forest projects tends to be difficult, and mixed results ensue because of the complexity of the issues involved. Of a set of 40 projects

that were examined for the "World Bank Forest Strategy: Review of Implementation" (Contreras-Hermosilla and Simula 2007), it was found that 16 contained activities that were highly relevant to poverty alleviation, while 12 had activities that were substantially relevant. Eight other projects were moderately relevant in their consideration of forests and poverty alleviation; in three projects the consideration was negligible.

KEY ISSUES

Donor engagement in forestry with a direct or indirect aim of alleviating poverty concentrates mainly in three areas:

- Increasing local users' participation in forest management to make management more responsive to their needs, and to increase benefits flowing to them
- Supporting management strategies that include growing trees on farms
- Exploiting income-generating opportunities from production and trade in forest products in the nonfarm rural economy

Activities in these areas have had mixed results. Much donor attention has been placed on local participation—often resulting in false perceptions of participation rather than true participation. Tree-growing schemes have resulted in little additional planting taking place, in some cases

---

Box 1.2   The Role of Forests in Benefiting the Rural Poor: An Example from the World Bank's China Loess Plateau Watershed Rehabilitation Project

This watershed rehabilitation project included activities in the forest sector among its several project components. More than 1 million farmers in the project area directly benefited from the project, with annual grain output raised from 427,000 tons to 698,600 tons and fruit production from 80,000 tons to 345,000 tons. Farmers' annual incomes per capita also increased from 360 Chinese yuan to 1,263 Chinese yuan (about US$43 to US$152).

The various project components contributed to the significant reduction of poverty and tripling of net incomes by addressing a range of short-, medium-, and long-term income-generating and income-stabilizing measures. The project supported diversification of production to reduce variability in income. For example, trees were used to provide an income buffer during difficult times.

Large tracts of land in the project area were severely degraded and past agricultural practices were clearly unsustainable as a result of uncontrolled grazing, fuelwood gathering, and cropping on slopes that were too steep for sustainable farming. The project succeeded in taking a large proportion of these areas entirely out of production for natural regeneration and in planting trees and shrubs on unstable slopes to protect soils and provide sustainable returns. This practice secured long-term productivity of those areas and raised incomes for the local people.

Source: World Bank Loess Plateau Watershed Rehabilitation Project (P003540). Board approval: May 26, 1994; closed: December 31, 2002.

Direct short-term poverty alleviation impacts were substantial in this project, which financed approximately 5,000 person-years of local villager employment to implement many field interventions. The budgets of households participating in project activities increased by an estimated 30 percent annually.

The quality and productivity of forest and pasture land managed under the new plans by the newly created resource user associations improved to such an extent that commune families quickly began deriving income from forest and pastures (including fuelwood, fodder, nontimber forest products, some grazing, and the like) that had been seriously degraded bush before project-supported investments.

Of significance is evidence that some commune and family investments in resource management (for example, active protection of areas from grazing, fencing, tree planting, and erosion control intervention) continued even after project support ceased, indicating that the shift to improved land-use practice brought about by the project is likely to be sustainable. This unexpected level of success led to identification of the need for the Albanian government to further develop its skills and capacity to provide communes with silvicultural and other technical guidance that will be necessary as their forests mature, and to approach the World Bank with a request for a follow-up project that would scale up and expand the coverage of communal forest and pasture management throughout the country.

Source: World Bank Albania Forestry Project (P008271). Board approval: April 16, 1996; closed: June 30, 2004.

because communities have their own strategies for coping with wood shortages. Activities focused on processing and trade often proved to be susceptible to changes in market requirements, to domination by intermediaries, and to shifts to domesticated or synthetic sources of supply, and few proved to be sustainable. Considerable room remains for improving the contribution of forests to poverty alleviation.

IMPROVED PERFORMANCE FRAMEWORK FOR FOREST INTERVENTIONS. An improved performance framework is necessary to enhance pro-poor benefits. A clear understanding of what forestry can and cannot do to alleviate poverty is essential to enhancing effectiveness of poverty-related interventions at all levels within the forest sector. To give greater emphasis to poverty alleviation within forestry, it is necessary to acknowledge that the greater part of the rural populations that benefit from forest products are located outside forests as normally defined. Thus, forestry interventions need to encompass all tree stocks and activities based on them to contribute significantly to poverty alleviation, rather than be confined to forests and forest-dwelling households. Forest sector interventions also need to recognize the different wealth levels among rural poor households and need to be appropriately structured to target the population of concern (see note 1.3, Indigenous Peoples and Forests).

HARMONIZATION OF ACTIVITIES WITH OTHER SECTORS. Harmonizing poverty alleviation activities in the forest sector with what is happening in other sectors is equally important. This harmonization requires recognizing and considering the implications of broader changes, such as market liberalization and structural adjustment for rural development (additional discussion on this is found in chapter 6, Mainstreaming Forests into Development Policy and Planning: Assessing Cross-Sectoral Impacts).

TRANSPARENCY AND ACCOUNTABILITY IN GOVERNANCE. Transparent and accountable governance is critical to fostering pro-poor growth and essential to ensuring that this natural resource wealth is managed wisely (see chapter 5, Improving Forest Governance). A pro-poor growth strategy for rural areas must build on natural resources and facilitate management of these resources for the long term to provide the fuel for economic development to relieve poverty. It also must grant secure and equitable access to assets—which requires development of property rights (see note 1.4, Property and Access Rights) and efficient land administration.

PROPERTY RIGHTS AND LAND ADMINISTRATION. Allocation of property rights and efficient land administration are critical to pro-poor growth in rural areas. The process of developing statutory property rights influences the pro-poor potential of forest activities (see note 1.4, Property and Access Rights, and note 1.3, Indigenous Peoples and Forests). Customary rights over forest resources often exist, and where these are codified and made statutory, they are seldom causes for conflict. However, in areas where customary systems of forest management and ownership have been disregarded or overruled, many local communities, poor households, and women have lost access to forest resources. In these cases, government policies have awarded favored groups concessions, licenses, and permits, limiting (or in some cases denying) the rights of poor local inhabitants. This is evident in places where creation of government forest reserves and protected areas have reduced households' access to common property resources. The need of the poor for continued access to a common pool biomass resource to sustain predominantly subsistence-based coping strategies can also increasingly conflict with the interests of better-off households and outsiders (Arnold 2001).

The transition to pro-poor forest tenure and property rights occurs through a combination of strategies—both reforms fostered by political elites and reforms demanded by civil society and community organizations. These efforts should, to the extent possible, move beyond transferring limited rights to forest resources to communities. For example, in India participatory forestry is restricted to degraded or poorer areas of forests, and there are widespread restrictions regarding rights over timber and other commercially valuable forest products.

POTENTIAL OF COMMUNITY-BASED FOREST MANAGEMENT. Community-Based Forest Management (CBFM) offers a vehicle for reducing poverty among forest-dependent households (see note 1.2, Community-Based Forest Management, and note 1.3, Indigenous Peoples and Forests). Commonly, forest-dependent people who live in or near forests tend to be politically weak or powerless. Formally recognized forms of CBFM can empower these households and individuals through recognition of their rights to sustainably manage, control, use, and benefit from forest resources. CBFM can also offer a competitive advantage for unorganized producers through economies of scale. Community engagement in forest management has been increasing as forest sector policy reforms give greater weight to participation of communities in forest management. Examples of CBFM are found in joint forest management, participatory forest management, community forestry, and other similar schemes in numerous Bank client countries. The performance of CBFM initiatives has been mixed, revealing the importance of the political, institutional, governance, and capacity elements in such initiatives. There are, however, several successful examples of communities that organized and thus gained financially and politically (for example, Mexico and Nepal; see boxes 1.11 and 1.13 in note 1.2, Community-Based Forest Management).

ENGAGEMENT OF THE PRIVATE SECTOR. Private sector engagement in forest activities is increasing (see chapter 2, Engaging the Private Sector in Forest Sector Development). Communities need to link with the private sector in forest activities to further enhance forests' contribution to poverty reduction. The growing demand for timber for processing into pulp and paper as well as for fuelwood (for example, from tea companies in Kenya) creates opportunities for communities to benefit from these private investments. Community-company partnerships can take various forms, including outgrower schemes or arrangements for community provision of management services (such as thinning, pruning, fire maintenance, and the like). Community-company partnerships are distinct from arrangements in which private entities (normally concessionaires) compensate communities for the use of forests. In partnerships, communities enter into legal contracts with companies and provide specific services.

POTENTIAL FOR FOREST-BASED SMALL AND MEDIUM ENTERPRISES. Small and medium forest enterprises (SMFEs) make up a large percentage of forest enterprises, with far-reaching poverty-alleviation potential. In many forest countries, forest-based SMFEs account for 80–90 percent of all national forest enterprises. Approximately 20 million people worldwide are employed in SMFEs. These enterprises generate a gross value added of about US$130 billion per year (Macqueen, Armitage and Jaecky, 2006). In countries with SMFEs, often more than 50 percent of total forest-related employment is in these enterprises. Numerous factors influence the feasibility, appropriate structure, and suitable direction of an SMFE program (see note 2.2, Small and Medium Forest Enterprises). Moreover, in many countries policies need to be developed to create an enabling framework for SMFEs. Nevertheless, where there is demand and potential, these enterprises offer room for managing forests and alleviating poverty.

ACCESS TO MICROFINANCE SCHEMES. Access to microfinance schemes can help small-scale forest enterprises build material goods, increase income, and reduce vulnerability to economic stresses and external shocks. Microfinance can assist in covering capital costs to improve productivity and quality as well as working capital to purchase equipment and materials. Access to credit and other microenterprise supporting services are often limited for poor, forest-dependent households. Commercial financiers seldom lend money to the rural poor because of the associated transaction costs, and the limited collateral, especially when rural poor households do not have secure tenure and access rights. Often poor households borrow from private lenders at unreasonably high interest rates to obtain money they urgently need. This often results in households having to exploit resources unsustainably to pay interest charges. The high interest rates often result in households either never repaying or slowly paying back the capital.

ACCESS TO TECHNICAL AND MARKETING SERVICES. Small-scale enterprises also need access to technical and marketing services. Given the low incomes of households involved and the low unit value of fuelwood and nontimber products, provision of conventional technical services may not be feasible. In such cases, facilitating the exchange of information among villagers through various channels can be beneficial.

GREATER MARKET ACCESS FOR FOREST PRODUCTS. Increasing market access for forest products can enhance forests' contribution to alleviating poverty. Small timber producers need to be more competitive with large timber companies, both in niche and domestic markets. This requires small timber producers to address challenges, such as lack of economies of scale. Creating arrangements that would facilitate smallholder marketing of timber would enhance that sector's contribution to income generation. Some simple changes include reversing the existing forestry regulations that tend to discriminate against small farmers and microenterprises by having fewer and simpler regulations and less paper work (see note 1.5, Making Markets Work for the Forest-Dependent Poor).

In some countries and regions, aggregate demand for fuelwood, wood for charcoal, and for commercially valuable nontimber forest products (for example, bushmeat) is growing. These are often peri-urban markets that can be profitable, making it economically attractive for farmers to plant trees and produce or harvest the needed commodities. There are also growing markets for furniture and housing materials, including construction timber and poles. Support for producing and marketing better quality products as well as improved infrastructure for accessing these markets could provide more employment and better remuneration, particularly if domestic per capita income grows. Such support can be provided through microenterprise development activities that provide attention to the associated natural resource issues and ensure a sustainable supply of raw material.

Another rapidly expanding market is that of environmental services provided by forests (see note 2.3, Innovative Marketing Arrangements for Environmental Services),

including carbon sequestration (see the World Bank's Carbon Finance Unit Operations Handbook at http://carbon finance.org/Router.cfm?Page=DocLib&ht=34&dl=1). These markets need to be accessible to forest-dependent households if they are to serve the purpose of engendering sustainable resource use and land-use practices. Creating the enabling conditions will require, among other things, clear and secure rights over forests and woodlands.

IMPORTANCE OF FOREST AND TREE COMPONENTS IN AGROFORESTRY. Forest and tree components will often become more important where there is greater reliance on agroforestry. This can happen in the following instances:

- where changes in the availability of land, labor, and capital favor tree crops as low-input land uses where labor is the limiting factor (for example, in multistory "home gardens" that increase land productivity), or as low-cost inputs into farm systems (for example, in place of purchased fertilizer)
- where growth in agricultural incomes can lead to increasing local commercialization of subsistence goods, such as fuelwood and other forest products
- where improved rural infrastructure gives farmers greater access to markets for forest fruits and other products of trees that can be grown as part of farm systems

REVERSING EXISTING TOP-DOWN APPROACHES. The contribution forests could make to rural development, forest conservation, and economic growth has been undermined by conventional top-down approaches to forestry. Transparent and accountable governance is critical to fostering pro-poor growth and essential to ensuring that this natural resource wealth is managed wisely. There is also a need to remove or relax regulatory provisions that reinforce the structural and scale advantages that the state possesses as producer of many forest products. The relationship between the forest department and small local producers would also benefit from separation of the regulatory function of the former from involvement in forest management and delivery of support services (see note 5.2, Reforming Forest Institutions).

IMPORTANCE OF LOCAL LEADERSHIP, INSTITUTIONAL CAPACITY, AND HUMAN RESOURCES. Activities oriented toward poverty reduction call for exceptional local leadership, institutional capacity, and adequate human resources in implementing agencies. These are not always available on the sustained basis required for operations that typically span several years.

Institutional development of capacity takes time. Thus, long-term technical assistance appears to be an indispensable part of future poverty-oriented interventions. Experiences in Brazil and Mexico suggest that options for the delivery of technical assistance should include consideration of training of rural producers and careful exploration of the tradeoffs involved in privatizing technical assistance because the latter can reduce the possibility of building up institutional capacity of government agencies.

Often, investments by national governments in rural areas are low. This is partly due to an inadequate understanding of poverty rates and poverty density in forest areas. Poverty Reduction Strategy Papers (PRSPs) have become the main mechanism for governments in developing countries and some middle-income countries to define their budget and policy priorities and discuss those priorities with the international community. Unfortunately, however, in the initial PRSPs, interim PRSPs, and National Forest Programs (NFPs), the pivotal role of forests in sustaining rural livelihoods, especially those of the poor and marginalized, has been neglected. There has been relatively little analysis of the contribution of forests to rural livelihoods, nor of the measures required to capture or expand the potential. Forest and tree products, particularly nontimber forest products, often fall between sectors with neither forestry nor agricultural agencies collecting data on household collection, use, and sales (see note 1.1, Mainstreaming the Role of Forests in Poverty Alleviation: Measuring Poverty-Forest Linkages).

FUTURE PRIORITIES AND SCALING-UP ACTIVITIES

In many regions the issues of natural resource management, poverty reduction, and local empowerment are loosely intertwined and cannot be tackled in isolation. Most of the linkages between forestry and rural poverty are also closely associated with what is happening in agriculture and the rural economy. For example, conversion of forests to either temporary or permanent agriculture can contribute to poverty alleviation. Forestry and agriculture activities need to be closely aligned with components of rural development strategies and programs.

This could be done through the following:

- Adapting forestry and agriculture interventions to changes being introduced in forestry, agriculture, and rural economies. For example, agroforestry, tree crop plantations, and scattered trees on farmland can potentially assist with poverty alleviation while conserving forests. Forest and tree components will be more important where changes in agriculture result in greater reliance on agroforestry; this could occur as a result of the availability of land, labor, or capital favoring tree crops; agricultural income increasing local commercialization of subsistence goods such as fuelwood; or improved rural infrastructure providing farmers with greater access to markets.

- Exploiting opportunities that rural development interventions create for forest-based activities. The growing importance of nonfarm rural activities as a source of rural household income and the share of nonfarm total income accounted for by forest product activities make this an important avenue by which forests can contribute to poverty alleviation.

- Understanding and taking into account information on cross-sectoral impacts of forest-based poverty situations.

For forest activities to have pro-poor impacts and reduce poverty, future activities must focus on better distribution of resource rights, both property and procedural. Control over and access to resources critical to growth and livelihoods is the main governance issue for rural people, including Indigenous Peoples and other communities with customary rights. There is a need for greater commitment to ensure that the rights of communities and forest-dependent households are entrenched in appropriate legislation and regulations, that mechanisms exist to implement them, and that these mechanisms are functioning properly. This includes establishing ownership and precisely defining rights, which will provide incentives for the poor to invest in forest management. Equally important is the need for forms of governance for common pool resources that can address the weaknesses in many existing comanagement systems (see note 1.3, Indigenous Peoples and Forests, and note 1.4, Property and Access Rights).

Timber harvesting must become more pro-poor. Local access to and management of natural forests, smallholder tree growing, and small-scale enterprise development as strategies to avoid capture by local elites in CBFM are central to a more pro-poor use of timber (see note 1.2, Community-Based Forest Management). There is a need to remove regulatory barriers and excessive state regulation to facilitate CBFM in areas other than degraded forests and enable management of forests for multiple purposes. From an analytical standpoint, there is a need for more research into pluralistic systems of comanagement that really do function effectively and equitably and for pilot testing of those models that show promise.

Frameworks, regulations, and encouragement are needed to make natural resource markets work for the poor. This requires responding to market failures and imperfect competition and identifying new opportunities that allow the poor to take advantage of their available assets. The collection and sale of timber and nontimber forest products are important for the poor. There is a need to look into their value-added potential and improved marketing strategies. Additionally, strategies need to ensure that the poor are not negatively affected by increasing commercialization (see note 1.5, Making Forests Work for the Forest-Dependent Poor). Studies should also be undertaken to determine whether growing urban domestic markets for forest products have significantly benefited the poor.

Similarly, payment for environmental services, such as carbon sequestration, biodiversity conservation, hydrological benefits, and forest-based tourism, is a potentially important source of revenue. It is important for the structure of such payments to allow for benefits to flow to the poor as well as for maintenance of services (see note 2.3, Innovative Marketing Arrangements for Environmental Services).

There is a need to create and enhance the role of forest-dependent communities and households in SMFEs and to foster forest partnerships between communities and the private sector. This will require incentives, regulations, and actions at the national level that facilitate these arrangements. Technical support must be provided to communities, and private entities must be required to look beyond logging and the timber processing industry to the long-term sustainability of forest resources (see chapter 2, Engaging the Private Sector in Forest Sector Development).

To promote forest uses for poverty alleviation, forest activities that primarily address biodiversity conservation need to be refocused to take a balanced approach that includes poverty alleviation. Conservation objectives for forests of value to local people will need to be revised from being predominantly protection oriented to encouraging sustainable systems that produce livelihood benefits. The increased recognition of Indigenous Peoples rights to their land and natural resources should also be further enhanced in biodiversity conservation activities (see note 1.3, Indigenous Peoples and Forests).

National forest programs can provide a broad platform with which to engage in a poverty reduction agenda by working toward coherent sector policies—and forests need to be integrated into a comprehensive rural development strategy (see note 6.4, Assessing Cross-Sectoral Impacts: Use of CEAs and SEAs). Such integration will be facilitated by improved knowledge and understanding of the extent to which the very large numbers of poor people living in or near forests depend upon those forests for their livelihood—a matter of significance to poverty alleviation outcomes in general in some countries (see note 1.1, Mainstreaming the Role of Forests in Poverty Alleviation: Measuring Poverty-Forest Linkages). It is important to gather information on whether the depletion of forest resources has had a negative impact on poor people, and whether the poor have been able to find alternatives to forest safety nets and gap fillers (see also note 1.3 on the particular risks and impacts to Indigenous Peoples). Equally important is a comprehensive examination of how existing World Bank data systems and records could be used to improve knowledge about the forest dependency of people dwelling in or near large natural forest resources in World Bank client countries. This needs to be developed through the appropriate networks of the World Bank in collaboration with Country Departments.

SELECTED READINGS

Angelsen, A., and S. Wunder. 2003. "Exploring the Forest-Poverty Link: Key Concepts, Issues and Research Implications." CIFOR Occasional Paper No. 40. Center for International Forestry Research, Bogor, Indonesia.

Chomitz, K. M., P. Buys, G. De Luca, T. S. Thomas, and S. Wertz-Kanounnikoff. 2006. *At Loggerheads? Agricultural Expansion, Poverty Reduction and Environment in the Tropical Forests.* Washington, DC: World Bank.

Sunderlin, W. D., A. Angelsen, B. Belcher, P. Burgers, R. Nasi, L. Santoso, and S. Wunder. 2005. "Livelihoods, Forests, and Conservation in Developing Countries: An Overview." *World Development* 33 (9): 1383–1402.

Sunderlin, W. D., S. Dewi, and A. Puntodewo. 2006. "Forests, Poverty, and Poverty Alleviation Policies." Background paper. World Bank, Washington, DC.

World Resources Institute (WRI) in collaboration with United Nations Development Programme, UNEP, and World Bank. 2005. *World Resources 2005: The Wealth of the Poor—Managing Ecosystems to Fight Poverty.* Washington, DC: WRI.

REFERENCES CITED

Angelsen, A., and S. Wunder. 2003. "Exploring the Forest-Poverty Link: Key Concepts, Issues and Research Implications." CIFOR Occasional Paper No. 40, CIFOR, Bogor, Indonesia.

Arnold, J. E. M. 2001. "Forestry, Poverty and Aid." CIFOR Occasional Paper No. 33. CIFOR, Bogor, Indonesia.

Contreras-Hermosilla, A., and M. Simula. 2007. "The World Bank Forest Strategy: Review of Implementation." World Bank, Washington, DC.

Macqueen, D., N. Armitage, and M. Jaecky. 2006. Report of a meeting of participants of the UK Tropical Forest Forum on small enterprise development and forests. Royal Botanic Gardens, Kew 26 September 2006. IIED, London.

Mallik, R. M. 2000. "Sustainable Management of Nontimber Forest Products in Orissa: Some Issues and Options." *Indian Journal of Agricultural Economics* 55 (3):383–97.

Monela, G., S. Chamshama, R. Mwaipopo, and D. Gamassa. 2004. *A Study on the Social, Economic and Environmental Impacts of Forest Landscape Restoration in Shinyanga Region, Tanzania.* Draft. Dar-es-Salaam: The United Republic of Tanzania Ministry of Natural Resources and Tourism, Forestry and Beekeeping Division, and the World Conservation Union, Eastern Africa Regional Office.

Ndoye, O., M. Ruiz Pérez, and A. Eyebe. 1999. "Non-wood Forest Products Markets and Potential Forest Resource Degradation in Central Africa." In *Current Research Issues and Prospects for Conservation,* ed. T. C. H. Sunderland, L. E. Clark, and P. Vantomme, 183–206. Rome: FAO.

Pinedo-Vasquez, M., D. J. Zarin, K. Coffey, C. Padoch, and F. Rabelo. 2001. "Post-Boom Logging in Amazonia." *Human Ecology* 29 (2):219–39.

Poschen, P., and M. Lougren. 2001. *Globalization and Sustainability: The Forestry and Wood Industries on the Move.* Report for discussion at the Tripartite Meeting, "Social and Labour Dimensions of the Forestry and Wood Industries on the Move," Geneva, Switzerland, International Labour Organization, September 17–21.

World Bank. 2001. *World Development Report: Attacking Poverty.* World Bank, Washington, DC.

World Bank Carbon Finance Unit. n.d. Operations Handbook. http://carbonfinance.org/Router.cfm?Page=DocLib&ht=34&dl=1. World Bank, Washington, DC.

Vedeld, P., P. Angehen, E. Sjaastad, and G. K. Berg. 2004. "Counting on the Environment: Forest Incomes and the Rural Poor." Environmental Economics Series, Paper No. 98, World Bank, Washington, DC.

CROSS-REFERENCED CHAPTERS AND NOTES

All notes in Chapter 1: Forests for Poverty Reduction

Chapter 2: Engaging the Private Sector in Forest Sector Development

Note 2.2: Small- and Medium-Scale Enterprises

Note 2.3: Innovative Marketing Arrangements for Environmental Services

Note 5.2: Reforming Forest Institutions

Note 6.4: Assessing Cross-Sectoral Impacts: Use of CEAs and SEAs

Mainstreaming the Role of Forests in Poverty Alleviation: Measuring Poverty-Forest Linkages

Forests provide a significant portion of forest dwellers' subsistence goods and services, and income. Yet the contribution of forests to income and the level of forest dependence are seldom systematically documented. Income streams from forests and the role of forests as safety nets are underestimated and the potential of forests to alleviate poverty is often unexploited. The lack of quantitative and readily available information on the role of forests in contributing to poverty reduction is a major constraint to mainstreaming the use of forests in poverty alleviation. A consequence is that the role of forests in poverty reduction is not reflected in any significant way in national-level strategies, such as the Poverty Reduction Strategy (PRS) process. In the same way, those countries that have been developing NFPs (NFPs; see note 6.1, Using National Forest Programs to Mainstream Forest Issues) have not tended to explicitly link forest issues to poverty reduction or to the achievement of the MDGs. If PRSPs fail to incorporate forestry, national efforts to reduce poverty and vulnerability will undercount the critical role that forest resources currently play—and the potentially greater role they could play—in the livelihoods of the poor.

There are two constraints to improving measurement and mainstreaming of linkages between forests and poverty. First, most countries have little data available to illustrate how forests contribute to the livelihoods of poor households. The Living Standards Measurement Surveys (LSMS; www.worldbank.org/lsms) have a variable on fuelwood consumption, but owing to the logistical and cultural challenges of surveying forest-dwelling and forest-reliant households in remote areas, the data associated with this variable are limited. It also is difficult to accurately measure and attribute the cash value of extracted forest products to households residing in high-population-density areas and forest-agriculture mosaics (Chomitz et al. 2006).

The second challenge is that the data that do exist are rarely presented in ways that are meaningful to those designing PRSPs and NFPs. Forest specialists are more familiar with reporting forest information about physical resources (trees planted, forest cover improved, or timber sold) than livelihoods, with the exception of quantifying the number of people employed in the forest sector. Poverty experts and macroeconomists are unfamiliar with the use of forests and NFPs and tend to underestimate the contribution of forests and off-farm natural resources to livelihoods.

OPERATIONAL ASPECTS

There is little knowledge about how rural households depend on forest and tree resources to meet their daily needs—and even less about the potential of these resources to reduce poverty. This failure stems in part from the fact that forest products, especially nontimber forest products, fall through the cracks of sector-specific data collection, with neither forestry nor agricultural agencies collecting data on household collection, use, and sale of forest products. A simple methodology is needed to capture this contribution and to demonstrate its ultimate relevance to many of the MDGs. This is what the Poverty-Forest Linkages Toolkit offers (box 1.4). This section provides a summary of key steps for measuring poverty-forest linkages and mainstreaming this information, based on the approach detailed in the toolkit.

Only at the national level can current country processes for poverty data gathering be identified and understood and effort invested in enabling these to take forest data into account. And only through local enquiry can a picture be developed of the two key ways in which forests have an impact on the lives of the poor—positively through livelihood support, and negatively if use of forests is formally illegal. To this end, the toolkit lays out a step-by-step process to gather and analyze the necessary information, detailing

Box 1.4   Poverty-Forest Linkages Toolkit

The Poverty-Forest Linkages Toolkit[a] is designed to meet two objectives. First, it aims to increase knowledge about how rural households depend on forest and tree resources to meet their daily need, and the potential of this resource to reduce poverty. Second, the Toolkit assists in engaging in a process of mainstreaming this information into national planning processes, including PRSPs. The Toolkit provides a framework for gathering and analyzing information to provide a clear understanding of the current and potential role of forest and tree products for poverty reduction. It includes social, institutional, and environmental concerns, in the context of local and national planning processes. An integral part is the identification of the most forest-dependent communities, and the impact of current and potential policies and programs.

The Poverty-Forest Linkages Toolkit may be used by forestry departments, local governments, and nongovernmental organization (NGO) facilitators to deliver the following:

- Local-level "snapshot data" on forest reliance and the livelihood and poverty reduction contribution of forests
- A documented case for the contribution of forests to the livelihoods of the poor
- Analyses of how forestry regulations promote or hinder the livelihoods of the rural poor
- Strengthened agency and institutional capacity to identify opportunities and constraints
- An assessment of issues (for example, inappropriate regulations) that need to be resolved if poverty

reduction is to be effectively addressed by forestry officials

The toolkit provides a complete set of tools, methods, examples, and case studies for the task, including the following:

- An explanation of the PRSP process and identification of the strategies needed for influencing it (including potential entry points for forestry)
- A set of rapid appraisal methods to gather information on cash and subsistence contributions from forests to households, particularly the poor
- Methods for analyzing field data for the potential role of forests in reducing poverty and vulnerability, and policy options for improving the contribution of forests to rural livelihoods
- Suggestions for how to frame the results, so as to be relevant to the planners, government agencies, and other institutions and organizations at both local and national levels
- A series of case studies that illustrate the contribution of forest resources to households and an analysis of the impact of forestry policies and programs

Included are annexes on the tools, with instruction for their use; a series of examples of all the tools, illustrating the data they generate; an explanation of how to analyze documents collected; and an example of a short document that might be written for distribution to government officials when explaining the purpose of the toolkit.

Source: Authors' compilation using PROFOR forthcoming a.
a. In May 2004, with PROFOR support, the World Conservation Union (IUCN), Overseas Development Institute, Centre for International Forestry Research (CIFOR), PROFOR, and Winrock International formed a working group partnership with the intent of consolidating and building upon the growing knowledge base from fieldwork and research efforts on the different ways in which forests can benefit the poor. The result was the draft Poverty-Forest Linkages Toolkit, which was piloted in four countries prior to finalization.

activities to be undertaken at the national, district, and local levels.

UNDERTAKING A NATIONAL-LEVEL ANALYSIS. The purpose of a national-level analysis is to find out whether the contribution of forests to poverty reduction is already being mainstreamed into current national policies, programs, and laws, and whether poverty issues are being taken into account in forest sector processes. If they are, the aim is to understand how, and if not, to identify country-specific pathways by which they could be.

The toolkit explains how the relevant natural resources ministries need to be involved and how to find out what the relevant entry points might be for more focus on the contribution of forests to the livelihoods of the poor (box 1.5). Tasks include identifying the main ministry hosting the PRS process, the main donors to the process, other important players (civil society groups, NGOs, and so forth), and the key documents that have been produced. These might include household, rural, or living standard surveys; a national census; or the drafting of an NFP. National-level analysis makes it clear whether the efforts to measure poverty-forest linkages can proceed with the support of the forest ministry or those responsible for the PRS.

GATHERING INFORMATION AT THE VILLAGE OR COMMUNITY LEVEL. After the national-level analysis has been completed, the next step is to collect data to identify forest–household use linkages at the local level. The results generated will be used at both the district and field levels and at higher (provincial and national) levels to underline the contribution of forests and trees to the livelihoods of the poor, and sometimes to highlight ways in which the presence of anachronistic, anti-poor forest policies or laws are an impediment to poverty reduction. The toolkit details several tools for identifying users (and nonusers) of forest resources, the level of dependency on and contribution of forest and tree products, existing resources and products, and key constraints of the existing system (see boxes 1.6 and 1.7).

PREPARING AND PRESENTING DATA FOR DIFFERENT AUDIENCES. Data gathered need to be analyzed and prepared in different formats for presentation to district and higher levels. Information should be presented in user-friendly forms (for example, diagrams and charts) that

accurately represent what is occurring at the local level, highlight essential livelihood information and critical factors (such as access and tenure, markets, and status of resources), and satisfy the needs of users of the data. The information should be debated at the district level and reframed, with the assistance of local officials, to fit with district-to-national reporting requirements. District officials' views on the incorporation of forest contributions to incomes into data-gathering systems should be written up and submitted to the national-level body responsible for collecting poverty data or to the forest ministry, or to both. At the national level, this information is further streamlined to fit with the formats needed for the PRSP process, the NFP process, and others as relevant (see box 1.8). Furthermore, many countries have found that disseminating a simple guide to the results of the assessment makes a large difference to the extent to which ideas are understood and acted upon.

The progress a country has already made in drafting its PRS and developing data-gathering and monitoring instruments should inform the planning of analysis and data gathering of poverty-forest linkages. If a country already has data-gathering systems in place at the local level and collates the data at the national level, the focus of the exercise will be on linking forest and poverty data by, among other processes, learning whether forest product contribution is recorded and integrated into income and livelihood assessments and, subsequently, discussing with the appropriate bodies ways of inserting forest data into national poverty data collection systems and poverty data into national forest data collection systems. If, however, no such national data-gathering systems exist, the Toolkit outlines forest-focused participatory poverty assessments to generate a national-level picture of the contribution of forests to poverty through "snapshots" from different forest contexts around the country. The Toolkit further describes how to collate collected data for discussion and planning purposes within the PRS process.

LESSONS LEARNED AND RECOMMENDATIONS FOR PRACTITIONERS

A participatory approach to measuring poverty could provide more detailed information on the informal and formal uses of forest resources. Informal uses are often overlooked because they are not easily valued—but these uses reflect the important role of forests as safety nets.

Without a comprehensive understanding of forest dependency, policies and investments may discriminate

1. Wealth Ranking (village leadership).

    Aim: to select participants who are representative of the local population for the Toolkit exercises

2. Local Landscape Situation Analysis (toolkit team plus selected villagers)

    Aim: to understand the way in which local resources are used by members of the village.

3. Timeline and Trends (village plenary)

    Aim: to record a short history of the community against which to project a picture of changes in forest resources, in agriculture, in local livelihood strategies and sources of income. This tool can also be used at the district and national levels.

4. Livelihood Analysis (in groups selected by gender and wealth category)

    Aim: to discover the extent of cash and subsistence reliance on forest resources and the proportion of the total annual livelihood (from all sources) from forest resources. This tool can also be used at the district and national levels.

5. Tree and Forest Product Importance (in groups selected by gender and wealth category)

    Aim: to rank forest products by importance for cash and subsistence uses. This tool can also be used at the national level. If time is limited, information gained by the use of this tool can be deduced from tool 4.

6. Users, User Rights, User Responsibilities, and User Benefits (in groups selected by gender and wealth category)

    Aim: to have local people list all forest stakeholders, the benefits they derive from the forest, and the rights and responsibilities they exercise.

7. Forest Problem and Solution Matrix (in groups selected by gender and wealth category)

    Aim: to identify and rank the main forest problems, and suggest potential solutions. Problems include those related to policy, rules and regulations, tenure, and access. This tool can also be used at the district and national levels to focus on higher-level issues.

8. Final Plenary

    Aim: to present the main findings from the subgroups in plenary so that key emerging issues can be summarized.

Source: PROFOR forthcoming a.
Note: People from whom information is sought are listed in parentheses.

Box 1.7   Livelihood Analysis in Busongo, Tanzania

Livelihood analysis can be used to discover the extent of reliance on forest resources and the proportion of their contribution to annual cash and noncash incomes. In groups selected by gender and wealth category, participants are asked to distribute beans or stones across a list of forest products (for example, gum, charcoal, timber), allocating more where cash income sources are more important. The exercise is repeated for farm produce (crops and livestock), other sources, such as petty trade, and for noncash income sources. Participants are then asked to list sources of cash for different kinds of expenditures and identify whether the forest is used for investment. This exercise can show forest contributions to the achievement of the MDGs. For example, in eradicating extreme poverty and hunger (goal 1), villagers in Busongo cite 20–29 percent of livelihoods comes from forest contributions and that charcoal, fuelwood, ghee and milk, livestock, gum, thatch, and fodder grass contribute directly and indirectly to the meeting of these goals.

Source: PROFOR forthcoming b.

against the forest-dependent rural poor. A lack of understanding of the scale and scope of forest dependence can result in governments giving private companies and large farmers preferential access to publicly owned forest resources, conservation policies that deprive poor families access to forest resources, or governments expropriating villagers' rights over local forests.

Communities often invest the income generated from formal and informal uses of forest resources. Detailed information on forest resource use and how it is invested can provide insight into community priorities (for example, in Busongo, Tanzania, communities used cash revenue from forest resources, including gum and charcoal, to help primary-age children access schools, and village forests were used to construct staff housing and extra classrooms for primary schools).

When proposing a forest-related action in a PRSP, it is important to have a clear rationale for selecting the action as a priority. Integration of forest issues into PRSPs will require a quantitative causal link between forests and poverty. It is therefore crucial to include important forest environmental income sources in poverty assessments and PRSPs.

To effectively integrate forest-poverty information into PRSPs, it is useful to be familiar with the poverty analysis process used in PRSPs (available in the Poverty Reduction Strategies Sourcebook).

SELECTED READINGS

CIFOR. Poverty Environment Network. http://www.cifor.cgiar.org/pen/.

Hudson, J. 2005. "Forestry's Contribution to Poverty Reduction and Trends in Development Assistance. *International Forestry Review* 7 (2):156–60.

Klugman, J. 2002. "Overview." In J. Klugman, ed. *A Sourcebook for Poverty Reduction Strategies.* Washington, DC: World Bank. http://go.worldbank.org/TL225F9JC0.

Vedeld, P., A. Angelsen, E. Sjaastad, and G. K. Berg. 2004. "Counting on the Environment. Forest Incomes and the Rural Poor." Environmental Economics Series Paper No. 98, World Bank, Washington, DC.

REFERENCES CITED

Chomitz, K. M., P. Buys, G. De Luca, T. S. Thomas, and S. Wertz-Kanounnikoff. 2006. *At Loggerheads? Agricultural Expansion, Poverty Reduction and Environment in the Tropical Forests.* World Bank: Washington, DC.

Klugman, J., ed. 2002. *A Sourcebook for Poverty Reduction Strategies.* Washington, DC: World Bank. http://go.worldbank.org/3I8LYLXO80.

PROFOR. Forthcoming a. "Poverty-Forest Linkages Toolkit." PROFOR, World Bank, Washington, DC.

———. Forthcoming b. "Poverty Forest Linkages: Synthesis Report and Case Studies." PROFOR, World Bank, Washington, DC.

CROSS-REFERENCED CHAPTERS AND NOTES

Note 6.1: Using National Forest Programs to Mainstream Forest Issues

Community-Based Forest Management

An often overlooked trend in the world is a doubling of community tenure in the past 15 years. During this time, the area under private but collective ownership has increased from 143.3 million to 246.3 million hectares of forests. Similarly, the estimated area under public but collective administration has increased from 18.5 million to 131.4 million hectares. In sum, community-owned and administered forest totals at least 377 million hectares, or at least 22 percent of all forests in developing countries and three times as much forest as is owned by industry or individuals (White and Martin 2002). Poverty alleviation strategies in the forestry sector have emphasized local participation to make forest management more responsive to local needs and to increase benefits flowing to forest users. As more of the world's forests come under community tenure, community-based forest management (CBFM) practices are continually being promoted as playing an important role in poverty alleviation, good governance, and sustainable use of the environment.

Involving communities in sustainable forest resource use is not a new concept. In 1977, the World Bank Forestry Sector Review (World Bank 1977) noted that many forestry projects failed without the collaboration of local residents and that their collaboration improved environmental outcomes. It stressed the need to learn more about how to support policies that successfully give management and benefits to smallholders and the need to better understand local use, forestry-related practices, and traditional institutions. Learning from these lessons and the growing evidence of positive outcomes of CBFM, the current World Bank strategy focuses on, among other goals, using forests for poverty alleviation and strengthening local governance and transparency to address corruption. CBFM can be an important entry point for achieving these goals. It can also be an outcome of good policy related to poverty, governance, and the environment.

CBFM includes the empowerment of, or in some cases, the recognition of the rights of, local communities to sustainably manage, control, use, and benefit from local forest resources (see boxes 1.9 and 1.10). It implies a legal, political, and economic framework that puts local people at the center of forestry. Community objectives for managing forest land can include conservation, sustainable use, local control, economic development, and mixes of these objectives. While the state and large private operators have a role to play in the management of forests, in many instances, improved effectiveness, equity, and efficiency are outcomes of community-based approaches.

Community management of forests and other lands is larger in scale and more intensely linked to other sectors than is commonly acknowledged. From a management and use perspective, essentially all forests, however remote and seemingly physically unoccupied, have traditional owners and users. The assumption should not be a need to impose outside management over "unmanaged" or vacant lands but a need to carefully assess traditional systems, owners, and users of forests. Recent work in Gabon, a highly forested and lightly populated country, shows that even there traditional use zones abut one another and there is no "unclaimed" forest land. Frequently, the issue is recognition of existing or traditional local rights rather than transfer of new rights to the local level, as is illustrated in the India case study (see box 1.12; also note 1.3, Indigenous Peoples and Forests).

A variety of outside interventions can be used to support CBFM, including grants and loans, policy support programs and projects, global environment funds, and biodiversity conservation activities. However, CBFM is *not* the use of communities to achieve the objectives of outsiders, no matter how laudable these objectives may be. CBFM is the empowerment of communities to use and manage forests to achieve their own objectives.

Box 1.9 Community Forestry Models around the World

Many types of community forestry have been implemented in different parts of the world. In Latin America, there have been three main types:

- Communities with clear rights given by their national governments to participate in commercial timber harvesting, such as in Bolivia, Guatemala, Honduras, and Mexico.
- Communities that manage extractive reserves, such as in Brazil, where the government gives them clear rights over the land and forests, while limiting the amount of forest to be cleared for agriculture and prohibiting commercial logging. Communities earn money by selling nontimber forest products.
- Countries where the territorial rights of Indigenous Peoples over the areas that they have traditionally managed have been recognized.

In China, villagers are being given more control over heavily degraded lands if they agree with local forestry officials on how to rehabilitate the forests while also using them for their own subsistence. In India and Nepal, limited rights to what are still officially considered public lands have been devolved to local communities to manage and benefit from forests. Revenues from commercial forestry activities are shared with the government.

In Southeast Asia and the Pacific, partnerships are developed between communities and logging companies to ensure that the communities share in the benefits and that logging companies do not damage the resources the communities would like to protect.

Several models exist in Africa:

- Community forest programs that protect wildlife for tourism and sport hunting in return for a share of the fees paid by the tourists and hunters. Examples of this model can be found in Zimbabwe and Botswana.
- Projects focused on increasing villagers' incomes through sale of their fuelwood and charcoal, as in Mali and Niger.
- Programs designed to recognize the rights of communities over their forests, as in Tanzania and Mozambique.
- Programs designed to allow communities to sell timber commercially, if supported by a logging company or donor project. In Cameroon, this has greatly limited the number of communities involved.

Source: Kaimowitz 2005.

OPERATIONAL ASPECTS

THE ROLE OF NATURAL RESOURCES IN ECONOMIC GROWTH AND GOOD GOVERNANCE. Natural resources play a fundamental role in the economic growth of poor countries and poor populations and in the development of democracies and good governance. Some specific steps for consideration include the following:

- Understand the different perspectives that government, communities, private operators, and other stakeholders have of devolution and its mode of implementation. A shared framework, more accountable to local livelihood needs and peoples' rights to self-determination, is required. Redefining issues of wider "public interest" forms part of this process, as does a careful analysis of the motivations and the negative incentives.
- Consider and support, if appropriate, the shift of priorities in programs, budgets, and plans toward greater investment and integration of natural resources across the board in agricultural and poverty reduction programs, in national and donor budgets, in decentralization programs, and in other initiatives, at the policy, national planning, and forestry project levels.
- Develop pathways for more transparent information and communication that are locally accepted and that are adaptable for community through national political and donor levels.
- Create a baseline of biophysical and socioeconomic factors. There are several methodologies, including those detailed in the Poverty-Forest Linkages Toolkit (see note 1.1, Mainstreaming the Role of Forests in Poverty Alleviation: Measuring Poverty-Forest Linkages) and through CIFOR's Poverty Environment Network (http://www.cifor.cgiar.org/pen/). In addition, the International Forest Resources and Institutions (IFRI) Research Program describes a comprehensive methodology for measuring

the biophysical resource through forest plots and overall forest condition, as well as for developing data on local use, economic and market value, rules of use, and all levels of relevant institutional arrangements (for more information, see Clay, Alcorn, and Butler 2000).

DISTRIBUTION OF RESOURCE RIGHTS. Better distribution of resource rights, both property and procedural, is needed. Common attempts at decentralization of forest resources (see note 5.1, Decentralized Forest Management) are often compromised; they often do not go far enough in the recognition of the rights of, or transfer of rights to, local people, or if appropriate policy exists, it often is not implemented or implementation is skewed toward specific groups (see boxes 1.10 and 1.14). Furthermore, in many cases, effective handover has been either limited to badly degraded forests or under institutional arrangements that are impractical or conflict with local organization. Organizational models that devolve authority directly to disadvantaged resource users are more embracing of local interests and priorities than those that allocate control to higher levels of political or social organization. An equally important outcome is the decreased inequality and improved political and social articulation of local people.

Potential specific steps to enhance devolution of resource rights include the following:

- Understand motives for participation by identifying incentives and constraints in CBFM at community and national levels. Many more forestry projects fail as a result of negative incentives for community members than as a result of lack of education on how to manage forest resources (see box 1.12). It is important to understand who will foster and who will block an initiative and how to create a supportive environment for the required changes.
- Support strong local organizational capacity and enhance political capital outcomes for local people by enabling them to mobilize resources and negotiate for better benefits. NGOs, donors, federations, and other external actors have a key role in moving devolution policy and practice toward local interests.
- Identify traditional institutions and rules influencing property and use of resources and endogenous pathways for resolving conflicts and their effects on formal land rights. Allow communities to handle these issues and to propose mechanisms accepted by all key stakeholders that foster sustainable management and conflict resolution.

Some countries, including India and Nepal, have devolved limited rights to local communities to manage and benefit from forests that are still officially considered public land. This process is also under way in most of the African continent, with more complete transfer of rights present in Cameroon, The Gambia, and Tanzania. These arrangements, known by such terms as "joint forest management" and "comanagement" do not alter state ownership and can be revoked by the state at any time, making them a much weaker form of property rights than the rights provided by private community-based ownership. In Brazil, for example, where some 75 million hectares of state-owned lands have been set aside for indigenous communities, the communities have no right to harvest their timber, even under sustainable management regimes. Some other countries are beginning to adjust traditional industrial logging concession arrangements to include indigenous and other local communities. In British Columbia, Canada, the provincial government recently agreed to allow Weyerhaeuser Limited to transfer its concession rights to a new business venture with a coalition of indigenous groups as the lead partner. The coalition now has majority ownership of use rights to a portion of its ancestral homelands—but not to the land itself. The Guatemalan government has granted timber concessions to local communities rather than to large industries, and the early experience is positive. In the Lao People's Democratic Republic (Lao PDR), the government has launched a similar participatory management pilot program involving 60 villages under 50-year management contracts.

Source: IUCN and World Wildlife Fund 2004.

- Consider the need for a special good governance program at the community level to address such issues as elite capture and increased transparency (see box 1.11).

FRAMEWORK AND REGULATION FOR NATURAL RESOURCE MARKETS TO BENEFIT THE POOR. Natural resource markets will work for the poor only with the development of frameworks, regulations, and enforcement. If commodity chains are biased against the poor (and remain so), increasing

Nepal has a great deal of experience to offer in understanding the benefits and concerns of locally managed forests. It was the first country to have a national forestry policy allowing communities to form forest user groups (FUGs) that, after they elect leaders and develop a constitution and management plan, can be assigned control of and benefits from specific forest plots. To strengthen their groups against potential challenges as forest productivity and value increase through management, the groups have formed a federation.

Elite capture is a key issue to be addressed during decentralization, as was the case in some situations in Nepal. How local control impacts equity in asset distribution, and whether local groups can develop the transparency and other mechanisms necessary to avoid corruption, are important considerations.

An NGO, Women Acting Together for Change, worked closely with the FUGs on equity, democracy, and transparency through a process that included household visits to FUG members to discuss good governance of forest resources. The community then carried out community resource, social, and economic assessments, and workshops in which the leaders and members identified what good governance would mean in their group and identified very specific goals with clear indicators that they designed into posters to monitor progress. An evaluation of this project found that many groups rewrote their constitutions and management plans giving special advantages to poorer members, and established open group audits. They elected lower caste and women members to some of the leadership positions, often for the first time, and identified totally new goals.

At the Fourth National Community Forestry Workshop in Nepal (2004), regional directors and researchers noted that at that time leadership in the FUGs and their federation were the only democratically elected bodies in the country, forming a basis for future democracy.

Lessons from this example include that in a country with very stratified social traditions, even when there is positive legal support, it takes skilled facilitators and group analysis with democratic approaches to mitigate elite capture and lack of transparency and to create positive outcomes for the poor.

Source: Women Acting Together for Change 2004.

the poor's market integration may increase poverty, not reduce it (see box 1.13). This issue is further discussed in note 1.5, Making Markets Work for the Forest-Dependent Poor.

Some specific steps for consideration include the following:

- Facilitate the organization and legal recognition of local groups for collecting, processing, transporting, and marketing natural resources.
- Analyze commodity chains and market weakness and develop strategies that benefit the poor.
- Support market studies and locally managed market information systems so that the full range of forest products and outputs are considered.
- Create simple management plans in which local users make at least some of their own rules related to use of forest products.
- Support systems of regular user monitoring, and sanction rule conformance of other users backed by the government.

USE OF SCIENCE AND TECHNOLOGY TO SUPPORT AND EMPOWER LOCAL FOREST MANAGEMENT INITIATIVES AND OBJECTIVES. Too often, an unintended consequence of using complex scientific and technical plans and institutions has been the exclusion of local people from planning and managing, or marginalization of local technical, social, and institutional knowledge. This is evident in the common practice of demanding complex, costly, and sophisticated forest management plans from local communities. Such misuse of science and technology should be reversed.

Some specific steps that can be taken include the following:

- Develop minimum management standards directly related to forest and poverty outcomes rather than abstract management procedures.
- Develop locally adapted tools that are understood and manageable by local actors themselves regarding evaluation and quantification of natural resources and shared use by communities.

Box 1.12   Andhra Pradesh Community Forestry Management Project

India is a leader in involving communities in tree planting and forest improvement on state-owned forest land through a strategy called Joint Forest Management (JFM), with a portion of the benefits from community collaboration going back to participating communities. JFM has taken different forms and has had contrasting outcomes in the 27 states of India where it has been applied. Its methods and biophysical and social impacts have interested policy makers from around the world. The World Bank has encouraged expanding JFM and moving it toward community forestry.

In 2001, the World Bank supported taking a step further toward community forestry to better address the Bank's antipoverty, anticorruption, and improved governance goals. The Community Forestry Management Project in Andhra Pradesh stressed that the primary focus would be on improving the livelihoods and the physical, social, and financial assets of rural communities through sustainable tree and forest management. Increased benefits from the improved resource were to go to strengthening communities in a pro-poor strategy. Local community groups were to be legally supported to take over control, their institutions were to be strengthened, and the processes made more transparent. It was recognized that success could be reached only with changes in forestry institutions, laws, and regulations and the recognition of tribal land rights. In early discussions, the government and other partners indicated their willingness to support such changes.

The project has made good progress on technical matters and needs to further advance institutional improvements. Additional training is needed for service providers, including NGOs, support agencies, and front-line staff to enhance their ability to work effectively with local groups in a participatory manner. Community user groups need to strengthen and form federations and partnerships to gain power.

A number of nontimber forest products (NTFPs) provided small increases in incomes to some communities, and where past plantings were ready for harvesting, some communities reinvested in the resource. However, the government has yet to make the required legal amendments to the Forest Code; liberalize trade regulations for NTFP harvesting, processing, and marketing; simplify procedures; require more transparent audits; or make conflict resolution procedures more balanced. The government of Andhra Pradesh withdrew resources previously allocated to the project. The World Bank reviews stressed the need to address the above issues and to continue to focus on livelihoods and pro-poor approaches.

The World Bank Report on India (World Bank 2005) noted the handicap to improving local incomes when forest resource rights are held by the government in spite of proposed legislation to return land that had been taken from tribal groups. The legislation has since been approved in Parliament, opening opportunities for increasing the contribution of forests to local incomes.

Source: Authors' compilation from World Bank 2002a.

- Elaborate appropriate tools for continual follow-up on how the management system works and the effects of management by communities.
- Identify different user groups in each area and their interactions under the participatory development framework.
- Use simpler management plans in which local users make at least some of their own rules related to use of forest products and control over encroachment.

CBFM is complex, can be costly, and involves many stakeholders and vested interests that may support or oppose CBFM activities. (See, for example, Clay, Alcorn, and Butler 2000; Borrini-Feyerabend and others 2004.) The following should be noted:

- Successful CBFM is a slow process and needs to be based on informed participation, capacity building, and trust.
- Enhancement of land and resource tenure of Indigenous Peoples tends to improve CBFM and sustainable management of forests (see note 1.4, Property and Access Rights).
- Without addressing overt as well as hidden power relations and vested interests through clear roles and responsibilities, availability of information, transparent and equitable decision-making processes, and monitoring, Indigenous Peoples and other forest-dependent communities may be worse off as a result of project activities (for example, access to natural resources in their areas may have been opened up to other stakeholders, but they do not share in the benefits).

Box 1.13   The Forest Sector in Cameroon

The World Bank has been involved in the forest sector in Cameroon since 1982, and has helped put forest sector issues at the center of policy debates and encouraged a multisectoral approach. A review of the World Bank's engagement between 1982 and 1999 found that interventions have appropriately focused on policy and institutional issues, and some forest product marketing has been liberalized. However, overall the results of the interventions have not been up to expectations. At the time, the establishment of a transparent, efficient, and equitable forest management system was compromised by lack of government commitment and capacity, the resistance of key actors in the sector (including logging companies and parliament), implementation strategies that were not compatible with the underlying political and socioeconomic dynamics, and lack of policy implementation. In addition, forestry interventions were isolated from broader rural development concerns (agriculture, for example), and permanent mechanisms for local participation in decision making were not developed.

In Cameroon, tropical timber wealth is concentrated in a small group of economic agents. The sustainability and equity of the sector is largely deter-

mined by the structure of the industry, ownership patterns, industry investment, employment, and linkages with the rest of the economy. The structural underpinnings of the sector have been little affected and local communities have been left out of the reform process despite a declared objective to include them. The World Bank recommended that communities be actively involved in forest management and in 1994 a law was passed to this effect. However, because rights and responsibilities have not been specified, there are no clear mechanisms for limiting elite capture and the sharing of taxes has not been fully implemented. Results, therefore, have been mixed.

Some lessons learned include (i) the need for broadly based government support and avoiding relying solely on the executive branch to deliver on reforms because other powerful individuals or institutions may have motivation to block changes; (ii) knowledge and information are essential for policy making and implementation, as are clarity and specificity of terms and mechanisms for implementing laws and regulations; (iii) local institutions are needed for success and sustainability; and (iv) overdependence on technical assistance does not always overcome institutional weakness.

Source: World Bank OED 2000.

- Methods to enhance communities' ownership and active collaboration should be assessed for the given project context. Participatory mapping exercises, using mapping tools appropriate for the local communities, should be included.
- Capacity building is needed for local communities, government staff, and other involved stakeholders.
- Efforts to combine local practices (bottom-up) and government or private approaches (top-down) are essential.

LESSONS LEARNED AND RECOMMENDATIONS FOR PRACTITIONERS

Task managers need to keep in mind not only the technical aspects of forest management but the dangers and limitations of a top-down technical approach, the complexity of forest dynamics, as well as local use and rights (both formal and informal). In all cases, an understanding of the motivations of the different actors to support or block the desired changes is helpful in knowing if the donor-facilitated changes will actually take place.

Control over and access to forests not only facilitate economic growth and poverty reduction but also empower local people to articulate themselves socially and politically. The spillover effects of local control over forests, as in India, Mexico, and Nepal, can be quite large and impact a range of sectors and decision-making arenas. Because forests can be such an important share of a poor community's asset portfolio, control over and access to forests is not a trivial governance concern.

At the same time, it should be noted that not all community management results in positive outcomes. There are areas with strong migration where transfer of rights to communities has not resulted in sustainable management of forest resources (for example, Ghana and Côte d'Ivoire). In other countries there is a need to revisit the definition of community and distinguish between traditional communities managing forests and management of forests by more recently formed communities.

In many developing countries, significant attempts at decentralization have taken place, which, in theory, could greatly facilitate CBFM, local benefits, and empowerment

Box 1.14   Community Forestry in Mexico

Mexican community forestry has perhaps reached a scale and level of maturity unmatched anywhere else in the world. It has demonstrated that where there has been greater community power over forest management there has been greater transparency and less corruption, better forest use and protection, and improved livelihoods for local people. Regions of greatest deforestation are where traditional social structures have been seriously weakened (Bray, Merino-Perez, and Barry 2005).

An estimated three-fourths of Mexican forests are communally owned either by *ejidos* (agrarian reform communities) or indigenous communities. Mexican forest management is rich in indigenous forms of common property management overlaid by massive agricultural reforms from the violent Mexican revolution in the second decade of the 20th century. However, across the country there is great contrast in resource quality; indigenous groups and their approaches to organization, equity, and resource use; as well as in state and local leadership. Efforts to support local management have met with mixed results. The World Bank has worked to improve forest management for environmental protection and quality of life for local people, starting with pilot activities in 1990 and then redesigning a project expanding to other regions, many of which have needed specially crafted approaches.

The Project for Conservation and Sustainable Management of Forest Resources (PROCYMAF) aimed to support community forest development, with a primary focus on Oaxaca but with some program work in Guerrero and Michoacan. PROCYMAF was a community-driven development project. PROCYMAF II retained the environmental and economic aims but focused on (i) strengthening local capacity and management; (ii) strengthening capacity of the local private sector to provide forestry services; (iii) promoting timber, nontimber, and nontraditional products; and (iv) strengthening federal and state institutions working in forestry conservation and development.

A more diverse and multisectoral staff supported existing or new community management groups to expand social capital and helped form federations to be able to carry more weight in addressing local issues, including increased transparency and fair returns. Community members as well as professional foresters were trained so that technical issues could become understood locally, putting communities in a better position to negotiate and understand what to require of specialists and, in some cases, become specialists themselves. The project initiated community-to-community extension and, because there are areas in which there are either inter- or intra-community conflicts, promoters were trained in conflict management. The projects did studies on expanding the options and markets for economic use of forest products, including such items as mushrooms, bottled water, and resin as well as timber. Communities selected activities they found promising.

Devolution of public and private forestlands to local communities with common pool resource regimes and clear tenure status can create economic equality, social peace, and democratization of power, addressing corruption and at the same time improving the forest ecosystem (Bray, Merino-Perez, and Barry 2005).

Source: Authors' compilation using World Bank 2003.

(see note 1.4, Property and Access Rights). However, the ways in which local people realize the benefits of devolution differ widely, and the negative tradeoffs are most commonly borne by the poor. Community control and management over natural resources is often limited by continual government intervention and the government's insistence on complex management plans.

It is extremely important to facilitate a change in paradigm among forest officials and extension service providers. This can help in transforming the forest department culture and can be brought about by providing capacity building in participatory and community forest management and for provision of formal services. Such paradigm changes should be accompanied by appropriate incentives to forest staff and adequate budget.

In many cases, CBFM can be a lever for wider pro-poor change and reform; in others, basic conditions must be present for it to flourish. The following elements should be considered in community forestry programs:

■ Bureaucracy and paper work necessary for communities to have the right to manage their forests should be limited. Communities often do not have the money or the skills required to produce professional management plans, resulting in overdependence on donors and logging companies.

- Community forestry programs should make rich forest resources available to communities for their use, not just heavily degraded forests (see box 1.14).

- Transparency in payments to communities is critical. Governments or companies should make sure that villagers are informed of payments made to traditional village leaders, of amounts paid, and of the intended use for the payments, to limit corruption.

- Both communities and government should benefit from community forestry projects. Community benefits are more likely to accrue in situations where commercially viable forest resources, including NTFPs, are available. Governments benefit from expanded collection of taxes and forest fees and from cost savings resulting from a reduction in enforcement.

- Solid feasibility studies and business plans need to be in place, and communities should be familiar with market conditions. While financial returns should be quick to materialize, this should be balanced with longer-term needs of investing in infrastructure, natural resource conservation, and at times primary and secondary processing of wood and marketing of end products. Local knowledge, science, and institutions are often ignored or treated with derision by outsiders, making it difficult to incorporate local knowledge into activity design.

- It is essential that markets be made to work for the poor and that market failures, such as monopolies, collusion, segmentation, asymmetrical information, and power, are overcome. This means responding to market failures and imperfect competition and identifying new opportunities that take advantage of the assets of the poor, such as labor and natural resources.

- Project support should include management capacity building for the community administration. In addition to technical skills, training should cover participatory planning, monitoring, and periodic updating of community development plans.

- Individual families should be supported. Collective activities are not always the best approach for community forestry, especially tree planting activities—smallholder farmers should be supported in this process.

- In addition to traditional management of highly stocked forests, secondary forests and low-density woodlands offer good opportunities for community management, because they offer multiple agroforestry services and higher flexibility for forest management.

- Customary claims and particular rights of Indigenous Peoples and other forest-dependent communities should be addressed.

SELECTED READINGS

Agrawal, A., and C. Gibson, eds. 2001. *Communities and the Environment: Ethnicity, Gender, and the State in Community-Based Conservation.* Piscataway, NJ: Rutgers University Press.

Gibson, C. C., J. T. Williams, and E. Ostrom. 2005. "Local Enforcement and Better Forests." *World Development* 33 (2): 273–84.

Ostrom, E. 1999. "Self Governance and Forest Resources." CIFOR Occasional Paper No. 29. Bogor, Indonesia.

Ribot, J. 2002. *Democratic Decentralization of Natural Resources: Institutionalizing Popular Participation.* Washington, DC: World Resources Institute.

USAID (U.S. Agency for International Development), with CIFOR, Winrock International, WRI, and International Research Group on Wood Protection (IRG). 2004. *Nature, Wealth, and Power: Emerging Best Practice for Revitalizing Rural Africa.* Washington, DC: USAID.

REFERENCES CITED

Borrini-Feyerabend, G., M. Pimbert, M. T. Farvar, A. Kothari, and Y. Renard. 2004. "Sharing Power. Learning by Doing in Co-management of Natural Resources Throughout the World." CENESTA, Tehran: IIED and IUCN/CEESP/CMWG.

Bray, D. B., L. Merino-Perez, and D. Barry, eds. 2005. *The Community Forests of Mexico: Managing for Sustainable Landscapes.* Austin, TX: University of Texas Press.

Clay, J. W., J. B. Alcorn, and J. R. Butler. 2000. "Indigenous Peoples, Forestry Management and Biodiversity Conservation." Report to the World Bank, prepared by WWF-US, Washington, DC.

IFRI. 2000. International Forestry Resources and Institutions Research Program. Indiana University, Bloomington, IN. http://www.indiana.edu/~ifri/.

IUCN and WWF. 2004. "Who Owns, Who Conserves, and Why It Matters." *Arborvitae: The IUCN/WWF Conservation Newsletter*, Vol. 26, September.

Kaimowitz, D. 2005. "The International Experience with Community Forestry." In *Proceedings of the First International Workshop on Community Forestry in Liberia, Monrovia, 12-15 December 2005,* 17–19. Bogor: CIFOR.

OED (Operations Evaluation Department). 2000. *Cameroon: Forest Sector Development in a Difficult Political Economy.* Washington, DC: World Bank.

WATCH (Women Acting Together for Change). 2004. Homepage http://www.watch.org.np/.

White, A., and A. Martin. 2002. *Who Owns the World's Forests? Forest Tenure and Public Forests in Transition.* Washington, DC: Forest Trends.

World Bank, 1978. *Forestry*. Sector Policy Paper. Report No. 11021. Washington, DC.

———. 2002. Project Appraisal Document, Andhra Pradesh Community Forest Management Project (P073094). Report No. 24184. World Bank, Washington, DC.

———. 2005. "Unlocking Opportunities for Forest-Dependent People in India." Sector Report No. 34481, World Bank, Washington, DC.

World Bank OED (Operations Evaluation Department). 2000. *Cameroon: Forest Sector Development in a Difficult Political Economy.* Washington, DC: World Bank.

CROSS-REFERENCED CHAPTERS AND NOTES

Note 1.1: Mainstreaming the Role of Forests in Poverty Alleviation: Measuring Poverty-Forest Linkages

Note 1.3: Indigenous Peoples and Forests

Note 1.4: Property and Access Rights

Note 1.5: Making Markets Work for the Forest-Dependent Poor

Note 5.1: Decentralized Forest Management

NOTE 1.3

Indigenous Peoples and Forests

It is estimated that worldwide 60 million Indigenous Peoples are highly dependent on forest resources for their livelihoods. Forests and other natural resources are the foundation for most Indigenous Peoples' livelihoods, social organization, identities, and cultural survival, which are based on a strong and deeply rooted historic relationship with their ancestral lands and natural resources. This relationship has cultural, socioeconomic, and spiritual dimensions and has influenced customary institutions and practices for managing land and resources.

The identities and cultures of Indigenous Peoples are inextricably linked to the lands on which they live and the natural resources on which they depend. This deeply rooted link informs their livelihoods, social organization, identities, and cultural survival. It also informs their perceptions of poverty, well-being, and "the good life," which often differ from those of mainstream society as well as of other rural communities. Their patterns of land use and relationship with land and resources may also translate into different goals and models for development—for example, developers may want to extract natural resources for economic gain, while indigenous communities may want to leave the environment and resources intact, providing them with their livelihoods and spiritual links to their ancestors.

Indigenous Peoples have specific rights relevant for forest-based projects. The rights and concerns of Indigenous Peoples have been internationally recognized, foremost through International Labour Organization (ILO) Convention 169. The convention affirms the way of life of indigenous and tribal peoples, recognizes the need to safeguard their customary rights to land and natural resources, and stresses that they should benefit equally from economic and social development and that they and their traditional organizations should be closely involved in the planning and implementation of development projects that affect them.

Specifically concerning biodiversity and sustainable natural resource management, Agenda 21, adopted by the United Nations Conference on Environment and Development (UNCED) in 1992, as well as the Rio Declaration, recognize the actual and potential contributions of indigenous and tribal peoples to sustainable development. The 1992 Convention on Biological Diversity (CBD) calls on contracting parties to respect traditional indigenous knowledge with regard to the preservation of biodiversity and its sustainable use. The CBD has been a key vehicle for enhancing Indigenous Peoples' rights to their resources and their participation in biodiversity conservation and management. Indigenous Peoples are represented in the Conference of Parties of the CBD, which recognizes traditional knowledge and cultural heritage as conservation values.

In October 2007, the United Nations' General Assembly adopted the UN Declaration on the Rights of Indigenous Peoples. The declaration, while nonbinding, sets international standards for the protection and promotion of the individual and collective rights of Indigenous Peoples, including their rights to land and natural resources, and advocates a human rights–based approach to development as it applies to Indigenous Peoples.

These and other international conventions and agreements, along with the World Bank's Indigenous Peoples policy (OP 4.10), provide an important context for World Bank–assisted, forest-related projects affecting Indigenous Peoples. Through OP 4.10, the World Bank recognizes the rights of Indigenous Peoples as addressed in international and national law and agreements. The policy acknowledges the vital role that Indigenous Peoples play in sustainable development, and calls for special considerations when projects affect the close ties that they have to land, forests, water, wildlife, and other natural resources. Specifically for projects supporting parks and protected areas, the policy states that the World Bank "recognizes the significance of

[Indigenous Peoples'] rights of ownership, occupation, or usage, as well as the need for long-term sustainable management of critical ecosystems" (OP 4.10 paragraph 21). OP 4.12 on Involuntary Resettlement also includes provisions for participatory natural resource management as well as mitigation measures for impacts from involuntary restrictions of access to legally designated parks and protected areas. (See section II of this sourcebook for more guidance on application of the World Bank's safeguard policies.)

Forestry projects, including policy-based lending, investment projects, and other types of projects affecting forest areas where Indigenous Peoples live, are particularly sensitive given the special relationship between Indigenous Peoples and their lands and natural resources. Forests can play a vital role in relation to livelihoods, sustainability of cultures, and development of Indigenous Peoples. In turn, Indigenous Peoples represent important stakeholders in the sustainable management of forest areas, and their involvement entails a range of challenges and opportunities that need careful assessment, often in a site-specific context. Finally, forest projects, if not properly designed and implemented, can have a variety of adverse impacts on the livelihoods and cultures of Indigenous Peoples. It is thus essential that any forest-related project in areas with Indigenous Peoples thoroughly assess and address any issues pertaining to them and involve consultation with these communities.

OPERATIONAL ASPECTS

A key aspect of forest activities involving Indigenous Peoples is to acknowledge that development practitioners should not assume that indigenous world views about land and natural resources, as well as development priorities, are the same as those that may be commonly held by government and development agencies. The analysis of and approach to development in indigenous contexts must, therefore, take into consideration the specific understanding of the natural world among Indigenous Peoples and be based on meaningful consultation with, and participation of, local communities.

INDIGENOUS PEOPLES' RELATIONSHIP TO LAND AND NATURAL RESOURCES. Indigenous Peoples' special relationship with their lands and natural resources often makes them vulnerable to development efforts. The special relationship that Indigenous Peoples have with their land and natural resources, along with their historical marginalization, may also result in significant impacts from development activities, which, again, may vary substantially from those on other rural communities. Indigenous Peoples historically have experienced unequal and inequitable development and have frequently been economically, politically, and socially marginalized. They often lack entitlements in national legislation and development processes as well as respect for their cultures, lifestyles, livelihood models, and natural resource management practices.

Moreover, Indigenous Peoples are often present in, and claim ownership of, areas with rich forest and other natural resources, leading to potential conflicts over such resources. They may endure proportionally high impacts from increased pressures on the land and resources as a result of development interventions as well as from general trends of agricultural expansion and resource extraction. In addition to the risk of losing land and access to natural resources, the languages, world views, social organization, cultures, and values of Indigenous Peoples are in danger of further erosion or disappearance when development interventions fail to recognize the close link between Indigenous Peoples and their lands and natural resources.

Forest-based projects and programs should be planned with these opportunities, differences, and risks in mind. They require special attention and measures to ensure that the unique ties between Indigenous Peoples and their lands are given full weight in the design of projects and programs. This may result in specific activities to support and protect Indigenous Peoples' rights and well-being, developed in consultation with the affected communities.

USE OF POLICY ANALYSIS IN INVESTMENT AND POLICY LENDING. World Bank operations, both investment and policy lending, involving forests and Indigenous Peoples require careful policy analysis. This analysis frequently identifies reform initiatives that would improve the overall policy framework. Key policy issues for Indigenous Peoples include tenure, harvest and marketing policies, governance issues, fiscal policies, decentralization, attitudes of the dominant culture toward forest uses, environmental and social policies, and technical guidelines. Some of these are discussed below (see also chapter 6, Mainstreaming Forests into Development Policy and Planning: Assessing Cross-Sectoral Impacts).

- *Tenure not only of forest land but also of rights to the use of forest products.* Indigenous Peoples' cultural attitudes toward claims of natural resource ownership and associated stewardship responsibilities are important, as are considerations involving individual versus community forms of tenure, and existence of and requirements for tenure adjudication and documentation. Policy analysis of tenure issues also needs to take into consideration the broader political economy and phasing of policies or institutions affecting the sector (see further discussion on tenure below).

- *Harvesting and marketing of forest products.* Where communities in forest areas are interested in economic use of forest products, the objective of harvest and marketing policies should be to maximize returns from forest products to Indigenous Peoples and other forest-dependent communities on an environmentally and fiscally sustainable basis (see note 1.5, Making Markets Work for the Forest-Dependent Poor, for points on what policy reform should address).
- *Governance.* Governance policies on transparency, accountability, grievance mechanisms, and independent review modalities are important to forest operations involving Indigenous Peoples. Forest-rich countries, where forest resources are being "mined" or exploited extensively and exported, often involve significant rent-seeking and revenue leakage. Efforts to address these challenging governance issues and associated vested interests can be especially beneficial to most Indigenous Peoples in forest areas, and inattention to these issues can be especially harmful (see chapter 5, Improving Forest Governance).
- *Fiscal policies.* Government services and programs targeting Indigenous Peoples in remote forest areas are often poorly funded. In addition, the unit cost of service provision is frequently higher, and there is limited availability of expertise tailored for Indigenous Peoples contexts. Public expenditure review and reform should address these problems caused by market and policy distortions, streamlining fund flow mechanisms, adjusting budget parameters, providing incentive payments, and correcting incentive distortions where necessary (see note 5.4, Strengthening Fiscal Systems in the Forest Sector).
- *Community institutions and decentralization.* Policies on indigenous community institutions are important to CBFM. Where indigenous communities are culturally homogeneous with strong social cohesion, key issues usually involve the extent to which the official structure reflects and acknowledges traditional decision-making systems and the extent of delegated authority and autonomy. Where they involve heterogeneous groups and interests, institutional systems and decentralization efforts also need to include effective modalities to negotiate the differing perspectives and relative levels of empowerment.

- *Values and attitudes of mainstream culture.* Some countries regulate forest use based on the attitudes and values of the mainstream culture in ways that do not accommodate traditional uses by Indigenous Peoples. Typical issues of contention include communal ownership, recognition or nonrecognition of sacred sites in forest areas, regulation or prohibition of hunting, and prohibition of shifting cultivation. Policy reforms may be needed to recognize, and improve the level of understanding by the majority culture of, Indigenous Peoples' resource use and management practices. Improvements in traditional practices that enhance sustainability and natural resources while still recognizing Indigenous Peoples' rights and cultures may be contemplated.

USE OF SECTOR ANALYSIS IN INVESTMENT AND POLICY LENDING. Sector analysis on Indigenous Peoples and forests may provide useful information and dialogue opportunities to inform investment and policy lending. The interactions of Indigenous Peoples and forests have been increasingly taken into consideration as part of broader country economic and sector analysis and the development of country assistance strategies. The Independent Evaluation Group (IEG, formerly the Operations Evaluation Department) has included Indigenous Peoples issues in forest sector country case studies for Brazil (Uma and others 2000), India (Kumar and others 2000), and Indonesia (Gautam and others 2000), all noting the importance of access to land and natural resources for Indigenous Peoples. More recently, analytical efforts have also been associated with poverty reduction strategies, as well as World Bank–wide reviews and formulations of strategies on forests, rural development, environment, and Indigenous Peoples. The degree of focus on forests and Indigenous Peoples has varied considerably across countries, depending on their relative extent and importance, the receptivity of governments to policy dialogue on these issues, World Bank staff expertise and capacity, and the concern and commitment of regional Bank management relative to other development issues. However, given the important role that Indigenous Peoples can play in the forest sector, and the risks to which they may be exposed, it is essential that forest sector analysis include analysis of Indigenous Peoples for countries where they are present.

INFORMED PARTICIPATION OF INDIGENOUS PEOPLES. Informed consultation with and participation of Indigenous Peoples are essential for successful forest-based activities. Their particular rights, circumstances, and needs often render standard development approaches and assumptions inadequate or inappropriate. Thus, development projects affecting Indigenous Peoples need to be prepared in full consultation with affected communities and their informed participation should be ensured during project implementation (see OP 4.10, paragraph 1, and chapter 12, Applying OP 4.10 on Indigenous Peoples, in section II of this sourcebook).

IEG evaluations of community participation in World Bank–assisted projects have found that when primary stakeholders—individuals and community-based organizations—participate in World Bank activities, development relevance and outcomes improve. Project-supported activities tend to be more sustainable, and there is less corruption because processes are more transparent and government officials are held accountable to the people they serve (World Bank OED 2001, 2005). Specific benefits concerning Indigenous Peoples include the following:

- Project development recognizes Indigenous Peoples' rights to be consulted on, and participate in, development efforts that affect them, whether positively or adversely.
- Participation increases the likelihood of active engagement by affected communities and community ownership of project activities.
- Indigenous Peoples are enabled to make informed decisions on projects that will affect them.
- Project design and implementation are based on the realities of particular communities and their involvement with forest-related project activities, and the project is more likely to provide culturally appropriate benefits.

Consulting with Indigenous Peoples can be demanding and time consuming. The consultation process should include participatory methodologies to ensure participation and voice of marginalized social groups within affected communities, to build community consensus, to enhance transparency, and to ensure local ownership of the process (see box 1.15). Use of traditional decision-making processes that are familiar to local communities, along with skilled facilitation and capacity-building activities, will usually enhance the process and outcome (see chapter 10, Consultation and Communications in Forest Activities, in section II of this sourcebook).

MECHANISMS FOR ONGOING PARTICIPATION OF INDIGENOUS PEOPLES. Detailed arrangements for ongoing participation of Indigenous Peoples and OP 4.10 complaint mechanisms should be included in project design. Local communities' participation must be clearly spelled out in project preparation and implementation plans, describing the roles

---

> ### Box 1.15 Brazil Santa Catarina Natural Resource Management and Rural Poverty Reduction Project
>
> This project, aiming to empower local communities to better manage their natural resources, used innovative methods to consult with affected Indigenous Peoples during project preparation. Initially, an interinstitutional committee, including representatives from government, NGOs, and academia began working on project design with Indigenous Peoples. A two-phased approach was developed to carry out consultations in a way that facilitated the communities' informed participation in designing the project. For the first phase, expert facilitators already familiar with the specific indigenous groups were contracted to develop dissemination materials together with indigenous students and to visit villages to present the project and the ideas for working with Indigenous Peoples. This laid a solid foundation for understanding the proposed project and activities specifically for Indigenous Peoples.
>
> The second phase of the consultations was a series of larger formal meetings between representatives selected by the Indigenous Peoples, in the location of their choice, with representatives of the project staff. Thanks to the initial field work that disseminated project information using culturally appropriate methods, including indigenous languages and specially designed graphics, the formal meetings were very productive. The Indigenous Peoples' representatives had had information and time needed to better understand the project, to form their opinions, and to make suggestions and recommendations for project design. As a result, the Indigenous Peoples felt their voices had been heard, and project staff received detailed feedback on how best to reflect Indigenous Peoples' concerns in the project design and Indigenous Peoples Development Plan (the project was prepared under OD 4.20).
>
> *Source:* Authors' compilation using World Bank 2002a.

---

and responsibilities of various stakeholders (see chapter 12, Applying OP 4.10 on Indigenous Peoples, in section II of this sourcebook). Activities to build the capacity of local communities to participate may be necessary. In projects involving Indigenous Peoples and forests, communication and conflict management measures help to build understanding, manage expectations, and address grievances. Given the range and variation of stakeholders, this frequently involves the development and implementation of a communication strategy that takes into account various audiences, culturally appropriate forms of communication, and provisions for two-way communication flows. Conflict management involves capacity and skill development. Grievance procedures frequently build on existing mechanisms and consideration of informal customary mechanisms is particularly important.

Indigenous Peoples' organizations, NGOs, academics, and others with appropriate experience and skills may play an important facilitation role in developing participatory processes and addressing social and environmental concerns related to Indigenous Peoples. If appropriate Indigenous Peoples' organizations or local NGOs cannot be identified, it may be necessary to consider arranging for services from national or international Indigenous Peoples' organizations or NGOs, building the capacity of existing local Indigenous Peoples' organizations and NGOs, or hiring consultants with comparable skills. It is important to be aware of external organizations that may claim to represent Indigenous Peoples and to confirm their legitimacy and acceptance by the affected communities. Irrespective of the entity contracted, it is important that it is acceptable to the affected communities, and is able to facilitate trust and cooperation. Good communication, coordination arrangements, and strategies that encourage ongoing learning and evolution in relationships will be key to successful partnerships with Indigenous Peoples' organizations, NGOs, and other civil society institutions.

SOCIAL ASSESSMENTS IN PROJECT DESIGN FOR INDIGENOUS PEOPLES AND FORESTS. Detailed social assessment of issues pertaining to Indigenous Peoples and forests is needed to inform project design. Forest projects provide opportunities as well as risks for Indigenous Peoples. These should be assessed thoroughly during project preparation, as part of the social assessment and as part of free, prior, and informed consultation processes, and addressed in project design and the design and implementation instruments used to address Indigenous Peoples' concerns. The specific relationship between Indigenous Peoples and the environment in the project area should be investigated, including aspects of natural resource use practices that may enhance or diminish biodiversity and natural resources, keeping in mind that sometimes assumptions about such practices can be misguided, politically motivated, or based on values of the dominant cultural model rather than the reality in specific situations. It is important that interventions be based on reliable facts obtained with the participation of local communities and through field-based biological and social assessments.

The social issues concerning Indigenous Peoples and forests are extensive and complex. Key issues include rights to, and conflicts over, forest resources, local livelihoods and natural resource management practices, social organization and sociocultural diversity, indigenous knowledge, gender and intergenerational issues, social and political risks, and vulnerabilities of local communities. (See World Bank 1997, World Bank 2005, and section II of this Sourcebook for more details on social analysis in natural resource management projects.)

INSTITUTIONAL AND STAKEHOLDER ANALYSIS. Institutional and stakeholder analysis helps identify opponents and proponents of project activities. It also identifies norms, rules, and behavior that may enhance or hinder successful project implementation. Forest management involves multiple stakeholder interests. In most countries, balancing competing interests and objectives is and will remain a constant challenge in forest management. While often one can find "win-win" solutions, at other times addressing these various interests involves inherent tradeoffs and significant risks to project outcomes.

The interests, values, capacities, and dependency on forest resources of Indigenous Peoples' communities vary. There can be a variety of indigenous groups or subgroups that have different experiences and capabilities in forest management. Levels of cultural homogeneity, social cohesion, social inclusion, familiarity with and management skills in a cash economy, ability to defend interests in forests, and forest management practices may vary. All these differences lead to different priorities regarding forest management that have to be negotiated and addressed in project design and implementation. Adding to this complexity, many Indigenous Peoples today live in mixed communities together with, or in close proximity to, other social groups.

RECOGNIZING CUSTOMARY TENURE SYSTEMS. Community resource management mechanisms under customary tenure systems are recognized as having great potential in helping mitigate negative social and environmental impacts of development. Customary tenure is supported through growing recognition of legitimate rights to land and natural resources of Indigenous Peoples and other forest-dependent communities (see also note 1.4, Property and Access Rights).

Indigenous customary tenure structures are generally communal, indigenous rights are usually collective rights, and Indigenous Peoples more often than not claim some form of collective tenure. Separating indigenous community territory into individual plots, which may be attempted through forest and land use planning exercises, runs the risk of adversely affecting the livelihoods and social cohesion of indigenous communities. (See, for example, the Asian Development Bank-financed poverty assessment for Lao PDR [State Planning Committee 2000].) Individual tenure arrangements should be developed with care and only with the informed participation of the local communities.

IMPORTANCE OF LAND AND LONG-TERM RESOURCE USE RIGHTS. Most Indigenous Peoples see resource use tenure as essential for their livelihoods and cultural survival. Land tenure and long-term access to natural resources are essential for forest-related projects that affect Indigenous Peoples. Lack of, or insecure, tenure or short-term tenure or use rights arrangements are likely to prevent positive project outcomes and intensify degradation of forests. In contrast, secure land tenure and long-term tenure arrangements are likely to empower local communities to manage forests in sustainable ways.

While international law recognizes Indigenous Peoples' rights to ancestral land and natural resources, and some countries have begun to recognize these rights in national law, the situation is far from uniform. Many countries in Latin America (for example, Bolivia, Brazil, Colombia, Mexico, and Nicaragua) and the Philippines have assigned Indigenous Peoples large territories or enacted legislation recognizing their rights. Most other countries do not legally recognize indigenous land and resource use rights, and those that do, do not always protect such rights in practice. The situation is compounded by the fact that most indigenous areas have never been demarcated or titled, or lack documentation of such official conventions. Accordingly, ancestral lands as well as areas of current occupation and resource use (if these differ) are often without legal recognition or protection.

Forest-based projects should support land and long-term resource use rights of Indigenous Peoples where relevant. In countries with legislation supporting Indigenous Peoples' land and resource use rights, projects should incorporate activities that formalize and regularize them. Where the customary lands of Indigenous Peoples are legally under the domain of the state, or where it is otherwise inappropriate to convert traditional rights into those of legal ownership, alternative arrangements should be implemented to grant long-term, renewable rights of custodianship and use of forest areas to Indigenous Peoples (see OP 4.10 for more details). Where Indigenous Peoples are weak relative to private commercial interests, it may be useful to combine government ownership of forests with use rights to forest products for Indigenous

Peoples. Such a combination could help to protect Indigenous Peoples' interests as well as prevent conversion of forest land to nonforest uses in the short term. As needed, legal reforms should also be supported to enhance the recognition of land and resource use rights of Indigenous Peoples.

HISTORICAL AND POLITICAL CONTEXT TO ADDRESSING RIGHTS. To address the land and resource use rights of Indigenous Peoples, it is important to understand the historical and political context in the country and local area. Indigenous Peoples have varying cultural values regarding tenure over forest land and forest products that need to be understood and addressed in project design. The belief system of some Indigenous Peoples does not encompass the concept of natural resource "ownership" at all, which can affect the way they address customary tenure claims and rights as well as daily management of resources. Views on individual and collective tenure also vary. The extent to which tenure rights are linked to stewardship responsibilities also varies from group to group.

Historical, cultural, and socioeconomic studies combined with participatory methods and community mapping exercises can help build a good understanding of local communities, their cultures, resource use, and customary land and resource tenure arrangements. They may also help to build trust and avoid conflicts over land and resource use, provided that findings are incorporated into project design, including measures that recognize Indigenous Peoples' customary rights and continued access to sustainable resource use.

USE OF PARTNERSHIPS FOR ENHANCING PROTECTION AND SUSTAINABILITY. In the context of CBFM, work with Indigenous Peoples to enhance efforts to manage forest resources. Building efforts on current relationships between the environment and Indigenous Peoples can lead to win-win situations that enhance the protection of biodiversity and natural resources and at the same time support the cultures and sustainable livelihoods of local communities (see chapter 9, Applying Forests Policy OP 4.36, and chapter 12, Applying OP 4.10 on Indigenous Peoples, in section II of this sourcebook, and note 1.2, Community-Based Forest Management).

Experience has shown that true partnerships are difficult to attain for various reasons, such as continued focus on top-down approaches, conflicting interests, corruption, and limited capacity. Despite such difficulties, however, collaborative arrangements are gaining ground quickly because they can help resolve conflicts, foster learning during implementation, enhance management of forest resources and biodiversity, and support the livelihoods and cultures of local communities. They require time, resources, and a flexible approach that recognizes that while consensus is a useful goal, conflicts are likely to occur and management arrangements and grievance procedures should be enabled to address such conflicts. Collaborative arrangements and enhanced participation of local communities require capacity building as well as arrangements that institutionalize participation and representation of local communities in decision-making processes and bodies.

INDIGENOUS KNOWLEDGE AS A BASIS FOR CBFM. Indigenous knowledge and management practices should be the starting point for CBFM where appropriate. Indigenous Peoples' forest and natural resource management approaches vary in methods, complexity, and quality. Most often, though, Indigenous Peoples have managed natural resources soundly, providing their communities with food and other products without depleting the resource base. Their knowledge and practices should be the starting point for project activities, in combination with modern approaches appropriate for the local context. (See box 1.16.)

HUMAN RIGHTS IN FOREST CERTIFICATION. Certification schemes should include, in addition to sustainability principles, the rights of Indigenous Peoples. The voluntary forest certification system should cover human rights, including rights of Indigenous Peoples to land, resources, and cultural sites as well as their free, prior, and informed consent. This often goes beyond national forest regulations. (See chapter 11, Forest Certification Assessment Guide: Summary on Use, in section II of this sourcebook.)

IMPORTANCE OF SHORT-TERM AND EQUITABLE BENEFITS. Indigenous Peoples and other forest-dependent communities are likely to benefit from forest-related projects that address the issues discussed in this note. However, these benefits may materialize only in the long term if forestry production or improved natural resource management practices are implemented. In many cases, activities are needed to improve the livelihoods of local communities and ensure equitable benefits in the short term.

These activities commonly consist of culturally appropriate assistance in improving agricultural production, sustainable harvesting and processing (including organization and legal recognition), market access, and the value of forest products (for example, market studies, strategy development, and organization); and support to small businesses and to joint ventures selling cultural products or forest-

Box 1.16	India Andhra Pradesh Community Forestry Management Project

This project aims to reduce rural poverty through improved forest management, with specific community participation by tribal forest-dependent communities to assume full responsibility for the development of forest areas. One of the three main components is community development to improve village infrastructure and livelihoods, through forest- and nonforest-based income-generation activities. A tribal development plan is an integral subcomponent in preparing investment proposals. The tribal development plan includes activities to narrow the gap in the levels of tribal and nontribal development through deliberate actions for tribal socioeconomic development. This includes community investments (for example, community halls, wells) and creation of wage labor, both for work within the protected area (fire management, habitat restoration) and other conservation activities. At several other protected areas in the country, specific programs target tribal and special-needs groups: a tribal trekkers program at Periyar, ropemaking skills at Pench, and community agriculture at Gir.

Source: World Bank 2002.

based products, through employment in conservation activities and through ecotourism.

Improving forest-based livelihoods through better multicropping in swidden cultivation fields and sustainable use of nontimber forest products are useful approaches to providing benefits to Indigenous Peoples. Experiments in markets for environmental services are under way and should be extended to include Indigenous Peoples. The World Bank's BioCarbon Fund (BiCF) may support forest-dependent communities in earning revenues through carbon credits for planting and managing forests.

Work is ongoing to extend the benefits to Indigenous Peoples of the newly established Forest Carbon Partnership Facility (FCPF), which will support policy approaches and programs with positive incentives for reducing emissions from deforestation and degradation. The facility will also develop concrete activities to reach out to poor people who depend on forests to improve their livelihoods. Ongoing efforts and consultations with Indigenous Peoples and forest-dependent communities are developing appropriate mechanisms to ensure that these communities benefit from the FCPF.

LESSONS LEARNED AND RECOMMENDATIONS FOR PRACTITIONERS

The following summarizes lessons learned to date:[1]

- Tenure over land and resources is the most important element of Indigenous Peoples' survival and needs to be assessed and addressed in forest projects. Indigenous Peoples' rights to land and resources should be recognized and, if needed, appropriate legal frameworks should be developed to guarantee such rights.
- Effective management of forest resources is best accomplished through local participation. It should be built on finding common ground, allowing sufficient time for mutual understanding and acceptance of goals and strategies, creating and maintaining transparency throughout the process, and recognizing that goals will change and that collaboration does not mean consensus.
- For Indigenous Peoples, survival is cultural survival. Forestry activities are a means toward that end, not an end in themselves. For example, the survival of local languages is key to the maintenance of local ecological knowledge and values. Indigenous Peoples should participate in activities supporting their intellectual property rights and bioprospecting.
- Too often, Indigenous Peoples have been seen only as laborers, park guards, or gatherers or producers of raw materials. Small businesses and joint ventures in which Indigenous Peoples retain an equity share in products as they move through the market chain should be supported.
- Efforts should be focused on sustainable timber management because ecotourism, nontimber forest products, bioprospecting, the sale of intellectual property, or even the sale of carbon rights will not generate the same levels of income for Indigenous Peoples in the short to medium term as logging.
- Alternative development efforts need to be designed to match or complement local skills. These efforts need to place equal emphasis on income generation and sustainable resource use in addition to addressing the steep learning curves of groups that are often only now entering the market economy.

Lessons have also been learned from Inspection Panel cases involving forest activities affecting Indigenous Peoples in Cambodia and Democratic Republic of Congo. These include the need to (i) analyze the current situation of Indigenous Peoples, not only in project areas, but in the country as a whole, to assess ongoing support and outreach efforts, as well as to undertake dialogue on any policy or legal reforms that

affect them; (ii) identify early on any potential impacts on, and benefits to, Indigenous Peoples, including any special needs and targeted poverty reduction activities; (iii) ensure a well-developed plan for consultation and participation of affected Indigenous Peoples and other forest-dependent communities; (iv) address adverse impacts from forest activities (for example, restrictions of access to, or logging in, areas of indigenous resource use and cultural sites), which may result equally from investment and policy lending activities; (v) undertake capacity-building activities in traditional and other sectors that are relevant to and that engage Indigenous Peoples.

A number of Bank-assisted projects have supported forest-based activities with Indigenous Peoples' communities. The Brazil Indigenous Lands Project supported the conservation of natural resources in indigenous areas and the well-being of Indigenous Peoples through regularization of indigenous lands in the Legal Amazon, and improved protection of Indigenous Peoples and their land. It has been innovative in improving technical quality and Indigenous Peoples' participation in and control of the processes of regularizing, protecting, and managing their lands. A methodology for ethno-ecological assessments of indigenous lands was developed to combine traditional knowledge with scientific information and provide a practical and flexible tool for investigating human-environment interactions. Some of the challenges the project confronted included securing involvement of the right experts; difficulties of organizing work in remote locations and timing it with seasonal conditions; and institutional weaknesses of Brazil's National Indian Foundation (FUNAI), the agency responsible for Indigenous Peoples. Involvement of multiple agencies, uncertainties concerning the legal aspects of natural resource use in Indigenous Peoples' areas, and conflicts between Indigenous Peoples and local and national stakeholders (for example, neighboring ranchers and conservation organizations) hampered progress on protecting Indigenous Peoples' lands and limited sustainable development efforts to enhance Indigenous Peoples' well-being (see World Bank 2007 and Lisansky 2004).

Lessons from the Colombia Natural Resource Management (NRM) Program, supporting improved natural resource management through CBFM and land titling activities, include local participation in NRM activities takes time, often requiring changes in the overall climate between different groups; Indigenous Peoples' organizations can play a significant role in monitoring the actions of government agencies; and collective land titling often faces resistance from government and other stakeholders (see Clay, Alcorn, and Butler 2000).

The Mexico Community Forestry Projects are excellent examples of the benefits that supporting CBFM activities with Indigenous Peoples can offer. Sophisticated forest management, product processing, and marketing have enhanced participating communities' livelihoods and improved natural resource management (box 1.17).

RECOMMENDATIONS FOR FUTURE ACTIVITIES. This note has discussed some of the operational aspects and lessons learned concerning forest-based projects affecting Indigenous Peoples. These can be summarized into the following key recommendations for future forestry activities involving Indigenous Peoples:

- Recognize Indigenous Peoples' rights to their land and natural resources, and to benefits from development activities, as well as the need for consultation and participation throughout the planning, implementation, monitoring, and evaluation processes.
- Base project preparation and implementation on well-prepared and well-executed consultations with Indigenous Peoples and sound social and institutional analysis providing a thorough understanding of the local context and affected communities.
- Ensure that project activities affecting Indigenous Peoples are based on a sound process of free, prior, and informed consultations with affected communities leading to broad community support.

- Support CBFM, emphasizing community ownership and collaborative arrangements (see note 1.2, Community-Based Forest Management).
- Support livelihood activities and ensure equitable benefits to affected Indigenous Peoples.
- Pay attention to the requirements of the Bank's Indigenous Peoples policy (OP 4.10) early on in project preparation, and make clear agreements with the borrower well before project appraisal.

NOTE

1. To inform the World Bank's Forest Policy Implementation Review and Strategy Development Framework, an independent study was undertaken to assess how the Bank has addressed the issue of Indigenous Peoples in selected World Bank and GEF-funded forestry and biodiversity conservation projects in Colombia, Indonesia, Mexico, Papua New Guinea, and Siberia (Clay, Alcorn, and Butler 2000). The lessons learned and recommendations are drawn from that study.

SELECTED READINGS

Beltran, J. ed. 2000. "Indigenous and Traditional Peoples and Protected Areas: Principles, Guidelines and Case Studies." IUCN and Cardiff University, Cardiff, Wales.

Box 1.17   Mexico First and Second Community Forestry Projects

The objectives of these two Community Forestry Projects (also titled PROCYMAF I and II) are to assist Indigenous Peoples' communities and *ejidos* (communal land owning units) in different priority regions of Mexico to improve the management and conservation of their forest resources and to generate alternative sources of income in a sustainable manner. Lessons from these projects suggest that community forestry is an effective instrument for sustainable rural development, building on existing local economic, social, and biophysical conditions and encompassing the development of social capital (based on traditional forms of governance), a minimum base of natural capital (forest resources with commercial value), and the development of technical and administrative capacity (human capital) at the community level to enhance decision-making powers.

The first project focused its community forestry activ-

ities on diagnostics and participatory planning aimed at self-management, including the financing of Participatory Rural Appraisals, enabling indigenous communities to take a more active role in natural resource management decisions based on an improved understanding of their needs, capabilities, and interests. In this way the project was successful in empowering local communities to improve management of their forest resources and expanding their options for income generation.

While the first project helped increase the competitiveness of community forest enterprises and opened up new markets for certified forest products from Mexico, a key lesson learned was the need to include significant funding for productive activities, particularly for processes that add market value to forest products and achieve economies of scale through community associations and strategic partnerships with the private sector.

Source: World Bank 2004. See also box 1.13 for discussion of the Community Forestry Project in Mexico (Project for Conservation and Sustainable Management of Forest Resources).

Borrini-Feyerabend, G., M. Pimbert, M. T. Farvar, A. Kothari, and Y. Renard. 2004. *Sharing Power: Learning by Doing in Co-management of Natural Resources Throughout the World*. CENESTA, Tehran: IIED and IUCN/CEESP/CMWG.

Clay, J. W., J. B. Alcorn, and J. R. Butler. 2000. "Indigenous Peoples, Forestry Management and Biodiversity Conservation." World Bank, Washington, DC.

Collier, R., B. Parfitt, and D. Woollard. 2002. "A Voice on the Land: An Indigenous Peoples' Guide to Forest Certification in Canada." National Aboriginal Forestry Association, Ottawa, and Ecotrust Canada, Vancouver.

Cruz, M. C. J., and S. H. Davis. 1997. "Social Assessment in World Bank and GEF-Funded Biodiversity Conservation Projects: Cases Studies from India, Ecuador, and Ghana." Working Paper No. 18176, World Bank, Washington, DC.

Davis, S. H., J. Uquillas, and M. Eltz. 2004. "Lessons of Indigenous Development in Latin America: The Proceedings of a World Bank Workshop on Indigenous Peoples Development." Sustainable Development Working Paper No. 20, World Bank, Washington, DC.

International Working Group for Indigenous Affairs. Not dated. "Indigenous Peoples, Forest, and Biodiversity." International Alliance of Indigenous-Tribal Peoples of the Tropical Forest, and International Work Group for Indigenous Affairs, Copenhagen.

Ortega, R. 2004. "Models for Recognizing Indigenous Land Rights in Latin America." Environment Department Working Paper No. 99, World Bank, Washington, DC.

Reichel-Dolmatoff, G. 1996. *The Forest Within: The Worldview of the Tukano Amazonian Indians*. Dartington, U.K.: Themis Books.

Stevens, S. ed. 1997. *Conservation Through Cultural Survival: Indigenous Peoples and Protected Areas*. Washington, DC: Island Press.

REFERENCES CITED

Clay, J. W., J. B. Alcorn, and J. R. Butler. 2000. "Indigenous Peoples, Forestry Management and Biodiversity Conservation." World Bank, Washington, DC.

Gautam, M., U. Lele, H. Kartodihardjo, A. Khan, I. Erwinsyah, S. Rana. 2000. *Indonesia. The Challenges of World Bank Involvement in Forests*. OED Evaluation Country Case Study Series. Washington, DC: World Bank.

Kumar, N., N. Saxena, Y. Alagh, K. Mitra. 2000. *India. Alleviating Poverty Through Forest Development*. OED Evaluation Country Case Study Series. Washington, DC: World Bank.

Lele, U., V. Viana, A. Verissimo, S. Vosti, K. Perkins, S. Arif Husain. 2000. *Brazil. Forests in the Balance: Challenges of Conservation with Development*. OED Evaluation Country Case Study Series. Washington, DC: World Bank.

Lisansky, J. 2004. "Fostering Change for Brazilian Indigenous People during the Past Decade: The Pilot Program's Indigenous Lands Project." In S. H. Davis, J. Uquillas, and M. Eltz, "Lessons of Indigenous Development in Latin America," 31–43. World Bank, Washington, DC.

State Planning Committee and National Statistical Centre. 2000. "Poverty in the Lao PDR: Participatory Poverty Assessment." Vientiane: State Planning Committee.

World Bank. 1997. "Introduction to Environmental and Social Assessment Requirements and Procedures for World Bank-Financed Projects." Environment Department Report No. 26115. World Bank, Washington, DC.

———. 2002a. Project Appraisal Document, Natural Resource Management and Rural Poverty Reduction Project—Santa Catarina (P043869). Report No. 23299. World Bank, Washington, DC.

———. 2002b. Project Appraisal Document, Andhra Pradesh Community Forest Management Project (P073094). Report No. 24184-IN. World Bank, Washington, DC.

———. 2004. Implementation Completion Report for Mexico Community Forestry Project. Report No. 29582. World Bank, Washington, DC.

———. 2005. "Social Analysis Guidelines in Natural Resource Management: Incorporating Social Dimensions into Bank-Supported Projects." Social Development Department, World Bank, Washington, DC.

———. 2007. Brazil Indigenous Lands Project. ICR0000338. World Bank, Washington, DC.

World Bank OED. 2001. "Participation in Development Assistance." Precis No. 209, World Bank, Washington, DC.

———. 2005. *The Effectiveness of World Bank Support for Community-Based and -Driven Development: An OED Evaluation*. Washington, DC: World Bank.

CROSS-REFERENCED CHAPTERS AND NOTES

Note 1.2: Community-Based Forest Management

Note 1.4: Property and Access Rights

Note 1.5: Making Markets Work for the Forest-Dependent Poor

Chapter 5: Improving Forest Governance

Note 5.4: Strengthening Fiscal Systems in the Forest Sector

Chapter 6: Mainstreaming Forests into Development Policy: Assessing Cross-Sectoral Impacts

Section II: Guide to Implementing Forests Policy OP 4.36

Property and Access Rights

In many countries, most of the forest estate remains publicly owned and managed, despite legitimate local claims to the forests, extensive occupation by agrarian people, and the limited ability of governments to protect these vast resources. Legal frameworks and rural land-use policies often discourage or deny local people's rights to own, use, and trade their forest products and services. A current dilemma is the complementarity between these frameworks and policies and environmental laws and regulations, which may evolve with limited attention to tenure and rights implications.

Development projects promoting agriculture expansion, large-scale irrigation, and industrial (and mining) development have often impinged on forest areas and forest inhabitants. Often, indigenous and forest-dependent communities do not directly benefit from these activities. Similarly, forestry projects that deal with industrial and logging concessions, government-controlled logging quotas, protected area enlargements, and plantation developments can, if not appropriately designed and planned, affect tenure and customary rights of indigenous and other forest communities. Most of these forestry projects affect traditional forest users, those with ancestral forest rights, shifting cultivators, and NTFP gatherers (such as in Cambodia, Lao PDR, and Vietnam). Operationally, it is difficult to avoid these undesirable impacts in absence of clarity on tenure and property rights (see note 1.3, Indigenous Peoples and Forests).

Emerging payment schemes and markets for ecosystem services, such as water flow and biodiversity conservation, present both similar and special sets of issues for forest tenure and property rights. Unless done properly, poor people are less likely to participate in these markets because of their inability to assume risk, the lack of organization to create economies of scale, limited land and investment capital, and often unclear property and use rights. These emerging markets can be a means for government and local communities to enhance forest rights in a pilot watershed credits or a carbon credits scheme and provide complementary technical support, as well as providing additional returns to poor producers managing forests on the margin. If not done sensitively, they can, however, also set dangerous precedents by introducing new uncertainties—deeming shifting cultivation or other traditional practices unacceptable, establishing long-term contracts in regions where forest tenure is contested, extinguishing traditional use and access, and raising the price of forests beyond the reach of local people.

Clearly defined rights are essential if the forest-dependent poor are to improve their income and well-being. If individuals, communities, and businesses are to invest in forest resources, take responsibility for their conservation, and participate regularly and openly in the marketplace, they need to be confident of their property rights. Growing evidence from around the world demonstrates that recognizing local rights and improving local governance is politically feasible. It is also a cost-effective strategy for rural poverty alleviation.

Emerging trends show that more countries are now actively engaged in reforming their forest land and management practices. Many communities and Indigenous Peoples are asserting their rights to manage their forests, and some governments are introducing substantive changes to forest tenure and to policies and rules governing markets, and linking these to agrarian and related sector policies. The forest sector is now undergoing important reforms, arguably the most important set of policy and market shifts since the end of the colonial era, and these present historic opportunities for, and sometimes threats to, the well-being—livelihoods, rights, freedom and choices, and culture—of the 1.6 billion poor people who live in and around forests. These reforms affect the way in which forest people manage and conserve forests and affect the provisioning of forest environmental goods and services that benefit society as a whole.

In what are considered public forest lands, there has been recognition of community or collective and individual property rights in some forests, including special rights of Indigenous Peoples, and elaboration of comanagement arrangements for other public forests. Complementary to introducing reforms in forest and land tenure, governments across the world are now beginning to reassess legal and regulatory frameworks and the way in which they allocate subsidies, provide privileged access to publicly owned forests, and monitor the resulting impacts. Many countries are also engaged in a process of decentralization.

In Canada, India, Indonesia, Malaysia, Nicaragua, and the Philippines, recognition of indigenous and community rights has at times been the subject of major national debate and conflict, though each country has also had examples of notable progress in dealing with these issues. Similar issues have occurred in Bolivia, Brazil, Chile, Ecuador, Guatemala, Honduras, and Peru. In many of these countries significant forest areas have been recognized as indigenous territories or reserves, and increasing areas of public forest are considered for community concessions. One of the most recent notable advances can be found in Guatemala.

Designation of public forests as community forest is expanding in Africa—as in Burkina Faso, Cameroon, The Gambia, Mozambique, Rwanda, Senegal, Tanzania, Uganda, and Zimbabwe—but effective handover has been extremely limited, either by severely degraded forests or under institutional arrangements that are impractical or conflict with local organization. Even in countries with the most extensive forest areas in public concessions—Canada, Cambodia, Democratic Republic of Congo, Republic of Congo, Lao PDR, and the Russian Federation—tenure shifts are under discussion. China's allocation of more than 100 million hectares of collective forests, and plantation success in these forests, supports deepening of collective rights and extending favorable policies to local communities.

OPERATIONAL ASPECTS

There are multiple dimensions to tenure security, which go beyond the simple recognition of property rights. Policies have failed to differentiate between tenure to recognize the nuances of private, public, collective, and common property, and open access (see box 1.18). Often, government statistics on land ownership mask or distort reality, leading to disregard for important property and use rights and tenure patterns, or poorly designed regulatory frameworks and permit controls.

DEVOLUTION OF RIGHTS. Devolution of rights to forest land and resources is severely impeded in many places by the remnants of colonial legal frameworks and by a system of subsidies and incentives; these need serious reform if tenure rights are to become meaningful to poor forest communities. Some operational steps to consider in cooperation with client governments include the following:

- reforming models of forest conservation to genuinely include populations living in and around protected areas
- considering and recognizing grazing rights and other agropastoral systems in forested landscapes
- reforming adverse systems of direct and indirect subsidies to plantations, industry, and intermediate marketing agents, which have adversely affected local producers and community enterprises
- reconsidering regulations that impede forest smallholders' entry into markets and that impose costly procedures (see note 1.5, Making Markets Work for the Forest-Dependent Poor)

MULTIPLE CHARACTERISTICS OF TENURE SECURITY. Tenure security has multiple characteristics, especially in the case of common property (see box 1.19). Institutional gaps can undo otherwise positive tenure reform (as was seen in Cameroon and Ghana) if permitted legal forms of community forests are complex, and customary or informal arrangements are seldom recognized, resulting in few communities effectively taking over management.

ANALYSIS OF TENURE STATUS, ACCESS RIGHTS, AND USE RIGHTS. Tenure is in transition in many developing countries. Particularly where land administration reform and land reform are ongoing, a gap can develop between the forest tenure dialogue and the overall land administration dialogue. Effective projects in such situations must be based on analysis of tenure status, access rights, and use rights. Such an analysis must be sensitive to the variety of tenure arrangements that exist between the two extremes of pure public property and pure private property. For example, a number of indigenous use arrangements and rights regimes coexist with the total state ownership of forest resources on paper. In a number of places the state has devolved partial to substantial use rights to communities without changing the status of property ownership, while in others communities exercise substantial control of the resource without state recognition. Each of these variations in tenure offers a

Box 1.18 Typology of Property Rights

Property rights can be viewed as reflective of social relations. Property rights are rules that govern relations between individuals with respect to property and they should therefore be defined by the community or the state to which such individuals belong. Property rights need to be clearly defined, well understood, and accepted by those who have to abide by them—and strictly enforced. Property rights need not always confer full "ownership" and be individual; depending on the circumstances it may be best if they are bestowed on the individual, in common, or to the general public. Most important for sustainable development is that property rights are deemed secure (van den Brink et al. 2006).

No single typology of tenure or property rights is universally accepted. Some typologies distinguish between legal tenure and customary tenure, others between *de facto* and *de jure* rights, while others distinguish among property regimes. Property rights are also often seen as a bundle of rights that include the right to access and withdraw, manage, exclude, and alienate (Schlager and Ostrom 1992).

Legal tenure is recognized as legitimate under the policies and laws of the state, while customary tenure is recognized as legitimate by the traditions and customs of a society but has not been formally codified in the law. Customary tenure systems exist in many countries with significant populations of rural poor, where land allocation and use are determined through longstanding "customary" methods that, in many countries, operate outside the formal legal system. Such customary tenure systems are dominant in many indigenous areas where traditional social structures are largely intact. Customary systems are associated with traditional land administration institutions and customary laws that define how rights are governed, allocated, and preserved. The systems are effective because they respond to a community's social, cultural, and economic needs and because they are enforced by local

leadership. Customary tenure systems typically possess both collective and individual dimensions. In part, the collective aspect relates to the community as compared with outsiders. Internally, the collective element relates to community land and resources, while the individual dimension concerns transactions, successions, and exchanges of family plots between community members. While it is reasonable to consider that both collective and individual tenure have their place in forest activities, introducing individual tenure from outside includes risks.

There are cases where customary rights have been legitimized but are still identified as customary rights. In such cases, the term "customary" helps identify the origin of the right. *De jure* rights are given lawful recognition by formal, legal instrumentalities, while *de facto* rights are rights that resource users continuously work cooperatively to design and enforce.

A common typology of property rights distinguishes among private, common, and public or state property rights:

- Private property rights
  - individual or "legal individual" holds most if not all the rights
  - property can be leased under a contract to a third party
- Common property rights
  - group (for example, community) holds rights
  - group can manage property and exclude others
  - rules are important to manage and distribute resource
- Public property or state property rights
- State holds the bundle of rights

Open access results from the ineffective exclusion of nonowners by the entity assigned formal rights of ownership.

Source: Authors' compilation using Molnar and Khare (2006) and Jensby (2007).

different set of opportunities for communities to use and protect their resources with varying outcomes (figure 1.1).

While government statistics and information available from land administrations are usually a good starting point, greater insights concerning evidence of historical use and dependence, as well as customary laws and rights, are often gathered through participatory mapping.

IMPORTANCE OF PILOTS. Pilot activities can be important to expanding the range of possibilities, demonstrating the viability of rights-based forestry approaches to improve livelihoods, generate income, or advance conservation. The objective is to build on a multisectoral analysis of forest tenure and access without limiting the recognition or devolution of rights where reform is ongoing.

Figure 1.1   Toward Tenure Security: Actors and Actions

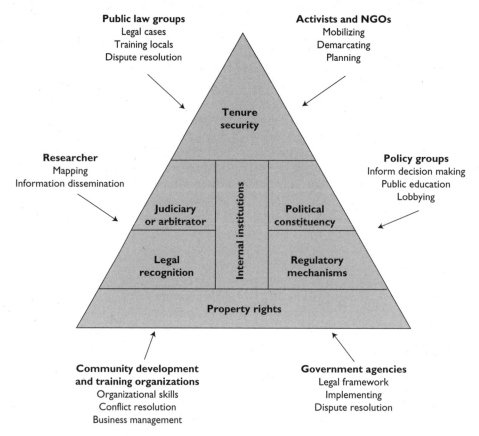

Source: Ellsworth and White 2004, Ellsworth 2004.

PARTICIPATION IN COMMERCIAL MARKETS. The ability of forest rights holders to manage and make use of their resources is linked to their level of, and opportunities for, participation in commercial markets (see note 1.5, Making Markets Work for the Forest-Dependent Poor). Forest tenure cannot be analyzed in isolation from world market trends, which both drive demand and create pressures on existing forest regimes. Newly created market opportunities for poor forest producers and forest owners can only be realized if the blend of tenure and other policies and regulations create the enabling environment. Changing long-established patterns of governance and industrial behavior inevitably entails a degree of political, economic, and environmental risk and adjustments in forest product supply and demand. Clear and secure tenure rights are necessary but not sufficient to engender these changes. Experience in Papua New Guinea shows that local landowners failed to manage enterprises for the long term when short-term returns were not high enough to encourage a change in behavior. Furthermore, technical and organizational support in early stages is essential. Mexican *ejidos* and communities have faced strong market competition from imports and subsidies to private plantations, requiring stronger enterprises and more flexible forest regulations to survive. Assistance in meeting these challenges will determine whether development and forest investments have pro-poor outcomes (box 1.20).

LESSONS LEARNED AND RECOMMENDATIONS FOR PRACTITIONERS

The transition to greater forest tenure and property rights occurs through a varied combination of strategies—both reforms fostered by political elites and bottom-up reforms demanded by civil society and community organizations. Development organizations have enabled reform processes through PRSP dialogue, but unless well linked to organic processes of civil society and empowered decentralization, these usually fail to make timely changes. Lessons from a variety of countries on successful strategies for change are listed in box 1.21.

Box 1.19 Characteristics of Secure Community Tenure

Security of community tenure encompasses a number of characteristics:

1. *Requires that there is clarity as to what the rights are.* Confusion about one's rights can significantly undermine the effectiveness and enthusiasm with which rights are exercised.
2. *Requires certainty that rights cannot be taken away or changed unilaterally and unfairly.* In almost any situation, of course, there are circumstances where it may be appropriate for rights to be taken away or diminished, but conditions for doing so need to be fair and clearly spelled out, the procedures fair and transparent, and compensation addressed.
3. *Is enhanced if the duration of rights is either in perpetuity or for a clearly spelled-out period that is long enough for the benefits of participation to be fully realized.* If rights are to be in force only temporarily—as in some comanagement arrangements or community forestry leases—care should be taken to ensure that agreements are at least as long as is realistically required to reap the appropriate degree of benefits.
4. *Means that rights need to be enforceable against the state* (including local government institutions)— that is, the legal system has to recognize an obligation of the state to respect those rights.
5. *Requires that the rights be exclusive.* The holders of rights need to be able to exclude outsiders or control the access of outsiders to the resource over which they have "rights." A corollary to exclusivity is that there must be certainty both about the boundaries of the resources to which rights apply and about who is entitled to claim group membership. A second corollary to exclusivity where comanagement concerns government land is that the government entity entering into the agreement must have clear authority to do so, authority that the responsible entity is empowered to fulfill.
6. *Requires that the law recognizes the holder of the rights.* The law should provide a way for the holder of the rights to acquire a legal personality, with the capacity to apply for credits and subsidies, enter into contracts with outsiders, collect fees, and so forth.
7. *Requires accessible, affordable, and fair avenues for seeking protection* of the rights, for solving disputes, and for appealing decisions of government officials.

Source: Lindsay 1998.

Box 1.20 Examples of Potentially Pro-Poor Approaches to Tenure Reform in Forests

- Overarching forest sector reform programs (Uganda, Ghana, Guyana, and South Africa)
- Titling of indigenous territories in Latin America and the Philippines
- Collectively managed community forests in Latin America—from extractive reserves to social forestry, to *ejidos* (Brazil, Guatemala, and Mexico)
- Recognition of community rights in Africa (The Gambia and Tanzania)
- Devolution of state and collectively owned forests to individual households (China and Vietnam)
- Joint forest management and collaborative management, where communities are given greater control over degraded resources, with the purpose of rehabilitating the resource (Cambodia, India, and Nepal)
- Decentralization of some decision making over forests (Indonesia) opening political spaces for local communities
- Some ethnic minority control over forests through peace negotiations (Myanmar, the Philippines, and Northeast India)
- Outgrower schemes where large-scale plantations have become politically untenable (Indonesia and South Africa)
- Comanagement in protected areas

Source: D. Kaimowitz, personal communication, in Hobley 2005.

- Support anticorruption and justice reform activities at national levels, through local and national legal groups.
- Nurture local organizations to help them act more effectively as advocates, while helping them to develop legal and mapping tools to better stake their claims.
- Support workshops on tenure where ideas are exchanged, and where lessons learned from the field can be translated into ministerial priorities.
- Strengthen emerging leaders and organizations who represent communities or indigenous peoples by fostering learning and opportunities to discuss their issues directly with the government.

- Build successful field models, recognizing these require time and patience. Avoid promoting pilot models that represent the lowest common denominator acceptable to government and undermine efforts at more meaningful reform.
- Mobilize civil society through effective activist and grassroots organizations with the capacity and will to champion a cause.
- Create linkages between local leaders at the global level, helping to sharpen their advocacy strategies.
- Support federations and associations in communities that are attempting to exercise their tenure rights, and support NGOs to build informed grassroots organizations.

Source: Ellsworth and White 2004.

The following topics should be considered in PRSPs and in project identification and design:

Overall land tenure, zoning, and land use arrangements have an impact on sound forest management and forest access for the poor. Particular attention should be paid to overlapping areas for private land adjudication and public or communal forests in frontier regions, and overlapping rights to Indigenous Peoples' lands and territories for above-soil and subsoil resources. Patterns of ownership should be mapped before project implementation, and instruments for resolving conflicts extra-legally or legally should be considered.

Tenure and policy frameworks create incentives or disincentives for forestry management, and control forest and forest market access for low-income producers. To minimize the harmful consequences of these frameworks on the forest-dependent poor, interventions should avoid regulatory frameworks that inadvertently place high burdens on the poor; tax and tariff polices that distort market participation; environmental regulations that low-income producers cannot afford to comply with, and therefore become "criminals" by ignoring; and barriers to low-income producers from outside the sector, such as small business regulations and lack of access to technical training or financial support. Existing and proposed protected-area regimes can support local rights and livelihoods by zoning for co-management and protecting local residents from incursions

by outsiders or extractive activities. They can hamper rights if overly restrictive or if they cause overlapping claims.

Industrial and infrastructure subsidies, and indirect subsidies, to processing industries, plantations, and transport create an unequal playing field for small and medium enterprises that do not qualify for such subsidies. Tax and tariff policies that affect domestic industry, imports, and exports can also be key drivers of distortions. These and other market and trade trends should be analyzed, with special consideration for the overlap of informal markets and trade and conflicted forest resources claims, as well as the impacts of commercial-scale plantations on land ownership patterns.

Ecosystem service payments or market schemes can offer opportunities to secure tenure for low-income producers as a reward for sustainable resource management. However, payment schemes must be carefully reviewed to ensure that existing local tenure and resource use rights are not threatened.

There are multiple mechanisms to monitor progress and influence the pace and quality of implementation of tenure reforms. These range from participatory monitoring to independent outside review, and should assist in adjusting processes (through changes either in projects or in project designs) to changing conditions over time.

With devolution of responsibility to communities and low-income producers, dependency on outside professionals must be reduced and local institutions and capacity for forest management must be strengthened.

SELECTED READINGS

Alden Wily, L. 2004. "Can We Really Own the Forest? A Critical Examination of Tenure Development in Community Forestry in Africa." Presented at "The Commons in an Age of Global Transition: Challenges, Risks and Opportunities," the 10th Conference of the International Association for the Study of Common Property, Oaxaca, Mexico, August 9–13.

Clay, J. W., J. B. Alcorn, and J. R. Butler. 2000. "Indigenous Peoples, Forestry Management and Biodiversity Conservation." Report to the World Bank, prepared by WWF-US, Washington, DC.

Ortega, R. 2004. "Models for Recognizing Indigenous Land Rights in Latin America." Environment Department Working Paper No. 99, World Bank, Washington, DC.

White, A., and A. Martin. 2002. *Who Owns the World's Forests? Forest Tenure and Public Forests in Transition.* Washington, DC: Forest Trends.

REFERENCES CITED

Ellsworth, L. 2004. *A Place in the World: A Review of the Global Debate on Tenure Security.* Washington, DC: Ford Foundation.

Ellsworth, L., and A. White. 2004. "Deeper Roots: Strengthening Community Tenure Security and Community Livelihoods." Ford Foundation, New York.

Hobley, M. 2005. "Where in the World Is There Opportunity for Tenure Reform?" Rights and Resources Initiative, Washington, DC.

Jensby, S.E. 2007. "Indigenous Peoples and Forests." Note submitted to World Bank as input to *Forests Sourcebook.* Unpublished. World Bank. Washington, DC.

Lindsay, J. M. 1998. "Creating Legal Space for Community-Based Management: Principles and Dilemmas." Paper presented at the International Workshop on Community-Based Natural Resource Management, World Bank, Washington, DC, May 10–14.

Macqueen, D., N. Armitage, and M. Jaecky. 2006. Report of a meeting of participants of the U.K. Tropical Forest Forum on small enterprise development and forests. Royal Botanic Gardens, Kew 26 September 2006. IIED, London.

Molnar, A. and A. Khare. 2006. "Note on Property and Access Rights." Note submitted to World Bank as input to *Forests Sourcebook.* Unpublished. World Bank, Washington, DC.

Schlager, E. C., and E. Ostrom. 1992. "Common Property and Natural Resources: A Conceptual Analysis." *Land Economics* 68 (3): 249–52.

van den Brink, R., G. Thomas, H. Binswanger, J. Bruce, and F. Byamugisha. 2006. "Consensus, Confusion, and Controversy: Selected Land Reform Issues in Sub-Saharan Africa." Working Paper No. 71, World Bank, Washington, DC.

CROSS-REFERENCED CHAPTERS AND NOTES

Note 1.3: Indigenous Peoples and Forests

Note 1.5: Making Markets Work for the Forest-Dependent Poor

Making Markets Work for the Forest-Dependent Poor

Improving market access of forest-dependent communities could enhance the contribution of forests to rural livelihoods. With 25 percent of the world's forests currently under community control, the expansion of agroforestry, and the development of community forest plantations, indigenous and other small communities own more than three times as much forest in developing countries as do private firms and individuals (see chapter 3, Meeting the Growing Demand for Forest Products). This creates new opportunities in commercial forestry that could serve a broader vision of meeting demand for forest products and forest conservation in ways that also address the livelihood needs of rural poor low-income producers (see note 1.2, Community-Based Forest Management, and note 1.3, Indigenous Peoples and Forests). Furthermore, changes in market structure, new market instruments, and forest companies' new interests in business partnerships with local people are opening market niches for which local producers have or could develop a competitive advantage. Environmental sustainability concerns are also creating new markets for certified forest products and environmental services.

Low-income forest producers[1] have potential competitive advantages for important segments of commercial forest markets. Forest dwellers located near population centers have lower transport costs, are more familiar with local preferences, and have the flexibility to supply small quantities of forest products as needed by local traders. Furthermore, they have an advantage in branding for specialty markets, enabling them to target socially responsible market niches. For example, the Rainforest Alliance supports Brazil nut-product organizations to enable them to access such market niches.

Community forest owners, comanagers of public forests, and farmers in forest-scarce locations near rapidly growing inland population centers can be competitive suppliers of commodity wood for construction and fuelwood. Further-more, community forest owners with high-quality, accessible timber, strong community organization, and good marketing and management skills can profitably sell tropical hardwoods as well, such as that sold from community forests in certain regions of Mexico. High-value timber can also be profitably sold by farmers from agroforestry systems. Benefits can also be gained from certified wood markets if there are established contracts or agreements with certified wood users or market intermediaries. For example, in Brazil a pulp and paper company assists small-scale farmer producer groups to obtain certification and to supply the local furniture company demand (Scherr, White, and Kaimowitz 2003, 2004).

Many local producers will benefit from preprocessing of forest products to reduce waste, increase quality, or reduce transportation costs, as well as from production of furniture and commodities for poor consumers in growing rural or urban markets. Small-scale sawmilling will also be viable in markets where there is no competition with high-efficiency, industrial mills. Additionally, in densely settled, forest-scarce countries with large markets for pulp, farmers or communities near mills could supply industrial pulpwood, especially on lower quality lands. Mondi Ltd. pulp and paper company in South Africa's Eastern Cape provides technical assistance and start-up capital to communities organized in common property associations.

NTFPs represent economic potential for those low-income producers or collectors of products with inelastic demand. In Cameroon, the demand for some NTFPs has grown dramatically in the past two decades as a result of increasing urbanization and a growing international market. Innovative marketing arrangements for environmental services also offer a market niche for those forest dwellers in areas with high levels of biodiversity or other values such as watershed protection or carbon sequestration (Scherr, White, and Kaimowitz 2003, 2004; also see note 2.3, Innovative Marketing Arrangements for Environmental Services).

Historically, low-income producers have been at a disadvantage in accessing markets, leading to a need to address this issue by jointly building on local human and natural capital assets, and building the institutional framework for good governance and distributive aspects of growth over time (see figure 1.2; Dürr 2002; Scherr, White, and Kaimowitz 2003, 2004; Sunderlin, Dewi, and Puntodewo 2006).

OPERATIONAL ASPECTS

There are many opportunities for forest management models to scale up the benefits they deliver for forest conservation and the rural poor or low-income producers. However, large gaps exist in information and experience and there are major challenges in finding the right market niches, supporting local forest businesses, and reforming policies to enable profitable market participation by local people. Addressing these challenges will require coordinated action by governments, international institutions, conservation and development organizations, and community producer organizations. Such action is necessary to level the playing field for low- income producers and give them a real chance to succeed.

Two areas that would benefit from interventions in collaboration with client governments are removal of policy barriers and development of forest businesses.

Potential measures for removing policy barriers include the following (based on Scherr, White, and Kaimowitz 2003, 2004; Sunderlin, Dewi, and Puntodewo 2006):

- Secure forest access and tenure rights of local people (see note 1.4, Property and Access Rights).
- Remove state monopolies and other controls on harvest and marketing that are common in several Bank client countries. However, decisions on the extent and phasing of deregulation need to carefully consider potential impacts on Indigenous Peoples and other forest-dependent communities and provide for capacity-building initiatives to avoid adverse effects and enhance their benefits from deregulation.
- Remove or revise regulatory barriers and excessive regulation that limits local forest producers from using their own or public forests. For example, in some regions of India, 10 separate permits are required for community forest producers to complete a timber sale. In other countries, indigenous communities have long-term rights to extensive tracts of natural forest, but they do not have the right to commercially exploit them.
- Revoke policies that discriminate against small producers (see box 1.22). For example, in Bolivia forest policy reforms have included formal recognition of indigenous groups' forest rights, lowered concession fees for small-scale forest producers, and simplified the process for accessing municipal forests.
- Facilitate the creation of forest user associations or producer groups to create economies of scale and to increase bargaining power (see note 2.2, Small and Medium Enterprises).
- Actively involve local producers in forest policy negotiations with private industry, government agencies, and

Figure 1.2   Forest Market Development Strategy for Low-Income Producers

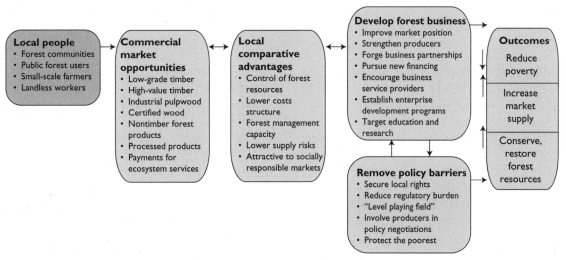

Source: Scherr, White, and Kaimowitz 2004.

environmental groups to produce more practical, realistic, and lower cost laws, market regulations, and development plans.

■ Create mechanisms that protect the poorest by, for example, ensuring that local forests retain their diverse cultural roles and their safety net functions without sacrificing others' potential income gains from commercialization of public forests.

Potential measures for developing forest enterprises include the following (based on Scherr, White, and Kaimowitz 2003, 2004; Sunderlin, Dewi, and Puntodewo 2006; USAID 2004):

■ Improve the market position of small producers by enabling them to respond to consumer preferences and to develop market strategies. This may mean improving production and marketing technology, product quality. or reliability of supply. Examples include drying forest fruits to improve product quality or chemically treating rattan to prevent fungal damage and staining.

■ Strengthen producer organizations through technical support and capacity building so that they can make cap-

ital investments, pursue new sources of financing, engage in value-added processing, negotiate deals, and establish product-quality or conservation controls.

■ Increase the contribution of commercially valuable NTFPs by enhancing community organization to increase the market power of NTFP producers and processors and decrease their vulnerability to external shocks (see box 1.23); build capacity in the areas of technical knowledge and organizational skills to ensure resource management and harvesting, domestication where appropriate, and improved product processing; and build business capacity of potential entrepreneurs and develop links between producer communities and fair trade organizations to improve marketing and add value to the products.

■ Promote strategic partnerships between communities and businesses (see box 1.24 and note 2.1, Community-Private Partnerships).

■ Adapt certification of forest products for small-scale and indigenous forestry (see note 1.3, Indigenous Peoples and Forests, and note 3.2, Forest Certification Systems).

■ Establish business services through NGOs or government extension for low-income producers that include

---

Box 1.22 Overcoming Barriers to Pro-Poor Forestry in Honduras

In Honduras, a number of factors, including excessive regulation, disadvantage small-scale forest producers, forcing many into illegality. An estimated 80 percent of the timber trade in Honduras is illicit. Securing management plans, harvesting permits, and commercial licenses is costly. In addition to formal charges, applicants may need to make informal payments for officials to facilitate the process. These, plus the costs of production and transportation, mean that local producers might make a profit of only 15 percent on the factory gate price for raw mahogany. Some of this profit may go toward debt repayments to local intermediaries, given the lack of liquidity to meet up-front production costs. But even discounting the costs of compliance, the returns to small-scale forest producers are limited by the small volumes they are permitted to harvest. And, because of insufficient capacity to produce high-quality timber and the lack of alternative marketing channels, many are locked into the domestic market—already saturated with cheap, illegal timber.

Source: Brown and others 2002.

There is, however, growing political recognition of the role of forests in rural poverty alleviation and of the need to provide equal opportunities for community-based forest producers. In 2000, Honduras launched a review of its forest sector through the Honduran Forest Agenda (AFH). The AFH is a forum established by the government and NGOs in 1996 for dialogue and coordination among a broad range of stakeholders, including producer groups, industry representatives, and indigenous peoples. The AFH review process secured a new national forest policy and law. At the time of drafting this note, the law was still being finalized for submission to Congress, but one of its main objectives was to secure a more equitable basis for community participation in forest management, including support for small enterprise development. In addition, the AFH is framing a new National Forest Plan, which will include a Community Development Program. The PRSP, which was jointly formulated with civil society, also makes provisions for participatory forest management.

Box 1.23   Market Analysis and Development in Community Forests of The Gambia

The Gambia has 264 Community Forest Committees (CFCs), 22 of which are developing their markets and managing their forests using the Market Analysis and Development (MA&D) methodology through a joint project of the Gambian government and the Food and Agriculture Organization. The MA&D program is a three-phase program that trains and empowers community members to identify and develop successful forest enterprises and learn to manage them independently. MA&D enables communities to link forest management and conservation activities directly to income-generating opportunities, and in the Gambian case it has also encouraged substantial diversification of marketable forest products. The program emphasizes sustainable institutional development for the community enterprises and extensive networking between businesses and local organizations. In The Gambia, 22 CFCs

have used MA&D methodology to develop 72 community enterprises.

Some of the communities now involved in successful enterprises have been entitled to commercialize community forest products since 1992 but, before the MA&D training, were hesitant to do anything other than protect their forests, or were repeatedly cheated by middlemen or Forestry Department staff.

The communities produce 11 different products from their forests, including fuelwood, logs and timber, honey, palm handicrafts, Netto fruits, oil palm fruits, and tree nurseries. Through program-sponsored artisan workshops, community members have learned skills to craft new products from their forests, especially beds, sofas, and chairs that are then sold to local ecotourism lodges and hotels in the coastal tourism area. Profits from beekeeping are expected to account for 15 percent of their total yearly profits.

Source: Molnar and others 2006.

management services, organizational support, and technical assistance, to link conservation of forest resources with processing of forest products (see box 1.23), market information, insurance, and marketing and financial assistance (see box 1.25).

- Conduct research, education, and training so that community forestry enterprises can better adapt to new trends in production, processing, and management.
- Improve government support and extension services for forest smallholders.

Box 1.24   Strategic Partnerships in Southern Africa

In the remote district of Rushinga in northeastern Zimbabwe, an individual runs a company called Creative Oils that produces oil from the seeds of the baobab. Creative Oils currently purchases six tons of seed per month from 60 rural producers. Rural producers can earn as much as $180 in a season, which is double their income from cotton, the staple cash crop. The owner of Creative Oils earns nearly $9,000 a season from the 360 liters of oil the company produces a month.

This success is due largely to an involvement with PhytoTrade Africa, the Southern African Natural Products Trade Association. In 2003, PhytoTrade Africa signed a joint venture agreement with a French company specializing in the production of derivatives from

natural plant oils for sale as cosmetic ingredients. The French company purchases baobab oil from Creative Oils, which it then processes and sells to the multinational company Bergasol, for incorporation into a new sunscreen for sale in Europe.

There are many products like baobab oil, derived from indigenous plant species in rural Africa and having significant commercial potential. For small-scale producers, however, the barriers to developing markets for these products are formidable. The owner of Creative Oils has successfully overcome these barriers by pooling resources with producers from across southern Africa and helping create a powerful trade association to represent their interests.

Source: Campbell and others 2004.

Box 1.25 Medicinal Plants as NTFPs in India and Nepal

The Pangi Valley is a remote, high-altitude area in the Chamba district, in northwest Himachal Pradesh. Most of the residents in the region subsist on single-season cash cropping, animal herding, road building, and most recently, collection and sale of medicinal plants and herbs from the region's forests.

More than 86 percent of residents surveyed in the Pangi Valley collected some medicinal plants and herbs from the forest during the collecting season of mid-June to mid-October. In most villages, income from medicinal herbs is between 10 and 20 percent of total cash income per household. Generally, those who engage in the most medicinal herb collection are individuals with fewer opportunities for income, less land available for cultivation, and fewer local labor opportunities.

This case contrasts with the situation in far western Nepal, also in the Himalayas, where multidonor support to a market and technical network organization, Asia Network for Sustainable Agriculture and Bioresources, and Nepali forest user groups led to better markets for essential oils and medicinals, investment in a NTFP paper-processing enterprise, and better resource extraction and management.

Source: Molnar and others 2006.

LESSONS LEARNED AND RECOMMENDATIONS FOR PRACTITIONERS

Potential actions that can be taken by international institutions, such as the World Bank, in partnership with government and other stakeholders, include the following:

■ Organize global and national initiatives to promote market and institutional reforms to enable greater participation of low-income producers in international trade and to protect their interests against trade rules and initiatives that would create unfair competition against them.
■ Develop new financial mechanisms to promote forestry investment for low-income producers, using domestic investment protocols and export guarantee systems to favor forest businesses that adopt business models supportive of low-income producers. Develop global norms of behavior for international companies who partner with local communities.
■ Generate the research and information needed to understand present levels of market participation by different groups of low-income producers, incomes generated, business profitability, and actual competitive advantages. Also develop partnerships with others who will enable the development of institutions to achieve these goals (Scherr, White, and Kaimowitz 2004).

Improved commercial markets may not improve the livelihoods of rural communities and farmers with low-quality forest resources and poorly developed market infrastructure. In these situations it remains important to focus on the subsistence and environmental values of forestry development.

Small-scale producers must be able to compete with low-cost industrial producers, as well as with producers who clear land or illegally extract forest products. The marketing strategy should complement the comparative advantages of the different forest "zones." (For example, people in remote areas may be able to make money from harvesting high-value timber. which compensates for high transportation costs. Closer to urban areas where forests are scarce, low-income producers who plant trees in agroforestry systems can benefit from the proximity to urban markets when selling their timber.)

Many attempts at NTFP commercialization from natural forests and agroforestry systems have failed to deliver the expected benefits because marketing and trading strategies for NTFPs have been neglected.

It is essential that opportunities are provided for women to be more involved in strategies to improve the successful commercialization of NTFPs because women often depend on NTFP sales as a source of household income. A study in West Bengal, India, reported that three times as many women as men were involved in gathering NTFPs, which accounted for 20 percent of household income (Scherr, White, and Kaimowitz 2004).

NOTE

1. Low-income forest producers include indigenous and other community groups who manage collectively owned forest resources; local individuals or groups who comanage or harvest products from the forest; smallholder farmers who manage remnant natural forests or plant trees in or around their crop fields and pastures; individuals or groups who engage in small-scale forest product processing; and employees of forest production and processing enterprises

(Scherr, White, and Kaimowitz 2003). This note focuses on markets for low-income producers.

SELECTED READINGS

Angelsen, A., and S. Wunder. 2003. "Exploring the Forest-Poverty Link: Key Concepts, Issues and Research Implications." CIFOR Occasional Paper No. 40, CIFOR, Bogor, Indonesia.

FAO. 2006. *Microfinance and Forest-Based Small-Scale Enterprise.* FAO: Rome.

Pfund, J.-L., and P. Robinson, eds. 2006. "Non-Timber Forest Products between Poverty Alleviation and Market Forces." Intercooperation, Bern, Switzerland.

Scherr, S., A. White, and D. Kaimowitz. 2004. "A New Agenda for Forest Conservation and Poverty Reduction: Making Markets Work for Low-Income Producers." Forest Trends, Washington, DC.

Schreckenberg, K., E. Marshall, A. Newton, W. D. te Velde, J. Rushton, and E. Fabrice. 2006. "Commercialisation of Non-Timber Forest Products: What Determines Success?" ODI Forestry Briefing, Number 10, Overseas Development Institute, London.

Shanley, P., A. Pierce, and S. A. Laird. 2005. "Beyond Timber: Certification of Non-Timber Forest Products." Forest Trends, Washington, DC.

Sunderlin, W. D., A. Angelsen, and S. Wunder. 2003. "Forests and Poverty Alleviation." In *State of the World's Forests 2003*, 61–73. Rome: Food and Agricultural Organization of the United Nations.

World Bank, Carbon Finance Unit. n.d. Operations Handbook (online). http://carbonfinance.org/Router.cfm?Page=DocLib&ht=34&dl=1.

REFERENCES CITED

Brown, D., K. Schreckenberg, G. Shepherd, and A. Wells. 2002. "Forestry as an Entry Point for Governance Reform." ODI Forestry Briefing No. 1, Overseas Development Institute, London.

Campbell, B., P. Frost, G. Kokwe, G. le Breton, S. Shackleton, and D. Tiveau. 2004. "Making Dry Forests Work for the Poor in Africa: Building on Success." Forest Livelihood Briefs, Number 3, CIFOR, Bogor, Indonesia.

Dürr, C. 2002 "The Contribution of Forests and Trees to Poverty Alleviation." Series IC No. 3, Intercooperation, Bern, Switzerland.

Molnar, A., M. Liddle, C. Bracer, A. Khare, A. White, and J. Bull. 2006. "Community-Based Forest Enterprises in Tropical Forest Countries: Status and Potential." Report to the ITTO. Forest Trends/Rights and Resources Group, Washington, DC.

Scherr, S., A. White, and D. Kaimowitz. 2003. "Making Markets Work for Forest Communities." *International Forestry Review* 5 (1):67–73.

———. 2004. "A New Agenda for Forest Conservation and Poverty Reduction: Making Markets Work for Low-Income Producers." Forest Trends, Washington, DC.

Sunderlin, W. D., S. Dewi, and A. Puntodewo. 2006. "Forests, Poverty, and Poverty Alleviation Policies." Background paper. World Bank, Washington, DC.

USAID, with CIFOR, Winrock International, WRI, and IRG. 2004. *Nature, Wealth, and Power: Emerging Best Practice for Revitalizing Rural Africa.* Washington, DC: USAID.

CROSS-REFERENCED CHAPTERS AND NOTES

Engaging the Private Sector in Forest Sector Development

Sustainable forest management (SFM) requires substantial financial resources. Developing countries need to explore and encourage all sources and mechanisms of funding for the forest sector to achieve SFM. The private sector is expected to play the lead role in global economic and production activities. Private investment in the forestry sector in developing countries and countries in transition is estimated at US$15 billion per year, or up to nine times more than current official development assistance flows.[1]

To date, private investment in SFM has been concentrated in developed countries. Although this trend is changing, the need remains to motivate similar investment in developing countries to maximize the full potential of SFM, because investments required for harvesting and processing can be large (for example, establishing a modern pulp mill can cost the better part of US$1 billion). Investments on this scale can only come from global corporations or joint ventures involving local partners and development banks willing to cover the risk. Furthermore, ensuring that these large investments are made in a socially and environmentally responsible manner is essential to preventing destructive use of forest resources.

When discussing the need to attract investment to the forest sector in developing countries, many organizations and governments tend to focus on large-scale international investors. However, the majority of the markets are domestic: For example, as much as 86 percent of the wood harvested in the Brazilian Amazon is consumed within Brazil, and log exports from West and Central Africa account for only 20 percent of the 25 million cubic meters harvested per year. Although developed countries now consume approximately 70 percent of industrial roundwood, consumption growth in developing countries is narrowing the gap: The consumption of industrial roundwood in developing countries grew by 3.2 percent per year in 1996–97, in contrast to developed countries, where it grew by only 0.6 percent per year (Victor and Ausubel 2000). In the forest sector, it would be logical for much of the new global private investment to try to capture the financial gains from these rising domestic markets in developing countries, where the majority of the world's natural tropical forests are located. This aligns with global trends that show that while foreign direct investment remains important in developing countries for foreign exchange earnings and skills and technology transfer, the bulk of private investment remains domestic across all sectors (ITTO 2006).

The forest products industry supplies a wide range of essential products—from construction materials, paper, sanitary products, and specialty chemicals to watershed and soil conservation—from a renewable resource. It provides millions of jobs and supports thousands of local communities with an annual production of about US$750 billion (WBCSD 2006).

Considerable potential exists in these investments to deliver benefits to farmers, small forest owners, local communities, and Indigenous Peoples. Forest investment can involve small- and large-scale investments and can bring together communities and companies through partnership arrangements, build small and medium enterprises (SMEs), or enable socially responsible corporate investments. SMEs are a major potential source for off-farm employment in rural areas (Molnar et al. 2006).

PAST ACTIVITIES

The International Finance Corporation (IFC), the private sector arm of the World Bank Group, promotes sustainable private sector investment to foster economic development and reduce poverty. The IFC finances investments with its own resources and by mobilizing capital in the international financial markets. In addition to equity and loan financing, IFC also provides technical assistance to its clients, either funded by grants or by the clients themselves.

Between fiscal[2] 2003 and fiscal 2006, the IFC invested more than US$1 billion to help finance 25 forestry sector projects with a total cost of about US$4 billion (figure 2.1). The size of projects fluctuated between US$3 million (a packaging project in the Kyrgyz Republic) and US$500 million (a paper mill project in China). The pulp and paper industry accounted for 56 percent of the total, while 33 percent was directed at the wood-based panel and engineered-wood products industries, with some small investments made in sawmilling and furniture production. The share of forestry projects in private sector financing was 11 percent and on the increase. The IFC has not invested in projects requiring raw material from natural tropical moist forests. During this period, about half of IFC

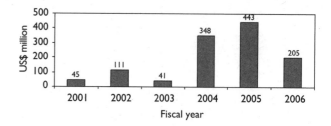

Figure 2.1   IFC Forest Sector Investments

projects included an integrated forestry component. IFC technical assistance was mostly targeted at specific projects but some sector work was also carried out.[3]

Geographically, Europe and Central Asia (ECA) attracted most IFC financing during the 2003–06 period followed by East Asia and the Pacific (EAP), Latin America and the Caribbean (LAC), South Asia (SAR), and the Middle East and North Africa (MENA) (figure 2.2). Only one African country appears in the IFC portfolio during the period.[4] IFC projects concentrated in 16 countries, and the Bank had forestry lending activities in 10 of them, indicating a considerable geographic overlap.[5]

The relatively high proportion of IFC investment channeled to the ECA region reflects the importance of the Russian Federation's forest industries and the emerging forest industrial investment opportunities in Eastern European transition countries. In both EAP and LAC, the IFC's main investments have been in rapidly expanding pulp and paper industries in China, India, and Brazil.

Although the link to poverty alleviation may not be direct in most IFC investments, the project companies often generate significant employment, ranging from a few hun-

---

Box 2.1   IFC Projects in the Forest Products Sector

The IFC has a Global Manufacturing and Services Department, within which there is a Forest Products Sector. The portfolio of projects from this sector spans a diverse group of pulp, paper, and converted products, ranging from linter and straw pulp to tissue, sacks, and various kinds of packaging. The sector involves dealing with sensitive political, social, and environmental issues. Among the greatest risks are severe environmental and human health impacts associated with antiquated technology and poor forest practices.

Subsector categories in this sector include plantations, wood fiber, and woodworking.

Source: http://www.ifc.org/ifcext/gms.nsf/Content/Forest_Products_Overview.

Figure 2.2   IFC Forest Investments Regional Distribution, 2003–06

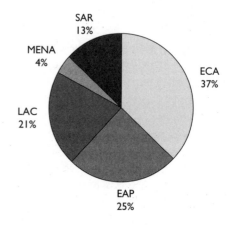

dred to tens of thousands of new jobs. Indirect employment impacts can be many times higher than direct employment, in particular when considering the forestry component.

While almost all the investments to date relate to large industrial projects, the IFC has a particular interest in supporting the expansion and sustainable management of upstream fiber sources. Greater IFC involvement in forestry can enhance the positive impacts of industrial development in environmental conservation, economic development, and poverty alleviation while possible negative impacts can be better mitigated.[6]

The International Development Association and International Bank for Reconstruction and Development arms of the World Bank Group have invested in enabling private sector engagement in the forest sector in different ways. In FY05, the Bank financed the Cameroon Forest and Environment development policy loan to help consolidate and scale up recent successful forest sector policy reforms, support capacity building, and strengthen forest and environment institutions. In this loan, a prior action for release of the second tranche included signed contracts with companies meeting requirements and implementation of appropriate measures, including the withdrawal of concession, if appropriate, for companies failing to meet requirements. Similarly, in the Lao People's Democratic Republic poverty support reduction credit, there were prior actions that included completing requirements for independent certification of sustainable forest management and establishing a forest sector monitoring system. The World Bank has also been investing in activities enabling payments for environment services (see details in note 2.3, Innovative Marketing Arrangements for Environmental Services).

In addition to lending, since 2004, the World Wildlife Fund (WWF) Global Forest and Trade Network (GFTN) has been involved in World Bank–WWF Global Forest Alliance activities by building up enterprise-level capacity for certification and linking responsible suppliers with buyers (for example in Ghana, Indonesia, Nicaragua, Peru, Russia, and Vietnam). In Nicaragua, the cooperation of the GFTN resulted in IFC support for local companies to achieve certification. A financing mechanism for forest concessionaires was developed in Peru. Development of timber tracking systems has been supported in Cambodia, Nicaragua, Peru, and in the Congo Basin countries. To promote responsible investment in forest management, PRO-FOR (Program on Forests) and the World Bank–WWF Alliance for Forest Conservation and Sustainable Use have organized three investment forums (a global forum in 2004, and regional forums in East Africa in 2004 and in South Africa in 2006) that have focused on the development of the SME sector in forest-based activities within the framework of poverty reduction.

KEY ISSUES

NUMEROUS PRIVATE SECTOR ACTORS. A variety of private sector actors, all with different interests, capabilities, and constraints, influence the forest sector, including

- large multinational companies,
- local companies of varying sizes,
- individual private investors (for example, conservation investments by philanthropists),
- community or cooperative enterprises applying SFM, and
- small-scale forest owners.

Primary manufacturers might include chainsaw operators or small sawmills, in addition to large corporations whose annual sales might be larger than the gross domestic product (GDP) of many developing countries. All have the potential to invest productively, create jobs, and expand—thereby contributing to economic growth and poverty reduction. Each type of business (or investment opportunity) can be affected differently by changes in international and domestic markets, as well as by changes in governmental policies and the general in-country business and investment environments (ITTO 2006).

FACTORS INFLUENCING PRIVATE SECTOR INVESTMENT. Factors that influence private sector decisions about forest-related investments include the following:

- *Returns.* Sufficient returns are a prerequisite; therefore, any factors that reduce the returns or profits from the investment can act as a deterrent.
- *Risks.* Weighing returns against risks, private investors generally demand much higher returns (typically 15 percent to 30 percent) from developing countries where risks are (or can be perceived as being) high.
- *Transaction costs.* High transaction costs can make investments less attractive. For example, evidence indicates that small investors in particular find it difficult to meet the additional costs associated with SFM (see note 3.2, Forest Certification Systems).

ELEMENTS OF AN ENABLING ENVIRONMENT. To encourage the private sector to invest in SFM with full confidence and commitment, an enabling environment has several dimensions, both national and international. Some of the factors may be outside the forest sector's control, yet they need to be addressed to promote investment in SFM. Key enabling actions include the following:

- Reducing domestic policy and institutional problems that restrain or discourage private sector engagement in SFM—for example, avoiding excessive and inappropriate regulations and bureaucracy that contribute to unduly high costs of registering companies and undertaking management.
- Seeking ministerial commitment for legislative and other policy reforms that will help to contain illegal logging and create a level playing field for responsible companies that are willing to invest in SFM (see chapter 5, Improving Forest Governance, and associated notes). The willingness of high-level political leaders and more responsible companies to engage in supporting such initiatives as the European Union– and World Bank-supported Forest Law Enforcement and Governance Program has been encouraging.
- Facilitating political stability necessary to assure investors.
- Assisting governments to engage private sector companies and local communities in dialogue regarding reforming timber allocation processes, achieving equitable revenue sharing, taxation and revenue collection systems, encouraging value added processing, and ensuring a secure supply of raw material.
- Assisting governments to develop transparent timber allocation procedures and concession policies that will help to ensure a secure supply of raw material for potential client companies, thus reducing the perception of risk for investors. Lack of security threatens the continuity of manufacturing operations.
- Ensuring stable and clear policies, institutions, and operating environments, including those related to tenure and concessions.
- Developing instruments or drawing upon existing instruments to hedge against excessive market fluctuations and seek mechanisms for better prices in international markets, and seeking ways to deter major markets from buying low-priced supplies from unsustainable sources that unfairly undermine responsible suppliers seeking to achieve SFM (see note 3.2, Forest Certification Systems).
- Ensuring relevant training and skills development and research for the forestry sector.

- Helping to expand the profit base of SFM investments through environmental services (see note 2.3, Small and Medium Enterprises).

POTENTIAL FOR RELATIONSHIPS BETWEEN COMPANIES AND COMMUNITIES IN THE FOREST SECTOR. With time and effort, some of the existing relationships between companies and communities could mature from superficial deals into real partnerships (Mayers and Vermeulen 2002; Howard et al. 2005; Nawir and Santoso 2005; Vermeulen and Walubengo 2006). These cover the full range of forest goods and services and a wide variety of partnership models, including the following:

- In outgrower schemes and sales or purchase contracts, small-scale farmers grow trees or NTFPs on their own plots with support from the company (such as technical advice, seed stock, fertilizers, pesticides, tools, harvesting) and with guaranteed purchase, sometimes at guaranteed prices.
- In joint ventures, companies and communities make capital coinvestments in goods or service projects, possibly sharing management. Often the community's capital investment is land or labor. In simpler lease models, the company pays a fee for use rights on community land over a fixed period and the community plays no part in management.
- In multiple land-use arrangements on land under company freehold or leasehold, communities are granted access rights and management rights to noncore goods and services, typically NTFPs in forest areas managed primarily for timber production.
- In social responsibility contracts, the forestry company negotiates a social license to operate within environmental and cultural limits set by the community; in return, the company receives the benefit of local investments, usually infrastructural. Globally, SMEs represent one of the faster growing industrial sectors in the world. Forest-based SMEs (SMFEs) account for 80–90 percent of all the forest enterprises in many countries (box 2.2). For many countries, more than 50 percent of total forest-related employment is in SMFEs, with approximately 20 million people employed worldwide. SMFEs generate a gross value added of about US$130 billion per year (Macqueen and others 2006). Greater awareness of the potential of SMFEs to contribute to essential subsistence needs and to poverty alleviation and economic growth is needed (see note 2.2, Small and Medium Enterprises). Such awareness should inform both forest policies and policies regarding market access, credit, and other relevant macro policies.

Since 1995, Brazilian small and medium enterprises have grown annually by 2.8 percent and 4.7 percent, respectively—much faster than larger enterprises—despite having a higher failure rate than larger companies, with 39 percent failing in Brazil within the first year (a reasonably average failure rate globally for small and medium enterprises (May, Da Vinha, and Macqueen 2003)). Logging by SMFEs in Guyana contributes almost as much to the revenue of the Guyana Forestry Commission as do large enterprises (Thomas et al. 2003). In China, more than 90 percent of the total value of wood products is generated by SMFEs (Sun and Chen 2003).

Source: ITTO 2006.

MARKETS FOR FOREST ENVIRONMENTAL SERVICES. Markets for environmental services need further development and may require the creation of an enabling environment for private sector investment in this area. This could be facilitated by providing greater clarity on the potential financial benefits of environmental services and greater certainty regarding the associated markets (see note 2.3, Innovative Marketing Arrangements for Environmental Services).

Consensus is growing that investment in the sector has to occur within a credible framework of safeguards and environmental assessment procedures. These have to motivate responsible investment and deter unsustainable and destructive activities. There is a need to address such issues as the identification and protection of forests that are a high priority for biodiversity conservation, protection of rights and resource interests of Indigenous Peoples and other forest-dependent people, certification and other systems of independent verification of forest management performance, and establishment and management of forest and agricultural tree-crop plantations (see note 1.3, Indigenous Peoples and Forests, and section II, Guide to Implementing, Forests Policy OP 4.36). The various safeguard initiatives also need to be harmonized and extended to a broader range of investing groups.

FUTURE PRIORITIES FOR ACTIVITIES

Increasing demand for forest products, especially in developing countries, indicates that investment in the forest sector will likely expand. Major prospects are in Brazil, China,

India, and Russia. To ensure that the growing private investment generates benefits for a wide range of forest users and forest-dependent households, some priority actions must be taken:

INCREASE AVAILABILITY OF AND ACCESS TO FINANCING FOR SMALL-SCALE FORESTRY AND WOOD PROCESSING. Opportunities that would provide funding for small-scale enterprises and mechanisms that would strengthen the supply chain for SMEs should be explored.

PROVIDE INCENTIVES FOR THE PRIVATE SECTOR to manage (rather than solely log) natural forests, to adopt a longer-term and broader view of forests (even for plantation forestry and the timber processing industry), take on emerging opportunities, and reduce perceptions of risk.

REMOVE CONSTRAINTS RELATED TO INVESTMENTS IN SUSTAINABLE MANAGEMENT OF NATURAL TROPICAL FORESTS. This should be done by the international community (the Bank and the IFC in cooperation with other donors and intergovernmental organizations [such as ITTO], nongovernmental organizations [NGOs], and the private sector) in collaboration with governments. The objective should be to enable policy reform to improve the investment environment and strengthen the policy and regulatory frameworks for responsible investment.

CONTINUE PROVIDING SUPPORT TO THE ESTABLISHMENT, AND ON-THE-GROUND IMPLEMENTATION, OF ENVIRONMENTALLY SOUND LEGAL AND REGULATORY STANDARDS AND CAPACITY, which are essential to creating the necessary preconditions for the sustainable operation of the predominantly downstream private operators. Because forest-based investments are usually made with a long-term time horizon, all means to mitigate risks are particularly important for private investors. Risk mitigation through enabling conditions is key in the decision making of responsible private investors.

BUILD CAPACITY AT ALL LEVELS TO ADDRESS THE LACK OF CAPACITY IN MANY DEVELOPING COUNTRIES to adequately implement environmental assessment procedures and safeguards. This increased capacity would develop multistakeholder institutional mechanisms for monitoring forest harvesting and management, especially where these are weak. The presence of visible and strong institutional mechanisms to implement monitoring of environmental procedures and safeguards can substantially contribute to project risk mitigation and would both encourage and support socially and environmentally responsible companies.

CONTINUE FURTHER COLLABORATION BETWEEN THE BANK AND THE IFC. IFC investments in an environmentally sustainable private company can demonstrate profitability within the framework of a Bank-supported regulatory structure (supply response), and it is at this intersection that the benefits of collaboration are strongest. Areas where the Bank and the IFC should increase collaboration include the following:

- promotion of investment in forest-based, small-scale enterprises;
- increased exchange of information at the country, regional, global, and research levels;
- further cooperation in areas where engagement has already been demonstrated to be beneficial (for example, the IFC could enhance the use of the GFTN of the World Bank–WWF Alliance in linking its investments with responsible buyers); and
- additional Bank economic and sector work and analytical and advisory activities, especially those related to governance reform, that can help create enabling conditions for IFC investment projects.[7]

NOTES

1. In 2002 the World Bank estimated that total forest sector private investment in developing countries and countries in transition was about US$8 billion to US$10 billion per year. This may underestimate actual private sector investment. According to the FAO (2005), the plantation area in developing countries is increasing at about 1.8 million hectares per year. This represents investments of US$3 billion to US$4 billion per year. Improvements in existing forest management should be added to this, but reliable estimates do not exist. In plantation-based projects, industrial investments represent 80–90 percent of the total. Applying this coefficient—with plantation investments being 20 percent of the total—total forest investment in developing countries should be at least US$15 billion.

2. The World Bank operates according to a fiscal year that begins July 1 and ends June 30.

3. As an example, there is ongoing work to prepare a strategic plan for the pulp and paper industry in Ukraine.

4. This appears to be due to the scarcity of companies that can meet IFC criteria for support.

5. The regional analysis is based on the projects with a total value of US$800 million. In two countries without the

Bank's forest lending, there are practically no production forests.

6. The upstream forestry activities have significant potential for rural poverty reduction. As an example, IFC projects in India have engaged 135,000 farmers or families in cooperative arrangements with pulp and paper companies, covering a total area of 128,000 hectares. Each family typically allocates 1 to 2 hectares to forest plantation to increase their income, demonstrating that primarily poor households are involved in these schemes. Similar arrangements are also being supported by IFC-financed projects in Brazil. IFC has also provided technical assistance to small-scale, forest-based operations in Central America through the LAC Project Development Facility in collaboration with the GFTN. The future impact of these investments can be significant for employment and local income, if such efforts move beyond technical assistance.

7. Several economic and sector work and analytical and advisory activity products developed under the World Bank's forest partnerships are directly related to this issue (see annex 2A to this chapter for a list of some products).

SELECTED READINGS

FAO (Food and Agriculture Organization of the United Nations). 2005. "Global Forest Resources Assessment 2005: Progress Towards Sustainable Forest Management." FAO Forestry Paper 147, FAO, Rome.

Mayers, James. 2006. "Poverty Reduction Through Commercial Forestry. What Evidence? What Prospects?" TFD Publication No. 2, School of Forestry and Environmental Studies, Yale University, New Haven, CT.

Mayers, J., and A. Vermeulen. 2002. *Company-Community Partnerships in Forestry: From Raw Deals to Mutual Gains?* Instruments for Sustainable Private Sector Forestry series. London: International Institute for Environment and Development.

Pagiola, S., and G. Platais. 2007. *Payments for Environmental Services: From Theory to Practice.* Washington, DC: World Bank.

REFERENCES CITED

ITTO (International Tropical Timber Organization). 2006. *Tropical Forest Update* 16 (2).

Howard, M., P. Matikinca, D. Mitchell, F. Brown, F. Lewis, I. Mahlangu, A. Msimang, P. Nixon, and T. Radebe. 2005. *Small-Scale Timber Production in South Africa: What Role in Reducing Poverty?* Small and Medium Forest Enterprise Series 9. London: International Institute for Environment and Development.

Macqueen, D., N. Armitage, M. Jaecky, 2006. Report of a meeting of participants of the UK Tropical Forest Forum on small enterprise development and forests Royal Botanic Gardens, Kew 26 September 2006. IIED, London.

May, P. H., V. G. Da Vinha, and D. J. Macqueen. 2003. "Small and Medium Forest Enterprise in Brazil." Grupo Economia do Meio Ambiente e Desenvolvimento Sustentável (GEMA) and International Institute for Environment and Development (IIED), London.

Mayers, J., and A. Vermeulen. 2002. *Company-Community Partnerships in Forestry: From Raw Deals to Mutual Gains?* Instruments for Sustainable Private Sector Forestry series. London: International Institute for Environment and Development.

Molnar, A., M. Liddle, C. Bracer, A. Khare, A. White, and J. Bull. 2006. "Community-Based Forest Enterprises in Tropical Forest Countries: Status and Potential." Report to the ITTO. Forest Trends/Rights and Resources Group, Washington, DC.

Nawir, A. A., and L. Santoso. 2005. "Mutually Beneficial Company-Community Partnerships in Plantation Development: Emerging Lessons from Indonesia." International Forestry Review 7 (3): 177–92.

Sun, C., and X. Chen. 2003. "Small and Medium Forestry Enterprises in China: An Initial Review of Sustainability and Livelihood Issues." Research Center of Ecological and Environmental Economics (RCEEE) and IIED, London.

Thomas, R., D. J. Macqueen, Y. Hawker, and T. DeMendonca. 2003. "Small and Medium Forest Enterprises in Guyana." Guyana Forestry Commission (GFC) and IIED, London.

Vermeulen, S., and D. Walubengo. 2006. "Developing Partnerships for Sustainable Management of Forests in Kenya: Review of Existing Models and Set of Options for Further Support." Report prepared for the Forestry Department, Government of Kenya, and PROFOR (Program on Forests), World Bank. International Institute for Environment and Development, London.

Victor, D.G., and Jesse H. Ausubel 2000. "Restoring the Forests." *Foreign Affairs* 79(6):127-144, November/ December 2000.

WBCSD (World Business Council for Sustainable Development). 2006. "Forest Products Industry." http://tinyurl.com/36fcrw.

CROSS-REFERENCED CHAPTERS AND NOTES

Note 1.3: Indigenous Peoples and Forests

Notes following chapter 2: Engaging the Private Sector in Forest Sector Development

Note 3.2: Forest Certification Systems

Chapter 5: Improving Forest Governmance, and associated notes

ANNEX 2A WORLD BANK ANALYTICAL AND ADVISORY ACTIVITIES AND ECONOMIC AND SECTOR WORK RELATED TO GOVERNANCE REFORM

Blaser, J., A. Contreras, T. Oksanen, E. Puustjarvi, and F. Schmithusen. 2005. "Forest Law Enforcement and Governance (FLEG) in Europe and North Asia (ENA)." Reference paper prepared for the Ministerial Conference, St. Petersburg Russia, Nov. 22–25, 2005.

Chen, H. K. 2006. *The Role of CITES in Combating Illegal Logging: Current and Potential.* Cambridge: TRAFFIC International.

China National Forestry Economic Development Center. 2006. "A Background Paper on Forest Law Enforcement and Governance in China." Draft.

Colchester, M. 2006. *Justice in the Forest: Rural Livelihoods and Forest Law Enforcement.* CIFOR Forest Perspectives 3. Bogor, Indonesia: CIFOR.

Contreras-Hermosilla, A. 2002. Law Compliance in the Forestry Sector: An Overview. WBI Working Papers. World Bank Institute, The World Bank 2002. Also available at: http://lnweb18.worldbank.org/eap/eap.nsf/2500ec5f1a2d9bad852568a3006f557d/c19065b26241f0b247256ac30010e5ff?OpenDocument.

Dykstra, D. P., G. Kuru, R. Taylor, R. Nussbaum, W. B. Magrath, and J. Story. 2003. "Technologies for Wood Tracking: Verifying and Monitoring the Chain of Custody and Legal Compliance in the Timber Industry." Environment and Social Development East Asia and the Pacific Region Discussion Paper, The World Bank, Washington, DC, 2003.

ECSSD/PROFOR. 2005. Forest Institutions in Transition: Experiences and Lessons from Eastern Europe. The World Bank, Washington, DC, February 2005.

Gray, J. 2002. Forest Concession Policies and Revenue Systems: Country Experience and Policy Changes for Sustainable Tropical Forestry, World Bank Technical Paper No. 522, The World Bank, Washington, DC, 2002.

International Union for the Conservation of Nature and Natural Resources (IUCN). 2006. *Illegal Logging: A Commitment to Change Through Tripartite Action.* Gland, Switzerland: IUCN.

Kishor, N. 2004. Review of Formal and Informal Costs and Revenues Related to Timber Harvesting, Transporting and Trading in Indonesia. World Bank informal note. 2004.

Magrath, W. B., R. Grandalski, J. Stuckey, G. Vikanes, and G. Wilkinson. Forthcoming. *Timber Theft Prevention and Forest Resource Security.* Washington, DC: World Bank.

PAF. 2004. Benchmarking Public Services Delivery at the Forest Fringes in Jharkhand, India. Public Affairs Foundation, Bangalore, India, October 2004.

Puustjarvi, E. 2006a. "Proposal for Typology of Illegal Logging." Draft. Savcor Indufor Oy, Helsinki

———. 2006b. "Guidelines for Formulating and Implementing National Action Plans to Combat Illegal Logging and Other Forest Crime." Draft. Savcor Indufor Oy, Helsinki.

Rosenbaum, K. L. 2005. Tools for civil society action to reduce forest corruption: Drawing lessons from Transparency International. PROFOR/FIN, The World Bank, Washington, DC, 2005

Savcor Indufor Oy. 2005a. "Ensuring Sustainability of Forests and Livelihoods Through Improved Governance and Control of Illegal Logging for Economies in Transition: World Bank Discussion Paper." Helsinki.

———. 2005b. "Action Plan to Combat Illegal Activities in Forest and Wood Processing Sectors in Bosnia and Herzegovina." Draft. Savcor Indufor Oy, Helsinki.

World Bank. 2003. Reforming Forest Fiscal Systems: An Overview of Country Approaches and Experiences. PROFOR, The World Bank, Washington, February 2003.

———. 2005a. "Going, Going, Gone: The Illegal Trade in Wildlife in East and Southeast Asia." Discussion Paper. Environment and Social Development, East Asia and Pacific Region, World Bank, Washington, DC.

———. 2005b. *East Asia Region Forestry Strategy.* Washington, DC: World Bank.

———. 2006a. Strengthening Forest Law Enforcement and Governance: Strengthening a Systemic Constraint to Sustainable Development. Report No. 36638-GLB, World Bank, Washington, DC.

———. 2006b. *Forest Law: Manual for Sustainable Development.* Washington, DC: World Bank.

COMPANY-COMMUNITY PARTNERSHIPS

Company-community partnerships in forestry are active agreements for the production of forest goods and services in which the parties share benefits, costs, and risks with the expectation of a mutually beneficial outcome. Companies are formal entities organized for making a profit, and range from large multinational corporations to small-scale local businesses. Communities include local farmers, households, and community-level units of social organization, such as producer groups or village councils.

Most partnerships to date have formed around production of industrial pulpwood (outgrower, joint venture, and lease schemes) and high-quality timber (mainly lease schemes). NTFP-based partnerships are most important in the case of high-value NTFPs (such as certain resins and medicinal plants). A niche is now growing for partnerships around forest ecosystem services, including carbon sequestration, watershed management, biodiversity, and ecotourism (see note 2.3, Innovative Marketing Arrangements for Environmental Services). The variety of partnership models are covered in table 2.1.

Both company and community partners have a variety of motives for entering into agreements. Immediate economic motives include access to niche markets, access to

Box 2.3 Outgrower Contract for Wood Production: Xylo Indah Pratama, Indonesia

The company Xylo Indah Pratama manufactures pencils for sale through Faber Castell, Germany. Because of wood supply shortages and the need to access wood from certified sources, the company set up an outgrower scheme in 1995 with local farmers, using low-value uncultivated land to grow *Alstonia scholaris*. Grower contracts over 11 years are based on a 50:50 profit-sharing ratio, with the company providing most inputs, but land-owning farmers free to sell to other buyers if the company is unable to absorb the harvest at current market prices. Farmers have benefited from early revenues through trimming, and at full harvest (from 2005 onward) returns are about US$450 per hectare to both company and community.

Sources: LATIN 2000; Nawir and Santoso 2005.

Table 2.1 Company-Community Partnership Models for Different Forest Goods and Services

| Forest good or service | Partnership model | | | |
	Outgrower or sales contract	Joint venture or lease on community land	Multiple land use on company land	Social responsibility contract
Timber and wood fiber	✓ (see box 2.3)	✓	—	✓ (see box 2.4)
Nontimber forest products	✓ (see box 2.5)	—	✓ (see box 2.6)	✓
Ecosystem services	—	✓ (see box 2.7)	✓	✓

Source: Vermeulen 2006.

Note: ✓ = Such partnerships are feasible. — = Not applicable.

Box 2.4   Social Responsibility Contract for Timber Production (with Lease of Use Rights and an NTFP Agreement): Bibiani Lumber Company and the Stool (Chief) of the Omanhene, Ghana

Ghanaian legislation requires logging companies to negotiate social responsibility agreements with communities as a condition for granting concessions. The agreement between Bibiani Lumber Company and the Stool of the Omanhene, Ghana, signed in 2000, requires the company to construct boreholes, latrines, and roads; to avoid all culturally significant sites and taboo days; to consult the community over planned logging routes and sidings; and to restore any accidental damage. The agreement also spells out terms for payment of stumpage fees and royalties to the community, for continued NTFP access and sale by the community and for dispute settlement.

Source: Yeboah 2001.

Box 2.6   Multiple Land Use on Company Land: Beekeeping and Mondi, South Africa

Mondi Fine Paper SA has an arrangement whereby 40 beekeepers from local communities are allowed to keep hives in Mondi-operated forests in the Port Dunford, Umfolozi, and Melmoth areas. Mondi has paid for each beekeeper to receive technical and business training. One beekeeper running 20 hives realizes about 12,000 South African rand (US$1,700) per season (February–July) through the sale of honey to local buyers. Mondi runs this scheme partially via the consortium SiyaQhubeka Forests, which is the first Black Economic Empowerment company to acquire significant shares in South African forestry, having successfully bid for 26,450 hectares of privatized forest land in Kwa-Zulu Natal.

Sources: www.siyaqhubeka.co.za; www.mondi.co.za.

Box 2.5   Purchase Agreement for Nontimber Forest Products: Vegext Limited, Kenya

Vegext processes and exports wattle tannin, but its factory is currently working far below capacity as a result of short supplies of wattle bark (*Acacia mearnsii*). Hence, the company, in partnership with a forestry NGO, has developed purchase agreements with wattle farmers. Vegext agrees to collect bark from any farm within 70 km of its collection yard at Eldoret and to pay a higher price than competitors; indeed, one of the company's objectives is to raise wattle prices so that farmers consider wattle an attractive alternative to other tree crops and seasonal crops. The NGO connects farmers with traders who will buy the debarked logs for charcoal production, further raising returns to wattle production.

Sources: Vermeulen and Walubengo 2006.

Box 2.7   Joint Venture for Ecosystem Services: Posada Amazonas Ecotourism, Peru

In 1996 the company Rainforest Expeditions signed a 20-year joint venture agreement with the Ese'eja community of Tambopata in southeastern Peru. The company and community agreed to jointly manage 9,600 hectares of land (to which the community has legal title) and a tourist lodge, sharing profits 60:40 between the community and the company, to reflect relative investments of land, labor, and finance. The company agreed to hand over all assets to the community at the end of the joint venture. The agreement came to an early close, satisfactory to both sides, when the community bought out the company's share using an international grant. The community has since built on its strengths, opening a research center at the site and winning the Conservation International ecotourism award in 2000.

Sources: Stronza 2000; Landell-Mills and Porras 2002; http://www.wildland.com.

inputs (communities), and cost savings (companies), while longer-term motives include social responsibility and securing land tenure or long-term use rights.

Company-community forestry partnerships have the potential to contribute to Bank objectives of SFM and rural development. A recent international review (Vermeulen and Walubengo, 2006) concluded that these partnerships can help communities reduce risk, achieve better returns on land use, diversify income sources, access paid employment, develop new skills, upgrade infrastructure, and enhance ecosystem management. They are also a mechanism for companies to practice SFM on their own land (Brody et al. 2006). However, company-community partnerships have not yet proved sufficient to lift people out of poverty and remain supplementary rather than central to income generation.

OPERATIONAL ASPECTS

CONTEXT AND CONDITIONS FOR PARTNERSHIPS. Experience shows that company-community forestry partnerships can emerge under a wide range of political and economic conditions. In considering whether partnerships may be appropriate—and what kinds of partnerships are likely to work—some important conditions to consider include the following:

- Production and markets
  - *Sound business*. Artificial promotion of partnerships for social gains will not work—an internationally competitive ratio of benefits to costs and risks must be demonstrated for specific forest products at the site level.
  - *Integrated land use*. Trees for fiber and fuel compete with food crops and grazing land and may or may not provide differential environmental services—partnerships will only work where a locally appropriate balance is achieved.
  - *Multiple use*. Opportunities for multiple land use at one site favor the use of partnerships (such as combining timber production, NTFP production, and ecosystem functions).
  - *Market maturity*. New production systems and new markets favor tight contractual partnerships while developed, open markets favor looser arrangements.
  - *Access to technology and information*. Insufficient technical and market knowledge among communities is a major disincentive to formation of partnerships.

- Policy and governance
  - *Land tenure*. Changes in land and resource tenure (such as the privatization of state forests or securing of collective land title) often precipitate partnerships because partners need new deals to access forest production.
  - *Forest sector incentives*. In some countries, specific policy statements encourage partnerships (such as the comanagement requirements for state forest land).
  - *Extra-sectoral incentives*. Some policies are generally pro-partnership, such as those that encourage decentralization (see note 5.1, Decentralized Forest Management) or provide incentives to indigenous or small-scale business, while particular policies encourage different types of partnership (for example, environmental tax breaks favoring ecosystem service partnerships).
  - *Governance*. Implementation and survival of partnerships require considerable backstopping, including functional courts and efficient systems for legal recognition of representative bodies (see note 5.4, Strengthening Fiscal Systems in the Forest Sector).[1]
  - *Private-sector policy*. Multinational corporate policies can precipitate transfer of partnership models internationally.

CONTRACTUAL ARRANGEMENTS. Partnership models may be based on successful arrangements elsewhere—and initial negotiations often depend on an external moderator. Typical agreements, verbal or written, include terms for financial and technical inputs, loan repayments, and benefit-sharing. Partners involved can benefit from advice and oversight on contractual terms (see Mayers and Vermeulen [2002] for guidance), and options for making the most of external incentive schemes should be explored, including carbon credits, certification, or business compacts.

TIME REQUIREMENT FOR FORMING PARTNERSHIPS. It takes continual investment over long periods to build partnerships. Experience to date reveals three broad scenarios for the development of company-community forestry relationships: (i) little constitutive change over long periods, with the company partner taking the lead in directing the partnership; (ii) strengthening of the community partner's position, such as renegotiation of benefit sharing or the community forming a company; and (iii) dissolution of the partnership (see "Ending a Partnership" below). A move toward tighter partnerships is not always desirable—in buoyant, competitive forest product markets, looser arrangements that are sensitive to demand and price trends will be much more sustainable.

IMPORTANCE OF RISK AND OPERATIONAL FLEXIBILITY. Partnerships are a means to share risks, particularly those associated with production and markets. Adaptability has proved to be key to the success of company-community partnerships. Best practices include allowance in contracts for flexible technical features (for example, partial early harvesting of timber, annual reassessments of NTFP offtake, variable levies for tourism or other ecosystem services), flexible loan repayment terms, provisions for alternative avenues for marketing in the event of over- or under-harvest, well-defined terms for managing any disputes, and renegotiating the contract on a regular basis.

TRANSACTION COSTS AND POWER SHARING. Dealing with a large number of scattered farmers or groups is a major challenge, not only for technical reasons (extension, harvesting, transport) but also for collective decision making. Power sharing is critical for both equity and resilience of partnerships (Ashman 2001). For communities, the solution is to create economies of scale and raise bargaining power by joining or forming farmers' groups, cooperatives, and other coalitions. Even small associations have been successful in saving costs and improving marketing—but so far there are few examples of communities improving partnership terms through collective bargaining.

ENDING A PARTNERSHIP. Some partnerships have disintegrated amid bad faith and litigation. However, termination does not necessarily mean failure, and conversely, close partnerships may outlive their utility. As priorities and market opportunities shift, partners may make strategic choices away from formal collaboration toward looser working relations. For the community, the partnership may be a steppingstone to developing viable independent enterprises, while for the company, the increased business acumen within the community provides reliable new opportunities (to develop and supply high-quality products and services, for instance).

LESSONS LEARNED AND RECOMMENDATIONS FOR PRACTITIONERS

Company-community partnerships take a long time to establish—they are built on trust gained through experience. The World Bank and other third parties can play a cru-

cial role in enabling and supporting company-community partnerships for the benefit of local livelihoods and SFM.

■ Existing local organizations are an important route to building deal-brokering capacity in communities. These local organizations often have the institutional flexibility to service community needs independent of external influences and the potential to provide equitable representation and a forum for equitable negotiation.

■ Empowerment must be an explicit objective of partnership schemes. Often the poorest people are only participants as contractors to those with land. To enable community empowerment, arrangements for revenue sharing, sharing ownership in downstream processing, and other broader joint ventures are important. Empowerment must be an objective if partnerships are to substantively raise people out of poverty.

■ Greater attention must be given to forming enterprise partnerships with entities other than limited liability companies. Partnership structures, such as cooperatives, should also be explored.

■ The details of benefit sharing and cost and risk sharing should be examined closely to ensure that the term "partnership" describes arrangements that are equitable for all parties.

■ Local communities may often need legal assistance to clarify their land ownership rights and in negotiating such rights.

■ There is a risk that benefits may only accrue to a small section of the community (for example, outgrower households) while the community at large may suffer loss of land rights and resource access (livestock households, for instance), leading to a need to examine both business projection and local tenure arrangements (legal and customary) to ensure such outcomes are avoided.

EXPLORE CURRENT OPTIONS AND FUTURE SCENARIOS FOR PARTNERSHIPS. This includes supporting work toward increasing understanding of practical arrangements for efficient and equitable community-company partnerships. It is important to build understanding in the community of practice of the impacts of corporate social responsibility and the cooperative movement. Equally important is to exploit the willingness of companies to network on company-community partnerships (for example, in Indonesia and South Africa). Leading companies can continue to exchange experiences and to experiment with innovative tools that promote equitable company-community arrangements, such as ethical supply chain management and transparent corporate reporting. These companies lead the way by going beyond legislative requirements to explore pioneering partnership models.

PROMOTE ACCESS TO INSURANCE, CREDIT, AND LEGAL AND BUSINESS SERVICES. Community partners would gain much from mechanisms to mitigate risk independently, outside the partnership. Such mechanisms can be developed by investing in insurance schemes that explore alternative policies for small-scale producers and strengthening safety nets for community members who may lose if a partnership ends. Communities involved in partnerships would also benefit from independent arbitration and assistance with legal aid in the event of legal actions. There have been advancements in small-scale finance schemes, yet more support is needed. Business information and advisory services for partners also still need support.

SUPPORT CAPACITY BUILDING FOR BUSINESS SKILL DEVELOPMENT. The performance of community partners would improve further through support to capacity-building in business (for example, understanding organizational and contractual models, market niches and market standing, technology and innovation, management of costs, and future trends). The capacity of community institutions and individuals needs to be strengthened in negotiation skills, negotiation of contractual terms, and business development. Greater support for development of community entrepreneurship is also important.

ENSURE POLICY COHERENCE AND ACCESSIBILITY. Partnerships are influenced by government policy and service provision across several sectors (for example, land, tax, trade, agriculture, forestry). Companies, communities, and their supporters repeatedly raise the need for national and local governments to coordinate and clarify relevant incentives, regulations, and agencies (Howard et al. 2005; Vidal 2005a, 2005b). While industry standards can help, governments and international bodies need to guard against stringency that favors the largest players in the industry at the expense of smaller, locally owned companies. To ensure this, members of representative community bodies should be included in policy dialogue at the national level. Governments would gain from support in development of complementary or alternative partnership facilitation services.

SUPPORT THE DEVELOPMENT OF VALUE ADDED PRODUCTS AND SERVICES. Few company-community partnerships go beyond production or site management. Community partners can reap far greater benefits if they are able to capture a share of value added operations, such as timber sawmills, downstream processing of NTFPs, or add-ons to ecosystem management (tailored tourism facilities, for instance; see box 2.5 and box 2.7 for examples). Supporters could also facilitate new business links that help communities secure a larger share of the value chain (for example, Fair Trade). New initiatives that include multiple roles for the community can help to bring benefits to the poorest members of the community who are otherwise excluded (by providing employment to landless people, for instance).

SUPPORT COMMUNITY NETWORKS AND THEIR REPRESENTATION. Associations and coalitions continue to be the most effective routes for communities to raise bargaining power. Support to networks and associations of community interests and emerging small businesses will help, as will efforts to increase meaningful representation by small-scale providers of forest goods and services in existing platforms for the forestry industry. Existing bodies that represent community interests are both legitimate and dynamic and may be forest specific or formed around agriculture.

NOTE

1. An ongoing IIED-supported program currently operational in 10 countries is supporting strengthening of bargaining power of local communities that are in the course of negotiating fair prices and legally enforced safe working conditions.

SELECTED READINGS: REVIEWS

Mayers, J., and A. Vermeulen. 2002. *Company-Community Partnerships in Forestry: From Raw Deals to Mutual Gains?* Instruments for Sustainable Private Sector Forestry series. London: International Institute for Environment and Development.

Nussbaum, R. 2002. "Group Certification for Forests: A Practical Guide." ProForest, Oxford.

Scherr, S., A. White, and D. Kaimowitz. 2003. "Making Markets Work for Forest Communities." *International Forestry Review* 5 (1): 67–73.

Vermeulen, S., A. A. Nawir, and J. Mayers. Forthcoming. "Rural Poverty Reduction Through Business Partnerships? Examples of Experience from the Forestry Sector." Environment, Development and Sustainability.

Wunder, S. 2005. "Payments for Environmental Services: Some Nuts and Bolts." CIFOR Occasional Paper No. 42, Center for International Forestry Research, Indonesia.

SELECTED READINGS: COUNTRY CASES

Ashley, C., and Z. Ntshona. 2003. "Transforming Roles but not Reality? Private Sector and Community Involvement in Tourism and Forestry Development on the Wild Coast." Overseas Development Institute, U.K., and University of Western Cape, South Africa.

Howard, M., P. Matikinca, D. Mitchell, F. Brown, F. Lewis, I. Mahlangu, A. Msimang, P. Nixon, and T. Radebe. 2005. "Small-Scale Timber Production in South Africa: What Role in Reducing Poverty?" Small and Medium Forest Enterprise Series, Discussion Paper No. 9. London: International Institute for Environment and Development.

Mayers, J. 2006. "Poverty Reduction Through Commercial Forestry. What Evidence? What Prospects?" TFD Publication No. 2, School of Forestry and Environmental Studies, Yale University, New Haven, CT.

Vermeulen, S., and D. Walubengo. 2006. "Developing Partnerships for Sustainable Management of Forests in Kenya: Review of Existing Models and Set of Options for Further Support." Report prepared for the Forest Department Kenya and PROFOR (Program on Forests), World Bank. International Institute for Environment and Development, London.

Vidal, N. 2005. "Forest Company-Community Agreements in Mexico: Identifying Successful Models." Forest Trends, Washington, DC.

REFERENCES CITED

Ashman, D. 2001. "Civil Society Collaboration with Business: Bringing Empowerment Back." World Development 29: 1097–1113.

Brody, S. D., S. B. Cash, J. Dyke, and S. Thornton. 2006. "Motivations for the Forestry Industry to Participate in Collaborative Ecosystem Management Initiatives." Forest Policy and Economics 8: 123–34.

Howard, M., P. Matikinca, D. Mitchell, F. Brown, F. Lewis, I. Mahlangu, A. Msimang, P. Nixon, and T. Radebe. 2005. "Small-Scale Timber Production in South Africa: What Role in Reducing Poverty?" Small and Medium Forest Enterprise Series Discussion Paper No. 9. London: International Institute for Environment and Development.

Landell-Mills, N., and I. T. Porras. 2002. *Silver Bullet or Fools' Gold? A Global Review of Markets for Forest Envi-* *ronmental Services and Their Impacts on the Poor.* Instruments for Sustainable Private Sector Forestry series. London: International Institute for Environment and Development.

LATIN (Lembaga Alam Tropika Indonesia). 2000. "Corporate Community Partnership Between PT Xylo Indah Pratama and the Local Community in Musi Rawas District, South Sumatera, Indonesia." LATIN, Bogor, Indonesia, and International Institute for Environment and Development, London.

Mayers, J., and A. Vermeulen. 2002. *Company-Community Partnerships in Forestry: From Raw Deals to Mutual Gains?* Instruments for Sustainable Private Sector Forestry series. London: International Institute for Environment and Development.

Nawir, A. A., and L. Santoso. 2005. "Mutually Beneficial Company-Community Partnerships in Plantation Development: Emerging Lessons from Indonesia." *International Forestry Review* 7 (3): 177–92.

Stronza, A. 2000. "'Because It is Ours': Community-Based Ecotourism in the Peruvian Amazon." Unpublished thesis, University of Florida at Gainesville.

Vermeulen, S. 2006. "Company-Community Partnerships." Note submitted to World Bank as input to *Forests Sourcebook.* Unpublished. World Bank, Washington, DC.

Vermeulen, S., and D. Walubengo. 2006. "Developing Partnerships for Sustainable Management of Forests in Kenya: Review of Existing Models and Set of Options for Further Support." Report prepared for the Forest Department Kenya and PROFOR (Program on Forests), World Bank. International Institute for Environment and Development, London.

Vidal, N. 2005a. "Forest Company-Community Agreements in Brazil: Current Status and Opportunities for Action." *Forest Trends,* Washington, DC.

————. 2005b. "Forest Company-Community Agreements in Mexico: Identifying Successful Models." Forest Trends, Washington, DC.

Yeboah, R. 2001. "Short Report on Social Responsibility Agreements in Ghana." International Institute for Environment and Development, London.

CROSS-REFERENCED CHAPTERS AND NOTES

Note 2.3: Innovative Marketing Arrangements for Environmental Services

Note 5.1: Decentralized Forest Management

Note 5.4: Strengthening Fiscal Systems in the Forest Sector

Small and Medium Enterprises

SMFEs are business operations aimed at making profit from forest-based activity. They are commonly defined by employment (between 10 and 99 full-time employees), by annual turnover (US$10,000–US$30,000,000), or by annual roundwood consumption (3,000–20,000 cubic meters) (Macqueen and Mayers 2006).

SMFEs can offer a trajectory out of poverty. SMFEs play a critical role in securing poor people's basic needs, spreading wealth locally, enabling local innovation, and preserving cultural identity and practices (Macqueen 2005; Macqueen and Mayers 2006). SMFEs grouped together in clusters or associations can reduce transaction costs for the poor, develop strategic alliances, and shape the policy environment through lobbying on behalf of the poor (Macqueen, Figueiredo et al. 2005; Macqueen, Vermeulen et al. 2005).

SMFEs are diverse and complicated to deal with. SMFE diversity is linked to a number of factors, including that they span both timber and NTFPs, and include rural producers, suppliers to large firms, primary and secondary processors, and forest service providers. It is difficult to make generalizations regarding SMFEs; thus, it is important to consider the following:

- how supportive the policy and institutional environments are toward SMFEs (Macqueen 2005)
- whether the market structure offers real opportunity or merely options of last resort
- whether the business structures adopted by SMFEs are those of profit-driven companies, democratically accountable social cooperatives, or something in between (Macqueen 2006)
- whether SMFEs are isolated entities or an integral part of a broader network

SMFEs tend to be underrepresented in policy initiatives and development programs. This could be on account of the following:

- the complexity of linking with diverse SMFEs in multiple locations—even when they are grouped into associations (there are 2,000–3,000 forest-based associations in Uganda; Kazoora et al. 2006)
- the constitutional diversity of these enterprises, which diminishes the likelihood of common agendas, lesson learning, and diffusion of relevant solutions (Saigal et al. 2006)
- the small individual scale of each enterprise, which reduces both per unit impact (that is, the perceived benefit to the development agency) and comparative human and financial costs of compliance (that is, the perceived benefits to the enterprise)
- The lack of formal incorporation and collateral through which SMFEs become visible to public bodies and private sector investors. For example, the informal economy makes up 41 percent of gross national income in developing countries (Schneider 2002) and is highest where incomes and assets are not evenly distributed (Becker 2004)

Despite their potential, it can be challenging to make SMFEs sustainable. Exploitative SMFEs can easily go unchecked. Informality, insecure tenure, low investment, and low profitability may reduce scope for social or environmental benefits. Lack of management capacity in SMFEs may lead to resource depletion. Risks are highest in "distress diversification," where SMFEs seek refuge in low-skill activities and seasonal migration for products without long-term prospects. High risks often lead policy makers and decision makers to marginalize SMFEs, but perhaps because of this, many self-help solutions have evolved around local enterprise associations and networks. Responsive support to these local institutions in areas such as market information, secure resource access, sustainable management, design and technology, and financial and business administration can make all the difference.

Due consideration should be given to the different values recognized by different types of SMFEs. The diversity of SMFEs is paralleled by a diversity of values. For example, profit-driven SMFEs may place economic values above social or environmental concerns (Macqueen 2006), while local or indigenous forest groups attribute up to 13 different values to forests (Brown and Reed 2000), of which "commercial values" used by economists in cost-benefit analysis or internal rate of return calculations represent only 6 percent of the sum of scaled forest values (Rowcroft, Studley, and Ward 2006).

SMFEs have variable social impacts. Depending on enterprise type, management disposition, and circumstances, SMFEs may differ in their social impact. Distress diversification or "SMFEs of last resort" often fail to deliver increasing social welfare. Particular care is required where outsourcing to SMFEs is prevalent (Clarke and Isaacs 2005), and greater benefits are evident in "upwardly mobile" SMFEs (Arnold and Townson 1998; Belcher, Ruiz-Perez, and Achdiawan 2005). For some products and services, market opportunities expand with the SMFE's increasing income, and the economic distance between SMFEs and large enterprise technologies, and employment standards, start to fall. Identifying which is which—whether the SMFE is of last resort or upwardly mobile—is a critical first step for appropriate intervention.

SMFEs have variable environmental impacts; enterprise type, management disposition, and the policy environment largely determine environmental impacts. SMFEs may cut environmental corners in the search for economic competitiveness, especially if the underlying legal and regulatory framework and government capacity for implementation are weak. Informality of operations, insecure tenure, inadequate investment, and low profitability may reduce environmental benefits. For example, SMFEs face great difficulty with third-party certification (Higmann and Nussbaum 2002) despite group schemes designed to accommodate them (Forest Stewardship Council 2004). For many SMFEs, local accountability for environmental impacts can enhance environmental quality, especially at the landscape level (Clay, Alcorn, and Butler 2000; Scherr, White, and Kaimowitz 2004; Durst and others 2005).

OPERATIONAL ASPECTS

Annex 2.2A to this note provides a checklist of key issues to consider to determine SMFE program direction and feasibility. This section discusses some of these issues in more detail.

STRENGTHEN TRANSPARENT ACCESS TO LAND AND RESOURCES FOR SMFEs. There are no cure-alls that will ensure transparent access to land and resources, and neither individual title, nor, conversely, community forest management, strengthens SMFEs in all cases. In some cases, clear land titling helps. In others, it is the democratic involvement of marginalized groups in decisions over common land that is critical. A priority is to identify and address, jointly with SMFEs, ill-developed or poorly understood codes and institutions that govern these rights (see note 1.4, Property and Access Rights). Many forest products or services with SMFE potential come from common property resources, which cannot be privatized, thus collective rather than individual decisions are required.

SUPPORT LOCAL SOVEREIGNTY AND ORIENT SMFEs PRIMARILY TO LOCAL PRODUCT OR SERVICE MARKETS. SMFEs can flourish in situations where they respond to civil society concerns about where products are originating, how they are produced, and who is profiting.[1] With regard to wider applicability, it is worthwhile to support SMFEs in identifying demand in local markets that are not yet highly competitive, local skills that can be used, options for specialization over time, and nonperishable products, unless excellent infrastructure exists. See box 2.8 for examples from India and Guyana.

IDENTIFY "SUPERIOR" PRODUCTS OR SERVICES FOR WHICH DEMAND RISES WITH INCREASING INCOME. Products that are only useful as subsistence safety nets or seasonal gap fillers

> ### Box 2.8 Local Sovereignty, Markets, and SMFEs in India and Guyana
>
> In India, the Madhya Pradesh Minor Forest Produce Cooperative has successfully developed a task force on ayurvedic herbal medicines with a retail outlet and consultations to support primary NTFP medicinal plant collection and processing societies (Saigal and others 2006). In Guyana, the Surama Eco-tourism Enterprise has developed a tourism package to showcase Makushi cultural identity and natural resources—a win-win combination for culturally sensitive development and the environment (Ousman and others 2006). An important lesson is that, unless ethical market niches or a unique world-class resource exists, it can be unwise to target export markets.

must be distinguished from products and services that can be critical steppingstones out of poverty.

IMPROVE INFORMATION FLOWS. SMFEs generally suffer from poor market information, and global communication technology and market access favor large multinationals, often to the detriment of SMFEs. Timely market information, through local radio networks or electronic media, can shift the balance back in their favor. For some products, local cultural tastes and the origin of production still count, which gives SMFEs local competitive advantages.

HELP BREAK UP MARKET MONOPOLIES. Market monopolies tend to exclude SMFEs—especially where large enterprises and government officials collude. In India, for example, the negative impact on small-scale producers of government marketing corporations has been well documented. Systematic attempts to break up monopolies (and associated collusion and corruption) require action at many levels. Mobilizing local legal support groups or independent forest monitoring can be useful tactics.

SUPPORT APPROPRIATE ECONOMIC INCENTIVES OR CAMPAIGNS AGAINST UNREASONABLE SUBSIDIES AND TRADE BARRIERS—DEPENDING ON CIRCUMSTANCES. Free trade can be biased toward larger enterprises because of inequities in power and scale efficiencies. Depending on the context, it may be necessary to ensure that trade reforms and economic incentives do not result in accumulation of power in the hands of a few, marginalizing small-scale producers.

STRENGTHEN THE CAPACITY OF SMFEs TO ATTRACT INVESTMENT. Building capacity for accurate risk assessments, installing policy interventions to underwrite collateral, and developing financial administration all can serve to attract investment. Transaction costs hamper the attempts of financial institutions to reach SMFEs—who often rely on their own savings (Spantigati and Springfors 2005). In some cases, group forest certification has been a useful tool for unlocking credit (see note 3.2, Forest Certification Systems).

STRENGTHEN THE CAPACITY TO NEGOTIATE FINANCIAL DEALS WITH INVESTMENT AGENCIES AND BIG BUSINESS. The potential often exists to combine financial capacity development, group lending schemes, and market development (see box 2.9 for an example from Guatemala).

Seeking support through local institutions deserves wider application. Also, risk assessments should better reflect forest timeframes, seasonality, returns, and constraints so that banks are better able to do business with SMFEs.

BUILD CAPACITY IN PRODUCT OR SERVICE DESIGN. Specialization is often critical to ongoing success. Information about what customers want can be obtained through training courses in design, trade fairs, pooled market research within an association, benign middlemen, or specialized information services, such as market chain workshops. Consumer concerns for fairer trade and more sustainable forest management drive networks that specifically target SMFEs and build their entrepreneurial capacity—even if all of the final product or service is not distributed through such channels.

DEVELOP ECONOMIC INCENTIVES OR GRANTS TO SUPPORT THE NEEDS OF FOREST ENTERPRISE ASSOCIATIONS. Forest enterprise associations can help shape the policy environment, reduce transaction costs, and invest in adaptive strategies to take advantage of new opportunities. Specific administrative, financial, and technical training can be extremely useful if properly targeted through existing associations (see box 2.10 for an example from Brazil).

DEVOLVE CONTROL OVER FOREST MANAGEMENT TO LOCAL SMFEs TO REDUCE THE RISK OF FOREST CONFLICTS, which are endemic to many forested areas.[2] Insecure rights and inequitable resource use in remote forest areas breed

---

Box 2.9 Building SMFE Negotiating Capacity

In Guatemala, community forest enterprises in the heavily forested Petén region managed to obtain credit from two banks, Banrural and Bancafé. This achievement was based heavily on (i) support for clear tenure rights, such as the legal establishment of a community concession system; (ii) technical support from business development providers; (iii) strong partnerships (including advance payments) with the timber industry and a dedicated joint marketing company (Forescom); and (iv) an association, Forest Communities of Petén, that provided bridging loans.

Source: Macqueen 2006.

grievances—in more extreme cases providing the motive and means for financing conflict (Kaimowitz 2005). In certain circumstances, putting local resources into local hands may be most appropriate. Local SMFEs generally have a greater understanding of local social and political contexts, stronger links with local civil society, and a greater commitment to operating in a specific area than do large-scale enterprises. Inappropriate forest land allocation to large players (even if justified by more sustainable forest management) may undermine local control and its "silent social responsibility" and generate conflict (Ozinga 2004).

LESSONS LEARNED AND RECOMMENDATIONS FOR PRACTITIONERS

INVEST IN UNDERSTANDING SMFEs and, if appropriate, initially work with pilots. Information on SMFEs in developing countries is often inadequate, especially for NTFPs (Thomas and others 2003), and it takes time to collect information and assess the impact of policies on SMFEs in the field (Johnstone, Cau, and Norfolk 2004; Johnstone and others 2004). SMFE staff are also usually heavily time-constrained and risk averse. Hidden constraints can prevent expansion of forest product activities. Available time, cultural

roles, social priorities, and misconceptions or mistrust of the language of economic development can affect outcomes. Tools to get to know entrepreneurs are essential (Mangal and Forte 2005). Smaller trial interventions with a long time frame may be necessary for initial implementation.

ENSURE THAT INTERVENTIONS ARE BASED ON DEMAND-DRIVEN APPROACHES RATHER THAN APPROACHES TO SUPPLYING CAPACITY. Trying to make what sells is invariably better than trying to sell what can be made. Too often the focus of SMFE programs is supply driven—for example, trying to create employment or raise income levels (Artur and Kanji 2005).

PARTNERSHIPS BETWEEN LARGE FIRMS AND SMFEs CAN HELP TO OVERCOME SOME OF THE CAPACITY DEFICITS that constrain vertical adaptation and specialization. Fair deals that balance resource supply with technological exchange from the large firm is a model that has worked in instances where it is in the interest of both sides. However, it must be assumed that negotiations are stacked in favor of large firms; thus, specific tools and processes should be used to equip SMFEs for negotiating (Joaquim, Norfolk, and Macqueen 2005).

WORK WITH EXISTING ENTERPRISE ASSOCIATIONS. The vast majority of SMFEs link themselves in some way to associations that help to shape the policy environment, reduce transaction costs, and invest in adaptive strategies to take advantage of new opportunities. Good information can be found about what makes associations work well (for example, Agrawal 2001). Working with trusted intermediaries to support the specific training needs identified by associations is fundamental to SMFE support (Macqueen, Figueiredo et al. 2006; Macqueen, Vermeulen et al. 2005).

GIVE PREFERENTIAL SUPPORT TO FORMS OF ENTERPRISE THAT ARE DESIGNED TO ACHIEVE PROGRESSIVE SOCIAL AND ENVIRONMENTAL OBJECTIVES. For some enterprises, such as associations, cooperatives, and nonprofit companies linked to marginalized groups, these objectives are as important as profit, and it is worth providing preferential support to or procurement policies for such aims (Macqueen 2006). Tools such as Fair Trade already exist that favor cooperative forms of enterprise or particular marginalized groups (for example, black economic empowerment procurement policies in South Africa or equivalents for First Nations in Canada).

ESTABLISH CROSS-AGENCY COORDINATION TO SIMPLIFY, STABILIZE, AND IMPLEMENT PRO-SMFE POLICIES AND SUPPORT PROGRAMS. In many countries, the burden of overregulation falls most heavily on smaller enterprises (see box 2.11 on South Africa). Experience has shown that SMFEs require a range of policy and support services and that external intervention can help to ensure that there is some degree of dialogue between such services, both to optimize what exists and to identify gaps.

INSTITUTIONALIZE MECHANISMS TO COORDINATE SMFE ACTIVITIES ACROSS MULTIPLE GOVERNMENT AUTHORITIES. Multiple overlapping authorities with varying responsibilities can often tie up the SMFE sector in red tape. Developing strong and clear advocacy messages within broad coalitions can shift policies and institutions. For example, depending on the context, it may be useful to establish a cross-ministerial SME development council or administrative body to coordinate policies. This might be linked with sector-specific SME centers, including forestry. In turn, these might interact with SME investment companies and banks or technical and business support companies, including cooperatives and credit unions.

SUPPORT FOR SMFEs CAN BE CHANNELED THROUGH LEADERS OF LOCAL ENTERPRISE ASSOCIATIONS AND COOPERATIVES. Dynamic individuals (often necessary to the establishment of an enterprise association) can serve as useful contact points about how to channel support to SMFEs. Associations work best when they arise independently without political patronage; this should be supported rather than creating new institutions (Agrawal 2001).

TRACK AND SUPPORT EXTENSION NETWORKS OF LOCAL ACTIVISTS WHO SUPPORT SMFEs. Experience has shown that SMFE support programs run by local groups and activists with long track records of community engagement can be successful and overcome the problems of centralized extension and support services that often bypass SMFEs (see box 2.12). Local networks can build administrative and technical capacity. It is vital that such local institutions, and the SMFEs they support, are known and understood; thus, data on SMFEs and their supporting institutions need to be collected. Such data could inform the option of catalyzing and rolling out programs area by area.

NOTES

1. While this is the starting point for most communities and for many this is the market focus that remains, some communities and some products could have export opportunities, especially for some commercially valuable NTFPs.

2. Reduction of forest conflicts through devolution of control is partly contingent on efficient land and forest tenure.

SELECTED READINGS

Auren, R., and K. Krassowska. 2003. "Small and Medium Forestry Enterprises in Uganda: How Can They be Profitable, Sustainable and Poverty Reducing?" Uganda Forestry Sector Coordination Secretariat (FRSCS) and International Institute for Environment and Development (IIED), London.

Box 2.11   South African SMFEs and the Burden of Bureaucracy

In many countries the burden of overregulation falls most heavily on smaller enterprises. For example, in South Africa the paperwork involved with value-added tax management, contributions to the Unemployment Insurance Fund, district municipality levies, and training levies can stretch small firms. Many useful support programs exist. For example, the Centre for Small Business Promotion (policy), the Ntsika Enterprise Promotion Agency (nonfinancial services), Khula Enterprise Finance Limited (financial services), and the Forest Industry Education and Training Association (training) all provide useful services. However, overall leadership and coordination is lacking and might be provided by some cross-ministerial SME development council or brokering bodies that could coordinate policies, interact with investment sources, and provide business support.

Source: Lewis and others 2003.

Box 2.12   Supporting Local Activists Who Support SMFEs in Guyana

In Guyana the North Rupununi District Development Board has successfully supported a range of local initiatives, including a logging cooperative, an agricultural producers association, a revolving development fund, a women's revolving loan scheme, a credit and development trust, community natural resources management projects, and the Bina Hill Training Institute (Ousman, Roberts, and Macqueen 2006). Local development of these initiatives followed methods documented elsewhere (Tilakarnata 1980; Albee and Boyd 1997).

Boyd, G. 2001. "Guidelines for a Poverty Focused Community Assistance Service." Caledonia, Edinburgh, Scotland.

Carter, J.. and J. Gronow. 2005. "Recent Experience in Collaborative Forest Management: A Review Paper." CIFOR Occasional Paper No. 43, CIFOR, Bogor, Indonesia.

FAO. 2005. *State of the World's Forests 2005.* Rome: FAO.

Global Witness. 2005. "Independent Forest Monitoring: A Tool for Social Justice?" Power Tools Series, Global Witness, London, and International Institute for Environment and Development, London.

Fisseha, Y. 1987. "Basic Features of Rural Small-Scale Forest-Based Processing Enterprises in Developing Countries." In *Small-Scale Forest-Based Processing Enterprises,* ed. FAO. Rome: FAO.

IIED (International Institute for Environment and Development). 2004. *Making Land Rights More Secure: Proceedings of an International Workshop.* Ouagadougou, March 19–21, 2002. London: IIED.

ILO (International Labour Organisation). 2001. *Globalization and Sustainability: The Forestry and Wood Industries on the Move.* Geneva: ILO.

Lecup, I., and K. Nicholson. 2000. "Community-Based Tree and Forest Product Enterprises: Market Analysis and Development." FAO and RECOFT, Rome.

Macqueen, D. J., S. Bose, S. Bukula, C. Kazoora, S. Ousman, N. Porro, and H. Weyerhaueser. 2006. "Working Together: Forest-Linked Small and Medium Enterprise Associations and Collective Action." Gatekeeper series, IIED, London.

May, P. H., V. G. Da Vinha, and D. J. Macqueen. 2003. *Small and Medium Forest Enterprise in Brazil.* London: *Grupo Economia do Meio Ambiente e Desenvolvimento Sustentável* (GEMA) and IIED.

Opoku, K., and E. Yaw Danso. 2005. "People's Law: Ideas for Resource Rights Campaigners." Power tools series, Forest Watch Ghana, Accra, Ghana, and IIED, London.

Phi, L. T. 2005. "Better Business: Market Chain Workshops." Power tools series, Non-timber Forest Products Research Centre, Hanoi, Vietnam, and IIED, London.

Redfern, A., and P. Snedker. 2002. "Creating Market Opportunities for Small Enterprises: Experiences of the Fair Trade Movement." SEED Working Paper No. 30, International Labour Office, Geneva, Switzerland.

Salafsky, N., B. Cordes, J. Parks, and C. Hochman. 1999. "Evaluating Linkages Between Business, the Environment, and Local Communities: Final Analytical Results from the Biodiversity Conservation Network." Biodiversity Support Program, Washington, DC.

Scherr, S. J., A. White, and D. Kaimowitz. 2004. "A New Agenda for Forest Conservation and Poverty Reduction." Forest Trends, Washington, DC.

Schreckenberg, K., E. Marshall, A. Newton, J. Rushton, and D. W. te Velde. 2006. "Commercialization of Non-Timber Forest Products: Factors Influencing Success." UNEP World Conservation Monitoring Centre, Cambridge, U.K.

Sun, C., and X. Chen. 2003. "Small and Medium Forestry Enterprises in China: An Initial Review of Sustainability and Livelihood Issues." Research Center of Ecological and Environmental Economics (RCEEE) and IIED, London.

Vantomme, P. 2004. "Extraction of Nonwood Forest Products." In Challenges in Managing Forest Genetic Resources for Livelihoods: Examples from Argentina and Brazil, ed. B. Vinceti, W. Amaral, and B. Meilleur, 51–69. Rome: International Plant Genetic Resources Institute.

REFERENCES CITED

Agrawal, A. 2001. "Common Property Institutions and Sustainable Governance of Resources." *World Development* 29 (10):1649–72.

Albee, A. and Boyd, G. 1997. "Doing it differently - networks of community development agents." Caledonia, Edinburgh, Scotland.

Arnold, J. E. M., and I. Townson. 1998. "Assessing the Potential of Forest Product Activities to Contribute to Rural Incomes in Africa." Natural Resource Perspectives No. 37, Overseas Development Institute, London.

Artur, L., and N. Kanji. 2005. "Satellites and Subsidies: Learning from Experience in Cashew Processing in Northern Mozambique." IIED, London.

Becker, K. F. 2004. "The Informal Economy. Fact Finding Study." Sida, Stockholm. http://www.sida.se/publications.

Belcher, B. M., M. Ruiz-Perez, and R. Achdiawan. 2005. "Global Patterns and Trends in the Use and Management of Commercial NTFPs: Implications for Livelihoods." *World Development* 33 (9):1435–52.

Brown, G., and P. Reed. 2000. "Validation of a Forest Values Typology for Use in National Forest Planning." *Forest Science* 46 (2):240–7.

Clarke, J., and M. Isaacs. 2005. "Forestry Contractors in South Africa: What Role in Reducing Poverty?" IIED, London.

Clay, J. W., J. Alcorn, and J. Butler. 2000. "Indigenous Peoples, Forest Management and Biodiversity Conservation." World Bank, Washington, DC.

Durst, P. B., C. Brown, H. D. Tacio, and M. Ishikawa, eds. 2005. *In Search of Excellence: Exemplary Forest Management in Asia and the Pacific.* FAO and RECOFT, Bangkok, Thailand.

Figueiredo, L.D., Porro, N. and Pereira, L.S. 2006. "Associations in Emergent Communities at the Amazon Forest Frontier, Mato Grosso." Instituto de Pesquisa Ambiental da Amazônia (IPAM) and the International Institute for Environment and Development (IIED), London.

FSC (Forest Stewardship Council). 2004. "SLIMF Streamlined Certification Procedures: Summary." FSC-POL-20-101. http://www.fsc.org/slimf/docs/FSC-POL-20-101%20SLIMF%20streamlined%20certification%20procedures.PDF.

Higman, S., and R. Nussbaum. 2002. "How Standards Constrain the Certification of Small Forest Enterprises." Pro-Forest, Oxford. http://www.proforest.net/ index3.htm.

Joaquim, E., S. Norfolk. and D. Macqueen. 2005. "Avante consulta! Effective consultation." Power Tools Series, Terra Firma, Maputo, Mozambique, and IIED, London.

Johnstone, R., B. Cau, and S. Norfolk. 2004. "Forest Legislation in Mozambique: Compliance and the Impacts on Forest Communities." Terra Firma, Maputo, Mozambique, and IIED, London.

Johnstone, R., B. Cau, S. Norfolk, and D. J. Macqueen. 2004. "The Good Average Bad (GAB) Framework for Scrutinising and Improving Legislation." Terra Firma, Maputo, Mozambique.

Kaimowitz, D. 2005. "Forests and Armed Conflict." *EFTRN* [European Tropical Forest Research Network] News 43–44: 5–7.

Kazoora, C., J. Acworth, C. Tondo, and B. Kazunga. 2006. *Forest-Based Associations as Drivers for Sustainable Development in Uganda.* London: Sustainable Development Centre and IIED.

Lewis, F., J. Horn, M. Howard, and S. Ngubane. 2003. "Small and Medium Enterprises in the Forestry Sector in South Africa: An Analysis of Key Issues." Institute of Natural Resources, Forestry South Africa and Fractal Forests, and IIED, London.

Macqueen, D. J. 2005. "Small Scale Enterprise and Sustainable Development: Key Issues and Policy Opportunities to Improve Impact." IIED, Edinburgh, U.K.

———. 2006. "Governance Towards Responsible Forest Business: Guidance on Different Types of Forest Business and the Ethics to Which They Gravitate." IIED, Edinburgh, U.K.

Macqueen, D. J., L. Figueiredo, F. Merry, and N. Porro. 2005. "Stronger by Association: Small and Medium Scale Forest Enterprise in the Brazilian Amazon." *Participatory Learning and Action* 53: 31–36.

Macqueen, D. J., and J. Mayers. 2006. "Forestry's Messy Middle: A Review of Sustainability Issues for Small and Medium Forest Enterprises." Unpublished, IIED, Edinburgh, U.K.

Macqueen, D. J., S. Vermeulen, C. Kazoora, F. Merry, S. Ousman, S. Saigal, S. Wen, and H. Weyerhaeuser. 2005. "Advancement Through Association: Appropriate Support for Associations of Small and Medium Forest Enterprises." In *How to Make Poverty History—The Central Role of Local Organisations in Meeting the MDGs,* ed. T. Bigg and D. Satterthwaite, 79–98. London, IIED.

Mangal, S., and J. Forte. 2005. "Community Tradeoffs Assessment: For Culture-Sensitive Planning and Evaluation." Power Tools Series, IIED, London.

Ousman, S., G. Roberts, and D. Macqueen. 2006. "Development from Diversity: Lessons from Guyana's Forest Based Associations." Guyana National Initiative for Forest Certification and IIED, London.

Ozinga, S. 2004. "Time to Measure the Impacts of Certification on Sustainable Forest Management." *Unasylva* 55 (219): 33–8.

Rowcroft, P., J. Studley, and K. Ward. 2006. "Eliciting Forest Values for Community Plantations and Nature Conservation." *Forests, Trees and Livelihoods* 16 (4): 329–58.

Saigal, S., and S. Bose. 2003. "Small-Scale Forestry Enterprises in India: Overview and Key Issues." Winrock International India and IIED, London.

Saigal, S., S. Bose, P. Lal, M. Verma, and P. S. Pareek. 2006. "Small and Medium Forest Enterprise Associations in India: A Brief Overview." IIED, London.

Scherr, S. J., A. White, and D. Kaimowitz. 2004. "A New Agenda for Forest Conservation and Poverty Reduction." Forest Trends, Washington, DC.

Schneider, F. 2002. "Size and Measurement of the Informal Economy in 110 Countries around the World." Presented at a workshop of the Australian National Tax Centre, 17 July 2002, Australian National University, Canberra, Australia.

Spantigati, P., and A. Springfors. 2006. *Microfinance and Forest-Based Small-Scale Enterprises.* FAO Forestry Paper No. 146. Rome: FAO.

Thomas, R., D. J. Macqueen, Y. Hawker, and T. DeMendonca. 2003. "Small and Medium Forest Enterprises in Guyana." Guyana Forestry Commission (GFC) and IIED, London.

Tilakarnata, S. 1980. "Organisation of the Poor. Lessons from Sri Lanka." http://www.caledonia.org.uk/siritila.htm.

CROSS-REFERENCED CHAPTERS AND NOTES

ANNEX 2.2A CHECKLIST OF KEY ISSUES TO DETERMINE SME PROGRAM DIRECTION AND FEASIBILITY

Checklist of Key Issues

Key issue	Possible intervention
Resource and infrastructure	
1. Natural forest resources are insufficient to support enterprise development.	Consider alternative investment programs or options linked to cultivation.
2. Natural forest resource ownership and access rights are not secure, nor accessible to SMFEs.	Consider support for land and natural resource reform programs, including education and awareness raising of current land tenure anomalies and potential for remedial reforms.
3. Basic business infrastructure does not exist (telecommunications, energy, transport).	Consider infrastructure development (bearing in mind potential environmental consequences).
Market structure issues	
4. Baseline diagnostics of SMFEs have not been carried out in-country.	Start by commissioning an adequate baseline survey.
5. An entrepreneurial target group has yet to be selected for further assistance.	Conduct a selection process, drawing on criteria from Poverty Reduction Strategy Papers, national strategic plans, and so forth.
6. Specific market surveys for potential products or services have yet to be carried out.	Identify specialized products and services whose demand rises with increasing income.
7. No overseas ethical market niches or unique world-class products suited to export have been identified.	Focus on developing products and services tailored to the local market.
Social and environmental safeguard issues	
8. There is a lack of information about the sustainable management of the natural resource in question.	Consider investing in baseline biological and ecological research and in associated education and awareness raising.
9. Target groups are not using business forms that guarantee distribution of benefits (for example, cooperatives).	Actively support such enterprises—or strengthen local governance enforcement.
Business structure issues	
10. Products or services are not specialized (beyond subsistence or seasonal gap-filler activities).	Start by short-listing possible products or services for specialization (for example, using FAO's MA&D).
11. There is a lack of business capacity within the target group.	Ensure that capacity is developed and disseminated over a specified period.
Financial and technological issues	
12. Target groups are unaware of market trends, design, technology, and the like.	Catalyse an information system that meets these needs (for example, buy trade magazines).
13. Target groups have inadequate financial services and lack collateral to take out loans.	Organize a mutual loan facility or develop forest-aware bank credit guarantee systems.
Networking issues	
14. Target groups lack the organization needed to collectively reduce costs, adapt strategically, and lobby.	Introduce the idea of creating an association, based around principles of group success.
15. There are no small enterprise support networks that connect SMFEs with service providers.	Develop a communication platform to link SMFEs with support services and customers.
16. Specific product-based market support networks for the entrepreneurial targets do not exist.	Consider support networks, such as Fair Trade, or push for government procurement contracts.
Policy and institutional issues	
17. SMFEs are not formally constituted (or evidence regarding this is inadequate).	Analyze the major bureaucratic and cost implications of formality, and simplify legislation.
18. Surveys of policy and institutional constraints for SMFEs have yet to be carried out.	Invest in an analysis of the main policy constraints.
19. Subsidies to small and large enterprises are inequitable.	Lobby for judicious subsidies or a level playing field.
20. Laws are not developed and/or enforced in a transparent and equitable manner.	Bring in independent monitors to expose corrupt practices and strengthen judicial capacity.

Innovative Marketing Arrangements: Payments for Environmental Services

Forests can provide a wide variety of benefits outside their boundaries. The main categories of such benefits are as follows:

- *Watershed protection.* Forests play an important role in regulating hydrological flows and reducing sedimentation. Changes in forest cover can affect the quantity and quality of water flows downstream, as well as their timing, in both positive and negative ways. A clear understanding of these impacts is crucial for ecologically sound forest land use planning.
- *Biodiversity conservation.* Forests harbor an important part of the world's biodiversity. Loss of habitat (such as forests) is a leading cause of species loss.
- *Carbon sequestration.* Forests and forest soils contain large stocks of carbon, sequestering it from the atmosphere and playing a vital role in climate regulation.

Because these are benefits enjoyed by people outside the forests, forest managers—whether local communities or logging companies—have no external financial incentive to take them into account in forest management decisions.

Forest loss or degradation can cause adverse impacts on those who benefit from these forest services—creating scope for arrangements in which the users of the services compensate forest managers for managing forests in ways that generate the desired services. This is the basis of the Payments for Environmental Services (PES) approach.

The PES approach is a market-based approach to conservation financing based on the twin principles that those who benefit from environmental services (such as users of clean water) should pay for them, and that those who contribute to generating these services should be compensated for providing them. The approach thus seeks to create mechanisms to arrange for transactions between service users and service providers that are in both parties' interests, thus internalizing what would otherwise be an externality. The basic logic of the approach is illustrated in figure 2.3.

Figure 2.3   The Simple Economics of Payments for Environmental Service

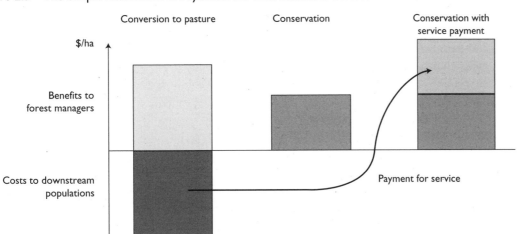

Source: Pagiola and Platais (2007).

The PES approach is attractive in that

- it generates new financing, which would not otherwise be available for conservation;
- it is likely to be sustainable because it depends on the mutual self-interest of service users and providers and not on government or donor funding; and
- it is likely to be efficient, in that it conserves services whose benefits exceed the cost of providing them and does not conserve services when the opposite is true.

PES programs are not limited to forests and can be used, in principle, to help induce the adoption of any land use that generates external benefits. The majority of PES programs to date have focused on forests or agroforestry, however.

There has been considerable experimentation with PES and other market-based approaches in recent years. Latin America has been a particularly fertile ground for such experimentation. Costa Rica established an elaborate, nationwide PES program, the *Pago por Servicios Ambientales* (PSA) Program, in 1997. Mexico created a similar program, the *Pago por Servicios Ambientales Hidrológicos* (PSAH) Program, in 2003. Both of these programs focus on forests. There have also been a wide range of subnational initiatives, with municipal water supply systems, hydropower producers, irrigation water user associations, bottlers, and other water users paying for the services they receive, either through national programs, such as Costa Rica's PSA or through self-standing PES mechanisms. Pilot efforts are also emerging in other regions.

The World Bank has been active in supporting PES programs. In fiscal 2007, several projects had explicit PES components under implementation or preparation (table 2.2).

The prospect for implementation of PES projects varies across the main services generated by forests:

HYDROLOGICAL SERVICES. Water services are often the most promising for actually generating payment streams. The users of water services are typically easy to identify, receive well-defined benefits, and stand to suffer substantially if water services were to be curtailed. However, water services are very site specific, meaning that some areas will have substantial potential for payments, and others almost none. Water users do not use generic "water services"; they are interested in very specific ones. Depending on the nature of the user, some will be primarily concerned about water quality, others about dry-season flow, and others about flood risk or sediment loads. This often eases the task of

understanding service provision in individual cases because efforts can focus on the specific dimensions of interest.

BIODIVERSITY CONSERVATION. The potential for PES for biodiversity conservation is limited because of the difficulty of identifying service users and of charging them. Nevertheless, biodiversity conservation has been a major theme of many PES projects, usually with support from the Global Environment Facility (GEF). This has usually taken the form of helping finance the up-front costs of establishing PES mechanisms that will then depend on payments by water users, as such mechanisms are also likely to generate biodiversity benefits. Although GEF cannot provide the long-term funding stream that is necessary for PES, in some cases it has supported the establishment of trust funds that can generate such funding.

CARBON SEQUESTRATION. Carbon sequestration has limited potential, because of the restrictions imposed on land-use and land-use change (LULUCF) projects under the current rules of the Clean Development Mechanism (CDM). The Bank's BioCarbon Fund has been working to develop CDM-compliant LULUCF projects, as well as emerging and new approaches. Carbon sequestration projects will not be discussed further in this note, but are addressed thoroughly in a separate sourcebook on the topic (World Bank Carbon Finance Unit, n.d.).

SCENIC BEAUTY. Payments for scenic beauty may potentially be generated from "users," such as the tourism industry, but this has not been done to date. This potential is being explored in the Mexico PES project.

OPERATIONAL ASPECTS

The process of designing a PES mechanism for forests can be broken into several steps:

- identifying and quantifying environmental services
- charging service users
- paying service providers
- creating an appropriate organizational and institutional structure

Identifying and quantifying environmental services

Implementing PES approaches requires that the services that are desired are clearly identified and that the effect of different land uses on these services be understood and quantified to the extent possible.

Table 2.2 World Bank Projects with Explicit PES Components

Country, project	Total cost	World Bank loan (US$ million)	GEF grant	Main features
Completed projects				
Costa Rica: *Ecomarkets*	49.2	32.6	8.0	Effective 2001–05. Supported the country's PSA program.
Projects under implementation				
Colombia/Costa Rica/Nicaragua: *Regional Integrated Silvopastoral Ecosystem Management*	8.45	—	4.5	Effective 2002. Piloting the use of PES to encourage adoption of silvopastoral practices.
South Africa/Lesotho: *Maloti-Drakensberg Transfrontier Conservation and Development*	33.1	—	15.2	Effective 2003 (separate but coordinated projects). Includes a PES pilot.
South Africa: *Cape Action Plan for the Environment (CAPE)*	49.6	—	9.0	Effective 2004. Uses PES to encourage conservation in the Cape Floristic Region.
Mexico: *Environmental Services*	156.6	45.0	10.0	Effective 2006. Will consolidate and ensure long-term financial sustainability of country's PES program.
Costa Rica: *Mainstreaming Market-based Instruments for Environmental Management*	90.3	30.0	10.0	Approved 2006. Will consolidate and ensure long-term financial sustainability of country's PES program.
Kenya: *Natural Resources Management*	78.0	68.5	—	Approved 2007. Will explore the potential for PES mechanisms to contribute to improved water and forest resource management.
Projects under preparation				
Brazil: *Espirito Santo Biodiversity and Watershed Conservation and Restoration Project*	12.5	—	4.2	Will use PES as part of package of measures to improve watershed management.
Kenya: *Agricultural Productivity and Sustainable Land Management*	12.4	—	10.0	Will pilot use of PES for watershed protection.
Panama: *Rural Poverty and Natural Resource Management II*	50.0	36.4	6.0	Will include pilot PES program for local communities and specific watersheds.
República Bolivariana de Venezuela: *Canaima National Park*	24.5	—	6.0	Will develop PES mechanism with hydropower producer to protect Río Caroni watershed.

Sources: Pagiola 2006.
Note: — = Not available. Projects noted as under preparation if PCN has been approved; other projects are in identification.
Amounts shown for projects under preparation are preliminary and subject to change; for projects with PES components, amounts reflect overall project costs, not PES-specific costs.

HYDROLOGICAL SERVICES. While forests are widely believed to provide a variety of hydrological services, the evidence is often far from clear (see box 2.13). This partly reflects the diversity of conditions encountered: hydrological services, for example, depend on the rainfall regime, on the type of soil, and on topography. Deforestation and afforestation can have multiple, often contradictory impacts, making the net impact on water services hard to determine. For example, infiltration can be reduced, but water use can also be reduced through evapotranspiration. The net impact of these changes (both in total and within a year) depends on the balance between these effects. Moreover, much depends on post-logging land use. The objectives also influence the analysis: Efforts to regulate waterflows to avoid flooding and dry season deficits may require different interventions than efforts to maximize total water volume, and the measures required to conserve biodiversity may be different from either. Moreover, even if the kind of benefit that a forest generates is known, one must also know how much of that benefit is being generated. Maintaining or regenerating forest cover imposes opportunity costs from the forgone land use and may also impose direct costs (for example, for reforestation). Without estimates of the amounts of benefits that would be generated, determining whether these costs are worth bearing is difficult.

BIODIVERSITY CONSERVATION. Although in some ways biodiversity is much harder to measure than water services, adequate indicators can be developed relatively easily in practice. These can include, for example, counts of the number of species of conservation interest, or of species that are particularly sensitive to ecosystem conditions, and of the number of individuals within these species.

Charging service users

It is sometimes asserted that water users will never pay for services. This assertion is manifestly false. In Costa Rica, a variety of water users (hydroelectric producers, bottlers, municipal water supply systems, agribusinesses, hotels) are paying to conserve the watersheds from which they draw their water, generating about US$500,000 annually in payments. Other examples exist throughout Central and South America, and in South Africa. In Kenya, the Nairobi Water Company has indicated its willingness in principle to pay for watershed protection. The principal challenge is to demonstrate to users that they will, in fact, benefit from making such payments, by reducing or avoiding costs from reduced water services. Nairobi Water, for example, is currently spending about US$150,000 a year in additional water treatment and desilting costs at its Sasumua treatment plant as a result of upstream degradation.

In general, the primary interlocutors in such discussions are not the ultimate consumers of the water services but the companies and public agencies that generate hydropower, provide domestic water services, or distribute irrigation water. In many cases, funding for payments comes from the existing budgets of these agencies. Thus, Nairobi Water would finance payments for upstream conservation from the savings resulting from reduced costs at its treatment plant. Only in rare instances is it necessary to increase fees to consumers to pay for PES. In those instances, experience has shown that this can be achieved with public support if the need for and use of the revenue are clearly explained.

As noted above, charging biodiversity users is difficult if not impossible. Most available funding from biodiversity users (for example, from the GEF) is short term, limiting its use to paying for the up-front costs of PES mechanism establishment or to capitalization of a trust fund.

Paying service providers

For PES to have the desired effect, the payments must reach the land users and do so in a way that motivates them to change their land use decisions. This is not easy. The historical record is replete with examples of efforts to induce land users to adopt particular land use practices, for a variety of reasons and using a variety of payment mechanisms. Most have very little to show for their efforts.

In general, several principles are clear:

PAYMENTS NEED TO BE ONGOING. The benefits being sought are generally ongoing benefits, which will be enjoyed year after year as long as appropriate land uses are maintained. For this to occur, land users must receive payments as long as they maintain the land use. All too often, payments have been frontloaded into a few years. Predictably, however, when payments cease, any leverage over land users' behavior also ceases.

PAYMENTS NEED TO BE TARGETED. Environmental services depend on both the kind of land use and its location. An undifferentiated payment system that pays everyone the same will be much more expensive than a targeted scheme. It will also make it difficult to tailor interventions to the particular requirements of given situations.

PERVERSE INCENTIVES NEED TO BE AVOIDED. Particular care needs to be taken to avoid perverse incentives. For example, payments for reforestation can encourage land users to cut down standing trees so as to qualify.

Creating the institutional framework

SCALE OF PROJECT. A critical initial question concerns the scale of the PES mechanism. There are, in principle, three broad scales at which PES could be implemented: (1) nationwide, (2) at the scale of a river basin, and (3) locally, usually at the scale of a microwatershed. In practice, although there are some high-profile national systems (in Costa Rica and Mexico), almost all existing mechanisms are at the local scale. There are no river basin–scale programs. Nationwide systems may appear attractive because they can cover large areas quickly and can have relatively low costs because of economies of scale. Experience has shown that such systems tend to be very inefficient, however. They are easily distorted by political considerations and exhibit low transaction costs mainly because they sidestep the difficult questions. Local initiatives are more likely to be efficient because they tend to be closely tailored to local needs and conditions. However, they often are constrained by limited local capacity. The El Salvador Environmental Services Project is exploring an intermediate approach, in which local mechanisms are being developed under a nationwide umbrella.

LEGAL FRAMEWORK. PES programs are often thought to require a specific legal framework. They only do so if they are to be based on public financing, in which case a legal framework is desirable so that the payment program is not wholly at the mercy of annual budgetary decisions. Relying on public financing is, however, generally an undesirable approach to PES. PES programs that are based on payments from service users do not require any specific law, other than general contract law. There may be a need for legal reform to remove obstacles, however. For example, public utilities may be restricted in their ability to charge consumers for the costs of conservation, or in their ability to use available funding in PES mechanisms.

FUNCTIONS TO BE ACCOMPLISHED. Systems of payments for environmental services require a supporting institutional infrastructure. This can take many forms, but several common functions must be accomplished (see figure 2.4). Organizationally, the most complex task to be undertaken is paying service providers because agents must be sent into the field, with all the logistical issues that entails. This task can often be subcontracted to NGOs or other agencies that already have a field presence, but sometimes it may be necessary to establish new organizations to undertake this task.

Ensuring the poor benefit

PES programs are not poverty-reduction instruments, but given the often high spatial correlation between areas that provide environmental services and areas of high poverty, PES programs may contribute to poverty reduction, at least locally. Guidelines are available on how to design PES programs to maximize their positive impact on the poor and minimize any potential negative impacts. For example, in some countries, even within a community, benefits may be captured by local elites at the expense of the poor. To address this issue, capacity needs to be built to empower the poor and vulnerable groups in the community.

Because some participants may be indigenous groups, it may be necessary to prepare an Indigenous Peoples Plan (IPP) or an Indigenous Peoples Planning Framework (IPFP). However, because PES programs are largely voluntary, these safeguards are triggered mainly in cases with collective decision making on land use and the use of PES revenues (see chapter 12, Applying OP 4.10 on Indigenous Peoples, in section II of this sourcebook).

Other operational considerations

PROJECT TYPE. PES projects can generally take two forms:

- Projects entirely dedicated to PES, which typically work on a nationwide basis (as in Costa Rica and Mexico).
- PES components within a broader project. Such PES components could be part of a variety of projects. Obvious examples include watershed management and sustainable land management projects (as in the Kenya KAPSLM (Kenya Agricultural Productivity and Sustainable Land Management), but there is also significant potential to undertake PES as part of institutional reform projects or water infrastructure projects (the Brazil Espirito Santo Project is partially blended with a domestic water supply project in the town of Vitoria).

AVOIDING PERVERSE INCENTIVES. PES projects do not support any clearing or degradation of forests or other natural habitats. On the contrary, they are intended to promote the conservation and restoration of forests and other natural habitats. PES projects, therefore, are usually fully compatible with both the World Bank's Natural Habitats OP/BP 4.04 and the Forests OP/BP 4.36.

Figure 2.4   Institutional Elements of a PES Mechanism

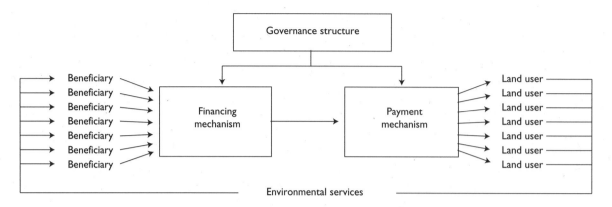

The main risk is of unintended, perverse consequences, such as land users clearing forest to qualify for reforestation payments or moving into previously intact ecosystems to claim payments for managing them correctly. These problems can generally be avoided by instituting appropriate eligibility criteria for participation, setting appropriate conditions for payments, and instituting effective monitoring systems (see box 2.14).

LESSONS LEARNED AND RECOMMENDATIONS FOR PRACTITIONERS

PES programs are not a universal answer to all forest conservation problems. Even when PES approaches are warranted, the details of their application will differ substan-

tially from case to case, in light of local technical, economic, and institutional conditions.

Identifying the services sought is critical, and most effectively done by focusing on the demand for services and asking how best to meet it, rather than on the supply. Beginning from the supply side carries the risk of developing mechanisms that supply the wrong services, in the wrong places, or at prices that buyers are unwilling to pay.

The land uses that can generate the services sought must then be identified and their impact quantified to the extent possible.

Monitoring effectiveness is essential to documenting to buyers that they are getting what they are paying for and to adjusting the functioning of the mechanism should problems arise. At the same time, excessively burdensome monitoring requirements can discourage potential suppliers without necessarily further reassuring buyers. Finding the right balance between information and compliance costs is an ongoing concern, as seen in the case of markets for certified timber and agricultural products.

PES mechanisms must also be sufficiently flexible to respond to changing demand and supply conditions and improvements in knowledge about how forests generate services.

SELECTED READINGS

Pagiola, S., A. Arcenas, and G. Platais. 2005. "Can Payments for Environmental Services Help Reduce Poverty? An Exploration of the Issues and the Evidence to Date from Latin America." *World Development* 33: 237–53.

Pagiola, S., and G. Platais. 2007. *Payments for Environmental Services: From Theory to Practice.* Washington, DC: World Bank.

> **Box 2.14   Avoiding Perverse Incentives in PES**
>
> Contracts under the Regional Silvopastoral Project specify that land users who switch any of their land to less environmentally desirable uses (as measured using the project's environmental services index) will not receive payment. Induced perverse incentives outside project areas may be more subtle. The Regional Silvopastoral Project had intended to only pay for improvements over baseline conditions, but ultimately decided to make nominal payments for preexisting baseline services to encourage current nonparticipants to undertake such improvements even before they were formally in the PES program.
>
> *Source:* Pagiola 2006.

Wunder, S. 2005. "Payments for Environmental Services: Some Nuts and Bolts." CIFOR Occasional Paper No. 42, CIFOR, Bogor, Indonesia.

REFERENCES CITED

Bruijnzeel, L. A. 2004. "Hydrological Functions of Tropical Forests: Not Seeing the Soil for the Trees?" *Agriculture, Ecosystems and Environments* 104 (1): 185–228.

Calder Ian R., 1999. *The Blue Revolution: Land Use and Integrated Water Resource Management.* London: Earthscan.

Chomitz, K. M., and K. Kumari. 1998. "The Domestic Benefits of Tropical Forests: A Critical Review Emphasizing Hydrological Functions." *World Bank Research Observer* 13 (1): 13–35.

ITTO. 2006. *Guidebook for the Formulation of Afforestation and Reforestation Projects Under the Clean Development Mechanism.* ITTO technical series No. 25. Yokohama: International Tropical Timber Organization.

Pagiola, S. 2006. "Innovative Marketing Arrangements for Environmental Services." Note submitted to World Bank as input to *Forests Sourcebook.* Unpublished. World Bank, Washington, DC.

Pearson, T., S. Walker, and S. Brown. 2005. *Sourcebook for Land Use, Land-Use Change and Forestry Projects.* Washington, DC: Winrock International.

WBCFU (World Bank Carbon Finance Unit). n.d. "Operations Handbook." http://carbonfinance.org/Router.cfm?Page =DocLib&ht=34&dl=1. World Bank, Washington, DC.

CHAPTER 3

Meeting the Growing Demand for Forest Products: Plantation Forestry and Harvesting Operations in Natural Forests

As a result of significant increases in demand for wood, the global wood market is undergoing rapid changes, putting considerable and increasing pressure on the world's remaining natural forests. Without significant investment in promoting sustainable forest management (SFM) efforts and in plantation management, it must be expected that, especially in many World Bank client countries, increasing demand for wood will lead to further degradation and fragmentation of forests and permanent deforestation. To successfully change this situation, international wood demand must be met through sustainable wood production from natural forests and plantation management. To facilitate such a process, markets must increasingly adopt mechanisms that not only ensure sustainable forestry and conservation, but also provide satisfactory livelihood opportunities for forest-dependent communities, and promote sustainable economic development for all nations, including countries with low forest cover. Therefore, the sustainable production of wood to meet increasing demand will continue to play a predominant role in the discussion of how to achieve global targets for forest management.

Economic processes have always relied on wood, and access to and exploitation of it have shaped economic structures. The exploitation of wood for subsistence uses for energy or construction material, or for commercial use in local, regional, and global markets, were among the first objectives of managing forest resources through human intervention. See box 3.1 for definitions of several commercial wood products.

Even though managing forests has become more complex over the past decades because of a wider range of management objectives than just wood production (for example, biodiversity conservation, carbon sequestration, recreation, and tourism), the core problems and challenges often remain similar. The exploitation of wood for subsistence use and commercialization at nonsustainable levels leads to forest degradation and destruction, which frequently constitutes the first step toward conversion of forests to other land uses and, thus, permanent deforestation dynamics (see figure 3.1).

This sequence of events has become a major concern to resource managers in recent years because the constantly growing demand for wood, particularly by emerging economies like Brazil, China, India, and South Africa, is strongly affecting forests and forest-dependent people in producer countries. For example, in China total forest-product imports rose from 40 million cubic meters (m^3) to almost 150 million m^3 between 1997 and 2005. It is expected that demand, both domestic and from outside the country, will continue to rise, and forest-product imports to China are likely to double within the next 10 years.[1] This development has strong impacts on markets in other countries in which forest management standards often are not yet as stringent as generally required by consumer countries.[2] Many of these countries are World Bank client coun-

Wood includes roundwood, wood fuel, industrial roundwood, sawnwood, veneer sheets, and plywood.

Roundwood is wood obtained from removal, harvesting, and felling from forests and trees outside forest. It includes roundwood generally classified as wood fuel (fuelwood and charcoal) and industrial roundwood (sawlogs and veneer logs; pulpwood, round and split; and other industrial roundwood).

Wood fuel is roundwood used for fuel consumption such as cooking, heating, or power production.

Industrial roundwood is roundwood used for industrial production of other goods and services except as a source of energy. It includes several products: sawlogs

and veneer logs (production of sawnwood or railway sleepers and veneer sheets, respectively); pulpwood, round and split (pulp, particleboard, or fiberboard); and other industrial roundwood (for tanning, distillation, poles, and so forth).

Sawnwood is wood that has been produced from domestic and imported roundwood, either by sawing lengthways or by a profile-chipping process.

Veneer sheets are thin sheets of wood of uniform thickness, peeled, sliced, or sawn.

Plywood is a panel consisting of an assembly of veneer sheets bonded together with the direction of the grain in alternate plies, generally at right angles.

Source: FAO 2005b.

---

tries, and supporting these countries in meeting international standards for responsible forest management and good governance constitutes one of the biggest challenges for World Bank operations in the forestry sector. For example, forests in eastern Siberia in the Russian Federation are the primary suppliers of wood to meet China's rapidly growing demand. Because many of the traditional supply markets are starting to experience resource shortages, the growing demand for wood currently focuses on the exploitation of the last remaining natural reserves, for example, in the Congo Basin and the Amazon. It is therefore very likely that roundwood production in tropical countries will still increase in regions with natural forests.

If demand for wood cannot be met through sustainable supplies, forest degradation and deforestation will continue or even accelerate; thus, other management objectives, such

as biodiversity conservation, carbon sequestration, and poverty alleviation are equally threatened. The increase in demand for wood and the resulting policy uncertainties and other sensitivities, paired with an increase in market prices, triggers another important factor contributing to these negative trends: illegal logging (see note 5.5, Addressing Illegal Logging, for further discussion), which is a serious threat to sustainable management of forest resources and, hence, to sustainable development in general. Between 1997 and 2002, estimates of illegally harvested timber in Southeast Asia alone amounted to more than 80 million m^3. Based on the factors presented in box 3.2, the global demand for wood is expected to continue to grow in the years to come.

While there has been little or no recent change in Europe and North America, deforestation is of great concern in many other parts of the world, especially in many African countries. According to the Food and Agriculture Organization (FAO) of the United Nations, the annual global deforestation rate is presently estimated to be about 0.2 percent (FAO 2006). In the period 1990–2000, this translated into a net loss of 95 million hectares (ha) of forests—an area larger than the República Bolivariana de Venezuela. The loss of 161 million ha of natural forests to deforestation was somewhat offset by 15 million ha of afforestation (the deliberate creation of forests where none existed), 36 million ha of natural expansion of forests, and 15 million ha of reforestation. These trends are critical because they lead to a decreasing supply of wood from natural forests, especially considering that productivity rates of natural forests are declining, too, because of overexploitation and insufficient management

Figure 3.1   Pathways of Deforestation and Land Cover Conversion

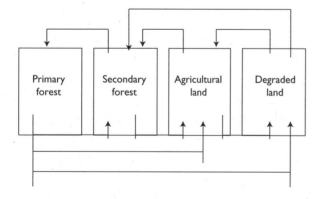

Subsistence use of wood (wood fuel, construction material)
- population increase
- increase of absolute number of people living in poverty, especially in rural areas
- increased role of forests as safety nets in emergency situations (for example, harvest failures caused by effects related to climate change dynamics)

Domestic wood use (charcoal, especially in Africa, but also South Asia and Eastern Europe)
- population increase
- continued urbanization
- macroeconomic reforms, for example, tariff increases in the electricity sector

Pulp and paper and industrial wood products
- population increase
- economic development in emerging-market and developing economies

High-value timber products
- increasing economic development, particularly in emerging-market economies (for example, Brazil, China, India, and South Africa)
- decrease of production forest area (natural forests), resulting in traditional net exporters turning into net importers of timber and timber products (for example, Malaysia, the Philippines, Thailand)
- population increase

Niche products (for example, nontimber forest products [NTFPs], such as medicinal plants)
- population increase

Source: Sander 2007.

interventions. Without further investments in improving the productivity of natural forests and establishing plantation forestry to meet future demands, it can be expected that supplies are only available for a limited number of years. Table 3.1 presents such estimations for selected countries.

The projected impact of the increase in the global demand for wood—especially from emerging economies[3] as major new processing and consumption markets—is, however, only one factor causing forest degradation and deforestation. At present, the conversion of forest land to other land uses, such as agriculture and urbanization, is by far the biggest factor for the continued degradation, fragmentation, and destruction of natural forest area in World Bank client countries and has a strong impact on the reduction in wood supply (illustrated in figure 3.1). While such dynamics are generally discussed with regard to their impacts on global forest market developments, their impacts on local and regional markets are equally important, with strong negative effects on local livelihoods and provision of local and global environmental services.

The global demand for wood fibers has complemented the increase in the demand for roundwood and timber products, with industry alone expected to need 1.9 billion m³ per year by 2015. Fast-growing plantations will be relied upon as a key element in meeting future demand for fiber. This shift of focus from natural forests to plantations for

pulpwood production is partly due both to their greater economic competitiveness and to environmental concern over declining natural forest cover.

Another significant contributor to the increase in roundwood consumption emerges from local and regional use of wood fuels, that is, fuelwood and charcoal. This aspect deserves particular attention because of its strong poverty link in many World Bank client countries (see table 3.2).

At the global level, the number of people living on less than $1/day is about the same as the number of those lacking access to commercial energy: 2 billion people (FAO COFO 2005). According to the World Bank (2004), about 575 million people depend on wood fuels as a source of energy in Sub-Saharan Africa. The use of wood fuels is pre-

Table 3.1 Estimated Number of Years Left of Economically Accessible Timber, by Country

Country of origin	Years
Russia (far eastern region)	> 20
Papua New Guinea	13–16
Myanmar	10–15
Indonesia	10
Cambodia	4–9

Source: Forest Trends 2006.

Table 3.2	Wood Fuel Data for Selected World Bank Client Countries, 2005		
	Total forest area (thousand ha)	Population (thousand)	Wood fuel consumption (thousand m³)
Chad	11,921	8,823	4,088
Ethiopia	13,000	69,961	108,879
Kenya	3,522	32,447	24,256
Madagascar	13,023	17,332	6,433
Malawi	3,402	11,182	5,617
Mozambique	19,512	19,129	20,297
Sudan	70,491	34,356	19,514
Tanzania	35,257	36,571	25,200
Uganda	3,627	25,920	42,041
Zambia	42,452	10,547	8,798
Zimbabwe	17,450	13,151	10,381
Total	301,358	1,359,140	278,976

Sources: FAO 2006; FAO 2007.

dominant in both rural and urban locations, accounting for approximately 70 percent of total and 90 percent of household energy use. On average, women carry 20 kilograms of fuelwood five kilometers every day. Commonly, a large number of traders are involved in buying, transporting, and reselling wood fuels; this is often where most of the value added is obtained in this mainly informal sector.

As a consequence, with one of the primary causes of deforestation being exploitation of forests for wood fuels, the use of wood fuels constitutes one of the most pressing challenges for achieving SFM in almost all Sub-Saharan African and other World Bank client countries (including in South Asia, East Asia, and Central America). The most important factor that will cause this challenge to persist for years to come is the considerable population growth in these countries (see box 3.2 for other factors). For example, Sub-Saharan Africa has one of the world's fastest growing populations (increasing by about 2.2 percent a year) and is expected to be home to more than a billion people by 2025 (compare with numbers in table 3.2). It is estimated that if current trends continue, many areas, especially the Sudano-Sahelian belt, will experience a severe shortage of fuelwood by 2025. Again, it must be emphasized that while the wood fuel challenge is most apparent and urgent in Sub-Saharan Africa, it applies equally to other regions where forest resource management is an important component in the World Bank's investment portfolio for achieving rural development and poverty alleviation. Even though some of these trends may be compensated for through the adoption of alternative energy sources, such as natural gas and biofuels, it is expected that the overall trend will lead to increases in wood fuel consumption over the next

15 to 20 years. It is also important to acknowledge that the wood fuel challenge generally exists in countries that are commonly not regarded as important forest countries for World Bank operations, but countries with low forest cover or low forest resource stocks and productivity rates (for example, savannah woodlands, Miombo forest ecosystems).

As a result of the increase in demand for wood, market pressure has been increasingly directed toward plantation forestry. Countries such as Argentina, Brazil, Chile, China, Indonesia, and South Africa are expected to become increasingly important world producers of pulpwood and industrial softwood for mass consumption through plantation forestry with exotic, fast-growing tree species.

In addition, wood fuel production in particular, but also larger-scale industrial production of wood, can be achieved through bottom-up approaches such as community woodlots, agroforestry, outgrower schemes, and company-community partnerships instigating economic opportunities at the household level (see notes 2.1, Community- Private Partnerships, and 2.2, Small and Medium Enterprises). Many of these interventions can also help regain degraded lands for economic productivity with positive effects reaching beyond sustainable wood production, for example, provision of environmental services. However, at this moment, certain wood, especially high-value timber species, can only be produced from natural forests; plantation forestry cannot yet be substituted for these sources of supply. Given the long production process wood requires, it is obvious that the stage has to be prepared right now for addressing—and meeting—future supply shortages from natural forests through plantation forestry. Another management intervention for increasing the wood supply in the future is to increase the production level of secondary and primary forests, providing the possibility for secondary forests to redevelop into primary forest–like ecosystems (see figure 3.1).

Last, a newly emerging factor is anticipated to have an impact on wood supply in the future: climate change. Changing climate regimes are expected to shift the current allocation of forest areas, leading not only to changes to and potential decline of natural forest areas, but also changing regimes for plantation establishment. Under climate change, production from plantations that have been established to date could decrease significantly, for example, through increasing climate variability and a higher probability of extreme climate events, such as droughts, initiating forest fires and increasing the vulnerability of trees to insects and disease. These effects are largely theoretical, but need to be explored and closely monitored in coming years to develop appropriate adaptation strategies.

In summary, the global market for wood is characterized by considerable and increasing pressure on the world's remaining natural forests. Without significant investment in promoting sustainable management of natural forests and in plantation management, especially in many World Bank client countries, further degradation, fragmentation, and destruction of natural forests can be expected. To successfully change this situation, the wood market must be transformed into one that ensures sustainable forestry and conservation, provides satisfactory livelihood opportunities for forest-dependent communities, and promotes sustainable economic development.

The Global Vision for Forest 2050 Project, which brought together leading experts, nongovernmental organizations (NGOs), industry representatives, and donor institutions, yielded the scenario depicted in figure 3.2 for a global closed-forest area of 3 billion ha in 2050. This would result in an increase in community-owned and -managed forests and a significant increase in protected areas as defined by the World Conservation Union (more formally known as the International Union for the Conservation of Nature and Natural Resources, or IUCN). The area of state and private production forests under intensive management would remain roughly the same as at present, and industrial plantation forests would increase slightly, from 95 million to 100 million hectares.

Figure 3.2   A Possible Global Forest Scenario for 2050

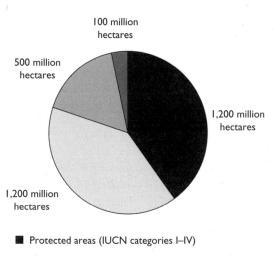

100 million hectares

500 million hectares

1,200 million hectares

1,200 million hectares

■ Protected areas (IUCN categories I–IV)

☐ Multiple use forests under community-based forest management

▨ State forests and private woodlands managed primarily for timber production

▧ Plantation forest management primarily for fiber and timber production

These developments will have a significant impact on how the World Bank—together with its development partners—can engage in forest management to develop feasible solutions to address these challenges. In a broad sense, this engagement can be put into practice in two ways: (i) through operational work directly supporting governments and industry in their efforts to use the potential of sustainable wood production from natural forests and plantations to foster economic development and achieve poverty alleviation, and (ii) through analytical work, ensuring up-to-date knowledge management and dissemination.

PAST ACTIVITIES

The initial rationale for the World Bank to engage in the forestry sector in the 1970s was based on addressing worldwide declining wood supplies and the dependence of the rural poor on wood energy. To meet these objectives, early projects promoted industrial-scale forest plantations with an emphasis on forest engineering components (plant breeding, fast-growing species, plantation establishment, and the like). One common feature during this period was that the forest service was assigned a policing and controlling role, enforcing forest laws with the main objective of keeping people out of state-owned forest reserves and plantations. The involvement of rural people in forestry was limited to being a source of labor.

The early 1980s began with a shift toward greater participation by stakeholders and community involvement. The World Bank started to promote the importance of community mobilization in stabilizing forest resources and improving the incomes of forest-dependent communities. The main objective of this change was to link investment in forestry with poverty alleviation and environmental protection efforts.

Following a period of strong criticism from civil society organizations, especially environmental NGOs, who regarded World Bank investments as strong contributors to global deforestation dynamics, the Bank's engagement in productive forest management decreased significantly. As a consequence, in the 1990s the World Bank's forest policy and Bank operational activities focused mainly on projects aimed at the conservation of biodiversity.

In 2002 the World Bank adopted its current forest policy, which provides the opportunity to reengage in industrial-scale forest management when such investments are certified under an independent forest certification system that is acceptable to the World Bank.[4] This development resulted from the intervention of environmental NGOs that considered it important to have the World Bank as an active stake-holder and partner promoting responsible forest management, especially given the scale of World Bank investments and the potential for addressing cross-sectoral issues of forest management and sustainable wood production.

Between 2002 and 2005, the World Bank ran approximately 29 projects with components that focused on meeting the growing demand for wood.[5] Total lending associated with these projects was approximately US$282 million, which constituted about 40 percent of the lending on forests during this period. Of this amount, a large portion was invested in projects involving community participation in plantation and commercial harvesting, approximately US$55 million was invested in projects involving mainstreaming biodiversity considerations, and approximately US$10 million was allocated to forest certification systems.

KEY ISSUES

Meet the increasing demand for wood. Plantation forestry will become more important in meeting the growing demand for wood (see note 3.3). From 1995 to 2000, global forest plantation area increased from 120 million ha to about 170 million ha (116 million of which are located in Asia).[6] In Brazil alone, forest plantation area increased from 500,000 ha in 1966 to 3.7 million ha in 1979, to 10.5 million ha in 2005 (Del Lungo, Ball, and Carle 2006). Over the past 15 years, the share of industrial fiber from plantations has grown from 5 percent to 30 percent compared to native forests, but in some countries the share is much higher (FAO 1995a).

Today, plantation forestry plays a significant role for wood production, especially in tropical countries, because of several important characteristics including high yield, short rotations, and accessibility. Although some plantations are for protection purposes, most are for production (FAO 2006), and plantations' share in providing roundwood to industry is growing. Plantation forestry is also increasingly changing from large-scale investments in monocultures to small-scale investments in which local households and communities are the principle owners of the means of production, not just employed as laborers (see chapter 2, Engaging the Private Sector in Forest Development, and its associated notes, and note 3.3, Forest Plantations).

Avoid cross-sector policy impacts on sustainable management of forests. Threats to the long-term sustainable management of natural forests have generally come from decisions regarding alternative land uses, not from a lack of technical knowledge about SFM (for example, in the agricultural sector and in infrastructure, such as building of roads and dams). Such cross-sectoral policy impacts must be further analyzed and increasingly brought to the attention of policy makers and relevant stakeholders so they can design and strengthen policy interventions at the macro level that address these issues (for example, agricultural policies, road building, and the like). In this context, projects primarily designed for improving forest management in World Bank client countries must increasingly have their cross-sectoral effects taken into consideration (see detailed discussion in chapter 6, Mainstreaming Forests into Development Policy and Planning: Assessing Cross-Sectoral Impacts), thus making cooperation with other sectors necessary. The World Bank concurrently should further improve the way in which forest considerations are integrated into projects developed in nonforest sectors (for example, the infrastructure and energy sectors). Last, the World Bank could enhance its engagement in international policy efforts that address these cross-sectoral impacts, perhaps by engaging proactively in international initiatives, such as the Roundtable on Sustainable Palm Oil and others.

Another example in which policies have negatively affected forest management in World Bank client countries is the tropical timber import ban executed by several Western countries in the 1980s and 1990s. The import ban exacerbated the problem it was trying to address by shifting the terms of trade away from products derived from natural forests, thus further reducing the incentive to avoid conversion to other land uses. Since then, innovative tools, such as independent forest certification, have been developed to permit access of wood and timber products to high-price consumer markets in Western Europe and North America if they are proven to be in compliance with internationally accepted management standards. The high prices gained from these markets make management interventions in natural and plantation forests requiring additional investments—such as reduced-impact logging or the rehabilitation of degraded forests—economically feasible and contribute to achieving sustainable wood production in the future. In light of these developments, future activities need to focus on reducing transaction costs for forest certification, especially for smallholder producers, and to supporting their efforts to increase the marketing potential for their products and their access to high-price markets. Independent certification may also lead, in some cases, to a reevaluation of export ban policies in producer countries for high-value certified roundwood if domestic prices cannot compete with prices that could be obtained in international markets. In this context, innovative marketing systems, auctioning of logs, for instance, need to be further developed and should include improvements in transparency and accountability.

DEVELOP INCENTIVES FOR SUSTAINABLE MANAGEMENT OF NATURAL FORESTS AND FOREST PLANTATIONS. In contrast to policies negatively affecting sustainable management of natural forests, policies can also be designed to provide economic incentives to invest in responsible forest management. For example, land tenure reform can play a significant role in improving the security of returns on investment in SFM, thus augmenting incentives to participate. This is especially important for motivating small-scale farmers and communities to make investments in forestry (see note 1.4, Property and Access Rights). Another example of such positive policy interventions are tax incentives for forestry operators that undergo independent forest certification, which may cause higher transaction costs for forest management. Providing a framework that facilitates secure contractual arrangements between various stakeholders in forest management can equally encourage investments in responsible forest management. Complementary investments in research and development also often provide the platform upon which improvements in the field can be realized (for example, silvicultural techniques, nursery improvements, species variations, knowledge generation on lesser-known species, and the like). Often, these costs are not taken over by private investors, but have to be taken up through public expenditures instigating improved and increased investments in forestry.

BALANCE WOOD PRODUCTION WITH DEMANDS FOR BIODIVERSITY CONSERVATION. Various benefits can be realized from integrating conservation and production (see note 3.1, Mainstreaming Biodiversity Considerations into Productive Landscapes). Three key benefits are (i) improving the feasibility of achieving conservation goals by using production and protected areas, (ii) increasing the benefits from conservation by conserving parts of forests adjacent to protected areas, and (iii) improving the overall ownership and understanding of conservation.

REDUCE WOOD PROCESSING OVERCAPACITY. In some areas, processing capacity has been created that exceeds the sustainable wood production of the region. This problem occurs mainly in southern countries, where raw material is often provided at subsidized, below-market prices to further promote investment in forest industries to create employment. This overcapacity has resulted in pressure to keep feeding the mills to make back the capital investment. Many of these facilities, however, are now being closed down.

USE SECONDARY FORESTS FOR INCREASING WOOD PRODUCTION. The management of secondary forests presents both a challenge and an opportunity. Tropical countries have seen an increase in wood production from secondary forests because these areas are increasing dramatically, and in some countries now exceed the area covered by primary forests. Reliance on secondary forests is expected to increase as larger primary forest areas are designated as protected forests. Secondary forests are a good source of wood fibers, NTFPs, social and environmental services, and other goods. The potential of lesser-known species has to be further explored,[7] and forest management should start to focus on these forests, steering wood production to shift gradually from primary to secondary forests. Secondary forests, therefore, have great potential to contribute to global wood demand (see figure 3.2).

INDEPENDENT CERTIFICATION OF FOREST MANAGEMENT. Independent certification provides proof that forest managers are using good management practices, adhering to internationally agreed principles and criteria (see note, 3.2, Forest Certification Systems). The development of forest certification systems and schemes emerged from strident attempts to ban imports of tropical timber, brought forward in the 1980s and 1990s by advocacy groups in North America and Western Europe. Certification was conceived as a market-based instrument, aimed at rewarding good forest management by improving or maintaining access to high-price consumption markets.[8] The final destinations for these products have, in the past, mainly been Western Europe, Japan, and North America, but increasingly, the emerging economies of Brazil, China, India, and Russia serve as destinations. Many of the emerging economies often only harbor the main processing and transformation facilities and export the final consumer products to high-value markets that increasingly demand certification as proof of good management practices. This is made possible by chain-of-custody certification, which, in most systems, complements forest management certification and provides a tool for tracking certified timber throughout the supply chain.

One of the key issues to address is the development of mechanisms to make certification economically attractive for small-scale forest management and timber processing operations (such as community-based forest management) that mainly produce for local and regional markets and do not necessarily have the ability to capture the benefits of high-value markets. Larger scale forest operations that do not produce for high-value market segments are another target.

ENSURE THAT PRODUCTION FORESTS PROVIDE ENVIRONMENTAL SERVICES WHILE SUPPORTING LOCAL LIVELIHOODS. With the amendment of the Kyoto Protocol in 2005, plantations are expected to increasingly act as carbon sinks in many carbon credit projects, so that in addition to improving markets for forest products, developing countries will benefit from the Clean Development Mechanism (CDM) under the United Nations Framework Convention on Climate Change (see note 2.3, Innovative Marketing Arrangements for Environmental Services, and note 3.1, Mainstreaming Conservation Considerations into Productive Landscapes). Brazilian eucalypts plantations provide a good example of an attempt to maintain biodiversity: High-yielding cloned stands are separated by strips and blocks of protected conservation areas along sensitive regions, such as creeks and rivers. NTFPs, of great importance to local people, also may be integrated into plantation forestry operations. NTFPs including medicinal plants, rattan and bamboo production, rubber tapping, resins, and beekeeping are often a significant component of the forestry operation. Again, facilitating independent forest certification, especially for smallholder forestry, for natural forest and plantation management will contribute to achievement of this goal, ensuring that multidimensional management objectives are simultaneously achieved (see note 3.2, Forest Certification Systems).

EMBED FOREST LAW ENFORCEMENT AND GOVERNANCE INITIATIVES INTO PRODUCTIVE FOREST MANAGEMENT AND TIMBER AND WOOD PRODUCT TRADE. Illegal activities, enabled and fueled by the absence of effective legislation and management or their enforcement, are a leading factor in the loss of forests and the degradation of the resources and thus seriously endanger sustainable development. (See chapter 5, Improving Forest Governance, and note 5.5, Addressing Illegal Logging.)

DESIGN APPROPRIATE CONTRACTUAL ARRANGEMENTS TO FACILITATE PARTNERSHIPS BETWEEN DIFFERENT STAKEHOLDERS. Reallocation of land ownership to smaller owners is expected to prevent large-scale wood clearing. However, in some countries, such as New Zealand and South Africa, planted forests have been privatized; several other countries

in Africa have also taken steps toward private and community engagement. Company-community partnerships are a promising approach and are expanding in the forest sector. Such partnerships can help to reduce risk, achieve better returns to land, diversify income sources, and much more—and therefore have the potential to contribute to the objectives of SFM and to economic development in rural areas (see note 2.1, Community-Private Partnerships).

Channeling economic potential to the local level can contribute significantly to poverty alleviation, especially when these benefits emerge not only as labor opportunities, but also as access to all means of production. Economic incentives should be created for smallholders to engage in forest management and make investments in sustainable forestry. Both traditional and innovative[9] economic mechanisms should be applied to capture the financial benefits and make them available at the local level. The growing worldwide demand for timber also presents an opportunity for the establishment of sustainably managed plantations with the participation of smallholders, taking environmental, ecological, and social requirements into consideration. Lessons learned from plantation forestry indicate that access to such land for poor rural households must be managed in a socially acceptable way to prevent the risk that the rural poor will not benefit. The same holds true for natural forest management. Approaches must be designed that make economic sense to the rural poor, given their constraints and preferences. In this context, future engagement by the World Bank is needed to establish participatory land use and land tenure systems as a precondition for sustainable plantation forestry (see boxes 3.3 and 3.4).

FUTURE PRIORITIES AND SCALING-UP ACTIVITIES

CONTINUE SUPPORT FOR COMMUNITY-BASED FOREST MANAGEMENT SYSTEMS. Pilot projects supported by others are important for the World Bank's operations, and demonstrate feasible approaches that can be scaled up to make a significant contribution to social, environmental, and economic objectives. The World Bank's support to community-based forest management systems is promising, with the aim of enabling local communities to manage their own resources, rehabilitate and protect forests, market forest products, and benefit from security of tenure. One of the positive projects in line with this strategy is the Forestry Sector Development Project for Vietnam, which involves small-scale farmers (see box 3.4).

Box 3.3   Global Forest and Trade Network

The Global Forest and Trade Network (GFTN), an initiative of the World Wildlife Fund (WWF), has supported the development of community-based forest management in Latin America (see also note 1.2, Community-Based Forest Management). Initiatives have included capacity building for chain-of-custody tracking in the lowland tropical hardwood forests of Peru, and the Nicaraguan Forest Finance Fund, a novel financial mechanism aimed at creating incentives for producers and processors dedicated to responsible forest management and trade. In Bolivia, the GFTN has been involved in developing a strategy for increasing the demand for responsibly produced wood products, primarily from indigenous communities, via responsible purchase policies and related market links to manufacturers and other members of the GFTN (for example, retailers in consumer countries).

Source: Authors' compilation using Sander 2007.

ENCOURAGE EXPANSION OF WOOD SUPPLY BY PRIVATE AND COMMUNITY FOREST OWNERS. Global fiber supply is shifting toward the southern hemisphere and China. Possibilities need to be explored for World Bank forestry projects and investment policies to support International Finance Corporation (IFC) private sector forest plantation investment in Argentina, Brazil, Chile, China, Ecuador, India, Indonesia, Mozambique, South Africa, Tanzania, Thailand, Uruguay, and Vietnam (see also chapter 2, Engaging the Private Sector in Forest Sector Development). Developing innovative approaches that facilitate certification of smallholder forest management, and improving access to high-price markets for certified small-scale producers, are regarded as important components.

FACILITATING SUSTAINABLE MANAGEMENT OF NATURAL FORESTS. Improving and extending responsible forest management according to the principles and criteria demanded by the World Bank's Operational Policy on Forests (OP 4.36) is the principal entry point and vehicle by which the World Bank can improve forestry outcomes. To meet future wood demand, the productivity of natural forests that serve production purposes must be improved. Securing appropriate structure, balance, and composition of the flows of resources into and out of the forestry sector is the most dif-

Box 3.4   The Forestry Sector Development Project for Vietnam

This project, financed by the International Development Association with cofinancing from the Global Environment Facility, the Netherlands, Finland, and the European Commission, was approved in 2004, and emphasizes the participation of smallholders in the establishment of plantations, aiming to ensure the sustainable management of plantation forests and the conservation of biodiversity in special-use forests. To this end, the project's scope includes the following aspects: (i) improvement of the environment for sustainable forestry development and biodiversity conservation; (ii) provision of attractive incentive packages to mainly poor farming households to plant trees on a sustainable basis to generate additional income and employment; (iii) making small, competitive grants available for effectively managing priority special-use forests of international importance; (iv) establishment of a credit line for participating farmers; (v) enhancement of capacity and capability at regional, provincial, and district levels; and (vi) establishment of support services to monitor and evaluate impact and outcomes. Implementation of the project started in 2005.

Source: World Bank 2004b.

ficult challenge to forestry in most World Bank client countries. Achieving sustainable management of natural forests requires significant reinvestment of revenues received from the extraction of wood. Meaningful stakeholder consultations also need to be maintained to ensure that socially endorsed goals and objectives are achieved (see also chapter 10, Consultation and Communications in Forest Activities, and chapter 12, Applying OP 4.10 on Indigenous Peoples).

ENHANCE TECHNICAL CAPACITY FOR NATURAL FOREST MANAGEMENT AND PLANTATION DEVELOPMENT. The technical capacity in many World Bank client countries is not sufficient to meet internationally acceptable standards for SFM. This is often evident even in the lack of timely collection and management of relevant and accurate data needed for forest management, such as forest area, forest types, resource stock inventories, growth and yield tables, biodiversity mapping, and so forth. Research on lesser-known species to increase management efficiency and productivity also needs to be extended in many countries. In addition, silvicultural knowledge as the basis for improving productivity of natural forest management is weak in many World Bank client countries and constitutes a key area for future intervention. Effective dissemination mechanisms need to be established, particularly when wood production is supposed to be increasingly channeled to smallholders.

IMPROVE COOPERATION WITH THE CONSERVATION COMMUNITY. Given the trend toward greater reliance on forest plantations, an agreement is needed between the conservation community and industry as to where and how plantation forests can be developed such that potentially negative social and environmental impacts are minimized. One way to achieve this cooperation may be by promoting the mapping of critical forest areas (for example, high conservation value forest [see note 3.1, Mainstreaming Conservation Considerations into Productive Landscapes] and related approaches) and independent forest certification of plantation management (see note 3.2, Forest Certification Systems).

DESIGN PLANTATIONS TO PROVIDE MULTIPLE FUNCTIONS. Plantations will need to be designed so that they are able to provide the multiple functions expected of SFM, in addition to supplying raw material to pulp and paper mills and other industrial processing. To achieve this objective, further research will be needed to improve knowledge on silvicultural techniques, especially on growth performance of indigenous tree species and approaches for creating mixed-species or uneven-aged plantation forestry that resembles near-natural forest ecosystems and, hence, has a higher degree of provision of environmental service functions, such as biodiversity conservation.

IMPROVE PROCUREMENT POLICIES OF WORLD BANK CLIENT COUNTRY GOVERNMENTS. Governments should be encouraged to increase the proportion of their forest product purchases that come from sources certified by systems and schemes that comply with internationally accepted criteria and indicators for SFM (see note 3.2, Forest Certification Systems).

SUPPORT UP-TO-DATE SYSTEMS FOR INDEPENDENT FOREST CERTIFICATION, INCLUDING CHAIN-OF-CUSTODY CERTIFICATION. Producers of tropical timber are under increasing pressure to be able to document the origin of their products, whether to demonstrate legality or achieve sustainability of forest management. Without this ability, producers may be excluded from key segments of the market. Related to this is the need to address "leakages" within the wood trade, such as through customs and other controls (see note 3.2, Forest Certification Systems, note 5.5, Addressing Illegal Logging, and chapter 2, Engaging the Private Sector in Forest Sector Development, and its associated notes).

NOTES

1. Different scenarios estimate that China's forest product imports will reach far higher levels, up to 600 million m^3, should imports continue to rise as they did from 1997 through 2005. Eventually the point may be reached when limited supply, coupled with rising prices for raw materials, will stem further increases in wood imports.

2. An increasing number of consumer countries—especially in Europe—are currently developing procurement standards for the import of wood and forest products that often demand independent management and chain-of-custody certification according to internationally recognized principles and criteria (see also note 3.2, Forest Certification Systems).

3. Emerging economies of particular interest in the context of this chapter include Brazil, China, India, Indonesia, Malaysia, South Africa, Thailand, and Vietnam.

4. For further information, please refer to the World Bank Forests Strategy (World Bank 2004a) and World Bank's Operational Policy on Forests (OP 4.36).

5. This included projects emphasizing biodiversity considerations in forest plantations and productive landscapes, project components that develop forest certification systems, and certification to prevent illegal trade of timber and forest products, arrangements for plantations, and so forth.

6. Successful (net) plantation area must be distinguished from total planted area. The failure rate is often in the range of 20–30 percent, or even higher; plantations in the Philippines have had a success rate of only 26 percent (FAO 2003).

7. Especially in Latin America and Southeast Asia, the knowledge about lesser-known species has improved significantly. In Africa, research and knowledge dissemination regarding these species needs to be further supported.

8. Many consumer countries have developed, or are currently developing, procurement guidelines that require certification of wood products.

9. In this context, "traditional" refers to technical support, provision of material, and the like, while "innovative" refers to payments for environmental services. See note 2.3, Innovative Marketing Arrangements for Environmental Services.

SELECTED RESOURCES

FAO Forest Products & Services (Trade). http://www.fao.org/forestry/site/trade/en/

FAO Forest Products & Services (Wood Energy). http://www.fao.org/forestry/site/energy/en/

FAO Forests (Facts and Figures). http://www.fao.org/forestry/site/28679/en/

International Tropical Timber Organization (ITTO). http://www.itto.or.jp

ITTO—Market Information Service. http://www.itto.or.jp/live/PageDisplayHandler?pageId=235

ITTO—Tropical Forest Update. http://www.itto.or.jp/live/PageDisplayHandler?pageId=243

GFTN (WWF)–Global Forest and Trade Network, World Wildlife Fund. http://gfta.panda.org.

The Forest Dialogue. http://research.yale.edu/gisf/tfd/

Forest Trends. http://www.forest-trends.org

World Resource Institute—Forest Management. http://www.wri.org/biodiv/about.cfm#ForestManagement

High Conservation Value Resource Network. http://hcvnetwork.org/

Forest Stewardship Council (FSC). http://www.fsc.org/en/

Programme for the Endorsement of Forest Certification schemes (PEFC). http://www.pefc.org/internet/html/

Forest Certification Assessment Guide (FCAG). http://www.worldwildlife.org/alliance/2006jul-fca.cfm

World Business Council for Sustainable Development (WBCSD). http://www.wbcsd.ch/ (click on "Forest Products")

SELECTED READINGS

Del Lungo, A., J. Ball, and J. Carle. 2006. "Global Planted Forests Thematic Study: Results and Analysis." Working Paper FP/38, FAO, Rome.

Evans, J. 1996. *Plantation Forestry in the Tropics.* Oxford, U.K.: Clarendon Press.

Kangas, K., and A. Baudin. 2003. "Modelling and Projections of Forest Products Demand, Supply and Trade in Europe." New York and Geneva, UN/FAO European Forest Sector Outlook Studies.

Whiteman, A., C. Brown, and G. Bull. 1999. "Forest Product Market Developments: The Outlook for Forest Product Markets to 2010 and the Implications for Improving Management of the Global Forest Estate." Working Paper FAO/FPIRS/02, FAO, Rome.

REFERENCES CITED

Del Lungo, A., J. Ball, and J. Carle. 2006. "Global Planted Forests Thematic Study: Results and Analysis." Working Paper FP/38, FAO, Rome.

FAO. 1995a. "Forest Resources Assessment 1990: Tropical Forest Plantation Resources." Forestry Paper No. 128, FAO, Rome.

———. 2005a. *State of the World's Forests 2005.* Rome: FAO.

———. 2005b. *Yearbook of Forest Products 2005.* Rome: FAO.

———. 2006. *Global Forest Resources Assessment 2005.* Rome: FAO.

———. 2007. *State of the World's Forests 2007.* Rome: FAO.

FAO COFO (Committee on Forestry). 2005. Seventeenth Session on Forests and Bioenergy, Rome, Italy, March 15–19.

FAOSTAT. 2005. http://faostat.fao.org/faostat/collections?version=ext&hasbulk=0&subset= forestry [last updated September 2005].

Forest Trends. 2006. *China and the Global Market for Forest Products: Transforming Trade to Benefit Forests and Livelihoods.* Washington, DC: Forest Trends.

Sander, K. 2007. "Meeting the Growing Demand for Wood. Sustainable Plantations and Commercial Harvesting Operations." Note submitted to World Bank as input to *Forests Sourcebook.* Unpublished. World Bank, Washington, DC.

World Bank. 2004a. *Sustaining Forests: A Development Strategy.* Washington, DC: World Bank.

———. 2004b. Project Appraisal Document for Vietnam Forestry Sector Development Project for Vietnam (P066051). Report No. 26767-VN. Rural Development and Natural Resources Sector Unit, East Asia and Pacific Region, World Bank, Washington, DC.

———. 2005. *East Asia Region Forestry Strategy.* Washington, DC: World Bank.

CROSS-REFERENCED CHAPTERS AND NOTES

Note 1.4: Property and Access Rights

Chapter 2: Engaging the Private Sector in Forest Sector Development, and associated notes

All notes in Chapter 3: Meeting the Growing Demand for Forest Products

Note 5.5: Addressing Illegal Logging and Other Forest Crime

Chapter 6: Mainstreaming Forests into Development Policy and Planning

Chapter 10: Consultation and Communications in Forest Activities

Chapter 12: Applying OP 4.10 on Indigenous Peoples

Mainstreaming Conservation Considerations into Productive Landscapes: Applying High-Conservation-Value Tools

Conservation has often been treated as a separate activity from production—protected areas were identified and set aside for conservation while production areas were largely ignored by those with a conservation agenda.[1] It is now widely recognized that a number of benefits can be achieved by integrating conservation and production.

First, conservation goals cannot always be fully achieved by using only protected areas. Critical biodiversity values and ecosystem services are also supported by many production forests. Many forests also have social and cultural values that may not be appropriately dealt with through exclusionary protection but can often be taken into account in production forest management. Forest-dependent communities are likely to have links to nearby forest areas so that the creation of a conservation area in another location brings few or no benefits.

Second, promoting conservation friendly practices in production forests surrounding protected areas can greatly enhance the benefits to conservation through a combination of reducing the threats to the protected areas and increasing the effective area covered. For example, threatened species within protected areas may be able to use adjacent land to supply some of their needs (such as food or shelter), thus increasing the overall population the area can sustain.

Third, addressing conservation within production areas makes conservation much more widely owned and understood. People involved in productive land uses begin to understand conservation and develop their own approaches to implementing it. In mainstreaming conservation, the separation between conservation and production is removed. Land users are mandated to consider how their actions can benefit conservation, both in their own land and in the broader context—a crucial extension.

Although there are major differences among countries in percentage of forests declared protected, existing coverage of protected areas globally[2] is widely regarded as inadequate to safeguard biodiversity for two reasons. First, the area assigned to protection is small. The total area set aside for conservation purposes is less than 12 percent of the earth's land surface (Brooks and others 2004). Second, protected areas are often created in areas where no other productive land uses are possible, meaning that protected areas tend to over-represent infertile, inaccessible, and often low-biodiversity areas, and under-represent highly diverse, productive ecosystems. They also often fail to take account of areas that provide irreplaceable livelihoods to forest-dependent peoples and are critical to the identity of unique human cultures.

Although these problems are recognized, pressures on land are already high, and in many places there are few opportunities to expand protected areas or increase the representation of protected habitats.[3]

Recently, the focus has shifted to improving the conservation of biological, social, and cultural values within a combination of protected and productive landscapes. The addition of production areas dramatically increases the area of land and the range of habitats in which some form of conservation can be practiced, providing more opportunities to address conservation priorities that are poorly represented in protected areas.

THE HCV CONCEPT—WHY IT IS USEFUL FOR INTEGRATING CONSERVATION AND PRODUCTION

The High Conservation Value (HCV) concept provides a framework for identifying forest areas with special attributes that make them particularly valuable for biodiversity or to local people (that is, High Conservation Value Forests, HCVF). The main objective of applying this framework is to design and implement appropriate management options for the area of concern. Strengths of the concept include the following:

- The concept is designed to integrate production and protection. Therefore, it does not preclude productive use of some or even all of the HCVF identified. Management prescriptions are developed based on the best way to protect the values identified.

- The methodology is not prescriptive, but provides a framework for systematic identification of values and planning for their protection. The HCV approach uses and builds on the findings of whatever conservation or land-use planning activities are already in place rather than replacing them. This makes it both more cost efficient and less threatening.

- The HCV framework places equal emphasis on environmental and social values and requires a consultative approach to identify critical values and areas and to reach management decisions.

- The concept is widely accepted and already integrated into the land-use planning frameworks of several nations or regions and within sustainable natural resource management standards and certification schemes.

The HCVF concept was initially developed for use in forest certification by the FSC in 1999.[4] Six generic HCVs that a forest may contain or maintain were identified (see box 3.5) and the identification and protection of HCVFs became a requirement for FSC certification. It quickly became apparent that the concept could be useful not only within forest certification, but also in a wider land-use context and it is now used for a range of situations.

The HCV approach is applicable to a wide range of natural resource management scenarios. It is used both within the certification context and more widely, to guide both SFM within production forests, and land-use planning for responsible production of natural resources. HCV is routinely applied for developing management prescriptions to support conservation goals in production forests under the FSC and Malaysian Timber Certification Council certification schemes. Outside of certification, it is mainly being used for land-use planning purposes, including identification of set-aside areas for total protection and plantation design.

For SFM in natural forests, the HCV approach has proved to be a robust tool for undertaking forest land-use planning that integrates conservation and production requirements. The output generally indicates areas needing total protection, areas needing specific management, and

---

Box 3.5   The Six Types of High Conservation Value Areas

High Conservation Value areas are critical areas in a landscape that need to be appropriately managed to maintain or enhance HCVs. There are six main types of HCV areas:

HCV1: "Areas containing globally, regionally, or nationally significant concentrations of biodiversity values (e.g., endemism, endangered species, refugia)." For example, the presence of several globally threatened bird species within a Kenyan montane forest.

HCV2: "Globally, regionally, or nationally significant large landscape-level areas where viable populations of most if not all naturally occurring species exist in natural patterns of distribution and abundance." For example, a large tract of Mesoamerican flooded grasslands and gallery forests with healthy populations of Hyacinth Macaw, Jaguar, Maned Wolf, and Giant Otter, as well as most smaller species.

HCV3: "Areas that are in or contain rare, threatened, or endangered ecosystems." For example, patches of a regionally rare type of freshwater swamp in an Australian coastal district.

HCV4: "Areas that provide basic ecosystem services in critical situations (for example, watershed protection, erosion control)." For example, forest on steep slopes with avalanche risk above a town in the European Alps.

HCV5: "Areas fundamental to meeting basic needs of local communities (for example, subsistence, health)." For example, key hunting or foraging areas for communities living at subsistence level in a Cambodian lowland forest mosaic.

HCV6: "Areas critical to local communities' traditional cultural identity (areas of cultural, ecological, economic, or religious significance identified in cooperation with such local communities)." For example, sacred burial grounds within a forest management area in Canada.

HCV Resource Network Charter (2006, pp. 2–3), adapted from the FSC.

areas that can be used more intensively without threatening maintenance of conservation values. For example, in the Russian Komi Republic, the HCV approach has been used to guide forest land planning exercises at the regional level, including rezoning concession areas based on public consultation and identification of social and biological HCVs. At the management unit level, the HCV approach can be used to guide ongoing management of natural forests. The presence or absence of each HCV is determined based on an analysis of existing information and the collection of additional information where necessary to fill gaps. The existing protection of, and threats to, the values, and the potential future threats (including those arising from the proposed activities) need to be identified to determine management prescriptions.

In areas zoned for conversion to agricultural or industrial forest plantations (for example, palm oil and pulp), HCV is also being widely used to identify areas that are low risk for conversion and those that must be maintained and managed as natural vegetation to preserve critical conservation values. It can also provide guidance on plantation planning and management to optimize conservation goals (see note 3.3, Forest Plantations). For example, the main industry standard for palm oil (the RSPO [Roundtable on Sustainable Palm Oil] Principles and Criteria)[5] includes a prohibition on conversion of HCV areas to oil palm plantations and a requirement to maintain HCVs within areas affected by oil palm plantations and mills. Also, outside of forest certification, at least one pulp company in Indonesia has made public commitments not to convert HCV forests to pulp plantations. In a conversion scenario, the HCV approach needs to be incorporated into an adequate safeguards framework, notably to ensure legal compliance, protect land use and tenure rights, address consent procedures, and ensure that the concept is not inappropriately used to justify conversion based on incomplete information.

Where the HCV approach is used for forest land-use planning involving conversion, identifying which areas of forest cannot be converted to plantations is a core part of this process, but management recommendations for other areas of forest are also extremely important.

Finally, the HCV concept has been invoked in the formulation of procurement and investment policies. A growing number of companies and governments are introducing purchasing policies that preclude the purchase of wood or wood products from forest areas where HCVF are not managed for their values. For example, members of the WWF's GFTN are committed to excluding material from HCVF, unless certified by the FSC. A number of investment organizations, particularly banks and screened pension funds, are making commitments to avoid investing in poorly managed HCVF.

OPERATIONAL ASPECTS

The HCV approach provides a systematic process for identifying critical conservation values—both environmental and social—within a forest tract or production unit, and for planning forest or land-use management to ensure that these values are maintained or enhanced (see examples in boxes 3.6, 3.7, and 3.8).[6] HCV forest is the area of forest that needs to be managed to protect its conservation values. The HCV approach is based on a three-step process:

1. Identify the *critical conservation values* that are present (the HCVs), and the areas where they occur.
2. Manage the HCVs by addressing the *threats* to the values, both now and in the future (including the threats posed by any planned activities).
3. Monitor the HCVs to ensure that management prescriptions are effective in maintaining or enhancing the values, and adapt the management regime to take account of any changes.

An ideal HCV process would follow the sequence illustrated in figure 3.3. The strength of the HCV approach is that it recognizes variations in countries and situations where it is applied (see box 3.9). Where existing protection is good and threats limited, the requirements will differ from those in a similar area where existing protection is poor and threats extensive. Although the HCV approach was originally developed for use at the scale of forest management units, it has increasingly been applied at various scales up to the landscape level.

HCV process: Implementing HCV assessment and defining management prescriptions

IDENTIFICATION OF THE PRESENCE AND LOCATION OF HCVs. For each of the six HCVs, a systematic process is required to establish whether it is present in the area of interest and, if present, the approximate extent.

A national interpretation of the HCVF toolkit, if it exists, is the first point of reference as the HCVs are defined for the national context and relevant data resources are listed. In the absence of a national interpretation, relevant information can be obtained from other regional interpretations. The HCVF toolkit provides generic guidance. The HCV

Figure 3.3   HCVF Identification and Follow-up: The Ideal Picture

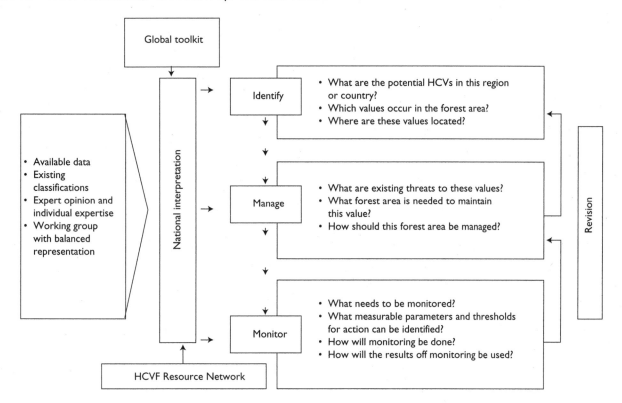

process draws on sources of data that are already available (box 3.10), which may take many forms.

Obtaining reliable maps is an important component of the process. The maps may include data on recent forest cover, hydrology, elevation, and slope, but many national mapping processes give further useful details on habitats, soil type, and current or planned land use. Existing data and maps can be combined with specifically commissioned surveys to build a picture of the location of the values.

Box 3.6   Identifying HCVFs in State Forests and Taking It to Scale: The Case of China

The WWF and IKEA Co-operation on Forest Projects selected two local forestry bureaus in northeast China as pilot sites for implementing SFM techniques. HCVFs were identified and assessed in the 420,000 hectares of forests managed by these two bureaus. The detailed work mapped out HCVFs as areas that should be set aside as nature reserves, areas where logging should be banned, and areas with important stands of Korean pine. It also led to these two forestry bureaus achieving the first FSC certification of state-owned forests in China. After their participation in this work, the two involved provincial governments firmly embraced the HCVF concept. The Jilin Forestry Department introduced HCVF identification into its five-year provincial forestry development plan, and in Heilongjiang province, the HCVF concept will be integrated into the provincial standard for identifying forests that provide key ecological benefits. Alongside this HCVF work, the projects also led to the identification of potential HCVFs at the landscape and regional levels within northeast China and Inner Mongolia. In 2006, China's State Forestry Administration incorporated the HCVF concept into the national guidelines on SFM planning. Thus, areas identified as HCVFs will be designated priority areas for sustainable management or protection. These guidelines are to be distributed to all provinces in China for implementation by local government or forest management units.

Source: WWF 2007.

In support of meeting the Global Forest Target of improving the management of 300 million hectares of production forests through forest certification by 2010 [http://www.worldwildlife.org/alliance/targets.cfm], WWF has developed a first draft of an HCVF toolkit for Papua New Guinea (PNG). By facilitating the identification of HCVFs, companies will be able to manage these according to FSC principles while maintaining their high conservation attributes, and pursue certification under this system.

The process of developing the HCVF national toolkit brought together government, NGOs, private industry, and land owners to develop consensus on the meaning of HCVF in PNG. After a first draft was circulated to stakeholders, comments were incorporated and a final version was made available online in February 2006 (see http://www.wwfpacific.org.fj/publications/png/HCVF_Toolkit_First_Ed.pdf).

PNG's ecological diversity posed a challenge to creating a national-level HCVF interpretation. At the time of preparing the technical progress report, large-scale industrial field testing had yet to be conducted, but testing had been conducted in smaller operations, and additional field trials were to be used to test whether monsoon forests, considered "fragile forests," should be excluded from logging and conversion activities altogether.

Other outputs of the project included the creation of coarse-scale HCVF maps and an effort to lobby the government to recognize HCVFs in provincial and national forest plans. At the time of drafting the technical progress report, it was indicated that the completed PNG HCVF national toolkit was to be adopted by the PNG FSC National Standards for compliance with the FSC's Principle 9.

Source: PNG FSC 2006.

MANAGING THE HCVs. The aim of HCV management is to ensure that the HCVFs identified are maintained or enhanced. The activities to achieve this aim can start with delineating areas that need total protection, areas requiring special management (for example, production activities that are consistent with conservation aims, managed to an agreed standard and monitored for any negative effects), and areas that do not require specific precautions.

This begins with knowing the area of forest that is required to maintain each relevant value. For example, to maintain or enhance an HCV1 area (containing a specified set of rare, threatened, or endemic species; see box 3.5), the area of forest required to support viable populations of those species needs to be defined. Thus, some knowledge of the biology of the species in question is required to define areas that are critical habitats or resources for breeding and foraging, areas that permit movement of individuals between these resources, or areas that protect these resources. A similar process needs to be applied to each HCV in turn, with equal consideration given to social, cultural, and ecological values.

The government of Bulgaria formally endorsed the national HCVF toolkit and adopted it as a methodology for biodiversity inventories. The toolkit will be included in the national standards for forest management planning in Bulgaria. This will ensure that more valuable forests will benefit from its stipulations and will be managed recognizing the HCVs. The toolkit is also being used by the United Nations Development Fund and a number of NGOs in Bulgaria for their biodiversity-related work and by the 10 nature parks in the country.

Source: WWF 2007.

In addition, management of HCVs requires understanding the present and future threats to the values, including those posed by any planned activities. Threats may be from proposed management activities, such as logging operations or plantation establishment, or from external activities, such as hunting of wildlife, encroachment for agriculture, planned conversion of land, or illegal logging. Examples of the type of methodologies for threat assessment that can be used in HCV management include the 5-S Framework for Conservation Project Management and the Participatory Conservation Planning tools developed by The Nature Conservancy.

Box 3.9   National Interpretation of HCV Guidelines

An important element of the HCV process is the national-level interpretation. Although it is possible to use the generic guidelines of the Global HCVF Toolkit, it is much more convenient for forest managers if the global HCV definitions are adapted for use in their particular country, region, or forest type. This step can be done by a specific HCV working group, drawing on existing groups working on related issues or groups working on defining or mapping forest values. This working group can interpret the HCV definitions to develop a national standard. Two types of processes can be used for creating national or regional standards:

- *A multi-stakeholder process that is consensus based.* Though more time intensive, this provides a definitive interpretation with wide-ranging support as the national or regional standard for HCV.
- *A technical adaptation process involving a technical working group or team.* This is often a practical way forward for projects in countries with no national standard. However, it must be made explicit that the objective is not national standard setting and that the outcome is not a definitive one.

Source: ProForest 2003.

The objective of national interpretation is to define HCVs and establish guidelines on management for specific cases. This includes deciding the relevant forest values, such as forest types, species assemblages, and the like, and specifying parameters to measure them. It also involves, for each forest value and parameter, defining thresholds for deciding when to designate a HCV (that is, a value that is significant at the global, regional, or national level). Thresholds can include actual locations, levels, numbers, or types.

A national interpretation serves two purposes:

- It facilitates on-the-ground application of the HCV concept by producing HCVs that are clearly defined, detailed, and straightforward in a manner that can be understood by nonspecialists and unambiguously assessed at forest levels. This ensures greater consistency in the way it is used.
- The process itself is useful because it brings together a range of interests and stakeholders and contributes to the development of a shared understanding of the best way to protect environmental and social values.

Box 3.10   Key Information Sources for HCV Identification

Specific guidance (all HCVs)
- Existing national or regional HCV interpretations (see www.hcvnetwork.org for a full list)
- Case studies
- Landscape-level HCV maps

Habitat and biodiversity information (HCVs 1, 2, and 3)
- Maps of known habitats
- Lists of threatened or endangered species and distribution maps
- Protected areas—location, status, threats, reasons for gazettement
- Conservation NGO information sources
- Forest inventories

Source: ProForest 2007.

Ecosystem service information (HCV4)
- Soil maps, topographic maps
- Watershed and catchment boundaries
- Fire incidence

Social and cultural information (HCVs 5 and 6)
- Maps of human settlement and community data
- Social studies conducted by industry, NGOs, or research institutions
- NGO projects and current campaigns on the communities or in the region

Finally, any existing protections, such as functioning protected areas or nature reserves can be considered.

The outcome of this process should be a documented plan, integrated into the operational management plan, that sets out management prescriptions, taking into account each HCV and the relevant threat assessments. Plans developed in this way for the protection of the same value in two different locations may be very different depending on the levels of threat and existing protections.

MONITORING THE HCVS. After management plans have been defined, a monitoring program needs to be in place to provide managers with up-to-date information on the HCVs for which they bear responsibility, as a basis for management intervention or ongoing adjustment of operational plans. Monitoring plans should be derived from management objectives and written into the management plan. Data gathered during the HCV assessment should be used to determine the generic and specific objectives of the monitoring program. The aim should be to develop a set of simple, measurable indicators for each key value. Monitoring activities can include social and biological surveys and direct and indirect observation of indicators, and are likely to involve detailed data collection over the long term.

There are a number of tools available to support the use of the HCV approach, all of which are available at the HCV Resource Network Web site (http://www.hcvnetwork.org):

- *The HCV Resource Network.* The network was formed by key organizations with an interest in the HCV concept to support and promote the consistent use of this concept across its range of uses.[7] The network's Web site provides a range of services, including general information on the HCV concept, information on HCVF projects and case studies, country-specific briefings, guidance and support material, contact details for HCV practitioners, details of conferences and training events, and links to relevant resources.
- *The Global HCVF Toolkit.* The toolkit (ProForest 2003) provides globally applicable information, but also contains sections that describe the process of defining HCVs at the national level and guidance for forest managers on how to identify and manage HCVs. The toolkit has been interpreted for several national contexts; it is available from the Web site.
- *Good practice guidelines for HCV identification management and monitoring.* Two documents (ProForest 2008a and ProForest 2008b) set out the process steps that are important to a credible HCV assessment process. The

Assessment, Management & Monitoring of High Conservation Values: A practical guide for forest managers (ProForest 2008a) is available from www.ProForest.net and www.hcvnetwork.org. *Good Practice Guidelines for High Conservation Value Assessments: A Methodological Approach for Practitioners and Auditors* (ProForest 2008b) is available from Proforest and www.hcvnetwork.org.

Good practice in HCV assessment and management

To ensure that an HCVF assessment is useful, some important elements should be considered.[8]

DATA REQUIREMENTS. Appropriate use of data is at the heart of the HCV assessment process. Identifying HCVs and planning appropriate management requires data to allow the assessor to know the values that are likely to be present and the potential impacts of different management scenarios. Preparation is therefore critical to ensure that the full range of applicable information is available. The impact and scale of planned operations, and the likely conservation importance of the assessed area, can only be properly understood with a solid knowledge base. These also help determine the team and stakeholder consultation requirements.

TEAM REQUIREMENTS. HCV assessments are typically carried out by small teams with practical conservation experience. Technical expertise (ideally, local expertise) in a relevant topic such as ecology, social issues, or environmental management is very important, but an HCVF assessment is also much more likely to be carried out successfully if it is undertaken by a team with a thorough understanding of the whole HCV process and experience in implementing it.

CONSULTATION REQUIREMENTS. Consultation is an essential part of the HCV process. Appropriate stakeholders, including industry representatives, conservation NGOs, local government, and local community representatives, have an important role to play in ensuring a successful outcome, both in identifying values and determining management options. Consultation serves a number of important purposes:

- To gather information on the social and environmental situation in the assessment area, to contribute to the HCV identification and decision making process
- To provide information on potential negative impacts of operations on HCVs

- To identify possible approaches for avoiding, mitigating, or compensating for negative impacts of operations
- To eliminate gaps in data, where information is held by stakeholders
- To avoid or significantly reduce conflicts arising from operations
- To ensure the transparency of the assessment process and the credibility of the decisions made

USE OF THE PRECAUTIONARY PRINCIPLE. Where data are lacking, it can be difficult to make management decisions. In the case of low- or medium-impact operations, if there is insufficient information for specific management of a given HCV, managers should aim to implement best operational practice and develop a monitoring plan that will detect changes in the status of an HCV and allow prompt action. The higher the potential concentration of values and the impact of the operation, the further the management plan should go toward protection and restoration. In the context of conversion, the land manager must try to reduce uncertainty, if necessary by commissioning surveys and field work to determine the limits and thresholds of HCVs, and secure these areas before any conversion. Stakeholder engagement is critical to a credible outcome; for example, the full range of stakeholders should be involved in defining what a sufficient area represents.

REPORTING AND TRANSPARENCY. The end product of an HCVF assessment should be management recommendations about forest that must be protected and forest that must be managed in a specific way. HCVF assessment reports should contain sufficient information for an expert third party to be able to judge whether the identification process and consultation were adequate to justify management decisions. This assessment should be done in a clear and consistent way, and include a final peer review and consultation process to guarantee quality control.

LESSONS LEARNED AND RECOMMENDATIONS FOR PRACTITIONERS

Although the HCVF concept was only developed in 1999, it has already been widely used and some key issues have emerged:

GOOD UNDERSTANDING OF THE CONCEPT AND TECHNICAL COMPETENCE ARE IMPORTANT FOR PROPER APPLICATION. The framework is relatively sophisticated and has multiple elements, as discussed earlier in this note. It requires a good understanding of the concept itself, as well as technical competence from practitioners, to be useful and to ensure that all the different interests and values are balanced.

PREDICTION OF COSTS. The cost of an HCVF assessment is closely related to the number of people involved and the time required, which, in turn, depend on the size and complexity of the forest area, the number of HCVs potentially present, the types of land use proposed for the area, the availability of data, and the complexity of the local situation. There are excellent examples of HCVF assessments carried out in a few days with a small team, or even internally by a company, and costing relatively little. At the other end of the scale, large assessments in complex situations, particularly involving forest conversion, can cost tens of thousands of dollars. Similarly, national interpretation processes can be relatively straightforward and cost only a few thousand dollars or be complex and involve significant costs.

FOLLOW-UP OF HCVF IMPLEMENTATION. Active stewardship of HCVFs is necessary for implementation. In Indonesia, in response to external pressure to protect the HCVFs in its concessions, the pulp and paper company APP committed to protecting the HCVF found in one of its concessions. In 2005, APP commissioned Smartwood to map HCVFs in three of its other forest management units in the area. On the basis of this mapping, APP announced that it would protect the HCVFs identified and signed an agreement with Smartwood to track how well it is managing its HCVFs over the next five years. However, recent monitoring reports showed that APP failed to protect these areas from fires and illegal logging, despite its earlier pledges. This case highlights the need for active stewardship of HCVFs if company commitments are to make a real difference in practice (WWF 2007).

A SYSTEMATIC FRAMEWORK FOR ANALYSIS. HCVF is not a panacea and cannot resolve every intractable land-use debate involving forests. However, it provides a systematic framework for analysis, gives consideration to a wide range of conservation values in an integrated process, and incorporates consultation and involvement of stakeholders in finding an appropriate solution, all of which combine to make it a very useful tool.

NOTES

1. It should be noted that in most countries regulations and silvicultural guidelines include conservation aspects.

However, these general rules are seldom sufficient to guide actions in particular sites.

2. IUCN World Commission on Protected Areas, http://iucn.org/themes/wcpa/.

3. The need to increase area under protection should be defined by each country and its particular conditions because in some World Bank client countries large shares of forests are already protected while in most others more is needed.

4. FSC Principles and Criteria: Principle 9: Maintenance of High Conservation Value Forests. According to Principle 9 of FSC, "management activities in HCVF should maintain or enhance the attributes which define such forests. Decisions regarding high conservation value forests shall always be considered in the context of a precautionary approach" (http://www.fsc.org/en/about/policy_standards/princ_criteria/11).

5. The Round Table on Sustainable Palm Oil (RSPO) Principles and Criteria are available at http://www.rspo.org.

6. This section draws heavily from the HCVF toolkit. All users of this note are encouraged to consult the detailed HCVF toolkit because it contains helpful checklists and concrete examples. The toolkit is available at http://www.hcvf.org.

7. The organizations making up the founding Advisory Group included the World Bank, World Wildlife Fund (WWF), IUCN, International Tropical Timber Organization (ITTO), WBCSD, Greenpeace, Forest Ethics, The Nature Conservancy, The Forest Peoples' Movement, Tetra-Pak, Mondi, and the FSC (HCV Resource Network 2006).

8. This section draws on ProForest 2003.

SELECTED READINGS

Dinerstein, E., G. Powell, D. Olson, E. Wikramanayake, R. Abell, C. Loucks, E. Underwood, T. Allnutt, W. Wettengel, T. Ricketts, H. Strand, S. O'Connor, and N. Burgess. 2000. "A Workbook for Conducting Biological Assessments and Developing Biodiversity Visions for Ecoregion-Based Conservation." Conservation Science Program, WWF, Washington, DC.

HCV Resource Network. 2007. Welcome to the HCV Resource Network (Web site). http://www.hcvnetwork.org.

Knight, A., R. Cowling, and B. Campbell. 2006. "An Operational Model for Implementing Conservation Action." *Conservation Biology* 20 (2): 408–19.

Nasi, R., and A. Fabing. 2001. "Integration of Biodiversity into National Forestry Planning: Synthesis Report." CIFOR Biodiversity Planning Support Programme, Bogor, Indonesia.

ProForest. 2003. *The High Conservation Value Forest Toolkit.* 1st ed. Oxford: ProForest. http://www.proforest.net/publication/pubcat.2007-01-19.4709481979.

———. 2008a. *Assessment, Management, and Monitoring of High Conservation Values: A Practical Guide for Forest Managers.* ProForest, Oxford.

———. 2008b. *Good Practice Guidelines for High Conservation Value assessments: A Methodological Approach for Practitioners and Auditors.* Proforest, Oxford.

REFERENCES CITED

Brooks, T. M., M. I. Bakarr, T. Boucher, G. A. B. da Fonseca, C. Hilton-Taylor, J. M. Hoekstra, T. Moritz, S. Olivieri. 2004. "Coverage Provided by the Global Protected-Area System: Is It Enough?" *BioScience* 54 (12): 1081–91.

HCV Resource Network. 2006. Welcome to the HCV Resource Network (Web site). http://www.hcvnetwork.org.

PNG FSC (Papua New Guinea Forest Stweardship Council). 2006. "HCV Forest Toolkit for Papua New Guinea." http://www.wwfpacific.org.fj/publications/png/HCVF_Toolkit_First_Ed.pdf]

ProForest. 2003. *The High Conservation Value Forest Toolkit.* 1st ed. (parts 1-3). Oxford: ProForest. http://www.proforest.net/publication/pubcat.2007-01-19.4709481979.

———. 2007. "Mainstreaming Conservation Considerations into Productive Landscapes: Applying High Conservation Value (HCV) Tools." Note submitted to World Bank as input to *Forests Sourcebook.* Unpublished. World Bank, Washington, DC.

———. 2008a. *Assessment, Management, and Monitoring of High Conservation Values: A Practical Guide for Forest Managers.* Proforest, Oxford.

———. 2008b. *Good Practice Guidelines for High Conservation Value assessments: A Methodological Approach for Practitioners and Auditors.* Proforest, Oxford.

WWF (World Wildlife Fund). 2007. "High Conservation Value Forests: The Concept in Theory and Practice." Forests for Life Programme, WWF International, Gland, Switzerland. http://assets.panda.org/downloads/hcvf_brochure_012007.pdf.

CROSS-REFERENCED CHAPTERS AND NOTES

Note 3.3: Forest Plantations

Forest Certification Systems

Forest certification has become of increasing consequence to forest management and policy in recent years, as consumers have become increasingly scrupulous about the source of their forest products. This note discusses the potential for certification not only to act as an investment safeguard and supplement traditional World Bank project monitoring, but also to provide a range of other benefits, such as market access and improved governance and stakeholder relations. The overarching goal of supporting the development and adoption of forest certification is to harness its potential while avoiding associated risks. This note describes how, in addition to providing an investment safeguard, certification can achieve less tangible benefits, such as resolving stakeholder conflict, providing forest surveillance where government capacity is inadequate, and enabling market access. This subject is interconnected with many of the notes within this sourcebook, including those on forest governance (chapter 5), illegal logging (note 5.5), and small and medium enterprises (note 2.2).

OVERVIEW AND CONSIDERATIONS OF INTEREST FOR WORLD BANK ACTIVITIES

Reliable information on social and environmental impacts of production processes becomes increasingly important for developing and maintaining business relations as markets become increasingly integrated at the global scale. Demand for such information originates from consumers, including governments, who are concerned about the negative consequences of their purchasing decisions as well as from a growing number of businesses that are interested in avoiding damage to their images, potentially triggered when engaging in socially and environmentally harmful activities.

Against this background, forest certification emerged as an instrument to provide information on forest management performance and thus assist consumers and businesses, predominantly in the timber products sector, with their purchasing decisions. Certification was conceived in the early 1990s as a market-based mechanism aimed at rewarding good management of forests with better market access and possibly price premiums—particularly to high-priced and environmentally sensitive markets in developed countries—for products from certified forests. Since then, the area under certified forest management increased considerably, from 30 million hectares in 2002 to approximately 250 million hectares worldwide today. The number of products bearing certification labels and the number of different certification systems in the marketplace have also proliferated.

OPERATIONAL ASPECTS

Generally, the first step of the certification process consists of a conformity assessment in which the quality of a production process (for example, its environmental impacts, social performance, technical aspects, efficiency) or special features of products or services are assessed against requirements specified in a standard. In the case of forest management certification, independent assessment provides an analysis of the applied management practices in relation to the standard requirements. If successful, a certificate is issued that can be used as assurance that the operation is in compliance with the provisions set forth in the applied standard. Continual conformance monitoring of the certified operation is carried out through repeated surveillance visits during the validity period of the certificate. In general, certificate holders are allowed to use a label and to make claims about their adherence to the standard requirements.

In addition, most certification systems developed rules for the handling of certified timber in downstream processing facilities, such as saw mills, paper mills, or furniture production, that allow certified timber to be traced throughout the supply chain to the end consumer. Application of these rules and the subsequent certification of the implemented processes in the timber industry are the basis for claims on the origin of products from a certified forest. This chain-of-custody certification is therefore an indispensable tool to link supplies from certified forests to consumer demand for certified products. It should be noted, however, that the scope of chain-of-custody certification is limited to the processes for control of certified and uncertified material flows and does not include the social or environmental quality of timber processing.[1]

The World Bank introduced certification as an important element of its safeguard policy on forests (World Bank 2004), making use of the control and surveillance mechanisms provided by certification systems to supplement the World Bank's own monitoring efforts. Certification under a system acceptable to the World Bank is required for enabling investments into commercial forest harvesting operations at an industrial scale. Alternatively, operations can adhere to a time-bound action plan accepted by the World Bank that is adequate to achieve certification under such a system within a defined time frame. The World Bank's policy more clearly defines the forest management standards a certification system should require (paragraph 10, OP 4.36) and the necessary minimum thresholds for the rules governing the operations of certification systems (paragraph 11, OP 4.36) for them to be acceptable to the World Bank.

Beyond this more narrowly focused perspective of certification as a safeguard tool are a number of reasons to use this instrument and related processes and institutions more proactively, including the following:

CONFLICT MITIGATION AND STAKEHOLDER DIALOGUE. Given the great potential of forests to deliver multiple products and services, interests diverge widely and conflicts over the use of forest resources are extensive in many forest regions. If properly designed, certification systems provide mechanisms for the involvement of stakeholders at the national level in the process of setting standards for forest management. In addition, local communities and other stakeholders are normally consulted during the certification audit and their concerns and opinions are considered in the certification decision. In the course of such processes, the available information is improved not only about forest management practices but also about the varying and conflicting interests of stakeholders. This increases transparency considerably and may contribute to better understanding between the different actors in the sector, and thus bears the potential to mitigate conflicts.

SUPPLEMENTING GOVERNMENT FOREST SURVEILLANCE. The certification process consists of an assessment of operations

according to a standard that at a minimum meets, and frequently exceeds, a country's legal requirements for forest management. Certification could therefore be used to supplement or in some instances even replace governmental surveillance mechanisms in the sector and thus contribute to more efficient use of scarce public resources.

PROVIDING A ROLE MODEL. To achieve certification under internationally acceptable standards, companies must have adequate management systems in place. In comparison with competing businesses, these companies often demonstrate better economic performance and can serve as a benchmark for SFM.

MARKET ACCESS. Maintaining or expanding access to export markets is critical to the economic viability of the forest sector in many countries. Particularly for timber from developing countries, market access can be hampered by consumer concerns about the negative impacts of forest harvesting. It is increasingly important for companies to be able to demonstrate the sustainability of their products and to be able to trace the source materials through the supply chain (chain of custody). Many certification systems can help provide this assurance.

LESSONS LEARNED AND RECOMMENDATIONS FOR PRACTITIONERS

Barriers to certification

In the past, a number of barriers particularly prevalent in developing countries became apparent, considerably hampering the development of certification schemes and their widespread application. The gap between then-current forest management practices and the performance level required by many standards resulted in high compliance costs and deterred many companies from pursuing certification. Furthermore, the kinds of institutions required for developing and conducting the processes for reliable certification are often not available or lack the capacity to perform the complex tasks involved. Experience has also shown that it is considerably more difficult for small-scale operations to achieve certification and access markets for certified products because of economies of scale that substantially decrease per-unit costs of certification for bigger enterprises. So far, only a limited number of timber processing companies in many developing countries have chain-of-custody certification, a situation that adds to the difficulties for primary producers to access certified supply chains.

The development of acceptable certification systems should form a key element of the World Bank's forest sector projects to overcome these barriers. This activity should receive increased support, for several reasons:

- In the absence of acceptable certification systems, the World Bank is not in a position to support a wide range of commercial activities involving key players and decision makers in the forest sector. This situation may contribute to unduly limiting the World Bank's influence to marginal fields and negatively impact the World Bank's potential role in improving performance in the sector. Integrating forests into sustainable economic development is an overarching goal for World Bank interventions and is greatly facilitated by the existence of appropriate forest certification systems.
- Small-scale operations potentially risk becoming further marginalized through certification activities because achieving certified status has proved to be particularly difficult for landholders with small areas and for community forest enterprises. Certification could therefore negatively affect the World Bank's overall goal of poverty reduction and the declared strategy to make use of forest benefits for the poor. More proactive World Bank support to the development of appropriate systems could help avoid these potentially adverse impacts of certification on the World Bank's overall goals (see also note 1.3, Indigenous Peoples and Forests, for particular issues concerning Indigenous Peoples).

Harnessing the potential of certification for improving forest sector performance and avoiding the risks to World Bank activities from a lack of adequate systems requires targeted activities to overcome the bottlenecks that are still widespread in many World Bank client countries.

Support to certification system development

The activities outlined below should be considered when providing support to the development of certification systems through World Bank–financed projects.

Assist standards development processes. Currently, the lack of appropriate standards presents one of the most important formal obstacles for the widespread application of forest certification. While international and national organizations may be available to implement other elements of certification (such as certification assessments), standards development has to be carried out by local initiatives that, in many countries, lack the funding, capacity, and staff

to conduct the tasks involved in managing participatory processes. The World Bank's provisions for standard setting, which clearly require locally adapted forest management standards developed with the participation of a wide range of stakeholders, provides further justification for supporting these processes.

Consensus-based decision making regarding contentious issues is often a lengthy process with a number of uncertainties. Progress may therefore not follow strict World Bank project deadlines or adhere to narrowly defined project targets. Furthermore, care should be taken to not unduly influence the process so that results not accepted by a number of the involved and affected stakeholders can be avoided. Eligibility of standard-setting initiatives for potential World Bank funding may best be based on the criteria defined in OP 4.36 and on the interpretation of these provisions outlined in chapter 9, Applying Forest Policy OP 4.36, and chapter 11, Forest Certification Assessment Guide: Summary on Use, in section II of this sourcebook.

Today, two certification systems are operating at the international level—FSC (http://www.fsc.org) and the PEFC (http://www.pefc.org). These umbrella organizations provide international framework standards for further elaboration through standard-setting initiatives at the national level. To maintain flexibility and to provide a basis for certification that can later be used by companies interested in either of the international systems, standard-setting processes should strive to adhere to the rules and regulations of both the FSC and PEFC. This approach could reduce conflicts that may arise from an early and potentially contentious selection of the system to which a national certification system may want to adhere to.

Build local certification capacity. The skills to implement and manage certification systems, particularly in the field of forest management, are underdeveloped in many World Bank client countries. Although international certification systems and certifying bodies provide services in these countries, the employment of expatriate personnel adds to the high costs for certification in developing countries. Establishment of local expertise for the tasks of certification assessment and possibly accreditation of certifying bodies would often reduce costs and, most of all, add to the maintenance of national ownership over certification and thus contribute to more widespread acceptance of the tool.

Assist small, individual operations in pursuing certification. Within its projects, the World Bank may finance investments directed at the improvement of forest management practices in selected enterprises. Given the decreased competitiveness that results from their structural disadvantages, small operations and community forestry are in special need of adequate funding. In this context, the time-bound action plan for certification foreseen in OP 4.36 and further outlined as a safeguard instrument in chapter 11, Forest Certification Assessment Guide: Summary on Use, can provide the conceptual basis for planning and monitoring assistance to individual companies.

Capacity-building efforts should be extended to downstream processing facilities to improve technical knowledge related to development and implementation of appropriate chain-of-custody systems. Again, these activities should focus on small and medium enterprises, which are important partners for smaller forest operations but in many cases lack the capacity to achieve certification of their processes for the control of material flows.

NOTE

1. The widely applied quality and environmental management systems set forth in ISO 9002 or ISO 14001 standards can provide the basis for chain-of-custody systems but, in general, require adaptation to the specific requirements of certification systems before products can be labeled as compliant with those systems.

SELECTED READINGS

Burger, D., J. Hess, and B. Lang, eds. 2005. "Forest Certification: An Innovative Instrument in the Service of Sustainable Development?" Deutsche Gesellschaft für Technische Zusammenarbeit, Eschborn, Germany.

Nussbaum, R., and M. Simula. 2005. *The Forest Certification Handbook.* London: Earthscan.

Richards, M. 2004. "Certification in Complex Socio-Political Settings: Looking Forward to the Next Decade." Forest Trends, Washington, DC.

REFERENCES CITED

World Bank. 2004. "The World Bank Operational Manual, Operational Policies OP 4.36 Forests." World Bank, Washington, DC.

CROSS-REFERENCED CHAPTERS AND NOTES

Note 1.3: Indigenous Peoples and Forests

Note 2.2: Small- and Medium-Scale Enterprises

Chapter 5: Improving Forest Governance

Note 5.5: Addressing Illegal Logging and Other Forest Crime

Chapter 9: Applying Forests Policy OP 4.36

Chapter 11: Forest Certification Assessment Guide: Summary on Use

Forest Plantations in World Bank Operations

Forest plantations can be highly effective for the production of fiber for wood and paper products, and may help in meeting the growing demand for wood identified in chapter 3. Managed properly, they may also be effective in the protection and conservation of soil and water resources, revegetation of degraded landscapes, rehabilitation of habitats, and for carbon sequestration. However, they have also been associated with conversion of natural forests, the destruction of habitat, and the marginalization of local and Indigenous Peoples. This note examines the potential for plantations to deliver a variety of goods and services and identifies the precautions necessary to avoid causing negative environmental and social impacts.

OVERVIEW AND CONSIDERATIONS OF INTEREST FOR WORLD BANK ACTIVITIES

Because of their efficiency in wood production, along with increasing restrictions on the use of native forests, wood supply from plantations has grown from 5 percent to 30 percent of the total share of industrial fiber over the past 15 years, and projections are that this will increase to 50 percent by 2040 (World Bank 2005). Today, most of the world's 140 million ha of plantations are established for productive purposes, with another 31 million ha established for protection (FAO 2006).

Trees have an excellent capacity to capture and hold, or "fix," atmospheric carbon and are now being employed for carbon sequestration to mitigate greenhouse gas effects and climate change. Carbon content in trees is a function of their density and volume. The faster the trees are able to grow, the more rapidly they fix carbon. The paradox is that many of the same exotic trees that grow rapidly and are most useful for sequestering carbon also pose increased risks for local environmental impacts because of their aggressive characteristics.

OPERATIONAL ASPECTS

In general, most productive plantations are characterized by uniform species composition and age-class distribution within stands, regular spacing between tree stems, and simple geometric configurations (blocks)—characteristics that enhance their utility and cost effectiveness. However, these same qualities, along with the use of mechanical and chemical treatments and occasional replacement of native vegetation, have led to concerns about plantations' impacts on the environment and biodiversity. Social issues can also emerge when large operations fail to address impacts on local populations or fail to include landowners' and other stakeholders' concerns in their operations. For these reasons, World Bank–financed operations need to ensure that both environmental and social concerns are considered early in the project design. In the end, productive plantations do not have to compromise the environment or biodiversity, or lead to social exclusion—in fact, they can favorably affect each of them, or at a minimum their impacts can be mitigated, and it is the World Bank's job to ensure that this happens within its investments.

SCALE OF ACTIVITY. World Bank operations involving plantations may be carried out at both national and local levels. Striking the balance between these very different approaches, or choosing one over the other, during project design requires a solid understanding of the country's needs and goals for the sector, as well as of local conditions in areas targeted for interventions. Conversely, most countries lack a strategic vision for forestry, and World Bank projects must frequently incorporate elements of strategic planning with more tangible activities that promote sustainable development, such as research, extension, and the promotion of best management practices. Stakeholder processes such as National Forestry Programs (see note 6.3, Identifying the Need for Analysis on Forests in Development Policy

Reforms) provide the framework for participatory development of national strategies and, where available, project preparation should draw on their work. Because forestry is a long-term endeavor, a correct focus and vision for the intervention is critical at the onset—it is a template for the future.

SPECIES SELECTION. Productive plantations are usually established for one of two purposes, sawtimber or pulp, and to a lesser extent for NTFPs, such as rubber, or in multiple-use agroforesty and silvopastoral systems. Plantations established for pulp usually emphasize high volumes of fast-growing trees with good pulping characteristics, particularly high specific gravity and long fibers (hardwoods) or tracheid (softwoods). Such plantations in developing countries are frequently established using exotic pines from the Americas, eucalypts from Australia, or acacias. Trees selected for sawtimber plantations must produce wood appropriate for the intended end use, which can be highly variable and includes wood for structural framing and construction, furniture, veneers, or crates and pallets, among others.

In all cases, species needs to be carefully selected to ensure that the desired end products (or services) are eventually obtained. At the same time, market demands and trends should be taken into account to ensure that the trees will be marketable at maturity. Planting programs that fail to take market factors into account can, and have, resulted in large areas of plantations with limited or negligible financial viability and consequent loss of investors in the sector. For many countries, this poses a paradox because they are unable to attract or develop wood industries until an adequate resource base is developed or assured. In such cases, planting programs with productive aims should carefully analyze projections of needs at local, national, and international levels during formulation to ensure their program gets off to the right start.

MANAGEMENT PRACTICE. Plantation productivity is normally much greater than that of natural forests. Well-managed plantations in some developing countries have annual growth rates in excess of 40 m³/ha. The most productive native forests (those of the southeastern United States) show internal rates of return (IRRs) of around 4–8 percent, whereas, *P. taeda* plantations in Brazil have achieved IRRs of 17 percent, and plantations of *Eucalyptus grandis* in Brazil have recorded IRRs of 24 percent (Cubbage et al., 2007). The large differences in returns between plantations and natural forests are attributable to the application of management practices, the selection of the best species for production, optimal stocking, and lower land and labor values in developing countries. Industrial plantations also benefit from site preparation techniques, the use of improved seeds, pest management, and higher levels of stocking over natural forests. Natural forests may not need these initial investments. If natural forests are managed as going concerns, they can be and often are economically viable.

USE OF NATIVE SPECIES. Because many species of trees grow much faster outside their native ranges, they provide improved opportunities for increased financial returns. This has given rise to an extensive use of eucalypts (from Australia) and southern yellow pines and Monterrey pine (from the United States) in industrial plantations and development programs. In the developing world, about 44 million ha of plantations are found in Asia, the bulk of which are located in China; 11 million in South America, mostly in Argentina, Brazil, and Chile; and another 10 million in Africa, in Côte d'Ivoire, Nigeria, Rwanda, and others. Smaller areas of exotic plantations are common throughout the rest of the developing world. While the use of exotics is popular from an economic perspective, concerns about their environmental impacts have been growing. A recent CIFOR study concluded that there are situations where plantations have affected critical habitats, but it also concluded that such claims may be exaggerated (World Bank 2003; Cossalter and Pye-Smith 2003). Still, the widespread use of exotics has led to an increasingly polarized debate concerning their use and potential impact on the environment. For World Bank projects, this means potential reputational risks, and the need for good public outreach and consensus building during project preparation and implementation, as well as safeguards monitoring.

While World Bank–financed projects should endeavor to use native species whenever possible, in reality, client countries and producers are more likely to favor the use of exotics over native species because financial returns on investments are frequently much higher. In such cases, finding a middle ground and ensuring that any impacts from the use of exotics is mitigated or avoided is essential. To achieve this, specific measures must usually be employed to integrate biodiversity conservation into exotic plantations. Examples of such techniques include maintaining biological corridors and integrating native species into plantations; establishing set asides for wildlife and biodiversity conservation; favoring smaller patches of plantations rather than large contiguous blocks of monocultures; avoiding invasive exotics; and generally following standard best management practices, which emphasize the control of nonpoint pollution from silvicultural activities, including site preparation, road building, and harvesting (Davis 2005). Research programs to promote knowledge building for the use and management of native species can also be helpful. With these tools at the disposal of the project team, World Bank operations stand to do a much better job of guaranteeing environmental sustainability than could be done under current industry standards, thereby ensuring that new programs get off to the right start.

COMMUNITY INVOLVEMENT IN PLANTATIONS. Planting trees to establish woodlots and agroforestry or other multiple-use systems can be important elements of community and local development. So can plantations for wood production, particularly those using short rotation systems. Such efforts generally focus on overcoming local population needs for building materials and fuelwood, increasing incomes (for example, through the sale of timber), and encouraging environmental sustainability of land holdings. The principles of working at the local level are similar to those outlined for larger-scale operations in technical terms—species and site selection; market, cost, and needs analyses; capacity building; and management practices. At the same time, because the rural poor are often challenged with day-to-day survival, it is critical that risks to their livelihoods are mitigated. Programs should be designed from the bottom up, and implemented in full cooperation and consensus with participants, in consideration of their particular situations. Frequently this means employing social foresters or other development specialists who work closely with the communities involved in a project (see also note 1.3, Indigenous Peoples and Forests, and chapter 12, Applying OP 4.10 on Indigenous Peoples, for particular risks and issues concerning Indigenous Peoples).

Pests and fires pose common threats to plantations; provisions for fire breaks and training and equipping fire crews in fire suppression can be important elements of World Bank–financed projects. Monoculture plantations, whether native or exotic, pose increased risks to investments because they may be more susceptible to pests and disease. Massive loss and near eradication of some tree species has occurred in the last 100 years. For example, one of the most important production trees in North America, the American Chestnut (*Castanea dentata*), was virtually eliminated in a matter of a few years by an introduced fungus, *Cryphonectria parasitica*. Thousands of hectares of exotic *P. radiata* plantations were infected and succumbed to infections of *Dothystroma pini* in the 1980s and *Cedrela odorata*, even in its native range, suffers from infections from *Hypsiphyla*

grandella when planted in monocultures. Despite the lessons learned from such experiences, monocultures are easier and more cost effective than mixed plantations—that is, until problems occur, causing devastating loss.

ESTABLISHMENT COSTS AND TECHNICAL CAPACITY. Two essential factors must be taken into consideration in the development of a plantation project—establishment costs, and the technical capacity required for planting and stand management. Initial investment capital for plantation establishment generally comes from three sources—land owners, loans, and government subsidies. With average establishment costs ranging from US$500 to US$2,000 per hectare, most small- and medium-scale producers are not able to finance their own plantations, nor do they have sufficient access to credit to guarantee loans.

Large areas of plantations may be required to guarantee sufficient raw material for major forest industries. For example, a large pulp mill with a capacity of 1 million tons per year will typically require a resource base of 100,000–200,000 ha of plantations to sustain its production over time (depending on growth rates and pulping characteristics of trees). In contrast, the resource base for sawtimber plantations rarely exceeds 20,000 ha, and could be substantially less for smaller operations.

Subsidies can play an important role in stimulating planting to encourage the development of an adequate resource base for industry (see note 5.4, Strengthening Fiscal Systems in the Forest Sector). To foster social inclusion within the sector, some World Bank projects either directly subsidize plantations through grants (usually for small farmers) or work with the government in the design and execution of subsidy programs for a wider range of producers. In theory, once the cycle of planting and harvesting has been completed, subsidies should be reduced or removed because producers will have the means to reforest with income derived from timber sales—and the economic incentive to do so.

While subsidies can sometimes be useful to mainstream small producers into the sector, and help to expand the resource base necessary to promote economic growth for other producers, they have to be approached with caution. Poorly designed or implemented subsidy programs can result in unintended environmental impacts when producers plant trees in environmentally sensitive areas, or cause habitat destruction and deforestation, as can happen when farmers convert native forests to plantations. They may also encourage planting without sufficient attention to end uses and markets. The management of subsidies also poses challenges to weak institutions, which may provide opportunities for corruption—for example, when planting subsidies are paid without sufficient field verification. Each case and country situation has to be reviewed carefully when entering into discussions on subsidies and considering their inclusion in the project design.

Outgrower schemes can also encourage plantation development. This approach involves mill owners providing subsidies and technical assistance to local land owners to ensure the availability of growing stock for the mill owners' production lines. In general, the World Bank would have a limited role in such cases because of the private-sector nature of these schemes, except in cases of IFC involvement. Still, Bank staff should be aware of the option and possibilities to interact with such schemes within the context of their project planning and implementation.

Carbon financing can provide about US$4 per ton of carbon sequestered. This is generally paid out in increments over an extended period, such as 20 years. However, funding available from carbon, may in some cases only be sufficient to pay a portion of the plantation establishment costs and, over the lifetime of the project, usually comprises only about 15–25 percent of the total costs of management. Consequently, carbon finance projects are building productive activities, including timber sales, into their projects. Thus, carbon financing can provide important subsidies for stimulating plantation development and carbon sequestration, but they are not viable economic endeavors in themselves. Despite these drawbacks, World Bank carbon projects are producing valuable lessons for future efforts, which may become vital as the climate continues to change and global warming continues.

TECHNICAL KNOW-HOW. Technical know-how is essential in plantation development—for site and species selection, plantation establishment, and carrying out management and harvesting activities. Technology transfer frequently involves the need for extension programs and training of agents to ensure that the required knowledge is transferred to producers and land owners. Existing extension programs may be strengthened through a World Bank intervention. However, client governments have been increasingly reluctant to finance the start up of new forestry extension programs through loan financing, World Bank projects may encounter problems with sustainability of such programs at closure, and government extension services can easily become encumbered by weak institutions.

One alternative to government-funded extension programs is to help countries establish private-sector extension services (see chapter 2, Engaging the Private Sector in Forest Sector Development, and associated notes). For example, Chile, which lacks a government extension service, has a booming forest industry, and exports US$2.3 billion in forest products annually. Here, a strong private sector developed, encouraged by a hands-off approach from the government and a supportive institutional system that enabled it to react quickly to market demand and to access the latest technologies. Numerous independent organizations also provide well-targeted advice and support to the sector. The result of this combination is an efficient, modern forestry sector that produces low-cost, high-quality timber products and is competitive in world markets.

LESSONS LEARNED AND RECOMMENDATIONS FOR PRACTITIONERS

Planted forests allow intensive production of industrial wood at a reasonable cost, which is important in countries with high population densities. Planted forests also offer economic opportunities for countries with natural competitive advantages and lands available for planting, such as Argentina, Brazil, Chile, China, Indonesia, Mexico, South Africa, Uruguay, and Vietnam.

In countries and zones where public land ownership is dominant, it is important to place plantation development within the framework of a transparent, accountable, and consultative land-use plan that specifies the extent of the permanent forest estate and locates land available for planted forests. Good governance and an enabling policy environment are necessary to ensure private investment in plantation development, which can be initially motivated by the World Bank's initial support.

To make plantation forestry economically viable, technical management standards frequently need to be raised. As happened in Chile and Brazil, the adoption of new innovative technologies relying on high-performance species, high-quality seedlings, and efficient planting practices can substantially improve productivity and economic profitability. Also, production technologies that depend on natural regeneration can offer cost-effective ways to conduct production forestry or to rehabilitate degraded lands. Furthermore, it has been observed (for example, in India and Vietnam) that plantations linked to industry tend to have higher levels of productivity.

Site and species matching must receive due attention to avoid adverse environmental and social impacts. In addition, because policy and market failures can create more formidable obstacles to viability than technical considerations, projects must be solidly based on sound policy and market organizational analyses. In particular, security of land tenure is key in fostering investments in plantation forestry.

In smallholder forestry, extension programs need to introduce improved technologies compatible with the maintenance of environmental and social values in plantation areas. These programs should be considered long-term undertakings and should not be limited to the plantation establishment phase. Effective linkages between silvicultural research and extension institutions are critical to successful technology transfer.

RECOMMENDED READING

Planted Forest Code. http://www.fao.org/forestry. The Planted Forest Code provides an excellent framework and concise synopsis of the major issues to consider in plantation projects. Recommended for anyone in the World Bank working with plantations.

Forest Stewardship Council. http://www.fsc.org. See the links concerning plantations to learn about the FSC standards and revision process under way for plantation certification. Subscribe to the plantations forum by e-mail at Plantationsforum_fsc.org to get a glimpse of the debate on plantation certification.

Marrakech Accord. http://www.unfccc.int/cop7/. The Marrakech Accord outlines the agreements and guidelines for eligibility of reforestation and afforestation activities for carbon financing.

Flinta, Carlos. 1960. *Practicas de Plantaciones Forestales en America Latina.* FAO Forestry Development Paper no 15. Rome: Food and Agriculture Organization of the United Nations. Though quite dated, this book contains a wealth of information on hundreds of species of trees, and detailed information required for their use and management in plantations.

Best management practices. http://www.stateforesters.org. State Foresters Association Web site for their silvicultural best management practices library and database. Multiple links to state best management practices guidelines.

International Union of Forest Research Organizations. 2005. Proceedings from the First International Union of Forest Research Organizations Conference on Biodiversity and Conservation Biology in Plantation Forests, Bordeaux, France, 26–29 April 2005. *Summary:* http://www.pierroton.inra.fr/IEFC/manifestations/ 2005 BPF/BPF2005.pdf. *Presentations:* http://www.pierroton .inra.fr/IEFC/affiche_page.php?page=manif_2005_bpf& langue=en.

REFERENCES CITED

Cossalter, C., and C. Pye-Smith. 2003. *Fast-Wood Forestry: Myths and Realities.* Bogor, Indonesia: CIFOR.

Cubbage, F. and others. 2007. "Timber Investment Returns for Selected Plantations and Native Forests in South America and the Southern United States." *New Forests* 33 (3): 237–255.

Davis, Robert. 2005. Argentina—GEF Sustainable Forestry Development Project. Project Brief. Washington, DC: GEF.

FAO (Food and Agriculture Organization). 2006. *Global Forest Resources Assessment 2005.* Rome: FAO.

World Bank. 2003. The Forest Investment Forum. Washington, DC, October 22–23.

———. 2005. "Report of the Forest Investment Forum." Washington, DC, World Bank.

CROSS-REFERENCED CHAPTERS AND NOTES

Note 1.3: Indigenous Peoples and Forests

Chapter 2: Engaging the Private Sector in Forest Sector Development, and associated notes

Note 5.4: Strengthening Fiscal Systems in the Forest Sector

Chapter 12: Applying OP 4.10 on Indigenous Peoples

CHAPTER 4

Optimizing Forest Functions
in a Landscape

The term "landscape" has permeated discussions regarding forest resource management during the past few decades. A landscape is often defined as a geographical construct that includes not only biophysical features of an area but also its cultural and institutional attributes (adapted from Farina [2006]). A landscape is not necessarily defined by its size; rather, it is defined by an interacting mosaic of land cover and land-use types relevant to the processes or services being considered or managed. Examples of forest landscapes can range from large tracts of forests used for multiple purposes (production; cultural, recreational, or environmental services; and the like) to mosaics of forests, home gardens, rice terraces, and villages that enable people to exploit mountain slopes in several countries in southeast Asia in ways that yield a diversity of crops, maintain soil fertility and watershed functions, and retain indigenous biodiversity.

Another definition of landscape is a dynamic, complex patchwork of overlapping political, economic, social, and ecological systems (Scoones 1999; Zimmerer 2000). The landscape is a heterogeneous area within which there can be a mosaic of land uses that are individually relatively homogeneous.

Recently the "landscape approach" has been incorporated in the conceptualization of geographical spaces of interest when defining a landscape.[1] A landscape approach is applied to a geographical space of interest. A landscape approach is a conceptual framework that allows for a structured way of viewing the broader impacts and implications of any major investment or intervention in the rural sector[2] (see box 4.1). It describes interventions at spatial scales that attempt to optimize the spatial relations and interactions among a range of land cover types, institutions, and human activities in an area of interest.

Forest landscape restoration, landscape planning, and ecoagriculture all build on landscape approaches and principles. Common among these landscape approaches is that they

- aim to restore a balance of environmental, social, and economic benefits from forests and trees within a broader pattern of land use;
- use a landscape-level view, whether for site restoration or for activities involving a mosaic of land uses (accordingly, site-level activities accommodate, or are nested in, landscape-level objectives);
- consider people as central elements of the landscape; and
- recognize that the dynamic nature of ecosystems and socioeconomic systems makes gathering complete information regarding any system unachievable (accordingly, explicit efforts are made to integrate and adapt plans, programs, and projects that are active in a landscape, including the sharing of new knowledge and information).

The World Bank's Forests Strategy aims to make the most of the multiple uses and values of forests. Forests are part of a diverse livelihood portfolio for a large number of rural

The landscape approach should incorporate the following elements:

- Builds understanding and a shared vision of desirable future landscapes
- Determines the factors that will shape the landscape in the future so that they can be mitigated or influenced
- Builds multidisciplinary teams to tackle these complex, intersectoral landscape-scale problems
- Explores possible future scenarios for the geographical areas in question and their peoples
- Provides a framework for negotiations between stakeholders who have different views of desirable landscape-scale outcomes
- Makes the knowledge, assumptions, and desires of different stakeholders more apparent and easily understood by other stakeholders

- Identifies key leverage points that can be used to get the ecosystem or landscape to change in desirable ways
- Establishes a flexible monitoring and evaluation system to monitor and measure impacts on the landscape to allow for changes to be made in implementation

Several approaches exist for implementing strategies that integrate management of land, water, and living resources and promote conservation and sustainable use in an equitable manner (for example, an ecosystem approach). The elements listed above are generic to several of these approaches and provide practical operational entry points.

Source: Authors' compilation using Sayers 2006.

poor. In addition, the productive use of forests can significantly contribute to economic development, while the management of biological and ecological services from forests can provide numerous local as well as global environmental benefits. As noted in the strategy, forests (and their users and beneficiaries) both have an impact on and are affected by policies and actions in other sectors, as well as by biophysical changes in adjoining or biologically linked areas (as examples, forest fires can result from land-use practices in agricultural lands, or macroeconomic reforms can affect the opportunity cost of land) (see chapter 6: Mainstreaming Forests into Development Policy and Planning). In this context, optimizing forest functions[3] in a landscape can unlock the full potential of forests.

A landscape-focused program can facilitate the assessment of broader, wide-ranging trends, influences, and management impacts to more adequately assess economic and ecological sustainability and identify the appropriate management strategies to maintain these resources for the benefit of all. In certain World Bank client countries where land conversion is a major threat to forests, a landscape approach can minimize site-specific activities negatively affecting or conflicting with each other. It can also enhance any synergies that otherwise may be overlooked. Similarly, in client countries where landscapes are a mosaic of land uses, an approach that takes the landscape into account can assist in

internalizing positive externalities and minimizing negative externalities from individual land uses.

While the global rate of deforestation has fallen from 0.22 percent in the 1990s to 0.18 percent in the 2000s, the development and conservation communities continue to bemoan the imminent loss of forests, biodiversity, and associated economic and environmental services. However, not all deforestation is inevitable and not all deforestation is necessarily bad because many countries are replanting native and/or exotic forests on former forest lands and in natural grasslands. These new forests are having landscape-, regional-, and global-level impacts although they do not provide significant biodiversity conservation and are not a substitute for natural forests. The landscape approach can aid in better understanding the tradeoffs and potential synergies among competing land claims and uses in forest zones. Thus, a balance would be attempted among pressures to increase protected areas; expand the area of independently certified and sustainably managed natural forest; and convert forests to sustainable agroforestry-based farming systems, timber plantations, commercial-scale agribusiness estates (such as soybean farming or cattle ranching), or crop-based biofuels manufactured from sugar or oil palm.

All of the multilateral environmental agreements now seek to achieve their objectives through the integrated management of natural resource systems at large spatial scales.

People and human societies are seen as being part of these systems. The words "landscape" and "ecosystem" are widely used in these agreements and in the general environmental policy discourse to convey the concept of integrated management of resources and human activities at the landscape scale. The World Bank's clients will or should be moving toward landscape and ecosystem approaches, and Bank lending should be designed in ways that encourage and nurture this process and facilitate the move in this direction.

This chapter (and associated notes) presents some of the key issues underlying implementation of the landscape approach and tools to assist with its application.

PAST ACTIVITIES

The study by Sayer and Maginnis (2005) showed that much contemporary forest management already uses many elements of the landscape or ecosystem approaches even though it may not be using those terms.[4] The World Bank has been involved in a number of watershed management projects, as well as sector projects with watershed management components. Boerma (2000) provides a review of the Bank's portfolio in this field between 1990 and 1999.

According to a review of the World Bank's activities based on project appraisal documents, 24 watershed management projects and 29 projects with watershed management components were reported on in the period 1990–2004. The project rationale and objectives for more than 80 percent of the watershed management projects were based on sustainable management of natural resources as a basis for agricultural production increase, which would lead to poverty reduction by increasing incomes. Simultaneously, institutional development and capacity building were addressed by more than 90 percent of the projects. In many projects, forest management was part of the spatial watershed management approach, with the twin objectives of maintaining or increasing forest cover and creating incentives for sustainable management by local people.[5] Investments were in both natural forest management and reforestation and afforestation.

KEY ISSUES

There is no single "landscape approach." There are, however, a number of underlying concepts that deserve to be more widely known and a number of useful techniques for developing a shared understanding of landscape-scale functions, for exploring landscape-scale scenarios, and for measuring landscape-scale outcomes (see note 4.2, Assessing Outcomes of Landscape Interventions). Thus, within the same geo-

graphical area, the landscape approach would be applied differently for interventions concerned with the preservation of rare plants and animals, the management of hydrological functions, the optimization of infrastructure investments, or the maintenance of scenic beauty. Not only would the area of interest be different for these different interventions, the methods used to address landscape issues would also be different.

DEFINE THE LANDSCAPE. The essential first step for most natural resource managers is to define the landscape so that (i) landscape patterns and management responses can be assessed and management adjusted according to anticipated tradeoffs and synergies, (ii) relevant institutional players can be identified and involved, and (iii) the approach can be suitably adapted. Linked to defining the landscape is explicitly delineating the boundaries of the landscape before undertaking activities at the landscape level. Boundaries need to be established through a clear definition of the purpose of operating at the landscape level, and should be agreed on by all main actors. To implement the landscape approach, it is useful to also spatially demarcate micro areas, or specific areas within the larger landscape. These units should be tractable, improve the understanding of interactions among different land uses, and assist in optimizing forest functions in the landscape. The objectives for these macro and micro areas should be harmonized and nested to the extent possible.

MOVE BEYOND SPATIAL PLANNING AND ESTABLISHING CORRIDORS. The rhetoric supporting large-scale approaches to forest conservation and management (including plantations) is ubiquitous in project and program descriptions. However, most systematic conservation planning approaches appear to be based mainly on spatial planning techniques. These approaches range from those that attempt to maximize the extent and connectivity of natural habitat and confine measures to improve local livelihoods to the residual land, to those that are highly technical and framed by mathematical optimization modeling that finds the landscape configuration that achieves specific environmental goals at minimum cost (see box 4.2). The premise underlying this chapter is that the planning associated with landscape approaches must incorporate the management of landscapes to provide flows of conservation and development benefits to stakeholders (see note 4.1, Integrated Forest Landscape Land-Use Planning). There can be a need to stimulate demand for such planning and to ensure that the planning process responds to community needs.

TAKE INTO CONSIDERATION THE DYNAMIC NATURE OF ECO-LOGICAL PROCESSES and livelihood strategies. The time lag between when an action is undertaken and when its impact on the forest resource and its users is manifested must be recognized. A temporally explicit framework is required to accommodate these important considerations.

RECOGNIZE THAT ECONOMIC FORCES ARE NOT SET UP FOR LANDSCAPE CONSIDERATIONS. Economic forces have a profound impact on both the long-term and short-term behavior of forest stakeholders and ultimately determine the balance between competing management objectives (see box 4.3). Such factors as location, accessibility, vegetation type, and management determine the value of forests for timber production versus environmental services. The adoption of ecosystem approaches currently provides limited financial rewards.

Box 4.2   Moving Beyond Optimization Models in Tri National de la Sangha

In the Tri National de la Sangha area of the Congo Basin, a World Wildlife Fund (WWF) initiative focused on determining the sort of landscape configuration that would be optimal for achieving two contrasting objectives—improving livelihoods and conserving biodiversity. The project used simulation models to determine the relative utility of different mixes of protected areas, logging concessions, and community lands. Models were developed in a participatory manner so that the model provided a framework for discussion and negotiation. Economic benefits to different stakeholder groups and employment created by different types of land management were quantified. Similarly, the costs of protection and the benefits from hunting safaris, bushmeat harvesters, and taxes paid to the government and local communities from these different activities were calculated.

Modeling exercises can result in counterintuitive conclusions. In this case, modeling showed that if the proportion of land under well-managed concessions increased, the funds allocated to conservation could be used to increase the intensity of conservation efforts in national parks. Overall biodiversity outcome in landscapes with high proportions of well-managed concessions might therefore be better than in landscapes with a high proportion of totally protected area.

Source: Sayer and others 2005.

Box 4.3   Incentives for Sustainable Forest Management in Fragmented Forest Landscape

The conservation project for sustainable development in Central America, implemented during the 1990s by CATIE (Tropical Agricultural Research and Higher Education Center, Costa Rica) and several local partners, demonstrated the feasibility of applying sustainable forest management to forest areas under 50 ha as an integrated component of diversified farming systems based on agriculture or livestock production. Communities in the Maya Biosphere Reserve in El Petén, Guatemala, could act as forest conservation agents but for them to do so required more sustainable and profitable agricultural systems and guaranteed legal access to forest resources. The project pioneered community forest concessions and was reinforced by subsequent initiatives. The community groups obtained legal access to forests by means of concessions that allowed them to protect and use the resource. In the process, the communities improved their organizational and management capacities, their silvicultural ability, and their environmental awareness.

Source: Campos Arce, Villalobos, and Louman 2005.

Innovative payments for environmental services (see note 2.3, Innovative Marketing Arrangements: Payments for Environmental Services) and other compensation arrangements can provide economic incentives for a more landscape-based approach to optimizing forest functions.

WORK ACROSS POLITICAL AND AGENCY BOUNDARIES. A landscape of interest often crosses multiple political (local or national) and agency boundaries, with government and community capacity and presence varying widely. Because legal governance authority is seldom available at the landscape level, consensus must be achieved among all relevant stakeholders and government agencies for implementation of natural resource and forest management plans on the landscape. Collaboration among these entities may be weak and might need to be strengthened to cost effectively supplement and complement landscape efforts. This can require convening and facilitating interaction among relevant stakeholder groups, working closely with these groups over time, and clarifying, or in some cases providing, the incentives for each of them to accept restrictions on the use of resources that would otherwise be unregulated.

ENCOURAGE STAKEHOLDER PARTICIPATION. By transcending political boundaries, landscapes encompass diverse users, managers, and decision makers. Stakeholder participation in the landscape approach is important to plan effectively across the landscape; understand landscape trends; integrate national, regional, and local perspectives in zoning decisions; promote the implementation of landscape activities; seek adoption of plans; and, finally, lay the groundwork for building in-country resource-management capacity.

ENSURE RESEARCH AND MANAGEMENT WORK IN CONCERT. Not all the desired data on the landscape and its resources will be available in sufficient detail. This is the case around the world, independent of financial and human resources available to the management authority. Management actions for landscape activities should be designed using existing data but within a learning context such that future management direction can be improved over time and updated as new information becomes available. It is beneficial to invest in prioritizing information and tracking these variables. Building an information base of these critical variables over time will facilitate addressing specific issues and questions that arise.

USE AN ITERATIVE APPROACH TO MONITOR IMPACTS AND UPDATE THE PROCESS. The approach adopted at the landscape level needs to be flexible and able to accommodate new information and changing contexts. This can require the use of approaches, such as adaptive management (see note 4.3, Using Adaptive Management to Improve Project Implementation), that link research and management. Management plans should be considered living documents, able to evolve with changing information, environmental conditions, and monitoring results. Conventionally systematic plan revisions happen on a periodic basis, usually after the current plan has been in effect for 5–10 years. During a plan revision, the entire plan is revisited, allowing for major revisions and changes to its content and objectives. Adaptive management, conversely, allows individual components of the plan to be amended or altered at any time because of changing resource conditions, social values, improved data, or in response to monitoring.

As part of the overall process, identifying suitable indicators and monitoring these interactions (using technological advances that facilitate continuous and periodic data collection) will help to fill data gaps during the course of the initiative. These data will need to be processed and presented in a manner accessible to stakeholders for updating the planning and implementation processes and for providing a better understanding of interactions among the various land uses and their impacts (see note 4.2, Assessing Outcomes of Landscape Interventions).

DEVOLVE MANAGEMENT TO THE APPROPRIATE LEVELS. A key principle of the landscape approach for forests is that management must be devolved to the appropriate level. Decentralization of decision making and support from national agencies and institutions is also important for a landscape approach. Devolution of management and decentralization of decision making, however, require ensuring accountability is built into the system and that the system complements the local context and, where possible, is based on existing and effective institutional arrangements and structures.

In landscapes where local institutions are characterized by elite capture, discrimination, or marginalization of vulnerable groups, the institutional arrangement adopted in the landscape approach must challenge these constraints and create a more equitable and participatory system, as described in box 4.4. New institutional arrangements, however, can also create new societal problems that may actually lead to further degradation of natural resources. Social cohesiveness and cultural norms are critical to fostering participatory approaches and must be understood before making assumptions about existing institutional arrangements.

STRENGTHEN LOCAL AND GOVERNMENT CAPACITY TO OPERATE AT A LANDSCAPE LEVEL. Working within a landscape approach requires skills in facilitation, conflict management and mediation, consensus development, linking qualitative and quantitative information, listening, synthesizing, and adapting ideas. This skill set is neither readily available nor easily acquired at conventional technical training programs. These skills also are not readily found in communities that are hierarchical or have traditionally suppressed the voice of minorities.

Building government and community capacity to engage in a landscape approach will be important to make the process effective, with long-term impacts. Developing the necessary capacity requires both broadening the skill set and developing an innovative and feasible method for implementing the landscape-scale approach.

DEVELOP NECESSARY METHODS AND MANAGEMENT SYSTEMS. Adaptive and flexible management systems are crucial to the effective implementation of the landscape approach. Existing methods must be adapted, or new ones developed, to, among other things

The Turkey Eastern Anatolia Watershed Rehabilitation Project aimed to "help to restore sustainable range, forest and farming activities in the upper watersheds of the three project provinces, reducing soil degradation, erosion and sedimentation in reservoirs as well as increasing productivity and incomes in this impoverished region of Turkey" (World Bank 2004: 1). The project exceeded its target on forestlands and the institutional sustainability of the project was substantial; however, the extent to which local institutions really changed is less evident.

A review of the project stated that the project could have "challenged the system" more in the areas of women's and poorer households' involvement. As part

of the effort to improve community involvement, the project used the existing system with the village *muktar* as the leader. While elected by the village and supported by elected (unpaid) elders, the *muktar* is paid a salary as a government servant. There are, therefore, inevitable loyalty tensions. He (it is invariably a man, although there have been a few women *muktars*) is very much a local politician. Many vote for him because he seems the most likely to pull in public funds. Indeed, in several community meetings with the mission, it was clear that government funding support, whether through a World Bank project or from other sources, was seen by rural households as a right and the *muktar* was expected to deliver on such entitled central support.

Source: World Bank 2004.

- incorporate spatial analysis to link objectives at differing scales into planning and decision making;
- integrate planning and management across site, landscape, region, and (perhaps) continental levels;
- predict responses of ecosystems to management activities;
- examine relationships and interdependencies of management actions taken on one spatial, temporal, and biological scale upon actions at another scale; and
- assess tradeoffs among multiple objectives and goals for the landscape (see box 4.5).

SUSTAINABILITY OF LANDSCAPE APPROACHES. Projects building on a landscape approach can draw significant lessons from several generations of watershed projects. An important issue is that high subsidies and other inducements should not be used to lower the real costs of participation for communities, distorting the true nature of demand. In many instances, this is a result of a mistaken assumption that what might be socially optimal for overall environmental improvements to a community will be privately optimal to the resource user. Such subsidization masks the sustainability of these initiatives (Boerma 2000).

FUTURE PRIORITIES AND SCALING-UP ACTIVITIES

Several successful projects in watershed management encompass the basics of a landscape approach. Successes in a few pilot microcatchment areas can generate demand for

appropriately scaling up the model. Incentives, constraints, and lessons learned will have to be documented, and processes streamlined, to facilitate such scaling up.[6]

FACILITATE THE APPLICATION OF LANDSCAPE APPROACHES IN DIFFERENT CONTEXTS. Landscape approaches to optimizing forest functions have boundless potential. Identifying effective applications of a landscape approach can benefit from a typology that distinguishes three forest landscapes: (i) forests beyond the forest-agriculture frontier,[7] (ii) frontier and disputed forest areas,[8] and (iii) forest-agriculture mosaics. In forests beyond the frontier, a landscape focus can help maintain large-scale environmental processes. For forests at the frontier, it is important to maintain landscape connectivity and to avoid irreversible degradation and negative externalities. In mosaic landscapes, a landscape focus can facilitate managing the forest for production, environmental services, and biodiversity.

ANALYZE THE POLICY CONTEXT AND ENABLING CONDITIONS. It is often stated that lack of ideal political and policy contexts should not constrain the use of a landscape approach. At the same time, improved government and community capacity and willingness to engage in a landscape approach and an enabling context would facilitate implementation of such approaches. Currently, additional analytical work would help to enable the policy context and institutional conditions necessary for implementing landscape approaches.

Successful employment of initiatives at the landscape level requires a clear understanding and identification of potential tradeoffs and opportunities for synergies. An improved understanding should lead to reduced power differentials among stakeholders, increased equity in outcomes, and minimization of losses suffered by specific stakeholder groups. Developing and adopting a suitable framework for identifying and assessing the various ecological, economic, and social tradeoffs would facilitate such understanding and decision making regarding which tradeoffs are acceptable.

ASB–Partnership for the Tropical Forest Margins (ASB) is a global partnership of research institutes, nongovernmental organizations, universities, community organizations, farmers' groups, and other local, national, and international organizations. ASB works at the nexus of two important problems: tropical deforestation and human poverty. ASB focuses on landscape mosaics (comprising both forests and agriculture) where global environmental problems and poverty coincide at the margins of remaining tropical forests. ASB applies an integrated natural resource management approach to analysis and action through long-term engagement with local communities and policy makers at various levels.

In the ASB matrix, natural forest and the land-use systems that replace it are scored against different criteria reflecting the objectives of different interest groups. To enable results to be compared across locations, the systems specific to each are grouped according to broad categories, ranging from agroforests to grasslands and pastures. The criteria may be fine-tuned for specific locations, but the matrix always comprises indicators for the following:

- two major global environmental concerns: carbon storage and biodiversity
- agronomic sustainability, assessed according to a range of soil characteristics, including trends in nutrients and organic matter over time
- policy objectives: economic growth and employment opportunities
- smallholders' concerns: their workloads, returns to their labor, food security for their families, and start-up costs of new systems or techniques
- policy and institutional barriers to adoption by smallholders, including the availability of credit, markets, and improved technology

Below is an illustrative example of an ASB Summary Matrix for the Forest Margins of Sumatra. This matrix provides information on benefits at different scales (based on rigorous analytical work). The matrix allows researchers, policy makers, environmentalists, and others to identify and discuss tradeoffs among the various objectives of different interest groups.

ASB Summary Matrix: Forest Margins of Sumatra

| Land-use | Global environment | | Agronomic sustainability | National policymakers' concerns | | Adoptability by smallholders |
| | Carbon sequestration | Biodiversity | Plot-level production sustainability | Potential profitability (at social prices) | Employment | Production incentives (at private prices) |
Description	Aboveground, time-averaged (tons/ha)	Aboveground, plant species/ standard plot	Overall rating	Returns to land (US$/ha)	Average labor input (days/ha/yr)	Returns to labor (US$/day)
Natural forest	306	120	1	0	0	0
Community-based forest management	136	100	1	11	0.2	4.77
Commercial logging	93	90	0.5	1080	31	0.78
Rubber agroforest	89	90	0.5	506	111	2.86
Oil palm monoculture	54	25	0.5	1653	108	4.74
Upland rice/bush tallow rotation	7	45	0.5	(117)	25	1.23
Continuous cassava degrading to *imperata*	2	15	0	28	98	1.78

Source: Alternatives to Slash-and-Burn, Policy Brief 05, http://www.asb.cgiar.org/PDFwebdocs/PolicyBrief5.pdf.

BUILD GOVERNMENT AND COMMUNITY CAPACITY TO ADOPT A LANDSCAPE APPROACH AND IMPLEMENT ADAPTIVE MANAGEMENT. Capacity needs to be built to undertake interinstitutional and interagency planning and coordination.

NOTES

1. The principles underlying a landscape approach are similar to those associated with an ecosystem approach. It recognizes that humans, with their cultural diversity, are an integral component of ecosystems. It is based on 12 principles endorsed by the Parties to the Convention on Biological Diversity (UNEP/CBD/COP/5/23 (see http://www.iucn.org/themes/CEM/documents/ecosapproach/cbd_ecosystem_approach_engl.pdf).

2. Many "production landscapes" link rural, urban, and coastal domains.

3. Forest functions are processes performed by a forest ecosystem, including photosynthesis, nutrient cycling, providing animal habitat, and so forth.

4. A landscape commonly refers to a heterogeneous land area composed of a cluster of interacting ecosystems. Understanding, quantifying, and managing the interactions among the component ecosystems is key in landscape-level approaches.

5. Although the watershed approach has elements of a landscape approach, inadequate attention to landscape-level tradeoffs can result in negative hydrological implications for downstream stakeholders outside the watershed but within the landscape. In addition, a long-term approach is needed to determine the system's sustainability.

6. The landscape approach seeks to assess optimal paths for achieving objectives and the limits that exist in scaling up as not all advantages can be derived through scaling up across ecosystems.

7. Forest areas beyond the frontier are those that have most of the world's forest area, few inhabitants, and no land scarcity.

8. Frontier and disputed forest areas are where agriculture is expanding and there are conflicts over forest use in "open access" areas.

SELECTED READINGS

Bonell, M., and L. A. Bruijnzeel. 2004. *Forests, Water and People in the Humid Tropics: Past, Present and Future Hydrological Research for Integrated Land and Water Management.* Cambridge: Cambridge University Press.

Calder, I. R. 2005. *Blue Revolution, Integrated Land and Water Resource Management.* Second ed. London and Sterling, U.K.: Earthscan.

Heathcote, I. W. 1998. *Integrated Watershed Management: Principles and Practices.* New York: John Wiley & Sons, Inc.

Kerr, J. 2001. "Watershed Project Performance in India: Conservation, Productivity, and Equity." *American Journal of Agricultural Economics* 83 (5): 1223–30.

Rhoades, R. E. 1999. *Participatory Watershed Research and Management: Where the Shadow Falls.* Gatekeeper Series No. 81. London: IIED.

Salafsky, N., R. Margoluis, and K. Redford. 2001. "Adaptive Management: A Tool for Conservation Practitioners." Publication No. 112, Biodiversity Support Program, Washington, DC. http://www.fosonline.org/Site_Docs/AdaptiveManagementTool.pdf.

U.S. Forest Service. 2006. "Guide to Integrated Landscape Land Use Planning in Central Africa." http://carpe.umd.edu/resources/Documents/USFS%20Landscape%20Guide%20Dec2006.pdf

WWF. "Guidance for Steps in the WWF Standards for Project and Programme Management." http://www.fosonline.org/Site_Page.cfm?PageID=156.

REFERENCES CITED

Boerma, P. 2000. "Watershed Management: A Review of the World Bank Portfolio (1990–1999)." Rural Development Department, World Bank, Washington, DC.

Campos A., J. Joaquín, R. Villalobos, and B. Louman. 2005. "Poor Farmers and Fragmented Forests in Central America." In *Forests in Landscapes: Ecosystem Approaches to Sustainability,* ed. J. A. Sayer and S. Maginnis, 129–46. London: Earthscan.

Farina, A. 2006. *Principles and Methods in Landscape Ecology.* Berlin: Springer.

Sayer, J. A., and S. Maginnis. 2005. *Forests in Landscapes: Ecosystem Approaches to Sustainability.* London: Earthscan.

Sayer, J. A., C. Ndikumagenge, B. Campbell, and L. Usongo. 2005. "Wildlife, Loggers and Livelihoods in the Congo Basin." In *Forests in Landscapes: Ecosystem Approaches to Sustainability,* ed. J. A. Sayer and S. Maginnis, 115–27. London: Earthscan.

Sayers, J. 2006. "Optimising Forest Functions at the Landscape Level." Note submitted to World Bank as input to *Forests Sourcebook.* Unpublished. World Bank. Washington, DC.

Scoones, I. 1999. "The New Ecology and the Social Sciences: What Prospects for a Fruitful Engagement?" *Annual Review of Anthropology* 28: 479–507.

World Bank. 2004. Project Performance Assessment Report, Turkey Eastern Anatolia Watershed Rehabilitation Project (Loan 3567-TR). Report No. 28274. March 19, 2004.

Sector and Thematic Evaluation, Operations and Evaluation Department, Washington, DC.

Zimmerer, K. 2000. "The Reworking of Conservation Geographies: Nonequilibrium Landscapes and Nature-Society Hybrids." *Annals of the Association of American Geographers* 90 (2): 356–69.

CROSS-REFERENCED CHAPTERS AND NOTES

All notes associated with chapter 4: Optimizing Forest Functions at the Landscape Scale

Note 2.3: Innovative Marketing Arrangements for Environmental Services

Integrated Forest Landscape Land-Use Planning

Forest landscape planning differs from other planning in that it plans at a larger spatial scale and can assess broader, more wide-ranging trends, influences, and impacts.[1]

Planning is the process in which stakeholders (community members, scientists, government representatives, private businesses, traditional authorities, and others) come together to debate and discuss how to manage lands for the benefit of current and future generations and to ensure ecological sustainability of lands and resources. The purpose of planning is to develop management and governance strategies that respond to scientific understanding of natural and social systems as well as changing societal conditions and values. The simple objective of any planning process is to promote decisions that are informed, understood, accepted, and able to be implemented.

Planning can be complex depending upon the number of issues internal and external to the planning area. Planning requires risk assessments and forecasts about anticipated and uncertain future events and conditions. Consequently, even the best plan will need to be altered to adjust to improving data and information; changing social, economic, or other conditions; evolving threats; or feedback from monitoring efforts (see note 4.3, Using Adaptive Management to Improve Project Implementation). Therefore, plans are adaptive in nature, and amendments or entire revisions will be an outcome of monitoring and other factors discussed in the plan.

Two predominant approaches to planning are the "threat-based" approach, and the "desired condition and zoning" model. The threat-based model addresses only current threats or those future threats that can be predicted by managers in designing management direction. It is limited in its ability to react to and consider unforeseen future threats that may evolve and does not account for nonthreat-based targets and objectives. The desired condition and zoning model, which is used by the U.S. Forestry Service (USFS) for its multiple-use planning for National Forest lands, outlines overall goals and objectives for the landscape, as well as more specific objectives within each macro-zone, to guide all future management decisions.

Through the setting of objectives, the desired condition planning model describes the compositional and structural characteristics of the biological and physical features desired across the landscape. It also accounts for the social and economic needs of stakeholders that depend on landscape resources and the social and economic elements needed to achieve the plan's long-term vision. In the desired condition approach, barriers or threats that may limit resource management ability to achieve or move toward the desired condition are specifically addressed in guidelines, regulations, and zoning concepts. Such an approach is flexible and adaptable and thus able to address not only existing threats, but also unforeseen future ones and nonthreat management targets.

The following section outlines important operational components of the landscape planning process and the landscape plan itself. These steps draw heavily from guidelines prepared by the USFS as part of the U.S. Agency for International Development (USAID) Central African Regional Program for the Environment (CARPE) initiative for guidance to implementing nongovernmental organizations (NGOs). These guidelines offer some key steps to be undertaken to effectively implement a landscape plan.

OPERATIONAL ASPECTS

Sometimes simpler plans are more effective, especially plans based on a participatory process. The likelihood that the plan will be more widely read and understood by local stakeholders, as well as the likelihood of their engagement in the process, will increase if the plan is relatively concise, focuses on what is important for the resource condition, and is light on scientific and legal jargon.

IDENTIFY PLANNING TEAM MEMBERS AND DEFINE INDIVIDUALS' SPECIFIC ROLES. The composition (see box 4.6) and size of the team should be based on a rapid needs assessment for successful landscape plan development. The roles and responsibilities of the planning team must be defined early to reduce confusion, focus staff time, avoid duplication of effort, and ensure that all aspects of the planning process are addressed. If any necessary skills are missing, it will be important to mention how these gaps will be filled and when.

The team may be distinct from or overlap with the team working on macro-zone plans. Any alteration in roles when working on the various plans should be expressed.

DEVELOP A PUBLIC PARTICIPATION STRATEGY. The planning team needs to develop a strategy for effective stakeholder participation for the plan and the landscape concept to be successful (box 4.7). Sound strategies for landscape planning will incorporate multiple opportunities for involvement and concurrence by local communities, government, relevant industry, and other stakeholders. Creating a sense of ownership among local community members and a wider audience of stakeholders by involving them in planning discussions and decision making improves the likelihood that the plan will be supported and its implementation will be successful (box 4.8). An important part of the strategy is stakeholder identification.

Box 4.6   Commonly Required Skills in a Planning Team

- team leader or program manager
- biologist(s)
- hydrologist(s)
- social scientist(s)
- economist(s)
- forester(s)
- mineral or mining specialist(s) (if mining activities impact the landscape)

It may not be necessary to have all of these specialists on the planning team throughout the entire process; rather, some could be brought in as needed to advise on certain issues.

Responsibilities and tasks must be assigned to each planning team member and new staff or consultants hired to fill voids.

Source: USFS 2006.

Box 4.7   Who Are the Landscape Stakeholders?

Landscape planning is broader in scope than site-specific planning and therefore requires a wide range of stakeholder perspectives to assess and develop priority strategies. Stakeholders can include:

- government representatives at the national, regional, and local levels
- government ministry representatives that have authority over lands in the landscape
- traditional leaders
- extractive industry representatives operating in or near the landscape
- local and international NGO representatives operating on the landscape
- marginalized groups that may not have a voice as part of the above groups
- military leaders
- individuals claiming ancestral rights to lands
- community members that are able to represent resource users
- local hunters and fishermen
- others to be determined

Source: USFS 2006.

Box 4.8   Participating in the Management of the Tongass National Forest

The Tongass National Forest, covering most of southeast Alaska in the United States, is managed under the guidance of the Tongass Land and Resource Management Plan, first completed in 1979, revised in 1997, and clarified and amended since then. Projects are planned with help from interested citizens: Proposed projects are listed quarterly in the district in which they will take place; contact people are provided to help citizens participate; and in some districts, draft documents are posted for review. All decisions are later posted for public viewing. All projects aim to foster the continued health of the forest and to provide commodities and experiences to people who depend on or visit the forest. Tongass employees work to balance multiple uses of the forest resources: fish and wildlife populations, clean water, trees to support local industry, and recreation opportunities.

Source: USFS 2007.

IDENTIFY EXISTING AND NEEDED INFORMATION ABOUT THE LANDSCAPE. Information should enable analysis of the demographic, political, and governance situation of the landscape, as well as its physical, biological, and ecological conditions, to determine the current condition and future trends. However, a lack of perfect information should not indefinitely delay progress with planning processes. Data gathering should be viewed as an ongoing process and new information should feed back into the adaptive management aspect of the landscape plan.

Processes for data gathering should include asking stakeholders to identify their existing resource use and interests on the landscape; threats, opportunities, or conflicts related to the landscape; and why and how the landscape is important to them. In addition to information within the landscape, planning teams should look at influences outside the landscape. Examine what is occurring outside the landscape that could affect the important values of the landscape. For example, are there plans to develop any infrastructure (roads, dams, and the like) that could affect values within the landscape? Is there potential for immigrants settling in the landscape because of displacement from another area?

An important step in the landscape planning process is identifying and evaluating existing applicable laws or any existing management plans associated with the landscape. Understanding legislation applied to any land unit in the landscape will help guide management decisions. It is important to monitor legislative changes throughout the landscape planning process so that adjustments to the planning process can be made if necessary. For example in the Democratic Republic of Congo, landscape planning teams need to monitor the forest concession conversion process because it can affect both the landscape land-use plan and the subsequent macro-zone management plans.

DEFINE WHY THE PARTICULAR LANDSCAPE WAS DELINEATED, AND WHAT FEATURES MAKE IT A PRIORITY. The objective of this description is to provide a focus for the planning process. This description should remain brief and focus on the key features that contributed to its designation as a priority landscape.

CHARACTERIZE THE LANDSCAPE, including the existing uses of the landscape and the different groups involved in those uses; the legal boundaries delineated within the landscape; and a general inventory of the resources and any information regarding their condition. This characterization should describe the physical, ecological, and socioeconomic conditions in a simple manner and identify influences outside the landscape that could affect the important values of the landscape, identify and evaluate applicable laws within the landscape, and identify key information gaps. This information will assist the planning team to define landscape vision and objectives, help inform zoning decisions and management strategies, and identify any knowledge gaps (see box 4.9).

Box 4.9   Baseline Data Needed on Aspects of the Forest Landscape

The following information is helpful in characterizing landscapes:

a. Physical
   i. Boundaries of landscapes
   ii. Topography, water courses, and other unique physical features
   iii. Maps and satellite imagery
   iv. Maps of boundaries of existing protected areas, community-based natural resource management areas and extractive resource use zones, and information on current status

b. Ecological—identify landscape features in regard to
   i. key wildlife resources
   ii. wildlife migration corridors
   iii. rare and under-represented plant communities
   iv. other floral and faunal resources that are of key importance to the landscape and its population
   v. forest standing stock
   vi. species composition within forests

c. Socioeconomic
   i. Identify villages, foot paths, transport routes, key economic centers within and around the landscape, agricultural activities, hunting and fishing areas, areas of subsistence-level timber extraction
   ii. Identify all stakeholders of the landscape (including populations outside the landscape)
   iii. Identify those resources and regions of the landscape used for subsistence purposes versus commercial trade
   iv. Map locations of economically desirable timber species or mineral deposits not currently in any concessions

d. Assess government management authority presence on the landscape and capacity to play a role in the planning process

e. Outline budget and timeline

Source: USFS 2006.

INVOLVE RELEVANT STAKEHOLDERS IN DEFINING DESIRED CONDITIONS FOR THE LANDSCAPE. The desired conditions will help provide context and direction for the rest of the planning process and should aim to maintain the landscape's unique features and significance, improve resource conditions on the landscape, and promote livelihood opportunities for those dependent on landscape resources (see box 4.10). The desired condition sets an idealized goal of what the landscape *should* be, what it should protect, and whom it should benefit.

DEVELOP LANDSCAPE OBJECTIVES THAT DESCRIBE THE FOCUS OF MANAGEMENT ACTIVITIES ON THE LANDSCAPE

over an extended period. Objectives are important because they support and describe the desired conditions for a given element or attribute of the landscape. The objectives should be unambiguous, measurable, and have a time line. It is essential to involve stakeholders in the development of objectives because different stakeholders may disagree about which objectives are or are not compatible with the shared view of the desired conditions. Objectives should be listed in order of priority, where possible.

Landscape objectives can be explored through simple discussions, but the process is much more instructive if tools are used to enhance understanding (see box 4.11). Visualization can be very valuable, with participants being encouraged to draw desirable and undesirable outcomes. If the resources are available, simple simulation models can be developed; these can be instructive in helping participants understand the full ramifications of landscape change (Ecoagriculture Partners and International Union for Conservation of Nature 2007).

IMPLEMENT AN ITERATIVE ZONING PROCESS. Zoning decisions are often considered the heart of a land-use plan and can be contentious. Zoning decisions should be based on all quantitative and qualitative information gathered. The planning process should include a validation step to confirm that the proposed location for each macro-zone reflects on-the-ground reality. The zoning process often has to follow an iterative approach because as data are gathered and stakeholder interests identified, the planning team refines zone boundaries to come up with a configuration that best responds to the vision, objectives, and priorities of the landscape.[3]

DEVELOP GUIDELINES (SIMILAR TO A SET OF RULES OR REGULATIONS) THAT DESCRIBE PERMISSIBLE OR PROHIBITED ACTIVITIES ACROSS A LANDSCAPE OR ZONES WITHIN A LANDSCAPE. Guidelines ensure that certain aspects of a landscape maintain their integrity and that various activities occur, or are prohibited, so as not to harm valued attributes. Guidelines should prohibit or permit specific activities or actions. If any exceptions to a guideline are to be granted, the guideline should explicitly describe the circumstances under which such an exemption would be granted and who has the authority to grant it. Existing laws in the country where the landscape is located may address issues or activities outlined in a guideline. Where appropriate, these laws should be referenced in the guidelines; however, the guidelines may be more stringent than the existing regulations. Guidelines are more often used at the macro- and microzone levels, but in some situations, it may make sense to establish landscape-wide guidelines.

Box 4.10 Participatory Mapping for Identifying the Landscape Value

Different people have very different understandings of the concept of a landscape and often have trouble articulating their differences. Getting stakeholders to draw the landscape on a large sheet of paper or white board as a facilitated group exercise helps to generate a valuable discussion of what people value in the landscape. This enables everyone to participate in planning and assessing conservation and development and is a valuable way of tapping into local knowledge. This approach can be valuable at the initiation of a project or during implementation. It is especially valuable in situations where there are upstream and downstream links that need to be made explicit or where connectivity of habitats is an issue.

To enable this process, a facilitator with artistic skills can encourage stakeholders to represent their perspectives of the landscape onto a map or sketch of the visible landscape. People will rapidly begin to argue and discuss the significance of different landscape features. The picture can then be improved by the facilitator, and eventually it should be possible to work toward a graphic representation of a desirable future landscape. The process is more effective if the images are edited digitally, which requires that the facilitator be able to use appropriate graphic software, such as Photoshop, Illustrator, or Paintbrush. Useful progress can be made in less than a day with a small group of stakeholders. Associated costs include the time of the participants and a facilitator.

Source: Sayer 2006.

Box 4.11   Tools for Integrating Various Viewpoints

The Bank's project in Natural Resource Management in Albania used a Participatory Microcatchment (MC) Planning Approach to collect information and data to fully understand the physical and socioeconomic conditions of the MC. This included collection of existing information (data and maps), data verification and updating, and supplementation of available information with further simple surveys. MC plans build on forest and pasture management plans for communal forestry and pasture activities and refer to the key actions they identify (if these plans have already been prepared).

To integrate various viewpoints in each village, the project conducted an exercise called Beneficiary-Centered Problem Census Problem Solving (BCPCPS). BCPCPS is a nonthreatening, focused discussion that uses small group dynamics to elicit (i) a complete and ranked census of the real and perceived problems of individual households, villages, and the commune as a whole; and (ii) the commune's proposed solutions to these problems. This approach provides a setting in which all members of the commune can contribute. No problem is rejected and all solutions are considered. The final ranking of problems and preferred solutions is performed by the villagers. The contribution of the team is limited to facilitating the creation of the

setting in which the BCPCPS approach can be conducted. The team does not take part in the discussion nor make promises. Project staff has to ensure that women and children are not marginalized in the BCPCPS process.

A "priority list of village problems" is developed by the team and the problems that are outside the mandate of the project are eliminated as the list is finalized. This list is used as the basis of a joint discussion of the solutions to the problems identified by the villagers. During this discussion, a suggested "menu of activities" prepared in advance by the team, is shared with the village community to contribute to solving the problems identified. The menu of activities often consists of rehabilitation activities and income-generation activities (or income-supporting activities).

Based on discussions, the villagers choose activities that meet their priorities. Often farmers make additional demands, particularly for income-generating activities. However, it was made clear to the villagers that the resources (money and time) available under the project were limited and that the project would support those activities and measures that focus most of the benefits at the level of the MC, that are cost effective, and that can be replicated in other parts of Albania.

Source: Cestti 2005.

a. This menu of activities is a basic tool in the planning process. The team determines on technical, economic, and institutional grounds which treatments are applicable in a particular MC and prepares the menu. The menu may vary in accordance with the agroecological and socioeconomic conditions of each village as well as the villagers' resources and needs. During the life of the project, it would be revised based on the experience with project implementation.

DEVELOP A WORK PLAN REFLECTING THE IMPLEMENTATION SCHEDULE. This work plan will provide prioritized action items with a timeline and a budget to accomplish the work. It is appropriate to include a description of how stakeholders will be involved. Most actions will be concentrated within the macro-zone management plans; however, important cross-zone issues and current conditions and future trends are better identified at the landscape scale. All implementation activities should be linked back to one or more of the landscape objectives. The schedule should specify what action items will be accomplished, by whom, and when, and the associated cost.

DEVELOP A MONITORING PROTOCOL. This protocol will help determine if the landscape plan and associated plans under

it are effectively contributing to the achievement of the landscape's desired condition and objectives. Monitoring will provide the feedback loop for evaluating and updating the plan (see note 4.2, Assessing Outcomes of Landscape Interventions). Landscape-wide monitoring is typically conducted to evaluate conditions and trends of specific resources on the landscape. The monitoring protocol should indicate the type and frequency of monitoring, as well as who is responsible for carrying it out and reporting on it.

LESSONS LEARNED AND RECOMMENDATIONS FOR PRACTITIONERS

This note's guidance on planning needs to be tailored to the specific context of the region in question and to the needs of implementing partners and involved government agencies.

Overall, the planning approach adopted at the landscape level needs to be flexible and able to accommodate new information, monitoring results, changing contexts, and resource conditions. An adaptive management approach may be adopted to allow for individual components of the plan to be amended or altered (see note 4.3, Using Adaptive Management to Improve Project Implementation).

While it is ideal to put a great deal of effort into each step of the planning process, implementation and monitoring activities and limited financial and human resources will prevent planning teams and authorities from meeting ideal levels of action. Therefore, it is important that the planning team prioritize. Honest assessments of available funds and costs of specific activities must be carried out by the planning team, in conjunction with stakeholders, to determine what can truly be accomplished with limited resources and which activities should be prioritized. The planners must also evaluate what other stakeholders are, or could be, doing to complement actions taken by the team and implementing partners.

Participatory processes succeed where there are common purposes that could interest all or most of the population, where the participatory process is flexible and provides for capacity building and genuine empowerment, and where there are income and livelihood incentives. The planning process has to allow for the inclusion of both community interests at the micro-zone level and the larger-scale objectives. Furthermore, while adopting a genuinely bottom-up approach to institutional development is essential, government commitment to landscape planning is critical to its success.

NOTES

1. This note was adapted from a guide developed by the USFS for the Congo Basin Forests of Central Africa as part of USAID's CARPE initiative. CARPE is a 20-year initiative with the objective of reducing the rate of deforestation and the loss of biodiversity in the Congo Basin Region of Central Africa. While the approach used in the USAID CARPE initiative is still under development, and thus cannot be pointed to as a success story just yet, it is hoped that the experience there can guide future successful planning efforts.

The first phase of CARPE (1995–2002) focused on research and capacity building in the region. CARPE's second phase introduced a more focused approach to program implementation, concentrating CARPE activities in 12 landscapes across the region. These landscapes were chosen for their biodiversity and conservation importance and established as foundations of regional conservation and sustainable natural resource use.

CARPE focuses on the larger landscape unit to maximize impact, to promote improved natural resource management over larger areas, and to broaden stakeholder involvement in land management activities. In light of this need for multiple-use management expertise of large landscapes, CARPE leadership has requested that the USFS take on a more strategic approach within the program to better benefit from USFS land management expertise gained from 100 years of experience in the United States. To that end, the USFS has been asked to develop planning guidelines for comprehensive landscape-level planning and the different use zones (as defined by CARPE) within those landscapes: protected areas, community use, and extractive use. The objectives of this landscape planning process are to (i) provide planning tools and standards to support the promotion of sustainable natural resource management in the landscapes by CARPE partners, host-country governments, and other stakeholders; (ii) highlight processes to encourage stakeholder involvement in land-use planning; and (iii) provide useful standards for CARPE management to monitor program progress.

CARPE landscape land-use planning prioritizes three types of zones to be delineated within the landscapes: Protected Area (PA), Community Based Natural Resource Management (CBNRM), and Extractive Resource (ERZ) use zones. These are referred to as macrozones. Each of these macro-zones will, in turn, also be zoned for differing uses and levels of resource protection. Additional USFS planning guides are available to assist in the development of management plans for these macrozones.

2. In the context of CARPE, landscape planning will define the CARPE implementing partner activities on each individual landscape that are needed to improve land management conditions across the landscape. The activities outlined in the landscape plans and the subsequent macro-zone plans will contribute to the long-term management and sustainability of forest resources in the region and thereby contribute to the development of livelihood strategies and economic development activities for those dependent upon these resources.

3. The advantage of this focused approach is that it invests the limited planning time and money on the areas considered critical within the landscape. As information is gathered and new trends or needs emerge, additional zones can be designated. To add a new zone, an abbreviated approach to the landscape planning process, focusing on stakeholder involvement, should be used.

SELECTED READINGS

Ashby, J. A., E. B. Knapp, and H. Munk Ravnborg. 1998. "Involving Local Organizations in Watershed Management." In *Agriculture and the Environment: Perspectives on Sustainable Rural Development,* ed. E. Lutz, 118–29. Washington, DC: World Bank.

Farrington, J., C. Turton, and A. J. James. 1999. *Participatory Watershed Development: Challenges for the Twenty-First Century.* New Delhi: Oxford University Press.

Kerr, J., G. Pangare, and V. L. Pangare. 2002. *Watershed Development Projects in India: An Evaluation.* Research Report 127. Washington, DC: International Food Policy Resource Institute.

Perez, C., and H. Tschinkel. 2003. "Improving Watershed Management in Developing Countries: A Framework for Prioritizing Sites and Practices." Network Paper No. 129, Agricultural Research and Extension Network, Department for International Development, London.

Turton, C., M. Warner, and B. Groom. 1998. "Scaling Up Participatory Watershed Development in India: A Review of the Literature." Network Paper No. 86, Agriculture Research and Extension Network, Department for International Development, London.

REFERENCES CITED

Cestti, Rita E. 2005. Albania Natural Resources Development Project. Aide-Memoire, Supervision Mission, November 7-11, 2005. Unpublished. World Bank. Washington, DC.

Ecoagriculture Partners and IUCN (International Conservation Union). 2007. "Principles of Engagement with Stakeholders in Negotiating and Measuring Landscape-Level Outcomes." Draft, Ecoagriculture Working Group, Cornell University, Ithaca, NY. http://ecoag.cals.cornell.edu/documents.html.

Jinapala, K., J. D. Brewer, and R. Sakthivadivel. 1996. *Multi-Level Participatory Planning for Water Resources Development in Sri Lanka.* Gatekeeper Series No. 62. London: IIED.

Sayer, J. 2006. "Optimising Forest Functions at the Landscape Level." Note submitted to World Bank as input to *Forests Sourcebook.* Unpublished. World Bank. Washington, DC.

USFS (United States Department of Agriculture Forest Service). 2006. "Guide to Integrated Landscape Land Use Planning in Central Africa." http://carpe.umd.edu/resources/Documents/USFS%20Landscape%20Guide%20Dec2006.pdf.

———. 2007. "Tongass National Forest: Projects and Plans." http://www.fs.fed.us/r10/tongass/projects/projects.shtml.

World Bank. Forthcoming. "Watershed Management Approaches, Policies, and Operations: Lessons for Scaling-up." Agriculture and Rural Development Department Economic and Sector Work, World Bank, Washington, DC.

CROSS-REFERENCED CHAPTERS AND NOTES

Note 4.2: Assessing Outcomes of Landscape Interventions

Note 4.3: Using Adaptive Management to Improve Project Implementation

Assessing Outcomes
of Landscape Interventions

Monitoring and evaluation systems are important for tracking performance against objectives and providing information to help managers with implementation (see chapter 7, Monitoring and Information Systems for Forest Management). For forest interventions, this can mean assessing externalities and measuring delayed impacts of the intervention. Monitoring and evaluation methods typically emphasize either the state of species (or ecosystems) or simply the effectiveness of providing project deliverables and outputs (Stem and others 2005). The approaches used often have limited ability to address where the balance between the different objectives from the forest landscape should lie.

The real challenge for landscape approaches is to assess the multiple functions of forests at the local and landscape levels. These are the levels at which management decisions are made and for which information on status and trends is required. The problems of assessment are further complicated where management is seeking to achieve multiple functions across a mosaic of forest and nonforest lands (Sayer and Maginnis 2005). Assessment and monitoring schemes in which tradeoffs are inherent in management require multidimensional tools, and progress must be measured across multiple axes (Sayer and Maginnis 2005). The methods should also provide platforms for negotiating tradeoffs. Tough questions need to be tackled, including the following: In areas of land shortage, how much natural forest might be sacrificed to provide additional agricultural options for local people; and, in areas with global environmental values, is placing restrictions on the development options of the poor justified? Forest agencies have often made unwarranted assumptions about what is desired by, or good for, local people. It is clear that more objective and equitable processes are needed.

OPERATIONAL ASPECTS

The development of a monitoring framework ideally should be initiated at the beginning of the landscape tracking process. The framework should be closely linked to the forest landscape land-use plan and should clearly identify how the monitoring information will be used to inform the decision-making process and implementation of the intervention.

USE A HIERARCHICAL FRAMEWORK FOR MONITORING. In the context of landscape activities, a hierarchical framework is often needed for relevance at different spatial scales and to be able to capture the impact of the activity, as well as to identify changes occurring over time.

CLEARLY ARTICULATE GOALS AND DESIRED OUTCOMES. Well-defined objectives for the forest landscape are important for monitoring performance (see note 4.1, Integrated Forest Landscape Land-Use Planning).

DEFINE CRITERIA. In the hierarchical monitoring framework, the broad goals are considered to be universally applicable. It is useful, then, to have subsidiary goals from the plan that serve as landscape performance criteria and that identify the desirable outcomes for the landscape (Buck and others 2006). There can be several performance criteria (subsidiary goals) associated with each goal. These specify the direction in which a healthy forest landscape ideally should be moving.

USE THE LANDSCAPE OBJECTIVES. The landscape objectives agreed on among stakeholders as part of the planning process should indicate the desirable future state of a landscape. This information is key to tracking changes in a landscape.

IDENTIFY APPROPRIATE INDICATORS. Indicators are often landscape specific. A participatory process of indicator identification can be useful for strategically selecting cost-effective indicators that can provide accurate information. Indicators can range from very broad to very specific. Furthermore, indicators may be layered such that an analysis begins with broad indicators and then adds increasingly specific indicators until the information needs are met (Buck and others 2006).

The selected indicators should be relevant, precise, sensitive, easy to understand, and measurable. Measurement indicators must be able to recognize tradeoffs (short-term versus long-term, at different scales, for different stakeholders) that need to be addressed in the landscape for the indicators to be credible. When employing a landscape approach, more than just the physical indicators should be measured; local livelihood outcomes also should be assessed (see box 4.12).

There may be multiple indicators associated with a specific criterion—some amenable to measurement at the landscape scale and others suitable for the site level. Similarly, indicators may vary by whether they are used to measure the state of a landscape or the impact of particular interventions on landscape performance (see box 4.13).

At the landscape level it is realistic for performance to be measured not by whether a desirable end condition has been achieved, but by assessing whether the combination of influences affecting change is moving the landscape in the right direction relative to stated performance criteria.

Box 4.12   Potential Indicators to Monitor

Biophysical indicators. Specific indicators will depend on the objectives that have been identified for the landscape, and may include, but are not limited to:
- species of concern
- human disturbances
- wildlife corridors
- infrastructure impacts
- external threats to the landscape
- ecological function and condition

These measures should give a sense of deforestation, drivers for change in the landscape, level of fragmentation, the condition of the forests, and the population of species of concern.

Livelihood indicators. Livelihood indicators can be based on the capital assets framework. These indicators can be applied to a sample of communities and then aggregated to a landscape scale. The capital assets framework has five types of capital: (i) financial, (ii) social, (iii) natural, (iv) human, and (v) physical.

Financial capital can include measures of:
- formal sector employment
- household income
- price changes in basic products
- number of local credit associations

Social capital can include measures of:
- community-based initiatives
- traditional governance effectiveness
- perceptions of levels of corruption
- state agency effectiveness

Natural capital can include measures of:
- deforestation rates
- frequency and size of fires
- extent of certified forests
- quality of land available for agricultural production

Human capital can include measures of:
- quality of clinics and health care
- quality of education
- number of qualified people
- infant mortality
- level and use of traditional knowledge

Physical capital can include measures of:
- household quality
- number of kiosks selling basic products
- sources of drinking water
- village accessibility

Specific monitoring activities will depend on the objectives that have been identified for the landscape, and may include, but are not limited to:
- development of local communities
- species of concern
- human disturbances
- wildlife corridors
- infrastructure impacts
- external threats to the landscape
- ecological function and condition

Source: Authors' compilation using USFS 2006 and Buck and others 2006.

IDENTIFY APPROACH FOR MONITORING. Multiple approaches are available for monitoring and evaluating interventions, and data can come from various sources (primary data; data from local laypersons, local experts, or outside technical experts using advanced technological tools and analytical methods). Identifying the most appropriate approach will require a clear understanding of the context, working within parameters such as available resources, and identifying approaches that will draw on readily available qualitative and quantitative information. (See box 4.14 for one approach.)

USE TECHNOLOGICAL TOOLS TO ENRICH THE DEBATE ABOUT FUTURE LANDSCAPE SCENARIOS. These same tools can also be used by special interest groups to excessively influence activities or processes. It is therefore important that technology not dominate or drive the process but be put at the service of stakeholders in an equitable and transparent fashion (Ecoagriculture Partners and IUCN 2007).

SPECIFY WHO IS RESPONSIBLE FOR MONITORING AND THE APPROPRIATE FREQUENCY AND FORMAT. The monitoring protocol should indicate the type and frequency of moni-

toring, as well as who is responsible for carrying it out and reporting on the monitoring.

LESSONS LEARNED AND RECOMMENDATIONS FOR PRACTITIONERS

Monitoring and assessment systems must be flexible to be able to function in a highly dynamic social and economic environment (see note 4.3, Using Adaptive Management to Improve Project Implementation). Consistent monitoring over time allows for changes to be tracked continuously. The indicators and means of measurement to be used must be chosen and used consistently over time; data sets are often rendered useless if they are too flexible.

Stakeholder perceptions of desirable outcomes will change with time, and the need for interventions to achieve desirable landscape conditions may also change. While flexibility is important, consistency over time is critical to tracking change meaningfully—the indicators and means of measurement must be enduring.

Monitoring should be continual and not simply consist of an update to the baseline information at the very end of

Box 4.14   Outcome Assessment Tracking

It is difficult to reach agreement among all stakeholders about what is wanted and what is likely to happen. The outcome assessment approach is based upon negotiations among all stakeholders on what they want the landscape to look like and what it is to deliver, that is, how they want the landscape to perform. Indicators then have to be selected that will measure change in the landscape and how that will correspond to the desired performance criteria. Indicators of changes in different categories of landscape values (natural, built, human, and social value categories) provide a basis for assessing the impact of interventions from a holistic perspective.

This approach is particularly useful in situations where an intervention is anticipated to impact a landscape mosaic, for instance, in determining and then assessing an appropriate balance between the amount of forest needed for conservation and the amount that might be converted to agriculture or other uses. Outcome assessment methodologies are consistent with commonly employed participatory techniques for planning and evaluating interventions; the techniques should thus be used early in project formulation to ensure clarity of desired project effects on landscape outcomes and establish the basis for measuring them.

The indicator sets can be developed in a few days during a multistakeholder meeting. A technical person, or small team, will then need to conduct the first, baseline assessment. This may require extensive field surveys and, depending upon the complexity of the situation and the availability of data, may take several months. The process will have to be repeated every year to track progress, so an annual meeting will be needed to review progress and adapt management as needed.

The costs associated with this approach include those of the facilitator for the first meeting and technical staff hired for several months to assemble data.

Landscape-scale outcome assessment approaches capture the broader impacts of any intervention—a policy change, financial incentive, new projects, and so forth—on the landscape. They could complement rates of return studies in negotiating possible externalities of an intervention and then measuring them.

Source: Sayer 2006.

---

the intervention. It should be an ongoing process through which periodic monitoring is used to modify, as necessary, the implementation of the project (see chapter 7, Monitoring and Information Systems for Forest Management).

SELECTED READINGS

Forthcoming. Landscape Measures Resource Center. www.ecoagriculturepartners.org.

Buck, L. E., J. C. Milder, T. A. Gavin, and I. Mukherjee. 2006. "Understanding Ecoagriculture: A Framework for Measuring Landscape Performance." Discussion Paper No. 2, Ecoagriculture Partners, Washington, DC. http://www.ecoagriculturepartners.org/documents/reports/discussionPapers/DiscussionPaperV2.pdf.

REFERENCES CITED

Stem, C., R. Margoluis, N. Salafsky, and M. Brown. 2005. "Monitoring and Evaluation in Conservation: A Review of Trends and Approaches." *Conservation Biology* 19(2): 295–309.

Buck, L. E., J. C. Milder, T. A. Gavin, and I. Mukherjee. 2006. "Understanding Ecoagriculture: A Framework for Measuring Landscape Performance." Discussion Paper No. 2, Ecoagriculture Partners, Washington, DC. http://www.ecoagriculturepartners.org/documents/reports/discussionPapers/DiscussionPaperV2.pdf.

Ecoagriculture Partners and IUCN (International Conservation Union). 2007. "Principles of Engagement with Stakeholders in Negotiating and Measuring Landscape-Level Outcomes." Draft, Ecoagriculture Working Group, Cornell University, Ithaca, NY. http://ecoag.cals.cornell.edu/documents.html.

Sayer, J. A., and S. Maginnis, eds. 2006. *Forests in Landscapes: Ecosystem Approaches to Sustainability.* London: Earthscan.

CROSS-REFERENCED CHAPTERS AND NOTES

Note 4.1: Integrated Forest Landscape Land-Use Planning

Note 4.3: Using Adaptive Management to Improve Project Implementation

Chapter 7: Information and Monitoring Systems for Forest Management, and associated notes

Using Adaptive Management to Improve Project Implementation

Conservation and development interventions take place in complex systems influenced by biological, political, social, economic, and cultural factors.[1] Project managers and practitioners operating within these complex systems must make important decisions, yet they often have limited information and are operating in the face of uncertainty. This complexity is compounded at the landscape scale, where a larger geographical space, including all functions and processes and additional institutions involved, needs to be considered. The approach adopted at the landscape level needs to be flexible and able to accommodate new information and changing contexts (see chapter 4, Optimizing Forest Functions in a Landscape). This note addresses the use of an adaptive management approach to project implementation, a method for making more informed decisions about strategies, testing the effectiveness of strategies used, and learning and adapting to improve the strategies (Lee 1993; Gunderson, Holling, and Light 1995).

OVERVIEW AND CONSIDERATIONS OF INTEREST FOR WORLD BANK ACTIVITIES

Adaptive management stands in contrast to traditional project and program management by requiring an explicitly experimental—or scientific—approach. Specifically, adaptive management is the integration of design, management, and monitoring to systematically test assumptions to adapt and learn (Salafsky, Margoluis, and Redford 2001). There are three main components to adaptive management:

■ *Testing assumptions.* Assumption testing involves systematically trying different activities to achieve a desired outcome and is distinct from a random trial-and-error process. It requires clearly and explicitly articulating assumptions underlying the way in which proposed activities will help achieve project goals and objectives to strategically select project actions. The outcomes of the activities are monitored to compare the actual to the predicted outcome. This enables the project team to understand what worked, but more important, why it was effective.

■ *Adaptation.* Several reasons may underlie the unexpected outcome of a project activity (for example, the project assumptions were wrong, the actions were poorly executed, the conditions at the project site changed, the monitoring was faulty—or some combination of these problems). Adaptation involves reviewing and, where relevant, changing assumptions and interventions to respond to the new information obtained through monitoring efforts.

■ *Learning.* Learning involves systematically documenting a project team's process and results. The aim is to avoid making similar mistakes in the future and to share lessons learned with the broader community of practice.

The *explicit* and *systematic* testing of assumptions is the key facet of adaptive management that helps project teams uncover *why* a project was successful or faced setbacks and whether it was due to poor theory and underlying assumptions, poor implementation, or a combination of the two (see figure 4.1).

There are at least two levels at which program managers could apply adaptive management: (i) at a high programmatic level, to help them determine the strategies and types of projects they should support and how well their portfolio of projects is doing; and (ii) at the project level, to help the initiatives they support go through an adaptive management process. This note focuses on the second of these levels, although the adaptive management process is important for both.

OPERATIONAL ASPECTS

For the purposes of explaining the adaptive management process, we use a cycle adapted from the Conservation Mea-

Figure 4.1　Necessary Ingredients for Project Success

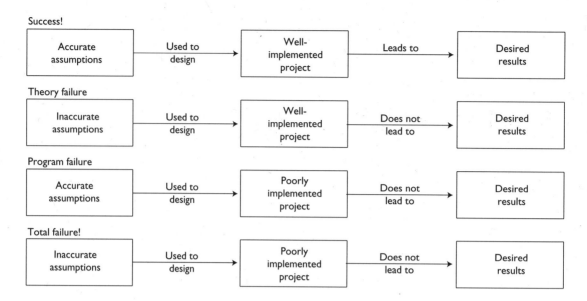

sures Partnership (CMP) (2004) that has several of the same elements of other project management cycles. Adaptive management is an integral part of each step in a project cycle. The main steps in adaptive management in a project management cycle are outlined in figure 4.2.

There are six major steps in the adaptive management process before the process may be repeated:

■ Clarify group's mission.
■ Design a conceptual model based on local site conditions.

Figure 4.2　General Project Management Cycle

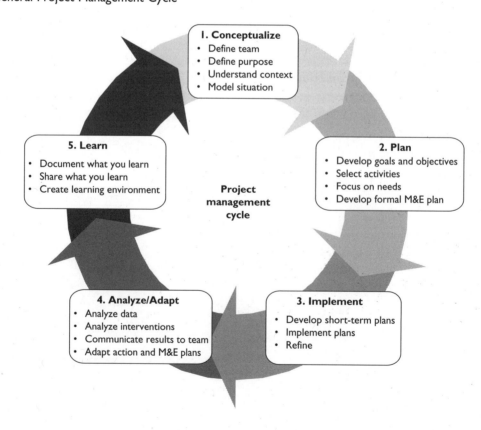

- Develop a project plan that includes goals, objectives, and activities.
- Develop a monitoring plan.
- Implement project and monitoring plans.
- Analyze data and communicate results.

Project teams that want to use adaptive management need to be explicit about who is on their team, where or on what they intend to work, and what is happening at their project site (see box 4.15). This information lays the groundwork for developing good goals and objectives, choosing the right strategies, and developing a sound monitoring and evaluation plan. Adaptive management requires that teams implement their action plans and monitoring plans, analyze the extent to which they are achieving their goals and objectives, and adapt based on what they learn. Thus, adaptive management is a continuous process that involves going through the project management cycle (or parts of it) multiple times.

Box 4.15 Conceptual Models: A Tool for Portraying a Site's Context and Determining Strategies

A *conceptual model* is a visual tool for depicting the context within which a project is operating and, in particular, the major forces that are influencing what the project is trying to achieve. A conceptual model is a diagram that uses a series of boxes and arrows to succinctly represent a set of causal relationships among factors that are believed to impact one or more targets (what one is ultimately trying to affect). Conceptual models are useful planning tools for project teams because they can help the teams determine what actions are needed to influence the factors at their site and what factors they should be monitoring to determine if those factors are changing with project implementation [Margoluis and Salafsky 1998; Morgan and Foundations of Success 2005 (see note in reference section)].

The following conceptual model schematic is adapted from a real-world conservation project at a watershed site:

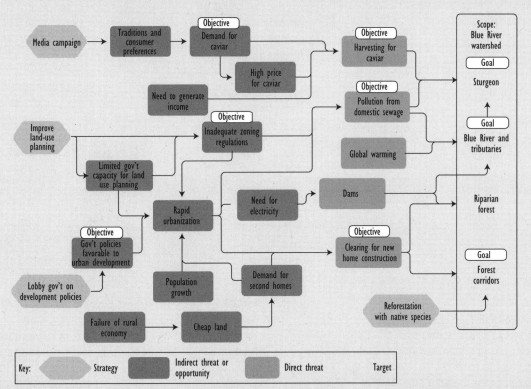

In this example, the team chose the strategy of "Improve land-use planning" because it would influence multiple factors at their site. The conceptual model helped the team be strategic about the activities they chose and those they omitted.

Source: Foundations of Success 2005.

USE TOOLS TO TEST ASSUMPTIONS UNDERLYING PROJECTS. Tools can include the conceptual model (see box 4.15), threat rating, and results chains (see box 4.16).[2] Often project teams will develop a project without fully understanding or describing the context within which they are trying to work. The selection of the project approach may be driven by factors other than ground realities, and may not be the optimal approach from a strategic point of view. Furthermore, when assumptions are not explicit, the project team cannot test them and learn over time whether the assumptions are valid.

The tools used to test assumptions should provide a succinct and powerful representation of what is happening at the project site. Thus, they can serve as excellent communications tools and important planning tools for the project team. Through the process of building the model together, the team should come to consensus on key forces influencing the objectives of the project and identify some high leverage points for intervention. The modeling process and model should also help teams determine where to set goals and objectives and what causal links they need to be testing (see Box. 4.17).

Box 4.16   Tools for Clarifying and Testing Assumptions: Results Chains

The results chain is a tool that clarifies assumptions about the way in which specific strategies are believed to lead to achieving a desired impact. In the conservation context, results chains show how strategies contribute to reducing threats and achieving the conservation of biodiversity or thematic targets. They are diagrams that map out a series of causal statements that link factors in an "if...then" fashion (Foundations of Success 2005). The basis for a results chain comes from a conceptual model, but, as illustrated in the example below, results chains build on that model to make the logic more specific and to change the boxes from neutral factors to results the team wants to see.

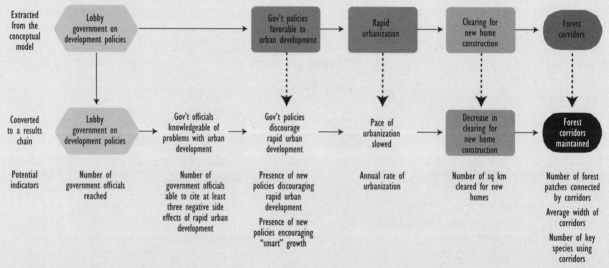

Source: Foundations of Success 2005.

Results chains are important tools for making assumptions explicit and facilitating their testing. In this example, one of the strategies this project team is undertaking is lobbying government to discourage policies favorable to urban development that have led to clearing of forest corridors for new home construction. The results chain shows the team's assumptions: "If we lobby government officials on development policies, then government officials will be more knowledgeable of the problems associated with urban develop-

ment. If they are more knowledgeable, they will develop policies that discourage rapid urban development. If they develop these policies, the pace of urbanization will slow...." The results chain lays out the logic step-by-step and provides a basis for developing indicators that will help the project team determine if the logic holds. If it does not, they will be able to quickly determine where in the chain their logic is faulty. Or, as illustrated in figure 4.1, they should investigate whether the project failure was due to poor implementation.

Another important and useful process for determining where to intervene and what action to take is a threat rating process (examples of threat rating processes are available in Conservation Measures Partnership 2007; Margoluis and Salafsky 1998; The Nature Conservancy 2006). This process involves rating the direct threats identified in a model to help teams determine which threats are the most important to address. This prioritization is particularly important in light of the fact that project resources are often limited and teams must make strategic choices.

DERIVE MONITORING INDICATORS FROM MODELS THAT MAKE PROJECT ASSUMPTIONS EXPLICIT. By explicitly specifying the most important factors affecting project sites and laying out the logic behind project activities, it is possible to narrow down a vast universe of data to the most important factors. In box 4.16, the example indicates that the main factor affecting forest corridors is clearing for new home construction. If this is the case, the project team should not be collecting data related to clearing for other purposes, such as agriculture or timber harvesting—unless, in going through the adaptive management process, the team learns that these are important threats. Likewise, the diagram in box 4.16 provides a concrete example of how a results chain would help a team identify indicators to test whether the strategies they chose are having an impact.

EXPLICITLY DEFINE THE TIME FRAME AND CHRONOLOGY OF EVENTS NECESSARY FOR ACHIEVING DESIRED IMPACTS. Results chains and other tools can help teams specify the chronology of changes that must occur to achieve their desired effect. As figure 4.3 illustrates, results take longer to materialize as one goes further down the chain. A results chain can help the team be very clear about when it is realistic to see changes as a result of their intervention and help them communicate this information to key stakeholders. For example, the project team for the watershed site should not commit that stakeholders will see any changes in clearing for new home construction as a result of their lobbying efforts until 2013.

Program managers often have their own project cycles for identifying, assisting, supervising, and evaluating projects. To encourage these projects to follow an adaptive management approach, program managers must be engaged as early as possible. Operationally, adaptive management support to projects might involve any of the following:

- *Help partners and stakeholders understand the value of the adaptive management process,* which might require that managers engage in awareness-raising about adaptive management.
- *Help project teams do adaptive management.* Specifically, help them use a systematic process to develop sound strategic plans that will allow them to monitor their project's progress and make adjustments during the course of the project. This might be done through
  - one-on-one technical assistance from the program manager, another staff person, or a contracted consultant;
  - facilitated planning workshops in which one or multiple project teams participate; or
  - a formal training course in strategic planning (in a classroom setting or online).[3]
- *View failures and challenges as learning opportunities.* This requires not penalizing project teams for poor performance, especially when they have been reflective and identified important lessons for current and future actions.
- *Allow projects to change as they proceed.* Adaptive management involves constant adjustments as teams expand their understanding of their sites and test their assumptions. Managers need to recognize the need for change and even encourage projects to change, as needed, when project teams make a good case for changing course.
- *Require that impact evaluations be based on the planning work project teams have done through the adaptive management process.* If an external consultant undertakes an evaluation of a project that has gone through a good adaptive management process, the consultant should use the assumptions teams originally documented (through tools such as conceptual models and results chains) and the goals and objectives they developed as the primary framework for the evaluation. However, there should be flexibility for situations in which project teams have not done a thorough job formulating their plans.

Figure 4.3   Timing of Outcomes and Impacts

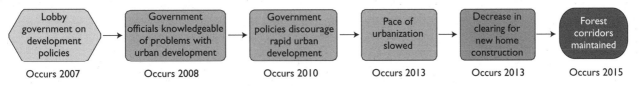

| Lobby government on development policies | Government officials knowledgeable of problems with urban development | Government policies discourage rapid urban development | Pace of urbanization slowed | Decrease in clearing for new home construction | Forest corridors maintained |
| Occurs 2007 | Occurs 2008 | Occurs 2010 | Occurs 2013 | Occurs 2013 | Occurs 2015 |

In the 1990s two organizations, Defensores de la Naturaleza in Guatemala and Línea Biósfera in Mexico, wanted to understand how effectively sustainable agriculture was reducing deforestation and the conditions under which it was effective. Like many conservation or development organizations, these two groups had been using sustainable agriculture under the assumption that it would reduce forest clearing for agriculture, yet they had no concrete evidence that the use of sustainable agriculture actually led to reduced deforestation. To explore this question, Defensores de la Naturaleza and Línea Biósfera partnered with the Biodiversity Support Program to implement a learning process to determine the utility of sustainable agriculture as a conservation tool.

As a first step, the organizations had to make explicit the assumptions they were using in promoting sustainable agriculture techniques. One of the main assumptions is articulated in the results chain in the figure:

The groups in both countries collected data related to each of the factors in the results chain and came up with some surprising conclusions. The assumptions in the first two rectangular boxes in the chain held, but there were differences regarding the third rectangular box, "Farmers reduce area planted." In Guatemala, farmers who used the sustainable agriculture techniques promoted by the project planted *more* area to maize than farmers who did not use sustainable agriculture. In Mexico, farmers who used the same sustainable agriculture techniques planted less area (thus, the assumptions in the results chain held true in Mexico). Through more analysis, the groups were able to determine that, in Guatemala, sustainable agriculture led to decreased investments in labor per hectare, and the farmers used the saved labor to increase the amount of area planted or to establish cash crops in forested areas.

In addition, access to land was an important factor affecting area planted and, thus, deforestation. In Guatemala, where land is relatively available, farmers lacked incentives to be efficient in their land use, so increased their maize production by increasing area planted. In Mexico, where land access is restricted, farmers were much more efficient in their use of land and increased maize production by increasing yield.

As a result of this work, the organizations concluded that sustainable agriculture programs that promote the same techniques used in these sites are unlikely to contribute to decreased rates of deforestation if access to land is not restricted. This is an important lesson—not just for the organizations carrying out this research, but for any organization working under similar conditions and using the same sustainable agriculture techniques to discourage deforestation. Adaptive management is about testing assumptions, learning, and adapting. When project teams can identify these types of general but nontrivial principles, they are helping to promote learning beyond their own project.

Source: Margoluis and others 2001.

LESSONS LEARNED AND RECOMMENDATIONS FOR PRACTITIONERS

Adaptive management should involve all team members, to the extent possible.[4] Plans developed by higher level managers or offices and handed down to field staff do not have buy-in from the field staff and do not represent the assumptions held by project teams familiar with the site.

Encouraging an adaptive management approach will help program managers overseeing multiple projects. If the projects they are supervising have followed good adaptive management practices, managers should be able to readily assess if a project is on track and, ultimately, how well the project performed. Obviously, there is an upfront investment in helping teams do adaptive management, but that investment can make overall portfolio management easier and more reliable for program managers.

Ideally, teams should integrate adaptive management into their projects from the beginning—as soon as they begin to conceptualize their project and think about who will be involved and where or on what they want to work. This helps them be explicit and systematic early on. Nevertheless, it is never too late to start doing adaptive management. Because of its iterative nature, adaptive management means teams are constantly revisiting steps in the project cycle. If a team decides to take an adaptive management approach midway through a project, the team should revisit each step and modify its action and monitoring plans, if necessary. Typically, teams find it enlightening to use tools like threat ratings to determine if they are addressing priority threats, conceptual models to determine what they should be doing, and results chains to determine if the logic for what they are currently doing makes sense. Together, these tools help teams evaluate whether they are currently taking the "right" actions or if they need to change course and undertake other, more strategic actions.

Although it may seem time-consuming, the process of identifying, agreeing upon, testing, and revisiting project assumptions is extremely important. Sometimes, members from the same project team will hold different assumptions about their project site and why they are doing a particular activity. It is only when they sit down together to specify their assumptions that the differences emerge.

To truly practice adaptive management, an open learning culture needs to be in place to encourage project teams to question their actions, share both successes and failures, and learn from their actions. Teams should not be afraid to admit mistakes, but at the same time, they should seek ways to remedy them and improve the project.

It is important to share lessons with the team and beyond. Lessons learned through adaptive management can improve not only the project under consideration but other projects operating under similar conditions and with similar goals.

Finally, adaptive management is not a trial-and-error process or a license to try whatever the team wants. Adaptive management requires a systematic and explicitly experimental—or scientific—approach to project management.

NOTES

1. This note focuses primarily on a couple of useful tools for testing assumptions—a key feature of an adaptive management approach. Those readers who are looking for more in-depth guidance on adaptive management or other tools should review Margoluis and Salafsky (1998) and visit the Web sites of Foundations of Success (http://www.fosonline.org/) and the CMP (http://www.conservationmeasures.org/). The CMP is a partnership of conservation NGOs that seek better ways to design, manage, and measure the impacts of their conservation actions.

2. For further information on these tools, review the Selected Reading and References and cited lists and also visit www.Miradi.org for updates on the piloting of Miradi Adaptive Management Software, which includes a component to help build conceptual models and rank threats.

3. Adaptive management requires that project team members execute the design, management, implementation, and adaptation.

4. The Open Standards for the Practice of Conservation (Conservation Measures Partnership 2004) provides an extensive list of guidance and principles for doing adaptive management.

SELECTED READINGS

Conservation Measures Partnership. 2004. "Open Standards for the Practice of Conservation." Conservation Measures Partnership, Washington, DC. http://www.conservationmeasures.org/CMP/Library/CMP_Open_Standards_v1.0.pdf.

Margoluis, R., and N. Salafsky. 1998. *Measures of Success: Designing, Managing, and Monitoring Conservation and Development Projects.* Washington, DC: Island Press.

Salafsky, N., R. Margoluis, and K. Redford. 2001. "Adaptive Management: A Tool for Conservation Practitioners." Publication No. 112, Biodiversity Support Program, Washington, DC. http://www.fosonline.org/Site_Docs/AdaptiveManagementTool.pdf.

The Nature Conservancy. "Conservation Action Planning Resources." http://conserveonline.org/workspaces/cbdgateway/cap/resources.

World Wildlife Fund (WWF). Guides for Implementing the WWF Standards of Conservation Project and Programme Management. http://www.panda.org/standards.

REFERENCES CITED

Conservation Measures Partnership. 2004. "Open Standards for the Practice of Conservation." Conservation Measures Partnership, Washington, DC. http://www.conservationmeasures.org/CMP/Library/CMP_Open_Standards_v1.0.pdf.

———. 2007. Miradi Adaptive Management Software. www.Miradi.org

Foundations of Success. 2005. "Basic Guidance for Tools: Results Chains." Resources for Implementing the WWF Standards, Worldwide Fund for Nature (WWF), Gland, Switzerland.

Gunderson, L. H., C. S. Holling, and S. S. Light, eds. 1995. *Barriers and Bridges to the Renewal of Ecosystems and Institutions.* New York: Columbia University Press.

Lee, K. N. 1993. *Compass and Gyroscope: Integrating Science and Politics for the Environment.* Washington, DC: Island Press.

Margoluis, R., V. Russell, M. Gonzalez, O. Rojas, J. Magdaleno, G. Madrid, and D. Kaimowitz. 2001. "Maximum Yield? Sustainable Agriculture as a Tool for Conservation." Biodiversity Support Program, Washington, DC.

Margoluis, R., and N. Salafsky. 1998. *Measures of Success: Designing, Managing, and Monitoring Conservation and Development Projects.* Washington, DC: Island Press.

Morgan, A., and Foundations of Success. 2005. "Basic Guidance for Cross-Cutting Tools: Conceptual Models." Worldwide Fund for Nature, Gland, Switzerland.

The Nature Conservancy. "Conservation Action Planning Resources." http://conserveonline.org/workspaces.

Salafsky, N., R. Margoluis, and K. Redford. 2001. "Adaptive Management: A Tool for Conservation Practitioners." Publication No. 112, Biodiversity Support Program, Washington, DC. http://www.fosonline.org/Site_Docs/AdaptiveManagementTool.pdf.

CHAPTER 5

IMPROVING FOREST GOVERNANCE

Forest sector governance refers to the ways in which officials and institutions (both formal and informal) acquire and exercise authority in the management of the resources of the sector to sustain and improve the welfare and quality of life for those whose livelihoods depend on the sector.[1] Good governance is fundamental to achieving positive and sustained development outcomes in the sector, including efficiency of resource management, increased contribution to economic growth and to environmental services, and equitable distribution of benefits.

Good forest governance is characterized by predictable, open, and informed policy making based on transparent processes, a bureaucracy imbued with a professional ethos, an executive arm of government accountable for its actions, and a strong civil society participating in decisions related to sector management and in other public affairs—and all behaving under the rule of law. Thus, key features of good governance include adherence to the rule of law, transparency and low levels of corruption, inputs of all stakeholders in decision making, accountability of all officials, low regulatory burden, and political stability (see also World Bank 2000).

The rationale for the World Bank to engage in improving forest governance in client countries is twofold. On one hand, broader governance reform processes, such as decentralization and devolution, and public sector reforms present direct opportunities to which the forest sector needs to respond. On the other hand, illegal logging, corruption, and other forest sector crimes, such as arson, poaching, land encroachment, trade in endangered fauna and flora, and evasion of legal taxes and royalties, indicate weaknesses in forest sector governance that need to be addressed. In developing countries, illegal logging in public lands alone causes estimated losses in assets and revenue in excess of US$10 billion annually, more than six times the total official development assistance dedicated to the sustainable management of forests. In addition, about US$5 billion per year is estimated to be lost to uncollected taxes and royalties on legally sanctioned timber harvests, as a result of corruption (World Bank 2004). The global magnitude of the problem as estimated by its direct monetary impacts is staggering.[2]

The associated physical, environmental, and social impacts resulting from poor governance are even more extensive and serious. They are characterized by the following:

- Violation of protected area boundaries threatens the conservation of forest resources and biodiversity.
- More than 350 million rural poor rely heavily on forests for their livelihoods, while more than 60 million depend almost exclusively on them for subsistence. Strong forest governance (including vesting tenurial rights with such communities) is essential for protecting their livelihoods and improving their well-being, and for protecting them from the consequences of illegal logging and unauthorized removals from the forest (World Bank 2006).
- Legitimate forest enterprises are subjected to unfair competition through price undercutting and discouraged from making socially and environmentally responsible investments in the sector.

- Forests are a global public good, and their degradation imposes global costs, such as climate change, environmental degradation, and species loss. Improving governance will help contain the negative environmental, economic, and social consequences at the global level.

- There are less visible—though highly insidious—costs resulting from the erosion of institutions, the spread of corruption across the economy, and lower growth. These spillover effects are the most far-reaching and significant aspects of the problem of poor sectoral governance. The problem originates in the forest sector but the impacts are transmitted through the economy, weakening governance and the rule of law, impeding investments in legitimate commerce, and undermining the overall governance structure.

Some of the complexities of these relationships and the magnitude of the task to improve forest governance are captured in figure 5.1.

The box in the center of the figure lists "entry points," or opportunities within the forest sector itself, directed toward reducing the means, motives, and opportunities for crimes and misdemeanors in the forest sector (see note 5.5, Addressing Illegal Logging and Forest Crime). The surrounding boxes indicate the "embedded" nature of the problem in the economy and of the need for other sectors, institutions, and actors to support and complement the within-sector efforts at improving governance and law enforcement. They elaborate on the roles of the overall political structure; of national and international checks and balances; and the contributions of civil society, media, the private sector, and local communities.

Figure 5.1 Identifying "Entry Points" and a Sustainable Reform Process to Improve Forest Governance

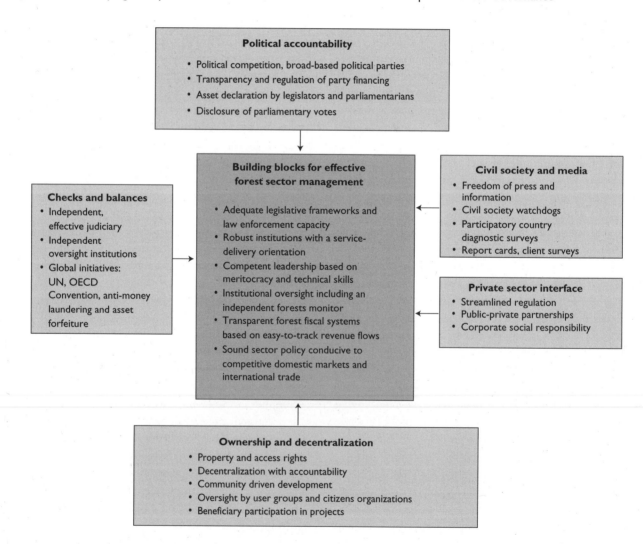

Improving forest governance and legislative compliance has been the focus of international attention for a number of years. For maximum effectiveness, the World Bank's efforts in this area need to be closely aligned with those of other partners, both in client countries and at the regional and international levels. This is especially important because effective action in this area requires collaboration among governments in producer and consumer countries, private sector operators, and civil society. Since 2001, regional Forest Law Enforcement and Governance (FLEG) ministerial conferences have been conducted in East Asia (2001), Africa (2003), and Europe and Northern Asia (2005). The resulting ministerial declarations are important tools that can be used in the dialogue with client governments, as well as in building alliances with the private sector and civil society actors. The World Bank has had a key role in facilitating these conferences and supporting their follow-up. Several multilateral, bilateral, civil society, and private sector initiatives have also originated from these efforts, which can provide traction for the World Bank's work in this area.

An independent and especially relevant initiative is the European Union (EU) Regulation and Action Plan on Forest Law Enforcement, Governance and Trade (FLEGT). An essential part of the EU FLEGT is the negotiation of Voluntary Partnership Agreements (VPAs) between the EU and interested timber-producing countries. VPAs aim to develop an agreement between producing and importing EU countries that only timber originating legally will be exported and allowed to be imported. If successful, the implementation of the VPAs will result in increasing demand for country-level financing in such areas as strengthening and reforming laws, regulations, and institutions in the forest sector; strengthening the capacity of indigenous and rural communities to manage forests sustainably; independent certification of sustainable forest management; implementation of timber tracking systems; forest products and trade-related information and statistics; and monitoring of forest cover changes to detect illegal activities. This will provide both the need and opportunities for improved collaboration between bilateral and multilateral financing institutions, including the World Bank.

The FLEG initiative enables the World Bank's project managers and task team leaders to incorporate FLEG into their projects using the political momentum and stakeholder coalitions it creates.

PAST ACTIVITIES

A review by the World Bank's Operations Evaluation Department of the performance of the World Bank's 1991 Forests Strategy (Lele et al. 2000) pointed to the failure to address governance issues as a serious gap in the World Bank's work in forestry and recommended that the World Bank help reduce illegal logging by actively promoting improved governance and enforcement of laws and regulations because poor laws and legislation and poor enforcement are fundamental failings in the sector. As a result, the World Bank placed forest governance and illegal logging high on the agenda in its 2002 Forests Strategy. Indeed, the World Bank committed itself to collaborate with borrower countries and partners to reduce by half the estimated annual financial losses from illegal logging by 2013. Likewise, the World Bank's 2001 environment strategy emphasizes the comparative advantage of the World Bank in supporting better governance, increased transparency, access to environmental information, and public participation in client countries (World Bank 2001).

The earliest explicit attention to forest crimes in Bank project design was in the Philippines in 1983 in the context of the Multisectoral Forest Protection Committees. These issues started to appear in a more systematic way in project design in the 1990s. Adjustment operations in Papua New Guinea in the 1990s supported the introduction of private sector administration of log export taxation. Work in Cambodia in the late 1990s involved the first use by the World Bank of forest law enforcement professionals in policy analysis and project design. Experiments in third-party independent monitoring of forest crime reporting, support for case tracking systems, and recommendations for timber theft prevention planning were among the innovations. In Africa, similar work, including independent forest monitors, was developed in Cameroon, and timber and postconflict issues are now being addressed in Liberia (see box 5.7).

COUNTRY ASSISTANCE STRATEGIES. To examine the extent to which FLEG and related issues are taken into account in Bank Country Assistance Strategies (CASs) today, a review of the most recent CASs for 18 forest-rich countries was carried out in 2006 (World Bank 2006). These 18 countries represent 75 percent of all forests in developing countries. Of these 18 CASs, 17 mention forestry, with 11 containing explicit forestry components. Nine CASs mention FLEG issues specifically, with at least seven outlining FLEG activities (both lending and nonlending) to be undertaken. Five CASs link deforestation to governance issues, and six describe links between poverty and deforestation.

LENDING OPERATIONS. A review in 2006 (World Bank 2006) found there are currently more than 50 active forestry projects in the World Bank's lending portfolio, with a total cost of

US$2.7 billion and total Bank commitment of US$1.6 billion. A recent assessment of these projects showed that some 35 projects have clearly identified FLEG components, totaling an estimated US$310.8 million. Thus, FLEG activities account for 11 percent of total project costs across all 51 forestry projects and 22 percent of total project costs for the 35 projects with forest governance components (also see table 5.1).

With regard to specific FLEG activities, some of the areas of forest governance addressed in World Bank projects include the following (see box 5.1 for country-specific examples):

■ development of national-level forestry policies and management plans;

■ capacity development for public agencies to better address forest crimes;

■ support for public awareness activities;

■ support for natural resource inventories, transparency in concession allocation, forest certification, and chain-of-custody verification; and

■ development of forest law enforcement reporting and monitoring systems and provision of equipment and capacity development for staff responsible for management of protected areas.

ANALYTICAL AND ADVISORY ACTIVITIES AND OTHER NON-LENDING ACTIVITIES. An essential and increasingly impor-

Table 5.1 FLEG Components in the World Bank Forestry Portfolio, by Region

Region	Total number of projects	Number of FLEG projects	Total cost (US$ million)	Cost as % of total forestry portfolio	Bank commitment (US$ million)	FLEG amount (US$ million)	FLEG as % of total forestry portfolio	FLEG as % of total FLEG
EAP	8	7	772.9	29	431.1	40.3	5	13
ECA	11	9	396.5	15	265.6	32.7	8	11
LAC	19	13	691.9	26	328.8	123.1	18	40
MENA	3	0	203.5	8	139.5	0	0	0
SA	1	1	127.1	5	108.2	5.8	5	2
SSA	9	5	515.1	19	289.7	108.9	21	35
Total	51	35	2,707.0	102	1,562.9	310.8	57	101

Source: World Bank 2006.

Note: EAP = East Asia and Pacific; ECA = Europe and Central Asia; LAC = Latin America and the Caribbean; MENA = Middle East and North Africa; SA = South Asia; SSA = Sub-Saharan Africa.

Box 5.1 Examples of Bank Support for Prevention and Detection Activities in Project Lending

Examples of FLEG prevention activities in the World Bank's portfolio:

■ Legal and regulatory reform in forest sector (Argentina, Bolivia, Bosnia and Herzegovina, Croatia, Georgia, Madagascar, Mexico, Romania)
■ Improving revenue collection and concession systems (Cambodia, Republic of Congo, Georgia, Ghana, the Russian Federation, Tanzania)
■ National-level forest management plans and protected-area plans (Bolivia, Cambodia, Ghana)
■ Demarcation of protected areas (Argentina, Brazil, Honduras, Ghana, the Lao Peoples' Democratic Republic [Lao PDR], Uganda, Vietnam)
■ Formalization of land tenure rights (Honduras, Vietnam)
■ Public awareness activities (Cambodia, Romania)

Examples of FLEG detection activities in the World Bank's portfolio:

■ Forest management information systems (Bosnia and Herzegovina, Georgia, Ghana, India, Lao PDR, Romania, Russia)
■ Certification systems (Armenia, Mexico, Russia)
■ Monitoring in the field (Peru, Uganda)
■ Guard houses, field inspection units, equipment for patrols (Bosnia and Herzegovina, Ecuador, Georgia, Lao PDR, Mexico)

tant part of the World Bank's contribution to development is the analytical and advisory activities[3] carried out for client countries. These activities provide a foundation for defining strategic priorities and informing policy dialogue and decisions on projects and programs and comprise economic and sector work, nonlending technical assistance, and knowledge management, as well as training and research services.

The World Bank also has prepared country-level forest sector reviews in several countries with a focus on FLEG. Furthermore, as part of its analytical and advisory work and as an integral part of its strategic approach to forest governance, the World Bank has actively supported international and regional initiatives on forest governance (see box 5.2), including the three regional ministerial FLEG conferences. At the country level, the World Bank has supported the development of national-level action plans related to controlling illegal logging and improving forest sector transparency for Albania, Armenia, Bosnia and Herzegovina, Indonesia, and Russia. In some cases, World Bank work related to investments in other sectors also involves issues of illegal logging and forest governance.

KEY ISSUES

Finding ways to improve forest governance is a challenging task. In addition, poor governance in the sector is often symptomatic of poor governance in the overall economy, compounding the problem. For example, illegal money generated from forest crimes often fuels "slush funds" for corruption in other sectors, including campaign financing, speculation, gambling, and human and drug trafficking, all of which have deep negative impacts on the economy at large. This access to illegal money also creates powerful vested interests, both within and outside the sector, which tend to benefit from the status quo and therefore strongly oppose any reforms.

Approaches to addressing forest governance and law enforcement must deal with, among other things, issues connected to land tenure arrangements, access rights (see note 1.4,

---

Box 5.2 Finding Synergies Between the World Bank Group's Efforts in FLEG and Its Broader Governance Reforms for Greater Impact

The forestry portfolio is nested within the World Bank's overall approach to governance and anticorruption and is consistent with a wide range of governance work being led by other sectors in the World Bank.

Some of the more relevant work of other parts of the World Bank Group on governance includes support to Poverty Reduction Strategy Paper processes and the alignment of the World Bank's CAS with these processes, work on governance diagnostics and integration of governance and anticorruption elements in the CASs, and the design of specific capacity-building programs based on the diagnostic surveys (Poverty Reduction and Economic Management Network and the World Bank Institute). Other relevant areas of the World Bank's work focus on anti-money laundering and financial investigation, the Extractive Industries Transparency Initiative, Justice for the Poor, and customs modernization. The World Bank's legal department has carried out important work in developing a benchmark study for assessing the quality of legal and regulatory frameworks. The Department of Institutional Integrity's investigative approaches to allegations of corruption in Bank-funded projects provide potentially powerful instruments to combat illegal logging and forest crimes. Similarly, some of the work with corporate social responsibility and social and environmental issues in the operations of the International Finance Corporation (IFC) (for example, investment safeguard policies) is extremely relevant to FLEG issues (see note 3.2, Forest Certification Systems).

The forestry work of the World Bank Group needs to be more consciously informed by and aligned with these initiatives. The expertise accumulated in these specialized fields is only now being brought to bear on the problems of forestry. Where it has been applied, for example, in anti-money laundering, it is clear that there is enormous potential to address problems in the sector. There are also potential advantages for these specialized initiatives to work with forestry because this can provide an important sectoral entry point on which to ground the specialized efforts.

Joint analytic work needs to be strengthened across the World Bank's organizational boundaries, specialists from other areas need to be familiarized with the special circumstances of forestry, and understanding among external stakeholders of the relevance of these tools needs to be improved. Transaction costs involved in working across sectoral lines can be significant and internal incentives need to be aligned to encourage cross-sectoral collaboration.

Source: World Bank 2006.

Property and Access Rights), overly complex laws and regulations biased against the poor (see note 5.3, "Strengthening Legal Frameworks in the Forest Sector), and transparency and stakeholder participation in decisions directly affecting their livelihoods. However, an increasing trend toward decentralization (both administrative and fiscal), coupled with increased willingness of governments to allow operation of multistakeholder processes, has created unique demands as well as opportunities for better and different forms of governance (see note 5.1, Decentralized Forest Management, and 5.2, Reforming Forest Institutions). These considerations have been complemented by the universal commitment to the Millennium Development Goals dealing especially with issues of equity and the rights of poor and indigenous forest communities. Thus, decentralization and participation are crucial issues that are extensively discussed in this sourcebook (see note 5.1, Decentralized Forest Management).

A forest fiscal system is needed that, in its broadest terms, influences revenue flows in and out of the sector as well as income distribution across various stakeholder groups within the sector. A well-designed and well-functioning fiscal system is an important instrument with which to address sustainable resource utilization and equity and rural development issues, and to minimize the risks of corruption (see note 5.4, Strengthening Fiscal Systems in the Forest Sector).

In addition, combating large-scale criminal activities requires targeted action to directly improve forest law *enforcement* so that criminals are apprehended and punished. Combating large-scale criminal activities would also include more fundamental changes to improve the broader governance environment in the forest sector and in society at large to help strengthen law enforcement efforts (see note 5.5, Addressing Illegal Logging and Other Forest Crimes).

In many countries, law enforcement capacity and expertise exists in other sectors and needs to be marshaled in new ways to support forest development. In others, specialized capacity needs to be developed within forestry agencies. Exploitation of new enforcement innovations and opportunities, made possible, for example, by the introduction of anti-money-laundering legislation, the adoption of the UN Conventions against Transnational Organized Crime and Corruption, and by other new legal and judicial innovations, will require new skills and capacity.

FUTURE PRIORITIES AND SCALING-UP ACTIVITIES

SUPPORT DECENTRALIZATION AND DEVOLUTION OF FOREST MANAGEMENT RESPONSIBILITIES. Decentralization and devolution based on the principle of subsidiarity, are means to promote more democratic and equitable management of forest resources and increase the contribution of the sector to poverty reduction. Decentralization and devolution processes can create imbalances and unforeseen negative consequences if they are not carefully managed and accompanied by sufficient capacity building, allocation of financial resources, and creation of mechanisms for downward accountability at the decentralized levels. Bureaucratic resistance to change at the central level, as well as powerful vested interests, can often swing the policy pendulum from decentralization and devolution back to re-centralization, reversing progress and resulting in incoherent policies and regulations.

PROTECT THE RIGHTS OF AND EMPOWER INDIGENOUS AND LOCAL COMMUNITIES THROUGH GOVERNANCE REFORM PROCESSES. Specific attention should be given to using governance reform processes to protect the rights of and empower indigenous and local communities. This can prevent unintended and potentially adverse impacts on forest-dependent livelihoods and traditional rights (see also note 1.3, Indigenous Peoples and Forests, and chapter 12, Applying OP 4.10 on Indigenous Peoples).

CONTINUE TO ENGAGE IN INSTITUTIONAL AND LEGAL SYSTEM REFORMS IN THE FOREST SECTOR. The World Bank, with its engagement in diverse sectors, helps governments tailor forest sector reform processes to the country context and effectively implement them. A model that works for a post-conflict country (for example, Liberia or the Democratic Republic of Congo) may be very different from what is possible in a country in transition from a centralized, one-party governance structure to a democratic model (for example, the experience of the former communist countries of Eastern Europe). (See note 5.2, Reforming Forest Institutions, for discussion on key principles and structures.)

ASSIST IN ENABLING AND DESIGNING FISCAL SYSTEM REFORMS THAT ARE ECONOMICALLY AND ADMINISTRATIVELY EFFICIENT. Fiscal system reforms that are economically and administratively efficient allow for appropriate rent capture. As part of this process, the World Bank should assist governments in assessing the appropriateness of structuring forest fiscal systems to achieve secondary objectives, such as equity and sustainable rural development.

CENTER FLEG ACTIVITIES AT THE COUNTRY LEVEL AROUND MORE EFFECTIVE INTEGRATION OF THE WORK IN THE FOREST

SECTOR WITH BROADER GOVERNANCE AND ANTICORRUPTION EFFORTS. Such instruments as anti-money-laundering and asset forfeiture laws, crime monitoring techniques, customs modernization, and governance diagnostics need to be brought into the picture to combat illegal logging and other forest crime. This will require both helping client countries to establish effective mechanisms for intersectoral coordination and collaboration and joint action (such as dedicated forest crime task forces) and joint work by the respective Bank departments and units.

WORK TO MOVE ACTIONS AGAINST FOREST CRIME FORWARD. Given the importance of international demand as a driver of illegal logging and other forest crime, the regional FLEG processes should continue to play an important role in creating political commitment and joint action by producer and consumer countries to address these issues. This work increasingly needs to become part of the agenda of existing international, regional, and subregional organizations and agreements to increase both its sustainability and impact. Significant work needs to be done to deepen the technical content of these processes and help them move from political declarations, to effective support, to action at the country level.

EXPLORE AND ENHANCE THE USE OF POLICY LENDING TO ENABLE FOREST SECTOR GOVERNANCE REFORMS as discussed in this chapter and associated notes. (For more information on the application of development policy lending for forest sector reform, see note 6.2, Prospects for Using Policy Lending to Proactively Enable Forest Sector Reforms.)

IDENTIFY NECESSARY FLEG MEASURES FOR ENABLING REDUCED EMISSIONS from avoided deforestation and degradation (REDD) while also exploring opportunities to mainstream FLEG considerations into country dialogue on REDD (see box 5.3).

NOTES

1. Officials and institutions may be either public or private, the first of which may be termed public sector forest governance and the latter corporate forest governance. This distinction is useful in developing a typology of reform measures.

2. How might a policy maker assess the state of forest governance in his or her own country? Systematic and objective quantitative and qualitative estimates of such activities can help benchmark the state of governance in the sector and identify critical areas for reform and can contribute to monitoring the progress of efforts to improve governance.

3. Analytical and advisory activities refer to activities that involve analytical effort with the intent of influencing client countries' policies and programs and comprise formal and informal studies of critical issues, either at the country level or for specific sectors (for example, economic and sector work, policy notes, and the like). This work has traditionally underpinned lending and investment operations. Nonlending technical assistance is the transfer of skills and knowl-

---

Box 5.3 REDD and Forest Governance

In response to growing awareness that deforestation and forest degradation are major sources of greenhouse gas emissions, many countries have expressed an interest in implementing payments for forest protection that achieves carbon storage. A UN Framework Convention on Climate Change (UNFCCC) mechanism to establish this is under discussion. The initiative is known as REDD, for Reduced Emissions from Avoided Deforestation and Degradation.

Proponents of REDD see it as a low-cost option for reducing global emissions that could also alleviate poverty and protect biodiversity. However, while much deforestation is a rational response to global and local economics and is the result of government planning, a significant proportion has been, and remains, illegal

and uncontrolled. Tackling this latter element of deforestation and establishing basic rule of law in the sector will be a critical prerequisite for governments hoping to achieve reduced deforestation or attract private sector investment in REDD projects, particularly in the early stages of the market.

Previous to the REDD concept, establishing legality in the sector has long been a priority for those working in forests, and it is important that synergies are recognized, continuity is emphasized, and political processes and tools designed to support improved legality in production forests are also used in support of REDD strategies where relevant. Beyond the need to establish legal control of the forest resource, it will also be necessary to tackle systemic issues.

Source: Saunders and Nussbaum 2008.

edge for development purposes and a key instrument for improving policies and project design, enhancing skills, and strengthening implementation capacity.

SELECTED READINGS

Kishor, N., and R. Damania. 2006. "Crime and Justice in the Garden of Eden: Improving Governance and Reducing Corruption in the Forestry Sector." In *The Many Faces of Corruption: Tracking Vulnerabilities at the Sector Level,* ed. J. Edgardo Campos and Sanjay Pradhan. Washington, DC: World Bank.

Lele, U., N. Kumar, S.A. Husain, A. Zazueta, and L. Kelly. 2000. *The World Bank Forest Strategy: Striking the Right Balance.* Washington, DC: World Bank.

Magrath, W. B., R. Grandalski, J. Stuckey, G. Vikanes, and G. Wilkinson. Forthcoming. *Timber Theft Prevention and Forest Resource Security.* Washington, DC: World Bank.

World Bank. 2000. *Anticorruption in Transition: A Contribution to the Policy Debate.* Washington, DC: World Bank.

———. 2000b. *Reforming Public Institutions and Strengthening Governance: A World Bank Strategy.* Washington, DC: World Bank.

———. 2002. "A Revised Forest Strategy for the World Bank Group." Draft April 2002. Washington, DC.

———. 2007. "Strengthening World Bank Group Engagement on Governance and Anticorruption." Washington, DC. http://www.worldbank.org/html/extdr/comments/governancefeedback/gacpaper-03212007.pdf.

REFERENCES CITED

Saunders, J., and R. Nussbaum. 2008. "Forest Governance and Reduced Emissions from Deforestation and Degradation (REDD)." Chatham House (The Royal Institute of International Affairs), London, England.

World Bank. 2000. *Reforming Public Institutions and Strengthening Governance: A World Bank Strategy.* Public Sector Group PREM Network. Washington, DC: World Bank.

———. 2001. *Making Sustainable Commitments: An Environment Strategy for the World Bank.* Washington, DC: World Bank.

———. 2004. *Sustaining Forests: A Development Strategy.* Washington, DC: World Bank.

———. 2006. "Strengthening Forest Law Enforcement and Governance: Addressing a Systemic Constraint to Sustainable Development." Report #36638-GLB, Sustainable Development Network, World Bank, Washington, DC.

CROSS-REFERENCED CHAPTERS AND NOTES

Note 1.3: Indigenous Peoples and Forests

Note 1.4: Property and Access Rights

Note 3.2: Forest Certification Systems

Note 5.1: Decentralized Forest Management

Note 5.2: Reforming Forest Institutions

Note 5.3: Strengthening Legal Frameworks in the Forest Sector

Chapter 12: Applying OP 4.10 on Indigenous Peoples

Decentralized Forest Management

Dissatisfied with centralized approaches to governance, many developing countries and countries in transition—it is estimated that 80 percent of them have embarked on some form of decentralization, transferring authority and responsibility for government functions from the central government to subnational governments or civil society and private sector institutions.

Given the right conditions, decentralization of forest management can lead to superior outcomes, improving the effectiveness of public forest institutions by matching the demand for public forest services with their supply by local governments. Decentralized local institutions of the public forest administration can be closer to local people, their demands, and priorities, and thereby offer opportunities for government to become more relevant to local conditions. By emphasizing subnational governmental autonomy, forest decentralization can promote democratic decision-making processes and free top executives of the public forest administration from many routine decisions. If decentralization leads to greater local voice and participation, it can contribute to greater accountability and to reducing forest-related corruption and government misuse of forest resources. Local participation can also induce design of and experimentation with creative and innovative programs that make use of local knowledge and that are tailored to local settings, moving away from the application of standardized actions designed by the central government. Furthermore, forest decentralization can help improve equity through greater capture and local retention, as well as democratic distribution, of forest management benefits. Because of this, decentralization can be instrumental in reducing local conflicts over the use of forest resources and the allocation of resulting benefits and costs among institutions and local people. Thus, decentralization can lead to better governance and improved efficiency, equity, and environmental management outcomes.

However, there are potential risks associated with decentralization. It is an extremely complex undertaking involving multiple levels of government, agencies with different functions, and stakeholders with diverse, sometimes incompatible, interests. Authority, responsibility, and financial and human resources as well as a variety of administrative functions can be decentralized to different degrees, thus creating countless possible pathways to decentralized forest administration. Decentralized forest institutions often cannot function adequately if they are not endowed with sufficient resources and authority. Imbalances in the allocation of authority and responsibility to the various levels of government, possibly because the process is still incomplete, also make efficient public forest service delivery difficult. Regardless of the path to decentralization, inadequate subnational capacity is almost always a limiting factor.

Some obstacles to effective forest decentralization have their origins in the drastic changes in power structures within the government apparatus that are associated with, and required for, effective decentralization, and that occur during the redistribution of authority and resources from the central government to subnational governments. Government officials at the center often resist these reallocations of power. Furthermore, when powers are redistributed to subnational levels, decentralization often also increases the possibility of regulatory capture by local interests. Local government officers and politicians can be even more subject to corruption than those of the central government.

In addition, unless some key functions of government remain at the center, such as defining national forest policy parameters, overall policy coherence in the sector may be lost. The challenge for forest sector planners is to shape and manage decentralization processes in a way that secures its potential benefits while avoiding associated pitfalls. Some of the main promises of decentralization and the corresponding limitations it faces are listed in table 5.2.

Table 5.2 Forest Decentralization: Potential Advantages and Dangers

Potential advantages	Potential dangers
There may be reduced bureaucracy and decision-making congestion at the center.	Coordination, implementation, and monitoring of national policies may be more difficult. Central government may be excessively weakened by the transfer of resources to subnational governments. Unclear division of powers may lead to increased conflicts between tiers of government.
There may be faster decision making, particularly in the case of routine decisions.	Economies of scale in implementing certain actions (for example, procurement) may be lost. Subnational government decision-making capacity may be inadequate.
Institution building at the local level may increase. There may be better understanding of local conditions, needs, and constraints. Information flows between tiers of government and between civil society, private sector, and governmental institutions may be enriched. There may be a better scope for establishing partnerships with organizations outside the government. Local knowledge can be exploited more fully.	The "bigger picture" of national forest management and development may be lost. Decisions may be conditioned by local objectives that may not coincide with national objectives. Decentralization may result in the allocation of central resources to regions, ethnic groups, or political associates, which may threaten social coherence. Decentralized organizations may have limited technical and managerial knowledge and lack institutional capacity to manage forest programs.
If decentralization leads to increased reliance on subnational sources of financing, subnational forest institutions will have a greater incentive to function as separate profit centers with decisions increasingly being subject to the discipline of the market. Subsidized operations will tend to be eliminated.	Decisions that are heavily influenced by financial considerations may not coincide with national or even local objectives, and financial incentives for accelerated forest exploitation may increase. These decisions may be socially or environmentally undesirable or unsustainable. Noncommercial national policy objectives may be lost.
It is easier to involve local populations, particularly if actions requested from them are linked to benefit sharing.	Local elites may control and use decentralized institutions for their own benefit. Decision making may be less transparent and less responsive. If local governments do not produce a substantial economic surplus, net transfers from the central government may be lost.
There may be a greater sense of local ownership.	Local ownership may be lost if benefit sharing becomes less equitable. Decentralized forestry offices may be controlled by special interests. Decentralization may increase arbitrariness and corruption.
Decentralization can lead to larger share of benefits remaining in localities and communities that generate them.	Central government may lose essential revenues and manpower. Local elites may gain control of benefits and create greater inequality and increase poverty. There may be overwhelming pressure to "mine" the forest for immediate local benefit.
There is potential for harmonizing local traditions and rights with formal governmental norms.	If formal norms were previously ineffective and de facto informal norms prevailed, decentralization may increase conflict between formal and informal norms.
Political meddling by central powers may be more difficult.	Local government officials with greater responsibility and power may use decentralized institutions for their own political and personal purposes. Political meddling by the central government may simply be replaced by local political interference and government capture by organized elites. Decentralization may be a vehicle for central political parties to penetrate the rural and forest economy.
Corruption may decrease if the discretionary power of central government officials is reduced. Those actions and powers of local officials can be more closely scrutinized, and downward accountability and transparency will tend to increase.	If centralized monitoring and control are loosened, particularly if decentralization is not accompanied by citizen participation, there may be more opportunities for corruption of local government officials by local elites.

Source: Contreras-Hermosilla. 2006.

OPERATIONAL ASPECTS

With decentralization being such a multifaceted process, there is no single "model" for forest decentralization. Different degrees of responsibility and authority can be transferred to one or more subnational units of government, and the central government may choose to retain a large or limited share of responsibility and authority. The potential benefits and disadvantages mentioned above will emerge depending on the functions being decentralized and on the local governance and institutional context.

ASSESS THE OVERALL DECENTRALIZATION CONTEXT. Forest decentralization will generally be part of broader decentralization initiatives involving the whole government, which will largely shape what can be done in the forest sector. Government-wide characteristics may impose limits as well as offer opportunities to decentralization in the forest sector. For example, some decentralized governments, such as that of Switzerland, have strong locally elected bodies that make local participation and downward accountability of local public forest administration to local populations and electorates easier to achieve. Other governments are not inclined to go this far and their levels of local participation and accountability may be lower. Project designers must evaluate the relative strengths and weaknesses of public and private sector organizations and their capacity to perform the forest management functions before drawing plans for forest decentralization interventions (see chapter 2, Engaging the Private Sector in Forest Sector Development, and note 2.1, Community-Private Partnerships).

Forest decentralization must be adequately linked to overall decentralization processes because of the multidisciplinary characteristics of forest administration and the numerous cross-sectoral influences that shape forest governance (see chapter 6, Mainstreaming Forests into Development Policy and Planning: Assessing Cross-Sectoral Impacts, and associated notes). For example, in Albania, a

Bank intervention observed that the Forest Administration was unable to control illegal logging except in selected areas where it was able to establish operational links with other decentralized agencies. In this case, an interministerial task force of various stakeholders at the national level was complemented by the creation at the prefecture and district levels of intersectoral task forces to organize collaboration (World Bank 2004).

GET THE LEGAL FRAMEWORK RIGHT. A critical operational consideration to making forest decentralization work is the existence of a clear and consistent legal framework guiding the distribution of responsibilities, resources, and authority at the different levels of government and the relationships between government and local communities and the private sector (see note 5.3, Strengthening Legal Frameworks in the Forest Sector). While this appears to be a self-evident aspect of good governance, experience shows that, in practice, forest decentralization often takes place in an environment of considerable legal uncertainty (see box 5.3). This legal uncertainty is a sure recipe for conflicts between tiers of government and government institutions as well as between public and private entities that defeat the potential governance benefits of decentralization. Legal regimes should provide local people and the private sector with enforceable rights to resources and enable them to play a meaningful

---

Box 5.4 Legal Uncertainty in Indonesia

In 1999 the Indonesian government approved legislation to decentralize government authority, resources, and responsibilities to provinces (second tier government) and districts (third tier). Districts, considered closer to the people and therefore more apt to promote democratization, were assigned primary responsibility for administrative and regulatory functions. However, drafted in haste, the decentralization laws were inconsistent or even contradictory with other laws. And in the midst of the instability that dominated the political scene after the fall of Suharto, corresponding operational regulations to the decentralization laws were slow to come, leaving much to interpretation and to the discretion of local public officials who were often inadequately prepared.

In the same year, the Basic Forestry Law was enacted. This law and its regulations contradicted significant parts of the decentralization legislation. A

decree issued a year later sought to clarify matters, limiting forest sector decentralization to marginal functions, and was resisted by some districts. Legal uncertainty surrounding the division of powers and responsibilities created a de facto movement toward forest decentralization and intense conflicts between the district governments and the center.

In these circumstances, and fearing appropriation or interference by other levels of government, forest resource–rich districts had a powerful incentive to accelerate resource exploitation, giving only secondary consideration to the long-term consequences of unsustainable practices. In some cases, legal uncertainty favored the creation of local alliances between powerful groups and government officials. To a great extent, the poor have yet to reap the benefits expected from forest decentralization.

Source: Contreras-Hermosilla and Fay 2005; Boccucci and Jurgens 2006.

role in decision making related to the management of forest resources. In most countries, the strength of legal frameworks is becoming more important as forest resources become increasingly scarce and thus the focus of conflicts between different stakeholders (Lindsay 2000).

General decentralization laws will provide most of the legal framework for the forest institutions of government, which must become aligned with those broader laws. An assessment of the legal frame of reference needed to make forest decentralization effective may be required. In most cases, the forest administration alone may be able to handle many of the desired regulatory changes without resorting to parliamentary sanctioning.

PARTICIPATION, EMPOWERMENT, AND POVERTY ALLEVIATION. An important requirement for decentralization processes to succeed and ensure transparency is the ability of local governments to work with local communities and other private sector and civil society stakeholders. The government's underlying political philosophy must allow local participation in the formulation of local plans and policies and the local forest administration must have capacity to manage these interactions. Government should be fully committed to involving local communities and other stakeholders in decisions related to implementation of forest programs. Adequate management of the interactions between local governments, communities, and private sector entities that may participate in joint schemes for the management of forest resources requires, in addition to capacity to handle technical matters, substantial changes to attitudes and institutional incentives. When these capabilities are not available, technical assistance to support intensive training of government officers, communities, and enterprises will be needed.

Participation mechanisms are likely to work better when government institutions and bureaucracy are exposed to incentives that reward participation; this often means accountability to local institutions and populations rather than exclusively to higher levels of government. In those cases where decentralization is based on local governments run by officials democratically elected by local constituencies, participation and bottom-up approaches to forest management are easier to integrate. But there are other complementary mechanisms as well, including joint projects (for example, comanagement schemes), planning advisory groups, monitored self-regulation of forest-related activities (particularly relevant for the private commercial sector), citizen appeals processes for government decisions, forest forums involving government and civil society, and

mandatory disclosure of forest administration records. Local citizen group participation, as observed in Bolivia, India, and Nepal, has contributed to ensuring that measures imposed by higher levels of government take local conditions and traditions into consideration.

Participation by communities and local populations in local government decisions and implementation of forest programs works better when there are clear and tangible benefits associated with such participation for all stakeholders. The flow of information between local governments and local groups must therefore be adequate to enable participatory decision making.

ADEQUATE BALANCE OF RESPONSIBILITIES, POWERS, AND RESOURCES AT EACH LEVEL OF GOVERNMENT. To function effectively and efficiently, each level of government and corresponding agencies must possess sufficient authority to fulfill the responsibilities allocated to them. While this balance is hard to determine with precision in practice, authority without a corresponding measure of responsibility fosters mismanagement and creates opportunities for corruption. In the same vein, responsibility without a measure of power to command resources and implement actions cannot be adequately discharged.

At the same time, power and responsibility are meaningless unless each level of government and each agency can count on adequate financial and human resources. There is no real local autonomy if higher levels of government have exclusive control over what programs and projects will receive financial support (see box 5.5). Transfers of financial resources to lower levels of government are normally needed to empower local levels of the public forest administration to carry out management activities. In some cases, local autonomy may require retention of forest revenues captured by local governments.

APPLY THE PRINCIPLE OF SUBSIDIARITY. Although there is no formula for deciding what degree of decentralization is optimal to ensure good forest governance, certain functions are best left at the central level and others can best be carried out locally. Subsidiarity, a fundamental concept behind decentralization, establishes that government functions should be carried out at the lowest possible level of government where capacity exists or can be readily created. The proper application of this principle requires an assessment of capacities at different levels of government and of institutions of civil society and the private sector that could assume responsibility for various forest management–related functions. Such assessment is a useful tool for judging the relative desirabil-

The 1997 Law of Municipalities assigned considerably expanded responsibilities to municipalities, together with greater administrative and political autonomy. However, municipal governments' capacity to discharge responsibilities was limited by an imbalance between the new obligations and the financial resources allocated to them by the central government.

Municipalities were entrusted with developing, conserving, and controlling the "rational use of the environment and natural resources…promoting local initiatives in these areas and contributing to their monitoring, vigilance and control…" (Larson 2001: 20). In addition, municipalities were to be consulted before central government approval of resource exploitation authorizations in both national and private lands. Also, municipal governments were to capture at least 25 percent of the revenues originating in these contracts.

Despite these formidable responsibilities, municipalities complained that they did not receive the tax revenues to which they were entitled. The central government on many occasions failed to consult with municipalities in awarding exploitation contracts or simply ignored them. In any case, the central government kept exclusive power to make key decisions over all natural resources.

Source: Larson 2001.

ity of decentralization options and for helping determine the responsibilities and powers of the various levels of government, including the central government (Anderson 1999).

ENSURE TRANSPARENCY AND ACCOUNTABILITY, PARTICULARLY DOWNWARD ACCOUNTABILITY. Closely linked to effective local participation in decision making and implementation of forest programs is the need to ensure that the actions of local government officers are transparent and that the officers themselves remain accountable to local populations for their actions (see box 5.6). The transfer of powers to local institutions may have worse outcomes than centralized management if accountability mechanisms to local populations are weak. When accountability has been mainly or exclusively to higher levels of government, local groups have no avenue to have their views heard and no power to influence policy design and program implementation. Local forest institutions are at risk of becoming simple extensions of the central government, which naturally tends to use them for promoting central agendas, thus defeating many of the opportunities of decentralization (Ribot 1998). Inadequate or nonexistent downward accountability facilitates control by local elites, often operating in association with local government institutions. This is a real danger, particularly when electoral accountability is weak and where there is a lack of nongovernmental watchdog organizations that can mobilize public opinion.

INDIGENOUS PEOPLES AND LOCAL COMMUNITIES. Forest decentralization should include adequate measures to improve community participation and to respect indigenous and traditional rights. In certain circumstances, transferring additional powers to local governments enhances the reach of government in areas where government presence was previously absent or weak. If government policy ignores ancestral rights, local community institutions, and community property, enhanced local government power is likely to lead to or exacerbate social inequality. Forest decentralization projects should therefore contain adequate measures to avoid potentially adverse effects on Indigenous Peoples and other vulnerable communities (see also note 1.3, Indigenous Peoples and Forests, and chapter 12, Applying OP 4.10 on Indigenous Peoples).

FOREST AND ENVIRONMENTAL VALUES. Forest decentralization may generate incentives for accelerated depletion of forest resources and loss of environmental values. These incentives are particularly intense if local governments are asked to raise a large proportion of their own financial resources to fund their operations and if rights of access to and control over forest resources by local governments, civil society, or the private sector are uncertain (see note 5.4, Strengthening Fiscal Systems in the Forest Sector).

LESSONS LEARNED AND RECOMMENDATIONS FOR PRACTITIONERS

CLARITY OF DIVISION OF RESPONSIBILITIES AND AUTHORITY. Experience acquired in supporting forest decentralization programs indicates that clarity in the distribution of

> **Box 5.6 Participation and Transparency in Bolivia**
>
> To ensure increased transparency in government decisions, the Public Forest Administration is empowered to consult with various groups of civil society. After decentralization and the reorganization of the forest sector administration, forest resources decisions are no longer at the exclusive discretion of bureaucrats, but are instead subject to public scrutiny and made with public participation. Thus, open auctions govern the allocation of all new concession contracts. Open auctions also rule the sale of confiscated forest products and equipment. Regulations allow the cancellation of previously granted rights only with due process, guaranteeing people's rights and fostering a balance between regulators and the regulated. Moreover, the forest administration must submit reports to the government twice a year, hold public hearings once a year to explain work carried out, and provide an opportunity for the public to raise questions about performance. Any citizen can freely request copies of official documents.
>
> *Source:* Contreras-Hermosilla and Vargas Rios 2002.

responsibilities and commensurate resources and authority are essential for quality decentralized governance. The problems faced by the rapid forest decentralization processes in Indonesia illustrate the importance of achieving a clear distribution of authority and responsibilities for various forest management functions (licensing, forest concessions, classification of forests) between the levels of government and between governments and civil society and private sector institutions (Boccucci and Jurgens 2006.

BUREAUCRATIC RESISTANCE TO CHANGE. Decentralization in India (Madhya Pradesh and Andhra Pradesh), Guatemala (Elias and Wittman 2004), Nicaragua (Larson 2001), and other countries shows that government executives are generally opposed to sharing power and resources with lower levels of government. Even when transfer of certain powers is mandated by law, in practice this has meant granting autonomy to manage only the least significant resources, keeping decisions about the use of the most valuable ones at higher levels. Furthermore, higher levels of government commonly have a tendency to maintain control over financial resources, thus effectively shaping the actions of lower levels of government or of local communities and other interest groups that require financial backing. This resistance to sharing power is one of the most critical threats to effective forest decentralization. In most cases, tackling this obstacle entails twin efforts aimed at (i) raising awareness of government officials based on clear and sound intellectual discourse and (ii) identification and support of key agents of change, as in Indonesia. Systems of institutional incentives must be geared toward rewarding progress in decentralization processes. This can be facilitated by democratic decision making schemes that enhance downward accountability of local government officials to local populations. (Resistance to change is also addressed in note 5.2, Reforming Forest Institutions).

CAPACITY BUILDING. Another lesson of experience is that lack of local capacity is often used as an excuse for reducing the pace of forest decentralization or for recentralizing. However, local capacity is unlikely to ever be created unless decentralization takes place. Thus, implementation of forest decentralization programs may require education and training programs for local governments and civil society institutions expected to play a role in the decentralized management of forest resources (World Bank 2004). If significant responsibility for forest resource management is transferred to local institutions, as in Indonesia, technical assistance will be required. Planning such assistance will require an institutional analysis of demands and capacities of the various levels of government and a coherent plan to fill in gaps. Improving the knowledge base and managerial capacity are long-term undertakings that may require sustained support for extended periods. As emphasized by a project in Nicaragua, World Bank interventions should pilot decentralization initiatives and be designed as a series of sequential building blocks as institutional and managerial capacity gradually develops over long periods (World Bank 1998).

SELECTED READINGS

Manor, J. 1999. *The Political Economy of Democratic Decentralization.* Washington, DC: World Bank.

Kaimowitz, D., C. Vallejos, P. Pacheco, and R. Lopez. 1998. "Municipal Governments and Forest Management in Lowland Bolivia." *Journal of Environment and Development* 7 (1): 45–59.

Larson, A., P. Pacheco, F. Toni, and M. Vallejo. 2006. *Exclusión e Inclusión en la Forestería Latinoamericana. ¿Hacia Dónde va la Descentralización?* La Paz, Bolivia: CIFOR/IDRC.

Ribot, J. C. 2002. "Democratic Decentralization of Natural Resources. Institutionalising Popular Participation." World Resources Institute, Washington, DC.

Parker, A. 1995. "Decentralization: The Way Forward for Rural Development?" Policy Research Working Paper No. 475, World Bank, Washington, DC.

Pierce Colfer, C., and D. Capistrano. 2005. *The Politics of Decentralization: Forests, Power and People.* London: Earthscan.

REFERENCES CITED

Anderson, J. 1999. "Four Considerations for Decentralized Forest Management: Subsidiarity, Empowerment, Pluralism and Social Capital." Food and Agriculture Organization of the United Nations, Rome, Italy.

Binswanger, H. 1994. "Agriculture and Rural Development: Painful Lessons." In *International Agricultural Development,* ed. C. K. Eicher and J. M. Staatz, 287–99. Baltimore, MD: Johns Hopkins University Press.

Boccucci, M., and E. Jurgens. 2006. "Reflections on Indonesia's Experience on Decentralization of Forest Management." Unpublished. Jakarta, Indonesia.

Contreras-Hermosilla, A., and C. Fay. 2005. *Strengthening Forest Management in Indonesia Through Land Tenure Reform: Issues and Framework for Action.* Washington, DC: Forest Trends and the World Agroforestry Center.

Contreras-Hermosilla, A., and M. T. Vargas Rios. 2002. *Social, Environmental and Economic Dimensions of Forest Policy Reforms in Bolivia.* Washington, DC: Forest Trends.

Contreras-Hermosilla, A. 2006. "Decentralized Forest Management." Note submitted to World Bank as input to *Forests Sourcebook.* Unpublished. World Bank, Washington, DC.

Elías, S. and Wittman, H. 2004. "State, Forest and Community: Reconfiguring Power Relations and Challenges for Forest Sector Decentralization in Guatemala." Paper presented at Interlaken Workshop on Decentralization in Forestry. Interlaken, Switzerland, 27–30 April 2004.

Manor, J. 1999. *The Political Economy of Democratic Decentralization.* Washington, DC: World Bank.

Larson, A. M. 2001. "Natural Resources and Decentralization in Nicaragua: Are Local Governments Up to the Job?" *World Development* 30 (1): 17–31.

Lindsay, J. M. 1999. "Creating Legal Space for Community-Based Management: Principles and Dilemmas." Food and Agriculture Organization of the United Nations, Rome, Italy.

Ribot, J. C. 1998. "Decentralization, Participation and Accountability in Sahelian Forestry: Legal Instruments of Political-Administrative Control." Center for Population and Development Studies, Harvard University, Boston, MA.

World Bank. 1998. "Project Appraisal Document. Nicaragua. Sustainable Forestry Investment Promotion Project." Report No. 18653-NI, World Bank, Washington, DC.

———. 2004. "Implementation Completion and Results Report." Albania Forestry Project. Report No. 28783, Washington, DC.

———. 2006. *Sustaining Economic Growth, Rural Livelihoods, and Environmental Benefits: Strategic Options for Forest Assistance in Indonesia.* Jakarta, Indonesia: World Bank.

CROSS-REFERENCED CHAPTERS AND NOTES

Reforming Forest Institutions

The World Bank has increased its attention to the processes of building and rebuilding sound public institutions. With respect to forest management, institutional reforms supported by the Bank have sought to take a broad view of the value of forests for the production of timber and nontimber products, as well as for biological diversity conservation and watershed management.

Every country has a different scope, pace, and outcome associated with its reform. Reform takes time and is often implemented in a step-wise manner to minimize risks and frictions among parties. In most cases, reforms are intro-

duced within the context of revisions of forest policy, strategies, and legislation. The latter may be catalyzed by factors outside the sector, including macroeconomic and structural reforms, and should occur in a transparent and participatory manner. The second phase of reform focuses on institutional issues. Considerations in the second phase include the capacity and functions of forest institutions. At this stage, as was done in many countries in western Europe, the roles of forest administration and management may be separated.

Reform processes have covered all the key functions in the forest sector (see box 5.7), including the following:

Box 5.7   Functions of Forest Organizations

When policy makers mandate that forest organizations are to deliver on certain tasks, and when multifunctional forest management is an explicit objective of policy, forest organizations (broadly defined) can be expected to have clear functions specific to the following areas:

Policy and legislation
- policy setting
- legislation and regulation
- enforcement of the legal framework

Forest management services
- forest management and planning
- fire and pest management
- forest inventory
- forest regeneration
- management for recreational uses
- management for conservation
- management for the provision of environmental services, such as watershed protection

Other services
- sale of timber and timber products
- sale of nontimber products
- marketing services (both timber and nontimber forest products)
- socioeconomic services to local communities, derived from state-owned forests (fuelwood, nontimber forest products, grazing resources, and so forth)
- forest extension services to private owners and users

These functions can be provided by multiple organizations, both within the public sector (forest departments, commissions, agencies, and state forest enterprises) as well as outside it, by the private sector and by civil society organizations. In most countries, harvesting, transport, and processing services are provided by the private sector, though often with mixed results.

Source: World Bank 2005.

- Management of forests (state and nonstate forests)
  - Forest management operations (silviculture, regeneration, harvesting, planning, and control)
  - Sales of timber and nonwood forest products
- Processing and marketing of timber and nonwood products
- Public forest administration
  - Formulation of policy and legislation
  - Control and enforcement
  - Development of forest information systems
  - Education and research
  - Extension

OPERATIONAL ASPECTS

REFORM PROCESSES VARY. Specific steps in a reform process will vary, depending on initial conditions. To initiate reform, all actors need to cooperatively create a basic understanding of targets and strategy for forest sector management. This policy should focus on equity, sustainability, biodiversity, and economics, and should include strategic

guidance for the main actors to determine their objectives and operational methods for using the resource in a sustainable and cooperative way. The main actors are

- national and local governments;
- commercial private sector;
- communities (including Indigenous Peoples) and smallholders, including cottage industries;
- civil society; and
- technical and financial assistance institutions, including research facilities.

POST CONFLICT CONTEXTS REQUIRE ATTENTION TO CAPACITY ISSUES. In postconflict countries, the capacity of different groups to engage in dialogue may need to be strengthened. This dialogue may need to be facilitated to ensure that all stakeholders start on a level playing field; thus, the process may need to be adapted accordingly (see box 5.8).

The major implementation challenges in reforming forest institutions include organizing a temporary minimal authority structure to deal with short-term necessities,

---

Box 5.8   The Liberia Forest Initiative: Institutional Reform in a Postconflict Country

In April 2004, the U.S. government sent a team to Liberia to initiate discussions with the provisional government and civil society representatives, and came to the conclusion that Liberia's forest sector was "utterly dysfunctional" (McAlpine, O'Donohue, and Pierson 2006) and that the Forest Development Authority (FDA) required a complete overhaul and adequate capacity and resources. The unique feature of the multidonor effort that followed was that although donor roles were coordinated to avoid duplication and ensure a strategic approach, each donor maintained a high degree of sovereignty over the allocation of its funds.

The Liberia Forest Initiative (LFI) was designed to promote and assist reforms in Liberia's forestry sector to create management transparency and ensure that forest resources are managed in an economically, environmentally, and socially sustainable way, to the maximum benefit of all Liberians, in accordance with Liberia's national policies and laws, and consistent with its international legal commitments. Although it was initiated by the U.S. Department of Agriculture in 2004 in response to concerns that proceeds from unsustainable logging were fueling the ongoing civil war, the LFI quickly came to involve a wide range of governmental

and nongovernmental organizations,[a] and has come to encapsulate a broad mandate. From the outset, the LFI recognized that thorough and effective reforms would require cross-cutting attention to the "3 C's" of forestry in Liberia: the commercial sector, conservation, and community forestry. As a priority focus, however, the LFI identified a few major components as critical to bringing the commercial sector back on line and addressing essential concerns of the UN Security Council:

- *Financial management and accountability.* There was a critical need to restore transparent financial management policies and practices as well as accountability in the forest sector (in particular, to timber products) and to implement transparent and equitable allocation of resources generated by the forest sector.
- *Institution building.* An FDA with the staff, skills, and means (financial and physical) to carry out its mandate needed to be established.
- *Forest allocation policy and practice.* There was a need to plan and initiate formal forest use in a balanced,

(Box continues on the following page)

transparent manner consistent with official Liberian policy and laws as well as with international obligations, including conservation and extractive uses, that is, sustainable forest management.

- *Legitimacy.* Legitimate Liberian authorities needed to be helped to establish control over forest resources.

The institutional reforms were part of a broader forest sector reform process under way in Liberia. Recent achievements of this process include the cancellation of all concessions, preparation of a Forest Policy, preparation and ratification of a completely revised Forest Law, a vision for a long-term governance structure, and the creation of the Forest Reform Monitoring Committee.

The World Conservation Union (IUCN) took the lead in consulting civil society organizations in developing a public communications strategy, involving workshops and various media, which proved effective in conveying the importance of the work of the LFI and garnering support for measures taken. Meanwhile, the UN Security Council renewed sanctions and passed a resolution that the LFI reform recommendations be adopted. This gave impetus to reform of the concession system, and triggered a multistakeholder review committee involving civil society. Similarly, a Forest Reform Monitoring Committee was also established, with a wide spectrum of stakeholders. However, this progress was stymied by the unwillingness of the provisional government to implement the committee's recommendations, and in response the donor community developed a Governance and Economic Management Assistance Plan for state-owned enterprises, including the FDA, that would impose outside controls and transparency.

The election of Ellen Johnson Sirleaf as president was a pivotal event. On February 6, 2006, soon after her inauguration, she adopted the recommendations and reforms proposed by the LFI, including the cancellation of existing concession permits.

With support from the LFI, the FDA started to reduce staff and select key personnel for carrying out high priority tasks, such as organizing and implementing a new concession and forest management system with the help of foreign expertise; designing the structure of community forests; implementing conservation activities; and setting up the long-term reform process for the FDA, beginning with providing crucial analytical and organizational know-how for strategic planning. In addition, financial and technical services required as supporting elements for the reform needed to be identified and quantified. To initiate these activities and raise knowledge and consciousness, three workshops were held on community forestry, forest policy, and institutional reform.

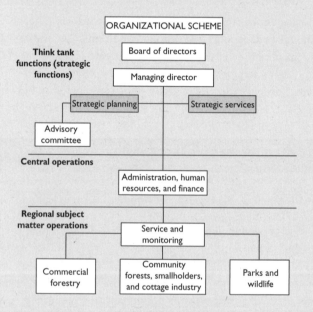

The activities in Liberia are a work in progress faced with enormous political and human resource obstacles. The future concept and structure of the FDA, proposed in October 2006 (see figure in this box) is generally accepted, but has yet to be finalized.

There are many aspects of the LFI model that could be used to create similar change in other countries, including the integration of forest sector reforms into broader governance and cross-sectoral reforms, the use of a diverse but coordinated partnership of donors, and provision for a strong role for civil society.

Source: Authors' compilation using material from http://www.fao.org/forestry/site/lfi/en/.

a. Organizations involved included the US Forest Service, the US Agency for International Development, and the US Treasury Department, as well as such NGOs as Conservation International and the Environmental Law Institute. Several multilateral organizations subsequently joined, including the World Bank, the European Commission, the Food and Agriculture Organization, the International Monetary Fund, IUCN, Centre for International Forestry Research (CIFOR), and World Agroforestry Centre (ICRAF) (LFI Web site).

such as designing a transparent concession system; establishing an accounting system; defining the role of each stakeholder in the sector; and setting up a strategic planning process to provide guidance for a future forest resource management system that is transparent, participatory, and analytical.

SEPARATING ADMINISTRATIVE AND MANAGEMENT FUNCTIONS. Efforts should be made to eliminate potential conflicts of interest and to ensure independence, transparency, and neutrality of the public forest administration. This can be done by removing direct administrative and financial links between entities responsible for public functions and state forest management (see box 5.9).

ACCOUNTABILITY OF FOREST INSTITUTIONS. A mechanism for ensuring accountability of forest institutions should be created, perhaps through the creation of a management board that supervises the activities of the entity managing state forests. The board should include representatives from different relevant government agencies or ministries, as well

as professionals with qualifications in forestry, environmental conservation, and corporate management.

Accountability also requires transparent budget procedures and accounting systems that match corporate standards (see box 5.10). These procedures, however, should be achievable and realistic.

CHANGE MANAGEMENT. A good strategy and structure are not sufficient to guarantee successful reform; it also requires people to align with the new direction, to bring life into the new structures, and to commit to strive for new goals. A strategic change-management approach can be a valuable investment for the future of an organization. Change management is a systematic approach to dealing with change from the very beginning of a change program and during all planning and implementation stages. Change management links the perspective of the organization with the perspective of the individual employee. Change management can increase the speed of implementation of a change project and decrease the costs. Effective change management requires that

---

Box 5.9   Reducing Conflict of Interest in Forest Management: An Example from Countries in Transition

In several countries in transition in Europe and Central Asia, earlier institutional arrangements in the forests sector suffered from conflicts of interest because the same body was both supervising and controlling its own operations. To remove this conflict, the proposed institutional structure separated these two functions. With this arrangement, forest administration, as part of its enforcement function, supervises and controls how forests are managed, whether owned by the state (and managed by the state forest enterprise) or by private forest owners (see box figure). A separate control activity for financial flows should also be maintained or set up, either through an independent government body or accredited private auditors, which typically are used in many Western European countries.

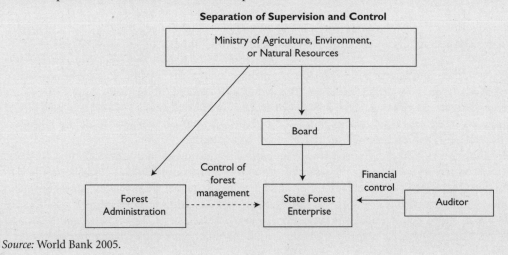

Separation of Supervision and Control

Source: World Bank 2005.

- the transformation process has leadership, top-level management commitment, and broadly based stakeholder participation;
- implementation is carried out through an independent and influential change team or steering committee;
- structure follows strategy: careful planning should set the foundation, but determination and speed are necessary for success during implementation;
- "quick win" achievable subtargets are set to help create and maintain momentum;
- people are actively engaged to build ownership from the very beginning of the change journey;
- second- and third-level management, key to success, adequately buy in; and
- communication and information, essential for both internal and external audiences, are professionally prepared.

CAPACITY CONSIDERATIONS. Reforms of forest institutions must be linked to building necessary capacity. The management objectives for service delivery organizations are to provide forest goods and services for forest industries and for households while maintaining the forest's ability to provide public goods (such as watershed protection and biodiversity conservation). Implicit in the idea of forest organi-

zations as service delivery institutions is that their services are provided to meet the demands of both private and community forest users. Some forest institutions may have the necessary capacity and simply require redeployment of these capacities. In most cases, however, the requisite capacity is not available, underscoring the importance of appropriate training.

ASSESSING SUCCESS. Measures should be in place to assess the success of institutional reforms. Measurement of success could be based on overall sectoral performance, including improved forest management, greater investment and job creation in the industry, stronger financial performance of both private and public institutions, better environmental protection, improved protected area management, and greater benefit for civil society. However, even in the best-run forest management organizations, these parameters are seldom assessed in any systematic way. Thus, innovative approaches to assessing performance must be introduced that enable policy makers to determine whether public expenditures are achieving desired outcomes (see box 5.11).

LESSONS LEARNED AND RECOMMENDATIONS

Box 5.10 Measures for Transparent Budget Procedures

Measures proposed for countries in transition in Europe and Central Asia to increase transparent budget procedures and enhance accounting systems include the following:

- To assign the responsibility for controlling forest harvesting and management to state forest administration.
- To determine appropriate funding for state forest management, physical targets for forest management and environmental conservation should be defined, and necessary investment requirements and operational costs assessed. Funding requirements may include ensuring cost efficiency of forest operations by using subcontractors from the private sector when possible; carrying out independent research on efficiency factors; establishing the transfer to the state budget based on a residual amount determined by deducting estimated costs from total

revenue (allowing efficiency gains to remain in the organization as an incentive for improved performance).
- Financial auditing through accredited third-party auditors should be arranged.
- An independent budget for the entity managing state forests should be established (to assist in increasing productivity and efficiency in state forest management). The budget should be associated with well-defined obligations toward the state budget, and development of salary schemes should be based on staff performance to reduce incentives for corruption.
- Marketing of timber and nonwood forest products based on competitive bidding should be arranged to establish fair, market-based prices; ensure open and equal access to timber and nonwood resources for potential beneficiaries at equitable conditions; and limit monopolistic features in resource supply.

Source: PROFOR 2003.

Box 5.11   Citizen Report Cards: Benchmarking Public Service Delivery

The Citizen Report Card (CRC) is a simple but powerful tool used to provide public agencies with systematic feedback from users of public services through sample surveys on service quality to enable public agencies to identify strengths and weaknesses in their work.

CRCs provide an empirical, bottom-up assessment of the reach and benefit of specific reform measures. CRCs identify the key constraints that citizens (especially the poor and the underserved) face in accessing public services and benchmark the quality and adequacy of those services as well as the effectiveness of the staff. CRCs aid in generating recommendations on sector policies, program strategy, and management of service delivery.

Citizen report cards can accomplish the following:

■ Help to convert individual problems facing the various programs into common sector issues.
■ Facilitate prioritization of reforms and corrective actions by drawing attention to the worst problems, and facilitate cross-fertilization of ideas and approaches by identifying good practices.
■ Provide a benchmark on quality of public services as experienced by the users of those services. Hence, CRCs go beyond the specific problems that individual citizens may face and view each issue from the perspective of other elements of service design and delivery, as well as in comparison with other services, so that a strategic set of actions can be initiated.
■ Suggest that dissatisfaction has causes that may be related to the quality of service (such as reliability of water supply), the type of difficulty encountered while dealing with the agency to solve service problems (such as complaints of water supply breakdown), and hidden costs in making use of the public service (such as investments in filters to purify drinking water). Therefore, CRCs delve into different aspects of performance to provide indicators of problem areas in public services.
■ Test out different options that citizens wish to exercise, individually or collectively, to tackle current problems (for example, whether citizens are willing to pay more, or be part of a group that has the responsibility for managing public water sources). Hence, CRCs are also a means for exploring alternatives for improvements in public services.

CRCs have gained credibility because the methodology involves systematic sampling across all subsections or segments—including those who are satisfied as well as the aggrieved—and presents a picture that includes all opinions.

Source: Public Affairs Foundation 2004.

FOR PRACTITIONERS

There are a number of lessons learned that merit attention in the implementation of institutional reforms:

■ The context should define the process of reform. Accordingly, it is important to distinguish between situations in countries in economic transition (for example, the Europe and Central Asia region, and China and other parts of Asia); countries recovering from crises (the Democratic Republic of Congo, Liberia), and countries responding to recent developments and having forests serve multiple functions (Kenya, Tanzania).
■ National forest policy and strategy should be the basis of institutional reforms—not vice versa.
■ Markets can be the best drivers toward sustainable forest management, but reliance on markets can be devastating if not coupled with necessary safeguards.
■ Sustainable forest management provides an appropriate framework for the assessment of policy options. Impacts should be quantified and properly evaluated before selecting the most desirable option.
■ Stakeholder participation and transparency are essential in assessing policy options and implementing institutional reforms.
■ Experience in large countries like the United States and Canada shows that decentralization in forest administration is an appropriate strategy within an adequate national legal and institutional framework, and that forestry development is best addressed at the local level (see note 5.1, Decentralized Forest Management). Decentralization reforms have to be coupled with strong organizations at the regional level and effective monitoring and control systems to prevent short-term political and economic interests from making uncontrolled use of forests and to reduce the potential for elite capture.
■ Where forests are large and diverse, a combination of institutional arrangements for forest management may

be required, including, among others, lease rights, concessions, and privatization of forest land.

■ Transaction costs tend to be high in countries where markets do not yet work effectively, corruption is common, risks and business protection costs are high, and other structural issues (uncertainties and frequent changes in taxation and other rules) increase costs to economic operators. High transaction costs significantly reduce the international competitiveness of the forestry sector and impede private investment. Institutional reforms should pay attention to the potential for reducing transaction costs.

REFERENCES CITED

McAlpine, J. L., P. A. O'Donohue, and O. Pierson. 2006. "Liberia: Forests as a Challenge and an Opportunity." *International Forestry Review* Vol. 8 (1): 83–92.

LFI. 2007. The Liberia Forest Initiative Web site. http://www. fao.org/forestry/site/ lfi/en/.

PROFOR (World Bank Program on Forests). 2003. "Institutional Changes in Forest Management: Experiences of Countries with Transition Economies, Problems and Solutions." Workshop proceedings. World Bank, Washington, DC.

Public Affairs Foundation. 2004. "Benchmarking Public Service Delivery at the Forest Fringes in Jharkhand, India." A pilot citizen report card. Unpublished. PROFOR, World Bank, Washington, DC.

World Bank. 2005. "Forest Institutions in Transition: Experiences and Lessons from Eastern Europe." Working paper no. 35153. ECSSD/PROFOR, World Bank, Washington, DC.

CROSS-REFERENCED CHAPTERS AND NOTES

Note 5.1: Decentralized Forest Management

Strengthening Legal Frameworks in the Forest Sector

The law is a powerful tool for shaping forest sector governance. Laws can create institutions and define institutional powers and responsibilities. Laws can set the bounds of acceptable behavior and set the punishment for crossing those bounds. Laws can change the allocation of money among government programs, and shift control over forest resources between central and local government and between government and other actors. Laws can define and strengthen property interests. Law can be part of the healing process that follows years of conflict (see box 5.12). In short, law plays a role in every forest governance issue (see chapter 5 for a definition of governance).

The legal framework applicable to forests has at least two areas that the World Bank may help to strengthen. The first, and most obvious, is the law itself—usually statutes and regulations—and the instruments created to operate under the law, for example, contracts. The second is the technical capacity to work within the legal system. This includes the legal knowledge of forest officers and the forest-related knowledge of legislators, prosecutors, judges, and others who help shape and implement forest laws. It also includes the capacity of citizens to understand and work under the law. Making communities, enterprises, and civil society effective users of law and active participants in its development boosts the rule of law and amplifies the benefits of improving the laws.

The usual focus of World Bank and donor legal framework projects is on the first of these areas, aiming to reform and strengthen the law. In the process, however, the projects also can strengthen capacity. For example, compiling an accurate set of the existing forest law is a first step toward writing new law, but the compilation process itself can also strengthen implementation of the present law. Public vetting of drafts of new laws is a way to improve the substance of reforms. It also gives officials hands-on training in deal-ing with the public, and gives stakeholders practical experience in policy making.

Strengthening forest legal frameworks typically requires legal advisers, but the task calls for skills that go beyond knowledge of the law. Lawyers working in concert with foresters, economists, policy experts, government officials, and stakeholders can build frameworks that promote both sustainable development and the rule of law.

OPERATIONAL ASPECTS

The ultimate goal of designing legal frameworks is to ensure the creation of responsive structures that are capable of adapting to changing needs and conditions. Writing a law that works is no easy task, and the stakes are high. A really bad effort can leave the country with a law that looks impressive but is of little practical use and may promote cynicism about government and dampen commitment to the rule of law. A really good effort can set the stage for more effective forest administration. More important, it can improve the transparency of forest governance, motivate under-represented stakeholders to get involved in forest policy, and encourage respect for the law.

Working with the law

WRITING FOREST LAWS. A good way to start is to consult two recent references on writing forest law. One, from the World Bank in collaboration with the Food and Agriculture Organization (FAO), is *Forest Law and Sustainable Development: Addressing Contemporary Challenges Through Legal Reform* (Christy, Di Leva, and Lindsay 2007). It is a comprehensive monograph on drafting forest law, with practical knowledge from experienced forest law drafters. Annex 5.3A to this note contains an outline of the monograph's contents that

Box 5.12 Reforming Forest Law in Postconflict Countries

The World Bank has supported modernization of forest law frameworks in several postconflict countries, including Cambodia, the Democratic Republic of Congo, Liberia, and Sierra Leone.

The task is sensitive because armed factions can, and do, divert forest income to support conflict. For example, in Cambodia during the early 1990s, the Khmer Rouge financed themselves through timber exports. In Liberia, the sale of timber and diamonds to fuel war was so notorious that the United Nations General Assembly placed sanctions on exports until the government could put appropriate financial controls in place (see box 5.8 in particular).

The task is challenging because it involves social as well as legal change. People who have known war and authoritarianism must embrace new ways to settle conflicts over resource use.

There are three broad avenues for settling conflicts: resort to power, as is typified in war; resort to rights, as is typified in litigation; and resort to interests, as is typified in voluntary negotiation. In most conflicts, power, rights, and interests all play some role. But in war-torn countries, rights and interests have taken a backseat to power.

Part of the healing process involves reviving the roles of rights and interests. This means promoting the rule of law, to allow people to appeal to the government to defend their rights, and it means promoting transparent and participatory government, to allow people to freely and fairly advocate their interests.

In Liberia, for example, the World Bank continues to be part of the LFI, which is assisting the government in forest sector reform. LFI supported the government's open review and resulting cancellation of existing forest concessions. Now the LFI is supporting government efforts to establish a chain-of-custody system for forest products. The system will track timber from harvest to export dock, to ensure the government collects all appropriate revenues. The LFI is also supporting development of a transparent planning system to allocate public forests among conservation, commercial, and community uses. A multistakeholder Forest Reform Monitoring Committee is vetting all reforms. The legal work includes drafting an amendment to the national forest law and regulations to support the chain-of-custody and land-use allocation systems, a new model forest concessions contract, and a model contract for community benefit sharing.

Source: Rosenbaum 2006.

---

can serve as a checklist of topics for the drafter to consider. The other reference, from the Development Law Office of FAO, is a paper listing six basic principles for forest law assistance projects (Lindsay, Mekouar, and Christy 2002). Annex 5.3B to this note contains a list from that paper of six principles for effective forest law. The ideas offered here largely come from those two sources.

Another important first step is to consider the dynamics of working with the lawyers and within a legal paradigm (see box 5.13).

Another challenge is to eliminate unnecessary regulation and circumscribe the discretion of forest officials. The motive goes both to improving governance and to reducing constraints on forest use. Layers of regulation and large amounts of official discretion create opportunities for waste and corruption. The ideal level of regulation conserves the resource while allowing people broad opportunities to enjoy resource benefits.

LIMITING POWER EXERTIONS. A further step toward good governance is to create checks on power exertion. These may include

- increased transparency, so that the press and public opinion can have a stronger influence on forest management;
- watchdog institutional structures, such as advisory boards, ombudsmen, or inspectors general;
- allowing citizen or community access to the courts to enforce rules or collect payments due the government;
- procedural steps, such as environmental impact assessments, that require the government to make a reasoned review of alternatives before taking action; and
- substantive standards in the laws to limit agency discretion.

PRACTICAL REFORMS. Finally, the legal adviser routinely faces the problem of making reforms practical. A system that is too elaborate risks overtaxing the technical capacity of a country and tying the forests down in lengthy procedures. The results may be frequent government shortcutting of the laws and resulting loss of the rule of law. Alternatively, the government could try to live by the letter of the law and end up mired in process, leading people to seek access to the forest through illegal means (see note 5.5, Addressing Illegal Logging). Practicality may demand simpler requirements or

Box 5.13   Working on the Law with Lawyers

Team leaders unaccustomed to working on laws with lawyers may wonder what to expect. Here are a few notes based on project experience.

Legal projects often require more than one lawyer because projects cross legal disciplines. A national consultant typically supplies essential knowledge of the existing national legal framework, while an international consultant brings knowledge of other areas, such as international standards, approaches to forest law reform, or legislative drafting.

Plan to give the lawyers some time to build working relationships with each other and with the team. The international consultant will need to learn about the existing national legal framework. The national consultant may need to learn about forest law. Both will need to gain a full grasp of the local forest context and the policy that the team is advocating that the government adopt.

Some team leaders worry whether lawyers will work well with technical advisers. Usually this is not a problem. The lawyer's role in society is to bridge people and the law, and to do that, the lawyer must be able to work with others on their own terms.

Still, technical advisers may find the process of legal reform to be novel and challenging. Just as writing a technical paper requires the writer to come to terms with the exact ideas that the writer wants to convey, writing a law requires the policy maker to come to terms with exactly what the policy means. Writing a law demands detailed consideration of practicalities and processes that might be glossed over in discussing the broader outlines of a policy.

Also, the law may require technical advisers to learn new terms and use old terms in new ways. A common example is the word "forest." To the forester, this may mean land bearing or capable of bearing tree cover. Strangely, the scientific definition may have little utility in the law, which might define forests in terms of land that the government has reserved or has placed in a particular class in a cadastral survey. In the end, these definitions are just tools for the accomplishment of particular tasks, and each task calls for the appropriate tool. The task of scientific forest management calls for the science-based definition, whereas efficient governance calls for the administratively derived definition.

Technical advisers may find legal language complex or awkward. At times, a legal drafter will sacrifice clarity in pursuit of precision. A good lawyer, with enough time, can be simple, clear, and precise. A lawyer faced with deadlines, or one who needs to follow old, complex phrasing to ensure that the local courts will interpret the new words like the old, may fall short of the ideal. Lawyers can be particular about language—words are their stock and trade. During training and practice, a lawyer encounters dozens or even hundreds of examples of inadvisably chosen words leading to legal disputes. Do not be surprised if a lawyer heavily edits any nonlawyer's attempts at legal drafting or if the lawyer suggests to others that they simply explain the policy more fully and leave the legal drafting to the lawyers.

Finally, some scientifically trained advisers are taken aback by the way lawyers think:

- A scientist is trained to look for truth, derived from objective facts. A lawyer is trained to advocate for what is good, often influenced by subjective values. Any practical adviser knows that good policy requires consideration of both facts and values. But the lawyer's focus on what is good can sometimes make the lawyer seem callous to the facts, just as a scientist's focus on what is true can sometimes make the scientist seem callous to human values.

- A scientist is taught to see the world through a lens of logic: induction and deduction. A lawyer is taught logic but also learns that law grows out of history: from precedent, politics, and practical experience. In fact, to the law, sometimes "a page of history is worth a volume of logic."[a]

- A scientist is taught to look for the mean: the average or expected. A lawyer is taught to think about the outliers: the criminal in society, the loophole in the law, the rare contingency that the law must anticipate, a precedent that might be set.

- A scientist sees proof as a matter of statistics. That which, 19 times out of 20, cannot be the result of chance alone is considered a significant event. A lawyer sees proof as a function of legal context. Some things may be presumed true before knowing any facts; some may be taken as true if they are more likely than not; some may only be considered true if they cannot reasonably be considered false.

These disciplinary differences are usually not as daunting as the cultural differences that project teams must bridge. As with cultural differences, the key is to be aware of your own practices and to be open to the practices of others.

Source: Rosenbaum 2006.
a. United States Supreme Court Justice Oliver Wendell Holmes, Jr., writing the opinion of the Court in *New York Trust Co. v. Eisner*, 256 U.S. 345, 345 (1921).

requirements that phase in over time, so that the government and forest users have the opportunity to adapt to the new regulatory system.

Improving capacity and law through good process

The process of reforming the law often gives the World Bank opportunities to address the other avenue of strengthening legal frameworks: increasing the legal capacity of government and stakeholders. These activities can be synergistic.

COMPILING EXISTING FOREST LAWS. A first step in legal reform is to compile the texts of the existing forest laws and, often, also property, administrative, criminal, and other general laws that affect forest management. In some countries, no one will have seen such a collection before. The forest laws may have been amended many times over the years, but no one may have published a version with all the amendments. The government may have produced many forest regulations but never have organized them into a single collection. The officials in the field charged with implementing and enforcing the law may have little idea what it looks like, and the forest-dependent people affected by the law may have no easy way to know what the law is.

UNDERSTAND LEGAL CONTEXT AND LEGAL PRACTICE LINKED TO FORESTS. A second step is to investigate the legal context of the country and the legal practices associated with the forests. This may expose any number of legal capacity issues, directly or indirectly linked to reform of the law. For example, forest officers may lack an understanding of basic policing skills and may not be properly preserving evidence of unlawful activities. Prosecutors and judges may lack a basic understanding of forest issues and may not be giving proper weight to the suppression of forest crimes. Land records may be incomplete or nonexistent, making it difficult to determine tenure rights. A law reform project is seldom tasked with addressing problems like these, but it can flag them for other projects and donors to address.

The most important capacity-building effort of a law reform project is typically also the most important step in improving the substance of the law: vetting proposals for the new law with government officials and local stakeholders.

LESSONS LEARNED AND RECOMMENDATIONS FOR PRACTITIONERS

THE FOREST LEGAL FRAMEWORK MUST BE RESPONSIVE TO CHANGE. History teaches that the social demands on the forest are slowly but constantly changing, and no one can possibly anticipate all the situations that will come before the law. It follows that for the legal framework to function, it must have flexibility.

INCENTIVES AND FEEDBACK MECHANISMS. Experience has demonstrated that the best legal systems achieve their goals through structures that contain incentive and feedback mechanisms. The hallmarks of those systems are transparency, accountability, and public participation. The true art of legal reform is to create a framework that is consistent with social change but that also drives institutions to change, striving for better governance of the forest.

REFLECTING CURRENT VALUES IS IMPORTANT. Forest law reform efforts typically share some common challenges. One is incorporating modern values into forest laws. Forestry as a profession has long embraced sustainability, but notions of what resources the forester must conserve have changed as society's knowledge and interests have changed. Now society may be as interested in biodiversity conservation and carbon sequestration as in fuel and fiber production, and ideally governments want their laws to reflect current values.

Values determine not only what resources the forester should conserve but who should have access to those resources. The present trend is greater recognition of indigenous, aboriginal, traditional, and community uses, which centralized forest management agencies have often marginalized. Writing modern standards that can coexist with uncodified traditional rights and expectations can be difficult. The drafter is often tempted to focus on commercial, large-scale forest use, but slighting traditional uses can promote conflict and disrupt forest-dependent communities. A project that hopes to combat poverty and promote the welfare of rural forest communities must consider their expectations and rights, including the particular rights of Indigenous Peoples (see note 1.3, Indigenous Peoples and Forests).

INVOLVE STAKEHOLDERS. Involving the public almost always strengthens the legal framework. Reviewers with multiple interests and perspectives shed new light on problems, exposing issues that a drafter listening only to government foresters might miss. Involvement also gives the public a sense of ownership of the law. A group that participates in the democratic process of lawmaking is more likely to respect the law than a group that has the law imposed upon them without consultation.

In addition, the process of public vetting builds capacity, both in the government and among stakeholders. Legislators and other elected officials bolster their knowledge of forest policy. Forest administrators, who often carry responsibility within the government for producing the first formal drafts of the law, learn how to tap stakeholder input. Being able to conduct a meeting where citizens feel respected and heard is a surprisingly rare skill. The technical skills of foresters often outweigh their social skills, but forest administrators have to master the social and political demands of public outreach. For their part, citizens, businesses, and civil society organizations must learn how to be effective participants, and like the government officials, they must learn to listen and not just make speeches. In the best of circumstances, all sides build trust, forge lines of communication, and learn patterns of dispute resolution that will continue to serve them for years after the new law is enacted, while the government implements the law (see box 5.12 for more about conflict and legal reform).

SELECTED READINGS

Christy, L., C. Di Leva, and J. Lindsay. 2007. *Forest Law and Sustainable Development: Addressing Contemporary Challenges Through Legal Reform.* Washington, DC: World Bank, in collaboration with the Food and Agriculture Organization of the United Nations.

Lindsay, J., A. Mekouar, and L. Christy. 2002. "Why Law Matters: Design Principles for Strengthening the Role of Forestry Legislation in Reducing Illegal Activities and Corrupt Practices." FAO Legal Papers Online #27, FAO, Rome, Italy. http://www.fao.org/legal/prs-ol/lpo27.pdf.

REFERENCES CITED

Christy, L., C. Di Leva, and J. Lindsay. 2007. *Forest Law and Sustainable Development: Addressing Contemporary Challenges Through Legal Reform.* Washington, DC: World Bank, in collaboration with the FAO.

Lindsay, J., A. Mekouar, and L. Christy. 2002. "Why Law Matters: Design Principles for Strengthening the Role of Forestry Legislation in Reducing Illegal Activities and Corrupt Practices." FAO Legal Papers Online #27, FAO, Rome, Italy. http://www.fao.org/legal/prs-ol/lpo27.pdf.

Rosenbaum, K. 2006. "Strengthening Legal Frameworks in the Forest Sector." Note submitted to World Bank as input to *Forests Sourcebook.* Unpublished. World Bank, Washington, DC.

CROSS-REFERENCED CHAPTERS AND NOTES

Note 1.3: Indigenous Peoples and Forests

Chapter 5: Improving Forest Governance

Note 5.1: Decentralized Forest Management

Note 5.5: Addressing Illegal Logging

ANNEX 5.3A   A CHECKLIST OF POTENTIAL ISSUES FOR THE FOREST LAW ADVISER

Note that in a given project, not every issue will rise to the point of demanding legal reform. This annex is based on Christy, Di Leva, and Lindsay (2007).

Tenure

Recognizing traditional and customary rights
Providing for rapid adjudication of disputed
   boundaries and claims
Delineating private property rights

Public forest management

Setting primary management goals beyond production
   of economic goods
Establishing inventory and planning requirements, with
   environmental impact assessments
Controlling concessions

Private forest management

Simplifying commercial regulation
Setting environmental standards

Decentralization and devolution of authority

(See note 5.1, Decentralized Forest Management)
Setting rules for community forestry
Delineating powers of local governments over forests
Public participation and transparency
   Requiring public access to agency plans, rules, and
      guidance
   Allowing public participation in agency planning,
      rule-making, and enforcement
   Creating efficient conflict resolution mechanisms
   Requiring public officials to disclose financial
      interests

Sustainability and environmental protection

Promoting noncommercial uses and values, such as
   environmental services
Creating reserves and parks
Creating standards or incentives for private forest
   stewardship

Commerce and trade

Regulating domestic transport and sales
Regulating mills and other processing of forest products
Regulating international trade associated with forests

Finance and taxation

Setting taxes and fees
Providing for collection of taxes and fees
Establishing dedicated uses of forest income, such as
   forest funds

Institutional reform

Establishing roles of ministerand forest agency
Assigning roles among competing ministries
Enhancing the public's role
Establishing commissions and advisory bodies
Defining the role of state forest corporations

Offenses and enforcement

Delineating the enforcement powers of officers
Defining criminal offenses and determining associated
   penalties
Defining civil wrongs and setting the associated
   measures of damages
Setting the process for prosecuting or compounding
   offenses
Setting rules of evidence and proof

ANNEX 5.3B   SIX DRAFTING PRINCIPLES FOR CREATING BETTER FOREST LAWS

From Lindsay, Mekouar, and Christy (2002).

Principle 1: Avoid legislative overreach

The new law should match the capacity, needs, and social context of the country.

Principle 2: Avoid unnecessary, superfluous, or cumbersome licensing and approval requirements

These can stifle private sector forest use. Do not create these without good cause.

Principle 3: Include provisions that enhance the transparency and accountability of forest decision-making processes

A broad range of mechanisms are available to accomplish transparency and accountability, including specific limits on the exercise of government discretion, requirements to seek public comment on plans and decisions, access to information rules, oversight bodies, and citizen access to the courts.

Principle 4: Enhance the stake of local nongovernment actors in the sustainable management of forests

The trend around the world is toward more local control of forest resources. The law can guarantee local actors secure rights while also granting them some flexibility in how they exercise those rights.

Principle 5: The drafting of law needs to be a broadly participatory process

Public participation improves the substance of law, and the process helps build support for law.

Principle 6: Increase the effectiveness of direct law enforcement mechanisms set forth in forestry legislation

Reformers should pay attention to both the penalties and the processes of law enforcement.

Strengthening Fiscal Systems in the Forestry Sector

Fiscal instruments encompass a wide range of mechanisms by which money flows between public and private sector institutions involved in the forestry sector. Flows from the private sector to the public sector (forest charges) can be broadly categorized as taxes, royalties, fees, and fines. Financial flows in the other direction (incentives) include tax incentives, grants, subsidies, and subsidized loans. Other fiscal instruments include temporary measures (such as performance bonds) and direct intervention by the state (for example, joint ventures, public shareholding, state marketing boards, and price restrictions). All of these instruments have different strengths and weaknesses (see box 5.14) and deciding on the right mix of instruments depends on the objectives that the forestry policy maker wishes to achieve.

The main objectives of fiscal instruments in the forestry sector are the same as in other parts of government. The two most important are to raise money for the state and to cover the costs of forest administration. In addition, a distinction should be made between raising revenue from the use of the forest resource (royalties) and general revenue collection (taxes).

Fiscal instruments (charges and incentives) can also be used as tools for policy implementation, either to promote

---

Box 5.14   Common Problems with Fiscal Systems in the Forestry Sector

Fiscal systems in the forestry sector generally suffer from three similar problems:

Inadequate rent capture. Charges for the harvesting of publicly owned forest resources often do not capture the full commercial value of the harvested products. Charges are often set administratively and are not updated frequently, so they rarely reflect true market values. The main consequence is that these artificially low prices distort markets, discourage efficient use of the resource, and result in lost revenues to the state. Inadequate charges may also encourage corruption, if government officials can capture some of the uncollected rent for themselves during the process of monitoring, controlling, and approving forestry activities.

Complexity. Fiscal systems in the forestry sector are often complicated, as a result of administrative processes (setting and collecting forest charges, for instance) that attempt to replicate market forces by the use of detailed schedules of charges according to product type, tree species, forest location, and total area of production. The main consequence is that such systems are often expensive to administer and administration costs can account for a high proportion of total revenue collected. Complexity may also present more opportunities for corruption.

Perverse or unintended effects. Fiscal systems also often have unintended effects, particularly with respect to environmental and social aspects of forest management. Incorrect pricing often leads to poor harvesting practices (for example, selective harvesting rather than harvesting of all commercial trees, thus leaving large amounts of roundwood as waste in the forest). Fiscal systems are also sometimes inequitable, especially where harvesting activities impose costs on people living in and around forests but provide them few benefits.

Source: Whiteman 2006.

forestry policy or to promote other government policies. Forestry policy objectives largely center on sustainable forest management (that is, the promotion of good forest practices and deterrence of bad practices). Broader policy objectives can include income redistribution, correction of externalities (nonmarket costs and benefits), strengthening of legal compliance, and encouragement of economic development (for example, through the creation of income, employment, and value added).

Three other issues should also be considered in the design of any system of fiscal instruments:

- *Economic efficiency.* Fiscal instruments often result in market distortions (they alter the costs and prices of inputs and outputs in the sector). These should be minimized wherever possible, unless introduction of such distortions is a specific policy objective.
- *Administrative efficiency.* The public costs of enforcement and the private costs of compliance with the fiscal policy should be appraised and minimized wherever possible.
- *Equity.* The impact of fiscal instruments on different income groups should be considered. All groups should face the same set of charges and incentives, unless income redistribution is an objective of the fiscal policy (to assist with poverty reduction, for instance) (see box 5.15).

OPERATIONAL ASPECTS

TECHNICAL AND POLICY CONSIDERATIONS CAN SHAPE FISCAL INSTRUMENTS. Fiscal instruments employed in the forestry sector encompass a wide range of different types of forest charges (see annex 5.4A to this note) and incentives. Operational aspects of the design of fiscal systems in the forestry sector fall into two broad categories. The first includes technical considerations, such as setting the correct level of charges and incentives and designing a system that is efficient and equitable. The second includes policy-related considerations: Does the system promote good forest management, good governance, and poverty alleviation? Box 5.16 presents a brief summary of some of these issues, which are further elaborated upon in this note.

SETTING FOREST CHARGES CORRECTLY. To ensure that forest charges are economically efficient and do not introduce unintended distortions in the markets for forest products, the correct levels of forest charges must be established. Because charges for services and materials (fees) should reflect their costs, and general taxes are largely outside the control of forestry administrations, the main concern of forestry administrations is usually to establish the correct level of royalty payments (that is, payments for the use of the resource).

Box 5.15 Informal Competition for Harvesting Rights in Fiji

Most natural forest resources in Fiji are owned by local communities (native landowners), but monitoring and control of forest harvesting is performed by the Forestry Department. The Forestry Department, along with the Native Land Trust Board, assesses and collects a variety of royalties and fees. Some of this revenue is retained by the two organizations to cover their administrative costs, but the majority of the revenue collected is distributed to individuals in local communities where harvesting has occurred.

To gain access to forest resources, forest operators have to obtain a license from the Forestry Department and (at least informal) approval from local communities where they wish to harvest. As part of the negotiations with local communities, it has become common practice for potential license holders to offer additional benefits (monetary or in kind, known as "commissions" or "goodwill") to communities where the harvesting will occur. Because of the infrequent revision of

royalty rates, these additional payments can be almost as much as the revenue collected through the royalty system.

Analysis of the total amount of revenue collection has shown that almost all the rent from forest operations is collected and that about 85 percent of this is paid to local communities (with the remainder retained equally between the Forestry Department, the Native Land Trust Board, and the forest operator). This high level of rent collection is no doubt due to the presence of the informal market mechanism on top of the official forest revenue system.

The success of this system is due to the following factors: a high level of competition for the resource; well-informed communities with a long tradition of community rights; a strong legal framework and institutions to support local communities; and the creation of an established norm to make informal payments on top of official royalties and fees.

Source: Whiteman 2005.

In theory, the royalty payment for roundwood harvested from the forest should equal the price that would be paid for standing trees (stumpage value) if they were sold in a competitive market. This price can be calculated as the value of the roundwood at the port or processing plant (determined by species, quality, product prices, and the efficiency of processing plants), less the costs of harvesting, extraction, and transport (determined by the efficiency of the producer and location-specific factors, such as terrain, forest stocking, and transport distance).

Royalty payments can be established through competitive means, such as competitive bidding in auctions or tenders, or they can be set by the forestry administration. In the latter case, consultation, negotiation, or calculation of the stumpage value (as described above), can be used to set the payment.

Because of the effort involved, infrequent revaluation of royalties is a major problem in many countries, although some countries regularly alter royalties according to predetermined formulae (for example, taking into account price indexes for the main operational costs and forest product prices). Another difficulty with setting royalties administratively is obtaining reliable information about costs and prices for the calculation of stumpage values. In addition, information about forest stocking is sometimes needed to calculate appropriate royalties (especially where royalties will be collected using area-based charges).

Traditionally, competitive mechanisms have mostly been used to establish royalties for relatively small, short-term sales of standing trees (especially from forest plantations). Royalties on production from longer, large-scale forest concessions have more commonly been established using administrative means. However, it is possible to combine both methods for forest concessions by, for example, setting volume- and area-based charges according to a predetermined formula and using a bidding process to set a license charge (World Bank 2003).

FISCAL INCENTIVES. Fiscal incentives are a subset of a broad range of measures that encourage others to act (FAO 2004). Incentives are most commonly used to promote activities that result in net nonmarket benefits (that is, production of goods and services, usually social and environmental, that have no value in the marketplace and are not, therefore, a source of revenue for the forest owner). In many countries, incentives are used to promote tree planting and afforestation in general, with a broad assumption that these actions will usually lead to net nonmarket benefits. However, with the development of payments for environmental services (PES) and funding mechanisms to support international conventions, incentives are gradually becoming more accurately targeted toward specific activities that result in specific nonmarket benefits (for further details, see note 2.3, Innovative Marketing Arrangements for Environmental Services).

The most common fiscal incentives in the forestry sector are reductions in forest charges (for example, provision of materials or services by the forestry administration at low cost or reductions in taxes and forest charges if operators build processing facilities). Other incentives include direct transfers from the public to the private sector if operators undertake certain activities (grants or subsidized loans for afforestation, training, or forest industry development, for instance). As with forest charges, effectiveness, efficiency, and equity are important issues that should be addressed as part of the design of any forestry incentive scheme.

TARGETING INCENTIVE SCHEMES. With respect to effectiveness, incentive schemes should be properly targeted toward both the objectives that it sets out to achieve and the individuals or institutions that it aims to influence. In this respect, it is generally better to offer direct transfers to support specific activities in the forestry sector rather than to reduce forest charges as an incentive.

Targeting and establishing the correct level of incentives are also important to achieving economic efficiency. Incentives should only be offered to support activities that result in net nonmarket benefits and the efficient level of incentives will be that which reflects the level of those benefits (as opposed to the cost of the relevant activities). Common problems in this area include the following:

- *Overpayment of incentives.* Overpayment occurs where a flat-rate subsidy or grant payment is used to encourage an activity. Inevitably, some recipients of such payments will receive more than would be necessary to make them undertake these activities. The difference between what is paid and what would be required is sometimes referred to as the deadweight of the incentive. This can be minimized by using competitive tendering for specific activities rather than flat-rate grant schemes.
- *Non-additionality.* This is an extreme form of deadweight, where recipients are paid to do something that they would have done anyway (without any incentive). This often occurs where an incentive is given to do something that is already required by law (for example, fiscal incentives to promote industry development where concessionaires are already required to build processing facilities as part of their concession agreements).
- *Displacement.* Displacement occurs when an incentive results in a change in behavior but little or no increase in the total amount of the desired activity. It is often associated with location-specific incentives, such as grants for tree planting that result in changes in the location of tree planting but little increase in total tree planting.

The issues just mentioned are starting to gain the attention of policy makers (for example, in the rules and procedures for investments for credits under the Kyoto Protocol) and again, direct transfers (as opposed to forest charge reductions) are likely to offer a better opportunity to improve targeting and efficiency.

POLITICAL CONSIDERATIONS. Fiscal policies in the forestry sector have a huge impact on the success of forestry policy. In addition, the administration of fiscal instruments often accounts for a significant proportion of the forestry administration's functions. Consequently, it is essential that fiscal policies support policy objectives and are administratively feasible.

Political consensus and broad stakeholder support must be built for fiscal policies in the forestry sector to be successfully reformed. An approach to revenue collection based on a social contract between government and the public, rather than coercion, is likely to be more sustainable in the long run. Consultation, transparency, and public disclosure of information during the establishment and collection of forest charges is likely to build support for the process and reduce the possibility for vested interests to block reforms. Coordination with policy makers in other parts of government should also assist in this respect.

ADMINISTRATIVE CONSIDERATIONS. Administration of fiscal instruments should be based on a stable framework, supported by legislation, that establishes the basic principles and procedures for forest charges and incentives but, at the same time, allows the forestry administration the flexibility to revise the instruments when required (in response to changing market conditions, for instance). The infrequency of revisions to forest charges is often a result of the requirement that the changes only happen through legislation. Thus, it is better to use primary legislation to establish the mechanisms and procedures that will be used to set forest charges, with appropriate mechanisms for regular reviews, oversight, and consultation.

In practical terms, fiscal instruments should be simple to administer and easy to enforce, and should minimize the need for discretion or judgment by forestry administration staff. A simple forest revenue system that can be easily enforced will be better than a more complicated system that is easy to evade. Where evasion is high, the partial enforcement of revenue collection can have a significantly detrimental impact on the equity of the forest revenue system and is likely to result in little public support for the forestry administration.

POVERTY ALLEVIATION CONSIDERATIONS. Because poverty alleviation is a major national priority in most developing countries, forestry policy (including fiscal systems in the forestry sector) should be designed with this in mind (see chapter 1, Forests for Poverty Reduction, and associated notes). Subsidies and other fiscal policies for nonforest activities can distort the incentive structure for community-based forest management. Government policies regarding revenue from taxes and fees on forest products and concessions can also undermine indigenous communities' interests in and claims on forest resources.

To make fiscal systems more advantageous to poor people, decision makers should gather and analyze information on the impacts of various policy and management options on the livelihoods of people living in and around the forest, for example,

- the ways in which commercial forest harvesting affects the availability of wildlife, nonwood forest products, and other forest services used by local people;
- the effect of protected areas or bans on hunting and collection of nonwood forest products on local livelihoods;
- the value of fuelwood and nonwood forest products lost if a degraded forest area were to be converted to planted forest; or
- the beneficiaries of financial incentives with regard to planted forest development.

NONFINANCIAL CONSIDERATIONS: In addition to the financial costs and benefits to forest owners and other stakeholders, nonfinancial aspects must also be considered. Many of these are local and can be detrimental to poor people, including degradation of soil and water resources, loss of access, and degradation or loss of forests that have cultural or spiritual value.

Fiscal systems that appear to be fair to stakeholders at the national level may have negative effects on poor communities if those communities bear the burden of some costs, but do not share the benefits of forest management. Thus, fiscal systems can attempt to compensate for some of these effects through revenue- or benefit-sharing arrangements (see below) or can be combined with incentives to support local participation in forest management or regulations to minimize the negative impacts of forest management on communities.

REVENUE SHARING. A recent trend in many countries is the development of revenue sharing or revenue retention mechanisms, or both. Revenue sharing occurs when part or all of the public revenue from forest operations is shared with individuals or local levels of government (usually in locations where production occurs). Revenue retention occurs where the forestry administration keeps some or all of the revenue collected and uses it to fund their operations.

The earmarking or hypothecation of government revenue is generally not recommended because it goes against the principle of good public financing that public revenue should be collected according to ability to pay and disbursed according to need. However, revenue sharing is often proposed as a mechanism to generate local support for forest protection and use. Revenue sharing and revenue retention are also suggested in situations where disbursement of public funds is slow and unpredictable.

Although the use of revenue sharing should generally be minimized, the above arguments may sometimes be valid. If so, the following should be considered:

- *Governance and administrative capability.* Any decision to automatically share revenue with lower levels of government (or communities) should consider whether the scheme will result in the desired effect. Lower levels of government are likely to have less capability to manage funds and, in particular, may be less qualified to properly assess and collect forest charges. In addition, it should not be automatically assumed that lower levels of government are more responsive to local people's needs (see note 5.1, Decentralized Forest Management).
- *Property rights.* In some countries, forest resources are managed by the government on behalf of local people (for example, where local communities own the land under forests or own the forests entirely). In such cases, revenue sharing is appropriate and the amount of revenue shared with local people should be determined on the basis of the value of their property rights.
- *Community forest management.* In some countries, complete (or nearly complete) control over forest management has been delegated to local communities. In such circumstances, the role of the forestry administration should be as a facilitator, to ensure that best practices in revenue collection are followed and to build capacity in local governance and administrative capability (see note 1.2, Community-Based Forest Management).
- *Forest administrations as service providers.* If the forestry administration is providing a good or service, it is performing the function of a state-owned enterprise and it

is reasonable to allow the administration to retain the revenue from charges it collects from such activities. Similarly, it is acceptable for forestry administrations to retain some revenue to cover the costs of administering the forest revenue system, when the costs of doing so can be clearly identified and quantified.

Revenue sharing is not a panacea for problems of weak governance and administration in the forestry sector at the national level. As with other aspects of fiscal policy in the forestry sector, any decision to implement revenue sharing should be based on a robust appraisal of what the problems are and how revenue sharing might address these problems.

LESSONS LEARNED AND RECOMMENDATIONS FOR PRACTITIONERS

Based on the lessons learned from countries' experiences with fiscal instruments, the following are recommendations for best practice in this area.

Policy and administration

- Fiscal policies in the forestry sector should support forestry policy objectives and the broader objectives of government. Negative impacts on efficiency and equity should be minimized.
- Fiscal policy reform requires political support and some degree of consensus and should not be viewed as a purely technical issue. Open debate and transparency in the procedures for revising and implementing fiscal policy are necessary to build this support.
- Administration of fiscal instruments should be as simple as possible and calculation of forest charges should be based on objective criteria. The need for discretion or judgment by field staff responsible for assessing and collecting charges should be minimized.
- The general framework for fiscal policies should be established in primary legislation, but forestry administrations should be empowered to revise the details of implementation. Automatic and regular reviews of fiscal instruments should be implemented according to clearly defined, rigorous, and objective processes and procedures.

Defining the mixture and level of fiscal instruments

- Wherever possible, market mechanisms should be used to establish the levels of charges and incentives rather than administrative means.

- When charges and incentives are set administratively, they should be based on a rigorous and objective calculation of costs and benefits. In particular, forest charges should be based on independent or aggregate information about forest product prices, and charges levied on individual operators should not be based on stated prices. Incentives should be based on the benefits of activities that are being encouraged rather than their cost.
- Incentives should be used to achieve clearly defined policy objectives; they should be properly targeted and regularly evaluated. Incentives in the form of direct transfers will generally be more successful than reductions in forest charges. Incentives should also be structured to maximize net benefit and minimize deadweight, nonadditionality, and displacement.
- There is a tradeoff between administrative efficiency and economic efficiency in fiscal instruments. More complicated instruments tend to be more economically efficient but more expensive to administer. Numerous charges should be avoided (especially where they are levied on the same item). However, in general, a mixture of different types of charges may be optimal. Thus, countries should not rely on volume-based charges alone, but should consider greater use of area-based charges and license charges.

Revenue sharing

- In general, hypothecation of forest revenue is not good practice in public finance and should be avoided. However, under some specific circumstances it can be justified. The first is where local people or communities have clearly defined property rights over some or part of the forest resource. The second is where the forestry administration is collecting charges to recoup costs for the provision of a good or service (which can include the cost of administering the forest revenue system). In such cases, revenue sharing should be based on an objective appraisal of the amount of revenue that should be shared or retained.
- Little evidence supports the hypothesis that revenue sharing alone will result in improved forest protection by local communities. In situations where conflict with local communities is an issue, it may be preferable to devolve complete responsibility for forest management (including revenue collection) to local communities. In such cases, the forestry administration's role becomes that of a service provider, to ensure that best practices in revenue collection and administration are followed.

- Any proposal to implement revenue sharing should consider local governance and the administrative capability of local communities or lower levels of government to implement such systems. Where governance and administration at the national level are weak, the situation is likely to be even worse at lower levels of government.

SELECTED READINGS

Gray, J. A. 1983. *Forest Revenue Systems in Developing Countries: Their Role in Income Generation and Forest Management Strategies.* Forestry Paper No. 43. Rome: Food and Agriculture Organization of the United Nations.

IUCN. 2000. *Financing Protected Areas: Guidelines for Protected Area Managers.* Best Practice Protected Area Guidelines Series No, 5. Gland, Switzerland: IUCN.

World Bank. 2003. "Proceedings of the International Workshop 'Reforming Forest Fiscal Systems to Promote Poverty Reduction, and Sustainable Forest Management.'" Washington, DC, October 19–21. PROFOR at the World Bank, Washington, DC.

REFERENCES CITED

FAO (Food and Agriculture Organization). 2004. *What Does it Take? The Role of Incentives in Forest Plantation Development in Asia and the Pacific.* RAP Publication 2004/27. Bangkok: FAO.

Gray, J. A. 1983. *Forest Revenue Systems in Developing Countries: Their Role in Income Generation and Forest Management Strategies.* Forestry Paper No. 43. Rome: FAO.

Whiteman, A. 2005. "A Review of the Forest Revenue System and Taxation of the Forestry Sector in Fiji." Forest Finance Working Paper FSFM/MISC/10. FAO, Rome.

———. 2006. "Strengthening Fiscal Systems in the Forestry Sector." Note submitted to World Bank as input to *Forests Sourcebook.* Unpublished. World Bank. Washington, DC.

World Bank. 2003. "Proceedings of the International Workshop 'Reforming Forest Fiscal Systems to Promote Poverty Reduction, and Sustainable Forest Management.'" Washington, DC, October 19–21. PROFOR at the World Bank, Washington, DC.

CROSS-REFERENCED CHAPTERS AND NOTES

Chapter 1: Forests for Poverty Reduction, and associated notes

Note 2.3: Innovative Marketing Arrangements for Environmental Services

Note 5.1: Decentralized Forest Management

ANNEX 5.4A A SUMMARY OF THE DIFFERENT TYPES OF CHARGES USED IN FISCAL SYSTEMS IN THE FORESTRY SECTOR

Gray (1983) lists different types of forest charges commonly used in the forestry sector. In addition to these, fines can also be considered a type of forest charge. A summary of the main features of 12 different types of forest charges is given below:

- *License charges.* License charges are a type of royalty or fee to cover the administrative cost of issuing licenses. They are usually lump-sum payments that may vary by the license area or duration and can be collected at the start of a license or annually. To be economically efficient, license charges should reflect the value of the security of wood supply conferred to the license holder or should cover the cost of administering the license (or a combination of the two). They may also be used to capture some of the value of production (that is, they may be part of the royalty on production) if this is not fully reflected in other charges. The costs of collection and administration are low and these charges are difficult to evade, so they are administratively efficient. License charges tend to have little impact on equity, but they can be used to redistribute income (by setting lower license charges for smaller operators, for instance). License charges are quite common in the forestry sector.

- *Annual area charges.* These charges are usually a type of royalty and are calculated as a fixed amount multiplied by the whole license area. Annual area charges are generally easy to administer and have little impact on equity. They can be economically efficient (that is, they can reflect the value of wood production), but it is often difficult to assess the correct level of charges because of the need for detailed information about forest stocking. Consequently, area charges are often used in combination with volume-based charges to collect royalties.

- *Charges based on standing volume, allowable cut, or property values.* These charges can be a type of royalty or can be used for general tax collection, or both. They are usually calculated as a fixed amount multiplied by standing volume or allowable cut or are related to property values. They are generally administratively efficient and have little impact on equity, but economic efficiency suffers from the same problems noted with annual area charges. The use of such charges as a component of royalty collection is not common, but these charges are sometimes used as a form of income tax on forest owners (mostly in developed countries).

- *Charges based on the area logged.* These charges are very similar to annual area charges, but are based on the area logged rather than the total license area. The main difference is that it is sometimes difficult to determine the area that has been logged. These charges are not commonly used.

- *Volume-based charges.* Volume-based charges are the most common type of royalty and are calculated by multiplying the volume harvested by a price. The prices used in this calculation can be derived in a variety of ways. A simpler version of this is per tree charges (where the number of trees is multiplied by a price). These charges can be economically efficient if the price reflects the true value of the wood produced, which is often not the case. The administrative efficiency of volume-based charges is often low because considerable effort (and cost) is required to monitor the level of production and to establish the correct price levels to use. Volume-based charges can be inequitable because they are often the same for all producers and do not account for location-specific differences in production costs (such as terrain or distance to market). However, they can be used as a policy tool, by adjusting charges to reflect policy objectives (for example, by deliberately lowering charges on lesser known species to encourage their use).

- *Charges on production of forest products.* These charges are similar to volume-based charges but are charged on the output of processed forest products and nonwood forest products. They are common and can be collected in addition to or in place of volume-based charges on roundwood. They can be used to support policy objectives (by deliberately setting low charges for nonwood forest products to promote rural income generation, for instance).

- *Charges on exports.* Charges on exports can be collected from exports of roundwood or processed forest products and are used in many countries. They have similar strengths and weaknesses to the charges on production of forest products but are generally more administratively efficient (because monitoring is usually easier and costs less). The purpose of such charges can be to collect additional royalties or general tax collection. A combination of low volume-based charges and export charges on roundwood is frequently used to promote domestic processing of roundwood by deliberately distorting the market (that is, reducing the domestic roundwood price to less than the international trade price).

- *Fees for services or materials provided.* These charges are common and are payments for services or materials provided by the forestry administration. They may or may not be voluntary, depending on whether the operator has a choice to request the service or materials. Their purpose should be to cover the costs of providing these services or materials, but they are sometimes used to collect additional revenue. They are generally administratively efficient and have little impact on equity (unless a significant proportion of these charges are paid by small, low-income producers). They can be economically efficient if they reflect the true value or cost of the services or materials provided, which is often not the case. They can also be used to promote other policy objectives.

- *Charges on equipment or workers.* Specific charges on equipment or workers are uncommon, but a number of countries collect charges for registration or permits to trade in forest products or to operate processing plants.

- *General taxes.* Companies operating in the forestry sector are also usually required to pay the same taxes as other industries (corporate taxes, income taxes, sales taxes, value-added taxes, and so forth). Their purpose is to collect government revenue, and responsibility for such taxes is usually outside the control of the forestry administration. However, in some countries, tax incentives are used to encourage certain forestry activities (afforestation, for example).

- *Profit-based royalties.* These types of charges (sometimes called "resource rents") are usually calculated as a proportion of the profits earned by companies working in the sector. They are common in other extractive industries (mining, for instance) but have rarely been used in the forestry sector.

- *Fines.* The main purpose of fines is to deter illegal activities in the forestry sector. Fines are usually fixed in legislation or regulations and are usually not based on any economic criteria, although they are sometimes based on a multiple of the value of illegal products seized or identified by the forest administration (called "compounding"). The administrative and economic efficiency of fines is generally low and could be improved in many countries. Similarly, if law enforcement is weak, the imposition of fines can be inequitable.

ADDRESSING ILLEGAL LOGGING AND OTHER FOREST CRIME

Forest crime—including illegal logging—and corruption are present throughout the world.[1] It is particularly troubling in developing countries, where illegal logging in public lands alone causes estimated losses in assets and revenue in excess of US$10 billion annually, more than six times the total official development assistance dedicated to the sustainable management of forests (World Bank 2004). Governments lose as much as US$5 billion annually from evaded taxes and royalties on legally sanctioned logging. 1.6 billion people depend upon forests for part of their livelihoods, and as many as 350 million people living in and around forests are heavily dependent on forests for their livelihoods and security (see chapter 1, Forests and Poverty Reduction, and associated notes). These vulnerable groups are at risk from illegal logging and removal of timber and nontimber products from the forests. Moreover, violations of protected area boundaries threaten the conservation of forest resources and biodiversity.

Illegal logging also subjects legitimate forest enterprises to unfair competition through price undercutting and discourages them from making socially and environmentally responsible investments in the sector. There are less visible—though highly insidious—costs resulting from the erosion of institutions, the spread of corruption across the economy, and reduced growth. Finally, forest crime creates negative environmental, economic, and social consequences at the global level as well. Forests are a global public good, and their degradation imposes global costs, such as climate change and species loss.

While illegal logging and other forest crime can, from a national point of view, be important in both small and large and high-forest and low-forest countries, from a global perspective it is possible to indicate where these impacts are likely to be most harmful. It is also possible to establish that the problems in the forest sector are closely linked to broader issues of governance (figure 5.2).

Trade has been identified as an important driver of illegal logging and other forest crime. The value of suspicious wood products worldwide may be as high as US$23 billion. Out of the total of illegal timber, it is estimated that about US$5 billion enters world trade, representing as much as 10 percent of the value of global trade in primary wood products. Trade in timber products is often routed through third countries, adding another trade-related dimension to the problem (China, for example, reexports about 70 percent of its timber imports). An economic analysis based on simulations from the Global Forest Products Model suggests that this illegal material depresses world prices by 7–16 percent on average (Seneca Creek Associates and Wood Resources International 2004).

Forest crime ultimately results from a failure of the rule of law. Two types of failure in the legal system lead to criminal behavior: *failures of law and failures of implementation* (see note 5.3, Strengthening Legal Frameworks in the Forest Sector). When laws themselves are flawed or contradictory, the focus of combating illegal logging and other forest crime should be on legal reform, whereas when the "right" laws are in place the focus should be on enforcement.

Fuelwood accounts for the largest single use of wood (by volume) around the world. In developing countries, most fuelwood is consumed for domestic and small-scale industrial uses and comes from family labor or informal supply systems that are often based on sources of supply outside officially recognized forest areas, such as farmland, brush and scrubland, and other scattered trees. A substantial portion of fuelwood collection takes place outside formal forest management and in some, perhaps in many, circumstances, is in violation of the law.

Other illicit activities are also associated with timber harvesting and trade, beyond cutting trees where and when it is proscribed. Such activities include irregular timber sales; corruption in the award of concessions and

Figure 5.2   Illegal Forest Activity and Its Link with Corruption

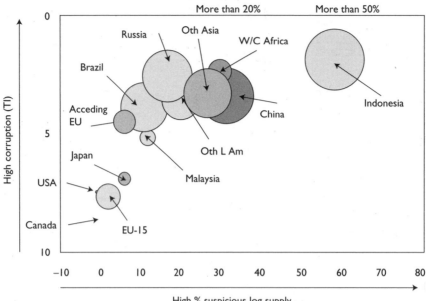

High % suspicious log supply

service contracting; evasion of taxes, royalties, and other fees by enterprises or by communities or private forest owners; circumvention of labor laws; and unauthorized wood processing. Although no reliable estimates are available, anecdotal evidence and stakeholder interviews suggest that in state-owned forests, financial losses from corruption can be as high as or even higher than those from stolen timber (Savcor Indufor Oy 2005). In practice, the distinctions between illegal logging and other timber-related crime become blurred. The same perpetrators may be responsible for outright theft or corruption-related illegal logging.

Corruption and other financial crimes often involve money laundering, adding another dimension to the constellation of what should be considered forest crime. In addition to the timber-related crimes, forest crime also includes such illegal activities as wildlife poaching, arson, and unlawful conversion of forest lands for other uses.

Despite the magnitude of the problem and existing measures to combat corruption (see box 5.17), there are few instances of prosecution and punishment. In fact, if there are prosecutions, it is the poor, looking to supplement their meager livelihoods, who are victimized and sent to jail, while large-scale operators continue with impunity. Arguably, this is the worst form of violation of equity and justice, arising from a clear failure of governance, and it needs to be addressed.

OPERATIONAL ASPECTS

Understanding causes of illegal logging and other forest crime

Reducing illegal logging and other forest crimes through Bank operations requires understanding the underlying causes and implementing actions that address these causes and complement national and local contexts. The ways that drivers behind illegal logging and forest crime operate are highly country and location specific, and depend on economic, social, and cultural factors as well as the type of forest resource and its ownership or tenure arrangements. An appropriate set of responses can only be defined at the country level in processes involving the key stakeholders who interact with the forest resources.

MEANS, MOTIVE, AND OPPORTUNITY CONSTRUCT. The "means, motive, and opportunity construct" (see annex 5.5A to this note) is useful to analyze the causes of crime. In this framework, persons motivated by greed, need, or other desires employ the tools (means) available to them to exploit the existing vulnerabilities (opportunities). Illegal logging and other types of forest crime take place when these three factors are in place simultaneously (that is, when there is a motive to act illegally, the potential illegal operators have the means to do so, and the context in which they operate provides an opportunity for illegal action) (figure 5.3). The responses to illegal logging and other forest crime then need

Several types of tools can be used to combat forest sector corruption in addition to the more standard institutional and administrative safeguards (for example, those related to procurement and institutional structures). Some of the more promising of these follow:

Diagnostics, such as (i) creating a forest sector corruption perception index; (ii) creating a forest corruption risk map; (iii) producing a forest sector citizens' report card; (iv) documenting government performance on forest-related tasks; and (v) creating a scorecard on forest law enforcement including arrests, prosecutions, convictions, and sentencing.

Awareness raising and access to information, such as (i) developing an internet-based clearinghouse for information on forest sector corruption; (ii) briefing and educating journalists on forest-related corruption; (iii) anti-forest-corruption advertisements and other media campaigns; (iv) creating a Web site on forest concessions and related information; (v) compiling a forest law and regulation reference book and making it available on paper and on the internet; and (vi) train-

ing law enforcers and judges on technical issues related to forest corruption.

Public institutional and business ethics, such as (i) establishment and implementation of model forest integrity pacts related to public contracting; (ii) defining and agreeing to codes of conduct through business associations; (iii) promoting forest certification; (iv) implementing whistleblower encouragement and protection programs; (v) establishing a safe channel for citizens' complaints and producing a public report on complaints received; (vi) developing a professional ethics pledge and encouraging public officials to sign it; and (vii) rewarding outstanding public service, perhaps through an awards program.

Structures and events for stakeholder participation and dialogue, such as (i) representative local and national stakeholder committees; (ii) specific conferences and workshops on professional responsibility and ethics; and (iii) best practices to combat forest sector corruption or any other key issues emerging from the above.

Source: Adapted from Rosenbaum (2005).

---

to focus on reducing the motivation for unlawful action, foreclosing the opportunities, and eliminating the means available to those operating outside the boundaries of the law.

The means, motive, and opportunity construct is of particular value in suggesting areas of comparative advantage

across potential partners in improving forest law enforcement and governance. For example, consumer countries and industry occupy particular niches in helping to reduce the motive for illegal logging by reforming markets and public procurement policies that discriminate against stolen

Figure 5.3   National Action and International Cooperation for Controlling Forest Crime

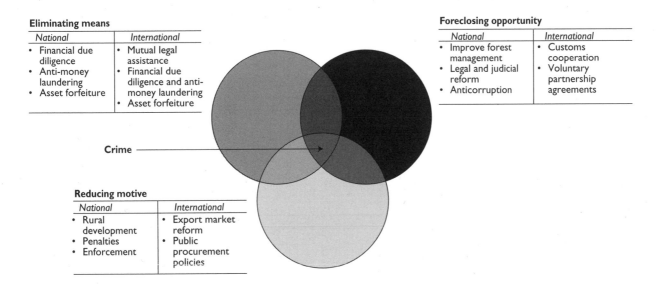

Eliminating means

National	International
• Financial due diligence • Anti-money laundering • Asset forfeiture	• Mutual legal assistance • Financial due diligence and anti-money laundering • Asset forfeiture

Foreclosing opportunity

National	International
• Improve forest management • Legal and judicial reform • Anticorruption	• Customs cooperation • Voluntary partnership agreements

Reducing motive

National	International
• Rural development • Penalties • Enforcement	• Export market reform • Public procurement policies

Crime

material. Governments and financial institutions can help limit the development of excess wood-processing plants and equipment by requiring and exercising due diligence in assessing wood supply and land availability in consideration of wood-based and agro-industrial investments. Producer countries have obvious priority with respect to improving forest management and control as an approach to reducing the opportunities available for illegal activities.

NEED-BASED VERSUS GREED-BASED CAUSES. Differentiating between illegal activities motivated by poverty (such as fuelwood and fodder collection needs, for example) and those resulting from outright greed and that often involve organized criminal activity (such as commercial logging in protected areas) is also helpful in formulating effective and equitable responses to address these complex problems.

Framework to combat illegal logging and other forest crime

An effective strategy to combat illegal logging and other forest crime combines elements of prevention, detection, and suppression in a way that helps to achieve both short-term gains (such as increases in forest revenue, or the apprehension and conviction of the most flagrant violators of laws) to maintain the momentum of the process, and longer-term systemic changes (legal and institutional reforms and reduction of possibilities for corrupt behavior).

PREVENTION. Prevention combines the promotion of good governance in and outside the forest sector in general with more specific actions focused directly on forest crime. Links to broader development (poverty reduction, land use, industrial development, rural development, institutional reform, and the like) and forest sector policies, strategies, and programs (such as national forest programs) are evident, as are links to legislation in other sectors. These links require coordination to avoid overlaps and missed opportunities.

Effective prevention of forest crime may need to address the following issues:

Supply-demand imbalances
- Improving the availability of legal wood (fuelwood, charcoal, and building materials) or substitutes (kerosene, solar energy, gas) to meet basic needs of rural and urban populations
- Improving the availability and reducing the cost of legal industrial roundwood (for instance, through industrial plantations; see note 3.3, Forest Plantations)

- Ensuring that proper due diligence on the availability of legal timber is carried out before authorizing or financing forest industry capacity expansion (see note 5.4, Strengthening Fiscal Systems in the Forest Sector)
- Restructuring industry and downscaling excess capacity

Quality of legal and regulatory frameworks within and outside the forest sector
- Securing forest land tenure and access rights of the local or indigenous communities to timber and wildlife (see note 1.4, Property and Access Rights)
- Ensuring recognition of the legitimate needs of different stakeholders in forest concession agreements
- Simplifying overly complex laws and regulations that are not in line with the capacity of the different groups of forest users to comply with the legal requirements (especially for community and small-scale private forest owners)
- Identifying and resolving conflicting legislation and regulations (central vs. decentralized levels, different sectors) (see note 5.1, Decentralized Forest Management)
- Reducing unreasonably high costs of compliance for legal operators (by streamlining administrative procedures and reducing processing time of contracts and permits)
- Increasing costs of illegal operators through adjustments in penal codes to ensure that these constitute effective deterrents to forest crime
- Including appropriate means to prevent crime in forest management plans in commercial concessions (for example, by closing roads after harvesting, employing routine patrols, and determining what sort of tree marking and log labeling systems are used)

Institutional structures and incentives
- Addressing broader governance failures, such as lack of transparency and accountability, and corruption (for example, by reorganization of the public forest administration, improvements in procedures for concession award and timber sales, improvements to financial audit systems and staff incentive systems)
- Promoting independent forest certification schemes and other demand-side measures related to corporate social responsibility (for example, third-party audited systems for verification of legal wood origin), especially in cases where demand for timber and other forest products is driven by export markets (see note 3.2, Forest Certification Systems)
- Creating positive incentives for those complying with legal requirements, especially in situations where they

initially have to compete with illegal operators (for example, reduced concession fees for producers certified by an independent third-party)

- Promoting partnerships with civil society, such as consultative groups and joint government–civil society structures for monitoring forest activities
- Creating and strengthening high-level, intersectoral coordination mechanisms to harmonize policies, minimize negative cross-sectoral impacts (for example, with agricultural policies), and ensure that broader reforms have important and positive law enforcement benefits in the forest sector
- Collaborating with financial institutions to establish means to foreclose opportunities to launder profits from illegal forest operations

Forest monitoring and information
- Improving information on forest resources and legal harvest at the forest management unit level (for example, forest inventories and management plans that are of appropriate technical quality and detail, and log-tracking and chain-of-custody systems) (see note 7.2, Establishing Forest Information Management Systems)
- Publicly disclosing information on forest cover change, forest concessions, management plans and harvesting quotas, logging and timber transport, and forest revenues; and making such information accessible (for example, by posting it on the internet) to minimize manipulation, self-censorship, and physical risk to those involved in law enforcement

Capacity building and awareness
- Improving capacity of both forest and judicial authorities to enforce forest legislation from detection to conviction, thus establishing an effective deterrent
- Conducting campaigns that inform the public about the provisions of forest law in local languages, thereby ensuring that users are at least aware of rights, restrictions, and prohibitions
- Indicating actions that the public can take to support law enforcement efforts (for example, ways to report illegal activity)

Because preventive measures target the fundamental problems underlying illegal logging, many of them can be expected to take effect only in the medium and long term.

DETECTION. Detection refers to various methods of collecting and processing information on forest crime and related trade with the objective of identifying illegal activities and facilitating the design of improved policies. Detection can entail the following:

- Monitoring and surveillance to determine if and where crime is occurring, to set priorities, and to evaluate other elements of the enforcement program. The kinds of information that are needed include the geographic incidence of different crimes, the types of crimes that are occurring, the types of perpetrators, and the apparent levels of crime.
- Using systems that include satellites, aircraft, and ground monitoring and surveillance personnel to document the location, type, volume, and if possible, the identity of violators involved in illegal logging activities. The procedures used to draw inferences for use with the rest of the law enforcement program are just as important as the sophistication of the data collection processes.
- Employing indirect methods to assess the prevalence of illegal activity (for example, comparisons of data on production, consumption, and trade in forest products often show significant disparities between trading partners' recorded exports and imports. These differences can indicate the potential magnitude of timber theft, smuggling, and transfer pricing).
- Establishing a process to determine if any institutional weaknesses exist that can create opportunities for timber theft (such as opportunities created by inadequate boundary marking, product marking, product measuring, product tracking, or an inadequate process of checking for revenue payments).
- Collecting evidence and documentation on a specific incident as the basis for arrests, judicial proceedings, fines, or other action. Specialized expertise is needed to employ techniques that are appropriate to the suspected crime and the national legal system.
- Establishing crime monitoring systems that collect data for evaluating the enforcement program's impact and efficiency, and for providing feedback to program planners.
- Increasing forest transparency and crime detection through independent forest monitoring, especially in countries with weak government systems prone to corruption.

SUPPRESSION. Suppression of illegal activity should be the last recourse in a forest law enforcement program, because it almost inevitably involves the use of force. Suppression measures pose risks to agency personnel, the public, and the lawbreaker. The indiscriminate use of force also poses risks to the public at large. Because the people involved in criminal activity at the field level are often simply laborers (and usually poor people with few alternatives) working at the direction of others, genuine ethical reasons exist to question the use of force. In any responsible suppression program, these risks need to be systematically considered in light of the probability of success, the accountability and transparency of the suppression effort, and the skills and training available to law enforcers. In addition, suppression is an area for which the World Bank has strict guidelines based on its mandate that define its level of involvement.

Effective suppression may require the following:

- Developing risk-success matrices to make appropriate preparations for safe conduct of suppression operations, or to determine when safe operations are a practical impossibility. Such matrices should be developed by law enforcement practitioners.
- Tailoring institutional arrangements for major suppression efforts or crackdowns to local circumstances (see note 5.2, Reforming Forest Institutions). However, these arrangements also clearly need to incorporate adequate provisions for accountability and transparency commensurate with the likely use of force and the need for security and confidentiality.
- Developing interagency arrangements in which the police, military, customs, and other law enforcement agencies frequently and effectively work together with natural resource agencies. These arrangements require resources, budgets, planning, and reporting provisions to be in place.
- Training staff members at all levels where extraordinary suppression efforts are needed, for example, in specialized skills such as investigating criminal activities, documenting crimes, handling evidence, and preparing judicial proceedings. In highly dangerous or specialized investigations, training appropriate for undercover operations, firearms safety, and other special expertise may be needed.

The complexity and risk of suppression efforts underscore the value of measures to avoid the emergence of a serious law enforcement problem through sound prevention and detection efforts. Where such efforts fail, or are not made, the problems of suppression can rapidly become nearly insurmountable.

Many of the specific interventions and tools discussed above can simultaneously contribute to more than one of the enforcement functions of prevention, detection, or sup-

pression. Issues of cost, risk, capacity, and commitment need to be addressed in the design of these programs.

Annex 5.5B to this note brings the drivers of forest crime (motive, means, and opportunity) together with the prevention-detection-suppression framework in several typical typologies of forest crime, and can be used as a tool to facilitate discussion in country contexts (for example, in the context of national-level action plans as discussed below).

National-level processes to combat illegal logging and other forest crime

NATIONAL AND LOCAL LEVEL FOREST LAW ENFORCEMENT PROGRAM. Forest law enforcement programs need to be formulated at the national and local levels, building on established laws, institutional arrangements, and the interests and capabilities of different stakeholders, and need to address the specific crime problems being encountered.

As a consequence of the FLEG processes (see chapter 5), some countries are beginning to address forest crime through concerted, coordinated, multistakeholder, national-level FLEG processes, resulting in national-level FLEG action plans. Experience with these processes has demonstrated that combating illegal logging and other forest crime is as much a political process as it is technical, and involves reconciliation of the various stakeholder interests in a manner that enables change. Where the economic stakes in illegal activities are high, powerful interest groups can forcefully protect the status quo even if the outcome is clearly negative from society's point of view.

STAKEHOLDER COALITIONS. Rarely is one stakeholder group able to push through a major change in the established power balance. Instead, successful change processes rely on coalitions of several interest groups with different capacities. Local and international NGOs have often managed to bring the problem of illegal logging out in the open and raise awareness among politicians and the general public of the need to act. Representatives from interest groups directly involved in timber production can wield considerable influence among their peers and colleagues. High-level political champions are also required who are able to fend off efforts to slow down the implementation of the proposed measures through behind-the-scenes maneuvering.

Partners willing to support FLEG can be found among many stakeholder groups. Ministries of finance and local municipalities are interested in the increased tax revenue that reduction of illegal activities could bring about. Forest enterprises may be motivated to join the effort because of market pressure or ethical reasons. Local people whose rights are trampled by illegal loggers are potential partners, as are NGOs concerned about protection of the environment, human rights, and democracy. In addition, there are always individuals in all stakeholder groups and institutions, including public forest administration, who need no other motivation than pursuit of fairness and justice. External partners can reinforce and support these progressive groups and, within the boundaries of their mandates, facilitate their work at the political and technical levels.

FLEG PROCESSES SHOULD BRING PARTNERS TOGETHER. The aim of a national FLEG process should be to bring all these partners together to enable them to reinforce each other. Although it is evident that there will not and should not be any standard model for such processes, some common elements seem to characterize the more promising initiatives currently under way:

- Establishment of a mechanism for interministerial coordination, and a forum for stakeholder participation
- Use of an analytical process for assessing the magnitude, scope, and dimension of the problems related to law enforcement and governance
- Creation of awareness, information sharing, and if necessary, whistle blowing, to "name and shame" the worst perpetrators of forest crimes
- Use of a consultative and consensus-building process to define the scope of actions and priorities
- Detailed definitions of the actions, responsible stakeholders, mechanisms of implementation, and financing (both internal and possible external sources)
- Obtaining political endorsement and support for the FLEG actions

LESSONS LEARNED AND RECOMMENDATIONS FOR PRACTITIONERS

General lessons

SUCCESSFUL CHANGE PROCESSES RELY ON COALITIONS OF SEVERAL INTEREST GROUPS WITH DIFFERENT CAPACITIES. Partners willing to support FLEG can be found among many stakeholder groups, such as ministries of finance and local municipalities, forest enterprises, local people, and NGOs. In addition, all stakeholder groups and institutions, including public forest administrations, house individuals who need

no other motivation than the pursuit of fairness and justice. External partners can reinforce and support these progressive groups and, within the boundaries of their mandates, facilitate their work at political and technical levels.

- Where the economic stakes in illegal activities are high, *powerful interest groups can forcefully protect the status quo* even if the outcome is clearly negative from society's point of view.

Country-level lessons

ADDRESS KEY DRIVERS BOTH WITHIN AND OUTSIDE THE FOREST SECTOR. Some governance issues relating to forest crime lie entirely within the forest sector while others affecting forests and forest-dependent people extend beyond this sector. Some of the governance work of other parts of the World Bank Group may help address these nonforest-sector issues, including support to Poverty Reduction Strategy Paper processes and the alignment of the World Bank's CASs with these processes, work on governance diagnostics and integration of governance and anticorruption elements in the CASs, and the design of specific capacity-building programs based on the diagnostic surveys (Poverty Reduction and Economic Management Network and the World Bank Institute). Other relevant areas of the World Bank focus on anti-money laundering and financial investigation (Financial Market Integrity group, Extractive Industries Transparency Initiative, Justice for the Poor, and customs modernization). The World Bank's legal department is carrying out important work in assessing the quality of legal and regulatory frameworks. Similarly, some of the work on corporate social responsibility and social and environmental issues in the operations of the International Finance Corporation (for example, investment safeguard policies) is extremely relevant to FLEG issues.

COMBINE ACTIONS WITH BOTH SHORT- AND LONG-TERM IMPLICATIONS IN A REALISTIC, STEP-WISE PLAN. Visible short-term impacts are often needed to create and maintain momentum, whereas long-term work on the structural drivers is necessary to ensure that these efforts are sustainable over time. Early "wins" (for example, significant increases in forest revenue) are important to motivating continued efforts.

ADDRESS BOTH FAILURES OF LAW AND FAILURES OF IMPLEMENTATION. First, ensure that the correct laws and policies are in place. Second, work to enforce the law. This two-pronged approach to legal compliance is the only way to ensure that the full range of motivations, opportunities, and means for illegal behavior are addressed.

STRENGTHEN SUPPLY-SIDE MEASURES WITH MEASURES TO CONTROL IMPORTS OF ILLEGAL TIMBER AND WOOD PRODUCTS. This is especially important in countries where export demand is a significant driver of illegal activities in the forest sector. It should be noted that—at least in principle— these measures could also be extended to other products (for example, wildlife or products derived from illegal conversion of forest lands).

INTEGRATE ANTI-MONEY-LAUNDERING AND ASSET FORFEITURE LAWS INTO THE FIGHT AGAINST FOREST CRIME AND RELATED CORRUPTION. These tools, along with the UN Conventions Against Corruption and Transnational Organized Crime, provide strong and effective regimes that governments can use to fight forest crime and related corruption.

Risks

Focusing more directly on illegal logging and other forest crimes will not always be a natural or comfortable role for development agencies, including the World Bank. Inevitably, development agencies will become involved in complex and controversial issues regarding the quality of laws, and at times these institutions will be put at odds with powerful interest groups, including high-level government officials, defending the status quo for personal gain. Consequently, there are two potential areas of risk for the development community:

- As with any complex and controversial issue involving different interests and actors, there are *reputational risks* related to work with FLEG. The World Bank and its partners need to be especially sensitive to issues related to human rights and equity in their work. Transparency and advocacy and support for participatory approaches are important means to avoid these types of risks.
- A more vigorous engagement with FLEG will also inevitably involve difficult issues related to national sovereignty in the management of natural resources. This *political risk* needs to be carefully managed.

Opportunities

Specific opportunities for action by the international community include the following:

- Address critical gaps in the understanding of the nature of the governance challenge. An illustrative list of important areas for focus follows:
  - Development of diagnostics to benchmark forest crime and the state of forest governance in high-priority countries, and identification of indicators to monitor the progress of proposed interventions
  - Advancements in the role of independent monitors in making forest operations more transparent and in providing legal operators with positive incentives
  - Institutional (and incentive-compatible) reforms of forestry agencies in Bank client countries that include gaining a better understanding of the role of incentives (including salary structure and so on) for civil servants
  - Development approaches to forest industry restructuring and retrenchment that will efficiently and effectively help address imbalances in wood supply and demand
  - Establishment of information management systems and use of geographic information systems for overall monitoring of the forest resource
- Deepen the technical content of FLEG processes at the international and national levels, mobilize opportunities for multilateral enforcement action, and integrate the regional FLEG processes into existing structures for regional cooperation
- Promote collaboration between the progressive elements of the industry, international financing institutions, and international NGOs involved in the FLEG process to develop, improve, and harmonize safeguards and due diligence on forest investments (see note 5.4, Strengthening Fiscal Systems in the Forest Sector). The aim should be both to ensure the legality of the timber used and to mitigate the risk for other forest crimes, such as poaching, arson, and encroachment of forest areas, resulting from forest industry investments.
- Ensure effective coordination between the implementation of the FLEGT Regulation and Action Plan and other FLEG efforts. The aim should be to strengthen the links between the voluntary partnership agreements envisioned in the FLEGT action plan and the lending and advisory operations of the international financing institutions, especially the World Bank.
- Explore the potential for initiatives similar to the Extractive Industries Transparency Initiative (EITI)[2] to increase transparency of forest sector financial flows in some key forest countries, especially where a relatively small number of companies operate large forest concessions.

NOTES

1. This note is based on World Bank (2006).

2. See EITI's Web site for more information: http://www.eitransparency.org/.

SELECTED READINGS

Kishor, N., and R. Damania. 2006. "Crime and Justice in the Garden of Eden: Improving Governance and Reducing Corruption in the Forestry Sector." In *The Many Faces of Corruption: Tracking Vulnerabilities at the Sector Level,* ed. J. Edgardo Campos and Sanjay Pradhan. Washington, DC: World Bank.

Magrath, W. B., R. Grandalski, J. Stuckey, G. Vikanes, and G. Wilkinson. 2007. *Timber Theft Prevention and Forest Resource Security.* Washington, DC: World Bank.

REFERENCES CITED

Magrath, W. B., R. Grandalski, J. Stuckey, G. Vikanes, and G. Wilkinson. 2007. *Timber Theft Prevention and Forest Resource Security.* Washington, DC: World Bank.

Puustjarvi, E. 2006a. "Guidelines for Formulating and Implementing National Action Plans to Combat Illegal Logging and Other Forest Crime." Draft. Indufor, Helsinki, Finland.

———. 2006b. "Proposal for Typology of Illegal Logging." Draft. Indufor, Helsinki, Finland.

Rosenbaum, K. L. 2005. "Tools for Civil Society Action to Reduce Forest Corruption: Drawing Lessons from Transparency International." PROFOR at the World Bank, Washington, DC.

Savcor, I. O. 2005. "Ensuring Sustainability of Forests and Livelihoods Through Improved Governance and Control of Illegal Logging for Economies in Transition: World Bank Discussion Paper." Helsinki, Finland.

Seneca Creek Associates and Wood Resources International. 2004. "'Illegal' Logging and Global Wood Markets: The Competitive Impacts on the U.S. Wood Products Industry." Report prepared for the American Forest & Paper Association by Seneca Creek Associates, Poolesville, MD, and Wood Resources International, University Place, WA.

World Bank. 2004. *Sustaining Forests: A Development Strategy.* Washington, DC: World Bank.

———. 2006. "Strengthening Forest Law Enforcement and Governance: Addressing a Systemic Constraint to Sustainable Development." Report No. 36638-GLB, Washington, DC.

CROSS-REFERENCED CHAPTERS AND NOTES

ANNEX 5.5A DRIVERS OF ILLEGAL LOGGING AND OTHER FOREST CRIME: MOTIVE, MEANS, AND OPPORTUNITY

Using the motive, means, and opportunity elements to analyze illegal logging and other forest crimes illuminates fundamental drivers of the problem (Magrath et al. 2007). This annex presents an overview of some of these drivers derived from a set of country-level studies and assessments.

Motive
- Overriding need to generate foreign exchange
- Imperative to finance military operations
- Poverty and lack of alternative income
- Lack of affordable fuel alternatives
- Denial of access by local people to resources they need for subsistence or livelihoods
- Indiscriminate (regarding legality of origin) demand for timber in neighboring countries
- Indiscriminate international demand for timber
- Economic factors and policies favoring forest conversion
- Low cost of illegal timber (that is, ineffective sanctions) and rent-seeking business culture in the forest sector companies
- Overcapacity in the wood processing industry
- Difficulty complying with legal regulations (especially by small-scale producers, concession holders, communities, and private forest owners)
- Bureaucratic laws related to forest management (cost of complying with laws is too high)

Means
- Roads, navigable rivers, harbors, and other transport infrastructure
- Labor in forest areas (often without alternative sources of livelihoods)
- Capital to finance illegal logging and other forest crime

Source: Modified from Puustjarvi (2006b).

- Equipment for logging and transport of timber and wood products
- Opportunities for money laundering to hide financial proceeds

Opportunity
- Weak governance in parts or all of the country (including areas affected by conflict and war)
- Breakdown of institutional controls and lack of accountability of public officials
- Rapid and disorganized decentralization and lack of institutional capacity at decentralized levels (see note 5.1, Decentralized Forest Management)
- Ambiguous forest land tenure (that is, lack of legal definition, overlapping uses, conflicting laws, and so on) (see note 1.4, Property and Access Rights)
- Inadequate or inappropriate legal framework (not based on a social contract with key forest users) (see note 5.3, Strengthening Legal Frameworks in the Forest Sector)
- Lack of or weak recognition of customary rights (of local and indigenous communities)
- Weak internal organization of these communities
- Inadequate or inappropriate prescriptions for forest management and use (regulations)
- Lack of reliable and up-to-date information on forest resources and their use
- Weak, poorly managed, or corrupt forest administration
- Ineffective or corrupt law enforcement
- Ineffective or corrupt judiciary
- Weak governance or contradictory policies in sectors related to forestry
- Weak control of illegal exports in producing countries or imports in purchasing countries

ANNEX 5.5B   TYPICAL CONTEXTS OF ILLEGAL LOGGING: DRIVERS AND POTENTIAL RESPONSES

Typical contexts	Potential drivers (motive, means, opportunity)	Potential responses	Type
Illegal logging Illegal logging for securing subsistence	• People unable to meet their basic needs	• Legalize illegal use or simplify regulations concerning access to public forest or wildlife resources	P
		• Create opportunities for income generation	P
	• Lack or high cost of alternative energy	• Offer alternatives to fuelwood as source of energy	P
Small-scale illegal logging to enhance livelihoods by • people without legal access to forest land • managers or owners of community forests • private forest owners	• Poverty	• Create opportunities for income generation	P
	• Complex legal procedures related to harvesting and access to forest resources	• Reduce bureaucracy and fees associated with legal timber harvesting	P
	• Disputes over land tenure rights	• Clarify land tenure, consider establishing local tenure of forest land	P
	• Poorly organized, under-resourced, and corrupt forest law enforcement	• Strengthen forest law enforcement	D+S
		• Improve internal control on law enforcement staff	D+S
	• Corrupt community leaders	• Improve internal control in communities	D+S
	• Criminal groups organizing illegal logging by recruiting rural poor	• Strengthen cooperation with police force and judiciary and target the organizers or financiers behind these activities	D+S
	• Inefficient legal procedures	• Amend forest-related legislation and penal code	P
		• Use money laundering and asset forfeiture laws	
Large-scale commercial illegal logging	• Poorly motivated staff in public forest administration or enterprises	• Reorganize public forest administration to increase staff motivation	P
	• High cost of legal timber	• Reduce bureaucracy and fees associated with legal timber harvesting	P
	• Capacity of wood processing industries exceeding legal supply	• Embark on phased program of capacity reduction in wood-processing industries	P
		• Increase supply by establishing plantations or adjusting forest management regulations	P
	• Export demand insensitive to legality of timber	• Collaborate with governments and private sector in importing countries to increase demand for legal timber and deter imports of illegal timber	P
	• Poorly organized and corrupt forest law enforcement and auditing system	• Increase resources and enhance independence of forest law enforcement	D+S
		• Enhance effectiveness of financial audits on public forest administration or enterprises	D
		• Provide support to patrolling networks among private forest owners	D
		• Use anti-money-laundering laws	
	• Inadequate monitoring data on timber flows and origin of timber	• Promote independent forest monitoring	D
		• Improve data management and transparency in public forest administration or enterprises	P
		• Promote responsible business practices (chain-of-custody systems, certification) in private industries	
	• Inefficient legal procedures	• Strengthen cooperation with police force and judiciary	S
		• Provide owners or managers of community and private forests with legal services	S
		• Amend forest-related legislation and penal code	P
Conflict timber	• High cost of armed conflict	• Focus on conflict resolution and management	P
	• Poor control of timber imports in recipient countries	• Improve controls on origin of timber	D
	• Ineffective international sanctions	• Promote international collaboration in sanctioning conflict timber	S

(continues on the following page)

Typical contexts	Potential drivers (motive, means, opportunity)	Potential responses	Type
Other forest crime Irregular timber sales, award of concessions and service contracting	• Low risk of sanctions	• Improve procedures for timber sales and awarding concessions to increase transparency and accountability	P
		• Increase proportion of timber sold or concessions awarded through competitive bidding	P
	• Poorly motivated staff in public forest administration and enterprises	• Reorganize public forest administration to increase staff motivation	P
	• Poorly organized and corrupt financial audit system	• Enhance effectiveness of financial audits on public forest administration or enterprises	D
		• Improve data management and transparency in public forest administration and enterprises	D
	• Inefficient legal procedures	• Strengthen cooperation with police force and judiciary	S
		• Amend penal code	P
Evasion of taxes, royalties, and other fees by enterprises	• Unreasonably high tax burden in relation to timber price and general tax level	• Adjust taxes as appropriate	P
		• Impose sanctions on enterprises found guilty of tax evasion	S
	• Poorly organized and corrupt financial audit system	• Enhance effectiveness of financial audits on enterprises	D
	• Inadequate accounting systems in private enterprises	• Oblige enterprises to provide required information in an easily accessible form	D
	• Inefficient legal procedures	• Strengthen cooperation with police force and judiciary to achieve minimum acceptable level of compliance	S
		• Amend penal code	P
Evasion of taxes, royalties, and other fees by communities or private forest owners	• Low risk of sanctions	• Adjust taxes, royalties, and other fees to levels at which most communities or private forest owners would make the payments voluntarily	P P
	• Inadequate accounting systems in private enterprises or communities	• Promote sound accounting practices in community forestry	D
		• Enhance effectiveness of external financial audits on community forests and private woodlots within the limits of available resources	D+S
	• Inefficient legal procedures	• Strengthen cooperation with police force and judiciary to achieve minimum acceptable level of compliance	S
		• Amend penal code	P
Circumvention of labor laws	• Indifferent attitude in enterprises toward labor laws	• Impose sanctions on enterprises found guilty of circumventing labor laws	P
	• Poorly organized and corrupt oversight	• Impose sanctions or disciplinary actions on companies proven to circumvent regulations	D
	• Inefficient legal procedures	• Strengthen cooperation with police force and judiciary to achieve minimum acceptable level of compliance	S
		• Amend penal code	P
Unauthorized wood processing	• Strong domestic and export demand encouraging unauthorized wood processing and illegal logging	• Enable an increase in authorized processing capacity by increasing legal timber supply	P
	• Excessive bureaucracy related to licensing	• Simplify licensing procedure	P
	• Poorly organized and corrupt oversight	• Impose sanctions or disciplinary actions on companies proven to circumvent regulations	D
	• Inefficient legal procedures	• Strengthen cooperation with police force and judiciary	S
		• Amend penal code	P
Wildlife poaching Wildlife poaching for subsistence needs	• People unable to meet their basic needs • Lack of or high cost of alternative sources of food	• Legalize illegal use or simplify regulations concerning access to wildlife resources	P
		• Create opportunities for income generation	P
		• Offer alternative sources of food	P

Typical contexts	Potential drivers (motive, means, opportunity)	Potential responses	Type
Wildlife poaching to engage in trade in animals and animal parts	• Poverty • Complex legal procedures for hunting of wildlife • Disputes over hunting rights	• Create opportunities for income generation, reduce bureaucracy and fees associated with legal timber harvesting • Clarify hunting rights with focus on rural poor	P P
	• Poorly organized, under-resourced, and corrupt wildlife law enforcement • Corrupt community leaders	• Strengthen wildlife law enforcement • Improve internal control of law enforcement staff • Improve internal control in communities	D+S D+S D+S
	• Criminal groups organizing illegal hunting by recruiting rural poor • Inefficient legal procedures	• Strengthen cooperation with police force and judiciary and target the organizers or financiers behind these activities • Amend forest-related legislation and penal code • Use anti-money-laundering and asset forfeiture laws	D+S D+S D+S
Arson			
Arson associated with subsistence-level slash-and-burn agriculture	• Poverty • Lack of viable alternative agricultural systems • Marginalization and disempowerment of Indigenous Peoples	• Land tenure reform • Agricultural intensification • Legal reform to decriminalize slash-and-burn agriculture	P P P
Arson associated with large-scale land clearing for commercial agriculture	• Biased policies and incentives • Weak regulatory controls of land development	• Policy reform based on strategic environmental assessment • Regulatory reforms to monitor and control land development	P P+D
Encroachment			
Conversion of forest land associated with subsistence-level slash-and-burn agriculture	• Poverty • Cyclical unemployment	• Land tenure reform • Agricultural development • Stabilization policies	P P P
Conversion of forest land associated with large-scale land clearing for commercial agriculture	• Distorted policies • Corrupt land access arrangements	• Policy reform • Anti-money-laundering and asset forfeiture laws	P S

Source: Adapted from Puustjarvi (2006a).
Note: P = prevention; D = detection; S = suppression.

Mainstreaming Forests into Development Policy and Planning

One of the targets under the Millennium Development Goals for ensuring environmental sustainability requires that countries integrate the principles of sustainable development into country policies and programs and reverse the loss of environmental resources. In line with this, macro policy reforms should give foremost consideration to ensuring enabling conditions for sustainable development, enhancing synergies and minimizing negative impacts on natural resources. For forests, the combined impacts of economic activities outside the forest sector are often significantly greater than those produced by economic activity within the sector itself.

Several policy areas can impact forests and forest development, including macroeconomic policies (fiscal, monetary, trade, privatization, and public expenditure policies); population and social affairs; agriculture, fisheries, game management, livestock; rural and regional development, land use planning, land tenure; infrastructure; industry; energy; environment[1]; and tourism. Macro policy reforms are central to strengthening an economy. Governments reform fiscal, exchange rate, and monetary policies, and make changes in trade policies, land reform, and privatization policies as part of adjustment packages to address economic imbalances, balance of payments, and structural weaknesses in their economy. Measures such as these—regardless of origin—can and do have significant impacts on natural resources in general. For example, real exchange rate depreciation (currency devaluation) favors the expansion of tradables (many agricultural, forest, and mineral

products) over nontradables (services, construction, and subsistence production). That generally encourages expansion of agriculture, logging, and mining. In addition, it can also boost sectors that use more land and labor and less imported capital and might, therefore, encourage more extensive agriculture. Conversely, exchange rate depreciation sometimes induces farmers to shift to export crops or production systems that require less land.

Fiscal policy directed at short-run stabilization, the implementation of growth and other long-term objectives, and decentralization policy (see note 5.1, Decentralized Forest Management) as a major instrument of national economic reform in many developing countries and countries in transition, all can affect forests and other natural resources. Such broadly based adjustments, which were often part of stabilization and structural adjustment policies recommended by the World Bank and, more often, the International Monetary Fund (IMF), have in the past been criticized for their negative impacts on the poor, on natural resources, and on the environment (see box 6.1). In the recent past, development policy decreased emphasis on restoring balance of payment and exchange rates, and focused on budget support geared toward domestic financing needs. The World Bank's development policy lending (DPL) portfolio has included promoting competitive market structures, correcting distortions in incentive regimes, establishing appropriate monitoring and safeguards in the financial sector, judicial reform, and adopting modern investment codes to create an environment conducive to

In 1997 the IMF and the World Bank provided an adjustment loan to Indonesia following the financial sector crisis in that country. The IMF began its negotiations with the government of Indonesia on an assistance package in October 1997. The original letter of intent focused on banking sector reform and other financial sector issues, and initially did not include environmental provisions. Information that forestry was the second largest contributor to Indonesian export income and was probably a sector that may survive the economic crisis better than others resulted in the IMF and the Bank incorporating specific forest sector conditions into the frameworks of these instruments.

By January 1998, the loan had become a US$43 billion assistance package, which included a set of environmental and forest sector reforms aimed at dismantling the forest product marketing monopolies that had dominated the sector and committed the government to implementation of a series of forest concession management reforms that the World Bank and other development agencies had been promoting in Indonesia for a considerable time.

In April 1998, the World Bank followed up on the IMF package with the first of two Policy Reform Support Loans (PRSLs), with a loan value of US$1 billion, which was followed by a second PRSL in the following year. The PRSL loans added detailed provisions calling for reform of regulations and legislation governing the award and management of concessions; an interim moratorium on any further conversion of forested lands to other uses; and moves toward stronger participation of local communities in the management and protection of forests, and ultimately recognition of traditional title to forest.

Lessons drawn from the Indonesian experiences are that (i) good, up-to-date analysis will allow for effective links between reforms introduced and outcomes for forests and forest-dependent people to be assessed, and (ii) careful monitoring of actual outcomes and follow-up with more focused and longer term operations (as was proposed but not pursued in the Indonesia case) are essential to good results.

Source: Douglas and Chandrasekharan Bher 2006.

---

private sector investment, thus promoting good governance, encouraging private sector activity, and mitigating short-term adverse effects of adjustment.

Independent of this evolution in DPL, some of the policy reforms can have unintended negative effects on forests or create opportunities for enhancing the forest sector. Where forests are a significant part of the economic and social resource base of a country, therefore, it will be necessary to mainstream forest considerations into development policies and planning processes, and to consider exogenous impacts.

Forests are part of the national capital base in most developing countries, and have important links to other natural resources, especially water, soil, and, in some cases, coastal marine assets. In developing countries, natural capital generally has a larger role to play in overall economic development than in wealthier countries. Therefore, alternative sources of capital for investment are scarcer, and the focus tends to be more heavily oriented toward natural resource utilization, through mining, forestry, agriculture, rural industries, and so on. The condition and sustainability of those resources is therefore of critical importance to the prospects for development and maintenance of economic growth at the national scale.

PAST ACTIVITIES

The World Bank's main engagement in macroeconomic reforms is through DPL. DPL is rapidly disbursing, policy-based financing that the Bank provides in the form of loans or grants to help a borrower address actual or anticipated development financing requirements that have domestic or external origins. These operations are large in scope and in their objectives. They support the policy and institutional changes needed to create an environment conducive to sustained and equitable growth. Typically, they will include improving the investment climate, diversification of the economy, employment creation, and support for meeting international commitments.

DPL was originally designed to provide support for macroeconomic policy reforms, such as in trade policy and agriculture. Over time it has evolved to focus more on structural, financial sector, and social policy reform and on improving public sector resource management. Development policy operations now generally aim to promote competitive market structures (legal and regulatory reform), correct distortions in incentive regimes (taxation and trade reform), establish appropriate monitoring and safeguards (financial sector reform), create an environment conducive to private sector investment (judicial reform, adoption of a modern investment code), encourage private sector activity (privatization and public-private partnerships), promote good governance (civil service reform), and mitigate short-term adverse effects of development policy (establishment of social protection funds).

Between fiscal years 2004 and 2006, the World Bank approved 258 development policy loans. Of those, 11 had forestry components with IBRD/IDA commitments totaling some US$94 million or 9 percent of the total IBRD/IDA commitment for those 11 projects. DPL has been most frequently employed in Africa. There were 50 additional DPLs with activities not formally classified as forest components but that included forest-related actions under a broader agriculture-forestry-fisheries classification. The other DPLs might have had effects on forests, but this information was not available in the program documents. Efforts are being made to use the policy lending instrument to generate positive outcomes for the forest sector. Examples include Brazil, Cameroon, the Democratic Republic of Congo, Gabon, Ghana and the Lao People's Democratic Republic (see boxes 6.12 through 6.14 in note 6.2).

The World Bank's experience in analyzing cross-sectoral outcomes in forests (or natural resources more generally) from lending activities, including the newer programmatic approach of DPL, is growing. Upstream analytical work, including country environmental analyses (CEAs) and strategic environmental assessments (SEAs) conducted before DPLs has increased. The Bank has also institutionalized a system whereby policy loans are reviewed by environmental, natural resource, and forest specialists at the concept stage to ensure that likely significant effects of the loan on the environment, forests, and natural resources are identified and measures are taken to enhance positive outcomes and minimize unintended negative impacts.

KEY ISSUES

DISTINGUISHING BETWEEN CROSS-SECTORAL AND MACRO-ECONOMIC IMPACTS.[2] Cross-sectoral impacts on forests can emerge from specific activities and investments in related sectors: rural development, infrastructure and transport, specific resource extraction projects, and so on. By and large, these are straightforward situations, and approaches

for identifying impacts and developing methods to ameliorate or eliminate them are available (see annexes to note 6.3 and suggested readings). A potential exception is the question of impacts on the forest-dependent poor because of the lack of knowledge on the numbers of poor in forests and the nature and extent of their dependence on forests. Macroeconomic policy changes can create shifts in the national exchange rate, in trade outcomes (and policies), and other major economic areas. The impacts on forests and other natural resources of large-scale economic changes and reforms will manifest themselves through a complex web of second- and third-round activities and associated responses. Identifying the nature of their eventual impacts on forests—or even whether there will be significant impacts—in specific cases is not straightforward.

UNDERSTANDING WHAT IMPACTS FOREST SUSTAINABILITY. The definition of forest sustainability and how best to achieve it have been widely debated in the forest community for more than two decades. The issue of the importance of exogenous influences on forests is critical to determining how to achieve forest sustainability. Practitioners concerned with mainstreaming forest considerations into policy dialogue, cross-sectoral impacts, and assessing impact of macro policy reform on forests will need to be kept informed of the status of this debate because the view taken on cause-and-effect in this area has direct relevance to the role that large-scale economic reform will have and, accordingly, potential entry points for introducing forest issues.

There are two distinct interpretations for the failure of sustainable forest management (SFM). The first interpretation focuses on problems of unbalanced vested interests and related inadequacies of sector governance, including the poor performance of public forest agencies and the private sector in many countries, and the lack of adequate title and access rights to forests by local communities. This interpretation assumes that if the highlighted problems are adequately addressed, the agencies and groups in society responsible for managing forests will have an appropriate policy basis, and adequate capacity, to address problems that may develop under broader economic change.

The second interpretation holds that many of the economic and social forces influencing forests and forest-dependent people are initiated a long way from the forest sector itself and can only effectively be manipulated by agents that operate well outside the sector; thus, attempting to deal with the resulting problems in forests through incentives and institutional issues within the sector may be necessary but will be insufficient to address the problems. In line with this thinking, many of the decisions on large-scale economic and social changes that are having an impact on forests are made by people with little or no involvement in the forest sector, and seldom contacted by forest sector specialists. Under this interpretation, the options for sustainability available to forest stakeholders are constrained. An avenue is for the donor agencies, in their dialogue with economic and social policy ministries on policy loans, to agree on supportive measures for the forest sector, such as training and education programs and consultative activities.

CREATING ENTRY POINTS FOR INTRODUCING FOREST ISSUES AND TIMING. Raising the profile and relevance of forest issues among ministers of finance and social programs will require rigorous analytical work to translate forest issues into economic issues. Analysis of the economic contribution of forests (or the impact of forest conversion or degradation

on the national economy) and forest-poverty links (see note 1.1, Mainstreaming the Role of Forests in Poverty Alleviation and note 1.4, Property and Access Rights) could create entry points for incorporating forest considerations in macroeconomic and sectoral policy dialogues. The process for informing relevant sector and finance ministries should be tailored to the country context to ensure credibility. Relevant analytical findings should be available at key intervention points in national policy processes.

INDIRECT EFFECTS. Changes in tree cover or access to forest resources are often the result of direct causes, such as logging and pressures to increase agricultural and pasture areas. Logging and forest conversion themselves, however, are the result of various economic factors. Angelsen and Kaimowitz (1999) provide a framework for understanding the indirect causes of deforestation. One step examines the immediate causes of deforestation and includes the parameters that influence an agent's decisions, such as prices, technology, institutions, new information, and access to services and infrastructure. The next level addresses the underlying causes of deforestation. These are the broader forces that determine the decision parameters and include the macroeconomic variables and policy instruments.

THE TEMPORAL FACTOR. In the case of large-scale policy lending, the temporal factor also comes into play: The impact of large economic and other changes that affect forests may take a considerable number of years to become evident at the field level in forests—long after disbursements under a policy loan or policy intervention that may have been a factor in the changes have been completed. Annex 6A to this chapter illustrates the temporal dimension of the potential impact of energy sector reform on forests.

COUNTRY CONTEXT. Recent efforts to assess cross-sectoral impacts have not been able to demonstrate an empirical connection between macroeconomic structural adjustment programs and deforestation (Pandey and Wheeler 2001). Because of the complexity of the issues, the indirect nature of many of the causal relations, and the wide diversity of situations, any attempt to generalize is inherently difficult. The study by Pandey and Wheeler (2001) suggests that the impacts of structural adjustment on forests could vary by country and may be related to the nature of their forest resource. Sedjo (2005) suggests that a country with a comparative advantage in forestry (usually a forest-rich country) that is already exporting forest products could see increased forest products exports in response to structural adjustment. In contrast, the forest sector in a country without a comparative advantage in timber production may face limited changes in response to structural adjustment. The World Bank publication on DPL and Forest Outcomes (2005) suggests that other country characteristics may also shape how macroeconomic reforms influence forest resource use and management.

IMPORTANCE OF POVERTY. Poverty issues must also be directly considered when assessing cross-sectoral impacts (see also chapter 1, Forests for Poverty Reduction, and associated notes). In addition to their role in underpinning environmental stability, forests play a direct role in poverty alleviation—the primary objective of World Bank involvement. It is evident from the World Bank's own assessment of this situation, as laid out in the revised Forests Strategy (World Bank 2004a), and from anecdotal evidence, field experience, and other studies and articles, that forests are extremely valuable to the livelihoods of large numbers of poor people.

The forests most subject to competition for the various forms of use and conversion that can arise from macroeconomic and other exogenous developments are often those of importance to significant numbers of rural poor. These will be forests located at the margins of current agricultural and other land-using developments, where the poor have tended to congregate because they have reduced access to other rural areas and production assets.

More systematic analysis and knowledge on the nature and level of dependence of these people on the forests for subsistence and income generation needs to be developed.

POSITIVE IMPACTS ON FORESTS FROM MACROECONOMIC REFORMS. Discussions of cross-sectoral impacts tend to focus, as this one has, on the avoidance of inadvertent harm because of the reputational risks and transaction costs involved. However, the literature is inconclusive regarding the directionality of the relationship. Some studies have found that structural adjustment can have negative outcomes and create pressure on the environment and forests (Angelsen and Kaimowitz, 1999; Sunderlin et al. 2000). Other studies have found ambiguous results, or in some cases, positive outcomes for income and environmental benefits (Gueorgieva and Bolt 2003; Munasinghe 2001).

Elements could potentially be identified to be included in policy lending and large cross-sectoral programs that could bring about positive outcomes for forests and forest-dependent people (Wunder 2003; box 6.3). For example, macro policy changes can be oriented toward creating an environment conducive to private sector engagement. If linked with community initiatives, such changes could enable community-company partnerships and create employment for forest-dependent households.

IRREVERSIBILITY. The well-known asymmetry in the forest-loss dynamic adds urgency to the need to address cross-sectoral impacts. In agriculture, or more generally, for economic development and social programs, poor outcomes from a given set of policy changes can be identified through monitoring and, in most cases, corrected within a reasonable time. In forests, however, impacts causing loss of forests or woodlands, and watersheds that depend on this form of vegetation, usually cannot be ameliorated so easily.

EVOLVING POLICY INSTRUMENTS. Policy instruments are beginning to change, putting more emphasis on financial

Community Forest Enterprises (CFE) in Mexico are widely known to be a product of institutional arrangements that decentralized forest management to *ejidos* (agrarian reform communities) and indigenous communities and enabled these groups to improve economic well-being through sustainable commercial use of forests. Recent work suggests that the transfer of natural assets to communities through an agrarian reform process laid the territorial and governance foundation for the establishment of a large community forest sector (Bray et al. 2005). It is argued that in Mexico the agrarian reform laws have been crucial in creating a larger number of CFEs than did specific forest legislation. Agrarian reform distributed forest lands to communities and provided a template for community governance that could later serve as an institutional platform for the development of CFEs (Bray et al. 2005).

Source: Authors' compilation.

incentives, persuasion, and procedures than on regulation. Timber labeling, for example, aims to influence the behavior of timber customers by making the external costs of products more transparent (see note 3.2, Forest Certification Systems). Another trend is to seek the voluntary agreement of forest owners for the establishment of nature protection zones by compensating them contractually for income losses. As measures become more effective because they are implemented by stakeholders that understand and agree on them, procedural and persuasive instruments are more widely used. Regional planning, Local Agenda 21[3], and other participatory and coordination mechanisms are important policy steering instruments in this context.

National forest programs (NFPs), promoted as planning instruments at the national and subnational levels to reach the goal of sustainable forest development, use a holistic approach that is much different from previous sector planning procedures. Within NFPs, intersectoral approaches are seen as a necessary core element (UN-CSD 1997). This reflects lessons learned from previous policy and planning instruments, in particular the Tropical Forestry Action Plan (TFAP). Experience with the preparation and implementation of the TFAP at the country level showed that many actions failed to halt deforestation because the objectives

and instruments concentrated too narrowly on the forestry sector (Humphreys 1996).

NEED FOR ADDITIONAL DATA. Data on the degree and nature of forest dependency of large numbers of people (many of whom will be among the poorest in a given country) are limited, imprecise, and often unclear in their implications for national policy. Moreover, the physical impacts on forests that most impinge upon the livelihoods of people living in or near them are not particularly well-identified by the broad and presently available parameters such as changes in forest cover and forest trade and market data.

As a result, the poverty implications of impacts upon forests are likely to be undervalued in broad national programs and objectives. Perverse incentives and misallocation of resources leading to forest removal or changes in the status of use and ownership of forests will be a risk factor from the poverty-alleviation viewpoint, and could be exacerbated by broader policy measures in a development policy loan designed without the necessary knowledge in this area.

MONITORING CROSS-SECTORAL IMPACTS. The temporal dimension and indirect nature of cross-sectoral impacts underscores the importance of effective systems for monitoring forest cover and changes in forests' contribution to forest-dependent households and the national economy. Macro policy reforms can change access to and use of forest resources, affecting their economic contribution and the quality and quantity of forests. A cost-effective monitoring system may have to combine spatial monitoring of the biophysical resource with periodic reviews of statistical information.

FUTURE PRIORITIES AND SCALING-UP ACTIVITIES

Developing good practice for identifying cross-sectoral impacts will revolve primarily around two subjects: (i) recognizing that many situations involving macroeconomic reform are not win-win and that there is a need to analyze tradeoffs and engage in a process that involves all stakeholders in determining the appropriate balance between conflicting objectives; and (ii) determining what might be done to improve knowledge about interactions between specific types of macroeconomic and cross-sectoral activities. Important to both is the need to further strengthen collaboration among sectors and between forest sector specialists and macroeconomists, both within countries and in development institutions.

Immediate measures

IDENTIFY PRIORITY COUNTRIES BASED ON ANTICIPATED POLICY INTERVENTIONS. Donor agencies and concerned stakeholders should identify countries, lending situations, and prior conditions that suggest forests may be vulnerable to policy reforms and related activities. For institutions such as the World Bank, the results of this analysis can be helpful during preparation of country assistance strategies, forest sector investments, and specific policy loans, to prioritize the specific programs and country situations where economic and sector work on potential impacts will be needed most. For example, if there are regional trends in macro policy reform (such as the trade agreement in Central America), it would be important to focus the analytical work on this change. An indexing system based on relevant data and the DPL pipeline can be used to identify the countries and situations where more needs to be known about prior conditions surrounding forests and forest people (see note 6.3, Identifying the Need for Analysis on Forests in Development Policy Reforms). This information would then be conveyed to appropriate departments and other networks in development organization involved in preparing the policy intervention, and further activities planned accordingly.

Medium-term measures

CONDUCT NECESSARY ANALYTICAL WORK ON CROSS-SECTORAL AND MACROECONOMIC IMPACTS. Analytical work should focus on identifying opportunities for policy loans to bring about significant improvements in the benefits flowing from forests for poverty alleviation, sustainable economic growth, and the global public goods aspects of forests, and minimize unintended negative consequences.

The World Bank's DPL policy paper (World Bank 2005) outlines a five-year program of implementation of environmental analytical work to support DPL operations. This includes CEAs and SEAs or other appropriate analytical work in countries where (i) DPL volume is large, (ii) adjustment lending makes up a large share of country GDP, or (iii) reforms are proposed in environmentally sensitive sectors such as forests, agriculture, natural resources, energy, mining, transport, and water supply and sanitation (OPCS 2004; Mani 2004).

ADAPT ANALYTICAL TOOLS FOR DUE DILIGENCE FOR FORESTS. CEAs and SEAs are seen as appropriate instruments for assessing the effects of development policy operations on the environment. However, some variations in their design and resource allocation may be required for

them to effectively identify situations where policy interventions have significant potential to have an impact on forests and forest people and then for implementation of the necessary upstream analyses (see note 6.4, Assessing Cross-Sectoral Impacts).

"Rapid CEAs" are already evolving in some areas of operations in the World Bank, and have value as a means for due diligence for forests, natural resources, and the environment. The Rapid CEA in Bosnia and Herzegovina (see box 6.4) proposes to use both historical data on the performance of previous structural adjustment operations in the area of environmental impacts, and recent environmental plans, to quickly identify which policies and sectors supported by the development policy credits pose significant risks to the environment, forests, and natural resources. This would appear to be precisely the objective of due diligence in these circumstances.

DESIGN ANALYTICAL STUDIES TO INFORM POLICY PROCESSES, SUCH AS POVERTY REDUCTION STRATEGY PAPERS, NFPS, COUNTRY ASSISTANCE STRATEGY DEVELOPMENT, POLICY LENDING, AND POVERTY REDUCTION STRATEGY CREDITS. Development practitioners need a detailed understanding of national policy processes before designing analytical studies on cross-sectoral impacts or impacts of macroeconomic reform on forests. The studies should, in addition to using rigorous analytical tools and reliable data, involve key stakeholders (see box 6.2) in an effort to enhance acceptance of the findings.

SUMMARIZING AN APPROACH FOR THE WORLD BANK. Mainstreaming forest considerations requires due diligence on forests with regard to cross-sectoral impacts, given the multiple objectives of the forest strategy, and the potential importance of forest outcomes for larger economic development and poverty alleviation objectives embodied in World Bank DPL and related lending. A sequence of activities should be followed to develop the capacity of World Bank staff to identify and deal with situations in which significant forest impacts from broad economic reform lending are possible:

1. The Poverty Reduction and Economic Management Network, the Sustainable Development Network, and the Development Research Group should undertake an initial evaluation of forest significance in countries where DPLs or large-scale, cross-sectoral activities are ongoing or planned, using the methodology outlined in note 6.3, Identifying the Need for Analysis on Forests in Develop-

A World Bank workshop on CEA and SEA in January 2005 recognized that a rapid form of CEA should be examined as one option for meeting the new provisions of Operational Policy 8.60 in Bosnia and Herzegovina. The core of the rapid CEA (RCEA) would be (i) prioritization of policies and sectors to be supported by the Programmatic Development Policy Credits regarding environmental implications and risks; (ii) an assessment of state, government entity, and local capabilities to mitigate negative effects; (iii) recommendations to fill key gaps; and (iv) a small set of recommended key indicators to track progress. The RCEA would be carried out in parallel with the final stages of fiscal 2005 Programmatic Policy Structural Adjustment Credit preparation, and would be amenable to updating as needed in subsequent fiscal years.

Background information: According to the National Environmental Action Plan, freshwater and air quality in rural areas are in fairly good condition, but because wastewater management, waste disposal, and industrial controls are generally below international norms, environmental risks are increasing. Bosnia and Herzegovina's goal of meeting the requirements of the environmental *acquis communautaire* of the European Union

means that considerable investment in both the technology for pollution control and institutions for monitoring and compliance will be required. The United Nations Economic Commission for Europe (UNECE) performed an Environmental Performance Review for Bosnia and Herzegovina (UNECE 2004), which outlined deficiencies and needs for improvements in the policy, legal, and institutional framework; public participation and access to information; water resources management (including drinking water quality); land use; agriculture and biodiversity; management of waste sites; and environmental aspects of tourism and energy development.

The RCEA will first "look back" to frame how past adjustment operations examined environmental implications. It will then "look forward" by building on the National Environment Action Plan, the Environmental Performance Review, and other studies to quickly identify which policies and sectors supported by the Programmatic Development Policy Credits pose the more significant risks to the environment, forests, and natural resources. New data will be collected by Bank staff and consultants on specific privatizations, new government permit programs, and the like.

Source: World Bank 2005.

ment Policy Reforms. This will provide an initial "watch list" of countries for which further exploration of the potential impacts of programmatic lending on forests is necessary. This list should be updated using information and methodologies outlined in note 6.4, Assessing Cross-Sectoral Impacts, as these become available; for example, better information on the numbers of poor people living in or near forests, and their level of dependency on those forests, will be highly relevant.

2. As countries and situations are identified as being of interest in this regard, country teams and managers, in cooperation with the Sustainable Development Network and the Development Research Group, should examine the scheduling and content of forthcoming Country Assistance Strategy (CAS), CEA, and SEA activities to determine whether these can and should be rationalized to allow focused forest impact analysis to be carried out under their auspices.

3. Even if this adaptation of policy instruments is not immediately possible, in countries and situations identi-

fied in step 1, DPL task managers should work with the networks on an initial assessment of whether the specific macroeconomic or broad cross-sectoral reforms intended under the DPL are likely to have flow-through impacts on forests, and, if so, the likely scale and nature of these impacts. Initially, it may be necessary to use qualitative and approximation approaches, as discussed in note 6.2, Prospects for Using Policy Lending to Proactively Enable Forest Sector Reforms, until more precise means of estimating impacts are available.

NOTES

1. Environment includes policies on environmental protection, soil conservation, water resources management, nature and landscape protection, and protected areas and national parks

2. The line between these two broad groups of impact sources can sometimes blur in project cases, creating the phenomenon labeled "Dutch Disease," in which exploitation

of or reforms in one sector provides the government with "easy money" and causes the government to lose control of fiscal expenditure. Elements of the safeguard and analytical approaches for World Bank investment lending projects may apply to aspects of these cases. These situations, however, will also have large secondary and tertiary impacts throughout the economy that parallel those associated with macroeconomic policy reforms.

3. Local Agenda 21 is a local-government-led, community-wide, and participatory effort to establish a comprehensive action strategy for environmental protection, economic prosperity and community well-being in the local jurisdiction or area. This requires the integration of planning and action across economic, social, and environmental spheres. Key elements are full community participation, assessment of current conditions, target setting for achieving specific goals, monitoring, and reporting. *Source:* http://www.gdrc .org/uem/la21/la21.html.

SELECTED READINGS

Schmithüsen, F., K. Bisang, and W. Zimmermann. 2001. "Cross-Sector Linkages in Forestry: Review of Available Information and Consideration on Future Research." Forest Policy and Forest Economics, Department of Forest Sciences—ETH, Zurich. http://www.fao.org/docrep/ 003/AA002E/Aa002e03.htm#6018.

World Bank. 2004. "Good Practice Note on Environmental and Natural Resource Aspects of Development Policy Lending." World Bank, Washington, DC.

———. 2005a. "Azerbaijan: Issues and Options Associated with Energy Sector Reform." Report No. 32371-AZ, World Bank, Washington, DC.

———. 2005b. "Development Policy Lending and Forest Outcomes: Influences, Interactions, and Due Diligence." Report No. 32724-GLB, Agriculture and Rural Development Department, World Bank, Washington, DC.

REFERENCES CITED

Angelsen, A., and D. Kaimowitz. 1999. "Rethinking the Causes of Deforestation: Lessons from Economic Models." *World Bank Research Observer* 14(1): 73–98.

Bray, D. B., L. Merino-Perez, and D. Barry, eds. 2005. *The Community Forests of Mexico: Managing for Sustainable Landscapes.* Austin, TX: University of Texas Press.

Douglas, J., and D. Chandrasekharan Behr. 2006. "Note #1: Prioritizing Where Cross Sector Impacts Matter." Note submitted to World Bank as input to *Forests Sourcebook.* Unpublished. World Bank. Washington, DC.

Gueorguieva, A., and K. Bolt. 2003. "*A CriticalReview of the Literature on Structural Adjustment and the Environment.*" Environment Department Papers No. 90. World Bank, Washington, DC.

Humphreys, D. 1996. "The Global Politics of Forest Conservation Since the UNCED." *Environmental Politics* 5(2): 231–57

Kaimowitz, D., C. Vallejos, P. Pacheco and R. Lopez. 1998. "Municipal Governments and Forest Management in Lowland Bolivia." *Journal of Environment and Development* 7(1).

Lampietti, J. 2004. "Power's Promise: Electricity Reforms in Eastern Europe and Central Asia." Working Paper No. 40. World Bank, Washington, DC.

Mani, M. 2004. "An Overview of Environmental and Natural Resource Aspects of IBRD Financed Development Policy Lending Operations in FY05." ENV-ESSD, internal note. World Bank, Washington, DC.

Munasinghe, M. 2001. "Special Topic I: Structural Adjustment Policies and the Environment." *Environment and Development Economics* 4(1): 9–18.

OPCS (Operations Policy and Country Services). 2004. "Good Practice Notes Relating to the Development Policy Lending OP/BP 8.60: Environmental and Natural Resource Aspects." World Bank, Washington, DC.

Pandey, K., and D. Wheeler. 2001. "Structural Adjustment and Forest Resources: The Impact of World Bank Operations." Policy Research Working Paper 2584. World Bank, Washington, DC.

Sedjo, R. A. 2005. "Macroeconomics and Forest Sustainability in the Developing World: Resources for the Future." Discussion Paper DP 05-47. World Bank, Washington, DC.

Sunderlin, W.D., O. Ndoye, H. Bikié, N. Laporte, B. Mertens, and J. Pokam. 2000. "Economic Crisis, Small-Scale Agriculture, and Forest Cover Change in Southern Cameroon." *Environmental Conservation* 27(3): 284–90.

UN-CSD (United Nations Commission on Sustainable Development). 1997. Report of the Ad Hoc Intergovernmental Panel on Forests. E/CN.17/1997/12. United Nations, New York.

UNECE (Economic Commission for Europe) 2004. Environmental Performance Reviews, Bosnia and Herzegovina. New York and Geneva: United Nations. http://www.unece. org/env/epr/epr_studies/bosnia_and_herzegovina.pdf

World Bank. 2004a. *Sustaining Forests: A Development Strategy.* Washington, DC: World Bank.

———. 2004b. "Azerbaijan Raising Rates: Short-Term Implications of Residential Electricity Tariff Rebalancing." Report No. 30749-AZ. Europe and Central Asia Region. Environmentally and Socially Sustainable Development. World Bank, Washington DC.

———. 2005. "Development Policy Lending and Forest Outcomes: Influences, Interactions, and Due Diligence." Report No. 32724-GLB. World Bank, Washington, DC.

Wunder, S. 2003. *Oil Wealth and the Fate of the Forest: A Comparative Study of Eight Tropical Countries.* London: Routledge.

CROSS-REFERENCED CHAPTERS AND NOTES

ANNEX 6A. TIMESCALE OF IMPACTS OF ENERGY SECTOR REFORM ON FORESTS AND FOREST INDUSTRIES

The table below illustrates different timescales of the impacts of energy sector reform on forests and forest industries. Although numerous policy objectives have short-term impacts, an equal number have medium-term impacts. This underscores the need to have an effective model for predicting these outcomes and monitoring them. A point that does not appear in the table is that any matrix of this kind would need criteria for weighting the importance of the links to provide comparable information.

Policy Area C: Energy					
Policy objective	**Policy instrument/ linkage**	**Impact on the forest and forest industries sector (particularly on the supply and demand of wood)**	**Scale of impact[a]**		
			Timescale[b]	**Supply**	**Demand**
1. Diversify energy sources (away from fossil fuel and toward alternatives)	Taxes on use of fossil fuels; subsidies and grants for research and development of alternative fuels	1 (a) increased afforestation as energy plantations	***		M
		(b) increased harvesting of thinnings, small-sized, and low-quality wood, including forest and logging residues, for use as energy	****		S
		(c) increased use of urban waste, notably waste paper, for heat and power		***	S
		(d) increased use of industry and post-consumption residues for heat and power		**	S
		(e) development of wood-based liquid and gas fuels for transport and other uses		**	L
		(f) fuller integration of electricity generated by wood-processing industries into national grids		*	M
2. Raise energy self-sufficiency and security	Subsidies and grants for research and development and use of domestically available resources	2 (a) as 1 above, esp. (a), (b), and (c)	****	****	M
		(b) develop wood use for local (community, institution, hospital, farm, military, and so on) heat and power generation		**	M
3. Improve energy conservation	Subsidies and grants for research, development, and use of energy-saving technology, equipment, buildings, and so on	3 (a) increased demand and production of sawnwood as low energy cost product	**	**	M
		(b) greater use of wood-based products, especially sawnwood, for insulation of buildings		**	M
...		...			
... (up to 5)		... (up to 5.c)			

Source: Peck and Descargues 1997: 79.

a. On a scale of * (= little impact) to ***** (= very significant impact). This is intended to show the possible extent of impact on wood supply and demand should policy be changed from its present direction.

b. This column is intended to show how soon after a policy change has been initiated an impact might begin to take effect: S = within 5 years; M = within 15 years; L = not before 15 years.

Using National Forest Programs to Mainstream Forest Issues

The NFP concept aims to promote forest sector reform and development as contributors to sustainable development and poverty alleviation (see box 6.5). It responds to global concerns about unsustainable exploitation of forests and deforestation and widespread discontent with the outcomes of earlier concerted efforts by the international community[1] to halt the destruction of predominantly tropical forests. The NFP expands the focus beyond the tropics, reflecting the principle of shared responsibility for the success of sustainable development, as defined during the United Nations Conference on Environment and Development (UNCED) in 1992.

The NFP refers to a process rather than a tangible program and operates on a set of procedural principles[2] that define how the exercise needs to be conducted. Its elements,[3] in turn, outline the scope of individual outputs—that is, what is to be accomplished. The NFP principles determine the concept's most characteristic features and underpin each country's sovereign entitlement to use its natural resources in a sustainable manner. While advocating donor coordination in support of sustainable forest sector development, the concept nevertheless emphasizes country leadership in NFP implementation. This sets the NFP apart from previous initiatives, which had been widely criticized for being donor driven, unnecessarily top heavy, and lacking in country ownership.

The World Bank's 2002 Forests Strategy calls expressly for a "multisectoral approach that addresses cross-sectoral issues and takes into account the impacts of activities, policies, and practices outside the sector on forests and people who depend on forests for their livelihoods"(World Bank 2004: 2). This programmatic requirement fits seamlessly with the NFP concept. Reflecting upon the specific usefulness of the NFP concept for these ends, the Forests Strategy concludes "…the motivation and coordinating framework will be based on a shared agenda for forests, so that all groups are able to focus their inputs on the same basic set of objectives in the sector. In many countries this framework will be provided by enhanced NFPs" (World Bank 2004: 9). This applies particularly to the World Bank's stated objective to build its forest sector interventions on blended financing arrangements.

The main objectives of the NFP are to

- introduce intersectoral planning approaches, involving all relevant partners, to resolve conflicts and generate effective policies and programs to address problems;
- raise awareness and mobilize commitments at all levels to address the issues related to sustainable forestry development;
- increase the efficiency and effectiveness of both public and private actions for sustainable forestry development;
- foster local, national, regional, and international partnerships;
- mobilize and organize national and (if necessary) international resources and catalyze action to implement programs and plans in a coordinated manner; and
- plan and implement how forests and the forestry sector could contribute to national and global initiatives, for example, the Environmental Action Plans and the actions agreed upon to implement the Forest Principles, Chapter 11 of Agenda 21, and the Conventions on Biodiversity, on Climate Change, and on Desertification.

The NFP, by definition, aims for cross-sectoral mainstreaming of forest issues. Such issues as livelihoods of forest-dependent people and their rights (particularly rights of access and resource tenure and equitable benefit sharing) call for broad stakeholder participation in forest policy formulation and legal as well as institutional reform (see note 5.3, Strengthening Legal Frameworks in the Forest Sector). The NFP specifically addresses these issues and promotes nonconfrontational and synergetic implementation. The development (or, rather, the adaptation) of national standards based upon international and regional processes,[4] and the establishment and operation of independent certification systems on a national scale, provide practical examples of how the NFP can serve as a transmission belt between the international policy dialogue and national implementation. In a similar way, the World Bank's need for baseline information and impact assessments of various kinds coincides with the need for systematic, structured information management as part of the NFP forest sector review.

Box 6.5 NFP in Uganda

NFPs can help raise the national profile of forest issues and mainstream forests within the larger policy context, as seen in Uganda. In 1997, Uganda was the first country to develop a poverty reduction strategy. During the NFP process, considerable effort was put into influencing the Poverty Eradication Action Plan (PEAP) and aligning the strategies for forest sector development with its pillars. As a result, the current PEAP document outlines in some detail the sector's contributions to the economy, the problems it faces, its potential to help alleviate poverty, and external influencing factors, such as land ownership, energy consumption, decentralization, and urbanization. It also makes reference to the NFP strategic framework and is consistent with the forest sector's new institutional setting.

In outlining forestry-poverty linkages, the NFP process analyzed significant amounts of data and commissioned studies to show that:

- forests provide an estimated 850,000 jobs, mostly in the informal sector related to the collection of domestic fuelwood;
- incomes from the sale of nonwood forest products are estimated at US$38 million per year, with poor households in forested areas earning up to US$75 to fill gaps in other income sources, such as labor and farm produce;
- more than 92 percent of Ugandans use fuelwood as their main or only source of energy, consuming 16 million tons of firewood and 4 million tons of charcoal each year;
- forests provide free goods that poor households rely upon for shelter, food, and medicines and that act as safety nets in times of emergency and sudden economic shocks; and
- forests can provide a source of income and development for many communities through ecotourism (MWLE 2002).

Using such findings in PEAP and NFP has raised awareness among policy makers and the public about the importance of forestry to the wider economy. The current PEAP notes that forests provide an annual economic value of US$360 million (6 percent of GDP), of which only US$112 million is captured in official statistics. It explains how trees (through fuelwood and charcoal) provide 90 percent of energy demands and are expected to still contribute 75 percent in 2015. The PEAP also describes the ecological services of forests: biodiversity, climate regulation, soil and water conservation, and nutrient recycling.

PEAP forest-related priorities regarding enhanced implementation of the NFP include the following:

- increased support to the Forestry Inspection Division for sector oversight;
- promotion of private sector investment in private forests through information and technical advice on forest management; permits to grow trees in central forest reserves with secure land and tree tenure; review of tax and other disincentives; continued operation of the Sawlog Grant Scheme and the establishment of a Tree Fund in accordance with the National Forestry and Tree Planting Act;
- increased support to District Forestry Services to provide forestry advisory services for private and community forestry to establish woodlots and planted forests and manage natural forests;
- development of the National Tree Seed Centre and decentralized seed production; and
- identification of potential markets for ecological services, such as carbon trading.

As in any iterative process, priorities for the sector have changed since forestry was included in PEAP, as a result of a review undertaken in 2002. After three years of persistent lobbying, PEAP now regards forestry not only as a sector, but as an "urgent short-term priority" for funding, which suggests that forestry could qualify for increased allocations.

Source: Adata et al. 2006; Geller and McConnell 2006.

Box 6.6   Basic Principles of NFP Preparation and Implementation

- *Sustainability of forest development.* The main purpose of the NFP is to ensure the conservation and sustainable development of forest resources.
- *National sovereignty and country leadership.* NFPs are national initiatives for which the country must assume full leadership and responsibility.
- *Partnership.* NFPs aim to bring together all stakeholders in a process to which they feel committed. The strength of this partnership will depend on its ability to draw upon the specific capacities of individual partners.
- *Participation.* In the NFP, issues, options, and the resulting policies, strategies, and programs are agreed upon through participatory decision making and consensus building among all interested partners.
- *Holistic and intersectoral approach.* NFP approaches forests as diverse ecosystems with interdependent elements in dynamic equilibrium producing a variety of goods and services; forestry includes trees in rural areas; forestry is practiced within the context of sustainable land management, environmental stability, and social and economic development. Forest dwellers are also part of this ecosystem.
- *A long-term iterative process.* The NFP is a cyclic process that includes planning as well as implementation, and monitoring and evaluation activities. It is also an iterative process that continually reflects changes in the environment and the acquisition of new knowledge even during implementation.
- *Capacity building.* Capacity building is an essential element of the NFP. Throughout the process, actions are taken to develop the planning and implementation capacity of the national institu-

tions and other key actors with a view to decreasing dependence on external assistance when necessary.
- *Policy and institutional reforms.* A priority of the NFP is to ensure that the policy and institutional framework is conducive to sustainable forestry development. Reforms must address policy and institutional issues in a comprehensive manner that recognizes the interdependencies between sectors.
- *Consistency with the national policy framework and global initiatives.* The NFP must link with national development plans and with regional and local strategies. They should be integrated in the land-use planning exercises at national and local levels and into broader programs, such as Environmental Action Plans and the actions to implement UNCED's Agenda 21 and related conventions and initiatives.
- *Raising awareness.* The NFP must raise the visibility of the forestry sector and its priority in national agendas. The full value of forests and trees must be recognized as should their contribution to social, economic, and environmental issues.
- *National policy commitment.* The national forest program must be backed by the long-term commitment of all national actors, particularly at political and decision-making levels.
- *International commitment.* The long-term commitment of the international community and its institutions is essential. These bodies should respect the policies, strategies, and programs approved by the countries and adapt their own priorities to the country priorities.

Source: FAO (http://www.nfp-facility.org/forestry/site/31811/en/).

The NFP approach is flexible and can be adapted to a wide range of situations:

- National governments may use this framework for the formulation of their forestry sector plans.
- Decentralized government authorities, as well as other national partners such as community-based organizations, nongovernmental organizations (NGOs), and the private sector, may use it to plan and implement their activities in line with the national framework.
- Concerned international institutions may use it to harmonize their actions, strengthen their cooperation in

forestry, and enhance the use of human and financial resources in an effective and efficient way.
- Subregional and regional organizations of different countries with the same interests can use this methodological framework to formulate and implement actions together.

OPERATIONAL ASPECTS

The preparation and implementation of the national forest program is guided by a series of basic principles, as listed in box 6.6. The application of these basic principles should be adapted to the specific national context (political, social, economic, environmental) of the country concerned.

There is no blueprint for launching an NFP—the process may embark from various entry points, depending on which problem or development goals are perceived as the highest priority. Designing and conducting an NFP involves four main phases: (i) organization of the process, (ii) strategic sector planning, (iii) program implementation, and (iv) revision and updating. NFP implementation is characterized by a sequence of management and learning cycles.

ORGANIZATION OF THE PROCESS. This first phase includes identification of all stakeholders in the forestry and related sectors, organization of coordination mechanisms, and development of a communication strategy to ensure transparency of the process and full participation by all actors. Partners in the process should include national partners and, where relevant, international partners. The national partners may include national- and subnational-level governmental institutions from the forestry sector and other sectors; training and research institutions; NGOs involved in development and conservation; community-based organizations; private interests; and user groups (including rural communities, farmers, settlers and Indigenous Peoples and other forest dwellers, private enterprises, and associations). International partners may include intergovernmental agencies and development banks, bilateral agencies, and international NGOs.

The coordination mechanism helps stimulate, lead, and monitor the NFP. Existing coordination mechanisms should be used. If necessary, existing mechanisms could be improved and strengthened through a capacity-building program. A communication strategy should be developed as early as possible to ensure that all stakeholders are informed about the process and its results and can participate in all phases.

STRATEGIC PLANNING. The second phase includes an evaluation of the current situation in the sector, identification of major problems, and possible immediate actions (see box 6.7). It also includes an in-depth sector analysis, strategic analyses, and formulation of the NFP. The strategic planning is aimed at the following:

- making the case for public investment in the forestry sector;
- identifying constraints, problems, and opportunities for forestry development in a cross-sectoral context;
- identifying and assessing development options;

- establishing sectoral goals and objectives, the long-term development strategy (20–25 years), and the overall program structure in the short term (5–10 years); and
- improving national capacity in policy formulation and sectoral planning.

Strategic planning choices should be a combination of professional analytical work and the result of public consultations through seminars, workshops, and other mechanisms that foster the involvement of all stakeholders. To ensure compatibility, strategic planning must be carried out within the broader context of the national planning framework and ongoing global initiatives.

Box 6.7   Recurring Key Issues in Forest Sector Reviews

Some recurring issues in forest sector reviews include the following:

- the need for policy, legislative, and institutional reforms;
- the assessment of the forestry resource and its economic potential (wood products, fuelwood and energy, nonwood products, and nonmonetary benefits) including such issues as demand and supply, trade, market prices and fluctuations, substitutes, and various other external factors;
- conservation needs and potential, including such issues as the need to develop a network of conservation areas, the protection of endangered species, biodiversity management in production forests, watershed restoration and protection, and soil conservation;
- the social functions of the forests, including such issues as employment generation, contribution to the local subsistence economy, cultural functions, special needs of indigenous groups, and benefit sharing; and
- the assessment of the environmental impact of forest management, wood production, industrial operations and trade, wildlife management and forest clearing, shifting cultivation, fuelwood collection, and extraction of other forest products.

Source: FAO (http://www.nfp-facility.org/forestry/site/31811/en/).

IMPLEMENTATION. The implementation of specific programs, activities, and projects is the responsibility of the national implementing actors with the support of external agencies when needed in the third phase of the NFP process. Implementation should be coordinated and closely monitored. The coordinating entity should also monitor. This phase may involve policy, legal, and institutional reforms and the implementation of financing strategies (including enhanced revenue collection). It will also involve provision of support to stakeholder organizations and the facilitation of partnerships for joint implementation. This phase is expected to increase stakeholder capacity and produce partnership agreements (such as sector-wide approaches; see box 6.8 on the use of this tool in Vietnam) and increase transparency and commitment.

REVISION AND UPDATE. The fourth phase of the NFP involves revising and updating. This requires selecting issues for monitoring and evaluation (M&E) and defining M&E criteria and indicators, followed by participatory monitoring and assessment of M&E results. The evaluation of NFP implementation should:

- review the relevance of the program targets and objectives in relation to changing conditions;
- provide information on its impact, for example, the extent to which program implementation has resolved

fundamental problems, such as deforestation, wood and nonwood product supply, and reforestation, and generated forestry sector contributions to social and economic development at various levels;

- assess the level of integration of the program with national development plans and its contribution to meeting national development goals;
- assess changes in policy, policy instruments, and the impact of institutional strengthening;
- assess environmental impact and the contribution of NFP-generated activities to global environmental issues;
- assess the contribution of the program to sustainable development;
- quantify the changes in activity in the forestry sector and their contribution to the national economy;
- appraise the involvement and performance of all partners, national and international, with regard to original commitments; and
- assess the efficiency and effectiveness of communications and information between all partners (national and international) (FAO http://www.nfp-facility.org/forestry/site/31811/en/).

Before updating the NFP, changes in country context should also be noted. The new NFP should follow the same process as the original program—the NFP is a cyclic process.

Box 6.8   Vietnam's 5MHRP: An Example of Success

Various developed countries promoted NFP processes in cooperation with developing countries (the Six-Country Initiative in support of the Intergovernmental Panel on Forests/Intergovernmental Forum on Forests (IPF/IFF) process, for instance) to gain first-hand experience, emphasize the concept's relevance beyond tropical forests and developing countries, and underline their commitment to shared responsibility in protecting the world's forest resources through sustainable management. In Vietnam, forest sector development is guided by the Five Million Hectares Reforestation Program (5MHRP), which runs until 2010. Aiming to facilitate implementation, the international community has provided support through the Forest Sector Support Program (FSSP) since 2001. To this end, more than 20 donor agencies and NGOs pooled and coordinated their contributions with the Vietnamese government by way of a sector-wide approach. The FSSP

seeks to actively involve all major stakeholders (including rural communities), addresses access and management rights and benefit sharing, and promotes sustainable forest management. Its operation is based upon a common work plan (which defines nine fields of action and applies agreed upon standards, set forth in a forest sector manual) as well as a multidonor forest fund. With a view to ensuring efficiency, effectiveness, complementarity, and poverty-orientation of the donors' activities, a joint M&E system was established, and common supervisory bodies (FSSP Partnership Group, technical committee) installed. By launching the FSSP, the original preoccupation of the 5MHRP with large-scale afforestation was reoriented toward sustainable forest management, poverty alleviation, and a more holistic approach to forest sector development. A constructive multistakeholder dialogue was successfully initiated and maintained.

Source: Sepp 2006.

LEARNING AND SHARING. Another operational aspect that warrants close attention is commonly referred to as learning and sharing. It includes progress reporting and systematic documentation and sharing of lessons learned in international and regional contexts.

Countries implementing the NFP concept are expected to report regularly to international forums (such as the United Nations Forum on Forests (UNFF) or the Committee on Forestry (COFO) of the FAO, or to regional frameworks, such as the Central African Forest Commission, the Amazon Cooperation Treaty Organization, or the Association of Southeast Asian Nations). Likewise, various donor organizations—including the World Bank and the FAO, among others—have undertaken to compile, assess, document, and share information about NFP implementation in various countries and settings, drawing on information furnished by individual partner countries. This process has recently been institutionalized through establishment of international and regional communities of practice.

LESSONS LEARNED AND RECOMMENDATIONS FOR PRACTITIONERS

Several attempts have been made recently to gauge the progress made in NFP implementation. Such undertakings have drawn on reports furnished by participating countries as well as upon feedback provided by numerous international experts and national practitioners alike, mostly in connection with high-level meetings of the UNFF or regional conferences and workshops (such as a UNFF-4 side event on achievement of the UNFF Plan of Action through NFPs).

THE NFP CAN RAISE PROFILE OF FOREST SECTOR. Past experience suggests that the NFP concept has been highly successful in raising the forest sector's political status in many countries. Awareness of the multiple functions and values of forests has improved markedly, as have participatory implementation and civil society and private sector involvement in forest sector development. In numerous countries, policy, legal, and institutional reforms (often including such cross-cutting issues as decentralization and devolution of administrative authority and land rights and resource tenure) have been successfully initiated (see chapter 5, Improving Forest Governance; note 5.1, Decentralized Forest Management; and note 5.3, Strengthening Legal Frameworks in the Forest Sector).

CHALLENGES AND FACTORS IMPORTANT FOR SUCCESS. A number of challenges and crucial success factors have been identified:

- There needs to be clear understanding and agreement among all stakeholders about the priority issues to be addressed in the course of the NFP.
- To ensure lasting commitment, equitable access to information and broad participation in discussion and decision making and the establishment of a focal point or secretariat as a clearinghouse structure and impartial moderator should be considered.
- Equitable participation hinges on identification of key stakeholder groups, support to stakeholder self-organization, and capacity building; communication and participation must be kept transparent and nonconfrontational.
- Cross-sectoral environmental and social assessments must be included in the NFP's analysis stage; adequate tools and techniques for data collection and assessment of information need to be communicated and applied.
- From the outset, macro policies and issues related to structural adjustment (for example, PRSPs) need to be integrated in strategic planning and decision making.
- Donor coordination should be promoted through partnership approaches and agreements—this also helps to ensure that the partner country's domestic resources are pooled and used in a transparent and efficient manner.
- Financing strategies need to coordinate and combine various types of financing instruments and sources of funding (donors, public budget, private sector, civil society) in the pursuit of sustainable forest sector development. Forest sector investment must be coordinated with commonly agreed upon goals and priorities; hence constituting a core area of discussion for overall strategy development and policy formulation.
- Science and research, professional education facilities, and public information services need to be included in the NFP with a view to ensuring systematic analysis and rationalized decision making, building management capacity, and promoting public discussion and awareness about the environmental and socioeconomic significance of forests and their sustainable use.
- NFP implementation needs to be monitored on a continuous basis. Because of the lengthy process, donor coordination should aim to ensure that assistance to forest sector development is provided on a continuous basis.

One additional, crucial lesson learned so far is the need for qualitative performance criteria, whereby the overall effectiveness and conformity of individual NFPs could be gauged. Such criteria would have to be sufficiently broad to allow for each country's different environmental, economic, and sociopolitical settings, while at the same time enabling objective summary conclusions about the NFP concept's progress and impact.

NOTES

1. Most notably, the TFAPs, as implemented throughout the 1980s, and Forestry Master Plans. By the mid-1990s, TFAPs had been discontinued.

2. National sovereignty and country leadership; consistency with the constitutional and legal frameworks of each country; consistency with international agreements and commitments; partnership and participation of all interested parties in the NFP process; holistic and intersectoral approach to forest development and conservation; long-term and iterative process of planning, implementation, and monitoring (Six-Country Initiative 1999).

3. National forest statement; sector review; policy, legislative, and institutional reform; strategy development; action plan; investment program; capacity-building program; monitoring and evaluation system; coordination; and participatory mechanisms, including conflict-resolution schemes.

4. For example, the Montreal Process, the Tarapoto Proposal, and the like.

SELECTED READINGS

In recent years, information about forest sector development, strategic forest sector planning, sustainable forest management, and the use of NFPs as implementation frameworks has multiplied at a startling rate. Concept papers, country reports, conference proceedings, and workshop presentations create a mind-numbing barrage of information. For quick reference and for keeping up with the dynamic development of the international forest regime as it continues to expand, online references may be the most convenient source of information. Here, the reader enjoys the benefit of regularly updated and selective reading.

European Tropical Forest Research Network. 2004. ETFRN News 41/42—National Forest Programs.

FAO National Forest Programme Facility: NFP Digests and Online Information Resource, available at http://www.nfp-facility.org.

Geller, S., and R. McConnell. 2006. "Linking National Forest Programs and Poverty Reduction Strategies." *Unasylva* 225 (57): 56–62.

Geller, S., and F. Owino. 2002. "Qualitative Assessment of National Forest Programs." LTS International, Edinburgh, Scotland. Available at http://www.fao.org/docrep/009/a0970e/a0970e13.htm.

Online resources provided by the United Nations Forum on Forests. Available at http://www.un.org/esa/forests/index.html.

Online resources provided by the Global Forest Information Service. Available at http://www.gfis.net.

REFERENCES CITED

Adata, M., S. Geller, R. McConnell, and G. Tumushabe. 2006. "Linking National Forest Programmes and Poverty Reduction Strategies." Report of FAO mission to Uganda 3 March 2006, Forestry Policy and Institutions Services, Forestry Department, FAO, Rome, Italy.

Geller, S., and R. McConnell. 2006. "Linking National Forest Programs and Poverty Reduction Strategies." *Unasylva* 225 (57): 56–62.

MWLE (Ministry of Water, Lands & Environment), 2002. "National Forest Programme." Kampala, Uganda.

Sepp, C. 2006. "National Forest Programmes and Forest-related Multilateral Environmental Agreements." Note submitted to World Bank as input to *Forests Sourcebook*. Unpublished. World Bank, Washington, DC.

Six-Country Initiative. 1999. "Practitioner's Guide to the Implementation of the IPF Proposals for Action." Prepared in Support of the UN ad-hoc Intergovernmental Forum on Forests (IFF). Second revised edition, Secretariat of the Six-Country Initiative, GTZ/TWRP, Eschborn.

CROSS-REFERENCED CHAPTERS AND NOTES

Chapter 5: Improving Forest Governance.

Note 5.1, Decentralized Forest Management, and 5.3, Strengthening Legal Frameworks in the Forest Sector.

Prospects for Using Policy Lending to Proactively Enable Forest Sector Reforms

At first glance, policy lending instruments (for example, DPLs and poverty reduction support credits [PRSCs]) seem well-suited to achieving basic reforms in forests. Forests, like all natural resources, are public goods and need to be managed in the interests of local people, the country, and the global environment. Effective management of forest resources involves difficult choices and reforms ranging from reshaping and enforcing taxation regimes (see note 5.4, Strengthening Fiscal Systems in the Forest Sector), curbing illegal logging (see note 5.5, Addressing Illegal Logging and Other Forest Crime), restoring the traditional rights of local populations (see chapter 12, Applying OP 4.10 on Indigenous Peoples), closing down parastatals, and reforming institutions (see note 5.2, Reforming Forest Institutions).

Despite this, there are mixed opinions in the World Bank on the effectiveness of using policy loans (versus investment loans) to address sectoral reforms in forest sector. There is no current consistent case evidence from Bank activities to support an unambiguous conclusion on this matter. This note presents key principles to consider when addressing forest sector reform through Development Policy Lending (DPL).

OPERATIONAL ASPECTS

COORDINATION BETWEEN ANALYTICAL AND LENDING ACTIVITIES. Independent of whether a policy lending instrument[1] is used to address forest sector reform, upstream analytical work, the development policy loan, and sectoral investments need to be coordinated so as to make the best use of the capacities of each of these instruments to bring about needed changes (see box 6.9).[2] Such coordination is especially critical where forests are both significant (important for economic revenue, poverty alleviation, and environmental services) and vulnerable to cross-sectoral impacts. Upstream analysis is a way to improve the World Bank's

ability to identify the appropriate sectoral reforms (or priorities) and, where relevant, anticipate and address potentially adverse forest impacts resulting from key sectoral and cross-sectoral macro policy reforms. This requires allocation of human and financial resources. In addition, it is important to integrate upstream analysis into ongoing work for PRSPs, CASs, and other Bank activities.

Development policy loans are usually issued in a single tranche, and consist of quick-disbursing assistance that can help restore balance of payments equilibria (and as such, are

---

Box 6.9 Mexico Environmental SAL: Making It Work

In an environmental structural adjustment operation in Mexico (Mexico Environmental Structural Adjustment Loan [ENVSAL] fiscal 2004), the objective was to mainstream environmental issues into key economic sectors. The policy loan was seen as effective in achieving its objective. It involved establishing a functioning intersectoral technical working group for each of the key sectors (water, energy, forestry, and tourism). The ENVSAL complemented investment loans that were focused on specific sectors. In the case of forestry, it was linked with the investment loan on community forestry and focused on complementary policy measures and fiscal instruments to enhance sustainability and betterment of livelihoods. A shortcoming of the Mexico ENVSAL is that the number of conditionalities was high and the triggers covered a broad range of developmental areas, which raised supervision and transaction costs significantly.

Source: Authors' compilation.

---

limited in the coverage and duration they can devote to sectoral reforms). They can also be designed as multiyear, multitranche operations that support sector-wide assistance programs in response to government requests when appropriate, and are associated with different types of conditionality (see box 6.10 and box 6.11).

The good practice principles proposed by the World Bank 2005 Conditionality Review are relevant for strong policy operations aiming to achieve forest sector reforms. These principles are reviewed in the following paragraphs:

OWNERSHIP. Success of sector policy reforms depends heavily on the ownership and institutional capacity of the agencies responsible for implementing the reforms. A realistic assessment of ownership must rely on the government's expressed policy intentions and its track record of reform. The nature of policy loans requires separating the reforms from the stakeholders responsible for implementation. Perspectives diverge on the implication of this for the utility of DPL for sectoral reforms. With DPLs, sector reforms often *must* be initiated and owned by central economic and policy ministries, thus broadening the group of agencies responsible for reform. Furthermore, policy loans can be more effective because disbursements are triggered by the delivery of tangible and measurable results. This can be an important incentive in achieving sectoral reforms that might not come to fruition under sector investment lending because of institutional inertia and unwillingness to venture into reform areas in the implementing agencies themselves (see boxes 6.11).

Separating reforms from the stakeholders responsible runs the risk of a disconnect between reform and implementation at the sector level, especially in cases where very specific sectoral objectives have been included in the DPL package. For example, in some countries energy sector reforms have been included in a series of DPLs over several years, with little impact on the sector program. When using DPLs for sectoral reforms, it can also be unclear where the funds required for costs of implementing triggers or prior actions for subsequent loans will be raised.

HARMONIZATION. Under the lead of country authorities, World Bank staff should reach an understanding with the government and other partners on a single and internally coherent framework for measuring progress under the government's program. These accountability frameworks are set out as policy matrices showing policy actions and expected results. These frameworks can serve to coordinate broader donor support, including technical assistance. Accountability

---

Box 6.10   Typology of Conditionality

Policy based loans are made available when the borrower accomplishes critical policy and institutional actions, or *loan conditions*. Actions to be met before an operation can be approved by the Board are referred to as *prior actions* and are listed in a schedule to the legal agreement, and all conditions for single-tranche operations are prior actions. In an operation with more than one tranche, the borrower complies with certain conditions after Board approval and effectiveness (in addition to any prior actions), termed *tranche-release conditions*. Unless all tranche-release conditions are met, a tranche can be released only if the Board approves a waiver of the unmet conditions.

In addition to the critical policy and institutional actions that are recorded as prior actions or tranche-release conditions in legal agreements, the World Bank uses *triggers* and *benchmarks* to review and describe progress under a programmatic series of loans.

- Triggers represent critical actions for achieving and sustaining the results of the medium-term program. Achievement of triggers normally indicates sufficient progress to move from one operation to the next. Triggers offer greater operational flexibility than using tranche-release conditions, because triggers can be adapted more easily to a changing program environment. Bank operations are expected to describe how triggers are adapted and modified to support program objectives before being converted into the prior actions of a follow-on operation.

- *Benchmarks* in program matrices describe the contents and results of the government's program in areas supported by the World Bank. Benchmarks are frequently used to describe steps in a reform process that represent significant, though not necessarily critical, progress markers for the implementation of the program. Although they help define an area of the Bank's policy involvement, they are not intended to determine disbursement of Bank loans or grants.

Source: World Bank 2005.

The fifth Poverty Reduction Support Credit (PRSC-5) for Ghana is the second in a series of annual operations supporting the implementation of the Ghana Growth and Poverty Reduction Strategy (GPRS II) covering the period 2006–09, in line with the 2004 CAS and the 2006 CAS Progress Report. This proposed operation will focus on three broad components of the new poverty reduction agenda organized under (i) accelerated private sector–led growth, (ii) vigorous human resource development, and (iii) good governance and civic responsibility. While the PRSC-5 support would translate primarily into funding for the implementation of the GPRS II, the PRSC-5 also focuses on cross-cutting issues related to private sector development and the strengthening of institutions related to governance, public sector reform, decentralization, and public financial management.

The first component of the proposed PRSC-5 reflects the objectives of the first pillar of the GPRS II, focusing on actions aimed at accelerating sustainable private sector–led growth. This first component also supports measures to improve the performance of the rural sector through policy actions aimed at strengthening government support to agriculture, and at improving the management of natural resources with a focus on forestry resources.

A forest condition was included as a prior action for PRSC-5. The proposed prior action was "conducting an inventory of plantation forests and providing the needed information for two auctions of timber utilization contracts in 2006." The inventory of plantation forests was carried out in early 2006, covering an area of 2,000 sq km, and provided the information needed to calculate the timber right fees (TRF) that were used to determine the value of the Timber Utilization Contracts (TUCs). Based on this information, a competitive bid on plantation timber resources was conducted in April.

The introduction of new policies for managing forestry resources, such as the conversion from timber area leases to timber utilization contracts, has proven to be much slower than expected. There have been delays in carrying out the inventory of trees in areas eligible for conversion, which are needed to calculate the TRFs that will, in turn, be used to determine the value of the TUCs. These inventories are time-consuming and expensive, making them difficult to carry out, especially given the lower-than-expected revenues coming from internally generated funds. Most of the internally generated funds for the Forestry Commission (around 50 percent) are derived from the export levy on timber, which was challenged in court by timber exporting companies.

The inventory of plantation forests carried out in early 2006 provided the required information for at least one TUC auction, completed in April that year. The inventory and auction implemented by the Forestry Commission should not detract from the fact that the budget execution rate of the Forestry Commission in 2006 was lower than in 2005, falling to 45 percent, down from 69 percent. The forthcoming PRSC-6 operation, therefore, has a trigger that supports the government's program to have in place a cabinet-approved financial framework Forestry Commission in 2007. This financial framework aims to ensure (i) that the forest revenues and the budget of the Forestry Commission are released in time to conduct its core functions; (ii) transparency and accountability in financial management, including budget execution; and (iii) the collection and distribution of revenue to stakeholders. In doing so, it expects to help ensure predictability of financing and allow the budget execution rate to increase.

Source: Authors' compilation using World Bank 2007a.

frameworks can be used flexibly to achieve different levels of coordination, responding to country circumstances.

CUSTOMIZATION. The accountability framework should be consistent with the government's expressed policy intentions and internal accountability mechanisms. The framework should not be used to add policy actions to the government's agenda. Several programs support reforms that are politically sensitive and require the government to make hard choices about reform. The program measures are usually derived from a government-led process of reform and the reform measures should be linked to an important objective in the government strategy document.

PRIORITIZATION OF CRITICAL ACTIONS. In establishing the conditions for lending, World Bank and country staff should choose from the agreed accountability framework policy and institutional actions that are critical for achieving the

In November 2005, the World Bank approved a US$15 million IBRD Natural Resources development policy loan to help Gabon design and implement reforms in the forest, fisheries, biodiversity and environment, mining, and oil sectors. In February 2006, it approved a US$35 million Forest and Environment development policy grant to help Cameroon consolidate and scale up recent sector reforms. Both operations represent World Bank contributions to national sector programs supported by multiple donors—the Cameroon grant is a joint IDA-Global Environment Fund (GEF) operation, while the Gabon development policy loan is an IBRD loan to be complemented by a parallel GEF grant.

Forests, biodiversity, and other natural resources are critical to rural livelihoods in both countries, where the majority of people live in extreme poverty. They are also central to economic development and stability, and are the focus of a number of international partnerships. While adapted to fit their specific country contexts, both operations focus on reforming sector incentive frameworks, improving governance, enhancing participation, and enforcing laws and regulations in the field. Their design is based on several principles: that natural resources are public goods to be managed in the interests of local people, the country, and the global environment; that sustainable forest management and fiscal and environmental responsibility must be integrated into the business model of the forest industry; and that government must assume full responsibility for the quality of management of the assets under its stewardship.

Well-designed, comprehensive forest operations tend to involve difficult choices and reforms ranging from reshaping and enforcing taxation regimes, curbing illegal logging, restoring the traditional rights of local populations, closing down parastatals, overcoming inertia, and reforming institutions. Two decades of Bank experience in providing assistance to the forest sector in Cameroon and Gabon revealed clearly the limits of traditional projects (called Sector Investment Loans, or SILs by the World Bank) in reforming forest sectors traditionally dominated by political patronage and vested interests. It also indicated that more successful reform programs can be pursued through sector-wide structural adjustments, if the programs are sufficiently broad, and endowed with flexible time frames and adequate resources for supervision.

A number of considerations led the World Bank to select DPL as the instrument for the new Cameroon and Gabon operations:

- DPLs directly involve central economic ministries, engaging high-level authorities to support fundamental changes in policy and its implementation. SILs, however, are often limited to sector ministries in which narrower interests tend to guard the status quo, leaving necessary policy changes in the hands of those most resistant to change.

- DPL disbursements are triggered by the delivery of tangible and measurable results, whereas SIL proceeds are used to reimburse eligible expenditures incurred by the client. SILs are based on the assumption that a strong direct link exists between expenditures and results, while DPLs focus more directly and uncompromisingly on results. DPL disbursements are far fewer in number and involve much larger amounts than SIL disbursements, making them significant to heads of state and central economic authorities who would otherwise likely overlook forest-related issues.

- DPL places a strong emphasis on defining results clearly and measuring achievements objectively, because these are at the core of legal agreements and key to World Bank loan and grant disbursements. This focus on results facilitates donor alignment and harmonization, joint donor supervision, public scrutiny, and independent monitoring.

For example, the joint adoption of the results matrix negotiated in the course of the preparation of the Cameroon Forest and Environment development policy loan, encouraged Canada, Germany, France, the Netherlands, the United Kingdom, the European Union, the African Development Bank, the World Bank, the FAO, the United Nations Development Programme (UNDP), the World Wildlife Fund (WWF), and the Netherlands Development Organization (SNV), to sign a partnership agreement that provides a clear framework for aligning their support to the forest sector.

- DPLs sharpen the focus of Bank-government dialogue on the achievement of larger results and the quality of processes. Dialogue surrounding SILs tends to revolve around individual procurement and financial transactions, leaving less time and fewer supervision resources for the operation's larger objectives and the underlying structural constraints that may be hindering procurement and disbursement processes. By providing for interministerial review of the results that disbursements are directly contingent upon, and requiring periodic audits of fiduciary processes, DPLs can more effectively and purposefully bring structural improvements to procurement and disbursement.

■ While DPLs are usually used as single tranche, quick-disbursing operations that can help budget support geared toward domestic financing needs, they can also be designed as multiyear, multitranche operations that support sector-wide assistance programs in response to government requests when appropriate. The timeframe for disbursement in the Cameroon and Gabon DPLs is comparable to those of SILs.

■ DPL components can be tailored according to Bank fiduciary concerns in a specific country, and be used to monitor compliance with the enhanced procurement and financial practices that have been previously agreed to with the World Bank in the context of its major assessments of the country's financial accounting, administrative, and procurement procedures. The Cameroon and Gabon DPLs include agreements that the government will use dedicated accounts for monitoring relevant resource flows, conduct external audits, and share the results with the World Bank, and use technical assistance as needed to improve procurement and financial management.

■ DPLs afford adequate flexibility to address any likely significant environmental and social issues

appropriately. While DPLs do not trigger World Bank safeguard policies, OP8.60 requires that the Bank determine whether policies it supports have any likely significant effect on the environment, natural resources, or forests, or any likely significant poverty and social impact. If there are any such likely significant effects, the World Bank needs to ascertain whether it has a clear understanding of how negative effects can be reduced or positive ones enhanced through the borrower's systems, drawing on relevant country-level or sectoral environmental and social analysis. Carrying out due diligence in the Cameroon and Gabon DPLs and related GEF operations, the Bank teams advised the governments to conduct full SEAs. In the view of World Bank staff, these assessments met the highest standards, including those set by Bank safeguard policies, and allowed staff to conclude that likely significant effects of the supported policies would be addressed appropriately during program implementation.

Are forest development policy loans suitable to all situations?

DPLs require particularly advanced policy dialogue on sector policy reforms and reform implementation. They can only be built upon strong collaboration between central economic and technical ministries, and in the presence of completed or unfolding national financial management, auditing, and procurement reforms. In the cases of Cameroon and Gabon, these conditions were created through long processes of intersectoral dialogue with the government and strong collaboration within the country team.

Source: Topa and Debroux 2006.

results of the program. Managing the size of program matrices is challenging, especially in harmonized donor settings, with different outcomes in different countries.

TRANSPARENCY AND PREDICTABILITY. In the context of medium-term World Bank support, progress should be reviewed regularly and in line with a country's M&E cycle, drawing to the extent possible on internal accountability

processes. It is equally important to be explicit about conditions, triggers, and expected results. In a programmatic series, it is possible to integrate a review of results into the next operation (see box 6.14). Aligning these reviews with government budget cycles is preferable.

MONITORING IMPACTS. An immediate challenge facing the World Bank and other institutions engaged in operations at

In the Lao People's Democratic Republic, a natural resource management component under public sector reform was incorporated into a structural adjustment operation (People's Democratic Republic of Lao Financial Management Adjustment Credit [FMAC], FY02). The overall objective of this component was to involve local communities in the management of forests and improve legislation on conservation. The project was under the control of the Minister of Finance, but the day-to-day implementation and monitoring was done by a high level interministerial coordination committee.

For release of the second tranche, Lao PDR had to accomplish two forest sector–related actions. A quality-at-entry review suggested that the inclusion of reforms in forestry regulations unnecessarily broadened the scope of the conditions. The objectives of the natural resource management subcomponent were partially achieved, but local participation was less than envisaged partly because of capacity limitations and political resistance. The implementation completion report states that the legal framework has established technically sound forest management with basic provisions for planning, mapping, consultation, and control.

Source: Authors' compilation.

The Republic of Armenia PRSC III is the third in a proposed series of four annual single tranche PRSCs intended to support policy and institutional reforms in furtherance of the government's PRSP. The PRSCs focus on four critical reform themes: (i) consolidating macroeconomic discipline and strengthening governance, (ii) sharpening competition and entrenching property rights, (iii) mitigating social and environmental risks, and (iv) modernizing the rural economy. Under the component on Reducing Risks in Natural Resource Management, the action taken under PRSCs I and II included adopting a national forestry policy and forest code, outlining the institutional restructuring plan for the sector, establishing a pilot system for monitoring illegal forest exploitation, and promoting community forest management. The Policy and Institutional Reform Actions under PRSC III included controlling illegal logging within agreed targets, and expanding community forest management. The trigger in PRSC II (as approved by the Board) was controlling illegal logging and forest removal within targets to be agreed with IDA by March 2006. As a result of political factors, the proposals for the structure, powers, and functioning of the illegal logging monitoring system were developed, but have not yet been adopted. The condition was deferred to PRSC IV.

Source: Authors' compilation using World Bank 2007.

the macroeconomic and larger cross-sectoral level will be to mainstream effective monitoring of forest outcomes into these operations, where these are identified as being potentially significant. Successful and effective monitoring of forest outcomes in policy lending operations will facilitate the implementation of "no fault" and relatively inexpensive monitoring of forest outcomes during implementation of lending operations. One of the primary uses of monitoring information on forest outcomes under development policy lending will be to develop more quantitative and analytical approaches to projection of likely forest outcomes.

LESSONS LEARNED AND RECOMMENDATIONS FOR PRACTITIONERS

DPL CAN FACILITATE SECTOR REFORM. DPL has not been generally thought of within the World Bank as an instrument

for specific sectoral reforms, yet it may in fact have more potential to effect the sort of fundamental changes in forest sector policy and practices than is available under traditional sector investment lending. Ministries of Finance are involved in implementing policy loans, and the inclusion of forest sector reform considerations in a policy loan can facilitate mainstreaming forest considerations into national policy dialogue and raise the profile of governance and institutional issues of concern in this sector.

PRIOR POLICY DIALOGUE. Development policy loans require particularly advanced policy dialogue on sector policy reforms and reform implementation. Such loans can only be built upon strong collaboration between central economic and technical ministries, and in the presence of completed or unfolding national financial management, auditing, and procurement reforms.

In the cases of Cameroon and Gabon outlined in box 6.12, these conditions were created through long processes of intersectoral dialogue with the government and strong collaboration within the country team. The results were not uniformly successful, and at times proved difficult and contentious, but some measure of reform was enabled by the process. This, however, needs to be viewed in a context where, in this region, two decades of World Bank experience in providing assistance via sector investment lending to the forest sector clearly revealed the limits of traditional sector investment projects in reforming forest sectors traditionally dominated by political patronage and vested interests.

GOOD GOVERNANCE AS AN ENTRY POINT. Good governance is a strong entry point for sector reforms (see chapter 5, Forest Sector Governance, and associated notes). Linking forest sector governance reforms with a broader extractive industries transparency initiative, or positioning them as part of the overall good public sector management effort (for example, an anticorruption, transparency, or improved governance component) can strengthen its hold in a policy loan. Done this way, forest sector reform could be included as a trigger or prior action, making the reform component binding and essential for release of a tranche.

AVOID MIXED RESULTS AND SIGNALS. When a client is performing well in general, and has achieved all the prior actions for a policy reform loan except those associated with forests, a decision needs to be made on whether to withhold the release of the tranche of one unfulfilled prior action. In some cases, the World Bank has employed a floating tranche, disbursable when particular conditions are expected in some way to be difficult, or more drawn-out than others in the policy matrix: the Cameroon structural operation is a case where this approach was applied to forest outcomes. In other cases (see box 6.9), the nature of the operation itself ensured that activities and measures undertaken complemented investment loans that were focused on specific sectors. It is sometimes possible to transfer policy objectives related to a single sector or related group of sectors into investment loans that are coordinated with DPLs, and can follow policy developments that are foreshadowed and perhaps initiated under a DPL, but require longer time frames for implementation.[3]

The primary requirement is that the World Bank remain internally consistent in its approach to dealing with forests and broader natural resource outcomes, in cases where these are important. If a sector-specific condition has not been achieved by a well-performing client, it is important to identify how to modify the condition rather than drop it. Natural resource and forest outcomes are not trivial adjuncts to economic reform objectives, but may play a significant role in the successful achievement of those objectives.

ANALYTICAL WORK SHOULD LOOK AT ALL INFLUENCES ON FORESTS. The use of analytical work should be carefully considered in the context of forests and DPLs. Essentially, what is required here is a broad scoping exercise that examines the status of DPLs, proposed forest sector or larger natural resource project activities, and other cross-sectoral developments that are indicated in CASs and business plans. Sector work should not be based simply on problems within the forests sector, as perceived by forest agencies in the country and the World Bank sector staff, but on a broader appreciation of all influences and changes likely to affect forests, and an analysis of what combination of macroeconomic, cross-sectoral, and within-sector measures are likely to produce the best outcomes from national economic, environmental, and social perspectives.

For forest outcome monitoring to be effective, the World Bank needs to undertake continuing research on how changes at the macroeconomic and broad cross-sectoral levels flow through the economic and social systems to manifest as impacts on forests.

OWNERSHIP MATTERS. Policy conditions in DPL, as in investment lending, are more likely to result in sector policy reform when there is clear borrower ownership, commitment, and demand at the sector level, and when the appropriate central ministry (such as the Ministry of Finance) is part of the dialogue and supports the agreements reached.

NOTES

1. For this note, a policy lending instrument will be called a development policy loan.

2. For further information on the points raised in this section, please refer to World Bank (2006).

3. There is some risk attached to this strategy, in that a government may successfully implement the DPL that foreshadows further policy changes under investment lending but then decides not to proceed with those investment loans.

SELECTED READINGS

Numerous relevant references are available at http://go.worldbank.org/4OJ07BWKQ0.

OPCS. 2004. "Good Practice Notes Relating to the Development Policy Lending OP/BP 8.60: Designing Development Policy Operations." World Bank, Washington, DC.

REFERENCES CITED

Topa, G., and L. Debroux. 2006. "The Use of DPLs to Support Natural Resources Management in Gabon and Cameroon." Note for internal circulation, World Bank, Washington, DC.

World Bank. 2005. "Review of World Bank Conditionality: Issues Note." Operations Policy and Country Services, World Bank, Washington, DC.

———. 2006. "Good Practice Principles for the Application of Conditionality: A Progress Report." Operations Policy and Country Services, World Bank, Washington, DC.

———. 2007a. Program Document for Ghana—Fifth Poverty Reduction Support Credit Project (P099287). Poverty Reduction and Economic Management, Africa Region. Report No. 39657-GH. World Bank, Washington, DC.

———. 2007b. Program Information Document for Armenia—Third Poverty Reduction Strategy Credit Project (P093460). Report No. 38358-AM. World Bank, Washington, DC.

CROSS-REFERENCED CHAPTERS AND NOTES

Chapter 5: Improving Forest Governance, and associated notes

Identifying the Need for Analysis on Forests in Development Policy Reforms

The combined impacts on forests of economic activities that originate outside the forest sector are, in most cases, significantly greater than those produced by economic activity within the sector itself. Macroeconomic change will almost always be a major component of these external forces. Therefore, if forests are a significant part of the economic and social resource base of a country, it will be necessary to consider such impacts when DPL, broadly based poverty alleviation programs, and related programmatic activities are being designed.

ASSESSING CAUSALITY IS COMPLICATED. The impacts on forests and other natural resources of large-scale economic policy changes and reforms will manifest themselves through a complex web of second- and third-round activities and responses that will be triggered as illustrated in figure 6.1 (World Bank 2005). Identifying the nature of their eventual impacts on forests—or even whether there will be significant impacts—will not be straightforward: Prior economic, environmental, and social conditions will have a major role in outcomes, and no general relationships or models to predict impact outcomes are, or are likely to become, available.[1]

Where forests are sufficiently important economically, or directly support the livelihoods of a large number of poor people, the impacts of broadly based growth could significantly compromise the broad goals of economic growth, poverty alleviation, and environmental sustainability of macro policy loans. Due diligence requires identification of cases where this is a potential risk to the overall implementation of the policy loan and making the necessary adjustments to program design.

A DEARTH OF DATA. There are currently relatively few comprehensive data sets on cross-sectoral impacts or impacts of macroeconomic reform; this imposes a significant operational constraint on development of good practice for managing the World Bank's engagement in this area. Good practice will, therefore, initially largely be a matter of developing guidelines and approximation methodologies for identifying cases where there is significant potential for important impacts to occur, and then applying economic and sector work in a timely and focused manner to those situations. Linked to the latter, there is a need to develop acceptable approaches and for the World Bank to adequately invest in assessing the potential impacts of particular economic changes in which it is involved in specific countries.

Figure 6.1   Indirect Impact of Fiscal Reform on Forests

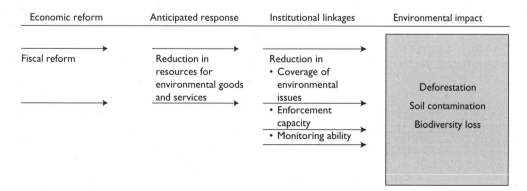

OPERATIONAL ASPECTS

Prioritizing those circumstances in which forest sector analytical work is important requires that countries and lending situations with significant forest interests be identified. A potential approach would include

- identifying countries where forests are important (for economic development, poverty alleviation, ecosystem services);
- identifying and screening the major macro policy reforms being proposed in each country;
- analyzing and developing, in the cases where the impact of the macro policy reform are directly or indirectly an issue, mechanisms for handling the cross-sectoral impacts; and
- identifying entry points for addressing the potential cross-sectoral impact.

This stepwise approach to prioritizing where detailed analysis may be needed is necessary for two pragmatic reasons. First, the resources needed to implement field analyses often will be limited; it is therefore unrealistic to propose a general application of analytical work to this task in all possible cases. Second, because uncertainty will inevitably surround the analytical process itself, at least in the early stages of application, it will be necessary to learn from and refine initial approaches along the way.

The actual approach can be applied at a regional or global level, depending on the need. The approach can also be applied at the national level and, as discussed in the following section, will require modifying the method. The main constraint to application of any approach is availability of data.

IDENTIFYING COUNTRIES WHERE FORESTS ARE IMPORTANT. A preliminary approach to identifying the countries and situations where forests are important, from an economic and poverty point of view as well as an environmental one, requires the development of appropriate indicator. A quantitative approach for the development of good practice could be initiated quickly following the approach in a recent study on policy loans and forest outcomes (World Bank 2005). This would allow task managers to compile a watch list of countries for which cross-sectoral impacts on forests from programmatic activities will need to be further examined in the field.

An index can be developed to identify where forests are important by characterizing forest significance. The forest significance index can be created using readily available data on the following:

- *Contribution of forests to the economy* (using data on production of wood fuel and production of roundwood, both from the FAOSTAT online statistical services, 2004). This measure picks up an element of forest output beyond the conventional measure of commercial logging, that is, the large amount of fuelwood that is used by local communities and frequently does not enter formal markets.
- *Forest-poverty linkage* (using data on the annual rate of change between 1990 and 2001 in the percentage of poor living on less than a dollar a day, and the percentage of poverty in 1996. Both of these measures use the Poverty Calculator (POVCAL) approach developed by the World Bank. It should be noted that the variable is a weak proxy for what is of interest here—some estimate of the prevalence of poor people who live in or near forests and depend on them greatly—but few alternatives are readily available.
- *Forest-conservation linkage* (using data on percentage of threatened bird species in 2000, percentage of threatened mammal species in 2000, and rate of change in forest cover over the period 1990–2000). These variables provide some reflection of biodiversity loss, as well as a gross measure of forest loss.[2]

A measure for forest-related governance was included in the index to assess where the prior conditions raise concerns about how cross-sectoral impacts are handled. This measure used data on the Rule of Law (which is a measure from Kaufmann, Kraay, and Mastruzzi's [2004] corruption indicators) and presence of democratic institutions. These are well-known and documented measures of governance. Their limitation as a proxy in this context is that they do not specifically reveal the state of governance in the forest sector itself, nor do they shed any light on how that is influenced by broader trends in the economy.

Each of the measures used in the index were weighted equally. The weighting can vary if the approach is to assist in examining a specific cross-sectoral impact (for example, impact of macro policy reform on the contribution of forests to poverty).[3]

More sophisticated vulnerability indicators can be developed to capture countries' performance in political and resource risks, policy and institutional failures (particularly in the resource sectors), weak regulation and implementation capacity, and lack of monitoring and enforcement. There is some merit to considering broadening the coverage of environmental policy and institutions in the existing Country Policy and Institutional Assessment index (used currently for IDA fund allocations). This could serve as a useful first cut in understanding country capacity in regulating the environment.

IDENTIFYING AND SCREENING MACRO POLICY REFORMS. The second part of the task of identifying and prioritizing situations where more intensive due diligence on forest outcomes is required involves examining the specific nature of those policy operations. Development policy operations come in many flavors, from macro scale to specific sectoral reforms. Moreover, they may mix reforms across different scales. Table 6.1 presents a list of typical reforms in World Bank development policy loans and potential forest linkages. However, this can only serve as a guide, and initial country conditions, such as the nature of its environmental problems, its resource endowment, and the policy and institutional setting, are critical in determining the direction and magnitude of effects of individual reforms on the environment.

There are certain sectoral macro policy reforms that immediately raise red flags. These include agricultural reforms, such as reforms in land markets and improved rural finance; reforms of government institutions, such as marketing boards, which can potentially strengthen resource management; energy price reforms; natural resource price reforms; changes in exchange rate regimes; and trade policy reforms. In contrast, closer assessment can be required for reforms with less apparent impacts on the forest sector, such as macroeconomic, public, and fiscal reforms that include tax policy reforms, reforms to promote foreign direct investment, and the like.

The sectors in which many World Bank policy operations are concentrated (such as Central Government Administration and the General Public Administration sector) do not immediately suggest a direct or indirect link with forest outcomes. However, a closer examination of the thematic

Table 6.1	Typical Reforms in Policy-Based Operations, and Potential Forest Linkages	
Sector	Reforms	Potential implications for forests
Energy	Typically encompass pricing, subsidies, ownership, and regulatory issues.	Fuel substitution could potentially push people to use biomass.
Agriculture	Reforms may span land markets, product markets, subsidies, rural finance, input prices, trade taxes, irrigation institutions, and reform of government institutions such as marketing boards and stabilization funds.	Extension of agriculture in forest-rich countries could potentially lead to deforestation.
Financial	Financial sector reforms cover privatization, writing down of bad loans, recapitalization of the banking system, and regulatory issues (among many possibilities).	Not much impact expected.[a]
Health, education	Reforms typically cover financing, resource allocation, level of access, and effectiveness of expenditures.	Not much impact expected.
Macro	Reforms	Potential to reduce or manage any negative outcomes
Public expenditures, public sector management	Reform programs embrace expenditure frameworks, budget transparency, financial management, accountability, priority setting, service delivery efficiency, and the skills, professionalism, and remuneration of the public service.	Could be detrimental if public expenditure for protecting forests is cut during major fiscal consolidation.
Tax reform	Reforms deal with tax incidence (income, assets, corporations, consumption), tax rates, exemptions, deductions, and the complexity of the tax system.	Will have an impact to the extent it involves taxation in forest or agriculture sectors.
Fiscal federalism and decentralization	Decentralization reforms aim to increase the efficiency of service delivery, accountability, effectiveness, capacity, and adequacy of regulatory frameworks at the local level; they may also embrace fiscal decentralization.	Provides opportunity for shifting forest governance to local levels.
Private sector development	Reforms deal with business climate issues—business taxation; regulation of entry, operation, and exit; bankruptcy procedures; protection of property rights; and operation of capital markets.	Will have an impact to the extent private sector involvement is envisaged.
Trade reform	Typically includes elimination of non-tariff barriers, reduction and simplification of tariff rates, reform of customs procedures, and regulations relating to foreign direct investment.	Reforms undertaken in the presence of preexisting market, policy, or institutional imperfections in the forest resource sector may lead to adverse effects.

Source: Mani 2004.
a. There are different schools of thought on this subject; note 5.4, Strengthening Fiscal Systems in the Forest Sector, suggests a different outcome.

orientation of the DPL operations can reveal areas of intervention in these categories that could potentially benefit or adversely affect forests. For example, 100 percent of a World Bank DPL operation proposed for Guatemala (in fiscal 2005) is allocated under the Central Government Administration sector. Thematically, this operation will focus on macroeconomic management and tax policy and administration—themes that could impact forest outcomes (see box 6.15 for other relevant themes).

Reviewing the most relevant effects of the reform and preliminarily assessing the environmental and social impacts are important to identifying where to focus a more detailed analysis. It is usually important to identify and consult key interest groups, public representatives, government officials, and other stakeholders at this stage. Analytical tools such as environmental balance sheets, checklists of possible effects of a particular type of policy, and a qualitative matrix can be helpful (see annex 6.3A to this note).

The review should produce a conceptual map that the team can follow during the assessment process. The exercise can also help distinguish between those effects that are most likely to occur and those that are severe and irreversible. The review only produces a strong indication of the eventual effects of the policy reform, but not evidence regarding the actual connection. The latter strong indications are important for informing the policy revision process.

Box 6.15   Themes Associated with World Bank Policy Lending Operations in FY05 and FY06 Relevant to the Forest Sector

- Environmental policies and institutions, regulation and competition policy, rural policies and institutions
- Macroeconomic management
- Environmental policies and institutions
- Rural policies and institutions
- Tax policy and administration
- Poverty strategy, analysis and monitoring, decentralization
- Public expenditure, financial management and procurement, infrastructure services for private sector development
- Regulation and competition policy
- Regulation and competition policy, small and medium enterprise support, trade facilitation and market access
- Rural services and infrastructure

Source: World Bank 2005.

SELECTING THE APPROPRIATE APPROACH FOR HANDLING CROSS-SECTORAL IMPACTS. A clear understanding of the relationship between policy reform and the forest sector is needed to analyze and develop mechanisms for handling the cross-sectoral impacts. Numerous analytical tools can help in this understanding. The appropriate analytical approach should be tailored to answer the questions as precisely as possible, show a good cost-benefit ratio, and be conducted with the available resources and accessible data. The analysis should be able to provide necessary information on links between the proposed reform and its impact on the forest sector. It should also provide options regarding measures to enhance positive impacts and mitigate negative ones. The formulation of mechanisms for handling cross-sectoral impacts should blend quantitative and qualitative information and bring in the outcomes of consultative processes.

To assess the key issues, the assessment team will have to collect relevant data on economic, social, and political conditions, as well as information about the environment, the natural resource base, and relevant institutions. This data will serve in the reevaluation of the outcome of the initial review. A central challenge will be to accurately understand and identify the economic, social, political, and environmental factors because the downstream effects are often indirect. Approaches such as the CEA or SEAs can be useful for this purpose (see note 6.4, Assessing Cross-Sectoral Impacts).

The fast-disbursing nature of DPL operations may not allow for a detailed CEA or SEA analysis in tandem with the lending cycle. However, to ensure that required due diligence on determination of "likely significant" effects is carried out, a number of rapid assessment tools may have to be used. For example, simple analytical tools (and elasticity estimates) can be used to assess environmental implications of raising tariffs in the electricity and water sectors or for analyzing the impact of relative price changes (often triggered by trade reforms) in agriculture and the implications thereof for forest depletion. Similarly, robust action-impact matrices can be developed to capture economy-environment linkages (such as fuel-switching implications of energy price reforms).[4]

If a rapid or preliminary assessment indicates that specific policy reforms supported by DPL operations are going to adversely impact forests or water resources, follow-up actions would need to be developed to help the borrower strengthen its institutional capacity and policy framework for environmental and natural resource management in these areas and monitoring of applicable indicators. A CEA or SEA would then be necessary.

SELECTING THE APPROPRIATE ANALYTICAL TOOLS. Appropriate analytical tools should be selected based on the objective, data availability, cost, and time constraints. Different analytical tools have different expertise requirements, and costs will depend on many factors and vary considerably. Table 6.2 provides some guidance on the requirements, significance, and costs of select analytical tools. As a general rule, the costs of national resource accounts, econometric modeling, and indicator frameworks will be relatively high, whereas impact and case studies or expert panels will be in the medium or lower range. In comparing the different strengths and weaknesses of alternative designs, the team should try to combine some of their relative advantages and informative value. Research could start with case studies and lead to quantitative impact analysis or to econometric modeling at a later stage. Qualitative studies can provide recommendations for quantitative monitoring over longer periods of critical effects that result from particularly relevant policy linkages.

Some standard tools include analysis of price changes, heuristic tools, such as checklists and action-effect matrices, and red flags (presented in annexes 6.3A and 6.3B to this note) that can be applied to better understand the nature and direction of environmental impacts. Most of these tools can be applied to analysis of potential risks, including a set of red flags that indicate potential problems. However, in a number of cases, policy reforms may also represent opportunities for better management of the forest resources.

DATA REQUIREMENTS. Relevant data is generally unavailable. Conventional economic statistics and social data collected by governments and other interest groups frequently either underestimate, or completely ignore, natural resource issues. Adequate resource allocation to data collection will be important. This will require gathering baseline data on the current state of natural resources, identifying trends in resource use and degradation, and obtaining data on the proposed reforms and on the actual effects from similar reforms.

Table 6.2 The Requirements, Significance, and Costs of Select Analytical Tools

	Requirements	Significance	Costs
National resource accounts	• Main linkages must be known. • Main linkages are with institutionalized and documented sectors. • Main linkages are quantifiable flows of resources, that is, high data quality needed. • Expertise in systems of national accounts.	• Stronger for intrasectoral linkages, less differentiated for cross-sectoral linkages. • Impact of variables can be estimated.	High
Econometric modeling	• Main linkages must be known. • Main linkages are with institutionalized. and documented sectors. • Main linkages are quantifiable flows of resources, that is, high data quality needed. • Econometric expertise.	• Complex linkages can be studied. • Impact of variables can be estimated.	High
Indicator framework	• Main linkages must be known. • Main linkages are quantifiable in single indicators, that is, medium data quality. • Expertise in measurement and statistics.	• Strong for monitoring a few linkages over time. • Estimation of the impact of single variables less precise than using an impact study.	High
Impact study	• Main linkages must be known. • Both quantitative or qualitative approaches are feasible, thus, flexible on data quality. • Expertise in quantitative data analysis and policy evaluation.	• Strong for illustrating linkages. • Estimation of the impact of single variables less precise than use of an indicator framework.	Medium
Case study	• Main linkages do not have to be known. • Linkages can but do not have to be quantifiable, thus, flexible on data quality. • Expertise in qualitative social research. • Field experience recommended.	• Strong for illustrating complex and indirect cause-and-effect relationships. • Estimation of the impact of single variables only rough.	Medium
Expert panel	• Only experts as source of information needed. • Expertise for selecting experts and staff for administration of panel needed.	• Less subjectivity through communicative validation. • Estimation of the impact of single variables only rough.	Low

Source: Schmithüsen, Bisang, and Zimmermann 2001.

Indicators are helpful in these situations because they assist in setting standards and thresholds, and enable comparison.

In collecting and working with data, the team must check for reliability, avoid double counting, and, where possible, indicate confidence limits or probabilities. Quantitative and qualitative data both have high value in these analyses and can complement each other.

IDENTIFYING ENTRY POINTS FOR ADDRESSING CROSS-SECTORAL IMPACTS. Identifying the links between the policy reform and potential cross-sector impacts is an important part of this overall approach. Equally important, however, is identifying entry points for addressing the potential cross-sector impacts. There are no specific good practices associated with this. However, policy loans are also the entry point for mitigating any negative cross-sectoral impacts as well as enhancing positive impacts. This is partly because some of the measures for mitigating or enhancing certain impacts can involve strengthening environmental laws, institutions, and enforcement mechanisms (see chapter 5, Forest Sector Governance, and note 5.5, Strengthening Legal Frameworks in the Forest Sector).

LESSONS LEARNED AND RECOMMENDATIONS FOR PRACTITIONERS

To date, there has been relatively little field analysis of actual forest or natural resource outcomes from specific structural adjustment or other programmatic forms of lending.[5] Literature and analyses of the relationship between large-scale economic changes and outcomes for natural resources or forests specifically do not allow consistent conclusions to be drawn across the range of country and field situations. Nevertheless, some key inferences can be drawn with regard to understanding the relationship between macro policy reforms and forest outcomes.

Economic and social forces originating outside forests generally have more impact upon those forests than do developments within the forest sector itself. Two broad lessons can be taken from this observation:

- It is evident that for forests to make their maximum potential contribution to economic growth and poverty alleviation, major policies and incentives from outside the sector that affect forests must be addressed—and policy lending instruments are appropriate to that task (see note 6.2, Prospects for Using Policy Lending to Proactively Enable Forest Sector Reforms).

- It is also evident that, where forests are determined to be significant for economic growth and poverty alleviation at the national level, policy loans and large cross-sectoral operations that have the potential to impact forests (either positively or negatively) must take that potential into account in their design and implementation.

As more policy loans are prepared, an immediate challenge facing donors, client governments, and other institutions engaged in operations at the macroeconomic and larger cross-sectoral levels, will be to mainstream effective monitoring of forest outcomes into these operations, where these are identified as being potentially significant with respect to forests.

Researchers with country or regional experience should be part of any team examining cross-sectoral impacts to make a meaningful selection of relevant cross-sectoral linkages, to carry out consistent document analysis, to organize expert interviews, and to collect and interpret the results.

Research methods need to be improved. Equally important is the need to launch specific case studies at national, subnational, and local levels to provide more empirical information on cross-sectoral successes as well as on drawbacks in a given social, economic, and political context. Quantitative research is needed as much as qualitative analysis to provide more information on the nature, structure, and functioning of different policies and cross-sector links. Research should also examine the actors and stakeholders involved, the instruments and procedures that influence their behavior, and the causal relationship between forest and other policy domains in both directions.

Ways to manage cross-sectoral impacts need to be further examined. This will require understanding how different agencies actually work together, what agencies have which resources, and the possibility of contradictory or overlapping competencies at the policy-setting and implementation levels.

New approaches in coordination mechanisms, as well as the likely limitations of coordination, need to be examined. More research is needed on how coordinating mechanisms, such as network management and interadministrative coordination, can be improved to contribute to reaching national forest policy goals. The current role of forest administrations and their ability to operate with success in a given policy and administrative setting needs to be reconsidered.

NOTES

1. In the World Bank assessment of cross-sectoral impacts of DPL is a due diligence requirement for DPLs as per Operational Policy 8.60.

2. The latter will have some relationship to the contribution of forests to the economy, in that it will provide a measure of whether the contribution, as currently constituted, is sustainable. Eventually, a more rigorous approach to estimating the sustainability of ongoing forest operations would be a useful ingredient in this overall measure, but it is not possible to implement this approach at present.

3. To assess the significance of forests relative to other sectors in a country, the variables used must compare the contribution of forests to poverty alleviation, economic development, and ecosystem services relative to other sectors (rather than compare these relative to other countries).

4. The Environment Department of the Social Development Network in the World Bank is developing a rapid assessment DPL toolkit that will assist task managers in identifying when a DPL operation could have likely significant impacts on the environment, forests, and natural resources. A final version of this toolkit will be available in FY08.

5. The lessons learned and recommendations also draw findings from Schmithüsen, Bisang, and Zimmermann (2001).

SELECTED READINGS

World Bank. 2005. "Development Policy Lending and Forest Outcomes: Influences, Interactions, and Due Diligence." Report No. 32724-GLB, World Bank, Washington, DC.

———. Forthcoming. "Rapid Assessment Toolkit for Due Diligence on Environment, Forest, and Other Natural Resource Aspects of Development Policy Lending." World Bank, Washington, DC.

REFERENCES CITED

Kaufmann, D., A. Kraay, and M. Mastruzzi. 2004. "Governance Matters III: Governance Indicators for 1996–2002." World Bank, Washington, DC. Available at http://www.worldbank.org/wbi/governance/pdf/govmatters3_wber.pdf.

Hamilton, K., and M. Mani. 2005. "Toolkit for Analyzing Environmental and Natural Resource Aspects of Development Policy Lending." Environment Department, World Bank, Washington, DC.

Iannariello, M. P., P. Stedman-Edwards, D. Reed, and R. Blair. 1999. "Environmental Impact Assessment of Macroeconomic Reform Programs." WWF Macroeconomics Program Office, Washington, DC. http://assets.panda.org/downloads/eia.pdf.

Mani, M. 2004. "An Overview of Environmental and Natural Resource Aspects of IBRD Financed Development Policy Lending Operations in FY05." ENV-ESSD, internal note. World Bank, Washington, DC.

Schmithüsen, F., K. Bisang, and W. Zimmermann. 2001. "Cross-Sector Linkages in Forestry: Review of Available Information and Consideration on Future Research." Forest Policy and Forest Economics, Department of Forest Sciences—ETH, Zurich. http://www.fao.org/docrep/003/AA002E/Aa002e03.htm#6018.

World Bank. 2005. "Development Policy Lending and Forest Outcomes: Influences, Interactions, and Due Diligence." Report No. 32724-GLB, World Bank, Washington, DC.

CROSS-REFERENCED CHAPTERS AND NOTES

Chapter 5: Improving Forest Governance

Note 5.5: Addressing Illegal Logging and Other Forest Crime

ANNEX 6.3A   SELECT TOOLS TO ASSIST SCOPING OF CROSS-SECTORAL IMPACTS

The information in this annex is based on prior work done by Iannariello et al. (1999).

Checklists

A checklist can assist in determining the effects that are likely to apply (table 6.3). This tool can be particularly useful if the list is focused on the most common and significant effects. The assessment team should review the checklist and provide a description and analysis of the relevant items.

Matrices

A matrix can assist in providing a clear summary of a qualitative review or an assessment, and can be easily used for comparing the various reforms and reform scenarios (table 6.4). The matrix can include such factors as direction of change, the severity or magnitude of the impact, reversibility, probability, duration, and potential mitigation measures. A matrix can be qualitative and descriptive or include quantitative information. Quantitative matrices rely on scoring techniques or other standardized measures that assess various factors such as the strength of environmental institutions.

Networks

Networks are diagrams that illustrate both the direct and indirect relationships between policies and the environment. Networks can show the sequences of causes and effects moving through the economic, social, and political spheres, and thus provide a useful tool for selecting points of entry. Quantitative networks can be translated into mathematical models for simulation purposes. Mathematical approaches can be useful when the assessment requires simple calculations with large data sets, when there are complex links among the elements, when processes are time dependent, or when the relationship can only be defined in terms of statistical probabilities.

Table 6.3   Sample Checklist for Devaluation

Effect	Probable	Investigated
Agricultural land (opening or abandonment)	x	x
Land degradation (increase or decrease)		
Logging and extraction of natural resources (increase or decrease)	x	
Industrial pollution (increase or decrease)	x	x
Water use (increase or decrease)		
Energy use (increase or decrease)	x	x
Encroachment on protected area (increase or decrease)	x	x
Wildlands and forests (increase or decrease)		

Source: Iannariello et al 1999.

Table 6.4   Sample Qualitative Matrix for Devaluation

Effect	Direction	Time frame	Reversible	Probability	Legal recourse
Land use	Negative	Long-term	No	High	Weak
Water use	Positive	Medium-term	Yes	Medium	Weak
Greenhouse gas emissions	Negative	Long-term	Yes	High	Medium

Source: Iannariello et al 1999.

ANNEX 6.3B TOOLS FOR RAPID ASSESSMENT OF CROSS-SECTORAL IMPACTS

This annex is based on Hamilton and Mani (2005).

Analysis of price changes

For reforms that will have a foreseeable effect on prices, it may be possible to carry out a partial equilibrium analysis of the effects of price changes, assuming that sufficient data and time for analysis are available. The prices of interest will typically be natural resource and energy prices because these will have the most direct effect on the environment and natural resources. Three forms of analysis are possible:

■ *Supply response.* Will the price change affect the supply of a good (timber, for example)? Can supply elasticities, including cross-elasticities, be estimated? How rapid is the supply response likely to be?
■ *Demand response.* Will the price change affect the demand for an environmentally sensitive good? Can demand elasticities, including cross-elasticities, be estimated (for example, will raising natural gas prices make coal relatively more attractive to consumers)?
■ *von Thunen analysis.* Will the price change affect the relative price of goods in such a manner as to change the location of economic activity? For example, will it make conversion of forested land to agriculture more profitable?

Heuristic tools

CHECKLISTS. When time and data limitations preclude the quantitative analysis of links between a policy-based operation and forests, one fallback is to pose a set of questions about the individual operation or the broader country pro- gram. This could be on the availability of adequate analytical underpinnings, policy and regulatory frameworks covering the forest sector, institutional issues, and issues relating to transparency and accountability (see Hamilton and Mani 2005). Depending on the answers to these questions, actions might be taken in the design of the operation, or within the country program, to enhance positive and mitigate negative effects of the operation.

ACTION-EFFECT MATRICES. A more structured nonquantitative approach to analyzing effects can be achieved through the use of action-effect matrices. Using an action-effect matrix, a given policy reform may be analyzed according to the likelihood of effects on the poor mediated by the environment, forest, and natural resources, and the likelihood of other effects on the environment (see Hamilton and Mani 2005). Based on this more structured analysis of the individual components of a policy-based operation, it may be possible to suggest design changes, mitigating actions, or indicators that should be monitored over time.

Red flags

Another nonquantitative approach to reviewing and analyzing policy-based operations is to look for "red flags"—issues that raise the likelihood of significant effects on the environment and natural resources. At the operational level these include energy price reforms, natural resource price reforms, and changes in exchange rate regimes. At the country program level, they could include economic, political, and resource risks; policy and institutional failures (particularly in the resource sectors); weak regulation and implementation capacity; and lack of monitoring and enforcement.

Assessing Cross-Sectoral Impacts: Use of CEAs and SEAs

Within the World Bank's Analytic and Advisory Activities, CEA and SEA were identified as key tools for informing country dialogue and more systematically addressing environmental concerns early in sectoral decision-making and planning processes, respectively.

In August 2004, the World Bank approved and updated its policy on DPL. Operational Policy 8.60 (OP/BP 8.60) emphasizes upstream analytical work—such as SEA, CEA, and other analyses done by the World Bank, the client country, or third parties—as a source of information for analyzing the likely significant effects of an operation on the borrowing country's environment and natural resources, and for assessing the country's institutional capacity for handling these effects.

Specifically, under OP/BP 8.60, the World Bank is required to determine for each development policy loan whether the specific country policies supported by the operation are likely to have significant effects on the country's environment, forests, and natural resources. For policies with significant effects, an assessment is required by Bank staff of the country's systems for reducing adverse effects and enhancing positive effects, drawing on relevant country-level or sectoral environmental analysis, a type of SEA.

This note describes CEA, SEA, and rapid assessment tools; the context of their use; the process of applying these tools for assessing cross-sectoral impacts or for due diligence in policy operations[1]; and finally, some examples of application in the forest sector.

OPERATIONAL ASPECTS

Country Environmental Analysis

CEA is a diagnostic analytical tool that can help to systematically evaluate the environmental priorities of client countries, the environmental implications of key government policies, and the country's capacity to address environmen-

tal priorities. The aim of CEA is to provide the analytical underpinning for sustainable development assistance. It has the potential to bring together the results of environmental, economic, and sectoral work and facilitate dialogue, both within a country and among development partners.

Specifically, CEAs have three main objectives:

- To facilitate mainstreaming by providing information and analysis of key environment, development, and poverty links in the country policy dialogue
- To guide environmental assistance and capacity building supported by the World Bank or other development partners through an assessment of capacity issues, especially in relation to specific environmental priorities
- To facilitate a strategic approach to safeguard issues by providing analysis and information about environment-development links at the earliest stages of decision making, thus shaping key lending and programmatic decisions at the country and sectoral levels and helping manage risks at the project level

BUILDING BLOCKS OF A CEA. CEAs consist of three main building blocks (see figure 6.2):

- *Assessment of the state of the environment and forest development priorities,* involving systematic evaluation of key environment-development priorities (highlighting trends, the links to poverty, and environmental indicators relevant for development policy and for the achievement of the Millennium Development Goals)
- *Policy analysis,* to identify key development policies that have potential implications for the environment, in particular, those linked to forests and environment-development priorities
- *Institutional capacity assessment,* to evaluate the country's institutional capacity to address key environmental priorities and respond to policy changes that have poten-

tial environmental implications, particularly those related to forests

LINK WITH WORLD BANK PLANNING AND LENDING. The programming of CEA preparation should be closely linked with the World Bank's annual business planning and budgeting process, and be based to the extent possible on the scheduling of PRSPs, CASs, integrative country diagnostic analyses (such as development policy reviews or country economic memoranda), or planned large DPL operations that may pose environmental issues. CEAs are most effective when carried out in advance of the preparation of these processes to allow environmental considerations to be introduced at the earliest stages of decision making.

Examples of CEAs that have provided input to CASs and PRSPs include the ones for Bangladesh. Nigeria, and Serbia and Montenegro. CEAs carried out in the context of a DPL portfolio include those conducted for El Salvador, Ghana, and South Asia (Bangladesh, India, and Pakistan). CEAs can be a basis for designing development policy loans, as was the Colombia CEA.

To date, the only CEA that includes forests as a specific focus area is the Ghana CEA (see box 6.16). Forest issues do appear in some CEAs, broadly linked with other develop-

ment concerns. For example, the Orissa CEA is a state-level environmental analysis in India that focuses on the government's program to generate growth from the mining sector. However, most of Orissa's mineral deposits are in forests that are inhabited by tribal populations and harbor numerous endangered and charismatic species. Mineral extraction, therefore, has disproportionately affected the forest-dwelling population, the environment, and forest ecosystems. The impact of mines upon natural ecosystems, biodiversity, and tribal livelihoods has been one of the principal concerns in Orissa and is often a source of conflict. Hence, a particular component within the Orissa CEA is a study to assess the consequence of mining on affected forest-dependent populations through a household survey.

In the near term, several CEAs with a focus on natural resource management issues are planned in the Sub-Saharan Africa region; these are expected to focus in more depth on forest issues. Full CEAs typically cost approximately US$200,000, but this number varies with scope and methodology. Experience with rapid CEAs, which provide a snapshot view in a stepwise approach to a CEA dialogue rather than a more detailed analysis, is limited, but these tend to cost about US$60,000–$70, 000.

Figure 6.2 Key Building Blocks of CEAs

COUNTRY ENVIRONMENTAL ANALYSIS		
STATE OF THE ENVIRONMENT AND PRIORITIES FOR DEVELOPMENT	POLICY ANALYSIS	INSTITUTIONAL CAPACITY ASSESSMENT
• Prioritization of environmental challenges (through available data, costs of degradation studies, stakeholder analysis, qualitative methods) • Environmental trends in priority areas • Poverty-environment linkages • Indicators • Data gaps	• Identification of key macro-economic and sector policies with potential environmental implications • Lessons from SEAs, relevant studies, and analytic work • Areas for new SEAs	• Assessment of policymaking, administrative efficiency, and implementation capacity • Methodology and process for priority setting and cross-sectoral coordination • EA capacity assessment • Public environmental expenditure reviews • Indicators for measuring public sector capacity • Areas for intervention

BUSINESS PLAN
• Stocktaking of and lessons from the World Bank's and development partner's past environmental assistance to client country
• Review of the World Bank's planned lending and nonlending activities in key sectors and their links with environmental priorities
• Review of development partners' ongoing and planned environmental support activities
• Assessment of the World Bank's comparative advantage vis-à-vis development partners
• Suggested World Bank assistance in the form of lending and nonlending assistance and partnerships

Box 6.16 The Forests Component in the Ghana CEA

The Ghana CEA specifically recognized the challenges facing the forest and wildlife sector. Building on an earlier study that focused on costs of degradation from the forest sector, the CEA undertook an analysis of the policy, legal, and regulatory framework; institutions (mandate, capacity, incentives); and a public expenditure review.

The analysis found that Ghana's natural resources are overexploited and continue to decline in both quantity and quality. Cocoa farming, gold mining, and the wood industry are threatening high altitude forests. Ongoing soil erosion undermines food and agricultural production, human activities are degrading wetlands, and silt accumulation and alien species threaten goods and services provided by Lake Volta. Indeed, it is estimated that the degradation of agricultural soils, forests, coastal fisheries, wildlife resources, and Lake Volta's environment accounts for losses of at least US$520 million annually (around 4.9 percent of Ghana's annual GDP).

The analysis also found the general policy and legislative framework to be adequate, and that significant progress had been made in recent years, but that severe challenges remained relating to the implementation and enforcement of policies and laws on forests, wildlife, protected areas, and habitat management. The CEA therefore stressed the need for (i) urgent attention to resolving the causes of forest degradation and habitat loss, and (ii) addressing underlying governance and institutional problems and insecure financial arrangements.

The CEA's principal recommendations were that (i) high priority should be given to an agreed on financial arrangement that provides secure and sustainable financing for the operations of all divisions of the Forestry Commission, including provisions for the costs of strengthened wildlife protected area management; (ii) government should demonstrate its support and commitment to improved log and wood tracking systems; (iii) contracts and benefit-sharing arrangements for all recently established plantations—however established—should be concluded and perfected; (iv) government should continue its policy commitments to competitive bidding and a better investment climate for private sector investment (whether in plantations, timber processing, or ecotourism), but it should be matched by improved transparency of allocation, a level playing field for all, conversion of timber leases into Timber Utilization Contracts, and a credible enforcement regime for payments of fees, including Timber Rights Fees, stumpage, and performance bonds; and (v) an extended policy dialogue on scenarios for industry reform should be reinvigorated and include the Ministry of Finance and Economic Planning.

Source: Ahmed, Loayza, and Mani 2006.

Strategic Environmental Assessment

Since the 1970s, environmental impact assessment (EIA) has been used to address environmental aspects of forest projects and activities. Strategic environmental assessment extends the application of environmental assessment from projects to plans, policies, and programs (PPPs). Policies influence social behavior and changes in behavior may result in significant indirect environmental effects. Programs leading to the implementation of several projects in a particular region or forest may have cumulative environmental impacts that are not accounted for in the individual EIA of each project. Unlike projects, PPPs, particularly policies, may be heavily influenced by political considerations. For these reasons, SEA has been developed as a specific approach different from, although related to, EIA (box 6.17).

SEA USES DIVERSE TOOLS AND APPROACHES. SEA can include a wide range of approaches and make use of a variety of different tools. Some SEAs can be stand-alone processes running parallel to core planning processes, while others can be integrated into the planning and policy- and

Box 6.17 SEA Definition

Strategic Environmental Assessment describes analytical and participatory approaches to integrate environmental considerations into policies, plans, and programs (PPP) and evaluates the interlinkages with economic and social considerations.

Source: OECD 2006.

decision-making processes. SEA may focus on environmental impacts or its scope can be the integrated consideration of all three dimensions of sustainability: environmental, social, and economic. SEA may be applied to predetermined PPPs or be integrated into PPP formulation, and may engage a broad range of stakeholders or be limited to expert analysts. SEA can be conducted in a short time frame or over a long period. Some SEA may consist of a quick analysis while others require detailed analysis. Environmental assessment can be the starting point of an SEA but SEA can also be fed into an existing process, such as policy analysis. Furthermore, SEA could be a finite, output-based effort, or a more continuous process that is integrated within institutional processes.

SEA PROVIDE A FLEXIBLE APPROACH. From an operational standpoint, SEA can provide a flexible approach that varies according to the complexity of the decision-making process. At one extreme, it focuses on impact assessment and, at the other extreme, it centers on institutions and governance (see chapter 5, Improving Forest Governance). Along the continuum that lies between these two, the decision-making process is more significantly influenced by political bargaining and the interaction of different interest groups and constituencies. Consequently, only a balanced institutional framework can capture and effectively take into account the rights and concerns of small communities, minorities, and stakeholders affected by environmental degradation. Therefore, as PPPs move up in the decision-making hierarchy for contributing to sustainability in development processes, SEAs focus more on building institutional capacity and strengthening governance than on assessing impacts.

IMPACT CENTERED SEA AND INSTITUTION CENTERED SEA. When political economy factors and political bargaining are not important in defining a PPP, the SEA is rooted in EIA experiences and methodologies involving technical processes. Some observers have called this the "impact-centered approach to SEA"[2] because it focuses primarily on predicting, preventing, and mitigating adverse environmental and social impacts, similar to EIA of projects and activities. Conversely, in PPPs significantly influenced by political economy and political factors, the SEA is rooted in policy, institutional, and governance analysis, involving multistage, nonlinear, iterative processes. Because of this focus, it can be called an "institutions-centered approach to SEA."

Although both types of SEA can be used in forestry PPPs, impact-centered SEAs are largely adequate in programs and

plans for reforestation, extraction, and processing of wood and nonforest products, and watershed protection. Typically, an impact-centered SEA consists of the following four stages[3]:

- First is establishing the context for the SEA, in which potential impacts are screened, the SEA's objective is set, and stakeholders are identified.
- Next is implementation of the SEA. It begins with establishing the scope of the SEA and the participatory approaches to bring in relevant stakeholders. Like EIA, in this stage baseline data is collected, alternatives are identified, and measures to mitigate adverse impacts and enhance opportunities are proposed. This stage includes an assessment of the institutional conditions needed to effectively implement the SEA recommendations. These results are circulated publicly during a consultation process and a final report is prepared.
- The third stage is informing and influencing decision making. It overlaps to some extent with the second phase because presentation of the draft and final reports are key points to influence decision makers. In this stage, decision makers become aware of the options open to them, the likely effects of particular choices, and the consequences if they fail to reach a decision.
- The last stage is monitoring and evaluation of the SEA.

Institutions-centered SEA is mostly appropriate for forestry policies, in general, and forestry reform, in particular. Forestry reform induces changes in property rights, institutional reform, and adjustment in the incentives regime to manage and use forests, and thus is likely to engender significant environmental and social effects and opportunities (see note 5.2, Reforming Forest Institutions). In this situation, SEA can only be successful if it influences the reform and policy process, which requires SEA to be fully integrated into the decision-making process. The SEA team should work along with the forestry policy team responsible for the reform. It should provide inputs on the potential environmental and social effects of the proposed policies and be responsive to the requirements of policy makers and planners when policies are being formulated and implemented. In box 6.18 a program SEA for the implementation of forestry policy in Cameroon presents key components of an institutions-centered SEA in the context of an impact-centered SEA. In box 6.19, an institutions-centered SEA on the Kenya Forest Act is described to illustrate how the SEA was integrated with the decision-making process and World Bank activities.

Considering the above issues, an institutions-centered SEA comprises the following three stages[4]:

- Identification of the potential significant environmental and social effects and opportunities that may result from an operation
- Assessment of institutional capacity to manage the environmental and social effects and opportunities, and to take into account interests of affected stakeholders
- Capacity building and governance strengthening for environmental sustainability

LESSONS LEARNED AND RECOMMENDATIONS FOR PRACTITIONERS

Country Environmental Analyses

There is considerable flexibility in CEA scope and design. CEAs can focus on all key environmental issues linked with

---

Box 6.18   The Sector Study of Social and Environmental Impacts of Forest & Environment Sector Program in Cameroon

Between 1992 and 1996, Cameroon established a New Forestry Policy, only partially implemented because of limited capacity of national institutions. The Forest & Environment Sector Program (FESP) was developed to address this gap and, therefore, focuses on strengthening national institutions responsible for sustainable management of forests. The Cameroon Ministry of Environment and Forests carried out a SEA of the FESP with the double objective of optimizing the environmental and social impacts of the program and verifying its conformity to the environmental and social policies of the World Bank. The SEA was undertaken by a multidisciplinary team of national and international consultants, and included an integrated impact assessment, general sector analysis work, and public consultation.

About 10 consultations were held with the local populations in six provinces. Two national workshops and four joint multidonor missions with the participation of NGOs were organized. Also, during the implementation of the FESP, a regular program of local consultation on the social and environmental impacts of the program were to be implemented.

The SEA shows that most of the negative impacts identified in the sector are not derived from forestry policy itself, but from the limited institutional capacity for implementation. If the program attains its objective, it will have large positive environmental and social impacts. However, the SEA brought out some environmental and social risks that will be associated with the implementation of the forestry policy. The main ones follow:

- *Environmental level.* (i) the risk of increased poaching activities following access to vast and previously inaccessible areas; (ii) the risk of overexploitation of agricultural and pastoral territories and other resources (firewood, water, and so forth)

- *Social level.* (i) the risk of reducing access to some areas and resources as a result of the landscape approach used and the classification of forests and protected areas; (ii) the risk of conflicts between investors and the administration on one hand, and some social groups on the other hand, if the distribution of forest revenue does not materialize; (iii) marginalization of Indigenous Peoples (Pygmies) resulting from lack of adaptation of compensation measures to their cultural specificities

The SEA also identified extra-sectoral social and environmental risks that may affect the FESP, such as strong population growth combined with extensive agricultural production systems, or the malfunctioning of the judicial system. It recommended that the program develop links with policies and programs external to the forestry sector, and act on the strategies of rural development, promotion of the rule of law, poverty reduction, and promotion of the private sector.

The SEA proposed the following plans to accompany program execution:

- A Master Plan of Access to Resources, to reduce the risk of loss of access to resources. It includes necessary procedures for public consultation and the maintenance of users' rights in all circumstances.
- A Development Plan for Pygmies, to ensure that the pygmies could fully draw on the opportunities offered by community forests, share charges and employment opportunities, and be guaranteed that the quality of their mode of life would continue
- The Permanent Environment Secretariat, to execute a monitoring and management plan for social and environmental impacts. The development of the Secretariat's capacity to implement this plan was to be supported by the PSFE.

Source: Derived from Ministry of the Environment and Forestry (2003).

The government of Kenya ratified a new forest bill in September 2005, an outcome of the Kenya Forestry Master Plan finalized in 1991. It intends to unlock opportunities for forest resources to contribute to economic development and poverty alleviation, and to enable socially and environmentally sustainable forest management and conservation. The bill embraces the concept of participatory forest management, a radical departure from the government's previous practice of assuming full management responsibilities. The bill also encourages the formation of forest community associations to be recognized as management partners. Commercial plantations will be open to lease arrangements by interested groups to supplement government efforts, with the aim of improving their productivity and increase availability of timber and other products and services to the country and for export.

In April 2006, the World Bank supported a SEA of the implementation of the Kenya Forests Act, focused on integrating environmental, social, economic, and institutional considerations of the act and strengthening the processes for its implementation. The act contains many innovative improvements, including a strong emphasis on partnerships, engagement of local communities, and promotion of private investment. The purpose of the SEA was to inform and influence the process of implementing the new Forests Act and indirectly inform the policy dialogue regarding sustainable use of natural resources for national development. The SEA examined current risks confronting both woodland and forest environments and the social well-being of communities relying on these resources. Evidence gathered through research and extensive consultation was used to identify the scope for improving institutional structures and governance processes under the planned forestry reforms; notably those relating to the Kenya Forest Service and the participation of communities and the private sector in forest management. The SEA recommends ways of enhancing the opportunities for environmental and social gain, which already form part of the overall goal of the Forests Act.

A crucial element of the SEA has been its reliance on the active participation of a wide range of stakeholders, which has been essential in identifying key issues and priorities for action. The SEA has also examined conditions within two forest areas to assess priority issues and consider the views of community forest associations and other local stakeholders.

Important characteristics of the SEA in Kenya include the following:

■ Reliance on rapid assessment of the political economy and analysis of existing publications to establish the background to implementation of the act
■ Strong emphasis on the role of stakeholder groups to help identify priority areas of concern and key intersectoral environmental and social linkages
■ Use of a case study to help identify potential winners and losers arising from implementation and the extent to which sustainable forest management benefits are likely to be shared throughout society
■ Development of a policy-action matrix that incorporates an accountability and transparency framework, to assist the government in charting out how to effectively implement the act

The SEA analyzed social, environmental, and economic risks and assessed opportunities, and examined potential weaknesses in institutional structure and governance. Through consultation and analysis, the SEA identified three priority areas for action: strategic management and planning of the Forest Service, enabling community participation and benefit sharing, and enabling investment in the forest sector.

Strategic planning and management of the Kenya Forest Service embraces a number of subsidiary themes, the most important of which are:

■ enabling proper governance (including transparency and accountability) of the Kenya Forest Service;
■ ensuring proper strategic planning of forest resources;
■ maximizing the economic value of these resources for the nation; and
■ achieving effective financial management and regulation of the forest sector.

Community participation and benefit sharing combines the following interlinked objectives:

(Box continues on the following page.)

- ensuring that all forest communities and those adjacent to forest areas are involved in decision making and implementation;
- equitably sharing associated costs and benefits among communities, the private sector, and government;
- protecting indigenous and customary access and use of forest resources by communities; and
- enabling equitable and fair partnerships.

Enhancing investment in the forest sector means ensuring the right mix of public and private to ensure sustainable forest management so that the sector contributes to the national goal of poverty reduction (see

Source: World Bank 2007.

note 2.1, Company-Community Partnerships). This involves:

- creating an enabling environment for forest sector private investment (both corporate and community);
- enabling and strengthening partnerships; and
- improving transparency and accountability of investment activities.

The SEA proposed main adjustments that were presented in a policy-action matrix that the government and other stakeholders could use to guide implementation of the act.

---

growth and poverty reduction or on a few priority issues. CEAs can also analyze broad institutional issues linked with environmental management or focus on institutional analysis in key sectors of the economy.

CEAs are most effective when carried out in advance of the preparation of PRSPs, CASs, or development policy loans to allow environmental considerations to be introduced at the earliest stages of decision making.

POLICY CONSIDERATIONS AT THE COUNTRY LEVEL WILL BE KEY TO THE TIMING OF THE CEA. For instance, a change in government, or opportunities arising from government planning processes, may signal the need for a CEA. Institutional changes in the country—such as the restructuring of government agencies—may also call for a CEA. Issues to consider include the following:

- Is there a planning and policy process that the national or state government is considering that requires analytical support on the environment? Is there a routine development planning process that could be influenced by the CEA?
- Is there a change in the government that could benefit from policy advice through CEA? Is the new government likely to take note of specific environmental concerns or is there a need for overarching guidance? Are there champions of environmental sustainability in the new government who could use the CEA for their efforts?
- Is there restructuring taking place in environmental or other ministries that would require institutional analyses?

Is there an opportunity to review the organizational structure that supports environmental management? Is there a demand for capacity building? Are there new laws and legislation that call for strategic attention to the environment?

- Is there a demand from the environment or other ministries for strategic environmental analysis? Do large reform programs take place that may have environmental implications? Are there transboundary issues that require cross-country coordinated environmental analyses? Is analytical support required to help the country meet the conditions of international agreements?

CEAS CAN STRENGTHEN COUNTRY LEVEL DIALOGUE. CEAs can also be prepared in a country to strengthen country-level dialogue on environmental development issues, to update existing work, or to reestablish dialogue with a client country in postconflict situations.

Strategic Environmental Assessments

SEAS CAN CONTRIBUTE TO THE ANALYSIS OF DEVELOPMENT ALTERNATIVES. The SEA will not identify alternatives for implementing PPPs, but it will provide key information and suggestions that contribute, among other factors, to the alternatives analysis and, therefore, to the decision-making processes. Another SEA strength is that in a systematic and orderly way, it can bring into the alternatives analysis the perspective of potentially affected groups and civil society, reinforcing the long-term feasibility of PPPs.

SEAs are useful for analyzing the cumulative and indirectly induced effects of PPPs. Cumulative effects are the combined effects of several projects or interventions within a project and development trends in a region or sector. Indirectly induced effects (behavioral effects) are adverse or beneficial environmental effects caused by changes in people's behavior resulting from economic and social processes induced or influenced by a specific PPP.

For an SEA to influence policy making, it must focus on the "target audience." In order to influence policy making, an SEA target audience can often include policy makers and policy constituencies or interest groups and other affected groups. Ministries of finance, for example, will be more receptive to analysis providing quantified estimates of the environmental effects (positive or negative) of various policy options (for example, as a percentage of GDP). Ministries and agencies mandated to reduce poverty will be receptive to analysis focusing the impacts of given policy choices on the most vulnerable groups, especially if that analysis results from consultation with affected groups. Elected officials, who tend to have short-term horizons, will be more receptive to information on the short-term impacts of given policy choices. The positive short-term impacts of proposed amendments to policy proposals should also be highlighted and, if possible, quantified.

Institution centered SEA should extend beyond identification environmental and social priorities. In an institutions-centered SEA, stakeholder participation goes beyond identification of environmental and social priorities to inform the formulation and implementation of PPPs. It also contributes to leveling the political playing field for stakeholders affected by or vulnerable to environmental degradation, and for their interests to be taken into account in the policy process. Sometimes this requires involving stakeholders and considering other sectors, because forestry reform may have environmental implications in other sectors, such as tourism, agriculture, hydropower, transport, mining, and so forth. Consequently, the apex of an SEA may be an intersectoral committee.

Likewise, in institutions-centered SEAs, the analysis of the institutional forestry framework cannot be constrained to the environmental institutions related to the sector. Other sector institutions, such as forestry concessions, taxes, community forestry rights (see note 1.3, Indigenous Peoples and Forests, and note 1.2, Community-Based Forest Management, and note 5.4, Strengthening Fiscal Systems in the Forestry Sector), and private contracts and arrangements, may have major implications in natural resource use, deforestation, and environmental degradation. Therefore, the scope of the SEA's institutional analysis must also comprise these institutions and their influence on environmental and social aspects of forest management. It is in this context that governance issues like community organization, access to the judiciary, transparency, access to resources, and accountability of decision makers for lost environmental services and environmental degradation also need to be considered in the SEA.

Capabilities for carrying out SEA can be strengthened and developed at the following levels:

- Enhancing the skills of SEA practitioners
- Improving the quality of SEA review
- Improving environmental management systems
- Promoting informed participation and dialogue within planning and policy processes to create opportunities for incorporating environmental considerations in the formulation and implementation of plans and policies

NOTES

1. CEAs and SEAs are not limited in their application to cross-sectoral impacts or due diligence in policy operations.
2. See, for example UNDP et al. (2005: 51).
3. For a detailed description of these stages see OECD (2006), chapter 4.
4. A more detailed explanation of these stages, methods, and techniques can be found on the World Bank's Web site in the section on Institutions-Centered SEA corresponding to the SEA toolkit: http://go.worldbank.org/XIVZ1WF880.

SELECTED READINGS

Ahmed, K., J-R. Mercier, and R. Verheem. 2005. "Strategic Environmental Assessment—Concept and Practice." Environment Strategy Note No. 14, Environment Department, World Bank, Washington, DC.

Asian Development Bank Country Environmental Analysis: http://www.adb.org/environment/cea.asp.

Hamilton, K., and M. Mani. 2005. "Toolkit for Analyzing Environmental and Natural Resource Aspects of Development Policy Lending." Environment Department, World Bank, Washington, DC.

OECD Environmental Performance Country Reviews: http://www.oecd.org/topic/0,2686,en_2649_34307_1_1_1_1_37465,00.html.

World Bank SEA Web resources: http://go.worldbank.org/ AMVQSQV7G0. SEA Toolkit: http://go.worldbank.org/ XIVZ1WF880. World Bank CEA Web resources: http://go.worldbank.org/OJM2I7S3L0. CEA Toolkit: http://go.worldbank.org/Z3F3QDPEF0.

REFERENCES CITED

Ahmed, K., F. Loayza, and M. Mani. 2006. "Tools for Due Diligence." Note submitted to World Bank as input to *Forests Sourcebook*. Unpublished. World Bank. Washington, DC.

Ministry of the Environment and Forestry. 2003. "Etude Sectorielle des Impacts Sociaux et Environnement Aux du PSFE." Final Report, Republic of Cameroon, E937, April 1.

OECD (Organisation for Economic Co-operation and Development). 2006. Applying Strategic Environmental Assessment: Good Practice Guidance For Development Co-Operation. DAC Guidelines and Reference Series. http://www.oecd.org/dataoecd/4/21/37353858.pdf.

UNDP (United Nations Development Programme), UNEP (United Nations Environment Program), IIED (International Institute for Environment and Development), IUCN (The World Conservation Union), and the World Resources Institute. 2005. "Assessing Environment's Contribution to Poverty Reduction." UNDP, New York.

World Bank. 2002. *Making Sustainable Commitments. An Environmental Strategy for the World Bank*. Washington, DC: World Bank.

———. 2007. "Strategic Environmental Assessment of the Kenya Forests Act 2005." Agriculture and Rural Development Department. World Bank, Washington, DC.

CROSS-REFERENCED CHAPTERS AND NOTES

Note 1.2: Community-Based Forest Management

Note 1.3: Indigenous Peoples and Forests

Note 1.4: Property and Access Rights

Note 2.1: Community-Private Partnerships

Note 5.2: Reforming Forest Institutions

Note 5.4: Strengthening Fiscal Systems in the Forestry Sector

CHAPTER 7

Monitoring and Information Systems for Forest Management

Information and monitoring systems for the forest sector are instrumental for effective policies and planning, prioritizing interventions, valuation of forest resources, efficient investments, and engendering accountability. Relevant forest information that is systematically and periodically collected can enable effective implementation of policies, inform decision making, and guide management (see box 7.1). Current and accurate information on forests also can help raise the profile of the sector and increase awareness of forest resources' potential. Abundant evidence points to how inadequate information on forests and weak monitoring capacity have resulted in poor forest policies, planning, and management; hampered efforts to reduce illegal and unsustainable extraction of forest resources and improve transparency; and resulted in undervaluation of forest resources. Such conditions, in turn, contribute to continuous decline in area, health, stock, and flows of forest resources.

Emerging financing opportunities for sustainable forest management under the climate change agenda will require effective systems for monitoring forest cover and carbon emissions and additional information on the resource base and drivers of change. More specifically, efforts to enhance the contribution of forests to reducing carbon emissions (through reduced emissions from deforestation and degradation [REDD] initiatives) will require participating countries to establish a credible reference scenario on REDD based on methodological guidance from the UN Framework Commission on Climate Change (UNFCCC). Most likely this will require assessments of historical emission

quantities and trends and establishment of a forest resource database. The assessments of historical emissions and trends can help identify a reference scenario. REDD pilot projects will be undertaken between 2008 and 2012 with the hope that REDD will be endorsed in the post-Kyoto climate protocol. Any country selected for the pilot initiative will have to design and implement a system that effectively monitors and verifies its REDD.

Payment for environmental services from forests requires that these services be properly valued, which, in turn, requires that the forest resource base and other resources (water, soil, and the like) be appropriately monitored. Such forest information and monitoring can also improve knowledge about the relationship between forests and other environmental services and facilitate opportunities to generate multiple benefits from forest resources. For example, ongoing discussions on the role of forests in climate change and the Convention on Biological Diversity (CBD) have stimulated efforts to include biodiversity benefits as a consideration when identifying forest sites for REDD. Information on forest cover and other relevant environmental benefits would assist in identifying forest areas with multiple benefits.

Better and more timely inventories and broader information collection on forest resources enables planning and implementing sustainable productive use of resources, including determining allowable cut and plantation and natural forest management. Information on forest use is needed for monitoring changes in the resource base and causes for change and identifying ways to integrate forest development efforts with overall sustainable development in the country. From a poverty standpoint, monitoring can provide more accurate information on how changes in resources and their uses are affecting the rural poor, and whether the pattern of resource use by the rural poor is sustainable (see chapter 1, Forests for Poverty Reduction).

Robust information on changes in quality and quantity of forest resources and periodic monitoring can assist in identifying factors driving forest change. Time series information generated through spatial maps of forest cover, roads, poverty levels, and property rights can help in the analysis of cross-sectoral relationships. Such monitoring

efforts can be used to understand the influence of external factors on forest resources, monitor illegal logging (see note 5.5, Addressing Illegal Logging), or assess carbon assimilated by forests. Innovative application of spatial and other monitoring tools can facilitate such uses (see box 7.2).

Periodic collection of, and public access to, relevant and robust forest information can enable better resource management. Other contributions to a new environment for decision making have included advances in understanding complex interactions, both within ecosystems and among ecosystems, human activities, and human well-being; improvements in information technologies and greater access to information as a result of computers and data systems; the changing paradigm of poverty; and ongoing policy and institutional reform. Multiple users in governments, the private sector, and civil society need better scientific information, such as that provided through technical assessments. Furthermore, the general public can make use of information found in assessments to hold decision makers accountable (Millennium Ecosystem Assessment 2003).

PAST ACTIVITIES

The World Bank has monitoring components in various investment projects, some of which are discussed in the notes associated with this chapter. It is estimated that approximately US$28 million has been invested in monitoring components of forest sector projects over 2002–05. This investment is nearly evenly distributed between creation of forest management information systems (FMIS), forest inventories, and development of capacity and tools for spatial monitoring. This component of forest activities is expected to increase as investments in governance increase (with monitoring of illegal logging activities) and as client country interest in avoided deforestation matures.

KEY ISSUES

TEMPORAL ASPECTS OF MONITORING. Forest monitoring is an assessment of the status of forests at different times, often including assessment of changes within established features (that is, changes within boundaries of protected areas, forest concessions, private properties, and so on). Forest monitoring thus requires systematic periodic assessment.

MONITORING SHOULD UPDATE FOREST MANAGEMENT. An effective forest monitoring system is much more than a technical set of data and techniques. A political process and the political will to integrate findings from forest information systems and to update management approaches and policies makes monitoring useful. An effective forest monitoring system is one that is tied to appropriate political processes that enable corrective actions.

NATIONAL FOREST INVENTORIES. Continuous or repeated forest assessments (or forest inventories) are often necessary to enable resource use planning and management. National forest inventories (NFIs) are an example of such assessments. NFIs provide information relevant for national-level decision making, policy formulation, and monitoring for forestry and related sectors, as well as for forestry planning in smaller geographical or political units at the subnational level (see note 7.1, National Forest Inventories). Because the results are an input to global forest assessments, there is also regional and global interest in high-quality national forest information. Several new methodologies and technologies can improve inventory, planning, implementation, analysis, and reporting of forest inventories (see table 7.1). Selection of tools or approaches should be informed by the characteristics of the activity being monitored and the availability of required capacity, hardware, and other supports.

BUILDING NATIONAL CAPACITY FOR GATHERING AND USING INFORMATION. Capacity to collect forest sector data and conduct forest inventories has declined since the 1960s. Currently, few national statistical organizations are strong enough to be of value in policy processes. The challenge at the local level is partly driven by poor links between information demand and supply (Holmgren and Persson 2002). In recent decades forest information seems to have been supply driven, partly because of the promotion of remote sensing rather than field work. The policy process, therefore, has been guided by what can be

Table 7.1 Areas Where New Methodologies and Technologies are Expected to Benefit NFIs

| Methodology or technology | Main phases of a national forest inventory | | | | |
	Planning	Implementation	Data quality and data management	Analysis (including modeling)	Reporting
Remote sensing		X		X	X
Satellite navigation systems		X		X	
Measurement devices		X			
Mobile information and communication		X	X		
Software and algorithms			X	X	X
Sampling options	X		X		

Source: Kleinn 2002.

collected via remote sensing rather than by a need for specific information. Changing this trend will require a close examination of how information is used in national and international policy processes and will require building the capacity to gather and use this relevant information.

In many countries, national statistical services are under-resourced and are unable to deliver reliable data in a timely fashion. Often, national statistical databases are filled with gaps or use imputed values that are prone to gross errors. This creates a vicious circle, with users dismissing the services of the statistical organizations, reducing the funding for these organizations, and causing them to continually perform poorly. Despite this reality, several national governments report on forest data, and some carry out periodic monitoring of forest resources.

More recently, donor programs have also concentrated on collecting information rather than building capacity, although this is slowly changing and investment in capacity is occurring. Recent donor initiatives include the Marrakech Action Plan for Statistics, which coordinates donor support for statistical capacity building and encourages countries to merge their own priorities for statistical development through the preparation and implementation of national strategies for development of statistics. There is still, however, room for further investment in capacity and infrastructure for monitoring and reporting.

SCOPE AND STATUS OF NATIONAL FOREST MONITORING EFFORTS. More detailed information on what different countries are doing in forest monitoring would be helpful for designing interventions in monitoring, as well as determining how a global monitoring system, compatible across countries, may be created. For example, the Forest Survey of India (FSI), an organization under the Ministry of Environment & Forests, was mandated in 1986 to monitor and map the country's forest cover on a biennial basis. Consequently, FSI has been carrying out assessments of the country's forest cover using satellite-based remote sensing data and has been publishing its findings in the State of Forest Report (SFR) every two years (see box 7.3).

Similar institutional arrangements for spatial monitoring exist in several other countries (for an example in Brazil, see box 7.4). There is a need to understand how these monitoring arrangements are set up; what technologies and methodologies are used; the periodicity with which information is collected; how the information is processed, analyzed, and reported; and who the end users are.

REDD: DETERMINING BASELINES (REFERENCE SCENARIOS). Discussions on the role of forests in climate change must distinguish between deforestation and degradation. This distinction is important because the appropriate tools for detecting deforestation (for example, remote sensing to capture clear-cuts) may not be as effective in detecting degradation. Furthermore, monitoring specific to REDD will need to satisfy UNFCCC and Intergovernmental Panel on Climate Change (IPCC) criteria, which are slightly different from conventional forest needs.

Box 7.3   Forest Assessments in India

The Forest Survey of India assesses the forest cover of the country on a two-year cycle using satellite data. The main objective is to present information on the country's forest resources at the state and district levels, and to prepare forest cover maps on a 1:50,000 scale. The first forest cover assessment of the country was made in 1987; eight more assessments have been made, with forest cover information at the district level being available beginning with the third assessment, in 1991. Before the fourth assessment, forest cover assessment for the entire country was generated through visual interpretation. After the eighth assessment in 2001, the entire country was assessed digitally.

The 2003 assessment, like the 2001, includes information on lands that are at least 1 hectare that have tree canopy density of at least 10 percent. The information does not differentiate land use or ownership, and all perennial woody vegetation—including bamboos, palms, coconut, and apple trees—were treated as trees; agroforestry plantations were also considered forests.

The findings of the assessments are published in the biennial State of Forest Report, which includes forest cover maps for the country, the states, and Union Territories. These maps, prepared with the use of remote sensing technology, are also used for carrying out other spatial studies, such as monitoring shifting cultivation, assessment of forest density, mining leases, wildlife habitats, forest fragmentation, forest fire affected areas, assessment of mangroves, and delineation of forest types.

Source: Authors' compilation.

Box 7.4   Monitoring Efforts in Brazil

Three significant monitoring efforts are occurring in Brazil: the Brazilian Space Agency project PRODES, the Amazon Surveillance System (SIVAM-SIPAM), and the government of the state of Mato Grosso's Environmental Control System on Rural Properties.

PRODES

Since the 1980s, the PRODES project has been monitoring the extent of gross and annual deforestation in the Brazilian Amazon based on interpretation of high-resolution satellite imagery (Landsat). Although highly automated, the deforestation mapping remains a labor-intensive process in which, each year, more than 220 satellite scenes are scanned, selected for minimum cloud coverage, geo-referenced, and prepared to run a predefined algorithm for analysis (for example, transforming vegetation, shade, and light features). Features are then classified and edited to derive deforestation and other maps by state (from a 1997 baseline). The thematic maps and Landsat imagery are made available to the Brazilian community.

The deforestation mapping has some limitations. Besides being labor intensive, the analysis is also dependent on the availability of cloud-free imagery. PRODES mapping also misses small plots of deforestation (3.0 to 6.5 hectares) caused by small disturbances to the forest canopy, such as those caused by selective logging, which is practiced extensively throughout the Brazilian Amazon. Enforcement of policy and regulation at the federal level remains fragile, yet such deforestation data can provoke significant public pressure, which often results in policy changes.

SIVAM-SIPAM

The Amazon Surveillance System project (*Sistema de Vigilância da Amazônia* in Portuguese) is a multi-billion dollar monitoring system that uses a sophisticated mix of fixed and mobile ground radar and airborne surveillance. SIVAM was conceived in the 1990s by the Office of the President, the Ministry of Justice, and the Brazilian Air Force, to defend the Legal Amazon and monitor illegal activity (drug trafficking, illegal logging, or burning). The system, later renamed the Amazonian Protection System (SIPAM) came into force in 1999.

SIVAM's infrastructure is able to acquire, process, and disseminate a variety of spatial information from various sources (radar, Landsat, SPOT [Satellite Pour l'Observation de la Terre], CBERS [China Brazil Earth Resources Satellite], and ERS-1 [European Remote Sensing Satellite]). This costly, state-of-the-art system offers a solid infrastructure and capacity for comprehensive monitoring; the data that can be acquired and processed could be applied to environmental monitoring, including vegetation cover, hydrology, human occupation, and fire monitoring. With all its potential, nevertheless, it appears that social buy-in for SIVAM has not consolidated completely.

Environmental Control System on Rural Properties

The State Environment Foundation of Mato Grosso (FEMA/MT)—the entity responsible for management of the state's environmental policy—developed the Environmental Control System on Rural Properties. This system uses monitoring as one element to enforce existing legislation, mitigate environmental liabilities, and protect environmental assets. The system focuses on large land holdings (1,000 hectares or more) in areas most affected by deforestation. FEMA uses Remote Sensing (RS)/Geographic Information System (GIS) technology to collect and manage land-use information—particularly agriculture and livestock—in the state, using visual interpretation of land cover and deforestation from detailed satellite images to prioritize field visits; identification of heat sources from National Oceanic and Atmospheric Agency (NOAA) satellite data to identify areas of incidence of fire and fire risk; GIS technology to generate maps, graphics, and tables to help field inspectors and planners to locate, quantify, and categorize environmental damage; its comprehensive GIS reference library of properties to pinpoint the precise location of licensed activities on properties; and a Global Positioning System (GPS) to guide FEMA field inspectors to locations where noncompliance is suspected. GPS is also useful to update and complement RS/GIS data with information from the ground.

The system has proven to be efficient and the role of RS/GIS has helped target and prioritize areas for field inspection. Over two months in 2000, for instance, 10 field teams carried out inspection and enforcement campaigns on almost 3,000 rural properties. For the same year, 50 noncompliant landowners were arrested; the number of identified heat sources was lower in relation to the previous year; and the demand for environmental licenses increased.

Source: Nuguerón and Stolle 2007.

Discussions and proposals on how to set a reference level have centered around identifying rates of deforestation or land conversion (historical hectares per year deforested) by looking at several years of deforestation data (most likely interpreted from satellite images). The deforestation rates would then be translated into a greenhouse gas emissions rate (a reference level). New annual "rates of deforestation" would be compared against the reference level. A reduction in the rate of deforestation would, therefore, also translate into a reduction in greenhouse gas emissions, which might then make the government or entity responsible for getting emissions reduced eligible for financial compensation.

Countries interested in REDD will need to, among other things, identify a baseline for carbon emissions and a rate of forest-cover change. While specific guidance will become available on determining baselines for forest cover and carbon emissions, a country will clearly need to be able to set a target that is based on a reduction from a certain reference level and quantify how much reduction in deforestation actually occurred if the government is to get credits. Historical data and projected deforestation rates will be important for determining baselines. Appropriately set baselines help ensure that REDD initiatives are capturing and covering the costs associated with reduced emissions but not creating perverse incentives.

NATIONAL AND INTERNATIONAL REPORTING OBLIGATIONS. Countries are obliged to report information related to their forest sectors to a variety of international and regional conventions, agreements, and bodies (Braatz 2002). There are 10 international instruments in force relevant to forests.[1] Parties to each of these instruments are asked to report on measures taken to implement their commitments under the instrument. In most cases, reporting consists of qualitative information on activities and means of implementation (for example, policy, legislative, or institutional measures). In a few cases, reporting also includes quantitative biophysical and socioeconomic data on forest resources or resource use. These reports, and associated efforts to monitor and assess status and trends in forest resources and progress in meeting international commitments, help orient national and international policy deliberations (Braatz 2002).

Accurate and consistent forest information at the global scale is still needed, specifically information on how much forest is lost annually and from where. The lack of such information is partly because previous efforts depended on inconsistent definitions of forest cover and used methodologies that could not readily be replicated or were very expensive and time consuming (see box 7.5).

The concern regarding national reporting burdens has been acknowledged in international forums for forest dialogue. Since 2000, various efforts have attempted to harmonize national reporting on biological diversity (specifically for CBD (Convention on Biological Diversity), CITES (Convention on International Traded in Endangered Species), CMS (Convention on Migratory Species), the Ramsar Convention, and WHC (World Heritage Convention). In April 2002, CBD, by Decision VI/22, adopted the expanded work program on forest biological diversity, which included as one of its activities to "seek ways of streamlining reporting between the different forest-related processes, in order to improve the understanding of forest quality change and improve consistency in reporting on sustainable forest management (SFM)" (Conference of the Parties [COP] Decision VI/22). These efforts all require reaching a common understanding of forest-related concepts, terms, and definitions.

MONITORING FRAMEWORK DESIGN. What is being monitored, how the information will be used and by whom, and the sustainability of a monitoring system should all inform its design. Monitoring systems should be designed to be flexible and able to respond to a dynamic context, which can change the scope and objective of monitoring. The monitoring system design must consider the end user and sustainability of the system. Engagement of end users in the design and implementation of the system increases their confidence in the system and ensures its utility.

MEASUREMENT FRAMEWORK. A measurement framework is helpful in designing the monitoring system. A measurement framework should have goals, criteria (the desirable endpoints), indicators for each criteria (how well each criteria is being fulfilled), and approaches (qualitative or quantitative) for measuring the indicators. The goals and desired outcomes should guide identification of specific indicators. In systems that integrate conservation and production, a hierarchy of goals can be established. Some may be broad, universal goals and others may be more specific (yet have some universal applicability).

When choosing a framework, various alternatives that have been tested and implemented should be considered, as should new ones. Ideally, preference should be given to the framework already in use in the country, for example, the Criteria and Indicators framework used by the nine regional Criteria and Indicators processes (including the Ministerial Conference on Protection of Forests in Europe), the Driver-Pressure-State-Impact-Response model, or the Services Model framework implemented by Millennium Ecosystem

Box 7.5   The Forest Resource Assessment Program of FAO

The UN Food and Agriculture Organization (FAO) has played a key role over the past 50 years in providing forest sector information at the global level, having recognized that reliable information and knowledge about forest resources is essential for sound policy development, forest resource management, and integration with overall sustainable development efforts in a country. Monitoring, assessment, and reporting on forests and forest products are some of the main activities of the FAO.

FAO's Forest Resources Assessment (FRA) program uses the concept of sustainable forest management and reports on six of the seven thematic elements common among the nine regional Criteria and Indicators processes. These elements include extent of forest resources, growing stock, biomass stock, carbon stock, forest health, forests under productive purposes, plantations, and removal of wood and nonwood forest products from forests (www.fao.org/forestry/fra). The Forest Sector Outlook studies (www.fao.org/forestry/site/5606/en), State of the World's Forests (www.fao.org/forestry/site/21407/en), and other FAO publications serve the seven thematic areas in achieving the overall mission of enhancing human well-being (see box figure).

Information from the FRA is accepted by international processes, conventions, and agencies, such as CBD, IPCC, and the United Nations Environmental Programme (UNEP), and by all countries. The FRA is a collaborative and participative effort of experts within and outside the FAO, and includes national experts in all countries (members and nonmembers of FAO). More than 800 such experts contributed to FRA 2005, and more than 170 officially nominated national correspondents provided and validated its contents.

The information compiled by FAO's FRA is the most comprehensive to date. It relies on aggregating national-level forest inventory information, which is reported by countries to FAO, to provide a global picture of forest cover and forest cover change every 10 years. Spatially explicit estimates of tree cover change based on repeated measurements would provide much needed information beyond what is readily available from the FRA. Such a spatial assessment would be useful in that it would provide comprehensive information that can be periodically updated, yield measures of change at the global scale, and help identify areas that need to be examined more closely.

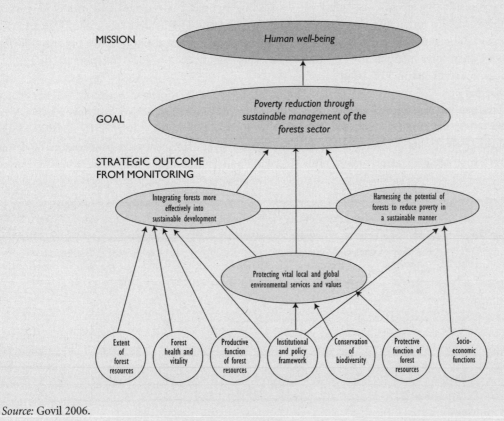

Source: Govil 2006.

Assessment (www.millenniumassessment.org). Another good framework, although still being piloted and not yet implemented at regional and global levels, is the "Manual for Environmental and Economic Accounts" (FAO 2004).

USING EXISTING AND NEW METHODOLOGIES. Advancements in methodology and technology are a constant phenomenon in forest monitoring, as evidenced by the advancements in remote sensing, a particularly useful tool for studying forest change comprehensively and uniformly across time and space. Remote sensing multiplies the value of field-plot data and permits complete, wall-to-wall analyses. Spatial images from Landsat have been a workhorse for scientists interested in measuring changes in the distribution and condition of forests. A number of satellites have come online since Landsat, several of which are useful for monitoring forests (USDA 2007). Other advancements in forest monitoring approaches have been based on imaging radar data, which works in all weather conditions. Methodological advancements, too, such as simplifying and automating mapping of forest disturbances (USDA 2007), have been important.

Older technologies, such as mobile data loggers and mobile communication, could be more effectively used for monitoring forest activities. Mobile telephone communication can serve two purposes: It can increase the safety of field crews by giving them access to communication in cases of emergency, while also enabling online data entry to a central database. Advancements in software, such as GIS[2], also offer many possibilities for presentation of results and improved access to information.

The use of some of the newer technologies is not without shortcomings. For example, the availability of reference data for digital image analysis or visual interpretation is one of the key problems in remote sensing–aided surveys. The parameters that can be estimated using remote-sensing surveys often depend on the intensity of the field sampling. Area of forests, other wooded land, and other land types, as well as their changes, can be adequately measured with available remote sensing–aided surveys. In contrast, tree stem volume and biomass, which are critical variables in determining the status of the world's forests, require thorough field measurements for their estimation. Such limitations are constantly being dealt with.

COST OF MONITORING. Cost is often an important driver in designing monitoring systems. A frequently asked question is when and whether satellite imagery–based forest cover mapping can substitute for forest inventory. Mapping studies cost less than field work (if the necessary hardware and software are available); need less planning, smaller teams, and less broad expertise; are partly independent of weather; and provide maps as the major product, which are usually more easily accepted and "marketed" than statistics and tables with error specifications.

The type of analysis required often influences the cost. High-resolution images are notably more expensive than coarse images. Tomppo and Czaplewski (2002) estimated costs for remote sensing under different resolutions and sampling options for regional and global surveys using remote sensing and field data (see tables 7.2 and 7.3). The costs have since changed significantly, but this information provides an indication of the differences in costs.

SELECTION OF INDICATORS. Assessing all benefits from forests over time is complicated, and only feasible if simplifications and approximations, such as indicators, are accepted. Several international processes have developed criteria and indicators for sustainable forest management.

Table 7.2 Example of Number of Images and Estimated Costs for a Remote-Sensing Survey with Different Resolution and Sampling Options

Region	Number of images needed				Imaging cost (US$ thousand)		
	MODIS full coverage	Landsat 10% coverage	Ikonos 0.1% coverage	Ikonos 1% coverage	Landsat 10% coverage	Ikonos 0.1% coverage	Ikonos 1% coverage
Africa	6	97	331	3,309	58	951	8,992
Asia	6	100	343	3,428	60	986	9,315
Europe	4	73	251	2,511	44	722	6,824
North and Central America	4	69	237	2,374	42	683	6,453
Oceania	2	28	94	943	17	271	2,564
South America	3	57	195	1,950	34	561	5,299
Total	25	424	1,451	14,515	255	4,174	39,447

Source: Tomppo and Czaplewski 2002.
Note: MODIS and Landsat are NASA satellite imaging programs; Ikonos is is a commercial Earth observation satellite.

Region	Land area (million ha)	Forest area (million ha)	Field plot area (ha)	Number of field plots	Estimated costs (US$ thousand)
Africa	2,978	650	13,692	69,221	30,457
Asia	3,085	548	28,540	30,010	13,205
Europe	2,260	1,039	28,268	44,751	19,690
North and Central America	2,137	549	27,814	27,421	12,065
Oceania	849	198	25,960	10,898	4,795
South America	1,755	886	21,648	49,035	21,575
Total	13,064	3,870	145,922	231,336	101,787

Table 7.3 An Example of the Number and Cost of Field Plots in a Global Survey Using Field Data Only

Source: Tomppo and Czaplewski 2002.

The criteria express the objectives of forestry, as negotiated in political processes, but the identification of indicators for national-level performance in meeting the criteria is more difficult.

Indicators are seldom optimal because they often need to be generated from a rapid process and, therefore, are identified based on the data that is available. Furthermore, indicators identified at an international level may not be considered equally valid or important among participating countries. This raises the need to agree on internationally accepted criteria, but also develop national indicators.

FUTURE PRIORITIES AND SCALING-UP ACTIVITIES

The following activities should be given priority:

- building capacity and investing in technology for effectively monitoring land-use change
- assistance in effectively measuring forest cover and carbon emissions at the project-intervention level and effective integration of this information into national accounting systems on carbon emissions
- supporting research to develop improved and affordable methodologies and technologies for national forest inventories
- supporting development and maintenance of national and regional networks of forest-related monitoring

NOTES

1. The United Nations Commission on Sustainable Development (CSD), the UN Convention to Combat Desertification (CCD), the UNFCCC, the CBD, CITES, the CMS, the Convention on Wetlands of International Importance especially as Waterfowl Habitat (Ramsar Convention), the Convention Concerning the Protection of the World Cul-

tural and Natural Heritage (World Heritage Convention), the UN Forum on Forests (UNFF), and the International Tropical Timber Agreement (ITTA).

2. A GIS is a collection of computer hardware, software, and geographic data for capturing, managing, analyzing, and displaying all forms of geographically referenced information. See http://www.GIS.com.

SELECTED READINGS

FAO. 2005. "Global Forest Resources Assessment 2005: Progress Towards Sustainable Forest Management." FAO Forestry Paper 147, FAO, Rome. http://www.fao.org/forestry/site/fra/en/.

Lange, G.-M. 2004. "Manual for Environmental and Economic Accounts for Forestry: A Tool for Cross-Sectoral Policy Analysis." Working Paper, FAO, Rome, Italy. http://www.fao.org/docrep/007/j1972e/J1972E00.htm#TOC.

International Tropical Timber Organization (ITTO). 2005. *Revised ITTO Criteria and Indicators for the Sustainable Management of Tropical Forests Including Reporting Format*. Yokohama, Japan: International Tropical Timber Organization. http://www.itto.or.jp/live/Live_Server/963/ps15e.pdf.

Ministerial Conference on the Protection of Forests in Europe (MCPFE). 2002. "Improved Pan-European Indicators for Sustainable Forest Management." MCPFE, Vienna, Austria. http://www.forestry.gov.uk/pdf/mcpfeindic03.pdf/$FILE/mcpfeindic03.pdf.

The Montréal Process. "Criteria and Indicators." http://www.mpci.org/criteria_e.html.

REFERENCES CITED

Braatz, S. 2002. "National Reporting to Forest-Related International Instruments: Mandates, Mechanisms, Overlaps and Potential Synergies." *Unasylva* 53/No. 210 (Forest Assessment And Monitoring): 65–67.

FAO. 2004. "Manual for Environmental and Economic Accounts for Forestry: A Tool for Cross-Sectoral Policy Analysis." Working paper. FAO, Rome.

Govil, K. 2006. "Monitoring Forest Sector Projects." Note submitted to World Bank as input to *Forests Sourcebook.* Unpublished. World Bank, Washington, DC.

Holmgren, P., and R. Persson. 2002. "Evolution and Prospects of Global Forest Assessments." *Unasylva* 210 (53):3–9.

Kleinn, C. 2002. "New Technologies and Methodologies for National Forest Inventories." *Unasylva* 210 (53):10–15. http://www.fao.org/docrep/005/y4001e/Y4001E03.htm#P0_0.

Lampietti, J. 2004. "Power's Promise: Electricity Reforms in Eastern Europe and Central Asia." Working Paper No. 40. World Bank, Washington, DC.

Millennium Ecosystem Assessment. 2003. *Ecosystems and Human Well-Being: A Framework For Assessment.* Millennium Ecosystem Assessment Series. Washington, DC: Island Press. http://www.ecodes.org/pages/areas/salud_medioambiente/documentos/ecosystems_human_well being.pdf.

Noguerón, R., and F. Stolle. 2007. "Spatial Monitoring of Forests." Note submitted to the World Bank as input to *Forests Sourcebook.* World Bank, Washington, DC.

Thuresson, T. 2002. "Value of Low-Intensity Field Sampling in National Forest Inventories." *Unasylva* 210 (53):19–23. http://www.fao.org/DOCREP/005/Y4001e/Y4001E05.htm#P0_0

Tomppo, E., and R. L. Czaplewski. 2002. "Potential for a Remote-Sensing-Aided Forest Resource Survey for the Whole Globe." *Unasylva* 210 (53):16–19.

United States Department of Agriculture (USDA). 2007. "Monitoring Forests from Space: Quantifying Forest Change by Using Satellite Data." *PNW Science Findings* 89:1–6.

CROSS-REFERENCED CHAPTERS AND NOTES

Chapter 1: Forests for Poverty Reduction, and associated notes

Note 5.5: Addressing Illegal Logging

Note 6.3: Identifying the Need for Analysis on Forests in Development Policy Reforms

National Forest Inventories

A basic element of planning and efficient investments in the forest sector is an inventory of forest resources. In several countries, the basic countrywide information on the current state of forests and other ecosystems is inadequate, fragmentary, or outdated—or all three. Often the existing data at the national level are speculative and largely based on reconnaissance-type inventories and unrealistic assumptions about forest production and the impact of human activities on the resource base.

In many countries, reliable estimates of forest and ecosystem resources, consumption rate, and real economic potential are still lacking. In such contexts, the awareness of forest values is low. The rates by which forest ecosystems change over time and the overall distribution of the lands supporting them is not precisely known. Furthermore, institutions for ensuring continued monitoring are weak and can require capacity building and access to current technology to facilitate inventory.

Implementation of national forest programs (see note 6.1, Using National Forest Programs to Mainstream Forest Issues) and national forest assessments requires monitoring to contribute to and guide the planning and implementation of forestry and natural resources–related programs and projects.

An up-to-date national forest inventory provides numerous benefits (see box 7.6), including the following:

- makes possible the calculation of the value of forest assets and monitoring of degradation and restoration trends, thereby enabling (i) improved decision making on forest-related public expenditure and revenue policies; (ii) improved understanding of the role of forests in past, current, and future national income accounts; (iii) improved environmental and governance management; and (iv) national reporting on important international conventions;
- improves the required planning and monitoring of the forest estate;

Box 7.6 Motivation for Forest Inventory in Bosnia and Herzegovina

A World Bank intervention in the forest sector of Bosnia and Herzegovina revisited the project's inventory component and requested approval for allocating additional resources to this component because both the government and the World Bank appreciated the importance of this activity for effective forest management. The initial efforts to undertake an inventory resulted in an increased focus on management for nontimber forest products (NTFPs), recreation, hunting, and tourism. These have the potential to significantly increase revenues on state and private forest lands. Currently, for each cubic meter of wood extracted (worth about US$50), forest enterprises earn only about US$1 on NTFPs, including recreation and tourism. This 50:1 ratio compares unfavorably to a 50:50 ratio (timber to NTFP) in Austria. Hence, there is much room for improvement.

Likewise, measures to reduce illegal activities in the forests, to instill good management and planning practices (that is, FMIS), and to certify forests and promote log tracking schemes would help to open the European Union market to Bosnian wood products, and thereby enable Bosnia and Herzegovina to obtain higher prices. Currently, Bosnian timber is locked out of portions of the export market because major buyers, such as IKEA, have adapted procurement policies that require good management and SFM certification. Forests inventories are a central component of FMIS (see note 7.2, Establishing Forest Management Information Systems).

Source: World Bank 2003.

- enables implementation of action plans to combat illegal activities in the sector;
- increases knowledge on the extent and location of the country's forest assets for potential private investors in wood-processing industries; and
- enables FMIS and state forest inventory use for decision making, monitoring, and planning, thereby helping to support the benefits of these tools.

OPERATIONAL ASPECTS

Operationalizing forest inventories requires great attention to detail as well as to the big picture in the forest sector.[1] Clarity of the objective of the inventory and an assessment of capacity to implement the inventory are central to designing a proper forest inventory and ensuring that all (or most) of the important components are covered (see box 7.7).

INVENTORY DESIGN. Areas to be included in the inventory must be clearly defined; for example, privately held forests, forests in areas that are considered nonforest, and tree resources on nonforest land (see box 7.8). It is equally important to determine whether the inventory will be "wall to wall," or based on samples. The objectives of the inven-tory and the sample should help confirm the statistical design and the required level of accuracy. The objectives also help determine how often inventory reports should be updated (annually, or every 5 or 10 years) and the way in which success will be measured. Success may not be solely a function of precision, but also depend on transparency and timeliness.

If the objective is to estimate status and trends in

- the area of forest land;
- the volume, growth, and removal of forest resources; and
- the health and condition of the forest;

important elements in a forest inventory will include

- sampling design—how to have a nationally consistent assessment;
- observations and measurements;
- using remote sensing applications effectively, perhaps for
  - initial plot observation,
  - stratification (see box 7.9);
- conducting remote sensing and GIS research, including
  - map-based estimation and internet (see box 7.10),
  - map-based sustainability analyses.

Box 7.7   Forest Inventory in Tanzania

The World Bank's intervention in Tanzania has an inventory component that includes

- setting up a specialized structure in the Forest and Bee Keeping Department (FBD) for data collection; updating of information; training of inventory personnel; developing norms and methods of inventories and assessments; helping define government policy in the area of knowledge generation, management, dissemination, and the like; and
- creating a new baseline of information, complete in scope and harmonized with existing information required by international reporting requirements (see box 7.12 for data collection model).

Objectives of the project:

- Strengthen capability of FBD to collect, analyze, and update the needed information on forests and trees for planning and sustainable management of the forestry resources.

- Prepare a national map based on harmonized classification of forest and land uses and related definitions.
- Undertake a national forestry resource assessment and develop a national database.
- Design specific and management-oriented inventory in priority areas and formulate projects.

Outputs:

- Harmonized forest and land use classification system and maps of state and changes of state produced based on remote sensing data.
- New baseline information, encompassing a wide range of data for both local and international users, generated and disseminated.
- Specific and management-oriented inventory in priority areas designed and projects formulated.

Source: FAO 2007.

If "forests on the edge" are to be included in the sample, a possible way of defining them would be to

- choose watersheds (approximately 1,000) with
  - at least 10 percent forest cover, and
  - at least 50 percent of forest in private ownership; and
- rank watersheds
  - by forest contributions,
  - by threats to forest contributions, and
  - by combination of contributions and threats.

The inventory could be focused on watersheds with a high rank.

Source: USFS 2007.

Internet map-based estimation methods involve

- selecting a map of forest attribute,
- drawing polygon of any shape, and
- developing a selection estimation type that could be
  - sample-based estimate and standard error, or
  - pixel-based estimate and standard error (for small or user-defined areas).

Within this process there are two relevant sets of images: (i) a "reference set," which is made up of satellite image pixels with associated plots, and (i) a "target set," which is the satellite image pixels without associated plots.

Source: USFS 2007.

PRACTICAL CONSIDERATIONS. Considerations to keep in mind when developing inventories include the following:

- difficulty of access to plots in large, remote areas;
- continuity of estimates when transitioning from a state-level inventory to a national level inventory; and

Initial plot observation and stratification can assist in identifying the areas that need to be measured and those that can be excluded. If initial plot observation indicates an area is obviously a nonforest area, it does not need to be observed in the field. This type of information can help classify satellite imagery into homogeneous strata to increase the precision of estimates.

When stratifying forests, stratification must be distinguished from classification. It is possible to have large numbers of classifications and few stratification, or vice versa. For example, there may be 21 classifications, stratified into forest and nonforest land; or the classification can be forest land and nonforest land, with four stratifications: forest, forest edge, nonforest edge, nonforest.

Source: USFS 2007.

- how to link the national inventory with (where available and relevant) existing stand (management) inventory.

It is helpful to identify regions where different sampling and attribute intensities can be applied, such as remote or reserved areas. The same level of precision is not required in such areas. If such an approach is adopted, it is important to

- decide whether aerial or ground sampling or both are to be used, by region;
- ensure that a core set of compatible results is available across all regions; and
- clarify the responsibilities of all groups involved.

COST OF INVENTORY. Cost is an important consideration in inventories. It is important when promoting forest inventories to

- determine the most cost-effective data collection and processing approaches;
- develop needed operational experience in the relevant department or unit so that the inventory can be scaled up on a cost-effective and timely basis; and
- provide an estimate of the cost for implementing the inventory.

Use of new technologies can help with cost concerns. However, cost should not be the sole driving force for selecting the technology. Technology selection should ensure that a balanced approach is taken with regard to use of remote sensing. The extent to which remote sensing is used should be based on a clear understanding of what it is good for, what its strengths are, and the overall efficiency of the inventory. For example, remote sensing may be effective in *identifying* change, but not in *classifying* it. Remote sensing may also assist with stratification to improve precision.

DATA INTERPRETATION. Data interpretation is a critical part of inventories. If spatial data are being used, interpretation is often preceded by field reconnaissance to develop an interpretation key. Interpretation of data can require the use of available historical air photographs; available thematic maps; photos taken during the field trips; and descriptions of the vegetation in selected representative sites and forest and land use classes in selected, geo-referenced sites. Image interpretation can be carried out digitally. Photo-interpretation and classification must be followed by validation by air, following selected transects all over the country.

CAPACITY TO CONDUCT INVENTORY. Capacity for executing an inventory is often lacking and can require additional support (see box 7.7). In cases where capacity needs to be strengthened, a field manual and training program can assist in implementing the inventory.

LINKING INVENTORY TO DECISION-MAKING. Considerations regarding integrating the inventory data into decision-mak-

ing processes should shape the inventory process from the beginning. Often inventories feed into larger forest management information systems (see note 7.2, Establishing Forest Information Management Systems).

LESSONS LEARNED AND RECOMMENDATIONS FOR PRACTITIONERS

PHASED APPROACH. Designing, coordinating, and conducting national forest inventories can pose numerous challenges. A phased approach, starting with inventories at a subnational scale, can help identify the most cost-effective and timely way of conducting a national-scale inventory.

DRAW ON GOOD PRACTICE. Drawing from good practice in countries where inventories are well-developed offers significant assistance. For countries in the Europe and Central Asia region, lessons from the United States, Canada, Sweden, and Finland could be used. The national inventories in the latter countries and other countries in the region provide a good foundation. However, inventories from other countries will not provide "off-the-shelf" approaches because of the details of the methods used. For example, plot densities may differ, and what can realistically be afforded may be different.

USE CURRENT AND WELL-TESTED TECHNOLOGY. It is important to draw on current and well-tested technologies, to the extent possible. These technologies and the latest science in inventories can assist in designing a cost-effective system

---

Box 7.11   Estimating Costs

Project cost estimations often require numerous assumptions. In Tanzania, the following assumptions were made for estimating the costs associated with mapping:

- The country is covered by 50 Landsat scenes.
- Procurement of the satellite images, training, and preparatory work for the mapping (equipment, manuals, interpretation key, preprocessing, and the like) require four months.
- One month of field reconnaissance is required at the onset of the project by three people—thus, three person-months of work.

- One person interprets one scene in three weeks, on average. This gives a total of 35 working months or up to 12 months work for 4 people.
- Field and air checking require two months of three people, or a total of six person-months.
- Revision and finalization of the map requires about three months of three people or nine person-months.
- Storage of the map in the database and reproduction of the map in hard copies will take two months for three people—or six person-months.
- The total person-months for mapping by technicians is 24 months × 3 people = 72 person-months.

Source: FAO 2007.

Box 7.12   A Data Collection Model

Data collection methods might combine multiple approaches. In Tanzania, two complementary methods were used for data collection. The first was from a network of field samples distributed along a systematic grid. The second was from mapping using remote-sensing techniques. The field sampling was arranged in sample sites composed of clusters. Each cluster contained four plots of 5,000 m². The plots were designed to monitor the dynamic of changes of the land-use systems and of the forest and tree cover in the country. It was a one-phase sampling for continuous forest inventory.

The data collection follows the model in the figure.

For each sample unit there were several levels of data collection, corresponding to different data sets. Data sets included local populations; forest and tree products and services, and users, which were tied to the land-use class; and land use–level data with information on protection status, vegetation coverage, environmental problems, and tree characteristics (species, height, diameter, health) attached to the plot where the trees were found.

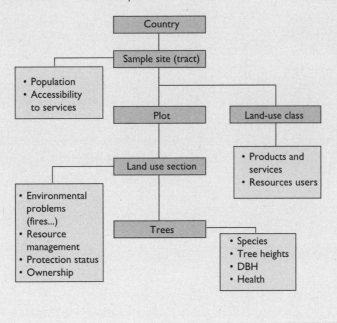

Source: FAO 2007.

with a high probability of successful implementation. At the beginning of the project, the project team should undertake the necessary consultations to find out the quality of the available data (for example, cloud free, right season), and at what cost. In some countries, much is already known about technical options, but the organizational and financial aspects are lacking. In implementing national forest inventories, it is important to clarify the objectives of inventories and articulate the responsibilities of the various groups involved.

ENSURE NEW AND PREVIOUS INVENTORIES CAN BE LINKED. The way national forest inventories are linked to previous inventories needs to be closely examined to ensure that the current inventories are seen as reliable and credible.

COUNTRY SPECIFIC CONSIDERATIONS. In some countries it will be important to develop a mechanism for handling forests under land mines.

NOTE

1. This section draws heavily on the United States Forest Service work on national inventories. For further information, Ron McRoberts (rmcroberts@fs.fed.us) and Chip Scott (ctscott@fs.fed.us) may be contacted.

SELECTED READINGS

USFS (United States Forest Service) National Forest Inventory and Analysis Web site: www.fia.fs.fed.us.

USFS Field Guides: www.fia.fs.fed.us/library/field-guides-methods-proc/.

USFS analysis tools: http://fiatools.fs.fed.us/fido/index.htm.

USFS (United States Forest Service). 2007. *Forest Inventory and Analysis: National Core Field Guide,* version 4.0 (October 2007). Washington, DC: USFS.

REFERENCES CITED

FAO. 2007. Trust Fund Agreement Between the Government of Tanzania and the Food And Agriculture Organization of the United Nations. Internal document. FAO, Rome.

World Bank. 2003. Bosnia-Herzegovina—Forest Development and Conservation Project, Project Appraisal Document. Report No. 25881. Washington, DC.

CROSS-REFERENCED CHAPTERS AND NOTES

Note 6.1: Using National Forest Programs to Mainstream Forest Issues

Note 7.2: Forest Management Information Systems

Establishing Forest Management Information Systems

Monitoring of projects, activities, and, more broadly, land-use practices has become more sophisticated, cost effective and, where relevant, participatory. The application and use of monitoring approaches in the forestry sector have been expanded to assess progress in projects and programs and to identify aspects that need modification (see chapter 7, Monitoring and Information Systems for Forest Management).

WHAT IS AN FMIS? An FMIS is an information technology (IT) system used as an aid for planning and monitoring forest management and conservation activities. The FMIS can potentially manage a wide range of spatial and alphanumeric data. Potential applications include its use in forest classification and mapping, rangeland and wildlife management, timber inventory (including projections of growth and yield), and for planning sustainable use and conservation of forest products and biological goods and services.

Integrating management processes and appropriate computer-based tools can greatly enhance the effectiveness of gathering and storing data and then transforming it (using models and analytical processes) into useful information for the sustainable management and conservation of forest resources. However, these tools also require great care and planning in their development because they are expensive and time consuming to develop and maintain. Start-up costs include hardware and software acquisition, staff training, and data entry, the combination of which could consume about 80–90 percent of project budgets.

WHO COULD USE FMIS AND HOW? Various users (private companies, state forestry agencies, ministries of agriculture or forestry, NGOs, scientists and academics, donor agencies, and more) would have different needs for an FMIS, including forest monitoring and research, as well as the more traditional forest management planning.

- Private industry uses FMIS to better manage timberlands and the fiber supply chain from the forest management unit (FMU) level onward. FMIS can also support multi-objective forestry as required by forest certification schemes, laws, or policies.
- Government agencies use FMIS to plan the management of forest lands for multiple uses (fiber supply, tourism, biodiversity conservation, watershed management, and other environmental services). Government uses for such systems (the focus of this note) will differ by institutional structure and land and forest ownership patterns.[1]

OPERATIONAL ASPECTS

FMIS ARCHITECTURE. Establishing an FMIS is not just "computerizing" existing hard copy systems of forest management. FMISs have a standard system architecture (see box 7.13), but the complexity and sophistication of this architecture can vary depending on whether the FMIS serves specific projects or small operations or is part of wider corporate tools for large industry or government use. The architecture of an FMIS should be compatible with organizational and management needs and, while recognizing the limitations of current management capability and data availability, should be flexible enough to allow for the incorporation of improved management processes, new data, and new technologies.

DESIGN AND SELECTION GUIDELINES. The FMIS is essentially a computer system, requiring hardware and software, as well as data, to be useful. Selecting the right hardware and software requires a good understanding of the system's needs and applications, as well as the frequency of use of the various applications. Consequently, technology and applications specialists are needed to help with the design, startup, and debugging of a system.

Box 7.13 System Architecture of a Standard FMIS

The following are the interconnected modules that would comprise a standard FMIS:

- *Forest Land Information Module.* This module would contain information on the current status of the forest, as well as information encapsulating the best current knowledge of how the forest develops and reacts to management actions and stochastic events (such as fire, pests, and disease). The module would normally include the following:
  - *Land-use database.* Basic attributes for various units of land, often including their location, area, legal status, administrative unit, land use/cover, and so forth. This relational database containing the attributes data would normally be linked to a GIS (map) database where the spatial data, in the form of polygons, are stored.
  - *Physical infrastructure database.* Information about the infrastructure (road network, bridges, dams) available for supporting forest management on the land base in question (these would normally be viewed as layers in the GIS database).
  - *Forest inventory system.* Information about each unit of land that is of concern. This information will include such data as forest cover type, tree species and vegetation, basal area, volumes, site class, terrain conditions, and any other forest information required for managing (analyzing, planning, and monitoring) the forest. The information would be periodically updated through interfaces with the growth and yield model, the operations tracking module, and the resource monitoring systems.
  - *Growth and yield models.* Models describing the natural development of forest types over time (growth) and the values (timber and nontimber forest products, revenues) that can be obtained at the various stages of development (yield). There are many kinds of growth and yield models, including stand-level models for a forest type in a specific geographic region, and single-tree models specific to a particular species. Single-tree modeling tends to be more flexible, but stand (or forest-type) models would usually be more appropriate for national-, regional-, or state-level forest management.
  - *Forest transition models* (or ecological scenario models). Models that describe the changes in a specific forest stand (or type, if on a national scale) as a result of some specific intervention (such as certain kinds of harvesting, stand establishment, and stand tending actions).
  - *Forest monitoring systems.* Although possibly included in the Forest Inventory System described in note 7.1, additional forest resource and biodiversity monitoring systems that may be required for purposes of administrative oversight, quality control, and compliance with the criteria and indicators of a forest certification scheme.

- *Forest Resource Planning Module* (also known as harvest scheduling module). Using much of the information in the Forest Land Information Module, the GIS and, in more sophisticated systems, the Operations Management module (described below), this module is used to forecast and plan the development of the forest and the flow of products and services (or forest values, including those related to ecosystem conservation). The planning is generally set up to cover a significant time horizon (often more than one rotation of the major tree species), thus allowing the resulting plan to be labeled "sustainable." The kinds of planning systems available range from simple forecasting models to simulation models through to optimization models. The model type appropriate to a particular situation depends upon management goals (strategic or tactical) as well as on the availability of good forest data.

- *Operations Management Module.* This is the mechanism for making changes to ongoing management activities and is well developed in commercial forest applications. This module is designed to facilitate stand-level planning, scheduling, and monitoring of all major forestry activities, including stand establishment, tending and harvesting, product sales and transportation, forest protection, and road construction. Costs, revenues, and production results should be gathered and used for this planning, although some or most of that information may come from an accounting or business information management system (described below). An operations management system should be capable of reporting on all relevant activities and operational results for purposes of management control, as well as to verify compliance with any regulations, forest certification, or quality control requirements that might apply.

Box 7.13   System Architecture of a Standard FMIS   (continued)

- *Business Information Management System (BIMS) Module.* This module would allow for the entry, storage, and processing of all data and information related to the basic business processes of the organization, such as accounting, invoicing, personnel management, and scheduling activities (job orders). It would normally be closely linked to the Operations Management module and may even provide much of the information needed for operational control.
- *Geographic Information System (GIS).* This would provide visual access to all of the cartographic information needed by the FMIS. GIS spatial analysis, modeling, and presentation capabilities are essential for good forest planning and management of large, complex forests, such as those on a national scale.

The overall system would have many types of users—from those who simply enter data to managers and forest analysts. Modules should be "co-designed" and linked so that the management processes they support are integrated and duplication of data entry is avoided.

Because some information may need to be considered confidential, and to accommodate the range of user needs, different access levels may be built into the developing system. Hence, while a system may be comprehensive and fully integrated, specific users would only have access to the information that they need to use for their own job. At the same time, it is critical that all the data are entered in standardized form so as to be compatible across the system for all users at all levels. Moreover, if jurisdictions charged with the management or administration of forests (countries, regions, provinces, or states) were to adopt such compatible systems, this would greatly help to standardize data and help make comparisons across countries easier to accomplish.

Source: Robak and Kirmse 2007.

Many on-line resources are available for software design, development, and implementation, as well as for the improvement of management processes.[2] Beyond these well-developed process rules, the following is a suggested protocol for macro-level FMIS design, development, and implementation. (See box 7.14 for an example of application of FMIS in Bosnia and Herzegovina.)

NEEDS ANALYSIS. This step, led by a management team task force, is critical for ensuring that the proposed investment will provide an integrated set of tools that meets the needs of everyone involved in the analysis, planning, monitoring, and control of forest management strategies, tactics, and operations. The task force should be educated about what the new FMIS might do for them before they are able to provide helpful input to the design process.

SYSTEM CONCEPTUAL DESIGN. The system strategy and vision would be developed by the forestry management team task force, working together with application, GIS, and IT specialists. All direct and indirect users should be consulted, while IT specialists should provide advice concerning capabilities and modalities. The needs definition and system design are most often iterative processes, as gaps or constraints identified in the system design phase reinforce the needs analysis.

DESIGN DOCUMENT. The design document should do the following:

- Articulate the vision, goals, and objectives (short- and long-term) of the system, as well as initial recommendations concerning development priorities and proposed timelines for the development phases.
- Identify and address all of the infrastructure and resources available and required to make the system useful and sustainable, including those related to data acquisition, communication technology, operating costs, training, and technical support.
- Articulate the physical, fiscal, and organizational constraints so that the IT specialists can design a system that can be implemented and supported. System designs should be based on structures, processes, and resources that are available beyond the life of the project (it would be appropriate to identify the compromises that have been made and the reasons for these).

Box 7.14   FMIS in Bosnia and Herzegovina

The following planning steps were employed in an FMIS project in Bosnia and Herzegovina that involved developing a unified network-based system:

a) Conduct a gap analysis of the planning capacity of the various enterprises and agencies.
b) Organize workshops to agree on approach with the stakeholders.
c) Organize an FMIS Working Group (FMIS-WG)—comprising foresters, IT specialists, business managers, and inspection and planning officers—who would function as a process advisory group to define the basic data (including the minimum data needs for central planning and control functions) needed by the Cantonal Forest Management Companies (CFMCs).
d) The FMIS-WG should organize a workshop to demonstrate the power of a comprehensive FMIS and to agree on the basic data needs and on the overall development process. State-of-the-art software providers (such as ESRI and Oracle), as well as users (for example, the Hungary forest enterprise association, the Polish State Forest Management Agency) should be invited to give presentations. Key representatives of the CFMCs and the ministerial and cantonal administrations should be invited to participate and the conclusions and recommendations should be recorded and disseminated. The main product of this workshop should be an agreed on concept of a centralized system as well as a process for developing that system. Agreement also needs to be reached as to the overall coordination of the process and on the "home" for the central database. Time required: three months planning and implementation. Coordinated by the Forest Development and Conservation Project's (FDCP) project implementation unit (PIU) with help from the FMIS-WG.

e) Designate the institutional coordinator for the FMIS development process and establish the institutional home for the central database. This is the responsibility of the ministry. All further development depends on this key step to designate and equip the "FMIS coordinator."
f) Prepare the tender package for designing the FMIS (international consultant, working with the FMIS-WG). At a minimum, the terms of reference (TOR) should include (i) an analysis of the existing situation and review of the data needs; (ii) a comparative analysis of international experience with similar systems to ensure the most cost-effective approach; (iii) the final design of the data module, the data format, and the presentational standards, taking into account any relevant government IT policy; and (iv) the programming, communications, hardware, and software customization. Time required: five months contracting and preparation. Coordinated by the FMIS coordinator, with input from the FMIS-WG.
g) Organize a follow-up workshop to agree on the FMIS tender package, and to seek funding sources. Invite possible donors as well as government officials to agree on the TOR and to secure funding. Coordinated by the FMIS coordinator, with help from the international consultant and the FMIS-WG.
h) Tender the development phase per the agreed TOR. Time required: eight months.
i) Design the database system. Time required: six months.
j) Tender the remaining hardware and software.
k) Install the system, including training.

In this case, the overall development process was estimated to take about two years.

Source: Robak and Kirmse 2007.

TECHNOLOGY SPECIFICATIONS. The specific technologies[3] to be employed depend on the conceptual design and performance specifications, which should, in turn, take into account the infrastructure and resources (human, technical, and financial) that are available to the organization, internally or from service organizations with a local (or, more often these days, online) presence. Additional considerations include the following:

- The programming language of the software should be one that is most appropriate and ideally, widely used.
- The databases and software should be able to handle the large number of transactions, ensure the security required in some applications, have the necessary long-term technical support, and not become obsolete in the short-term.[4]
- The total cost of operation, rather than the initial start-up costs, should be the focus over the life of the project.

If the application specifications are more complex, the most cost-effective approach would normally be to consider an already developed application or integrated multi-application system, where the provider is capable of adapting that system to the special needs of the client.[5]

- Developers or providers should not be forced to adopt one development environment. Instead, data interchange and interoperability rules should be adopted and enforced, allowing the replacement of old applications or addition of new ones in a "plug-and-play"[6] approach to system evolution.

SYSTEM DETAILED DESIGN AND DEVELOPMENT. The application of an iterative design and development process may be more effective in producing an end product that finds widespread acceptance in a large organization. Coupled with a well-thought-out prototyping approach or the use of mockups, the risk of large project failures is greatly reduced and the likelihood of end user buy-in is greatly increased.

SYSTEM IMPLEMENTATION AND TRAINING. For implementing complex systems in large forestry organizations, the application of a pilot area approach, followed by phased roll-outs of the tested system, seems to be an effective strategy. End users should be involved in the design and development process to facilitate their understanding of and sense of ownership in the software and reduce implementation problems and training time. Training of the end users (especially foresters and other professionals) should focus on the process that the system is supposed to support. If the system (and user interface) is well designed, a good understanding of the processes that it is meant to support will ensure that the system will be used properly.

LESSONS LEARNED AND RECOMMENDATIONS FOR PRACTITIONERS

FMIS has recently become a popular component of World Bank projects (such as in Argentina, Bosnia and Herzegovina, Kazakhstan, Russia, Romania), but the development and implementation of these systems has been slow. Hence, there is inadequate experience from which to build standard design, development, and implementation protocols or compilations of lessons learned within the context of World Bank projects. Previous FMIS projects in India (Madhya Pradesh and Uttar Pradesh) have a longer track record, although they were also plagued with missed milestones and eventual loss of focus. Some key lessons follow:

CONSTANCY WITH RESPECT TO FMIS RESPONSIBILITY WITHIN THE BUREAUCRACY. Given the frequency of personnel transfers in bureaucratic systems, it is helpful to develop a cadre of specialists to provide long-term technical support for FMIS implementation and operation.

UNDERSTANDING AND BUY-IN REGARDING MODERN FOREST MANAGEMENT AND ITS REQUIREMENTS AT CRITICAL LEVELS OF THE MANAGEMENT HIERARCHY. It is important that managers realize that an FMIS should not simply "computerize" the traditional management processes.

REASONABLE GOALS FOR THE INITIAL DEVELOPMENT PHASES. While it is always necessary to keep in mind the nature and capabilities of the FMIS that must be developed, eventually, to support good forest management, the goals of the project must recognize the constraints and capabilities of the organization. It is far better to set realistic near-term goals within the context of a well-articulated, long-term development plan than to attempt to turn around an entire bureaucracy in one go.

VISION OR AGREEMENT AS TO WHAT FORM SUCH SYSTEMS SHOULD TAKE. The focus should be on spatial decision making and not on acquisition and maintenance of data, that is, let the process drive the system design. Time and effort must be spent on formulating a vision and strategy for the IT system and the new management processes that it is intended to serve, and on defining very specific objectives. Only after those have been defined can a TOR be formulated (see annex 7.2B to this note) and the detailed design and development phase begin.

REALISTIC, PHASED DEVELOPMENT FOR A LARGE, COMPLEX SYSTEM. This is necessary for a bureaucracy to have time to adapt to new management processes and gain confidence from a series of "mini-successes."

Given the rapid development of FMIS technology, the development process should include two critical considerations: (i) the contracting of an FMIS specialist to lead the overall decision making and design process; and (ii) a comparison of the cost effectiveness of developing a system from scratch or adapting an already designed system (that is, procuring a turnkey system, in which the company would install the system and provide training). The turnkey approach would probably cost a fraction of what it would cost to develop a system from scratch and would take much less time, hence addressing some of the development problems mentioned above (see box 7.15). The value of a tested and client-rich system, which would also aid an organization (especially one new to the technology) in thinking "outside the box," cannot be overstated.

NOTES

1. Some World Bank client countries (the Russian Federation, Belarus, Bosnia and Herzegovina, Kazakhstan, Romania, and most all other Commonwealth of Independent States and Eastern European countries) operate like private companies because the governments own the forest and have their own enterprises (called *Leskhozes* in Russia, Kazakhstan, and Belarus, and Forest Management Units in Bosnia and Herzegovina) for management and harvesting operations. Thus, they are responsible for tactical as well as strategic planning. In Argentina, Chile, or Brazil, for example, where much of the productive forest is private, the public sector would, in fact, have less of a tactical role and would require mainly the strategic planning functions that a scaled-back FMIS would offer.

Box 7.15 Private Consulting or Software Firms That Have Developed Turnkey FMIS or Major FMIS Components for Customization to User Needs

Company	Country	Product	Web Site
American Forest Management Inc.	U.S.	Cypress, Harvest Scheduling Software	http://www.americanforestmanagement.com
Assisi Software	U.S.	Assisi Inventory, Assisi Compiler, Assisi Forest, AI Object Library, AF Object Library	http://www.assisisoft.com/
Cengea Solutions	Canada	Woodlands - The System	http://www.cengea.com
Cuesta Systems Inc	Canada	TIMS	http://www.cuestasys.com/
D.R. Systems Inc.	Canada	Phoenix, OPTIONS, SiLvIRR, DRS INVENTORY System, Forest EcoSurvey Professional	http://www.drsystemsinc.com/
Force/Robak Associates Ltd.	Canada	IFMS, ForMAX, OperMAX, OP-Plan/CTS, FIS	http://www.fra.nb.ca/
Geographic Dynamics Corp.	Canada	Volume Compilation System, SiteLogix, FloraLogix, CarbonLogix, Tactical Forest Planning Systems	http://www.gdc-online.com/index.htm
Indufor Oy	Finland	EnsoMOSAIC	http://www.indufor.fi
James W. Sewall Company	U.S.	WebFRIS	http://www.jws.com
LandMark Systems	U.S.	RTI	http://www.landmarksystems.org/
Larson & McGowin, Inc.	U.S.	ForestPro Manager	www.larsonmcgowin.com
pcSKOG AB	Sweden	pcSKOG family of products	http://www.pcskog.se/
Oy Arbonaut Ltd.	Finland	ARBNaut FDD	www.arbonaut.com
Remsoft Inc.	Canada	Woodstock, Spatial Woodstock, Stanley, Allocation Optimizer, Behave	http://www.remsoft.com/
Savcor Group Ltd. Oy	Finland	MekaERP	http://www.savcor.com/forest/
Silvics Solutions	U.S.	IFMS	http://www.metsyssolutions.com/
Spatial Planning Systems	Canada	Patchworks	http://www.spatial.ca/index.html
WoodPlan Ltd.	U.K.	Amenity Tree, Forecasting and Valuation, Operations Manager, Felled Timber, Prospect 3D	http://www.woodplan.co.uk/

For an alternate list of possible FMIS systems and components, see the Decision Support System Inventory developed by the U.S. National Commission on Science for Sustainable Forestry at http://ncseonline.org/NCSSF/DSS/Documents/search/complete.cfm.

Source: Robak and Kirmse 2007.

2. For example, the Capability Maturity Model® for Software (SW-CMM®) or its process-focused successor CMMI are used by many organizations in software and process improvement projects. Information concerning SW-CMM and CMMI can be found online at http://www.sei.cmu.edu/cmm/, while other models and protocols can be found by searching online.

3. Programming language or "development environment," database technology, special purpose programs, such as GIS, communication technology, and the hardware platforms.

4. This limits the usefulness of free and pirated databases and software.

5. Even if the initial cost of such a turnkey approach is higher, it may be more cost effective in the long term given the difficulty of maintaining a self-developed system in a bureaucracy that is likely to see a high turnover of skilled technical people.

6. The "plug-n-play" principle in large system design is one that says that the system should be built (and documented) in such a way that, as new, better technology components become available, the old component could be "unplugged" and the new one could be "plugged in" in a seamless manner. For example, the FMIS should be designed so that when a new forest inventory system becomes available, the developers of that new system would simply need to know the rules for exchanging data with other components (planning packages, GIS, and the like) and any other usage and security protocols, and develop an interface and "plug it in" to the FMIS.

SOURCES OF HELP

UN Food and Agriculture Organization. Mr. Magnus Grylle. Magnus.Grylle@fao.org.

USFS. Mr. Chuck Liff. cliff@fs.fed.us.

Forestry Tasmania. Dr. Martin Stone. Martin.Stone@forestrytas.com.au.

British Forestry Commission.

SELECTED READINGS

Bauer, M., T. Burk, A. Ek, and P. Bolstad. 2003. "Integrating Satellite Remote Sensing into Forest Inventory and Management." Environmental Resources Spatial Analysis Center, College of Natural Resources, University of Minnesota.

FAO. 2003. "A Case Study On: Computerized Forest Management Control and Forest Information Management System in India: An Application to Criteria and Indicators for Sustainable Forest Management." FAO-Forestry Department Working Paper FM/23, Rome, Italy.

Gallis, C., and E. W. Robak. 1997. "The Proposed Design for an Integrated Forest Management System for Greek Forestry." Paper presented at the IUFRO 3.04 Conference on Planning and Control of Forest Operations for Sustainable Forest Management, Madrid, Spain, June 16–20.

Jamnick, M., and E. W. Robak. 1996. "An Integrated Forestry Planning System." Proceedings of the Workshop on Hierarchical Approaches to Forest Management in Public and Private Organizations. University of Toronto, Toronto, Ontario, Canada, May 25–29. Petawawa National Forestry Institute Information Report PI-X-124, Canadian Forestry Service, 27–35.

Kilgour, B. 1991. "FRIYR: An Integrated and Computerized System for Forest Management and Yield Regulation." Proceedings of the Symposium on Integrated Forest Management Systems, Tsukuba, Japan, October 13–18.

Robak, E. W. and R. Oborn. 2000. "Design of an Integrated Forest Management System for Madhya Pradesh: Towards Sustainable Forestry." Invited presentation at the IUFRO XXXIII World Congress in Kuala Lumpur, Malaysia (unpublished, contact robak@unb.ca for an electronic copy).

Robak, E. W., and B. Rama Murty. 1999. "Forest Management Information System (FMIS): An Integrated Approach for Forest Management." GIS Development 3 (5):44–5.

Robak, E.W., and R. Kirmse, 2007. "Forest Management Information Systems." Note submitted to World Bank as input to Forests Sourcebook. Unpublished. World Bank, Washington, DC.

Rondeux, J. 1991. "Management Information Systems: Emerging Tools for Integrated Forest Management." Proceedings of the Symposium on Integrated Forest Management Systems, Tsukuba, Japan, October 13–18.

Tieying, S., Y. Zhengzhong, Z. Yuejun, Z. Wenchao, and F. Xiulan. 1991. "A Prototype Decision Support System for A Selection-Forest Management." Poster paper presented in the Symposium on Integrated Forest Management Systems, Tsukuba, Japan, October 13–18.

ANNEX 7.2A   MODEL TERMS OF REFERENCE

The TOR for a specific FMIS project should be drawn up only after the vision and strategy for the desired system have been developed. Nevertheless, the following may help form the basis of a TOR.

TERMS OF REFERENCE
DEVELOPING A NATIONAL FMIS

Summary and Instructions

This section should provide an executive summary of the project, including a description of the broad objectives and scope of the FMIS project; the sources and timing of financing; and the project management responsibilities and protocols.

Background

This section sets the broad context for the FMIS project and provides justification for the goals and scope of the FMIS project and the development approach to be taken. In most cases, an FMIS project is intended to do more than provide new IT support for existing forest management processes; it will require and support new management and decision processes. However, any intended "re-engineering" of management processes should be made explicit, otherwise resistance to change will be difficult to overcome and FMIS design will lack focus.

Specific Objectives of the Assignment

An FMIS project should normally be divided into at least two (and possibly three) phases and contracts that would involve

1) the identification of the forest management decision processes that the FMIS is intended to support, with a detailed description of the context that should inform the project management process and drive and constrain the design and development phases, and a broad description of the functionalities of the proposed FMIS;
2) a system design process resulting in clear design specifications that are justified in terms of that context and project goals; and
3) a system development and implementation process based upon the design specifications and the project management process.

OBJECTIVES AND CONTEXT—PHASE I. The first contract would manage the consultative process for developing the detailed objectives that the FMIS will support and clearly defining the context of the system. The contextual information that should be provided would include

a) a summary of the forest inventory, categorized and characterized in terms of uses, values, tenure, and management structures;
b) the status of current forest policies, strategies, and plans at the national, regional, district, and individual forest areas;
c) the current state of knowledge concerning the status and dynamics of the forest resources to be managed;
d) a summary of the major influences on and challenges to good management (including knowledge gaps, public policy trends, land use and tenure issues, public attitudes, and illegal activities);
e) current uses and values (economic, environmental, and social) of the forest and an identification of the beneficiaries and stakeholders;
f) the laws, regulations, and regulatory and management structures (including but not limited to the organization of the forest service) that influence and direct forest management;
g) the status of the communication and IT infrastructure (including data quantity and quality) in the country, classified by region and according to the forest service hierarchy;
h) internal and external technical support capabilities with respect to the IT and communication infrastructure;
i) human resources policies that may have an impact on developing an IT cadre in the forest service (even if much of the work is outsourced, there needs to be a core of management that understands and directs IT development over the long term); and
j) the current level of knowledge and capacities regarding forest management, business (or organizational) management, and information technologies in the forest service and other allied or support organizations that are involved in the analysis, planning, implementation, and control of forest resources and forest management activities.

Based upon the above context, the FMIS design objectives and project management modalities should be clearly described and explicitly justified. This work should include a description of functionalities, an identification of users (direct and indirect) and usage patterns and processes, as well as a description of the data requirements and data sources. If the FMIS development is to coincide with management process changes, the links between the FMIS project and process change initiative should be clearly delineated.

DETAILED DESIGN—PHASE II. The main tasks of this phase of the work are to

a) develop the detailed design specifications for the FMIS;
b) review and analyze existing FMIS and support technologies in relation to the specifications;
c) review possible methods for the development of the FMIS (adapting existing technologies, developing components "from scratch" using in-house or external expertise)[1];
d) recommend (with justification) the preferred development method (which may well include a combination of the above);
e) estimate the human resources requirements (including commitment from client personnel), time, and cost of the installed FMIS; and,
f) consolidate the above information into a document that outlines the critical elements of the Development and Implementation TOR.

In principle, it should not be the task of this consultant to recommend the specific development environment or database and support technologies to be used because the design specifications and the context description (especially those related to local IT capabilities) should be clear enough that any inappropriate technologies would not be proposed or, if proposed, would not be chosen. However, the design consultant should develop a draft Development and Implementation TOR that recommends the software development, quality assurance, and project management standards and protocols that should be used by the developer, including those that facilitate future system evolution and compatibility with other national and international forestry and environmental systems.

DEVELOPMENT AND IMPLEMENTATION—PHASE III. The following is a list of issues that would likely need to be addressed in the Development and Implementation TOR:

■ Software design specifications and performance criteria, including those related to specific functionalities; national and international data standards that must be followed (such as European numerical data standards); reports to be produced; spatial visualization and modeling capabilities; data entry protocols; security and access; description of users (including working language) and usage patterns (including multiuser and web-enabled capabilities); integration among FMIS components; interfaces and integration with existing or proposed non-FMIS systems; minimum data auditing and data recovery; and back-up and archiving requirements.

■ Characteristics of software technologies to be employed, including recommendations concerning which elements should be built from scratch and which should be adapted from existing technologies. This should also address issues concerning the flexibility and resiliency of any system being proposed, including its degree of adherence to "plug-n-play" principles and open source[2] standards.

■ Hardware specifications (including those related to operating environment, health, and ergonomics) and rules and regulations that govern hardware acquisition.

■ Description of data preparation work required, including (as appropriate) data migration and conversion; preparation of base and thematic maps; forest and land recharacterization; and acquisition, analysis, and incorporation of remote sensing imagery and data.

■ Description of the current forest management and IT knowledge of proposed users and internal IT support personnel, and the level that is desired. This means that, where appropriate, the TOR must specify the education and training required to use the system to maximize the benefits, not simply train people about "which buttons to push."

■ Minimum requirements related to implementation and training, technical and user documentation, and system support.

■ Minimum software and project management quality assurance protocols to be employed.

■ Description of the minimum level of long-term support that will be required to be provided by the development and implementation contractors.

■ Description of the commitment from the clients with respect to the engagement of its people in the development, testing, implementation, and training processes.

Evaluation Criteria

Tender documents should be evaluated according to the quality of the tender in relation to the requirements of the TOR and then according to the following criteria:

- expertise of the consultancy team
- experience and track record in similar FMIS projects
- proposed cost of development, implementation, and training
- estimated cost and requirements (especially those related to human resources) for continued operation of the system
- estimated ongoing maintenance and support costs
- technologies, protocols, and standards proposed (including facilitation of future development and evolution of the system)
- intellectual property ownership and rights
- realism of schedules
- realism and acceptability of commitment required of the client
- ability to provide long-term support

Specific tasks

Besides the work described above, specific tasks and operating methods are suggested as ways to increase the likelihood of success in an FMIS project. Most of these are related to education, communication, and participation.

PHASE I. Interview officials who are responsible for the strategic direction of the organization to gauge their clarity of purpose and understanding of modern forest management and the capabilities of IT. Undertake a review of the context in which the FMIS must fit. Based upon the results of these interviews and the evaluation of the context, design and hold a workshop that fills knowledge gaps and leads to a consensus on the objectives and strategies of the FMIS on the part of upper management. To ensure the outcomes of the workshop are appropriate:

- The various user groups in an organization need to be educated about what the new FMIS might do for them. Often they do not have a clear idea about how an FMIS might work and what it implies for their work processes.
- It needs to be made clear that the FMIS is not just about computerizing their existing manual processes. Existing work processes may need careful review and redesign as a prelude to the detailed design and development of the FMIS, which adds to the size of the task.
- The FMIS project design should recognize that the requirements of an FMIS will change over time, as will the technologies employed.
- It should be recognized that other government agencies (related to land and water management and agriculture,

for example) may maintain databases that could augment the FMIS and vice versa. It is not efficient, from an overall government perspective, to duplicate data-gathering and storage efforts or, even worse, to have agencies develop incompatible systems.

- After a consensus on objectives and strategies has been reached, present the conceptual design recommendations to upper management (articulating the needs, functionalities, and development strategy; estimating costs and time needed for the various development options and for the various functionalities; reviewing and disseminating information on the various turn-key options) for their approval. Upon receiving this approval, the conceptual design (with functionalities) should be presented to intended users of the FMIS, to get their feedback and suggestions for improvements. It is strongly recommended that a well-defined and stable user group sign off on the final design (and then monitor the development of the FMIS). An agreed on process of staged development and implementation is necessary to avoid future conflicts within the user group or between users and developers.

PHASE II. The design phase will require that interviews and workshops be held with all major user groups, first to help establish draft design specifications, then to gain acceptance of the final specifications and the major elements of the Development and Implementation TOR (including acceptance of their responsibilities in the development, testing, implementation, and training processes). Successful implementation of an FMIS will require, or will be undertaken in combination with, work process changes, which may necessitate a cultural change in an organization. The human resources management issues must be considered, both in terms of the FMIS requirements and their impacts upon the FMIS project.

PHASE III. An important element that should not be forgotten in the development, testing, implementation, and training phases is the ongoing communication and feedback processes that must be developed and maintained to ensure the best possible final product, reduction in lost time due to misunderstandings, and eventual buy-in from the users. It should be made clear to Phase III bidders that their proposals will be evaluated in part by how well they have responded to this requirement.

Process and Reporting Arrangements

Specify the line agency to which the consultants would report. That is, specify the agency that would be managing the overall development phase of the FMIS and, if different, the agency that would operate the system.

Implementation of this assignment should aim to be inclusive and transparent and should specifically seek to engage a broad range of stakeholders, including forest owners (public and private); forest managers (public and private); conservation and protected areas managers; the wood-using industries; the forestry consulting profession; researchers and academics; NGOs; regulators; relevant government ministries, such as finance and environment; and the international agencies supporting the forest sector.

Duration

Experience shows that the full development and installation (with training) takes much more time than planned. Although it would vary with the size and complexity of the system being contemplated, in general an FMIS developed "from scratch," using no or few existing FMIS components, would probably take five to seven years to full implementation, while the adaptation and installation of an already developed system may take two to three years. A good, well-used FMIS may never be "completed," but rather will evolve with a changing understanding of needs and with changes in technologies and technological capabilities within user and support groups.

Expertise Required

The Phase I consultancy should be led by a forester who has a clear understanding of modern forest management principles, processes, and information requirements. The Phase II consultancy should include a forester who has worked on the development of FMIS elsewhere, supported by an IT specialist with experience in developing standards for the management of large-scale IT projects. As is the case in the Phase I consultancy, the "FMIS forester" should have knowledge of the principles of modern, sustainable forest management and demonstrated experience in applying those principles in the design, development, and implementation of Management Information Systems and Decision Support System tools in a variety of contexts for forestry organizations.

In Phase III, the bidders (normally international FMIS consulting firms) should propose the mix of expertise and type and level of experience that they believe will best suit the achievement of the objectives.

NOTES

1. There is a tendency on the part of local and in-house IT specialists to want to develop a system in-house. However, World Bank experience shows that this is very time consuming and costly; more costly than adapting an existing system. Most firms that develop and market systems provide the implementation and training expertise needed to get their systems up and running.

2. Open source standards for software and data (including spatial data) are being developed in Europe and North America to reduce the likelihood that users are "trapped" by a specific manufacturer or technology. For example, for a long time ESRI used a proprietary data format that made it difficult (if not impossible or illegal) for other GIS or GIS component suppliers to tap into the ARC/Info data. So even when someone came along with a better technology, the user could not upgrade technologies without a huge and expensive effort. In general, "open-source" does not mean that developers cannot maintain their trade secrets—they do not have to show their source code—it just means that there is an agreement to adhere to codes and standards (for example, the use of metadata dictionaries) that ensure a client is not trapped by a particular technology.

Spatial Monitoring of Forests

Remote sensing (RS) has become part of most forest management strategy implementations. While the technology for RS has evolved, aerial photography has been in use for almost a century, and satellites have been recording forest change for more than 35 years. Landsat, launched in 1972, was one of the first satellites widely used for remote sensing. Since then, Landsat has been a workhorse for scientists interested in measuring changes in the distribution and condition of forests. Remote sensing (aerial flights, aerial photography, optical and radar satellite imagery) and GIS have aided forest mapping and forest inventories for many years.

Two trends have stimulated the rise of spatial monitoring. First, technological advances in RS/GIS make these tools more accessible; human capacity to manipulate this data has also increased while information has become more accurate, less expensive, and more freely circulated. In addition, there is a wider choice of satellites, prices of satellites have deceased significantly,[1] the Internet is widely used to share data, and more affordable and more user-friendly RS/GIS software is now readily available.

Second, in addition to these technical advances, a variety of needs are increasing demand for forest monitoring. The impetus to monitor comes from, among other things, the need to assess national-level compliance with international conventions, and measure global public goods (for example, carbon sequestration, area under protection for conservation purposes, and the like). RS/GIS technology provides the data and the tools needed for monitoring by enabling precise overlays between different time periods within specific boundaries, and by storing and analyzing the data. However, because inventories and mapping are frequently time intensive and expensive, they are often carried out only in specific regions or for specific purposes. To date, only six attempts to map forests worldwide exist.

Various local, national, and international entities systematically collect, examine, and disseminate data about forest resources throughout the world. Nevertheless, efforts at these different levels to systematically collect, examine, and disseminate data about forest resources are done independently of one another, and use different definitions and measurements. Accordingly, comparison of results is difficult, major knowledge gaps remain in large areas, and duplications exist in others. Only a few countries use spatial information for national forest inventories that are updated and suitable to address current environmental issues (see boxes 7.16 and 7.17 for examples).

Spatial monitoring has become increasingly important in the context of REDD. For REDD, even minimum requirements to develop national deforestation databases using typical and internationally agreed on methods will require using RS data. The data would help assess gross deforestation, possibly develop a map of national forest area, and present a visual representation of forest cover change. Spatial monitoring, in some cases, is already part of discussions for monitoring land use, land-use change and forestry (LULUCF) (see box 7.18).

Independent of demand, there are challenges to effective spatial monitoring of forests:

- *Availability of RS data.* Detailed data (that is, certain satellite sensors and aerial photographs) must be ordered in advance and may not be available in the short term. Clouds often hamper monitoring in the tropics and in mountainous areas, and can become a major problem, especially for data acquired with less frequency (for example, it can take more than a year to get a detailed resolution image with less than 30 percent cloud cover in Indonesia). Because higher temporal resolution satellites acquire data more often, they have better opportunities to acquire imagery with fewer clouds. Another alternative is the use of radar satellites because radar sensors "see" through clouds. Nevertheless, radar applications for forest monitoring are still uncommon.

Box 7.16   Forest Monitoring in Cameroon

Cameroon has made significant commitments and notable progress in monitoring forest-based activities. These commitments have launched initiatives to produce and compile forest information and improve the quality and availability of relevant forest data, in part to enable better decision making.

In 2005, a partnership that included the Cameroon Ministry of the Environment and Forests (MINEF), Global Forest Watch, the Limbe Botanical Gardens, and Cameroon Environmental Watch (the latter two are members of civil society) assembled the Interactive Forestry Atlas of Cameroon. The decision-support tool is a compact disc (CD) atlas that compiles and integrates GIS/RS data useful to forest monitoring. Key data sets presented in the atlas include roads, hydrological networks, logging concessions, vegetation, forest management unit statistics, and forested areas. Forested areas include boundaries of (i) state forests (protected areas such as game reserves, hunting areas, game ranches, wildlife sanctuaries, and buffer zones, as well as zoological gardens belonging to the state); (ii)

forest reserves (ecological reserves and forests allocated for production and research, as well as botanical gardens, plant life sanctuaries, and forest plantations); (iii) council forests; (iii) communal forests; (iv) community forests; and (v) private forests.

The CD tool has been widely distributed and used. Because it presents the data in graphic, user-friendly formats, the tool has been used in various ways including in prioritizing forest monitoring and enforcement of forest laws, and monitoring compliance by determining whether road construction is taking place within the boundaries of legally attributed logging areas and in compliance with approved management plans. MINEF and private companies use the tool to support land-use planning, assess impacts from forestry operations, and (because maps are unequivocal) inform dialogue and negotiation in conflict resolution.

The Interactive Forestry Map is currently being updated; a new version is expected to be released in the near future.

Source: Noguerón and Stolle 2007.

Box 7.17   Forest Monitoring in Indonesia

In a 2004 forest sector paper, the Center for International Forestry Research (CIFOR) identified the lack of reliable and timely information on forests as the foremost origin of poor public and private forest policies. The Ministry of Forestry of Indonesia (MoF) also recognized this lack of information as a major obstacle for sound decision making and development of appropriate policies; this recognition has paved the way toward better forest governance in Indonesia.

In 2005, the MoF established a National Forest Sector Monitoring and Assessment Process (FOMAS). The overall goal of FOMAS is to promote good forest governance to ensure the optimal contribution of forest resources to poverty reduction, economic growth, and sustainable forest management and conservation. To achieve this goal, FOMAS will enable transparency and accountability, which are the essential foundations for effective forest governance. The specific objective of FOMAS is to establish the conditions for transparency in the forest sector by

- making relevant, reliable, accurate, and up-to-date forest sector information available to decision makers inside the MoF on a continuous basis, as well as making key information accessible to the public; and
- supporting better decision and policy making based on this information.

A first and necessary step is to provide support and inform forest management decisions with updated and reliable maps of forest use and forest cover. FOMAS is using mapping technology as a tool within a comprehensive decision-making and policy reform approach. Thus, FOMAS will help the MoF in better carrying out its mandate of regulating and managing forest use and establishing an appropriate framework for a profitable forest sector in Indonesia that is socially and environmentally sustainable.

Source: Noguerón and Stolle 2007.

- *Availability of reference data.* Monitoring is effective when reference data (for example, type of forest, boundary of parks, roads, or populations) are available. The use of reference data facilitates monitoring and thus decision-making and enforcement processes. However, reference data often do not exist or are of insufficient quality.
- *Human capital.* Satellite imagery processing and interpretation can be time consuming and often requires an initial investment to set up the processing system.
- *Costs.* Costs depend on the satellite used and the accuracy needed. High-resolution imagery remains costly. Spatial accuracy and ground verification, at least in the initial stages to calibrate imagery interpretation, can add significant expenses.
- *Limited information.* Not everything can be detected with RS. Tree species cannot be determined unless data is collected at a very detailed scale. Spatial monitoring with RS/GIS can add to, and should not compete with, a detailed ground inventory.

OPERATIONAL ASPECTS

RS/GIS REQUIREMENTS. Forest monitoring using RS/GIS requires the following:

- Technological capability to generate, store, and update the RS/GIS data; this often requires high computer capa-

bilities and specialized software for imagery and GIS analysis, interpretation, and manipulation.
- Human capital to generate, manipulate, apply, and interpret the data, as well as capability to translate data in user-friendly format to end users.

EFFECTIVE AND FUNCTIONAL FOREST MONITORING. Effective and functional forest monitoring involves the following:

- An initial assessment of existing information and identification of data gaps to reconcile data with features of interest: Forest change in a national park cannot be monitored if there is no information on the boundaries of the park. This assessment includes an evaluation of the quality and accuracy of the data: Extraction of a valuable species cannot be effectively monitored if the forest composition data is inaccurate or outdated.
- Filling out data gaps by creating the data needed (that is, digitizing features from satellite imagery; purchasing satellite imagery) or identifying and defining surrogate indicators to assess features data (for example, using incidence of fire as an indicator of human activities in certain forest types).
- Establishing a baseline of (i) the spatial distribution of features of interest that are susceptible to change and (ii) the boundaries against which change will be periodically assessed.

Box 7.18   Using Geospatial Tools for LULUCF Projects

Geospatial tools can help shape LULUCF projects during the conceptual stages, and beyond, in the following ways:

The tools can be used in demonstrating and justifying the status of the land use before 31 December 1989 (deadline for the first LULUCF commitment period). Imagery will provide information on current land cover, and if past imagery is available then information about the past land cover can be derived. Land cover maps can then be drawn from these. Where digital information is not available (for example, when using only old aerial photographs), an old map can be digitized.

They can assess the changes taking place in forest canopy over time. Such change could be a result of forest restoration activity or tree removals (by logging, fires, disease, and the like).

They can demarcate and survey carbon asset boundaries in a project area. Such information, including land ownership, soil typology, drainage, elevation, and vegetation cover percentage, can then be stored and managed in a GIS.

Because GPSs are affordable and portable in the field, they can work in very remote areas and in difficult terrain. Locations can be georeferenced (*x* and *y* coordinates of the latitude and longitude), and coordinates can be directly stored in a computer system.

Advancements in the technology now make it possible to integrate geospatial information into a decision-making tool. For instance, remotely sensed data from an IKONOS spectral image can be analyzed through a GIS platform into different layers as needed. Such layers could include vegetation type, land with or without tree cover, water bodies, ownership patterns, roads, and so forth. This information then becomes a product that can help inform decision making.

Source: Kaguamba 2004.

- Information obtained through RS sources can be less detailed than intensive fieldwork; ground verification is usually needed to verify and calibrate the RS data. A combination of RS data and field work will produce the most accurate information.
- Conducting periodic assessments of the features of interest or surrogate indicators. Periodicity depends on the characteristics being monitored. Compliance with forestry law may only need yearly assessments of the extent and location of logging activity, while incidence of fires may need weekly or monthly monitoring.
- Effective venues to channel the information to end users in easy, user-friendly formats such as Web sites, paper maps, posters, or CDs. Critical information should be channeled in a speedy manner to allow rapid response and action.

In many situations, one or several of these ingredients exist. Many countries have some type of periodic assessment, or produce maps of reference data (boundaries of national parks, for instance). However, monitoring requires a well-thought-out, systematic approach to integrate all ingredients together in a methodic way. For example, between 1980 and 2000, four maps of forest resources in Indonesia were produced (1988, 1993, 1996, and 2000); however, they do not use consistent legends, units, scales, and time frames, and thus cannot be used effectively for monitoring.

SELECTING THE MONITORING APPROACH. There are many different applications of forest monitoring and an equally large number of approaches by which it can be done. For example, for measuring forest disturbance (selective logging, for example) and deforestation some methods are highly manual and others are highly automated. Some methods work at moderate resolution over large regions of forests. Many tools were designed using dated ideas, technologies, and methods.

Selecting the appropriate approach requires that the goals of the monitoring exercise be clearly articulated (see box 7.19). Factors to consider include the size of area to monitor, the level of detail required, budget constraints, and season of the year (because of cloud cover).[2]

Box 7.19   Selecting the Appropriate Approach and Tools

If the goal is to develop a country-scale monitoring program for deforestation, defined as clear-cuts of 20 hectares and larger, the rate-limiting step is not analytical methodology or data availability. Terra-MODIS satellite imagery is free and can perform the function, and the methods are simple and automated. The limitation is in training, exercise, and operational demonstration of the capability.

If the goal is to develop a country-scale monitoring program for deforestation with clear-cuts of one hectare and above plus selective logging, the rate-limiting steps are in both the analytical techniques and satellite data availability. With the loss of Landsat 7, the available data are from a 22-year-old Landsat 5 or from more expensive sources such as the French or Indian space agencies. This is workable if, and only if, such channels remain open.

The methods for fine-scale deforestation and logging monitoring are highly automated in some programs, such as the one coordinated at the Carnegie Institution of Washington.a This automated system currently works well but falls short in mountainous terrain and with some of the more noisy high-resolution sensors, and is still being improved for very small-scale disturbances. This automated system is the only one to deliver country-scale deforestation and logging maps, such as the first-ever large-scale deforestation plus logging map at sub-30 m resolution (see box figure for the Amazon). The information from this system can produce both extent and intensity of forest disturbance, where the latter is defined as the percentage of canopy opening and surface debris generation. Remote monitoring of forest damage levels is now straightforward, if the challenges presented by clouds and terrain are resolved.

Other groups mostly use manual techniques, resulting in long delivery times. Most methods produce forest and nonforest classes in their products. A few produce more information, such as fractional cover of the canopy.

In the figure below, showing land cover change in the Amazon, the medium gray is what the other "state-of-the-art" technology shows as deforestation (forest cover change). The dark gray shows what the automated system reveals—selective logging completely missed by other widely used RS systems. The dark gray currently shows a preview of what will be medium gray in two to four years.

(Box continues on the following page.)

Box 7.19   Selecting the Appropriate Approach and Tools (continued)

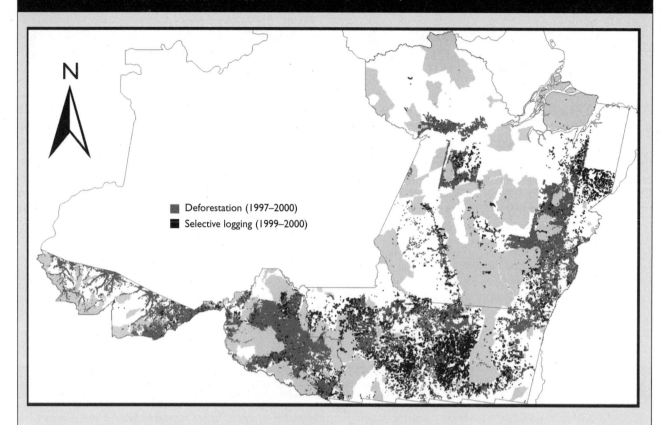

Deforestation (1997–2000)

Selective logging (1999–2000)

Source: Asner and others 2006 (copyright 2006 National Academy of Sciences, U.S.A.).
Note: This program is coordinated by Gregory P. Asner, Department of Global Ecology, Carnegie Institution of Washington, Stanford, CA, USA. This program required about US$2.5 million to develop the areas of signal processing, super-computing, canopy physics, and field ecology necessary to make such monitoring feasible.

SPATIAL AND TEMPORAL SCALE. Forest monitoring using RS/GIS can be carried out on different spatial and temporal scales depending on the features of interest for monitoring and the goal of the monitoring exercise. Forest monitoring using RS/GIS can include clear cuts, intensive selective logging, log yards, fires, road building, habitat fragmentation, biomass, and productivity. The monitoring of these features often requires different time steps and detail. A national overview of deforestation usually requires a one to five year time frame, while monitoring of fires in national parks may need more frequent updates (several satellites can detect fires in the forests, see box 7.20).

FOREST MONITORING METHODS. A number of different applications and methods for forest monitoring exist, and the choice of which to use will depend on the purpose of the monitoring and the desired spatial and temporal scales.

Table 7.4 lists the existing satellite remote sensors, and their applications and limitations for specific purposes. Table 7.5 lists currently available global forest maps.

An emerging RS/GIS application that merits special consideration is the MODIS-derived data set of percentage of tree coverage, produced by researchers at the University of Maryland and South Dakota State University. The new maps, based on the MODIS sensor operated by NASA, provide a consistent overview of the global distribution of percentage of tree coverage in a continuous gradient (0 to 100 percent). This allows flexibility so that the gradient can be adapted to different forest definitions. The MODIS satellite provides free global data coverage daily, allowing information to be compiled and processed in a relatively speedy manner. The speed of data availability, the relative low cost, and the flexibility to adapt to different forest definitions offer huge opportunities for international and global forest monitoring efforts.

Box 7.20   Using Remote Sensing for Real-Time Monitoring

Annual, and even quarterly, large-scale assessments are very possible using satellite data, if the imagery is being collected. However, there is no guarantee that the necessary imagery is being collected. The spatial resolution of MODIS is not high enough to be of real value—too much forest area needs to be cleared for it to be recognized by the free MODIS data. Landsat-like sensors, or better, are needed. Next-generation techniques and technologies are being developed.

Weekly or monthly assessments require a very specialized satellite capability (Quickbird imagery) or aircraft. Both are viable options with different budgetary implications:

- Quickbird satellite data are for smaller areas of forest (<10,000 ha) and expensive, and the images yield basic information, such as forest cover.
- Airborne platforms are extremely data rich (providing forest cover, detailed structure, diversity to some

degree, and so forth), can cover large areas (up to 250,000 ha per day), and are cheap in comparison with launching a satellite.

In general, satellites with a high temporal resolution (for example, daily over-pass) have low spatial resolution (250–1,000 meters), and satellites with higher spatial resolution (30 meters) have low temporal resolution (20–30 days over-pass). Thus, from the beginning the user has to choose between

- satellites with an overview scale (1 km to 250 meter spatial resolution), which provide a wide view (often 1,000 km) and high frequency (once or twice a day) (available from MODIS or NOAA); or
- more detailed data (5–50 meter spatial resolution) with a much narrower view (50–100 km) but less frequency (20–40 days) (for example, TM, SPOT, ASTER).

Source: Erick C. M. Fernandes, Senior Land Adviser, World Bank (personal communication); Noguerón and Stolle 2007.

PARAMETERS AFFECTING COST AND QUALITY. Several remote sensing technology parameters determine the quality of results as well as the costs. They include, but are not limited to scale, resolution, and color (panchromatic or multispectral) and whether a GIS component is to be added. Ground-truthing of some features and aspects—legality of identified logging, taxonomic identification of some species, determination of "forest" status (where it is not easy to differentiate, for example, between a dense shrub thicket and a degraded poor quality forest)—will inevitably remain necessary. However, the cost of ground-truthing will be kept low because it will be done selectively.

Depending on the objective, stratification approaches can assist in reducing costs. A gross assessment can provide guidance on which relevant locations require a more detailed assessment, providing guidance for stratifying the sample. Detailed mapping of more specific sites can reduce overall cost without compromising accuracy.

LESSONS LEARNED AND RECOMMENDATIONS FOR PRACTITIONERS

A well-thought-through monitoring plan with a choice of

the best combination of RS technologies (satellite, aircraft, ground GPS, GIS), with pockets of ground-truthing, and a resultant acceptable cost structure, should start operating from project identification, especially for projects such as LULUCF projects.

A cost-saving approach should be adopted for small-scale projects, or for projects involving many but small community afforestation or reforestation projects. Such an approach would use a centralized RS data acquisition and processing provider for the monitoring requirements.

An effective forest monitoring system using RS/GIS should be technically sound, but it should also have social buy-in. Technological advances in the RS/GIS field are not enough for effective forest monitoring; monitoring has to be driven by societal and political demands. Forest monitoring systems have to be collaborative and they have to be developed with the information end users want to ensure that the information meets their needs and is appropriate for managing resources, policies, and practices.

Monitoring systems must be firmly integrated into the decision-making process and must be supported by civil society. Monitoring should go hand-in-hand with transparency and better and accurate forestry and reference data.

Table 7.4 Existing Satellite Remote Sensors, their Applications, and Limitations for Forest Monitoring

Platform	Principal operator	Resolution (meters)	Scale	Frequency/ cycle	Temporal coverage	Costs	Applications	Comments
Overview satellites								
NOAA-AVHRR	USA	1,100, 4 km, and 8 km for older data	Continental, Regional	Up to daily	1982 to date	Freely available	Indices used to recognize droughts, state of vegetation, and others. Most known is the Normalized Difference Vegetation Index (NDVI).	NOAA has launched 14 satellites into orbit since 1980. Satellites 6–12 and 14 are still operational with the Advanced Very High Resolution Radiometer (AVHRR) sensor.
SPOT VEGETATION	Europe	1,000	Regional	3 days	2002 to date	Relative low cost	State of vegetation.	Large data storage requirements.
EOS AM-1	USA	250–1,920		1–2 days			Intended to measure canopy structure and state; photosynthesis and transpiration rates.	
MODIS	USA	250, 500	Continental, Regional	Up to daily	Up to twice daily	Relative low cost	Percentage of tree coverage.	Promising tool for monitoring deforestation.
Detailed satellites								
IRS	INDIA	2.5–180	Continental	24 days	1995 to date		Vegetation and land use.	
Landsat 5	USA	30–120	National/ Global	8 days	1970s to date		Forest types, land use changes, disturbances.	Aging.
Landsat 7	USA	15–120	National/ Global	8 days	Late 1990s	Relative low cost	Forest types, land use changes, disturbances.	Crippled by aging sensor component and failure in June 2003.
Radarsat-1 Radarsat-2	Canada	10–100	3–100	16–24 days	1995 to date			High power allows radar to peer through clouds and darkness.
ASTER	USA	15–90	Continental	16	1999 to date	US$60 per scene		Acquisition is on a task-by-task basis.
CBERS	China/ Brazil	20, 80, and 240	National	3–4 days	1999 to date		Vegetation mapping.	
SPOT	Commercial (France)	2.5–5	Regional National	3–26 days	2002 to date	Pricey, from base US$2,300 per image	Net primary productivity, seasonality, disturbances, land-use, disturbance.	Acquisition is on a task-by-task basis.
Super detail satellite								
Quickbird	USA	0.60–3.2 m		1–3.5 days	2002 to date	~22.5 $ x sq km	Landcover mapping, habitat mapping.	Large data storage requirements.
IKONOS	USA	1–4	Local	1–3 days	2000 to date	Pricey, depending on resolution, bands, and scale.	Intended uses include forest fire detection, vegetation monitoring.	Because of detail presented, spatial extent is limited. Many images are required for extended coverage.

Source: Noguerón and Stolle 2007.

Table 7.5   Global Forest Maps

Title	Author	Domain	Methods
International Geosphere-Biosphere Program (IGBP)	Loveland et al. 1999	Global	12 monthly vegetation indexes from April 1992 to March 1993
University of Maryland (UMD)	Hansen et al. 2000	Global	41 multitemporal metrics from composites from April 1992 to March 1993
TREES	Mayaux, Richards, and Janodet 1999 Eva et al. 1999	Humid tropics	Mosaics of single date classifications of cloud-free images (1992–93)
FRA-2000	FAO 2001	Global	Updated from the IGBP-DIS cover data set
MODIS-Land Cover	Friedl et al. 2002	Global	12 monthly composites of 8 parameters from October 2000 to October 2001
Global Land Cover (GLC) 2000	Eva et al. 2004 Mayaux et al. 2004 Stibig, Beuchle, and Achard 2003	Global	365 daily mosaics of 4 channels + 36 temporal vegetation indexes profiles for 2000

Source: Based on Mayaux et al. 2005.

NOTES

1. The widely used Thematic Mapper (TM) scenes—each covering 12,000 km^2—cost around US$5,000 per scene in the 1990s and now cost around US$500 per scene.

2. The choice of best options will be severely limited if imagery is required within a very short time. The time it takes to deliver an image will depend on the location of satellite sensors at the time the image is needed, ability of the image provider to handle the request, cloud cover, and ability to transmit the image via the Internet or by other quick delivery systems.

RECOMMENDED READING (INTERNET SITES)

Earthpace, LLC; Satellite Remote Sensing: Environmental Applications, Forestry. http://earthpace.com/resources/satellites_apps.html.

Environmental Analysis and Remote Sensing. http://www.ears.nl/EARShome/projects/txtfo.htm.

FAO
- Remote Sensing for Decision Makers Series. http://www.fao.org/sd/EIdirect/EIre0072.htm (3/10/06).
- Africover Initiative. http://www.africover.org/africover_initiative.htm.
- Global Observation of Forest Covers. http://www.fao.org/gtos/gofc-gold/.
- Global Terrestrial Observation System. http://www.fao.org/gtos/index.html.

International Union for Forest Research Organizations (IUFRO). http://www.iufro.org/.
- Division 4: Forest Assessment, Modelling, and Management. http://www.iufro.org/science/divisions/division-4/.

- Forest Resources Inventory and Monitoring. http://www.iufro.org/science/divisions/division-4/40000/40200/.
- IUFRO Conference on Remote Sensing and Forest. Monitoring http://rogow99.sggw.waw.pl/.

South Dakota State University, GIS Center of Excellence. http://globalmonitoring.sdstate.edu/.

UNEP, Global Resource Information Database. http://www.grid.unep.ch/activities/global_change/index.php?act=5.

University of Maryland
- Global Landcover Facility. http://glcf.umiacs.umd.edu/index.shtml.
- Deforestation Mapping Group. http://glcf.umiacs.umd.edu/research/.
- Landcover Change. http://glcf.umiacs.umd.edu/services/landcoverchange/.
- Monitoring Forest Dynamics in Northeastern China in support of GOFC. http://www.geog.umd.edu/research/projects/Sun_Forest.htm.

USDA Forest Service
- Forest Inventory and Analysis National Program. http://fia.fs.fed.us/ and http://fia.fs.fed.us/program-features/.
- Inventory and Monitoring Institute. http://www.fs.fed.us/institute/index.shtml.
- National Forest Health Monitoring Program. http://fhm.fs.fed.us/.
- Remote Sensing Application Center. http://www.fs.fed.us/eng/rsac/.
- International Programs Forest Monitoring, Remote Sensing and GIS. http://www.fs.fed.us/global/topic/welcome.htm#2.

Tropical Ecosystem Environment Observation by Satellite (TREES). http://www.geo.ucl.ac.be/LUCC/research/endorsed/14-trees/TREES.HTML.

Woods Hole Research Center

- INFORMS, Integrated Forest Monitoring System for Central Africa. http://www.whrc.org/africa/INFORMS/overview.htm.

- Satellite "Remote Sensing" Observations and Products. http://www.whrc.org/borealnamerica/our_work/satellite_rs.htm.

- Monitoring Landscape Properties. http://www.whrc.org/borealnamerica/our_work/monitor.htm.

REFERENCES CITED

Asner, G. P., E. N. Broadbent, P. J. C. Oliveira, M. Keller, D. Knapp, and J. N. M. Silva. 2006. "Condition and Fate of Logged Forests in the Brazilian Amazon." *PNAS* 103 (34): 12947–50.

Eva, H. D., A. Glinni, P. Janvier, and C. Blair-Myers. 1999. "Vegetation Map of Tropical South America, Scale 1/5M." TREES Publications Series D, No. 2, EUR 18658 EN, European Commission, Luxembourg.

FAO. 2001. "Global Forest Resources Assessment 2000 Main Report." FAO Forestry Paper No. 140. FAO, Rome.

Friedl, M. A., D. K. McIver, J. C. F. Hodges, X. Y. Zhang, D. Muchoney, A. H. Strahler, C. E. Woodcock, S. Gopal, A. Schneider, A. Cooper, A. Baccini, F. Gao, and C. Schaaf. 2002. "Global Land Cover Mapping from MODIS: Algorithms and Early Results." *Remote Sensing of Environment* 83 (1–2):287–302.

Hansen, M. C., R. S. Defries, J. R. G. Townshend, and R. Sohlberg. 2000. "Global Land Cover Classification at 1 km Spatial Resolution Using a Classification Tree Approach." *International Journal of Remote Sensing* 21: 1331–64.

Kaguamba, R. 2004. "Cost and Benefit of Remote Sensing Methods for Monitoring LULUCF Carbon Assets." Unpublished internal paper, World Bank, Washington, DC.

Loveland, T. R., Z. Zhu, D. O. Ohlen, J. F. Brown, B. C. Reed, and L. Yang. 1999. "An Analysis of the IGBP Global Land-Cover Characterization Process." *Photogrammetric Engineering and Remote Sensing* 65:1021–32.

Mayaux, P., T. Richards, and E. Janodet. 1999. "A Vegetation Map of Central Africa Derived from Satellite Imagery." *Journal of Biogeography* 26:353–66.

Mayaux, P., E. Bartholomé, S. Fritz, and A. Belward. 2004. "A New Land-Cover Map of Africa for the Year 2000." *Journal of Biogeography* 31:1–17.

Mayaux P., P. Holmgren, F. Achard, H. Eva, H.-J. Stibig, and A. Branthomme. 2005. "Tropical Forest Cover Change in the 1990s and Options for Future Monitoring." *Philosophical Transactions of the Royal Society B: Biological Transactions* 360 (1454):373–84.

Noguerón, Ruth, and Fred Stolle. 2007. "Spatial Monitoring of Forests." Note submitted to World Bank as input to *Forests Sourcebook.* Unpublished, World Bank, Washington, DC.

Stibig, H.-J., R. Beuchle, and F. Achard. 2003. "Mapping of the Tropical Forest Cover of Insular Southeast Asia from SPOT4-Vegetation Images." *International Journal of Remote Sensing* 24:3651–62.

CROSS-REFERENCED CHAPTERS AND NOTES

Note 7.2: Forest Management Information Systems

ANNEX 7.3A ELEMENTS FOR TERMS OF REFERENCE FOR DEVELOPING A NATIONAL SYSTEM FOR FOREST MONITORING AND INFORMATION

BACKGROUND. A national system for forest monitoring and information will enable a decision-making environment where reliable, accurate, and current information on forest and timber resources and related decisions are continuously and publicly available, and where authorities can take actions upon this information to combat illegal logging and strengthen law enforcement.

SPECIFIC OBJECTIVES. The specific objective of a national system for forest monitoring and information is to establish the conditions for transparency in the forest sector by

■ making relevant, reliable, accurate, and up-to-date forest sector information continuously available to decision makers as well as making key information publicly accessible; and

■ assisting decision makers in better decision and policy making based on daily use of better-managed information.

There are several steps to consider before such an activity can proceed. These include the following:

■ *Create and mobilize political support to generate continued incentives for action and establish a culture of transparency.* This may involve stakeholder consultations to build a constituency and attain official recognition.

■ *Make use of the best available forest monitoring and communication technologies and existing capacity in forest research and related technical fields in nongovernment sectors to increase effectiveness and reduce cost.* To do this effectively, it would be important to collect and compile existing forest-related data into a GIS database, to assess the availability and quality of forest data, and to identify data gaps. This should include a review of the new remote sensing–based forest cover change mapping approaches being developed by a number of organizations. With this information, a needs assessment can be carried out.

■ *Focus on improving high-impact forest sector decision making to address the most critical issues and ensure continued momentum for action.* This will require prioritizing information and decision support activities that are (i) most important for enabling policy change and (ii) most likely to rapidly result in successful outcomes.

■ *Enable public scrutiny and promote clean government.* This will require (i) developing a clear information disclosure policy and operational information disclosure mechanism to ensure public access to relevant information, (ii) training civil society to use this information, and (iii) gathering NGO and industry feedback to improve the policy.

Upon completion of these steps, the terms of reference for this activity can use elements of the sample TOR for FMIS (see Annex 7.2A to note 7.2, Forest Management Information Systems).

PART II

Guidance on Implementing Forests Policy OP 4.36

CHAPTER 8

Introduction to the World Bank Forests Policy

The World Bank has 10 key policies that are critical to ensuring that potentially adverse environmental and social consequences are identified, minimized, and mitigated, as well as a policy on disclosure. In the context of forests, the Operational Policy on Forests (OP 4.36) is proactive in both identifying and protecting critical forest conservation areas and in supporting improved forest management in production forests outside these areas.

The reader should note that this section covers only the policies relevant to World Bank investment projects. The World Bank also has an Operational Policy on Development Policy Lending (OP 8.60) that is relevant to the forest sector and Forests Strategy. Section 11 of OP 8.60 states:

> The World Bank determines whether specific country policies supported by the operation are likely to cause significant effects on the country's environment, forests, and other natural resources. For country policies with likely significant effects, the World Bank assesses in the Program Document the borrower's systems for reducing such adverse effects and enhancing positive effects, drawing on relevant country-level or sectoral environmental analysis. If there are significant gaps in the analysis or shortcomings in the borrower's systems, the World Bank describes in the Program Document how such gaps or shortcomings would be addressed before or during program implementation, as appropriate.

Guidance on handling the due diligence requirement in OP 8.60 with regard to forests is discussed in chapter 6 of the Forests Sourcebook, and its associated notes.

HISTORY OF THE WORLD BANK'S FORESTS POLICIES

The World Bank's original Operational Directive on Forestry (OD 4.36) was issued in 1993. It grew out of a concern (voiced by environmental nongovernmental organizations [NGOs] and other outside stakeholders, as well as within the World Bank) that World Bank–supported forestry operations need to be environmentally sustainable. As such, the policy was focused primarily on forestry activities. This Forestry Policy was controversial, both within and outside the World Bank, because it prohibited World Bank financing of commercial logging in primary tropical moist forests. This provision did not prohibit technical assistance and numerous indirect forms of support for such logging. Nonetheless, it had a chilling effect upon World Bank management and project staff, who were reluctant to support activities that were in any way linked to any kind of tropical forest harvesting, even when the expected outcomes would be highly positive from a conservation standpoint. Meanwhile, deforestation (driven more by agricultural expansion than by logging) was continuing and even increasing in many World Bank member countries, resulting in the concern that the World Bank's relative disengagement from forestry activities was counterproductive, from a poverty reduction as well as from a conservation perspective.

To promote a more proactive World Bank role in forest management and conservation activities in developing countries, the Board in 2002 approved a new Forests Policy (OP 4.36) and a revised Forests Strategy, following a long and extensive consultation process with numerous stakeholders, including environmental NGOs. The new OP 4.36 differs from the previous Policy on Forests in several key respects, including (i) a focus on all types of World Bank–supported investment operations that involve forests, not just forestry; (ii) emphasis on all types of forests in developing countries (including temperate and boreal forests), rather than principally tropical forests; and (iii) permitting World Bank support for commercial harvesting within tropical or other forests, provided that the forests in question are not critical forests (or related critical natural habitats) and the harvesting is carried out according to specific high standards, normally including independent certification (see below for further details). The new OP 4.36 has been rewritten to ensure consistency with the Natural Habitats OP 4.04, although the Forests Policy is more detailed with respect to forestry activities.

The following are three safeguard policies that apply to almost every World Bank–financed investment project[1] involving forests:

ENVIRONMENTAL ASSESSMENT. The World Bank's Environmental Assessment Policy (OP/BP 4.01)[2] governs the environmental assessment process that all World Bank–supported projects—that is, all investment operations, including those of the World Bank's debt financing (IBRD) and concessional financing (IDA) arms, as well as those involving the Global Environment Facility (GEF)—must follow. Most projects involving forests are classified as either Category A (requiring a full environmental impact assessment, EIA) or B (requiring an environmental analysis that is usually more limited in scope than a full EIA), according to criteria that are discussed further below.

FORESTS. The Forests Policy (OP/BP 4.36) covers all projects that affect natural or planted forests, whether positively or negatively (see chapter 9, Applying Forests Policy OP 4.36).

NATURAL HABITATS. The Natural Habitats Policy (OP/BP 4.04) covers projects that affect natural forests or other nonforest natural ecosystems, with special focus on those projects that might lead to significant loss or degradation of natural habitats (details below).

SCOPE OF THE FORESTS AND NATURAL HABITATS POLICIES

Because the Forests Policy was rewritten in 2002 in a manner that would ensure consistency with the Natural Habitats Policy, these two safeguard policies overlap extensively in (i) the types of ecosystems they cover, (ii) the types of projects that are subject to their requirements, and (iii) the main requirements that relevant projects need to follow.

TYPES OF ECOSYSTEMS OR LAND-USE SYSTEMS. Forests OP 4.36 applies to projects involving all types of natural (primary and secondary) forests (defined in OP 4.36, annex A, to include a rather broad range of wooded ecosystems), as well as forest plantations. Natural Habitats OP 4.04 applies to projects involving all types of natural ecosystems, including natural forests as well as the full range of nonforest natural ecosystems (terrestrial, freshwater, and marine). Thus, both of these safeguard policies apply to projects that somehow involve natural forests (broadly defined). However, only the Forests Policy would apply to projects with non-native plantation forests, if these are planted on land that does not (and did not recently) contain natural habitats. Conversely, only the Natural Habitats Policy would apply to projects affecting exclusively nonforest natural habitats (such as natural grasslands, freshwater lakes, beaches, or coral reefs).

TYPES OF PROJECTS. The new Forests OP 4.36 covers all forestry projects, as well as a broad range of other projects that may affect (positively or negatively, directly or indirectly) the health and quality of forests of any type. These projects can include, among others, investments in (i) transportation (highways, rural roads, large bridges, railways, airports, ports, river navigation works); (ii) electric power (hydroelectric dams, power transmission lines, wind farms on forested ridges, thermal power plants emitting air pollution harmful to forests); (iii) industry (mining, oil and gas, manufacturing industries requiring fuelwood); (iv) agriculture (crop cultivation, agroforestry, cattle and other livestock, fisheries involving mangrove or other forests, land administration and land reform involving forested areas); (v) water supply (reservoirs, canals, abstraction of ground or surface water affecting forests); (vi) urban development involving wooded areas; (vii) tourism (resort development, ecotourism in forested areas); (viii) telecommunications (transmission towers and access roads on mountaintops or other forested areas); (ix) privatization of state-owned forested lands; and (x) natural resource management and conservation, including all types of forestry, protected areas, and similar investments. The Natural Habitats OP 4.04 applies as well to all these types of investments, as long as they involve natural forests or other kinds of natural habitats.

As a practical, quick summary, the largely overlapping safeguards requirements of the Forests and Natural Habitats policies can be summarized as follows:

- If a nonforestry project complies with OP 4.04, it also automatically complies with OP 4.36.
- If a nonforestry project complies with OP 4.36, it also complies with OP 4.04, except where nonforest natural habitats are involved (in which case OP 4.04 needs to be specifically applied).
- All forestry projects (involving natural forests as well as plantations) are subject to the additional requirements in OP 4.36.

OTHER RELEVANT SAFEGUARD POLICIES

The remaining eight safeguard policies can sometimes apply to projects involving forests (for more information on each of these policies, please refer to the World Bank Safeguards Web site):

INDIGENOUS PEOPLES. The Indigenous Peoples Policy (OP/BP 4.10) specifies how Indigenous Peoples need to be consulted and involved in the design of projects that may affect them (positively or negatively). Many projects involving forests also involve Indigenous Peoples, who are important stakeholders in forest-based activities. Key requirements of OP 4.10 are social assessment; free, prior, and informed consultations leading to broad community support to the project; and development and disclosure of an Indigenous Peoples Plan or Planning Framework (see chapter 12, Applying OP 4.10 on Indigenous Peoples).

INVOLUNTARY RESETTLEMENT. The Involuntary Resettlement Policy (OP/BP 4.12) applies to projects involving either (i) the involuntary taking of (forested or any other) land for project purposes that leads to physical relocation, loss of assets, or loss of income sources or livelihoods for the affected persons; or (ii) the involuntary restriction of access to legally designated protected areas that leads to adverse impacts on the livelihoods of the affected persons. To address these impacts, the policy requires the preparation of (i) either a Resettlement Plan or Resettlement Policy Frame-

work in the case of involuntary land taking; and (ii) a Process Framework in the case of involuntary restriction of access to the natural resources within parks and protected areas. The policy does not cover restrictions of access to natural resources outside of formal protected areas, such as community-based natural resource management projects (OP 4.12, footnote 6), or the regulation of forests or other natural resources at a national or regional level (OP 4.12, footnote 8). (See the World Bank's Involuntary Resettlement Sourcebook, and for more details on the preparation of a Process Framework, see also "Guidance on Development of Terms of Reference Related To OP 4.36" in chapter 9.)

PEST MANAGEMENT. The Pest Management Policy (OP 4.09 and BP 4.01, annex C) applies to projects that (i) involve (through World Bank or counterpart funds) the procurement of pesticides or pesticide application equipment; (ii) would lead to substantially increased pesticide use; or (iii) would maintain or expand pest management practices that are unsustainable or risky from an environmental or health standpoint. Some forestry projects involve significant pest management issues (sometimes including pesticide use) in natural or plantation forests as well as in tree nurseries (for guidance on applying this OP, please refer to the Pest Management Guidebook).

PHYSICAL CULTURAL RESOURCES. The Physical Cultural Resources Policy (OP/BP 4.11) was issued in April 2006, replacing the substantially similar Management of Cultural Property in World Bank–Financed Projects OPN 11.03. This policy applies to projects that might affect sites and objects of archaeological, paleontological, historical, architectural, religious, aesthetic, or other cultural significance. Projects involving forests that might also trigger this policy include, among others, those with (i) civil works (including forestry roads, small buildings, and manual tree planting) that might uncover previously unknown relics; and (ii) forested sites of special cultural significance (including sacred forests identified by local communities).

PROJECTS IN DISPUTED AREAS. This policy (OP 7.60) prescribes special consultation and due diligence procedures for any projects proposed in geographic areas that are disputed between two or more countries. Many such areas are remote and forested.

PROJECTS ON INTERNATIONAL WATERWAYS. This policy (OP 7.50) covers projects that could appreciably affect international waterways, or the quantity or quality of water in more than one country. Some of these projects could also affect forests (such as through inundation by a reservoir or the loss of available water to riparian forests from upstream abstraction).

SAFETY OF DAMS. This policy (OP 4.37) applies to projects that construct, rehabilitate, or substantially depend upon large or high-hazard dams, whether these dams are for hydropower, water supply, or other functions (including mine tailings containment). Some projects involving dams also affect forests—whether through permanent flooding, water diversion, induced land-use changes, or other impacts. (For guidance on applying this OP, please refer to the Regulatory Framework for Dam Safety.)

This section of the sourcebook has four chapters following this introduction. Chapter 9 is on applying OP 4.36. Chapter 9 also includes a discussion of the main requirements of the Forests Policy, guidelines for implementation (including preparation requirements, appraisal requirements, and supervision requirements), definitions, and guidance on identifying critical forests and critical natural habitats through environmental assessment, which includes a discussion on protecting forests through conservation offsets. Chapter 10 is on consultation and communication in forest projects. Chapter 11 discusses the Forest Certification Assessment Guide. The Indigenous Peoples policy is covered in chapter 12.

NOTES

1. This may include technical assistance and grants, such as the GEF. Technical assistance that affects forests can be covered by safeguards. Development policy loans are not covered by safeguards. Development policy loans are subject to OP 8.60, which is discussed in chapter 6 and associated notes.

2. OP means an Operational Policy, which is approved by the Board and regarded as a requirement for projects to follow. BP means a World Bank Procedure, which is approved by Bank management. When used in this sourcebook, OP often refers as well to the accompanying BP for that safeguard policy.

REFERENCE CITED

World Bank. "Pest Management Guidebook." Available at http://go.worldbank.org/RJPAKAND00.

CHAPTER 9

Applying Forests Policy OP 4.36

Operational Policy (OP) 4.36 applies to all World Bank investment operations that potentially have an impact on forests, regardless of whether they are specific forest sector investments. It also encourages the incorporation of forest issues in Country Assistance Strategies (CASs), and addresses cross-sectoral impacts on forests. The policy provides for conservation of critical natural habitats and prohibits World Bank financing of any commercial harvesting or plantation development in critical natural habitats. It also allows for proactive investment support to improve forest management outside critical forest areas, with explicit safeguards to ensure that such World Bank–financed operations comply with independent certification standards acceptable to the World Bank, or operations with an agreed upon, time-bound action plan to establish compliance with these standards.

OBJECTIVE OF THE FORESTS POLICY

The objective of OP 4.36 is to assist clients to harness the potential of forests to reduce poverty in a sustainable manner, to effectively integrate forests into sustainable economic development, and to protect the vital local and global environmental services and values of forests. Where forest restoration and plantation development are necessary to meet these objectives, the World Bank assists clients with forest restoration activities that maintain or enhance biodiversity and ecosystem functionality. The World Bank assists clients with the establishment of environmentally appropri-

ate, socially beneficial, and economically viable forest plantations to help meet growing demands for forest goods and services.

Specifically

- The World Bank uses environmental assessments, poverty assessments, social analyses, public expenditure reviews, and other economic and sector work to identify the economic, environmental, and social significance of forests in borrowing countries.
- The World Bank integrates strategies into its CASs to address any potential significant impacts of the CAS on forests.
- The World Bank does *not* finance projects that would involve significant conversion or degradation of critical forest areas or other natural habitats.
- The World Bank does *not* finance projects that contravene applicable international environmental laws.
- The World Bank does *not* finance plantations that involve any conversion or degradation of critical natural habitats, including adjacent or downstream critical natural habitats.
- The World Bank *only* finances commercial harvesting operations or the purchase of logging equipment in areas that it has determined are not critical forests or related critical natural habitats.
- The World Bank *only* finances industrial-scale commercial harvesting operations in areas outside critical forest areas, where such operations are either certified as meeting standards of responsible forest management under

an independent forest certification system acceptable to the World Bank, or adhere to a time-bound, phased action plan acceptable to the World Bank for achieving certification to such standards.

- In areas outside of critical forest areas, the World Bank may finance harvesting operations by small-scale land-holders, local communities under community forest management, or entities under joint forest management. Such financing can be provided where these operations have either achieved a standard of forest management developed with the meaningful participation of affected local communities that is consistent with the principles and criteria of responsible forest management outlined in paragraph 10 of OP 4.36, or adhere to a time-bound action plan to achieve such a standard that has been developed with the meaningful participation of affected local communities and acceptable to the World Bank. All such operations must be monitored by the client, with the meaningful participation of local people who are affected.
- The World Bank uses environmental assessment to address the impact of all World Bank–financed investment projects on forests and the rights and welfare of local communities.
- The World Bank ensures that World Bank–financed investment projects involving the management of forests incorporate measures to strengthen the fiscal, legal, and institutional framework in the borrowing country to meet defined economic, environmental, and social objectives that address, among other issues, the respective roles and legal rights of the government, the private sector, and local people.
- The World Bank ensures that World Bank–financed investment projects involving the management of forests give preference to small-scale, community-level management approaches where they best harness the potential to reduce poverty in a sustainable manner.
- The World Bank ensures that the design of World Bank–financed investment projects that use forest resources evaluate the prospects for the development of new markets and marketing arrangements for nontimber forest products and related goods and services, taking into account the full range of goods and environmental services derived from well-managed forests.

TRIGGERS. The policy is triggered whenever any World Bank–financed investment project (i) has the potential to have impacts on the health and quality of forests or the rights and welfare of people and their level of dependence upon or interaction with forests or (ii) aims to bring about changes in the management, protection, or utilization of natural forests or plantations.

MECHANISMS FOR ACHIEVING POLICY OBJECTIVES. As noted above, the World Bank's objectives in forests are to assist clients to harness the potential of forests to reduce poverty, integrate forests into sustainable economic development, and protect vital local or global environmental services and values of forests. Mechanisms to achieve these objectives are described in the OP, and the World Bank procedures document, and include

- use of appropriate economic, environmental, and social assessments to identify the economic and environmental significance of forests and any activities involved in the World Bank-financed investment that may adversely affect the well-being of forests and the people who depend on them;
- assessment of the potential for activities proposed in a CAS that would significantly impact forests, and incorporation of strategies to address these impacts;
- use of information required from the client on policy, legal, and institutional frameworks in sector or project design to address priority poverty, social, and environmental issues needed to meet the economic, environmental, and social objectives of World Bank–financed investment projects;
- use in project design of assessments of the adequacy of land-use allocations for the management, conservation, and sustainable development of forests, including identification of any additional allocations needed to protect critical forest areas;
- use of clear standards of forest management certification to guide any investment support for harvesting operations, including time-bound action plans to achieve certification of acceptable standards of forest management; and
- use of market assessments to determine the full range of goods and services available from well-managed forests to enhance returns from forest management and give preference to small-scale, community-level management approaches where they best harness the potential of forests to reduce poverty in a sustainable manner.

CONSULTATION AND DISCLOSURE REQUIREMENTS (WORLD BANK POLICY ON DISCLOSURE OF INFORMATION). The World Bank requires clients to identify and consult the groups in forest areas likely to be affected by World Bank–financed investment projects in and beyond the forest sector.

The disclosure requirements set out in the Environmental Assessment (EA) Policy (OP 4.01) apply to all projects affecting forests. Aside from the required EA documentation, there is no freestanding document that is automatically required for all projects affecting forests. However, many forest-related projects will generate freestanding reports (such as Forest Management Plans), which should be made publicly available as a matter of good practice. Experience has shown that transparent decision-making processes are important for good forest governance and good development outcomes, and full disclosure of forest-related information should be encouraged wherever feasible. Additional requirements for consultations apply if the World Bank's Indigenous Peoples' or Involuntary Resettlement policies apply.

MAIN REQUIREMENTS OF THE FORESTS POLICY

OP 4.36 requires that all relevant types of projects must ensure that they avoid causing significant, unmitigated harm to natural forests or other natural habitats. These "do no harm" requirements can be summarized as follows (see the text of each policy for the full details):

AVOIDING SIGNIFICANT DAMAGE TO CRITICAL FORESTS AND OTHER CRITICAL NATURAL HABITATS. OP 4.36, paragraph 5 prohibits World Bank support for projects that would involve the *significant conversion or degradation of critical forests* or other types of *critical natural habitats* (see the definitions section that follows).

MINIMIZING AND MITIGATING DAMAGE TO OTHER (NON-CRITICAL) FORESTS AND OTHER NATURAL HABITATS. For proposed projects that would adversely affect *noncritical* forests and other natural habitats, the World Bank's Forests Policy has more flexible (but nonetheless rigorous) standards of compliance. Where feasible, the conversion (loss) or degradation of any forests and other natural habitats should be avoided through careful project siting and design. There is a strong presumption against any significant conversion or degradation of noncritical natural forests. However, the World Bank may still support a project that would lead to significant conversion or degradation of noncritical forests or other noncritical natural habitats if (i) there are no feasible alternatives for achieving a project's key objectives; (ii) comprehensive analysis demonstrates that the overall benefits from the project substantially outweigh the environmental costs; and (iii) the project includes mitigation measures acceptable to the World Bank. These mitigation measures must be technically justified and should

include, where appropriate, the establishment or strengthening of ecologically similar protected areas (see OP 4.04, paragraph 5; OP 4.04, annex A, item [e]; and OP 4.36, paragraph 5 for the full legal language).

FOREST PLANTATIONS. With respect to forest plantations, OP 4.36 (paragraph 7) specifies the following:

- The World Bank does not finance forest plantations that involve *any* conversion or degradation (whether "significant" or not) of critical natural habitats. Such conversion would typically take place when a native forest or natural grassland is replaced as part of plantation establishment. Under OP 4.36, all World Bank–supported forestry plantations must be sited away from critical natural habitats.
- In the case of noncritical natural habitats, the World Bank gives preference (as with other types of projects) to siting forest plantations on lands that no longer contain natural habitats, provided that these lands were not converted in anticipation of the World Bank–supported project.
- World Bank–supported forest plantation projects need to prevent and mitigate threats to natural habitats and biodiversity, including the potential spread of invasive species (such as the *Pinus* species in the natural grasslands of southern South America).

HARVESTING OF NATURAL FORESTS. With respect to the harvesting of natural forests, the Forests Policy:

- Prohibits World Bank financing for commercial or community-based harvesting in any areas containing critical forests or related critical natural habitats (OP 4.36, paragraph 8), with the exception that community-based harvesting (defined in OP 4.36, annex A, items [d] and [e]) may take place within multiple-use Managed Resource Protected Areas (Category VI in the standardized World Conservation Union [IUCN] international classification scheme for different types of protected areas), where such harvesting is an integral part of the management plan for the area.
- Requires that industrial-scale commercial forest harvesting can receive World Bank financing only if it is either (i) certified under an independent forest certification system acceptable to the World Bank as meeting standards of good forest management or (ii) adhering to a time-bound action plan acceptable to the World Bank for achieving certification of such standards. (These standards of good forest management are specified in OP 4.36, paragraphs 10–11.)

- In the case of forest harvesting by small-scale landholders or local communities (by themselves or under joint forest management arrangements), formal certification is not required for World Bank financing. However, these producers, who are generally small scale, must either (i) achieve standards of forest management consistent with the criteria outlined in OP 4.36, paragraph 10; or (ii) adhere to a time-bound action plan (developed with the meaningful participation of affected local communities and acceptable to the World Bank) to achieve these standards.

SMALL-SCALE LANDHOLDERS AND LOCAL COMMUNITIES. The forests policy does not require formal certification of the forest management practices of small-scale landholders and local communities, largely because of the typically high transaction costs for these small-scale producers to obtain such certification.

WHEN IS THE FORESTS POLICY TRIGGERED?

Strictly speaking, both policies (OP 4.36 and Natural Habitats OP 4.04) apply to any projects that affect forests or other natural habitats, whether positively or negatively. As explicitly stated in OP 4.36 (paragraph 3), the Forests Policy applies to all investment projects that (i) may have some impact on the health and quality of forests; (ii) may affect the rights and well-being of forest-dependent people; or (iii) seek to bring about changes in the management, protection, or use of natural forests or plantations. Although the emphasis is on the "do no harm" safeguard provisions, OP 4.36 also promotes "doing good" by pursuing opportunities for the conservation and sustainable use of forests and other natural habitats within World Bank–supported projects, analytical work, and policy dialogue.

Within the World Bank, the triggering of a particular safeguard policy is often understood to mean either (i) the need for due diligence to verify whether adverse impacts are expected, to ensure compliance with the policy's specific requirements; or (ii) the need for designing and implementing specific measures to prevent or mitigate adverse impacts. Under these rather narrow interpretations, both OP 4.36 and OP 4.04 would be triggered by those projects that have the potential to convert or degrade forests or other natural habitats, but not by those projects that are strictly conservation oriented and have no significant adverse environmental impacts (except that forestry projects always trigger OP 4.36).

In several World Bank project documents (including the Project Appraisal Document [PAD], Project Information

Document [PID], and Integrated Safeguards Data Sheet [ISDS]), it is necessary to indicate whether a proposed investment project triggers OP 4.36 or OP 4.04. In this regard, it is *recommended* as good practice to take a broad (and literal) interpretation of the full text of these policy statements, and thus to indicate that the project does trigger these policies if it would affect forests or other natural habitats in any way, positively or negatively. However, at a minimum, it is *required* to indicate that a project triggers (i) OP 4.36 if it is either a forestry project of any kind, or a nonforestry project with the potential for significant loss or degradation of any natural forests or related natural habitats; and (ii) OP 4.04 if it has the potential for significant loss or degradation of any natural habitats (including natural forests). For this particular reporting requirement, the potential to cause significant loss or degradation of forests or other natural habitats should be assessed in the (at least theoretical) absence of any planned project-specific screening or other measures that would serve to prevent or mitigate these adverse impacts.

ENVIRONMENTAL CLASSIFICATION OF PROJECTS INVOLVING FORESTS

Under the EA policy, all World Bank–supported investment projects are classified as Environmental Category A, (requiring a full environmental impact assessment); Category B (requiring a more limited environmental analysis); Category C (requiring no environmental analysis after the initial screening); or Category FI (involving on-lending through financial intermediaries). The Environmental Assessment OP 4.01 (paragraph 8) provides the generic criteria for environmental classification that should always be followed. The 1998 Good Practices Note (OP 4.01, annex B) suggests that Category A is normally the best classification for "forestry production projects," while Category B is generally most appropriate for watershed management or rehabilitation, protected areas, and biodiversity conservation. OP 4.36, paragraph 3, specifies that "a project with the potential for conversion or degradation of natural forests or other natural habitats that is likely to have significant adverse environmental impacts that are sensitive, diverse, or unprecedented is classified as Category A; projects otherwise involving forests or other natural habitats are classified as Category B, C, or FI, depending on the type, location, sensitivity, and scale of the project and the nature and magnitude of its environmental impacts." The Natural Habitats Policy (OP 4.04, paragraph 2) provides a similar (but not quite identical) approach: "[i]f, as part of the environmental assessment process, environmental screening indicates the potential for significant conversion or degradation of critical or other natural habitats, the project is classified as Category A; projects otherwise involving natural forests are classified as Category A or B, depending on the degree of their ecological impacts."

Guidelines for the environmental classification of projects that involve forests include the following[1]:

- *Category A* is the appropriate category for (i) nonforestry projects of any type with the potential to cause (directly or indirectly) the significant conversion or degradation of natural forests or adjacent natural habitats (such as new roads through forests, large dams, mining, oil and gas, large-scale irrigation or new land settlement, other large-scale civil works in forested areas, and industries dependent upon natural forests for raw materials); (ii) forest plantation projects that would lead to the significant conversion or degradation of noncritical natural habitats; and (iii) commercial forest harvesting that (because of intensive or high-impact management practices) would lead to significant ecological modification (with reduced native species diversity) of natural forests.
- *Category B* is the appropriate category for (i) natural forest management (including forest harvesting) that does not lead to significant ecological modification or degradation; (ii) forestry plantations that would not adversely affect natural habitats; (iii) most other types of natural resource management projects, including watershed management and protected area establishment or strengthening; and (iv) many types of nonforestry projects with some potential for adverse environmental impacts, but no significant loss or degradation of forests or other natural habitats.
- *Category C* is appropriate for some types of conservation-oriented projects with no civil works and no evident adverse environmental impacts, such as (i) environmental service payments to landowners to maintain their existing natural forest cover; or (ii) the establishment of conservation trust funds for the recurrent costs of protected area management.
- *Category FI* is appropriate for certain projects in which financial intermediaries would invest in subprojects, some of which might involve forests.

GUIDELINES ON IMPLEMENTING OP 4.36

PREPARATION REQUIREMENTS. The task team leader and client ensure that

- Terms of Reference (TOR) are reviewed and agreed upon for any social, environmental, and economic assessments required in OP/BP 4.36 and other relevant World Bank OPs/BPs;
- economic, environmental, and social analyses are undertaken to identify the economic, environmental, and social significance of forests and any activities involved in proposed CASs or World Bank–financed investments that may adversely affect the well-being of forests and the people who depend on them;
- inventories are undertaken at a spatial scale that is ecologically, socially, and culturally appropriate for the forest area in which the project or investment program is located to identify critical forest areas and assess the adequacy of land allocations to protect these areas;
- the linkages between any proposed forest sector activities and the poverty reduction, macroeconomic, and conservation objectives of the World Bank's country assistance program are clear;
- there is evaluation of the potential for developing markets for the full range of forest goods and services, giving preference to small-scale, community-level management approaches that best harness the use of forests for poverty reduction in a sustainable manner; and
- local people, communities, and the private sector are meaningfully involved in defining activities to be undertaken in the management, conservation, and sustainable utilization of natural forests or plantations.

APPRAISAL REQUIREMENTS. The task team reviews project preparation and any environmental or project management or monitoring plans to ensure that

- all necessary social, economic, and environmental studies are satisfactorily completed;
- government commitment is secured for any measures that may be required to strengthen the fiscal, legal, and institutional frameworks needed to meet the project's economic, environmental, and social objectives;
- adequate land allocations have been made for the management, conservation, and sustainable development of forests, including any additional allocations needed for the protection of critical forest areas or other critical natural habitats;
- procedures are in place to ensure that any harvesting operations or plantation development supported by World Bank financing are restricted to areas outside critical forest areas or other critical natural habitats;
- the certification systems or community-based forest management monitoring systems used to assess whether forest

harvesting supported by World Bank–financed investment projects meet appropriate standards of forest management and use conform with the standards for these systems (as defined in paragraphs 10 and 11 of OP 4.36);

- projects with time-bound action plans to improve forest management include clearly defined performance benchmarks and time frames for achieving appropriate forest management standards (in accord with OP 4.36, paragraphs 9–12), and that any time-bound action plans and their associated performance benchmarks are included in the PAD and made available to the public; and
- PADs include clear performance indicators that will enable the contribution of the project to the poverty reduction, macroeconomic, and conservation objectives of the World Bank's country assistance program to be assessed.

SUPERVISION REQUIREMENTS. The task team ensures that during project implementation

- monitoring and evaluation procedures are informed by the meaningful participation of locally affected communities and other groups interested in forest areas affected by World Bank–financed investment projects;
- the integrity of the boundaries of any critical forest areas or other critical natural habitats in or near areas affected by World Bank–financed investment projects is continuously monitored;
- the protection of the rights of access and use of forest areas by Indigenous Peoples and other local communities is monitored in accord with the requirements of OP 4.12 Involuntary Resettlement and OP 4.10 Indigenous Peoples, and that any necessary corrective actions are taken in accord with these policies;
- project performance is monitored against the indicators for the contribution of the project to the poverty reduction, macroeconomic, and conservation objectives of the World Bank's country assistance program defined in the PAD; and that
- the client specifically makes available to the public the results of all forest management assessments carried out under the independent certification systems and related time-bound action plans referred to in paragraphs 9–12 of OP 4.36.

DEFINITIONS

FORESTS AND NATURAL HABITATS. OP 4.36, annex A, defines "forests" rather broadly to include areas of at least 1 hectare, at any successional stage of tree growth, with tree crown cover of normally at least 10 percent and trees at least 2 meters tall (at maturity). This definition thus includes natural (primary or secondary) forests, as well as forestry plantations of native or nonnative species. The definition also takes into account intended land uses (not just actual tree cover, or the lack thereof) by (i) including areas dedicated to forest production, protection, multiple uses, or conservation (whether formally recognized or not) and (ii) excluding areas where other land uses not dependent on tree cover predominate, such as agriculture, grazing, or settlements.

OP 4.04, annex A, defines "natural habitats" as land and water areas where (i) the ecosystem is composed largely of native plant and animal species and (ii) human activity has not fundamentally altered the area's primary ecological functions. Natural habitats thus include natural forests of all types, as well as the full range of other kinds of natural terrestrial, freshwater, and marine ecosystems. Natural habitats often are not "pristine" but have been modified by human activities, such as logging, collection of nontimber forest products, hunting, fishing, or livestock grazing (on natural rangelands). However, areas that still maintain a majority of their original native plant and animal species should be regarded as natural habitats, notwithstanding some (light or moderate) degree of human modification.

In accordance with these definitions (as well as those in normal professional usage outside the World Bank), natural forests are a type of natural habitat. Other types of natural ecosystems (such as shrub lands, native grasslands, nonwooded wetlands, beaches, and coral reefs) are natural habitats, but not forests. Conversely, forestry plantations of nonnative species are forests, but not natural habitats.

CRITICAL FORESTS AND CRITICAL NATURAL HABITATS. OP 4.36, annex A, defines "critical forest areas" as the forest areas that qualify as "critical natural habitats" under the Natural Habitats OP 4.04. In summary, the Natural Habitats Policy defines "critical natural habitats" as those natural habitats that are either (i) legally protected or officially proposed for protection; or (ii) unprotected but of known high conservation value. In practical terms, critical natural habitats (including critical forests) can be regarded as relatively natural areas that are either legally protected or really should be, because of their conservation significance. In more specific and official terms, critical natural habitats comprise the following types of areas (see OP 4.04, annex A, for the full World Bank policy text):

EXISTING AND PROPOSED PROTECTED AREAS. Critical natural habitats include (i) existing protected areas that meet the standard IUCN criteria for Categories I–VI; (ii) areas officially proposed by governments as protected areas; (iii) areas recognized (before the proposed project) as protected by traditional local communities (such as sacred groves); and (iv) sites that maintain conditions vital for the viability of these protected areas.

UNPROTECTED AREAS OF HIGH CONSERVATION VALUE. Critical natural habitats include areas currently lacking status as existing or proposed protected areas, provided that they are recognized by authoritative sources as (i) areas with known high suitability for biodiversity conservation or (ii) sites that are critical for one or more rare, vulnerable, migratory, or endangered species. Critical natural habitats typically appear on lists prepared by conservation experts outside (and sometimes within) the World Bank. This helps to distinguish the genuinely critical areas from the noncritical ones. A critical natural habitat site may appear on a list that existed before the preparation of the project proposed for World Bank support. Alternatively, such a list might be developed during project preparation, as part of the environmental assessment process (discussed below). In other words, a site could be evaluated and classified as a critical natural habitat for the first time during World Bank preparation of a proposed project.

SIGNIFICANCE OF FOREST CONVERSION AND DEGRADATION. For the Forests Policy, "significant conversion" and "degradation" are defined in OP 4.04, annex A, paragraph 1 (c)–(d). (OP 4.36 cross-references OP 4.04 for this purpose.) This definition states that *"significant conversion is the elimination or severe diminution of the integrity of a critical or other natural habitat caused by a major, long-term change in land or water use. Significant conversion may include, for example, land clearing; replacement of natural vegetation (e.g., by crops or tree plantations); permanent flooding (e.g., by a reservoir); drainage, dredging, filling, or channelization of wetlands; or surface mining. In both terrestrial and aquatic systems, conversion of natural habitats can occur as the result of severe pollution."* In simple terms, conversion is essentially the loss of an area of natural habitat; determining the significance of a conversion may be more complex (see below).

OP 4.04 defines degradation as the "modification of a critical or other natural habitat that substantially reduces the habitat's ability to maintain viable populations of its native species." In this context, degradation is an environmental safeguards concept, rather than an economic one. Some land management or silvicultural treatments may be regarded as improvements from an economic perspective,

but as degradation from an ecological standpoint. For example, the systematic removal of dead or dying trees, or species of low economic value, might be considered a management improvement by providing more space to the trees of higher economic value; however, it could reduce the forest's biodiversity and remove the habitat of birds and other wildlife that depend upon snags. Further complexity is involved in choosing between the different wild species that benefit from different types of forest management interventions. While many species of conservation or other management interest depend upon primary or old-growth forests, some can survive only in logged, burned, or otherwise disturbed areas (such as young secondary forest, or grassy clearings). Good judgment is needed in choosing the appropriate, site-specific forest management techniques to optimize between economic, social, and a variety of different environmental objectives. The project team should seek to ensure that the management objectives for a forested area are explicit, transparent, and thoroughly discussed with the full range of interested stakeholders.

When is the scale of the proposed conversion or degradation of an area of forest (or other natural habitat) large enough to qualify as significant? Neither OP 4.36 nor 4.04 provide numerical threshold figures; there is thus some case-by-case flexibility, provided that decisions are well-justified from a technical and scientific standpoint. When evaluating the significance of a proposed conversion or degradation of forests or other natural habitats, it is important to take into account the cumulative effects of (i) multiple subprojects under the same project; (ii) World Bank–financed repeater projects; and (iii) concurrent projects financed by other sources. It is also necessary to consider the area of each specific forest (or other natural habitat) type to be affected, in relative terms and (for still very extensive ecosystems) in absolute terms as well. In relative terms, an informal rule of thumb, used at times in the World Bank, is to consider the area of conversion or degradation to be significant if it exceeds 1 percent of the remaining area of any specific natural habitat type within the same country. One percent also happens to be the threshold for requiring natural habitat conservation offset measures in the European Union's Habitats Directive, Article 6(4).

In absolute terms, the substantively very similar Wildlands OPN 11.02 that preceded OP 4.04 (and was in effect 1987–95) suggested 10,000 hectares as a threshold figure, above which the conversion or degradation should be considered significant, even for a very extensive ecosystem type within the same country (where the converted or degraded area would be well under 1 percent of the remaining area).

However, some of the World Bank's environmental and bio-diversity specialists now suggest a lower figure, such as 5,000 hectares. Although they provide no official threshold figure, both the Forests and Natural Habitats policies require the World Bank and clients to apply a precautionary approach (OP 4.36, footnote 4 and OP 4.04, paragraph 1). Thus, in borderline situations under scientific uncertainty, the proposed conversion or degradation should be considered significant, and the relevant safeguard measures applied (project redesign or inclusion of specific mitigation measures, as discussed above). The decision needs to be justified and documented in a scientifically credible manner (typically within the PAD and EA report).

It is important to remember that the significant conversion or degradation of forests or other natural habitats can occur as a result of both (i) the direct impacts of a project (such as the civil works "footprint"); and (ii) the indirect impacts of project-induced human activities. As stated in OP 4.04, annex A, paragraph 1(c), "Conversion can result directly from the action of a project or through an indirect mechanism (e.g., through induced settlement along a road)." The induced impacts of a project frequently account for more forest loss or degradation than the direct ones.

SMALL-SCALE LANDHOLDERS AND LOCAL COMMUNITIES. OP 4.36, footnote 13, notes that "'small-scale is determined by the national context of a given country and is generally relative to the average size of household forest landholdings. In some situations, small-scale landholders may control less than a hectare of forests; in others they may control 50 hectares or more." Organized communities may own or otherwise control much larger tracts of forest (for example, up to several thousand hectares for some forest communities in the mountains of Mexico). However, forestry by local communities can normally be distinguished from industrial-scale commercial forestry operations by some combination of (i) community land tenure; (ii) long-term residence in the forest area; (iii) traditional forms of social organization; (iv) dependence upon nontimber forest products (not just cash from the sale of timber); (v) low levels of capitalization; (vi) relative poverty, or other relevant characteristics.

GUIDANCE ON DEVELOPMENT OF TERMS OF REFERENCE RELATED TO OP 4.36

OP 4.36 requires that appropriate analyses be undertaken to identify the social, economic, and environmental significance of forests and any activities that may affect the well-being of forests and the people who depend on them. To

meet those requirements, several analytical studies may be necessary. This section provides guidance on what should be included in the terms of reference (TOR) for conducting assessments necessary under OP 4.36.

In developing the TOR, it is important to consult other World Bank policies that are triggered or relevant, including OP 4.04 Natural Habitats, OP 4.09 Pest Management, OP 4.10 Indigenous Peoples (see chapter 12 , Applying OP 4.10 on Indigenous Peoples), OP 4.11 Physical Cultural Resources, OP 4.12 Involuntary Resettlement, and Policy on Disclosure of Information.

Consultation and communication with stakeholders are essential elements for the development and implementation of forest-related projects. Indeed, under OP 4.01, EAs require public consultations for review of draft plans by stakeholder groups, and if Indigenous Peoples are affected (whether positively or negatively), OP 4.10 requires a process of free, prior, and informed consultation with affected Indigenous Peoples communities leading to their broad support to the project. The information in chapter 10, Consultation and Communications in Forest Sector Activities, about stakeholder consultation can help to shape all of the analyses discussed in this section on TOR. The communication elements discussed in that chapter can assist in disseminating analysis results, as well as generating local interest in and commitment to the project.

A TOR must have certain sections, including a summary and background section, and a scope of work section. The scope of work will be different for each project and will reflect the characteristics of the project. Likewise, the personnel requirements and the balance of national and international consultants will be unique. This section provides an indicative list of items for consideration in TORs for OP 4.36. A project would not necessarily require all the items described here, nor is the list intended to be exhaustive. The emphasis on specific activities in a TOR will depend on the objective of the project, site context, prior work done, and other project-specific factors.

Depending on the nature of the project and analyses required, the necessary analyses can be done independently or jointly. For simplicity, the key elements of each type of analysis are presented as distinct sections below. If questions should arise, please refer to OP 4.36.

SUMMARY AND BACKGROUND. This section should provide an executive summary of the project, including a description of: the rationale for the project; the broad objectives and scope of the project; an overview, including a summary of the project and a brief discussion of timing; and the project management responsibilities and protocols. Additionally, this section sets the broad context for the project and provides justification for the goals and scope of the project and the development approach to be taken.

POTENTIAL COMPONENTS. This section provides a list of possible elements of the three main types of analyses: (i) a Social Assessment (which also includes assessment of institutional issues), (ii) an Economic and Financial Analysis, and (iii) an Environmental Assessment.

SOCIAL ASSESSMENT

The objective of the Social Assessment (SA) is to examine various social and institutional factors influencing the livelihood of all forest-dependent social groups, including Indigenous Peoples, women and youth, and other vulnerable groups. As mentioned in OP 4.36. paragraph 14, this information should "address, among other issues, the respective roles and legal rights of the government, the private sector, and local people."

The stakeholder and socioeconomic analysis associated with an SA should assess likely positive or adverse impacts on stakeholders, including head loaders, cultivators, people dependent on grazing lands, wage laborers, seasonal migrants, women-supported households, and other forest-dependent people. It should also recommend ways that stakeholders can benefit from the project inputs. (For further information on consultation and stakeholder analysis, please see chapter 10, Consultation and Communication in Forest Sector Activities.) The institutional analysis should ensure that key actors in the project have the necessary capacity, commitment, and incentives to implement and sustain the operation, and that the operation will have a positive impact on the country's public institutions.

The consultant should focus on the following key components for this analysis:

STAKEHOLDER ANALYSIS

- Identify and describe key characteristics, and describe the relationships among stakeholders. Assess formal and informal, codified and uncodified, and socially shared relationships.
- Assess the stake or interest in the project for each stakeholder group. This may include an assessment of potential support or opposition, openness to change, and potential benefit from the project.
- Understand the underlying political economy by identifying and examining the relevant civil society organizations and groups, as well as private sector actors, and NGOs. What are their agendas, constituencies, and links with other institutions?

SOCIOECONOMIC ANALYSIS

- Examine people's relationships to the forest from a spiritual and social standpoint.
- Examine people's degree of economic dependence on the forest. Assess practices such as shifting cultivation, the sustainability of these practices, and livelihood alternatives for the affected forest-dependent communities.
- Examine how dependence upon forests creates conflicts at intra- and inter-community levels.
- Examine village-level land-use patterns, tenure, and customary rights of private and common properties, and issues of indebtedness and land mortgage.
- Document and analyze needs, opportunities, and constraints for marginalized, discriminated against, and most vulnerable groups and individuals (Indigenous Peoples and women, for instance). Assess how to minimize risk and enhance benefits for these groups and individuals.
- Explore how encroachments affect the study area with attention to socioeconomic status, traditional tenurial rights, and other issues.
- Explore public attitudes toward conservation and the environment, willingness to participate in resource management activities, perceptions of local people of legal and illegal forest-related activities, remedial measures, and mechanisms for resolving potential conflicts.
- Identify ways to enhance access of forest-dependent persons (especially marginalized and vulnerable groups) to forest resources and broader economic opportunities.
- Develop and incorporate specific indicators related to social impacts on marginalized and vulnerable groups into monitoring and evaluation mechanisms.
- Provide guidance, if adverse impacts on vulnerable groups or individuals are unavoidable, in accordance with the World Bank's safeguard policies, in particular OP 4.10 (Indigenous Peoples) and OP 4.12 (Involuntary Resettlement).

INSTITUTIONAL ANALYSIS (should be undertaken at national, regional, and local levels)

- Evaluate institutions for their organizational structures, capacities, track records, rules, budgets, interlinkages, and levels of participation.
- Examine the relationship between government forestry institutions and local governments and local people.

- Examine the formal and informal local-level institutions and their characteristics, specifically principles of recruitment, inclusion, stratification, authority structure, and links to other institutions.

- Conduct a legal analysis of issues related to encroachments on forestland, and regularization of title, with a view to resolving tenure disputes and resource access within the existing policy framework of the relevant forest-related legislation.

- Identify appropriate measures for transparent decision-making process, fund flow mechanisms, and dissemination of information, and increased downward accountability of implementing agencies. Suggest modifications to existing institutional arrangements to facilitate good governance by providing voice, transparency, and free flow of information.

- Where relevant, assess forest-related contracts, including identifying those with whom communities enter into contract, and for what purpose. Assess performance, social dynamics, decision-making processes, transparency, and sustainability of forest protection.

- Address issues of empowerment and voice with attention to potential for leadership by marginalized and vulnerable groups, including women and indigenous groups.

- Develop and incorporate specific indicators related to marginalized and vulnerable groups into monitoring and evaluation mechanisms.

POTENTIAL METHODOLOGIES (see box 9.1 for an example of a Social Assessment methodology)

- consultations with key stakeholders (for example, through workshops, focus groups, interviews)
- in-depth interviews
- focus groups
- rapid rural appraisals and other participatory rural appraisal methods
- review of secondary data sources
- stakeholder analysis
- gender analysis
- training needs assessment or human resources development needs assessment

POTENTIAL OUTPUTS

- *Participation strategy* identifies stakeholders who must be included in the process, links these stakeholders with the activities, defines how and when the stakeholders will be involved, specifies the methods for working with these stake-

holders, and details the communication tools used to successfully promote stakeholder participation (see box 9.2).

- *Participation framework* describes the approach and process used to consult with different stakeholder groups. It explicitly includes measures to involve vulnerable people affected by the project in decision making, in receiving a share of benefits, and associated monitoring (see box 9.3).

- *Stakeholder consultation workshops* will enable stakeholders to provide information and opinions regarding issues of concerns in the assessment. The workshops use approaches and tools to elicit stakeholder inputs.

- *Social impact report* details the main social issues and interventions and assesses likely positive and negative impacts, as well as mitigation measures (see box 9.4).

- *Poverty impact assessment* analyzes the distributional impact of policy reforms on the well-being or welfare of different stakeholder groups, with particular focus on the poor and vulnerable.

- *Process framework* for access restrictions to legally designated parks or protected areas. According to World Bank established practices (OP 4.12), the borrower prepares a Process Framework describing the participatory process by which affected communities will participate in designing the project or project component, determination of restrictions, eligibility criteria, mitigation measures to assist them maintain or improve their livelihoods, and conflict resolution mechanisms. The framework is publicly disclosed and transmitted to the World Bank for review before project approval.

- *Indigenous Peoples plans*. When Indigenous Peoples are affected, whether positively or negatively, OP 4.10 requires the development, in consultation with affected communities, of a plan to address adverse impacts and provide culturally appropriate benefits (see chapter 12).

- *Assessment of vulnerability and social risk.*

- *Operation manual* provides guidelines for the design of surveys, methods of facilitating stakeholder participation, conflict resolution techniques, collaboration with technical specialists, and so forth.

- *Communications strategy* with other groups and within the program, to ensure public and political support, to initiate the planning of the project, and to initiate and pave the way for a potential long-term program.

- *Policy, legal, and administrative framework* discusses the policy, legal, and administrative framework within which the project is carried out.

- *Training or human resources development plan.*

- *Legal analysis.*

Box 9.1   Methodology of Social Assessment

CRITERIA FOR SAMPLING IN A SURVEY

- social composition, with particular attention to caste and tribe subgroup dimensions
- degree of homogeneity and heterogeneity along other dimensions, such as known conflict and tension, and the like
- degree of legitimacy of tribal leaders versus other patterns of leadership
- poverty criteria, such as assets, land ownership, landlessness
- status of tenurial rights to forest lands, encroachments, and so forth
- geographic isolation, proximity to roads and markets, and other location dimensions
- presence of government departments other than the forest department, and availability of development schemes and basic services
- presence of NGOs or other organizations
- integration or coordination with other formal committees
- human development indicators, such as female literacy and maternal mortality rates
- vulnerability and risk, coping strategies, migration, and the like
- level of indebtedness and coping strategies

MAPPING PROJECT. Create social maps by charting name, clan, tribe, village, degree of legitimacy or conflict among other tribal and caste groups.

CLUSTERS MATRIX ANALYSIS using the following potential criteria:

- social homogeneity or heterogeneity
- degree of social capital
- patterns of leadership and degree of legitimacy;
- forest cover and degree of degradation
- market- and nonmarket-oriented approach

STAKEHOLDER IDENTIFICATION. The following outlines some ideas to effectively identify those stakeholders that should be involved:

Source: World Bank 2005a.

- assess the different groups overseeing, operating, or depending on the forests
- identify those groups that are central to the process, impact forest resources, or benefit from resources in forests
- consult with persons working in nonnatural resources–related fields that could contribute useful information or know of affected stakeholders (for example, health care worker or teachers) who could contribute to the process
- include stakeholder representatives from the various governmental, nongovernmental, religious, private sector, and other interest groups. The stakeholders invited should also represent the different levels of interest (national or ministerial, as well as local) and the different activities planned in forests or influenced by forest activities
- given priorities and trends, decide which stakeholders are essential to addressing forest priorities and making decisions

PARTICIPATORY RURAL APPRAISAL METHODS

- participatory mapping and modeling of resource maps of forests for water, soils, trees, pastures
- local histories of people's accounts of the past; ecological histories; histories of cropping patterns; changes in trends of population, migration, fuels used, and causes of these
- seasonal diagramming of rainfall; labor in agriculture, crops and harvests, food and fuel availability, marketing patterns; gender perceptions of labor, crops and harvests, food and fuel availability, marketing patterns
- livelihood analysis relating to seasonality, crises and coping, credit and debt
- matrix ranking for people identifying their priorities and options for action
- Venn diagramming for conflict identification and resolution.

All of the above may be selectively used in social and institutional assessments.

Box 9.2 Participation Strategy

To make the task manageable for a public participation strategy, it is important to (i) identify the relevant stakeholders (for example, distinguish between those stakeholders who are directly affected or benefit from the process, and those who are indirectly affected); (ii) quickly assess the political economy to ensure that the voices of commonly marginalized groups are heard and the feasibility of collaboration among various stakeholder groups is understood; and (iii) use tools for integrating the various viewpoints that underpin the initiative (for example, ranking tools; GIS to overlay the different social, institutional, and biophysical layers; or others such as those listed below).

Involving the stakeholders will require strategies equally as enterprising as those used to identify them. Some considerations for engaging different stakeholders include

- the type of interaction (for example, individual or group meetings and location);

- accommodation of the stakeholders' time constraints (and if key stakeholders are unable to attend meetings, considering keeping them informed through personal communication);
- the manner by which information will be exchanged;
- the purpose of such stakeholder communication (information sharing, data gathering, decision making, and so forth);
- coordination between the landscape planning team and stakeholder groups to ensure viewpoints are conveyed and received accurately;
- sharing of concepts and well-defined terminology with the stakeholder groups to minimize confusion in the planning process;
- use of an appropriate language and mode of communication; and
- ensuring all actors have an accurate picture of the process and their roles in it.

Source: World Bank 2005b.

Box 9.3 Participation Framework

Based on the stakeholder analysis, a participation framework with specific systems and procedures will be developed, which will describe the approach and process used to consult with different stakeholder groups to incorporate their views into project design and implementation, and to communicate with them about the project. The framework should identify ways and procedures in which the marginalized and the less vocal groups and individuals can best participate in the process of group formation and micro-plan development. A detailed communications strategy should also be developed for the project, largely based on the stakeholder analysis. The consultation process should be ongoing throughout the project's life; key stakeholders should continue to be consulted and involved. See note 1.4, Indigenous Peoples and Forests, and chapter 12, Applying OP 4.10 on Indigenous Peoples, for particular issues concerning Indigenous Peoples.

Source: World Bank 2005b.

Box 9.4 Social Impact Report

- Identify the main social issues related to the reforms supported by the project and, specifically, by the set of interventions envisaged under each of the components.
- Assess the project's likely positive and negative impacts—in quantitative terms to the extent possible—on key stakeholders, particularly the poor and most vulnerable social groups that depend on forest resources.
- Identify mitigation measures and any residual negative impacts that cannot be mitigated.
- Assess the key (formal and informal) institutions in the forestry sector that will be involved in the delivery of the mitigation measures, evaluate their respective roles, capacity, and training needs.
- Spell out the mechanisms for participation of all affected stakeholder groups in design, implementation, and monitoring of the social aspects of the reform and the project's implementation. The report will also formulate recommendations, taking into consideration the possibilities of participation of project beneficiaries in the monitoring and evaluation process.

Source: World Bank 2005b.

Box 9.5   Process Framework for Involuntary Access Restrictions

The World Bank Policy on Involuntary Resettlement (OP 4.12) is triggered when World Bank–assisted investment projects cause the involuntary restriction of access to legally designated parks and protected areas. For purposes of this policy, involuntary restrictions of access cover restrictions on the use of resources imposed on people living outside the park or protected area, or on those who continue living inside the park or protected area during and after project implementation. In such projects, the nature of the restrictions, as well as the type of measures necessary to mitigate adverse impacts, is determined with the participation of the displaced persons during the design and implementation of the project.

Given the potential impact of project activities that could result in the involuntary restriction of access to resources and livelihood for inhabitants of some of the areas covered by the project, a "Process Framework" (PF) is a condition of project appraisal. Usually a consultant or other entity is contracted to assist the government in preparing this document.

The draft PF is to be endorsed by the government and transmitted to the World Bank for review before project appraisal. The final PF must be made available in the borrowing country at a place accessible to, and in a form, manner, and language understandable to, the displaced or affected people and local NGOs. Important aspects of preparing the PF document are (i) the awareness of the national government of the risk of impact on the livelihoods of certain population groups and (ii) agreement with the national government on how to address these risks.

The process framework describes the participatory process by which

- specific components of the project will be prepared and implemented;
- the criteria for eligibility will be determined;
- measures to assist the displaced persons in their efforts to improve their livelihoods, or at least to restore them in real terms while maintaining the sustainability of the park of protected area, will be identified; and
- potential conflicts involving displaced persons will be resolved.

The PF describe the site and impact areas and the activities that are likely to restrict access to forest resources and thereby affect the livelihoods of some population groups. These may, for instance, include measures to curtail illegal logging, poaching, and hunting; fishing; restrictions on collecting other forest products, such as herbal plants and mushrooms; or using forest areas for grazing or farming. The PF will, to the extent possible, estimate the magnitude of the impact caused by the particular activity, including, for example, in the case of illegal logging, issues such as what is considered illegal logging by the law; what is the actual interpretation of this law by local officials; what is the enforcement record of their current interpretation; what are the chances for an effective elimination of illegal logging across the country; what would a clampdown on illegal logging really mean; what is the magnitude of the impact from the stakeholders' point of view; who does illegal logging; are there any regional disparities, ethnic patterns, and so forth; for what purpose do they do illegal logging (cooking, heating, subsistence, commercial); is it a seasonal or regular activity; what is the degree of dependence on the acquired wood (financial or in kind); what are other sources of income and how sustainable are they; what is the likely coping mechanism by those affected in the case of a successful or semi-successful clampdown on illegal logging; is a potential successful clampdown on illegal logging likely to force those affected to move to other areas, and if so, which areas; what other changes in regard to livelihood and behavior are likely to be triggered by government efforts to curtail illegal logging; and other pertinent issues.

Given the nature and magnitude of the impact, the PF can also suggest the likely mitigation measures that will be put into place, and the implementation process. But the thrust of the PF is the description of the participatory process by which these decisions will be made rather than the decisions themselves. The action and mitigation plans—their integration and coordination with other project components—are an iterative process and will evolve through the project. The PF also includes a description of the arrangements for implementation and monitoring the process and records of interagency and consultation meetings, including consultations with affected people on their views.

It would be useful to keep in mind that the review of the PF at the World Bank is based on five key criteria:

(Box continues on the following page.)

QUALIFICATIONS OF CONSULTANTS FOR SOCIAL ASSESSMENT. The consultant or team of consultants should have the following qualifications:

- practical experience in designing and implementing participatory natural resource management projects, in assessing and addressing interests of vulnerable people, and an ability to manage interdisciplinary teams
- detailed local knowledge of social issues related to natural resource management, including usage of forest and agriculture resources and community practices involving natural resources
- familiarity with the legal framework for usufruct rights and access
- experience with local forest or forest-related social issues
- operational experience in social survey methods
- ability to engage with local people and keep an open mind to new approaches
- ability to speak local languages

Additional qualifications might include the following:

- extensive experience in microenterprise development; familiarity with microfinance and revolving fund options, marketing issues, and regulatory climate
- experience with assessing structure, capacity, and inter-linkages of national and community-level organizations
- knowledge of national and local institutions
- extensive experience in community development and participatory planning

- operational experience in analysis and design of communication activities and dissemination materials
- extensive professional background in human resources development, including experience with training needs assessment, building analytical and problem-solving skills, and participative and interactive approaches to training

Economic and financial analysis

This analysis should examine the various economic and financial factors affecting a forest-related project to enhance the economic efficiency of the project and address distributional questions. An economic analysis compares economic and social benefits to the economy as a whole. The financial analysis compares revenue and expenses, like operations and maintenance costs.

It is important to understand the economic value of forests that are affected by the project. In addition to forest products and services, this valuation should include nonmarket uses of forests, such as environmental services, social uses, and subsistence uses.

In particular, the consultant should focus on the following key components for this analysis:

ECONOMIC IMPORTANCE

- evaluate direct use of forests arising from consumptive and nonconsumptive uses: timber, fruits, nuts, mushrooms, medicinal plants, forage, hunting and fishing, tourism and recreation, genetic resources, and educational uses

- evaluate indirect use of forests: watershed and soil protection, wind breaks, climate control, and nutrient cycling
- evaluate options values, including future direct and indirect uses
- evaluate off-site and on-site economic effects; also evaluate private costs and benefits versus social costs and benefits, with attention to market failures, policy-induced distortions, and externalities
- evaluate nontimber values like health, carbon sequestration, and alternative livelihood strategies
- assess the incremental or additional costs associated with transforming a project with national benefits into one with global environmental benefits, for Global Environment Facility projects

FINANCIAL ANALYSIS

- evaluate the financial viability of investments like reforestation, microenterprises, and so forth; also evaluate risk and market access

- conduct a financial analysis from the perspectives of various stakeholders
- undertake a cost-benefit analysis (see box 9.6)
- base decisions, to the extent possible, on a total economic valuation of forest resources, that is, an estimate of the value of all economic benefits that a society derives from its forests (see box 9.7)

POTENTIAL METHODOLOGY

- review of primary and secondary data sources
- rapid Rural Appraisal
- interviews, including stakeholder interviews, questionnaires, village-based surveys for livelihood analysis (including wealth ranking, group interviews, process analysis)
- Cost-benefit analysis
- Market analysis (see box 9.8)
- Contingent valuation
- Quantitative measures, including TEV, internal rate of return, net present value

---

Box 9.6   Cost-Benefit Analysis

A detailed cost-benefit analysis will be undertaken during project preparation, taking into account the issues of economic importance and financial analysis and using quantitative models. Incremental costs and benefits of project investments will be examined in detail, and economic and financial rates of return calculated. Cost-effectiveness analysis will be conducted on alternative plantation and protection techniques. The analysis will also include the preparation of indicative economic and financial models for participatory management of forests by locals, including analysis of alternative land uses. The economists will also undertake sensitivity analysis on key risks and discuss implications for project design.

The quantified cost-benefit analysis will be supplemented by an analysis of other environmental benefits not as readily conducive to financial quantification (for example, biodiversity, climatic changes), which, where appropriate, will take into account physical measurements and least-cost analysis of any associated marginal costs of interventions specific to those benefits.

Source: World Bank 2003a.

Box 9.7   Total Economic Valuation

TOTAL ECONOMIC VALUATION (TEV) is a method used to identify and estimate the value of all economic benefits that a society derives from its forests. As such, TEV extends well beyond the scope of financial analyses of forest values that concentrate almost exclusively on timber, to account for the great variety of other products and services provided by a forest system. The TEV of a forest is the sum its use and nonuse values. Use values are, in turn, divided into direct, indirect, and option values; while nonuse values include bequest and existence values. Examples of the various use values include

- Direct uses—timber, fruits, nuts, mushrooms, medicinal plants, forage, hunting and fishing, tourism and recreation, genetic resources, and educational uses
- Indirect uses—watershed and soil protection, wind breaks, climate control, and nutrient cycling
- Option—future direct and indirect uses

Source: World Bank 2003a.

POTENTIAL PRODUCTS. The economic and financial analysis could include the following elements:

- *Cost estimate.* A realistic, reliable estimate of all costs for proposed forestry investments (see box 9.9).
- *Cost-benefit analysis.* An examination of incremental costs and benefits of project investments. Calculates economic and financial rates of return. Includes indicative economic and financial models for participatory management of forests by locals, analysis of alternative land uses, and undertakes sensitivity analysis on key risks. It should be supplemented by analysis of less quantifiable environmental benefits (for example, biodiversity, climatic changes).
- *Market analysis.* An assessment of current and potential market conditions for forest and rangeland products and the associated policy reform ramifications.
- *Local public goods assessment.* An assessment of environmental services and potential payment arrangements, which may include special adjustments to ensure inclusion of women and vulnerable groups, and reward good performance.
- *Incentive framework.* A description of arrangements and policy incentives to ensure ongoing economic decision making (see box 9.10).
- *Poverty impact analysis.* An analysis of the project impact on poverty (opportunity, empowerment, and security) that addresses household income, stakeholder groups, loss of access to forest resources, and seasonal vulnerability (see box 9.11).
- *Economic monitoring.* An estimate of with- and without-project scenarios that provides the basis for full baseline

measurements and subsequent monitoring of project and control results (see box 9.12).

- *Fiscal impact analysis.* Includes an assessment of the fiscal impacts of the project—both expenditure and revenue aspects—within the context of a public expenditure and revenue review of the whole forestry sector (see box 9.13).

Box 9.11   Poverty Impact Analysis

The economic analysis will also include a special focus on the impact of the project on poverty, considering opportunity, empowerment, and security. This would include analysis of the size and timing of impacts (both benefits and costs) on household income, and variations in impacts on different social groups (women-headed households, unemployed, herders, and so forth). Special attention would be paid to any impacts resulting from loss of access to forest resources. The models would also reflect the impact on seasonal and other factors of vulnerability, and assess the likely asset transfer as a factor in empowerment and in improving livelihoods. Potential project impacts on both winners and losers will be quantified to the extent feasible.

Source: Mott 2003.

Box 9.13   Fiscal Impact Analysis

The fiscal impact analysis will include an assessment of the fiscal impacts of the project—both its expenditure and revenue aspects—within the context of a public expenditure and revenue review of the whole forestry sector. Links with government wide cross-sectoral fiscal analyses and reforms would be considered. The financial analysis would also include an assessment of the financial sustainability of the project interventions, taking into account the proposed institutional (policy and organizational) framework and arrangements, including plans for the postproject period. Opportunities for cost recovery, revolving funds including postharvest reinvestment arrangements, role realignment, and other mechanisms that would facilitate self-financing would be identified.

Source: Mott 2003.

Box 9.12   Economic Monitoring

Projectwide indicative estimates of with- and without-project scenarios will be made, building on preliminary assessments based on initial surveys and secondary data. These estimates would provide the basis for full baseline measurements and subsequent monitoring of actual results in the project areas and carefully selected control areas at project start-up, midterm, and closing. Preparation work will include the design of this monitoring agenda.

Source: Mott 2003.

QUALIFICATIONS OF CONSULTANTS FOR ECONOMIC AND FINANCIAL ANALYSIS. The consultant or team of consultants should have the following qualifications:

■ extensive operational experience with skills in cost-benefit analysis modeling, environmental economics, nonmarket valuation techniques, participatory rural appraisal, policy analysis, and reform

■ experience in analysis of forestry or tree crop cost-benefit analysis, poverty impact analysis, market analysis, financial expenditure trend analysis, project cost estimation

■ proven track record in effective teamwork

■ experience in data collection and analysis, ability to access local data sources, and ability to work as part of a team

■ ability to speak local languages

■ ability to work closely with local economists to build local capacity for economic and financial analysis, and develop a program for training

■ knowledge and experience with capacity-building activities in economic analysis, forest product marketing, incentive frameworks, fiscal management, market opportunities, appropriate involvement of local people and the private sector, as well as an understanding of the resources, incentives, and accountability needed for decentralization of forest management

Environmental assessment

The EA (under OP 4.01) is the World Bank's officially recognized system for determining what areas constitute critical forests or natural habitats. An EA should examine the positive and negative environmental impacts of the project; compare these with feasible alternatives (including a "no-project" option); and recommend measures to prevent, minimize, mitigate, or compensate for adverse impacts, and to improve the environmental conditions and impact management performance. The EA should focus special attention on developing guidelines and procedures for identifying and measuring conservation and sustainable-use objectives.

The document should be prepared according to World Bank guidelines, as set out in OP 4.01 (see World Bank, Environmental Assessment Sourcebook).

This information is not intended to supersede EA guidelines presented elsewhere, but instead to supplement those guidelines with information specific to forest-related projects.

In particular, the assessment could examine the following key components:

- *Assess the key environmental concerns in the forestry sector.* The assessment should focus on key environmental concerns in the forest sector that are relevant to the proposed project.
- *Identify and describe critical forests or critical natural habitats.* (See the section of this chapter titled Identifying Critical Forests and Critical Natural Habitats through Environmental Assessment). Describe ecosystem type(s), species of conservation concern, natural or cultural features, existing or proposed legal protection, threats, and other information relevant to decision making.
- *Assess critical ecosystems and recommend a program for their conservation and management.* This might also include supporting community-driven conservation initiatives, integrating conservation components into participatory forest management and forest development, and supporting participatory biodiversity monitoring.
- *Develop quantitative indicators and a baseline for monitoring changes.* This is to monitor changes in the natural environment (both positive and negative) that may result from project activities. Define a methodology for data collection and assessment (see box 9.14).
- *Assess threats to cultural heritage* (archaeological, religious, and cultural properties and resources). Evaluate the potential to improve protection of such resources, and monitoring and screening methods to be implemented in project areas.
- *Assess the impact of the project on the natural environment.* Evaluated impacts might include the benefits to soil and water regimes, species conservation and diversity, and ecological stability. From a negative perspective, the EA should evaluate the potential impacts of project

interventions on the physical and biological environments. In addition, the EA should include an analysis and understanding of the issues related to wildlife habitats and populations in the project areas, and the implications of shifting populations of wild animals on tribal communities and their access to forestry resources.

- *Review legal, administrative, and institutional frameworks* relevant to the proposed project.
- *Involve communities in planning, implementing, and assessing the results and impacts of the project.* Stakeholders (including people affected by the project, NGOs, and other relevant groups) should be incorporated throughout the project, both in planning and implementation.
- *Strengthen capacity at local, entity, and state levels for biodiversity conservation and sustainable management practices.* The project could finance professional development, management training, ranger training, business planning, and forest management planning at the ecosystem level, and capacity building for national ministries.
- *Where relevant, identify, establish, or expand sustainably managed protected areas (PA).* For all PAs, the project should establish a biodiversity monitoring system at the site, entity, and state levels.
- *Improve local benefits originating from protected areas.* Involve and provide incentives (possibly through small grants) for stakeholders living in and around PAs to ensure long-term sustainability through the development of alternative, environmentally sensitive income-generation based on sustainable resource use that would bring economic benefits to local people.

Box 9.14 Quantitative Analysis and Baseline Monitoring

Tools to develop quantitative indicators and a baseline for monitoring changes in the natural environment (both positive and negative) that may result from project activities and define a methodology for data collection and assessment should be implemented. Elements of the natural environment that should be taken into consideration include: flora and fauna, natural habitats and ecosystems (including animal habitats), wetlands, soils, minerals, water resources, and hydrological patterns.

Source: World Bank, Environmental Assessment Sourcebook and Updates.

POTENTIAL METHODOLOGY

- *Impact analysis.* Assesses potential positive and negative impacts of the proposed study. Impacts might involve changes to soil and water regimes, species conservation and diversity, and ecological stability (see box 9.15).
- *Field visits.*
- *Background information from other publications and electronic databases.* Documents provide lists, brief descriptions, and map locations for critical natural habitat sites.
- *Consultation with experts.* Consult experts knowledgeable about the locations and significance of critical forests and other critical natural habitats within a country or a proposed project area.
- *Stakeholder workshops.* Hold workshops to solicit stakeholder input and provide opportunities to incorporate local knowledge. Inclusion of all stakeholder groups promotes transparency, builds coalitions, and ensures inclusion of vulnerable groups, such as Indigenous Peoples.
- *Public consultations.* Conduct two public consultations as required by the World Bank for a Category B Environmental Assessment to review the draft environmental management plan (EMP) document to the satisfaction of affected local groups and NGOs.

POTENTIAL PRODUCTS

- *Environmental Management Framework (EMF).* Serves as a tool to identify and manage potential environmental concerns; also provides practical operational procedures and guidelines for environmental screening, for assessment and approval of subprojects or investments, and for the management of any potential impacts (see box 9.15).
- *EMP.* Details site-specific plans for mitigation, monitoring, capacity development, and implementation (as outlined in annex C to OP 4.01) (see box 9.16).
- *Review of baseline conditions.* Describes the physical, biological, and socioeconomic environment, including information on climate, human environment, health, environmentally sensitive areas, critical natural habitats, and vegetation.
- *Assessment of environmental impact and proposed mitigation and enhancement measure guidelines.* Assesses positive and negative environmental impacts of proposed project. Provides information and identifies processes for monitoring and evaluation to maximize the project's intended environmental benefits. The guidelines should encompass tangible natural resource benefits, environmental services, and ecological functions, as well as insti-

tutional and capacity development, particularly at the village or microplanning level (see box 9.17).

- *Monitoring and evaluation plan.* Provides realistic procedures for participatory monitoring involving the communities in assessing the results and impacts of the project.
- *Stakeholder workshops.* Hold workshops to discuss findings and implications with community members and other interested stakeholders, including government officials.
- *Policy, legal, and administrative framework.* Reviews or describes the relevant national, regional, provincial, communal, or World Bank safeguard policies that pertain to environmental reviews and impact assessments.

Please note that some projects combine the environmental and social analyses and produce an Environmental and Social Management Framework (ESMF) (see box 9.18).

Box 9.15 Environmental Management Framework

The EMF should provide practical recommendations and guidance on minimizing and mitigating any potential environmental impacts of project-related interventions, and measures for enhancement and improvement of environmental conditions in the project area. The EMF will include guidelines for identifying conservation and sustainable-use objectives, incorporating them into the microplanning process, maximizing the intended environmental benefits of the project as a whole, and providing information and procedures for monitoring and evaluating the implementation of environmental actions and their impacts. The EMF will specifically include (i) criteria and procedures for screening of project investments on the basis of their potential environmental impacts and benefits; (ii) a list of negative activities (those that will not be financed under any circumstance) for the proposed project, and ecologically sensitive areas where project investments should not be implemented; (iii) draft technical guidelines that incorporate environmental concerns for each of the major potential types of project investments; (iv) proposed institutional arrangements for environmental oversight, review, and management at different levels; (v) proposed arrangements for independent monitoring, audit, and consultation in the implementation of the EMF; and (vi) identification of specific capacity-building and training objectives for implementation of the EMF.

Source: World Bank 2005a.

Box 9.16 Environmental Management Plan

Develop an environmental management and monitoring plan for project implementation that addresses all key environmental quality indicators and includes institutional roles, responsibilities, capacities, and training requirements, in accordance with annex C to OP 4.01. The EMP should include mitigation measures, institutional strengthening, training, and monitoring, as follows:

- *Mitigation of environmental impacts.* Recommend feasible and cost-effective measures to prevent or reduce significant negative impacts to acceptable levels. Estimate the impacts and costs of those measures. Consider compensation to affected parties for impacts that cannot be mitigated. The plan should include proposed work programs, budget estimates, schedules, staffing, and training requirements, and other necessary support services to implement the mitigating measures.
- *Institutional strengthening and training.* Identification

of institutional needs to implement EA recommendations. Recommend any additional support that should be provided to the PA management institutions, the project implementation units, the relevant ministries, and others, to strengthen or expand them so that the management and monitoring plans in the EA can be implemented. The institutional needs should be presented separately for the two entities.
- *Monitoring.* Prepare detailed arrangements for monitoring implementation of mitigating measures and the impacts of the project during construction and operation. Include in the plan an estimate of capital and operating costs, and a description of other inputs (such as training and institutional strengthening) needed to carry it out.

It should be noted that the EMP must be incorporated by reference in the legal agreement for the project. As a result, the EMP must be clear and coherent to support any efforts to determine compliance with the EMP.

Source: World Bank 2003b.

Box 9.17 Assessment of Environmental Impacts and Proposed Mitigation Measures

Determine the potential positive and negative environmental and social impacts of the project with respect to the proposed PAs, including already defined and proposed expansions. (Description of any social impacts should be based on the results of the Social Assessment.) These impacts should include any future development of the villages and settlements within each PA, as well as impacts from construction of any PA infrastructure (visitor centers, headquarters facilities, latrines, and the like), rehabilitation of access roads and hiking trails, and changes in land use or vegetative cover. Propose an environmental screening process for activities to be financed by the small grants program during project implementation.

Source: World Bank 2003b.

QUALIFICATIONS OF THE CONSULTANT FOR THE ENVIRONMENTAL ASSESSMENT. The consultant or team of consultants should have the following qualifications:

- extensive experience in the environmental field, preferably at the international level, and in the preparation of environmental management plans according to international standards
- practical experience in biological surveys and assessment in the country in question or a similar country
- proven ability to write clear and concise reports
- field experience in environmental assessment in the country in question or a similar country
- extensive experience in the management of forest pests
- basic understanding of cost-benefit analyses
- ability to speak local languages

IDENTIFYING CRITICAL FORESTS AND CRITICAL NATURAL HABITATS THROUGH ENVIRONMENTAL ASSESSMENT

The World Bank's officially recognized system for interpreting the definitions above and determining what areas con-

The consultant is expected to develop an environmental and social management framework (ESMF) that establishes methodologies for environmental and social impact assessment within the project preparation, approval, and implementation processes, including the preparation of an environmental mitigation plan and a resettlement action plan. Specific activities include the following:

- Providing the description of the environmental and social characteristics of the PA and description of the biophysical and socioeconomic environment. Identifying links between different types of livelihood and sustainable environment management in the PA.
- Outlining the provisions under national legislation, policies, and regulations regarding the environmental and social impacts that are relevant to the characteristics of the PA. Assessing the consistencies of these with the standards and procedures of the World Bank regarding environmental and social safeguard policies.
- Designing and clearly outlining methodology for preparation, approval, and execution of subprojects. The consultant is expected to provide information for project preparation from design process to approval.
- Assessing and documenting the implementation capacity of collaborating institutions at the local, regional, and national levels; proposing ways of strengthening the capacity to manage and provide training; and providing an estimate of the costs for implementing the environmental and social control plan.
- Developing an elaborate ESMF, which would include recommending feasible measures for preventing or reducing impacts, such as a resettlement action plan and other mitigation measures as identified during the ESMF.

- Developing a resettlement action plan that establishes
  - potential impacts of the project on people and properties;
  - regulatory and institutional context for land tenure;
  - evaluation of assets and rate of compensation;
  - complaint system management;
  - identification, assistance, and provisions to be included in the resettlement plan for vulnerable groups;
  - consultation and diffusion of information, describing the consultation framework for preparation of the resettlement plan and the framework for its diffusion to stakeholders;
  - responsibilities for implementation; specifically
- Describing the institutional setting for the implementation of the resettlement plan.
- Proposing the composition and tasks of a joint committee for liaison between the affected communities and local structures in charge of implementation of the resettlement plan.
- Designing a clear communications strategy for information dissemination to all stakeholders.
- Developing a participatory monitoring and evaluation plan for the implementation of the proposed mitigation measures. The plan should clearly indicate
  - the link between the impacts identified in the EMSF report, the indicators for measuring these impacts, data collection methods, and the time plan for monitoring and evaluating these impacts; and
  - institutional responsibilities for monitoring indirect and direct impacts, as well as responsibilities for supervision, the frequency of monitoring and reporting mechanisms, and the budget for the monitoring and evaluation plan.

Source: World Bank 2006.

stitute critical forests or other critical natural habitats is the EA process under OP 4.01. The EA report required of all Category A, B, and FI projects should be used to identify any critical natural habitats within the proposed project's area of influence. It is thus essential for the EA TOR to direct the EA study team to identify those forests and other natural habitats within the proposed project area that should qualify as

critical natural habitats, in accordance with the above-mentioned criteria of OP 4.04 and 4.36. For any areas that appear to qualify as critical forests or other critical natural habitats, the EA report should indicate

- the official and common names for the site;
- ecosystem types;

- map location(s);
- approximate surface area;
- size of the proposed project-affected area, relative to the same ecosystem type(s) within the same country;
- species of conservation concern or special management interest known (or suspected) to occur, and (if known) their estimated populations (in absolute terms and relative to the rest of the country or world);
- special concentrations of migratory or other species;
- other natural or cultural features of special interest;
- land ownership;
- existing or proposed legal protection (if any);
- on-the-ground protection and management (if any);
- who controls and influences land- and water-use decisions;
- types and intensity of current or recent human uses;
- existing and potential future threats to the natural habitats; and
- other information relevant to decision making.

In the course of project preparation (before appraisal), the World Bank interprets and evaluates the findings of the EA report—along with any supplementary sources of relevant information—and determines which project areas (if any) indeed qualify as critical forests or other critical natural habitats, in terms of applying the safeguards requirements of the Forests and Natural Habitats policies. In cases where the World Bank's judgment differs from the recommendations of the EA report, the former overrides. It is thus important that this decision be made with inputs from technically qualified World Bank staff and other specialists (as needed), in a manner that is credible and convincing from a scientific standpoint.

COMPLEMENTARY MEANS OF IDENTIFYING CRITICAL FORESTS AND CRITICAL NATURAL HABITATS. Although the EA process is the official, World Bank–endorsed mechanism for identifying critical forests and other critical natural habitats, there are complementary sources of information that project teams (World Bank staff as well as their government or NGO counterparts) should use. These additional sources of information are important (i) for preliminary assessment of the presence, nature, and extent of critical forests and other critical natural habitats before the EA report is available; (ii) to help verify the validity and completeness of the EA report with respect to this issue; and (iii) to provide, as needed, supplementary information useful for decision making regarding project design. Broadly speaking, these complementary information sources comprise

experts to be consulted, and useful publications and electronic databases. This type of complementary information should be backed up by up-to-date, project-specific field studies (as needed) during the EA process.

EXPERTS TO BE CONSULTED. As part of the EA process, and also to obtain independent verification, it is essential to consult experts knowledgeable about the locations and significance of critical forests and other critical natural habitats within a country or a proposed project area. The types of experts who should normally be consulted include the following:

- *Regional Safeguards Unit within the World Bank* should be a useful first point of contact for advice about the possible presence and significance of critical forests and other critical natural habitats within a proposed project area.
- *Government agencies* (at the national or subnational level) responsible for protected areas, natural resource management, or the environment in general, which usually have up-to-date lists of existing and officially proposed protected areas. Some also have authoritative information on unprotected areas of high conservation value.
- *Conservation NGOs* (national or international), which often have high-quality information about critical forests and other natural habitats. They are frequently also project stakeholders and sometimes partners.
- *Expert individuals* with specialized knowledge about sites of interest, who can often be found in universities and research institutions, at the national or international level.
- *Public consultation,* which is primarily a vehicle to ensure stakeholder participation in the decision-making process, but can provide information about critical natural habitats not obtained from other sources. For example, the World Bank first learned that the site proposed for a solid waste landfill on the Caribbean island of Grenada was the habitat of the critically endangered Grenada dove (Leptotila wellsi) as the result of a public consultation held in 1994, even though the initial EA report for the Organization of Eastern Caribbean States (OECS) Solid Waste Management Project failed to mention this issue.

USEFUL PUBLICATIONS AND ELECTRONIC DATABASES. A variety of documents and Web sites provide lists, brief descriptions, and map locations for critical natural habitat sites—including many outside existing protected areas—in a large number of countries. These information sources should be regarded as useful "first approximations" of the locations and characteristics of many, though not all, critical natural habitats. Geographic sites that do not appear on any of these lists might still qualify as critical forests or other critical natural habitats, based on the above-mentioned criteria and the World Bank's review of the EA report and other relevant information during project preparation. The following is a partial list of some useful publications and electronic databases (see the Selected Readings list for this chapter for full bibliographic information).

WORLD BANK PUBLICATIONS

- *Ecologically Sensitive Sites in Africa* (World Bank 1993);
- *Protected Areas Systems Review of the Indo-Malayan Realm* (with maps showing existing and proposed protected areas in East and South Asian countries; MacKinnon 1997);
- *Critical Natural Habitats in Latin America and the Caribbean* (World Bank n.d.); and
- for marine critical natural habitats proposed for protection, A *Global Representative System of Marine Protected Areas* (four volumes covering the world's oceans and seas; Kelleher, Bleakley, and Wells 1995).

Important Bird Areas. Important Bird Areas (IBAs) are sites that are of global significance for bird conservation, particularly of threatened species. They can be regarded as a very significant subset of critical natural habitats, because sites important for bird conservation tend also to be important for the conservation of other biodiversity as well—although not all critical natural habitats also qualify as IBAs. BirdLife International and its national partner organizations have recently published a number of books (as hard copies and sometimes also as compact discs) that list and briefly describe all the currently known IBAs at a national and regional level, including, among others,

- *Áreas Importantes para Aves en Panamá* (Panama Audubon Society 2003);
- *Áreas Importantes para la Conservación de las Aves en Argentina* (Aves Argentinas 2005);
- *Áreas Importantes para la Conservación de las Aves en México* (CIPAMEX 2000);
- *Important Bird Areas in Africa and Associated Islands: Priority Sites for Conservation* (Fishpool and Evans 2001);
- *Important Bird Areas in Europe: Priority Sites for Conservation* (Heath and Evans 2000);

- *Important Bird Areas of the Tropical Andes,* covers Venezuela, Colombia, Ecuador, Peru, and Bolivia (Boyla and Estrada 2005);
- *Important Bird Areas in Zambia* (Leonard 2005); and
- *Key Sites for Conservation in Cambodia* (2003).

The list of IBAs by country can also be accessed electronically via www.birdlife.org.

Alliance for Zero Extinction Sites. The Alliance for Zero Extinction (AZE) is an alliance of international NGOs, including the World Wildlife Fund, Conservation International, The Nature Conservancy, Wildlife Conservation Society, BirdLife International, American Bird Conservancy, and numerous national-level conservation NGOs. AZE sites are discrete areas where most or all of the population of a critically endangered or endangered animal or plant species occurs (all or part of the year). As such, AZE sites are among the most critical of endangered natural habitats (including forests). Around 700 AZE sites worldwide have been identified; they are listed by country at www.zeroextinction.org. A link to Google Earth became operational in October 2006, which enables users to view the site in reasonable detail on their computers.

Wetlands and Marine Habitats Directories. Wetlands that are likely to qualify as critical natural habitats (including wooded freshwater swamps and mangroves that would qualify as critical forests) are listed and described in several published wetlands directories, including the following

- *Directory of African Wetlands* (Hughes and Hughes 1992);
- *Directory of Asian Wetlands* (Scott 1989); and
- *Directory of Neotropical Wetlands,* covers Latin America and the Caribbean (Scott and Carbonell 1986).

Those wetlands that have been designated as Wetlands of International Importance under the Ramsar Wetlands Convention are listed and mapped in the *Ramsar Sites Directory and Overview* (Wetlands International 2005), available online at www.wetlands.org.

Marine coral reefs (most of which would qualify as critical natural habitats) are covered in *Coral Reefs of the World* (Wells 1988).

National-Level Directories and Databases. Some countries have published lists and descriptions of their critical natural habitats, or broadly comparable areas. A good example is the detailed *Biodiversidade Brasileira* book published by Brazil's Environment Ministry (2002).

High Conservation Value Forests. Note 3.1, Mainstreaming Conservation Considerations into Productive Landscapes, discusses the (optional) planning methodology for designating High Conservation Value Forests (HCVFs). According to the HCVF Toolkit (available online at www.hcvf.org), HCVFs are those forests considered to be "of outstanding significance or critical importance," according to six High Conservation Value (HCV) criteria. Three of these six criteria (HCV 1, 3, and 6) correspond very closely to the above-mentioned OP 4.36 criteria for critical forests. Thus, forests designated as HCVFs under the HCVF methodology are likely to also qualify as critical forests under the Forests Policy. Moreover, if their selection as HCVFs was made according to HCV criteria 1, 3, or 6, then they would almost certainly qualify as critical forests under OP 4.36. As noted in Note 3.1, while many HCVFs are likely to be placed under strict protection, some HCVFs may be subject to limited timber harvesting or other direct resource uses—so long as the particular HCVs that are characteristic of those forests would be maintained or enhanced, and not degraded or lost. This is consistent with OPs 4.36 and 4.04, which do not prohibit natural resource utilization within critical forests or other critical natural habitats—only their conversion or degradation (as defined above).

PROTECTING FORESTS THROUGH CONSERVATION OFFSETS

The Forests and Natural Habitats policies require, under some circumstances, the establishment or strengthening of ecologically similar protected areas to compensate for, or "offset," the project-related conversion or degradation of noncritical forests and other natural habitats. Conservation offsets can be a valuable tool to leverage the funds from infrastructure or other large-scale development projects (that convert noncritical forests or other natural habitats) to achieve "win-win" outcomes that represent net gains from a conservation standpoint. Compensatory protected areas provide an opportunity to turn a negative project feature (natural habitat loss) into something environmentally positive (new or strengthened protected areas). In response to this requirement of the Forests and Natural Habitats policies, some important forested areas are being effectively conserved—whereas, without the project, they would have remained unprotected and vulnerable to loss or damage from other, often imminent, threats. Through the prudent

application of conservation offsets, many potentially controversial development projects can yield significant net environmental benefits and even turn some, though not all, NGO project opponents into supporters.

One recent example of a large-scale conservation offset supported by the World Bank is the extensive and biologically valuable Nakai-Nam Theun National Protected Area in the Lao People's Democratic Republic, which is receiving much needed on-the-ground support for its protection and management as an offset for the inundation of a much smaller, and generally less ecologically valuable, forested area by the Nam Theun II hydroelectric dam. The protected area was set up after the World Bank worked with the government to develop a law that established a national protected areas system and included the Nakai-Nam Theun National Protected Area by reference through government decree.

When protected areas are established or strengthened to compensate for the loss or degradation of noncritical forests or other natural habitats, the funding for these compensatory areas should come from the same project causing the conversion or degradation. The Global Environment Facility (GEF) does not fund activities intended to mitigate or compensate for the environmental damage from IBRD- or IDA-supported projects. However, the GEF will support biodiversity-related or other qualified environmental enhancement activities (including protected areas), if these clearly go above and beyond the project mitigation required by national laws and World Bank safeguards policies.

Under the Forests and Natural Habitats policies, compensatory protected areas should be ecologically similar to, and ideally no smaller than, the forest or other natural habitat area that is converted or degraded under the overall project. However, it is acceptable (and desirable) to conserve as an offset an area that is ecologically somewhat different, if it is of greater conservation value. For example, under Brazil's Ceara Integrated Water Resources Management Project, the flooding of some relatively common dry forest with water supply reservoirs was compensated for with support for improved conservation of several moist forest areas (of higher conservation priority) in the Sierra de Baturite and Chapada da Araripe.

See box 9.19 for an indicative list of the main steps involved in creating new protected areas (regardless of whether they serve as conservation offsets). Among the basic issues to consider in the establishment or strengthening of protected areas as conservation offsets are the following:

- *Fundamentals of protected area components.* If they are to be more than empty promises, components involving compensatory protected areas (or virtually any other environmental mitigation measures) all need, before appraisal, (i) an implementation schedule; (ii) a clear division of institutional responsibilities; (iii) an itemized budget; (iv) an identified source of funds, for investment as well as recurrent costs; and (v) the legal framework to support the establishment and protected status of the area.

■ *Interinstitutional coordination.* In most infrastructure projects with natural habitats components, the institution in charge of protected areas is different from the executing agency for the main civil works. The protected

areas component should be implemented as soon as possible in relation to the main civil works, to ensure that (i) the conservation area is fully implemented within the life of the project and (ii) the main civil works do not damage (directly or indirectly) the conservation area before key protection and management measures are in place.

■ *Multiple uses of protected areas.* Most protected areas allow various kinds of direct human uses. Different categories of protected areas allow different types of nonconsumptive, and sometimes consumptive, uses of natural resources.[2] Protected areas should typically have a

---

Box 9.19   Typical Procedures for Establishing New Protected Areas

Phase I: Verifying the Feasibility of Establishing a Protected Area

1. *Documenting the conservation value.* This ecological evaluation (or similarly named) report should verify that the proposed protected area is (i) of high conservation value for biodiversity or other environmental criteria (fishery habitat, flood protection, or the like); and (ii) if a conservation offset area, ecologically similar to, or of even greater conservation value than, the area that would be lost or degraded under the overall project.

2. *Documenting land tenure, use, and occupation.* This land tenure and socioeconomic report should indicate (i) who owns all the land comprising the potential protected area, (ii) who has any concessions or use rights, and (iii) who is currently occupying or using the land (even if they lack legal rights).

Phase II: Choosing the Boundaries and Management Category of the Protected Area

3. The two reports produced during Phase I determines whether a protected area is feasible. If the protected area is feasible, the ecological evaluation and land tenure and socioeconomic reports are used to decide, in consultation with local residents, conservation NGOs, and other key stakeholders, (i) the precise boundaries (shown on a map) and (ii) the official management category of the new protected area.

Phase III: Legal Establishment of the Protected Area

4. A decree (executive order) or law is approved to establish the new protected area. The decree or law

should specify the precise boundaries and official management category of the protected area.

Phase IV: On-the-Ground Implementation of the Protected Area

5. *Physical demarcation.* The protected area boundaries are marked in the field, using signs, concrete monuments, cleared paths, or fences (as appropriate).

6. *Basic infrastructure and equipment.* Much of this should be provided during the first year of protected area implementation and itemized in the first Annual Operating Plan (AOP), which should be finalized before the first year.

7. *Protected area staff.* The needed personnel (including government employees, contracted local people, NGO staff, volunteers, and other) should be specified in each year's AOP, as well as in the management plan.

8. *Management plan.* Normally, the terms of reference for producing the management plan should be prepared before the first year, and the plan itself should be prepared during the first year (with ample stakeholder consultation) and implemented in subsequent years. The management plan should ideally be viewed as a living document, subject to revision from time to time.

9. *Recurrent cost funding.* The commitment of a government agency or NGO to provide long-term funding for the recurrent costs of protected area management (mostly salaries and fuel) should be secured at the earliest possible date.

Source: Edec 2006.

a. A law may be preferred because in many countries, while a law may take more time and expense to prepare, it may also be more difficult to reverse than a decree.

management plan—prepared in a participatory manner with all major stakeholders—that specifies which activities are allowed, in which zones.

- *Land tenure.* In general, new protected areas are easiest to establish on public (state-owned) lands. Under the right conditions, protected areas can also be established on communally owned indigenous lands, or on large individual landholdings (with legal safeguards to ensure long-term management and recognition of Indigenous Peoples and other community rights). The World Bank Financing OP 6.00 (approved in April 2004) authorizes the use of IBRD and IDA funds for land acquisition for a wide range of project purposes, including protected area establishment and consolidation. For details, see the "Guidance Note on World Bank Financing of Land Acquisition for Protected Areas," an internal World Bank document available from the Operations Policy and Country Services intranet site http://opcs.worldbank.org/eligibility/1guide.html.

- *Social safeguards.* World Bank–supported protected areas need to be established and strengthened in a manner consistent with the Indigenous Peoples OP 4.10 and the Involuntary Resettlement OP 4.12 (see chapters 8 and 12 for a brief summary of their requirements).

NOTES

1. The environmental classification of any investment project should be justified and explained in the ISDS and PAD.

2. The World Conservation Network (IUCN) protected area categories are a standardized classification system for similar types of protected areas that may have very different names in different countries. For example, a "forest reserve" in one country may mean an area of strict preservation (Category I), while in another it might mean a production forest suitable for commercial logging (Category VI). The IUCN categories relevant to the Natural Habitats OP 4.04 and Forests OP 4.36 are as follows: I: Strict Nature Reserve/Wilderness Area (protected area managed for science or wilderness protection); II: National Park (protected area managed mainly for ecosystem protection and recreation); III: Natural Monument (protected area managed mainly for conservation of specific natural features); IV: Habitat/Species Management Area (protected area managed mainly for conservation through management intervention); V: Protected Landscape/Seascape (protected area managed mainly for landscape/seascape conservation and recreation); and VI: Managed Resource Protected Area (protected area managed mainly for the sustainable use of natural ecosystems).

SELECTED READINGS

Angehr, G. 2003. *Directory of Important Bird Areas in Panama/Áreas Importantes para Aves en Panamá.* Panama Audubon Society.

Aves Argentijas. 2005. *Áreas Importantes para la Conservación de las Aves en Argentina.* Buenos Aires: Aves Argentinas.

Boyla, K., and A. Estrada. 2005. *Important Bird Areas of the Tropical Andes.* Cambridge: Birdlife International.

CIPAMEX (Sección Mexicana del Consejo Internacional para la Preservación de las Aves. 2000. *Áreas Importantes para la Conservación de las Aves en México.* Hidalgo, Mexico: CIPAMEX.

Environment Ministry of Brazil. 2002. *Biodiversidade Brasileira.* Brasília, Brazil.

Fishpool, L. D. C., and M. I. Evans. 2001. *Important Bird Areas in Africa and Associated Islands: Priority Sites for Conservation.* Newbury and Cambridge: Pisces Publications and BirdLife International.

Heath, M. F., M. I. Evans, and D. G. Hoccom. 2000. *Important Bird Areas in Europe: Priority Sites for Conservation.* Cambridge: BirdLife International.

Hughes, R. H., and J. S. Hughes. 1992. *Directory of African Wetlands.* Gland, Switzerland: IUCN.

Kelleher, G., C. Bleakley, and S. Wells. 1995. *A Global Representative System of Marine Protected Areas.* Four volumes. Washington, DC: Great Barrier Reef Marine Park Authority, World Bank, and IUCN.

Leonard, P. 2005. *Important Bird Areas in Zambia.* Lusaka, Zambia: Zambian Ornithological Society.

MacKinnon, J. R. 1997. *Protected Areas Systems Review of the Indo-Malayan Realm.* World Conservation Monitoring Centre: Cambridge.

Scott, D. A. 1989. *Directory of Asian Wetlands.* Gland, Switzerland: IUCN.

Scott, D. A., and M. Carbonell. 1986. *Directory of Neotropical Wetlands.* Gland, Switzerland: IUCN.

Wells, S. M. 1988. *Coral Reefs of the World.* Gland, Switzerland: IUCN.

Wetlands International. 2005. *Ramsar Sites Directory and Overview.* Wageningen, The Netherlands: Wetlands International.

World Bank. "Critical Natural Habitats in Latin America and the Caribbean." Unpublished. Latin America and Caribbean Environment Unit, World Bank, Washington, DC.

World Conservation Monitoring Centre. 1993. *Ecologically Sensitive Sites in Africa.* Seven volumes. Washington, DC: World Bank.

REFERENCES CITED

Edec, G. 2006. "Safeguards and Due Diligence in Forest Activities." Note submitted to World Bank as input to *Forests Sourcebook.* Unpublished. World Bank, Washington, DC.

World Bank. n.d. Environmental Sourcebook and Updates. http://go.worldbank.org/LLF3CMS1I0.

————. 2003a. Kazakhstan Forest Protection and Rehabilitation Project (P078301). PHRD Grant, Suggested Draft Terms of Reference, Component D: Economic and Financial Analysis. Internal document. World Bank, Washington, DC.

————. 2003b. Bosnia and Herzogovina—Forest Development and Conservation Project (P079161). Environmental Management Plan (EMP) Framework, Draft Contract. Internal document. World Bank, Washington, DC.

————. 2005a. Jharkhand Participatory Forest Management Project (P077192). Draft TORs for Social Assessment. Internal document. World Bank, Washington, DC.

————. 2005b. Bosnia and Herzogovina—Forest Development and Conservation Project (P079161). Development of Standard Procedures for a Comprehensive Consultation Process, Social Assessment, Process Framework, Participation Plan, and Operational Sourcebook. Draft Contract. Internal document. World Bank, Washington, DC.

————. 2006. Western Kenya Community–Criven Development & Flood Mitigation Project. (P074106). Consultancy on Formulation of Environmental and Social Management Framework Draft contract. Internal document. World Bank, Washington, DC.

CHAPTER 10

Consultation and Communication in Forest Sector Activities

Forests are the meeting point for the diverse interests of a wide variety of stakeholders. For the private sector, forests are a lucrative source of income and opportunity for investment. For the state, forests are a source of revenue and power. For forest-dependent households, the resource base is an important element of the household portfolio. For conservation entities, forests are repositories of biological diversity and critical habitat or ecosystems. This makes forest sector projects complex and multifaceted. The projects potentially have issues of conflicting vested interests, states unwilling to relinquish control of the resource, livelihood issues involving local forest uses and indigenous groups, as well as problems of illegal extraction and much more.

Consultation and communication in forest sector projects are important to build coalitions, manage risk, create transparency, and formalize mechanisms for participation and responses to stakeholder concerns. Consultation enables the involvement of indigenous groups and other marginalized and vulnerable groups (including women and youth). A well-designed communications strategy facilitates transparency while contributing to the long-term sustainability of a project. The two strategies are intertwined. Consultation requires communication and communication enhances and is reinforced by consultation.

The first section of this chapter addresses consultation in forest sector projects. The second section addresses communication. Although there are times when consultation and communication may be stand-alone components of a project, they are generally part of an integrated approach in which safeguards play a critical role (see chapter 9, Applying Forests Policy OP 4.36). Furthermore, the terms of reference (TOR) provided in chapter 9 may be helpful in developing consultation and communication approaches. Chapter 12 describes the additional requirements when Indigenous Peoples are affected, including the need for free, prior, and informed consultations with affected communities leading to their broad support for the project.

CONSULTATION

In this chapter, consultation refers to the inclusion of all representative groups of stakeholders. Another form of consultation is consultation among donors—sharing information and harmonizing projects. Though consultation among donors is an important part of a successful project, it is not addressed here.

Consultation with stakeholders in forest sector projects is not just a requirement—it is a strategic tool. Consultation creates opportunities to identify key issues that, if left undetected, can threaten the long-term success of a project. Consultation helps project teams, donors, government agencies, and project beneficiaries elaborate on and understand realities at the site. Consultations are opportunities for project designers to capture and build upon local knowledge by involving stakeholders in the design of the project. Furthermore, consultation is a way to ensure that indigenous and other vulnerable groups are involved in projects, and to ensure that equity issues are addressed.

The complex and multifaceted nature of forest sector projects can make them risky. Forest sector projects often have to address such issues as local access to the resource, the rights of indigenous groups, and other related livelihood issues. In such cases, consultation offers a means to manage these risks by creating transparency and clearly representing the approach and objectives of a project. Through proper consultation, stakeholders can be involved in project design, generating local commitment to the process and project. Stakeholders have a means to express concerns constructively, and an opportunity to help design solutions (box 10.1). In short, consultation builds a coalition (see box 10.2).

The benefits of consultation are not without costs, both human and monetary. Consultation requires trained personnel and takes time. The time and budgetary constraints can be managed with proper planning. Because the consul-

tation process and the project design should be shaped by and respond to stakeholder concerns, the consultation process can and should be flexible. The benefits of consultation far outweigh the costs, in spite of the additional planning and accommodation that consultation requires.

CONSULTATION WITH WHOM? No successful consultation can take place without first identifying key stakeholders. Stakeholders are individuals or groups directly affected, indirectly affected, or with an interest in the project. Though deceptively simple sounding, stakeholder identification is an essential step, and many long-term problems can be averted by identifying and including all key groups.

Once stakeholders have been identified, the next step is to undertake a stakeholder analysis (see chapter 9, Applying Forests Policy OP 4.36). This process groups stakeholders into categories on the basis of their relationship to the project (policy makers, potentially adversely affected people, Indigenous Peoples or tribal organizations, donor agencies,

---

Box 10.1   Liberia Forest Initiative: A Strategic Partnership that Enables Consultation

"Strategic communications and civil society consultations can help manage risks."
—Communications Officer,
External Affairs, Communication, and Network
Anchor (EXTCN)

The Liberia Forest Initiative (LFI) is a partnership of government and international organizations and NGOs to support the rehabilitation and reform of Liberia's forest sector and enhance cooperation and coordination of activities in Liberia for the promotion of sustainable forest management. Liberia is a post-conflict nation with many forest resources. These forest resources are in high demand to serve the nation's economic growth through a process that accounts for community rights and equitably addresses distribution and environmental issues.

Actions in Liberia are under close scrutiny by national and international groups because there is a great deal at stake. In the recent past, an international NGO wrote a letter to the Forest Development Authority (FDA) of Liberia, a member of the LFI, expressing concern that the draft National Forestry Reform Law of 2006 failed "to adequately address the important issues of community rights and participation in decision making, forest management, and land tenure."

Source: Adapted by author.

The managing director of the FDA prepared a response highlighting how the LFI has helped in making the process highly consultative. "We, too, are extremely concerned about these issues, and as a result we have been studying and debating them since the debut of this legal reform process in 2003... Currently, all actors involved in the forest sector reform process have been diligently working in a collaborative fashion to achieve this objective, and we strongly believe that the content of the draft law provides a far greater recognition of community rights and many more formal avenues for participation of communities in decision making about the use of Liberia's forest resources than ever encountered in this nation's history."

Having the structure of the LFI in place allowed the international parties and the government to handle this situation in a constructive manner that did not escalate or paralyze the project. The framework for consultation was already in place. The LFI provided a place for outside parties to express concerns and a venue for response—thus assuaging fears and creating transparency. Ultimately, the external party was offered the opportunity of continued involvement and was folded into the project.

Meaningful public consultation typically takes place at three different levels: conveying information to the public, listening to the opinions and preferences of the public, and involving the public in making decisions. The nature and size of the project, combined with both the nature and number of stakeholders and the status of national legislation, will largely define when, where, and what level of public consultation is required for an Environmental Assessment (EA) and its Environmental Management Plan.

For instance, if the aim is to inform the public about a project or important issues, the initial number of people to contact will be large, but the interaction may be limited. If public preferences are being sought, closer contact and dialogue will be required, but with a smaller number of people. If the public's direct input to decision making is being sought, ongoing discussions with a small group of representatives of stakeholder groups will likely be held. Site-specific factors, such as a history of local opposition to similar projects in the area, will also be important in determining the level of consultations.

Source: World Bank 1999.

media, NGOs, other interest groups, and so forth) (see box 10.3). For each category of stakeholders, three categories of information should be developed:

- *Defining characteristics,* including social dimensions, organizational strength, formal or informal power and authority, organizational capacity, and so forth.
- *Stake or interest in the project,* and the stakeholders' potential support or opposition to the project. This may include degree of commitment to the status quo, openness to change, and an assessment of whether the proposed project is aligned with the interests of the concerned stakeholders.
- *Influence* of each stakeholder group, and whether potential opposition from each of them—and the groups collectively—constitutes a high, substantial, medium, or low risk to the project outcomes.

WHAT IS A GOOD CONSULTATION PROCESS? A good consultation process is one that is carefully planned, with clear goals

and responsibilities agreed to by all institutions involved. The sequence of consultation steps should be well-planned from the beginning; public consultation should begin—where possible—before major decisions are made. Each stage of the project may require different consultation measures (see table 10.1). The scope of the consultation should also be appropriate to the project. For example, long-term projects involving diverse stakeholders may require consultation processes specific to each stakeholder group and repeated consultations during the course of the project.

Ultimately, a project's success depends on stakeholders understanding the project's purpose and committing to a plan for its success. Appropriate goals will vary by project and by phase within a project. For example, during the site selection phase of a protected area establishment, the goal might be to identify the concerns of local stakeholder groups regarding potential sites. During the implementation phase, consultation could contribute to identifying potential mitigation approaches to the challenges associated with implementation (see table 10.1 for a summary of consultation objectives at different project phases).

To ensure positive outcomes, responsibilities must be clearly defined and agreed to by all implementing institutions—whether international, national, or local. The consultation plan should clearly delineate who is responsible for particular monitoring and evaluation exercises, as well as for specific outputs.

To produce effective results, good consultation requires the provision of adequate resources before embarking on a project activity. Planning—skills required, scope, and level of consultation—should fit the budget. Budget constraints can lead to the temptation to conduct insufficient or cursory consultation, but inattention to stakeholder concerns can threaten the success of a project.

Furthermore, a successful project is sensitive to local issues. It builds upon existing networks (for instance, donor coordination groups or forest user groups). It identifies latent conflicts and deals with them proactively (see boxes 10.3 and 10.4). The consultation process should be designed to accommodate both national laws and international conventions. It should also consider site-specific sensitivities; for example, political and cultural issues like ethnic prejudice or restrictions on women, as well as geography, can have an impact on the process, so plans must be made accordingly. Values, particularly those of minorities, such as Indigenous Peoples, sometimes conflict with national ones (see box 10.5). For example, national desire for foreign exchange from timber sales can be at odds with use of forest resources for equitable improvement of local livelihood or sociocultu-

"Listen to your critics and learn from them."
—Communications Officer, EXTCN

Lessons can be drawn regarding the importance of consultation and a clear communications strategy from the World Bank project in Cambodia on forest concession management that started in 2000. The project focused on (i) forest concession planning and inventory, (ii) forest concession control, (iii) forest crime monitoring and prevention, and (iv) project management and institutional strengthening. An inspection panel case on this project identified some shortcomings—including overlapping claims on timber and resin trees, lack of effective concessionaire controls over subcontractors, and restriction of access to livelihood resources—and provided some guidance on how these could have been addressed. These lessons are useful for projects with complex natural resource management issues.

Shared Vision and Engagement with Other Stakeholders
- In projects that address national resource management issues, it is important to map stakeholders' varying and, at times, conflicting interests and engage them early and throughout implementation.
- Advisory groups could be useful for ongoing feedback and guidance.
- Interactions with stakeholders should be managed

with great care—ensuring expectations are clear, materials are available early and in an appropriate format, neutral facilitators are employed if necessary, and existing mechanisms such as technical working groups are used for ongoing dialogue with a range of stakeholders.

Role of Local Communities, Including Consultations with Affected Communities
- The World Bank should play a proactive role in encouraging early and sustained involvement of local communities in project design and implementation.
- Many crucial issues can be more effectively addressed at an earlier stage, thus lowering tensions and apprehensions on all sides and speeding the process of reform.
- When project implementation involves community consultation, the World Bank should work with the implementing agency to ensure appropriate identification of affected communities, the associated area of impact, and appropriate third parties (free from conflict of interest) to carry out environmental and social impact assessments.
- Mechanisms for monitoring compliance with planned consultation procedures should also be agreed upon in advance, and results of monitoring efforts should be made publicly available.

Source: Adapted from IBRD and IDA 2006.

ral purposes. Where values conflict, the objective of the consultation process is for stakeholders to exchange information and perspectives and identify compromises.

PLANNING TASKS. Finally, there are some commonalities for successful consultation. Though every project will be unique in its needs, many (if not all) of these planning tasks will apply[1]:

- *Identify stakeholder groups* (see above).
- *Identify the key consultation issues.* One of the first critical steps is to identify the key issues around which the consultation will be oriented. Environmental and social issues, such as indigenous groups, resettlement, and spiritual uses of forests, often prove important.
- *Understand the decision-making process.* Next, understanding how environmental decisions are made is essen-

tial. Who makes which decisions at what point in the project cycle?
- *Determine the appropriate level of consultation.* (See box 10.2.) Consultation can occur at three different levels: conveying information to stakeholders, listening to stakeholder opinions, and involving stakeholders in decision making. How much consultation and at which level it should occur will depend on the scope and size of the project.
- *Identify timing for consultation.* Consultation before major decisions is essential. Consultation as part of research, planning, and development of mitigation plans is better. For the specific purposes of an EA, consultation is required at a minimum after an EA category has been assigned, and once a draft EA has been prepared.
- *Choose consultation techniques.* In general, it is essential to maintain good communication in consultations. Target

"Planning an effective consultation up front is easier than trying to 'catch up' or fix situations later."
—Lead Forestry Specialist, Africa Region.

Forests are ubiquitous in the Democratic Republic of Congo; they touch the cultural and economic life of most of the population and have enormous global environmental significance. After years of conflicts and mismanagement, reconstruction is critical to improving living conditions and consolidating peace. At the same time, better roads and trade bring risks—threatening forests and biodiversity by facilitating logging, land conversion, and the seizure of forest rights by vested interests. Anticipating these threats, in 2002, the transitional government started a priority reform agenda. This was a politically charged agenda with supporting and opposing views.

Source: Adapted from Debroux and others 2007.

A recent analysis assessing the soundness of the priority reform agenda provided a vehicle for strengthening the relationship among groups that previously opposed one another. The study involved a consultative process to sharpen the analysis and test consensus on initial conclusions. The process also included consultations with government, national and international NGOs, industry, forest people, and donors. Field visits and meetings with local groups took place in September 2003 in Equateur province, in February 2004 in Eastern province, and in December 2005 in North Kivu. This study also benefited from a number of thematic workshops and from two International Forest Forums held in Kinshasa in November 2004 and February 2006. The overall process improved the working relationship among more than 10 partners.

---

groups must be clearly notified about collaboration opportunities. Extensive records of consultation events should be kept. Feedback should be provided to the public, clearly explaining project responses to their concerns (see box 10.6) The most effective consultation plan will likely use a range of listening techniques, a variety of methods for involving stakeholders in decision making, as well as several methods of conveying information (see tables 10.2 and 10.3). (For more information about techniques, see World Bank 1999).

- *Develop a budget.* Consultation is not without costs, and it is important that the consultation budget reflect the size and scope of the consultation plan (see box 10.7).

- *Define a communication methodology* (see next section of this chapter).

COMMUNICATION

Development of a comprehensive communications strategy is essential to the long-term success of a project. Clear communications are especially important in challenging governance environments because they create transparency. Consistent, open communication is instrumental in developing the public and political support required for the long-term success of a project. Furthermore, communication is important in every phase of a successful project: initiating, planning, and presenting results. Communication and consultation are tools that work hand-in-hand to build strong,

effective projects—consultation is one form of instigating communication and communication is an important outcome of consultation.

Communication is a term that incorporates information dissemination, dialogue, transparency, feedback, responsiveness, and engagement. Communication requirements can be broadly classified into external and internal needs. External needs involve engagement with the media, political leaders, and civil society to build trust, credibility, reputation, and support for the program. Internal needs involve communication directed at clients, stakeholders, or partners to generate understanding, participation, or ownership of the program (see box 10.6). Internal and external communication needs are mutually reinforcing: transparent, clear, open communication will help win political and civil society support, and a broad alliance will help to increase the effectiveness of a project and its ability to reach stakeholders.

WHAT IS A GOOD COMMUNICATIONS STRATEGY? In the interest of cohesion and transparency, the entire project team should discuss and eventually agree to the communication plan. The communications strategy should encompass and maintain oversight of all aspects of communications contained in the project—everything from speeches by government officials, to the information given to local people by local representatives of agencies responsible for investment in, and operation of, the development program. If this comprehensive aspect fails, disconnected communications

"The underlying issue was not actually the World Bank policy, but rather a local conflict."

—Retired Senior Social Specialist

All over the world, Indigenous Peoples and ethnic minorities have historically been pushed out of fertile flood plains into mountains and interfluvial areas where forests remain intact. Here they developed balanced and stable adaptations to forest environments, using resources in a relatively conservative fashion. Today, roads, globalized markets, and demand for timber, crop, and grazing land have pushed deep into forested areas and threaten the lifestyles of forest dwellers. At the same time, ethnic minorities—such as the Montagnards of Southeast Asia, the Pygmies of the Democratic Republic of Congo, many Indigenous Peoples of Brazil and the eastern Andes, and the Mayans and other Indigenous Peoples of Mexico and Central America—are undergoing economic and political awakening. International instruments such as the International Labour Organization Convention 169, the United Nations Declaration on the Rights of Indigenous Peoples, and the World Bank Safeguard Policies, have helped strengthen the rights of Indigenous Peoples and have created tools they can use to push the envelope with regard to their rights to land and resources. That said, local laws, regulations, and political processes are still the preponderant influences on how well Indigenous Peoples and other minorities fare in the defense of territorial and other rights.

This picture changes somewhat when a multilateral actor like the World Bank comes on the scene as the financier of a development project. World Bank projects in forested areas may have different objectives, but usually they are aimed at raising incomes, helping secure land rights, and ensuring sustainable resource use. World Bank intervention carries the relatively new international charter of indigenous and minority rights. Indigenous Peoples and the organizations that support them are aware of this and use the policies of multinational organizations as leverage in their struggles for control over their land and resources. Often, however, the picture is more complex. Local conflict may not be articulated simply in terms of "the developers versus the natives." Other issues may underlie the complaint, such as local political conflicts in the form of electoral politics, and intercommunity, interethnic, and even interpersonal rivalries and conflicts.

Indigenous Peoples often claim to occupy a higher moral ground as the primeval defenders of a pristine environment against the depredations of developers. These claims are powerful in national and international discourse on the use of forests, creating a strong bias in favor of the stands taken by Indigenous Peoples.

To comprehensively address concerns of Indigenous Peoples and preempt any local conflicts that may be manifested as a result of a forest project, it is important to do the following:

- Be aware of the *geographic and political context of Indigenous Peoples and minorities* in areas affected by a project. Pay attention to surrounding areas as well.
- Be familiar with the *legal framework,* especially in regard to rights to land and resources and help ensure compliance with these rights.
- Identify the *conflicts that exist in the project area,* being familiar with the actors and their political links. Upon becoming aware of a conflict or a potential conflict, be proactive in addressing it, even if it is not directly related to the project. This is the proverbial "ounce of prevention."
- Consider how the project's *interventions may create winners and losers* especially with regard to entitlements. Does it shift the balance?
- Try to ensure that *all legitimate representatives of Indigenous Peoples are included in consultations;* listen for sometimes poorly articulated demands and complaints, even if they do not appear to be related to the project. Keep in mind that "legitimacy" is a slippery concept and the task managers and their counterparts may not be the best judges of who legitimately speaks for a given group or faction.
- *Avoid consultants who give broad legal and historical surveys* and descriptive ethnographic tours but fail to describe the dynamics of what is happening on the ground.
- Read the consultant's report, question him or her closely, and insist on a *full account of conflicts that may be occurring or may be latent.*
- Seek the right balance between people-oriented and ecosystem-oriented solutions.
- *Write it all down;* capture the above points in the Project Appraisal Document and safeguard compliance documents.

Source: Gross 2007 (Daniel), consultant and former World Bank social safeguards specialist.

Communications methods should be transparent and open to review. Some general principles for achieving transparency and openness include notification, record keeping, and feedback.

NOTIFICATION. The target groups must be notified how, when, and where they can participate. In general, effective notification is highly visible to the target audience, delivered early, uses more than one medium to reach the target groups, and is repeated shortly before major events.

RECORD KEEPING. A record of the types of consultation activities held, the target groups and numbers reached, the information conveyed, and the stage at which the information was provided should be kept and analyzed to reveal

Source: World Bank 1999.

- summaries of views by type of stakeholder;
- a summary of points of agreement, disagreement, issues raised, and options discussed;
- analysis of the validity of the concerns and issues raised by different stakeholders;
- recommended responses to valid comments; and
- discussion of the implications and options for decision makers.

FEEDBACK. Feedback should be provided to the public, clearly explaining the responses to their concerns, describing the decisions made, why they were made, and how the information they provided was used. Otherwise, participants may feel that their input had no impact on the decision; some of the benefits of the process may be lost, and effective consultation may become more difficult in the future.

Providing adequate resources for a successful consultation depends on the complexity of the project, the diversity of the stakeholders, and the importance of the effects, as well as such constraints as the availability of skilled practitioners, availability of funds, and project deadlines. The principal cost elements vary widely according to the context of the project, but are likely to include some of the following:

- consultants' fees
- hiring and outfitting of meeting venues
- Public opinion surveys
- preparation and distribution of materials
- staff time preparing, attending, and keeping records of public meetings
- maintenance of channels of communication (telephone hotline, radio announcements, or other means)
- travel expenses

Source: World Bank 1999.

activities will, at best, fail to be of the highest possible quality and, at worst, cause confusion or mixed messages, undermining the effectiveness of the communications strategy (see World Bank 2005).

A successful communications strategy is based on research. As a first step, a team should undertake a comprehensive review of communications lessons learned from other programs in the country, as well as from relevant natural resource management projects in other countries. Information about stakeholder knowledge, attitudes, and practices informs the formulation of an effective communications plan. Further information about the link between communications, political analysis, and operational decisions is important to ensure that communication is a two-way street. Furthermore, expertise of outside consultants may be required when communications needs extend beyond skills available in-house (for example, reaching international mass media outlets, or generating video footage). Finally, an ideal communications strategy is developed in collaboration with stakeholders, perhaps through a workshop in which researchers summarize findings and stakeholders help to determine how to communicate them.

Though every project will be unique in its needs, a communications strategy and work plan comprises these planning tasks:

Table 10.1   Consultation at Various Stages of an Environmental Assessment Project

Stage in EA process	Consultation goals	Strategic consideration
Validation of environmental procedures and standards	Review national law and practice relating to consultation Ensure compatibility with World Bank requirements	Is there a need? Are there opportunities for capacity building?
Screening: Assign an EA category	Identify stakeholder groups; secure proponent commitment to consultation program Agree on extent and mode of consultation	Is there a commitment to consultation from project proponents and the relevant authority?
Scoping: Agree on EA TOR and schedule	Identify stakeholders Disclose relevant project information Determine stakeholder concerns and include them in the TOR	What resources are needed and available? Who is responsible for implementation and monitoring and evaluation? Are there potential conflicts between the needs of the developer and those of the public?
Environmental analysis and production of draft EA reports (including social assessment and resettlement plan, as appropriate)	Disclose information on study methods and findings Agree on proposed mitigation measures with stakeholders Let stakeholders determine whether their concerns are adequately addressed	What methods are appropriate for reaching different stakeholder groups?
Production of final report	Finalize mitigation plan and disclose to stakeholders	Are mechanisms in place to ensure ongoing consultation and compliance with agreements?
Implement the Environmental Management Plan (including environmental monitoring)	Inform the public about scheduling of potentially disruptive events Disclose results of environmental monitoring Maintain effective complaints procedures	What role can stakeholders play in monitoring?
Final evaluation	Assess effective consultation process Consult stakeholders for their assessment	Were any lessons learned that might be transferable to other projects?

Source: World Bank 1999: 2.

Note: This table, extensively abridged, was adapted from the World Bank's *The Public Participation Handbook* (1996), which contains a full version of the table and extensive supporting text describing each tool.

- *Identify goals.* This component should detail issues to be addressed and desired outcomes, as well as the feasibility of those goals. Goals will vary with the scope, size, and phase of projects.
- *Assess target audience.* What motivates them? What are their needs? What are their stakes in the project? This component has obvious overlap with consultation and the results of stakeholder analysis (see consultation section above).
- *Develop key messages.*
  - The *content* will be based on previously identified issues and desired outcomes.
  - The *scope and timing* for the plan will depend on the scale and phase of the project (for worksheets helpful for developing timelines for communication projects, see Module 9 of the World Bank's *Strategic Communication for Development Projects* [Cabañero-Verzosa 2003]).

- *Define roles and accountability.* Clearly establish divisions of responsibility for which tasks will be handled by which agency (see annex 10A to this chapter for a checklist). This may entail an assessment of client capacity for communications tasks and opportunities for capacity building. Specific areas of assessment might include communications planning and management, research, communications material development and production, monitoring and evaluation, liaison work with mass media, and liaison work with large-scale outreach networks. (See Cabañero-Verzosa 2003 for guide questions to assess institutional capacity [module 7] and for a model TOR [module 4].)
- *Identify allies,* barriers, options, and possible risks. This identification could potentially be accomplished with communications planning workshops with stakeholders, using participatory methods.
- *Outline initiatives and tactics for communications plan.*

Table 10.2 Listening to the Public

	Key Points	Advantages	Disadvantages
Survey techniques	• Interviews, formed surveys, polls, and questionnaires can rapidly show who is interested and why. • May be structured (using a fixed questionnaire) or nonstructured. • Experienced interviewers or surveyors familiar with the project should be used. • Pre-test the questions. • Open-ended questions are best.	• Show how groups want to be involved • Allow direct communication with the public • Help access the views of the majority • Are less vulnerable to the influence of vocal groups • Identify concerns linked to social grouping • Give statistically representative results • Can reach people who are not organized in groups	• Poor interviewing is counterproductive • High cost • Requires specialists to deliver and analyze • Tradeoff between openness and statistical validity
Small meetings	• Public seminars or focus groups create formal information exchanges between the sponsor and the public; may consist of randomly selected individuals or target group members; experts may be invited to serve as a resource.	• Allow detailed and focused discussion • Can exchange information and debate • Provide a rapid, low-cost monitor of public mood • Provide a way to reach marginal groups	• Complex to organize and run • Can be diverted by special interest groups • Not objective or statistically valid • May be unduly influenced by moderators
Large meetings	• Public meetings allow the public to respond directly to formal presentations by project sponsors. • Effective meetings need a strong chairman, a clear agenda, and good presenters or resource people.	• Are useful for medium audiences • Allow immediate response and feedback • Acquaint different interest groups	• Not suitable for detailed discussions • Not good for building consensus • Can be diverted by special interest groups • Attendance is difficult to predict
Conferences	• Technical experts and representatives of interest groups may be brought together.	• Impart specialized technical information • Promote data sharing and compromise • Resolve technical issues	• Time and effort needed to prepare • Cost, if experts are hired
Community organizers or advocates	• These work closely with a selected group to facilitate informal contacts, visit homes or work places, or simply be available to the public.	• Mobilize difficult-to-reach groups	• Potential conflicts between employers and clients • Time needed to get feedback

Source: World Bank 1999: 6.

Note: This table, extensively abridged, was adapted from the World Bank's *The Public Participation Handbook* (1996), which contains a full versios of the table and extensive supporting text describing each tool.

Table 10.3 Involving the Public in Decision Making

	Key Points	Advantages	Disadvantages
Advisory groups	*Task forces:* Set up task groups to focus on a single technical issue Define the limit of the group's authority and lifetime; ensure that all interests are represented and that contact with the public is maintained.	• Can address highly technical problems • Help prioritize and reach consensus	• Rarely represents all interested parties • May replace wider consultations • Often focuses too much on procedures
Problem-solving techniques	*Brainstorming:* Designed to enhance creativity and generate ideas quickly Selection of the facilitator and participants is critical.	• Help groups break out of the obvious • Provide insights for decision making	• Difficult to include a full range of views • May yield too many ideas to evaluate
Consensus-building techniques	*Unassisted negotiations, mediation:* Voluntary processes by which representatives of affected organizations make decisions by consensus, to be ratified by parent organizations. Parties either agree on decision-making procedures at the outset or use an experienced mediator.	• Provide a forum for jointly identifying solutions • Puts responsibility on the disputants to identify common ground • Can reach robust agreements with broad support • Can lead to quick resolution of contentious issues	• Not all parties will participate • Parties may drop out before the end • Requires good faith • May take too long • Highly skilled mediators are scarce
Arbitration	A process by which conflicting parties seek a solution through an impartial mediator. It can be binding, by prior agreement, or all sides may reserve judgment until the outcome.	• Provides impartiality from an uninvolved party • Is difficult to oppose the arbitrator's recommendations	• All parties must stand to gain • Difficult to identify an acceptable neutral party

Source: World Bank 1999: 13.

Note: This table, extensively abridged, was adapted from the World Bank's *The Public Participation Handbook* (1996), which contains a full version of the table and extensive supporting text describing each tool.

- *Preliminary research* should include data on how people get their information (newspaper, radio, town caller, and others).
- Tactics should identify *appropriate methods for reaching specific groups or specific locations.* The most effective mode of information delivery may vary from place to place. For example, one project used different strategies to reach male and female stakeholders in Mali. Another broadcast information from a speaker on a moped in Bangladesh—a method that proved more effective than conventional media (see table 10.4).
- In the interest of transparency and effective external communication about the project, a plan should include mechanisms, like press briefings, for *proactive disclosure* of project details and policies to identify and correct misperceptions (see box 10.8).
  - *Assess availability of resources* and other arrangements, including specialist advice and authority.
- *Create a communications implementation plan.* The implementation plan should detail specific events, measures for monitoring and evaluation, indicators, and potentially a training scheme and capacity-building component, as well as a budget and time line (see box 10.9). (For examples of communications plan budgets, see Module 10 of Cabañero-Verzosa (2003)). Plans should include feedback mechanisms for monitoring effectiveness of communications and adjusting as needed. (For indicators, see Module 3 of Cabañero-Verzosa (2003)). The proposed plan should be assessed to determine whether it is appropriate to the stated goals and whether it is feasible, given staffing, funding, and time.

- *Supervision during implementation.* Supervision should assess effectiveness, ensure adequate monitoring of inputs and outcomes, make corrective changes, and allow the plan to adapt to changing conditions. The supervision should involve experts and stakeholders. Key questions to be considered include the following: Are communications activities taking place? Are materials and messages reaching the target audience? Are they having the desired effect?

- *Evaluation.* An evaluation should address accomplishments, lessons learned, future improvements, and should evaluate and monitor results.

Table 10.4 Techniques for Conveying Information

	Key Points	Advantages	Disadvantages
Printed materials	*Information bulletins, brochures, reports:* Text should be simple and nontechnical, in the local language where possible, and relevant to the reader. • Provide clear instructions on how to obtain more information.	• Direct • Can impart detailed information • Cost effective • Yield a permanent record of communication	• Demand specialized skills and resources
Display and exhibits	• Can serve both to inform and to collect comments. • Should be located where the target audience gathers or passes regularly.	• May reach previously unknown parties • Minimal demands on the public	• Costs of preparation and staffing • Insufficient without supporting techniques
Print media	• Newspapers, press releases, and press conferences can all disseminate a large amount and wide variety of information. • Identify newspapers likely to be interested in the project and to reach the target audience.	• Offers both national and local coverage • Can reach most literate adults • Can provide detailed information	• Loss of control of presentation • Media relationships are demanding • Exclude illiterates and the poor
Electronic media	*Television, radio and video:* Determine the coverage (national or local), the types of viewer, the perceived objectivity, and the type of broadcast offered.	• May be considered authoritative • Many people have access to radio	• Time allocated may be limited • Costs can be high
Advertising	• Useful for announcing public meetings or other activities. • Effectiveness depends on good preparation and targeting.	• Retain control of presentation	• May engender suspicion
Formal information sessions	*Targeted briefing:* Can be arranged by project sponsor or by request, for a particular community group, firm, or industry association.	• Useful for groups with specific concerns • Allow detailed discussion of specific issues	• May raise unrealistic expectations
Informal information sessions	*Open house, site visits, field offices:* A selected audience can obtain first-hand information or interact with project staff. • Visits should be supported with more detailed written material or additional briefings or consultations.	• Provide detailed information • Useful for comparing alternatives • Immediate and direct • Useful when the project is complex • Local concerns are communicated to staff • May help reach nonresident stakeholders	• Attendance is difficult to predict, resulting in limited consensus-building value • May demand considerable planning • Field offices can be costly to operate • Only reach a small group of people

Source: World Bank 1999: 10.

Note: This table, extensively abridged, was adapted from the World Bank's *The Public Participation Handbook* (1996), which contains a full version of the table and extensive supporting text describing each tool.

"Transparency is essential."
        —Communications Officer, EXTCN

Strategic communications can help to manage risks in the forestry sector by making information about the project approach, collaborators, decisions, scope, and outcomes available in ways that are accessible and useful to people. This accessible information facilitates two-way communication and empowers local people, the media, parliament, and civil society to be actively engaged in the process and to provide feedback.

To this end, it is essential that a project have a clear, proactive communications strategy. Lessons learned in the World Bank project in Cambodia on forest concession management that started in 2000 (see box 10.3 for project details) provide important conclusions about development of a proactive communications strategy:

- Clear, consistent communications are essential in challenging governance environments.
- Teams should first clarify the formal links among communications, political analysis, and operational decisions to ensure external information and questions are fed back into operational decision making.
- The communications strategy should be discussed and endorsed by the entire project team—and shared with the larger country team.
- The strategy should include a proactive disclosure policy (including press briefings at agreed intervals), mechanisms to promptly identify and correct errors and misperceptions, and plans and resources to translate information into local languages and disseminate it through a variety of media.
- Involvement of communications specialists in project design and implementation will help to ensure effective engagement.

Source: Adapted from World Bank 2006.

Box 10.9   Communications Implementation Plan

The following are elements within a communications implementation plan:

- A *strategic approach defines* (i) the goal(s) identified as feasible and effective in supporting the project's purpose, (ii) the type of response desired, (iii) the target audiences, and (iv) methods (print, mass media, group encounters, interpersonal communications) that will be used.
- A *training scheme* in skills needed to carry out communications activities is critical to the strategy.
- *Monitoring and evaluation activities* are designed for continuous monitoring of communications strategy and activities to provide timely information to improve judgments about action.

- *The capacity-building component* is a plan to provide the infrastructure, staffing, and training on communications strategy development and management. It may investigate organizational systems, work performance indicators, and staff development opportunities that affect the quality of communications work.
- *Budget line items for critical elements* that affect the success of communications activities are needed, including the funding of communications research during the planning phase, as well as adequate funding for mass media dissemination costs and group communications activities.
- *Timelines* that allow for a participatory process of planning, implementing, and monitoring communications activities are necessary.

Source: Cabañero-Verzosa 2003.

ANNEX 10A   CHECKLIST FOR TASK MANAGERS

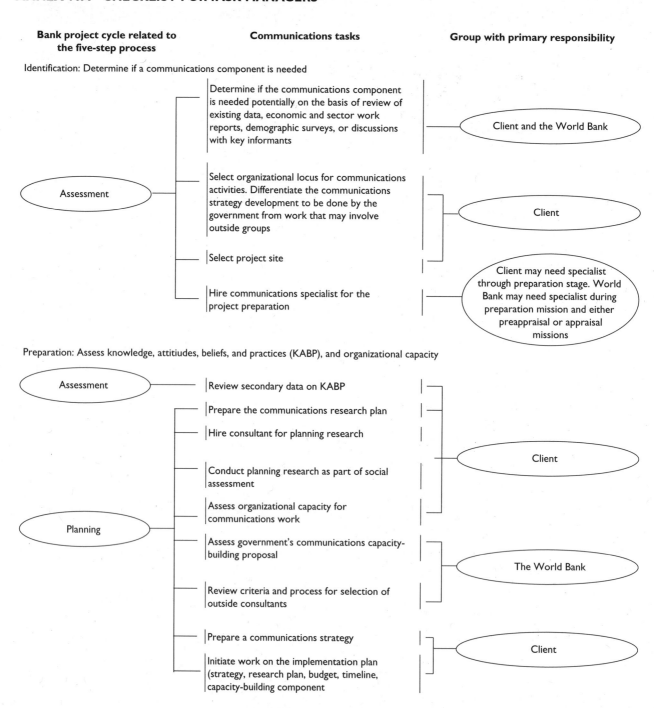

Bank project cycle related to the five-step process   **Communications tasks**   **Group with primary responsibility**

Identification: Determine if a communications component is needed

Assessment

Determine if the communications component is needed potentially on the basis of review of existing data, economic and sector work reports, demographic surveys, or discussions with key informants

Client and the World Bank

Select organizational locus for communications activities. Differentiate the communications strategy development to be done by the government from work that may involve outside groups

Client

Select project site

Hire communications specialist for the project preparation

Client may need specialist through preparation stage. World Bank may need specialist during preparation mission and either preappraisal or appraisal missions

Preparation: Assess knowledge, attitiudes, beliefs, and practices (KABP), and organizational capacity

Assessment

Review secondary data on KABP

Planning

Prepare the communications research plan

Hire consultant for planning research

Conduct planning research as part of social assessment

Assess organizational capacity for communications work

Client

Assess government's communications capacity-building proposal

Review criteria and process for selection of outside consultants

The World Bank

Prepare a communications strategy

Initiate work on the implementation plan (strategy, research plan, budget, timeline, capacity-building component

Client

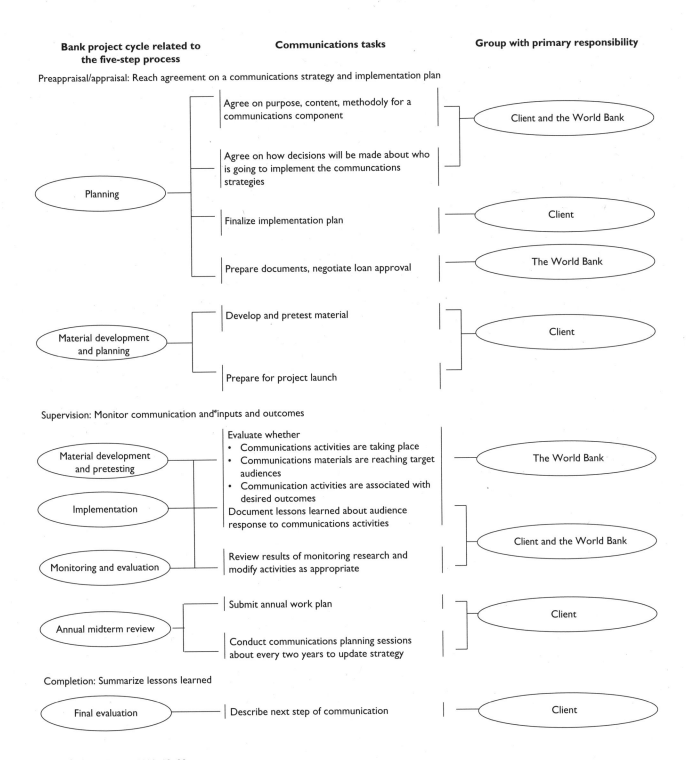

Bank project cycle related to the five-step process | **Communications tasks** | **Group with primary responsibility**

Preappraisal/appraisal: Reach agreement on a communications strategy and implementation plan

Planning
- Agree on purpose, content, methodoly for a communications component
- Agree on how decisions will be made about who is going to implement the communcations strategies

Client and the World Bank

- Finalize implementation plan

Client

- Prepare documents, negotiate loan approval

The World Bank

Material development and planning
- Develop and pretest material
- Prepare for project launch

Client

Supervision: Monitor communication and*inputs and outcomes

Material development and pretesting

Implementation

Evaluate whether
- Communications activities are taking place
- Communications materials are reaching target audiences
- Communication activities are associated with desired outcomes
Document lessons learned about audience response to communications activities

The World Bank

Monitoring and evaluation
- Review results of monitoring research and modify activities as appropriate

Client and the World Bank

Annual midterm review
- Submit annual work plan
- Conduct communications planning sessions about every two years to update strategy

Client

Completion: Summarize lessons learned

Final evaluation
- Describe next step of communication

Client

Source: Cabañero-Verzosa 2003: 19–20.

NOTE

1. For an example specific to environmental assessment that addresses the timing of these planning tasks, see World Bank (1999).

REFERENCES CITED

Cabañero-Verzosa, C. 2003. "Strategic Communication for Development Projects: A Toolkit for Task Team Leaders." World Bank, Washington, DC.

Debroux, L., T. Hart, D. Kaimowitz, A. Karsenty, and G. Topa, eds. 2007. Forests in Post-Conflict Democratic Republic of Congo: Analysis of a Priority Agenda. A joint report by teams of the World Bank, Center for International Forestry Research (CIFOR), *Centre International de Recherche Agronomique pour le Développement* (CIRAD), African Wildlife Foundation (AWF), *Conseil National des ONG de Développement du Congo* (CNONGD), Conservation International (CI), *Groupe de Travail Forêts* (GTF), *Ligue Nationale des Pygmées du Congo* (LINAPYCO), Netherlands Development Organi-sation (SNV), *Réseau des Partenaires pour l'Environnement au Congo* (REPEC), Wildlife Conservation Society (WCS), Woods Hole Research Center (WHRC), World Agroforestry Centre (ICRAF), and World Wide Fund for Nature (WWF). Jakarta: CIFOR.

Gross, D. 2007. Personal communication.

World Bank. 1996. *World Bank Participation Sourcebook.* Washington, DC: World Bank. http://www.worldbank .org/wbi/sourcebook/sbhome.htm.

———. 1999. "Public Consultation in the EA Process: A Strategic Approach." Environmental Assessment Sourcebook Update 26. Environment Department, World Bank, Washington, DC.

———. 2005. Jharkhand Participatory Forest Management Project (P077192). Draft TORs for Social Assessment. Internal document. World Bank, Washington, DC.

———. 2006. "Management Report and Recommendation in Response to the Inspection Panel Investigation Report." Report No. INSP/35556-KH. World Bank, Washington, DC.

Forest Certification Assessment Guide: Summary on Use

Paralleling the growing demand for wood products is the growing demand for the verification of the sustainability of the forest management from which those products are derived. With the introduction of the World Bank's Operational Policy on Forests in 2002 (OP 4.36), the World Bank made its support for commercial harvesting contingent on certification of operations under an acceptable system, with the exception of small-scale landholders and operations under community forest management and joint forest management. Alternatively, support can be provided under the condition of adherence to a time-bound action plan to pursue certification under an acceptable system within a certain time frame. Consequently, assessment of certification systems against World Bank requirements is a necessary step in the project appraisal process for this kind of investment. Assessment of certification systems for compliance with these Bank provisions requires an in-depth analysis of the standards and applied procedures.

In this chapter the available instruments for the assessment of certification systems and the lessons learned so far are described, and the application of time-bound action plans for certification are given consideration. A description of the elements that should be included in the terms of reference (TOR) for the assessment of systems and in the design and evaluation of time-bound action plans are provided in the annexes. This chapter is relevant for other notes in this sourcebook on the identification of high conservation value forests (note 3.1, Mainstreaming Conservation Considera-

tions into Productive Landscapes), which, in some certification systems, forms part of forest certification assessments; and that on plantations (note 3.3, Forest Plantations), as forest certification continues to expand its work to include this sector.

THE WORLD BANK–WORLD WILDLIFE FUND (WWF) FOREST CERTIFICATION ASSESSMENT GUIDE (FCAG): PURPOSE AND CONCEPT

Through an intensive process involving experts in this field and external stakeholders, and in close collaboration with the WWF, the World Bank developed an assessment framework for certification systems that includes elements deemed essential for reliable and independent certification of forest management. It allows for the evaluation of a system's compliance with the World Bank's principles, and can contribute to decisions about whether the system is acceptable in the context of Bank investments.

This section will examine the purpose of this initiative. Additional information on the background and the reasoning behind specific criteria may be obtained from the original document (World Bank–WWF Alliance 2006).

The World Bank–WWF guide for the assessment of forest certification systems was originally conceived to evaluate progress toward achieving the World Bank–WWF Alliance goal of having 200 million hectares of forests independently certified under an acceptable system by 2005. In addition to this, other useful functions of the guide include

- assisting WWF and the World Bank in providing guidance for the development of national standards and advice to governments and companies;
- serving as a diagnostic tool for WWF and the World Bank to identify and target capacity-building efforts to strengthen certification systems; and
- assisting the World Bank in the assessment of forest harvesting operations receiving World Bank investment support under its forests policies.

As a result of these different objectives and the different processes chosen for the development of the underlying principles, the elements of the guide are not entirely aligned with the principles for acceptable certification systems as defined in the OP 4.36 (World Bank 2004). The consequences of this for using the tool in the context of World Bank evaluations are further analyzed below.

In general, certification systems consist of three main components: standard setting, conformity assessment (including certification), and accreditation.[1] In most cases, they also encompass provisions for claims that can be made by certified operations. Specific rules guiding the work of the related bodies are available from the International Organization for Standardization (ISO) (ISO guides 62, 65, or 66 for certification; ISO standard 17011 for accreditation; and ISO guide 59 for standardization) (ISO/IEC 1994, 1996a, 1996b, 1996c, 2004). Further guidance is provided by the International Social and Environmental Accreditation and Labelling (ISEAL; http://www.isealalliance.org) alliance for standard-setting processes in the field of social and environmental standards (ISEAL Alliance 2004). The latter also takes into account relevant World Trade Organization agreements for avoiding trade barriers through standardization (WTO n.d.). The basic provisions set in these international standards provide an internationally agreed upon framework for the main operations of a certification system. They summarize the best available knowledge on the necessary procedures for conducting independent and reliable certification and standard setting. Hence, adherence to these rules is defined in the guide as a necessary prerequisite for acceptable certification.

The conformity of operations to the rules defined in international norms and standards is monitored in the case of standard-setting and accreditation bodies by international umbrella organizations through their membership requirements. If bodies for standard setting and accreditation operating under the assessed certification systems are members of these organizations—ISEAL Alliance, International Accreditation Forum, or the United Nations' Investment Advisory Facility (UNIAF)—they are subject to control for compliance with international norms and standards. In this case it can be assumed, based on evaluation and monitoring carried out by these organizations, that compliance with ISO and ISEAL standards is achieved and maintained over time. The assessment process should emphasize the actual scope of the monitoring procedures of international umbrella organizations, and whether the forest certification activities of standard-setting and accreditation bodies are actually covered. The operations of certification bodies are monitored by their respective accreditation bodies. Again, evaluation and subsequent surveillance of certification bodies has to be carried out to determine the body's performance specifically within the field of assessing forest management.

In the absence of appropriate surveillance mechanisms, the requirements defined in the guide have to be verified in a stand-alone evaluation of the standard-setting and accreditation bodies.

Although the above-mentioned international norms and standards provide a framework applicable to a wide range of sectors, they are insufficient to address the more complex social and environmental issues involved in forest management certification. Additional elements have been defined in the guide that deal with the content of standards and the standards-development process, as well as with guidance to assess, among other elements, the level of transparency and reliability achieved by each system's accreditation and certification operations.

USING THE GUIDE FOR WORLD BANK ASSESSMENTS OF CERTIFICATION SYSTEMS

This chapter describes how conformance with World Bank principles can be analyzed using either guidance included in international framework standards, such as ISO guides and the ISEAL Alliance Code of Good Practice, or the additional requirements in the World Bank–WWF guide. The chapter also presents elements that are not included in the World Bank–WWF guide, but are relevant to assessing compliance of certification systems with the World Bank's policy. It is understood that the guide developed by the World Bank–WWF Alliance is suitable as an interpretation of the respective provisions in Bank policy, but should not be applied as a normative document because, for the purpose of World Bank project preparation, the rules in the policy prevail.

INDEPENDENCE, AVOIDANCE OF CONFLICT OF INTERESTS, AND THIRD-PARTY CERTIFICATION. Independence of the operations carried out under a specific certification system is a key aspect of the World Bank approach to certification, and related requirements appear repeatedly in the policy. Consequently, personnel involved in audits and decision making have to be selected to avoid former or current relations with the candidate for certification or accreditation, which may influence judgment. It follows from these requirements that only third-party certification can be accepted because self-certification or certification among business partners cannot be considered independent. The same applies for the relationship between the certification body and the accreditation organization, which has to be designed to avoid undue influence on the outcome of the accreditation process.

Because independence is a fundamental principle comprehensively dealt with in all ISO guides and standards, it is not necessary to define additional criteria. According to ISO guidance, certification and accreditation bodies have to ensure that financial or commercial interests are not influencing operations and decisions. To this end, the certification body and all personnel involved in auditing or certification decisions, as well as senior executive staff responsible for finances, supervision, and policy implementation, must be free of any undue commercial or financial influence on its decisions. This also includes proving financial stability of the operation. Furthermore, auditing personnel are not permitted to be involved in certification decision making, and certification or accreditation bodies are prohibited from providing consultancy services to assessed operations. At the personnel level, conflicts of interest must be declared and bodies must exclude those with former or actual relations with the operation under assessment. Although subcontracting is generally permitted, it is limited to auditing tasks and subject to the same independence and impartiality requirements.

TRANSPARENCY OF CERTIFICATION DECISIONS. According to World Bank policy, an acceptable certification system must have transparent decision-making procedures. Requirements in the ISO and ISEAL guidance documents make it mandatory to publish basic information on the applied procedures, such as the processes applied for standard setting, certification or accreditation, the complaints and appeals mechanisms, and the evaluation and assessment procedures. In addition, standard-setting bodies have to make their work plan publicly available, produce a written synopsis of the comments received during the standard-setting process, and state how comments were addressed in the standard. For certification and accreditation bodies, it is obligatory to publish the results of the certification process,

normally through a publicly available list of the certificate holders or the accredited certification bodies, respectively. Proven compliance with these ISO and ISEAL rules therefore provides basic information about the conformance of a certification system with the World Bank's transparency requirement.

In addition, transparency demands that stakeholders external to the process be able to understand the rationale for the decisions made by certification, accreditation, or standard-setting bodies. The World Bank–WWF Alliance Forest Certification Assessment Guide therefore includes rules concerning publication of reports on evaluations and related decisions on certification and accreditation.

FAIRNESS OF CERTIFICATION DECISIONS. World Bank policy requires the decision-making procedures of a certification system to be fair. For standard-setting procedures, this can be achieved through balanced voting procedures, further outlined below. The most frequent cause for an unfair decision in certification or accreditation is granting or maintaining certified or accredited status where the operation does not comply with the standard. This is unfair to other certified or accredited operations that fully comply with the standard. However, all rules for independence, reliability, and credibility guiding certification were developed with the intent to avoid such incidences. Certification systems that follow ISO rules and comply with additional requirements described in the World Bank–WWF guide can be regarded as in conformity with the fairness requirement included in the World Bank policy.

PARTICIPATION IN STANDARDS DEVELOPMENT. Based on its overall principles on participation, the World Bank emphasizes in its policy the need for involvement of a wide range of stakeholders and interest groups in the standards-development process. According to the World Bank, the standards should be "developed with the meaningful participation of local people and communities; indigenous peoples; non-governmental organizations representing consumer, producer, and conservation interests; and other members of civil society including the private sector" (World Bank 2004). Identification of relevant stakeholders and proactive measures to engage interested parties in the process before commencement of standard-setting activities are basic requirements in the ISEAL code. The provisions also encompass other elements for broad stakeholder involvement, including the publication of draft standards, specification of an appropriate period for receiving comments, as well as procedures for handling comments received. The

ISEAL code also requires that an appropriate dispute resolution mechanism be in place.

While compliance with ISEAL ensures that basic provisions for stakeholder involvement are being followed, additional aspects should be evaluated to verify that the decision-making process allows for balanced participation of economic, social, and environmental interests. The World Bank–WWF guide describes voting procedures that should be applied when consensus cannot be reached so that a single interest group does not dominate the process.

In addition, the World Bank requires the meaningful participation of local people and communities. Because most standard-setting processes in the forest sector have a national-level focus, it is difficult to adequately address the representation of often widely differing local interests. Therefore, the system should have mechanisms that require, at a minimum, a standard be field tested in close consultation with adjacent people and communities before endorsement.

ATTRIBUTES OF FOREST MANAGEMENT STANDARDS. Standards are a basic element of certification systems because they describe the performance level that certified operations have to achieve, and provide the basis for the communication of these achievements. OP 4.36 lists in paragraph 10 the general principles that have to be covered by the standard, and, in addition, requires "objective and measurable performance standards that are defined at the national level and are compatible with internationally accepted principles and criteria of sustainable forest management." The content of a system's standards can be analyzed using provisions in the World Bank–WWF guide because compliance with requirements in the guide encompasses conformance with the World Bank's principles for forest management.

The provisions for the content of standards are set at a rather general level of overall principles of forest management. Therefore, the World Bank–WWF guide requires the development of more detailed indicators during their adaptation to national or regional circumstances. These indicators have to describe the performance level for each criterion, as highlighted in paragraph 11 of the World Bank's policy, and be measurable and objective.

To avoid trade distortions, national standards have to be based on a set of internationally applicable principles. The World Bank–WWF guide therefore includes the need for national standard-setting bodies to seek harmonization of national standards with those of neighboring countries, and to introduce an endorsement mechanism at the international level for the approval of national standards.

COST-EFFECTIVENESS. International norms and standards in the ISO or ISEAL frameworks for certification systems do not include specific rules guiding the economic performance of the operations and processes involved in the certification process, as required in OP 4.36. On the other hand, it is a basic condition for certification operations that costs are covered at all levels by their economic activities; otherwise, the systems would not be economically viable. Furthermore, it can be assumed that businesses in the sector will only participate in a certification system when either their monetary or nonmonetary benefits from the system outweigh the costs incurred to achieve certification or accreditation.

It is important to ensure that certification systems do not discriminate against operations according to their size, location, or forest type, particularly in terms of cost-effectiveness—that is, a certification system should not be so expensive that a small company automatically does not qualify. Most international systems extended their services to provide a global reach and are indifferent to location or forest type. However, it has proven to be difficult to make certification attractive to small landholders because of excessive per-hectare costs. Given the current trend of rapidly increasing the forest area under management by communities and smaller operations that are directly or indirectly supported by the donor community (including the World Bank), and the importance of these types of forest owners as custodians of the forest in many countries, it is of particular concern when certification systems are not accessible to these groups because of the size of their operations. Although economic efficiency implies that costs are covered by the beneficiaries of the system, it is particularly important for the World Bank that certification systems have procedures to ensure cost-effectiveness for these groups and facilitate their access to services. This can be achieved by reducing the intensity of evaluations for these groups or by waiving certain cost-intensive requirements, such as planning and documentation or landscape-level objectives mainly applicable to larger operations.[2] Corresponding requirements are included in the World Bank–WWF guide.

ASSESSING CERTIFICATION SYSTEMS

This section describes the limitations of the assessments carried out using the tools mentioned in the previous section and the lessons learned during the process of developing the World Bank–WWF guide (see annex 11A to this chapter for guidance on TORs). The Bank has yet to initiate a project that has required assessment of certification systems, but once more practical experience has been achieved through the application of the guide, it will be incorporated.

Certification systems are institutionally and organizationally complex, and their assessment requires considerable professional knowledge of forest certification, coupled with a profound understanding of international framework rules and insight into the specific roles of the different system elements and their interactions.

While the elements outlined above should be examined when considering certification systems, it is likely that at present no system is in full conformity with all requirements. Assessment of schemes as a first step will highlight strengths and weaknesses and deliver general information on the performance of each. Nonetheless, decisions regarding whether a certification system is consistent with World Bank policies should consider the impacts of the identified deficits in the particular country or project situation.

Although it is desirable to assess a system's actual performance, it is not always possible because internal procedures of bodies are, with certain exceptions, normally kept confidential, and operations can deny access to auditors outside the regular monitoring and surveillance structures. This makes analysis of the organizations difficult, and may preclude methodologically consistent and reliable assessments of the system's performance. In many cases, assessments must therefore rely on existing mechanisms provided by international organizations overseeing standard setting or accreditation, such as the International Accreditation Forum or the ISEAL Alliance.

Elucidation of the World Bank principles for forest management standards through development of indicators may at least partly overlap with provisions for Bank investments in the sector, which are included in other Bank policies (for example, OP 4.04 Natural Habitats, OP 4.10 Indigenous Peoples, or OP 4.09 Pest Management). However, the rules outlined in these policies are specifically tailored to the needs of World Bank project preparation and surveillance, and, as such, are not necessarily part of standards and related monitoring procedures of certification systems. Decisions on the acceptability of certification systems should therefore primarily be based on elements included in paragraph 10 of OP 4.36.

PROVIDING SUPPORT BEFORE CERTIFICATION USING TIME-BOUND ACTION PLANS

So far, performance of many forest management operations in World Bank client countries lags behind the level specified by the standards of certification systems that can com-

ply with the Bank's provisions and be deemed acceptable in the context of OP 4.36 (see annex 11B to this chapter for guidance on TOR). It is therefore likely that the alternative provided by the policy—to support operations on the condition of adherence to an acceptable time-bound action plan—will be used frequently. Measures included in this plan should be adequate to achieve certification under a system acceptable to the World Bank. Thus, the first step in developing a plan for improvement is the selection of a certification system accepted by both the World Bank and the client.

Identification of areas of nonconformance with the standard is part of the assessment work carried out by certification bodies operating under the selected system. In situations in which the operation is unlikely to achieve full compliance with the standard, the certification body should carry out a preassessment of the operation and provide a list of issues that need further improvement. Measures to overcome these deficits can be derived from this information either by the operation, the certification body, or through other external advice. In addition, the time frame set for achieving full certification should be realistic. The World Bank should refrain from supporting the operation if it is unlikely that full certification can be reached within the duration of the project.

To determine the feasibility of the action plan, the actual available capacity to implement the measures proposed within the specified time frame needs to be assessed. To this end, the World Bank should carry out an assessment of costs resulting from the implementation of measures in relation to the overall financial situation of the applicant operation, taking into account, if available, information on potential benefits through better market access or price premiums resulting from certified status. This analysis should also consider funds provided through the envisaged World Bank support.

Human resources available to the operation—numbers of staff and qualifications—are another critical aspect for its capacity to implement the measures defined in the action plan. Hence, evaluation of the overall capacity available to the applicant, and its adequacy for implementation of the action plan, forms another important component of the project planning phase. Experience has shown that the commitment of the owner and senior management to certification is an important success factor. Although this may be difficult to evaluate, the interim steps taken by the company to pursue certifiable forest management may indicate the sincerity of their intentions.

Depending on the nature and duration of implementation, it can be desirable not only to define the overall target, but also to consider intermediary phases using a step-wise approach. Progress could then be monitored against previously agreed upon milestones.

NOTES

1. Standard setting: The process by which a standard for forest management is developed.

Conformity assessment and certification: Assessment of forest management against the standards. If successful, this will result in a certificate being issued.

Accreditation: The procedure by which an authoritative body gives formal recognition that a body or person is competent to perform conformity assessment and certification.

2. The Forest Stewardship Council (FSC) has developed standards that give consideration to small and low-intensity managed forests, available online at http://www.fsc.org/slimf/.

SELECTED READINGS

Burger, D., J. Hess, and B. Lang, eds. 2005. *Forest Certification: An Innovative Instrument in the Service of Sustainable Development?* Eschborn, Germany: Deutsche Gesellschaft für Technische Zusammenarbeit.

Nussbaum, R., and M. Simula. 2005. *The Forest Certification Handbook.* London: Earthscan.

Richards, M. 2004. "Certification in Complex Socio-Political Settings: Looking Forward to the Next Decade." Forest Trends, Washington, DC.

REFERENCES CITED

World Bank. 2004. The World Bank Operational Manual, Operational Policies OP 4.36, Forests. World Bank, Washington, DC.

World Bank–WWF Alliance. 2006. *Forest Certification Assessment Guide—A Framework for Assessing Credible Certification Systems/Schemes.* Washington, DC: World Bank–WWF Alliance. http://www.panda.org/about_wwf/what_we_do/forests/publications/index.cfm?unewsID=81080.

ANNEX 11A MODEL TERMS OF REFERENCE FOR ASSESSMENT OF CERTIFICATION SYSTEMS

BACKGROUND. In its global strategy on forests, the World Bank recognizes the integration of forests into sustainable economic development as one major pillar of its investments in the sector, including enabling or directly supporting commercial use of the forest. At the same time, the World Bank must limit negative social or environmental impacts of forest use by setting preconditions for supporting commercial operations in the forest. The policy framework laid out in OP 4.36 stipulates that in order to receive Bank support, commercial harvesting of forests carried out on an industrial scale must be certified by a system deemed acceptable by the World Bank.

The forest management standards required by such systems and their operational procedures must conform to the elements further specified in paragraphs 10 and 11 of OP 4.36. The World Bank, in close collaboration with the WWF, developed an assessment guide that details the principles of the policy (World Bank–WWF 2006) and provides a framework to assess the quality of certifications systems. This instrument is recognized as the basis for the assessment of certification systems according to World Bank requirements.

The TOR listed in this document summarize the key steps in assessments carried out according to the World Bank–WWF guide on assessing certification systems. The assessment will provide information on the performance level achieved by certification systems in relation to World Bank principles and identify the gaps that may still exist in the system's standard requirements of operational procedures. This analysis can support decisions regarding the acceptability of systems, but further judgment will need to be exercised when certification systems do not fully comply with all requirements, and consideration be given to the potential impacts that may result from these deficits in a particular project environment.

TASKS. Different tasks can be performed depending on the background of the assessment. The issues listed under the first three tasks can be carried out in a stand-alone assessment that does not require a decision on the acceptability of systems. The fourth and fifth tasks are recommended if the assessment is to provide the basis for investment decisions under OP 4.36 and in cases where the assessment showed deficits in the system's standards or procedures.

The consultant shall perform the following tasks:

1. Analyze the respective certification system for its conformance with the OP 4.36 requirements using the World Bank–WWF guide as a reference document. This should include direct consultations with certification systems personnel on draft findings.

2. On the basis of this assessment, compile a list of required elements with which the system is not in compliance.

3. Compile a list of those elements for which an assessment was not possible due to a lack of information or lack of access to procedures or operations of certification, accreditation, or standard-setting bodies working under the system.

4. Analyze the identified deficits in the context of the overall project environment and conduct a risk assessment on the potential negative impacts of the identified deficits. This exercise can be supplemented by consultations with relevant stakeholders in the World Bank client country.

5. On the basis of the findings, produce a substantiated judgment on whether the system meets OP 4.36 requirements and can provide sufficient assurance that certificate holders fully comply with the World Bank's requirements for forest management certification listed in paragraph 10 of OP 4.36.

QUALIFICATIONS. The qualifications necessary for assessing the elements of a certification system may, in many cases, require the employment of an audit team rather than a single auditor. The assessor or the assessment team should have the following qualifications:

- practical experience and knowledge in forest certification
- profound understanding of the different elements of systems for accreditation, certification, and standard setting, and their various interactions
- broad knowledge of ISO guides 62, 65, and 66; ISO standard 17011; and practical experience in assessing bodies against the requirements set in these norms
- advanced degree in forest resource management or related field
- no conflicts of interest with regard to the certification system under assessment

For a judgment on the impacts of identified system deficits, the consultant(s) should have

- in-depth knowledge of the overall economic, ecological, and social environment, and the country's legal and policy context; and

- the ability to analyze certification systems and their impact in a given environment.

REFERENCES CITED

World Bank–WWF Alliance. 2006. *Forest Certification Assessment Guide—A Framework for Assessing Credible Certification Systems/Schemes.* Washington, DC: World Bank–WWF Alliance.

ANNEX 11B PROCEDURES AND TERMS OF REFERENCE FOR THE DEVELOPMENT AND ASSESSMENT OF A TIME-BOUND ACTION PLAN FOR CERTIFICATION

BACKGROUND. The World Bank supports investments in the forest sector under OP 4.36. To qualify for this support, operations involving commercial forest harvesting on an industrial scale must achieve certification under a system acceptable to the World Bank. Alternatively, operations can qualify by adhering to a time-bound action plan that is adequate to achieve certification within a specified time frame.

Preparation of investments in this area should therefore include the following steps:

- selection of a certification system
- assessment of the performance of the operation in relation to the forest management standard
- elaboration of a time-bound action plan
- assessment of the plan's acceptability under World Bank terms
- monitoring of the implementation of the plan

Each of these individual steps is associated with different responsibilities, tasks, issues to consider, qualifications required, and actors involved, which are outlined below.

SELECTION OF A CERTIFICATION SYSTEM. Selection of a certification system that conforms with World Bank requirements and is operational in the country of the applicant is a precondition for assessing the performance of the operation. Details describing the World Bank's approach to selection of certification systems are given in this chapter of the sourcebook. The decision has to be made by the applicant, but preferably in close collaboration with the World Bank's contact person for the project, normally the task team leader.

To prepare for the selection, the consultant will do the following:

- Identify the forest management certification systems that are operational in the country of the applicant.
- Assess the systems against World Bank requirements in accordance with the World Bank's instruments for assessment of forest certification schemes (annex 11A). The consultant should draw upon the results of assessments conducted for similar projects in the country, or previous assessments commissioned by other bodies, if available.
- If the certification systems are not entirely in compliance with World Bank requirements, the consultant will provide the World Bank with a list of deficits, together with a substantiated judgment regarding risks that could

potentially emerge for the project because of the identified system's deficiencies.

ASSESSMENT OF THE APPLICANT OPERATION. The assessment should highlight the strengths and weaknesses of the applicant in relation to the forest management standard of the certification system. Because the tasks involved are similar to those performed during normal audits, the assessment should be conducted by a team that is familiar with the regular audit procedures of the system and be selected according to the same criteria applied by the respective certification system. It is essential that team members have sufficient competence and local knowledge to analyze the legal framework, the ecological and social aspects of forest management, and its broader impact on the well-being of adjacent communities. During such a preassessment for certification, the consultant(s) will perform the following tasks:

- Assess the applicant's forest management practices for compliance with each element of the selected certification system's standards.
- Compile a list of issues where the company's performance falls below the requirements of the standard.
- If applicable to the selected certification system, group the deficits into minor noncompliance issues that could be resolved after certification has been awarded, and major noncompliance issues that would prevent the operation from obtaining immediate certification.
- Highlight the strengths and weaknesses of the operation.
- Identify appropriate measures to improve forest management to the level required for full certification.

DEVELOPMENT OF THE TIME-BOUND ACTION PLAN. On the basis of the identified deficits, the company should develop a plan detailing actions envisaged for improvement. Although external consultants can assist in this step, senior staff should play a leading role in this process to ensure a close connection between the company and the action plan.

Depending on the situation, it may be necessary to introduce a step-wise approach by defining interim performance levels to be achieved. This approach may be necessary depending on, among other issues, the previous record of the company applying for assistance, the commitment of senior management or the owner to implementation of the action plan, the time frame set for full compliance in relation to the duration of the project, as well as the gravity and number of identified instances of noncompliance with the standard.

In this step, the applicant will develop a time-bound action plan with the following elements:

- The list of deficits identified as being impediments to immediate certification (also referred to as preconditions).
- The measures proposed by the company to overcome the deficits and to achieve certification in the specified time frame. The measures should be suitable to address the identified deficits and consider the overall legal, political, and economic situation of the company, and feasible given the means available to the operation. The description should avoid the use of ambiguous terms.
- Each proposed action should be accompanied by an estimate of the time required for implementation and the expected time for achieving the performance level prescribed by the standard. The time frame should be realistically set given the overall resources of the operation and the commitment expressed by the management or the owner (see below).
- The plan should include a summary of the resources available to the company presented as the number and qualifications of personnel. In addition, the financial means dedicated by the operation to the implementation of the proposed actions should be described and analyzed.
- The plan should be accompanied by a clear statement from the executive director of the operation or the owner to accept and adhere to the measures defined.
- If a step-wise approach is considered necessary, the plan should define individual steps, including the achievements to be reached within a specified time frame.

ASSESSMENT OF THE PLAN FOR ACCEPTABILITY UNDER WORLD BANK TERMS. According to OP 4.36, the action plan has to be evaluated to determine its acceptability. Although the World Bank's policy does not provide further detail regarding what should be covered by the action plan, the elements listed in the previous section can provide a framework to apply on a case-by-case basis. The assessment must consider the plan's suitability, adequacy, and feasibility for implementing the proposed measures within the set time frame. To ensure independence and avoid conflicts of interest, the persons involved in the previous steps should not take part in this evaluation.

MONITORING OF IMPLEMENTATION. The monitoring procedures applied to the implementation of the plan can be sim-

ilar to the World Bank's normal mechanisms for project surveillance. The preparation of the time-bound action plan already describes the necessary elements for monitoring, such as the deadlines and achievements required, and the necessary resources. In addition, the monitoring schedule and intensity should reflect the level of risk involved with the project. Risk factors may include, but are not limited to, the potential impact on critical forests or critical natural habitats, the overall economic situation of the operation, and the effects of the project on adjacent communities or Indigenous Peoples. When a risk analysis shows that the impacts of the project are considerable, sanctions for nonconformance with the set deadlines should be incorporated into the loan agreement.

To comply with the standards of a certification system deemed acceptable to the World Bank, the operation has to develop its own monitoring procedures, through which information on key forest parameters is collected and analyzed (see also OP 4.36, paragraph 10[h]). In general, internal monitoring of certified operations provides information on the resource base (harvest rates, growth, and regeneration), status and changes of flora and fauna, and economic parameters, such as cost and efficiency. Consequently, an assessment of these procedures has to be carried out against the certification standard during the preassessment of the operation. For tailoring its own monitoring program, the World Bank can take into account the results from the preassessment under point 2 concerning the quality of the company's monitoring program. The World Bank's own monitoring can be limited to aspects insufficiently covered by these mechanisms.

REFERENCES CITED

ISEAL Alliance. 2004. "ISEAL Code of Good Practice for Setting Social and Environmental Standards." Bonn, Germany.

ISO/IEC (International Organization for Standardization/ International Electrotechnical Commission). 1994. "ISO/IEC Guide 59: Code of Good Practice for Standardization," Geneva, Switzerland.

———. 1996a. "ISO/IEC Guide 66 General Requirements for Bodies Operating Assessment and Certification/Registration of Environmental Management Systems." Geneva, Switzerland.

———. 1996b. "ISO/IEC Guide 62: General Requirements for Bodies Operating Assessment and Certification/Registration of Quality Systems." Geneva, Switzerland.

———. 1996c. "ISO/IEC Guide 65: General Requirements for Bodies Operating Product Certification Systems." Geneva, Switzerland.

———. 2004. "ISO/IEC 17011: Conformity Assessment—General Requirements for Accreditation Bodies Accrediting Conformity Assessment Bodies." Geneva, Switzerland.

World Bank. 2004. The World Bank Operational Manual, OP 4.36. World Bank, Washington, DC.

World Bank–WWF Alliance. 2006. *Forest Certification Assessment Guide—A Framework for Assessing Credible Certification Systems/Schemes*. Washington, DC: World Bank–WWF Global Forest Alliance.

WTO. 1995. "Agreement on Technical Barriers to Trade, Annex 3, Code of Good Practice for the Preparation, Adoption, and Application of Standards." Geneva, Switzerland. http://www.wto.org/english/tratop_e/tbt_e/tbtagr_e .htm#Annex%203.

CHAPTER 12

Applying OP 4.10 on Indigenous Peoples

Several World Bank safeguard policies emphasize that local sites may have special value, in particular for those who depend on them for their livelihood or their social, spiritual and cultural well-being. Operational Policy on Forests (OP 4.36) recognizes that many local communities depend entirely or primarily on forests and forest products and that these communities are an essential factor in forest conservation and management. The policy provides specific safeguards concerning Indigenous Peoples and other forest dwellers, specifically their rights of access to and use of designated forest areas. In World Bank–assisted commercial forest activities, the policy calls for a forest certification system, which respects "any legally documented or customary land tenure and use rights as well as the rights of Indigenous Peoples and workers," and includes "measures to maintain or enhance sound and effective community relations" (paragraph 10). The policy also stresses the need to develop the certification system "with the meaningful participation of local people and communities; Indigenous Peoples; nongovernmental organizations [NGOs]" (paragraph 11).

OP 4.11 Physical Cultural Resources, is also relevant for forest projects affecting Indigenous Peoples. The policy aims to protect physical cultural resources, defined as "movable or immovable objects, sites, structures, groups of structures, and natural features and landscapes that have archaeological, paleontological, historical, architectural, religious, aesthetic, or other cultural significance" (paragraph 1). These resources "are important as sources of valuable scientific and historical information, as assets for economic and social development, and as integral parts of a people's cultural identity and practices" (paragraph 2). These resources may include burial sites and spirit forests important to many forest communities, particularly Indigenous Peoples.

The World Bank's policy on Involuntary Resettlement (OP 4.12) applies to involuntary restrictions of access to legally designated parks and protected areas. The policy requires that such restrictions be determined in participation with affected communities and that adverse impacts be mitigated or compensated for. These arrangements are described in a process framework prepared as a condition for project appraisal (guidance on the application of OP 4.36, OP 4.11, and OP 4.12 is included in chapter 9).

The World Bank's Indigenous Peoples Policy (OP 4.10) is the key instrument to address Indigenous Peoples' issues for any type of World Bank–assisted investment project affecting Indigenous Peoples, whether the impacts are anticipated to be positive or negative. The policy recognizes the rights of Indigenous Peoples, which are increasingly being addressed under international and national law. It notes that their identities and cultures are inextricably linked to the lands on which they live and the natural resources on which they depend, and that this combined with their frequent marginalization and vulnerability often exposes them to particular risks and impacts from development projects. The policy recognizes the vital role that Indigenous Peoples play in sustainable development, which is especially relevant for most forest-related projects (see note 1.3, Indigenous Peoples and Forests).

IDENTIFICATION OF INDIGENOUS PEOPLES

Indigenous Peoples today reflect a great variety of histories and circumstances that defy a single definition. Accepted or preferred terms and definitions vary by usage among the groups concerned as well as by country and continent; terms used include "aboriginal," "native," "autochthonous," "tribal," "ethnic minority," and "first nations." Nevertheless, an international consensus has been emerging regarding the general identifying characteristics of Indigenous Peoples, consistent with those adopted in the World Bank's policy. OP 4.10 identifies (paragraph 4) Indigenous Peoples as "a distinct, vulnerable, social and cultural group possessing the following characteristics in varying degrees:

- self-identification as members of a distinct indigenous cultural group and recognition of this identity by others;
- collective attachment to geographically distinct habitats or ancestral territories in the project area and to the natural resources in these habitats and territories;
- customary cultural, economic, social, or political institutions that are separate from those of the dominant society and culture; and
- an indigenous language, often different from the official language of the country or region."

OBJECTIVES OF THE POLICY

OP 4.10 aims to protect the rights of Indigenous Peoples and supports the World Bank's mission of poverty reduction and sustainable development. The policy calls for the World Bank to provide project financing only when affected indigenous communities have provided their broad community support to the project through a process of free, prior, and informed consultation. Projects affecting Indigenous Peoples are designed to deliver culturally appropriate social and economic benefits to Indigenous Peoples and include measures to avoid, minimize, mitigate, or compensate for any adverse impacts.

KEY POLICY REQUIREMENTS

The World Bank's policy on Indigenous Peoples applies to all investment lending projects affecting, whether positively or adversely, Indigenous Peoples. The key procedural requirements of the policy follow:

- screening by the World Bank to determine whether Indigenous Peoples are present in, or have collective attachment to, the project area

- a social assessment by the borrower to evaluate the project's potential positive and adverse effects on Indigenous Peoples, and to examine project alternatives where adverse effects may be significant
- an inclusive, transparent, and continuing process of free, prior, and informed consultation
- the affected Indigenous Peoples communities' broad support to the proposed project
- preparation, and disclosure, of an appropriate planning instrument: an Indigenous Peoples Plan (IPP) or Indigenous Peoples Planning Framework (IPPF)

The level of detail and complexity necessary to meet the requirements of the policy are proportional to the complexity of the proposed project and the nature and scale of the potential effects on the Indigenous Peoples. The time needed for project preparation comprising consultations with affected Indigenous Peoples and the scope of social analysis also depends on the circumstances and vulnerability of affected communities. Technical judgment is essential in determining the appropriate approach.

Most forest-related projects do entail potential risks for Indigenous Peoples, and borrower and project teams preparing such projects should expect to pay significant attention to Indigenous Peoples' issues and concerns during project preparation and implementation. They should keep in mind that the particular rights, circumstances, and vulnerabilities of Indigenous Peoples often result in impacts and needed design features for Indigenous Peoples that are different from those for other communities living in or near forest areas.

SCREENING FOR INDIGENOUS PEOPLES IN THE PROJECT AREA. Early in the identification phase the project team should assess, in coordination with the borrower, whether Indigenous Peoples are living in or have collective attachment to the project area. Often the advice or input from qualified experts is needed during this screening process, and consultations with affected communities also may be needed.

SOCIAL ASSESSMENT. The main purpose of the social assessment is to evaluate the project's potential positive and adverse impacts on the affected Indigenous Peoples (and other affected communities). Critical to the determination of potential adverse impacts is an analysis of the relative vulnerability of, and risks to, the affected Indigenous Peoples' communities according to their distinct circumstances, ties to the land, and dependence on natural resources, as well as lack of opportunities relative to other social groups in their respective communities, regions, or national societies. Indigenous Peoples' vulnerability is multistranded. It is not only economic, social, and political, but also demographic (at risk of being numerically overwhelmed) and environmental (if access to natural resources is restricted and their subsistence and livelihoods affected). They are often excluded from political processes at all levels. They are often also more exposed to external shocks that have an impact on their lives, lacking the capacity to cope with such shocks or other external changes—including those realized through development projects (see box 12.1 for the policy's language on social assessment).

The assessment is also used to inform project design to ensure that activities are culturally appropriate, will enhance benefits to target groups, and are likely to succeed in the given socioeconomic and cultural context. The social assessment will usually include the establishment of a framework for consultation with and participation of the affected people throughout the project cycle. This usually includes the process of free, prior, and informed consultation with affected Indigenous Peoples, leading to their broad community support for the project. However, this process may be conducted partly or fully separate from the social assessment process, particularly for more complex projects requiring several rounds of consultations during project preparation that go beyond the timeframe of the social assessment.

A good social assessment will improve understanding of Indigenous Peoples' culture, social structure, institutions, socioeconomic characteristics, and the specific environment and social context in which they live. It will identify stakeholders and analyze the local and national institutional context and legal framework relevant to the proposed project and affected Indigenous Peoples, including legislation concerning customary rights, access rights to forests and natural resources, and participation of Indigenous Peoples or other forest-dependent communities in forest and development planning. It should also reveal any social risks and existing or potential conflicts. Combining analytical processes with field-based knowledge, the social assessment will aid efforts to design culturally appropriate and gender-inclusive projects that take into account affected Indigenous Peoples' views on the benefits that they can derive from a project, the role they can play in its implementation, and how adverse impacts can be eliminated, reduced, or mitigated.

The social assessment for forest-related projects, particularly those concerned with natural resource management, must assess the relationship between Indigenous Peoples and forests, including livelihoods, culture, and social organization. Mapping of traditional and existing land and natural resource use for livelihoods as well as for cultural and spiritual practices should be an integrated element of the assessment. Potential conflicts and disputed claims concerning access to land and natural resources should be identified—and ways to address them should be recommended.

Assumptions held by project developers and other stakeholders as well as by Indigenous Peoples about traditional resource use practices and their environmental impacts or benefits may not hold true. If based on mainstream cultural models rather than a full understanding of the local context, Indigenous Peoples' practices may be viewed with skepticism or outright prejudice, rendering them unsustainable, regardless of whether the assumption actually proves to be true. It is therefore important that interventions be based on reliable information obtained with the participation of local communities.

It is the borrower's responsibility to conduct the social assessment, which is usually done by contracting with a research institute, university, consultant (firm or individual), or NGO. The identified social assessment team must have the required expertise, including knowledge of Indigenous Peoples, and have the trust of the affected communities. The project team provides assistance and also approves the terms of reference and the composition of the team for the assessment.

In addition to the World Bank's *Indigenous Peoples Guidebook* (forthcoming), guidance on conducting social assessments can be found on the World Bank's Web site on social analysis (www.worldbank.org/socialanalysis), in the World Bank's *Social Analysis Sourcebook* (World Bank 2003), and the World Bank's *Social Analysis Guidelines in Natural Resource Management* (World Bank 2005a). (See also sections in this *Forests Sourcebook* on social assessment in chapter 9, Applying Forests Policy OP 4.36, and note 1.3, Indigenous Peoples and Forests).

FREE, PRIOR, INFORMED CONSULTATION. OP/BP 4.10 focuses on the importance of engaging Indigenous Peoples in a process of free, prior, and informed consultation (see box 12.2). Such a process has to be inclusive, including women, the poorest, and members of different generations. The consultation process should, in most projects, take place at each step in the project cycle—project preparation, implementation, and evaluation. This process includes the borrower, the affected communities, and Indigenous Peoples' organizations, if any, or other local civil society organizations identified by the Indigenous Peoples' communities.

Box 12.1   OP 4.10 on Social Assessment

OP 4.10 provides the following guidance on the elements of the social assessment (OP 4.10, Annex A):

1. The breadth, depth, and type of analysis required for the social assessment are proportional to the nature and scale of the proposed project's potential effects on the Indigenous Peoples.

   The social assessment includes the following elements, as needed:
   - A review, on a scale appropriate to the project, of the legal and institutional framework applicable to Indigenous Peoples.
   - Gathering of baseline information on the demographic, social, cultural, and political characteristics of the affected Indigenous Peoples' communities, the land and territories that they have traditionally owned or customarily used or occupied, and the natural resources on which they depend.
   - Taking the review and baseline information into account, the identification of key project stakeholders and the elaboration of a culturally appropriate process for consulting with the Indigenous Peoples at each stage of project preparation and implementation (see paragraph 9 of OP 4.10).
   - An assessment, based on free, prior, and informed consultation, with the affected Indigenous Peoples' communities, of the potential adverse and positive effects of the project. Critical to the determination of potential adverse impacts is an analysis of the relative vulnerability of, and risks to, the affected Indigenous Peoples' communities given their distinct circumstances and close ties to land and natural resources, as well as their lack of access to opportunities relative to other social groups in the communities, regions, or national societies in which they live.

   The identification and evaluation, based on free, prior, and informed consultation with the affected Indigenous Peoples' communities, of measures necessary to avoid adverse effects, or if such measures are not feasible, the identification of measures to minimize, mitigate, or compensate for such effects, and to ensure that the Indigenous Peoples receive culturally appropriate benefits under the project.

Source: World Bank 2005b.

Key elements of the consultations during the preparation phase follow:

- information about the proposed project and its intended benefits and possible adverse impacts
- achieving understanding of Indigenous Peoples' perceptions of possible project benefits and impacts, and possible measures to enhance benefits and avoid or mitigate adverse impacts
- incorporation of Indigenous Peoples' views, preferences, and indigenous knowledge into project design and the Indigenous Peoples instrument (Indigenous Peoples Plan or Indigenous Peoples Planning Framework)
- facilitation and determination of affected communities' broad support for the project
- development of a culturally appropriate framework or strategy for Indigenous Peoples' participation throughout project preparation, implementation, and monitoring and evaluation, which may involve particular methodologies to ensure participation of marginalized social groups,

to build community consensus, to enhance transparency, to ensure local ownership of the process, and to assess and ensure continued support for the project

While most of these elements can be encompassed within the social assessment process, keeping project-affected people informed should also be part of the borrower's ongoing communications with people in the proposed project area. The borrower and the project team should keep in mind that free, prior, and informed consultations with Indigenous Peoples will likely require more time than consultations with other affected communities and stakeholders. Consultations that may just require a few hours in an urban setting may take days with Indigenous Peoples. Moreover, the consultation process for ascertaining the community's broad support for project activities will require more time and may go beyond the time frame of the social assessment process, particularly for more complex projects. Many, if not most, projects affecting forests in areas with Indigenous Peoples would be considered complex (see note 1.3, Indigenous Peoples and Forests).

When a project affects Indigenous Peoples, the
project team assists the borrower in carrying out
free, prior, and informed consultation with
affected communities about the proposed project
throughout the project cycle, taking into consideration the following:

- "Free, prior, and informed consultation" is consultation that occurs freely and voluntarily, without any external manipulation, interference, or coercion, for which the parties consulted have prior access to information on the intent and scope of the proposed project in a culturally appropriate manner, form, and language.
- Consultation approaches recognize existing Indigenous Peoples' organizations, including councils of elders, headmen, and tribal leaders, and pay special attention to women, youth, and the elderly.
- The consultation process starts early, because decision making among Indigenous Peoples may be an iterative process, and there is a need for adequate lead time to fully understand and incorporate concerns and recommendations of Indigenous Peoples into the project design.
- A record of the consultation process is maintained as part of the project files.

Source: World Bank 2005b.

A number of aspects of consulting with Indigenous Peoples should be recognized. Consulting in the local language is often needed, particularly to ensure that all community members are heard and feel comfortable raising their ideas and concerns. Efforts to build trust may be needed to reduce frequently encountered mistrust of government, project developers, or outsiders in general, built up during years of exclusion. Other aspects that may affect the consultation process include traditional social structures and leadership patterns, representation of communities, decision-making processes (for example, through consensus building), and traditions of oral transmission of knowledge and culture. It is important to ensure that the team conducting or facilitating the consultations understands these aspects, has the required skills to conduct meaningful consultations with Indigenous Peoples and has their trust.

The use of independent entities that have the trust of the affected communities is often necessary to undertake free, prior, and informed consultations. Borrower involvement is needed to obtain the communities' broad support for the project because, in many cases, specific agreements will need to be negotiated between the affected communities and the borrower. Having an independent entity facilitate this process is usually preferred. For consultations to be meaningful, their results need to be processed and used to inform project design and implementation. The results should be described in the social assessment report, or in a separate report on the consultation process, and, as appropriate, in the Indigenous Peoples instrument used for project implementation.

In addition to the free, prior, and informed consultations with affected Indigenous Peoples, the borrower and the project team normally consult a number of other stakeholders. Table 12.1 provides a basic overview of a typical consultation process and the key stakeholders involved. It should be used only as guidance to inform the planning of the consultation process for a given project—the principles of the Indigenous Peoples' policy should be invoked as a basic guideline for eliciting practical solutions based on the sound judgment of qualified experts. Many forest-based projects require more than two rounds of consultations with affected Indigenous Peoples during preparation. The World Bank's *Environmental Assessment Sourcebook* section titled "Public Consultation in the EA Process: A Strategic Approach, 1999, Update 26" (World Bank 1999) provides general guidance on conducting public consultations. For more guidance on consultations with Indigenous Peoples, see the World Bank's *Indigenous Peoples Guidebook* (forthcoming) and "Participation and Indigenous Peoples" (Davis and Soeftestad 1995). (See also chapter 9, Applying Forests Policy OP 4.36, and note 1.3, Indigenous Peoples and Forests).

BROAD COMMUNITY SUPPORT. OP 4.10 requires that affected Indigenous Peoples' communities provide their broad support for a project before the World Bank can support the project. It is the responsibility of the borrower to achieve broad community support through the free, prior, and informed consultation process. Evidence of such support should be provided in a detailed report (which could be the social assessment report) documenting: "(a) the findings of the social assessment; (b) the process of free, prior, and informed consultation with the affected Indigenous Peoples' communities; (c) additional measures, including project design modification, that may be required to address adverse effects on the Indigenous Peoples and to provide

Table 12.1 General Consultation Process

When	With whom	Substance	By whom
Identification	Borrower	Possibility of Indigenous Peoples in the project area; World Bank policy requirements	Project team
	Experts on Indigenous Peoples	Identification and presence of Indigenous Peoples in the project area	Project team/ Borrower
	Borrower	If Indigenous Peoples are present, identify the process for addressing Indigenous Peoples' issues and OP 4.10 requirements, including terms of reference for the social assessment and consultations	Project team
Preparation	Indigenous Peoples, first phase	Information about the proposed project (preliminary design), its anticipated benefits, and possible adverse impacts	SA team/ Borrower
	Other stakeholders	Information about the project, its anticipated benefits, and possible adverse impacts	SA team/ Borrower
	Indigenous Peoples, second phase	On the proposed project (detailed design) and possible measures to address particular issues concerning Indigenous Peoples Obtaining broad community support and input to the Indigenous Peoples instrument	SA team/ Borrower
	Other stakeholders	Consultations on the proposed project (detailed design)	SA team/ Borrower
Appraisal	Borrower	Assessment of commitment and capacity of implementing agency concerning Indigenous Peoples' activities	Project team
	Indigenous Peoples, experts, and other stakeholders	Assessment of feasibility and appropriateness of Indigenous Peoples' measures	Project team/ Borrower
	Indigenous Peoples	Select field visits as needed to determine affected communities' broad support to the project and the feasibility of proposed measures	Project team
Implementation	Borrower Indigenous Peoples	On the implementation and monitoring of Indigenous Peoples' instrument Ongoing consultation on implementation progress through borrower monitoring and World Bank supervision	Project team Borrower/ Project team
	Experts and other stakeholders	Consultation and feedback on implementation progress as appropriate	Borrower/ Project team

Source: Jensby 2007.
Note: SA = Social Assessment.

them with culturally appropriate project benefits; (d) recommendations for free, prior, and informed consultation with and participation by Indigenous Peoples' communities during project implementation, monitoring, and evaluation; and (e) any formal agreements reached with Indigenous Peoples' communities and/or the IPOs [Indigenous Peoples' Organizations]" (OP 4.10, paragraph 11).

It is the responsibility of the World Bank to review the process and the outcome of the consultations to satisfy itself that the affected Indigenous Peoples' communities have provided their broad support to the project. The World Bank does not proceed with the project processing if it is unable to ascertain that such support exists (OP 4.10, paragraph 11). A mix of opinions, and sometimes disagreements, as to the overall desirability of the project should be anticipated. When considering the level of broad support for the project and the strength of the consultation process itself, the project team should ensure that all relevant and appropriate sectors and subgroups of the communities have been given opportunities to express themselves. If they have, and the broad majority is generally positive about the prospects of

the project, the finding that broad support exists would be reasonable. While a referendum may not be practical in most situations, there is a need for broadly based validation and documentation of what has been said, by whom, and how any specific agreements were reached and what they contain.

Broad community support does not mean that everyone has to agree on a given project. Nevertheless, consensus building is an important form of decision making among many Indigenous Peoples. Thus, consensus building should often be an element of the free, prior, and informed consultations that aim to facilitate broad community support for the project. A community's broad support may be based on specific agreements for benefit-sharing measures or mitigation of adverse impacts. As part of its due diligence in applying OP 4.10, the project team must ensure that such agreements are adequately reflected in project design and the Indigenous Peoples' instrument.

INDIGENOUS PEOPLES' INSTRUMENT. For projects affecting Indigenous Peoples, the borrower prepares an instrument containing specific measures to ensure that Indigenous Peoples receive social and economic benefits from the project in a manner that is culturally appropriate, and when potential adverse effects are identified, those effects are avoided, minimized, mitigated, or compensated for.

An Indigenous Peoples Plan (IPP) is required for a standard World Bank–assisted project with interventions affecting Indigenous Peoples identified at the time of appraisal. For projects with multiple subprojects or annual investment plans in which specific interventions are not known at the time of appraisal, an Indigenous Peoples Planning Framework (IPPF) is required. If the overwhelming majority of affected people are Indigenous Peoples, the project design itself (described in the Project Appraisal Document and subsequently in the Project Implementation Plan and/or Operational Manual) may make up the instrument. It should include the relevant elements of an IPP.

The instrument is intended to serve as a flexible and pragmatic implementation document; its activities are integrated into the design of the project and address the issues discussed in the social assessment and agreed to during the consultations (see annex 12A to this chapter for more guidance on the elements of an IPP or IPPF). The contents of the instrument will vary with the nature of the project as well as with the characteristics of the country and the Indigenous Peoples affected. Proportionality is crucial: The principle is to plan appropriately so as to include (and budget for) only those activities that are necessary to deal with the Indigenous Peoples' issues identified by the social assessment, with consultations proportional to the project impacts and benefits and the circumstances and vulnerabilities of affected communities.

For a project with no adverse impacts, it may suffice to include as the main part of the plan a strategy for targeting Indigenous Peoples and a participation and consultation framework to continue the free, prior, and informed consultation and to ensure the input and continued support from Indigenous Peoples on specific project activities during implementation. The strategy also should aim to ensure that the social and economic benefits of the project are culturally appropriate. Projects with adverse impacts would, in addition, include measures to avoid, mitigate, or compensate for such adverse impacts. Specific institutional arrangements and capacity-building activities may be necessary and efforts should be made to work with local organizations and institutions as appropriate.

Forest-based projects should assess and incorporate, as appropriate, indigenous knowledge and local resource management arrangements into the instrument and the general design of the project. Capacity building and strengthening of Indigenous Peoples' organizations at local and national levels should be considered to enhance project implementation as well as the affected communities' general ability to participate in, and respond to, development efforts. The monitoring and evaluation plan, including timing and methodology, should be designed to take into consideration any issues pertaining to Indigenous Peoples. It usually includes some form of independent or external monitoring. Complaint mechanisms should incorporate local and traditional methods as appropriate (see also note 1.3, Indigenous Peoples and Forests).

SPECIAL CONSIDERATIONS. The policy specifies particular areas, listed below, that merit special attention during preparation of projects affecting Indigenous Peoples. Each one of these is potentially a critical issue for forest-based projects, which the borrower and project team need to consider carefully during project preparation and address in the Indigenous Peoples' instrument.

- *Lands and natural resources.* Projects affecting the lands and natural resources of Indigenous Peoples should include measures to recognize land tenure and resource use rights. This may include recognition and regularization of customary rights to land and natural resources.
- *Commercial development of natural resources.* Projects supporting commercial development of natural resources should, in consultation with Indigenous Peoples, identify the affected communities' rights to the resources under statutory and customary law, the scope and nature of the proposed commercial development, and the potential impacts of such development on the communities' livelihood, environments, and use of such resources. The Indigenous Peoples should share equitably in the benefits.
- *Commercial development of cultural resources and knowledge.* Projects supporting commercial development of cultural resources and knowledge should identify, in consultation with the Indigenous Peoples' communities, their rights to such resources under statutory and customary law, the scope and nature of the proposed commercial development, and potential effects it may have on the Indigenous Peoples' livelihoods, environments, and use of such resources. World Bank assistance to projects supporting commercial development of cultural resources and knowledge of Indigenous Peoples is conditional on their prior agreement to such development.
- *Access.* Involuntary restrictions on Indigenous Peoples' access to legally designated parks and protected areas should be avoided or minimized. If not feasible, a process

framework should be prepared based on free, prior, and informed consultation with the affected communities and in accordance with OP 4.12 on Involuntary Resettlement (see chapter 9 for guidance on development of terms of reference related to OP 4.36). This should only be done in a manner that ensures that affected Indigenous Peoples share equitably in the benefits, and that prioritizes collaborative arrangements. The process framework should be developed in parallel with the Indigenous Peoples' instrument.

Disclosure, appraisal, and documentation. As soon as the draft Indigenous Peoples' instrument has been prepared, it should be disclosed, together with the social assessment report, in a form, manner, and language culturally appropriate to the Indigenous Peoples affected by the project. After the World Bank has reviewed the documents, and before appraisal, the borrower shares the revised instrument with the affected communities. If changes are made to the instrument as a result of project appraisal, the final document to be used for implementation should be publicly disclosed and shared with the affected communities.

The appropriate sections of the Project Appraisal Document should include a careful description of the processes of social analysis and consultation undertaken during project preparation, including the broad community support obtained, as well as the design features and special measures included to address particular issues concerning Indigenous Peoples during implementation. The implementation measures in the Indigenous Peoples instrument should be described in more detail in Annex 10 to the Project Appraisal Document (Safeguard Policy Issues). The World Bank's Project Information Document and Integrated Safeguard Data Sheet are disclosed at the World Bank's InfoShop along with the Indigenous Peoples' instrument before appraisal.

The appraisal mission should assess the project design with regard to policy requirements concerning Indigenous Peoples. The mission should usually include a social scientist familiar with Indigenous Peoples' issues and who has operational experience sufficient to evaluate the measures planned regarding Indigenous Peoples. The appraisal evaluates measures to address OP 4.10 requirements and Indigenous Peoples' issues as appropriate for the given project context, including the following:

- the adequacy of the free, prior, and informed consultation process
- confirmation that affected Indigenous Peoples have provided their broad support for the project based on free, prior, and informed consultations

- the feasibility and sustainability of the Indigenous Peoples' instrument, including participatory implementation processes, that is intended to provide culturally appropriate benefits and to mitigate any adverse effects on Indigenous Peoples
- if required, the feasibility of any proposals for regularizing land and resource tenure
- the adequacy of the enabling legal and policy framework for implementation of proposed project measures
- the capacity of agencies charged with implementation of the Indigenous Peoples' instrument and adequacy and timeliness of any capacity-building exercises during project implementation
- the capacity of affected communities and others who will participate in project implementation, including the adequacy of any capacity-building exercises during project implementation
- the adequacy of detailed budgetary and institutional arrangements for timely implementation of the Indigenous Peoples' instrument
- implementation schedules with measurable benchmarks for the Indigenous Peoples' instrument, coordinated as necessary with the overall project implementation schedule
- the results of public disclosure of the Indigenous Peoples' instrument
- arrangements for project monitoring and complaint mechanisms

The legal document includes a covenant requiring the borrower or the project entity to carry out in a satisfactory manner the Indigenous Peoples' instrument. It is often important, depending on the project, to include additional covenants concerning key actions or specific issues of the instrument. These can include, for example, actions required before the instrument can be implemented (such as staffing or other specific institutional arrangements, special studies, or further consultations); contentious or complex aspects of the instrument that should be highlighted to ensure they are fulfilled in a timely fashion (for example, regularization of land and resource tenure); or specific benchmarks, as part of the monitoring indicators, for monitoring timely implementation of the instrument. Disbursement may be made conditional on the implementation of such specific actions.

PROJECT IMPLEMENTATION

The importance of good monitoring and supervision of project implementation cannot be emphasized enough. The borrower's monitoring and evaluation team and the World

Bank's supervision team must include appropriate expertise and skills in understanding how Indigenous Peoples view development and how development efforts may affect them. Knowledge of the affected communities, local language competency, and skills in participatory assessment techniques should be valued.

Monitoring of measures for Indigenous Peoples should be integrated into the project's overall monitoring and evaluation system, but often with specific indicators and particular monitoring and evaluation activities. Monitoring requirements vary for different types of projects depending on their scope, interventions, the characteristics of the affected Indigenous Peoples, and the project's benefits to, and impacts on, them. For some simple projects with few Indigenous Peoples, and where project activities are primarily beneficial, the elements of the monitoring and evaluation system concerning Indigenous Peoples may be limited to disaggregating data by ethnicity or social groups. For projects with significant impacts on indigenous communities, an elaborate monitoring and evaluation system conducted by an independent entity focusing on measures for Indigenous Peoples may be needed.

Forest-based projects should, in most cases, plan to pay significant attention to Indigenous Peoples' issues during project preparation because of the particular vulnerabilities, views, and circumstances of Indigenous Peoples in forest areas. It is important to assess whether assumptions for project success are correct, whether there are any unintended impacts on affected Indigenous Peoples, and whether they are able to participate in project benefits or whether exclusion or other factors inhibit their participation. Finally, it is important to assess community satisfaction and whether the project continues to receive broad community support.

Qualitative and participatory data collection methods to monitor and evaluate project impacts on Indigenous Peoples are useful. Such methods may include workshops, focus group discussions, informal interviews, mapping exercises, and other participatory assessment tools. Special studies assessing specific implementation issues concerning Indigenous Peoples through qualitative methods and field work may also be useful. Participatory monitoring and evaluation differs from more conventional approaches by engaging beneficiaries actively in assessing the progress and achievements of the project; sharing control over the content, the process, and the results of the activity; and identifying corrective actions. When the people who are affected most by a project participate in its monitoring and evaluation, the project receives valuable input for improvements; account-

ability and transparency may be improved; acceptance is likely to be heightened; and beneficiaries' participation in, and ownership of, implementation is likely to be enhanced. It may also foster learning at the local level and contribute to organizational strengthening and empowerment of local communities.

A key element of World Bank supervision is assessing whether the Indigenous Peoples' instrument is carried out as agreed. Implementation of the instrument is a critical dimension in decisions on project performance ratings. The project team also assesses implementation of the borrower's monitoring and evaluation system and ascertains the extent to which monitoring information is used to strengthen project implementation and make needed adjustments— and whether it is able to include Indigenous Peoples' perceptions, concerns, and evaluations in the project feedback system. Key questions to consider during supervision missions include the following:

- Are the Indigenous Peoples' instrument and legal covenants being implemented? If not, what are the constraints? What should be done to rectify this? Is there a need to change the agreed on activities or project design more generally?
- Are the affected Indigenous Peoples participating in project implementation? If not, what should be done to enhance their participation?
- How are Indigenous Peoples benefiting from project activities? How are their socioeconomic circumstances changing?
- What project impacts are there on Indigenous Peoples? Are there any unanticipated impacts (given their characteristics and socioeconomic circumstances, unanticipated impacts are more likely for Indigenous Peoples than for other population groups)? Are impacts being avoided or mitigated or should new or additional mitigation measures be introduced?
- What are the risks concerning the affected Indigenous Peoples? Have those risks changed since project preparation or have new risks surfaced? How should they be addressed or mitigated?
- What are Indigenous Peoples' perceptions about the project, its benefits, and its impacts? Do the respective communities continue to provide their broad support to project activities? If not, how can this be changed?
- Does the project include new locations? Have they been screened for Indigenous Peoples?
- Is the capacity of the implementing agency and other involved stakeholders increasing with project implemen-

tation? Is there a need for (additional) capacity-building activities?

■ Is the monitoring and evaluation system working? Are the findings informing project implementation? Are Indigenous Peoples participating in the exercise?

At completion of a project, the project team should ensure that the Implementation Completion Report includes Indigenous Peoples' issues. The following should be assessed: "(a) the degree of Indigenous Peoples' partici-pation in the project cycle; (b) the impact of the project, both positive and adverse, on the affected Indigenous Peoples; (c) the achievement of the objectives of the relevant instrument(s), as relevant; and (d) lessons for future oper-ations involving Indigenous Peoples. If the objectives of the relevant instrument(s) have not been realized, the Implementation Completion Report may propose a future course of action, including, as appropriate, continued post-project supervision by the Bank" (World Bank Proce-dures 4.10, paragraph 13).

ANNEX 12A   ELEMENTS OF AN INDIGENOUS PEOPLES PLAN AND PLANNING FRAMEWORK

INDIGENOUS PEOPLES PLAN. OP 4.10 provides the following guidance on the elements of the IPP (OP 4.10, Annex B):

"1. The Indigenous Peoples Plan (IPP) is prepared in a flexible and pragmatic manner, and its level of detail varies depending on the specific project and the nature of effects to be addressed.

The IPP includes the following elements, as needed:

(a) A summary of the information referred to in Annex A, paragraph 2 (a) and (b).

(b) A summary of the social assessment.

(c) A summary of results of the free, prior, and informed consultation with the affected Indigenous Peoples' communities that was carried out during project preparation (Annex A) and that led to broad community support for the project.

(d) A framework for ensuring free, prior, and informed consultation with the affected Indigenous Peoples' communities during project implementation (see paragraph 10 of this policy).

(e) An action plan of measures to ensure that the Indigenous Peoples receive social and economic benefits that are culturally appropriate, including, if necessary, measures to enhance the capacity of the project implementing agencies.

(f) When potential adverse effects on Indigenous Peoples are identified, an appropriate action plan of measures to avoid, minimize, mitigate, or compensate for these adverse effects.

(g) The cost estimates and financing plan for the IPP.

(h) Accessible procedures appropriate to the project to address grievances by the affected Indigenous Peoples' communities arising from project implementation. When designing the grievance procedures, the borrower takes into account the availability of judicial recourse and customary dispute settlement mechanisms among the Indigenous Peoples.

(i) Mechanisms and benchmarks appropriate to the project for monitoring, evaluating, and reporting on the implementation of the IPP. The monitoring and evaluation mechanisms should include arrangements for the free, prior, and informed consultation with the affected Indigenous Peoples' communities."

INDIGENOUS PEOPLES PLANNING FRAMEWORK. On the elements of an IPPF, the policy provides the following guidance (OP 4.10, Annex C):

"1. The Indigenous Peoples Planning Framework (IPPF) sets out:

(a) The types of programs and subprojects likely to be proposed for financing under the project.

(b) The potential positive and adverse effects of such programs or subprojects on Indigenous Peoples.

(c) A plan for carrying out the social assessment (see Annex A) for such programs or subprojects.

(d) A framework for ensuring free, prior, and informed consultation with the affected Indigenous Peoples' communities at each stage of project preparation and implementation (see paragraph 10 of this policy).

(e) Institutional arrangements (including capacity building where necessary) for screening project-supported activities, evaluating their effects on Indigenous Peoples, preparing IPPs, and addressing any grievances.

(f) Monitoring and reporting arrangements, including mechanisms and benchmarks appropriate to the project.

(g) Disclosure arrangements for IPPs to be prepared under the IPPF."

REFERENCES CITED

Davis, S. H., and L. T. Soeftestad. 1995. "Participation and Indigenous Peoples." Environment Department Paper No. 021. World Bank, Washington, DC.

Jensby, S. E. 2007. "Indigenous Peoples and Forests." Note submitted to World Bank as input to *Forests Sourcebook.* Unpublished. World Bank, Washington DC.

World Bank. 1999. "Public Consultation in the EA Process: A Strategic Approach." Environmental Assessment Sourcebook Update 26. Environment Department, World Bank, Washington, DC.

———. 2002. "Social Analysis Sourcebook: Incorporating Social Dimensions into Bank-Supported Projects." Social Development Department, World Bank, Washington, DC.

———. 2005a. "Social Analysis Guidelines in Natural Resource Management: Incorporating Social Dimensions into Bank-Supported Projects." Social Development Department, World Bank, Washington, DC.

———. 2005b. "World Bank Operations Manual; OP 4.10 on Indigenous Peoples." World Bank, Washington, DC.

INDEX

forest monitoring, 275b
social and environmental impacts study, 242b
capacity building, 75, 176, 193
environmental assessment, 67–68
for data collection, 249–250
forest certification systems, 115, 116
SMFEs, 79, 79b
carbon financing, 120
carbon sequestration, 85, 86, 117
Carnegie Institution of Washington, 277b
CARPE, 137n
case studies, as analytical tool, 233t
CASs. *See* Country Assistance Strategies
causality, 229
CBD. *See* Convention on Biological Diversity
CBFM. *See* community-based forest management
CEA. *See* Country Environmental Analysis
Ceara Integrated Water Resources Management Project, Brazil, 314
Center for International Forestry Research (CIFOR), 275b
CFEs. *See* Community Forest Enterprises
chain-of-custody certification, 102, 102n, 114, 116n, 174b
change management, 169–170
charges, 181–182, 187–188
Chile, 120
China, 18b, 31b, 107b
forest product imports, 93, 102n
Citizen Report Card (CRC), 171
climate change, 96
clusters matrix analysis, 301b
Colombia Natural Resource Management (NRM) Program, 46
commercial development and Indigenous Peoples, 353
commercial outputs, 17b
common property rights, 51b
communication, 319, 325b
and strategy, 323, 325–326, 329
Cambodia example, 322b, 331b
checklist for managers, 332–333
implementation plan, 329, 331b
community empowerment, 74
Community Forest Enterprises (CFE), 208b
community forestry models, 31b
community forestry projects, PROCYMAF, 47b
community forestry, distinguishing from industrial, 298
community networks, supporting, 75
community ownership of forests, 3f, 56
community participation, 42, 97, 119
and benefit sharing in Ghana, 243b–244b
control over access, 35
decentralization of forest management, 159, 162
forest landscape planning, 133
forest management, 3, 3f
OP on Forests, 298
community rights, 50
community tenure, 30, 53b, 54b
community-based forest management (CBFM), 20, 22, 34–35, 100

and poverty reduction, 30
elements of, 36–37
India, 45b
indigenous knowledge, 45
Latin America, 101b
project examples, 46–47
community-company partnerships, 20, 71, 100
bargaining power, 74
important conditions, 73
models by goods and services, 71t
competition, unfair due to illegal logging, 189
conceptual model, 145b
conditionality, 222b
Conditionality Review, 222
conflict. *See* postconflict countries
conflict of interest, 169b
conflict, resolving, 174b
Congo Basin Forests, 137n
Congo, Democratic Republic of, 323b
consensus building, 328t
conservation, 10, 23, 125
and forest significance index, 230
coexistence with production, 3–4, 104
community agreement with industry, 102
conservation offsets, 314–316
consultation, 319–320, 321b, 325b
at various stages of EA project, 326b
Cambodia example, 322b
Democratic Republic of Congo example, 323b
LFI example, 320b
planning tasks, 322–323
process, 321–322
with Indigenous Peoples, 349–351, 351b, 352t
contracts, 66, 73, 100
Convention on Biological Diversity (CBD), 39
conversion of forest, 2, 94f, 106. *See also* deforestation
significance of, 297–298
corruption, 151, 154, 190, 191b
and forest crime, 190f
cost estimates, 306
cost-benefit analysis, 305b, 306
Costa Rica, 86
Country Assistance Strategies (CASs), 153
Country Environmental Analysis (CEA), 209, 238, 242, 244
building blocks, 239, 239f
Ghana, 240b
country identification of important forests, 230
CRC. *See* Citizen Report Card
Creative Oils, 59b
Criteria and Indicators processes, 253b
cross-sectoral impacts, 98, 208, 209, 232
identifying links with policy, 234
tools for assessing, 232, 236, 237
cross-sectoral mainstreaming of forest issues, 214–215
cross-sectoral outcomes, 205
cultural importance, 17b
customary rights, 51b

D

dam safety, 290
data, 27, 111, 182b, 248
  interpretation for forest inventories, 260
  lack of, 208, 229, 233–234
data collection, 28b, 261b, 355
de jure and de facto rights, 51b
decision-making environment, 248
deforestation, 2, 94f, 124, 157b. *See also* conversion of forests
  avoided, 4
  causes of, 2f, 206–207
deforestation maps, 251b, 277b, 278b
deforestation rate, 94, 252
degradation, significance of, 297–298
deregulation, 57
design document, 265–266
development, 5, 39
development policy loans (DPLs), 6, 65, 207
  conditions, 222b, 223b, 227
    prioritization of actions, 223, 225
  country identification, 209
  cross-sectoral impacts, 232
  dialogue requirement, 226–227
  flexibility and suitability, 225b
  Gabon and Cameroon, 224b–225b
  impact on natural resources requirement, 238
  Lao PDR, 226b
  portfolio of, 203–204, 205
  rapid assessment toolkit, 234n
  watch list, 210
development policy, integration with forest policy, 209–210
development projects, 49
directories and databases of critical habitats, 313
displacement, 183
donor engagement, 18–19
due diligence, 209
Dutch disease, 210n–211n

E

EA. *See* Environmental Assessment
EAP. *See* Environmental Assessment Policy
East Asia and Pacific, 8
ECA. *See* Europe and Central Asia
econometric modeling, 233t
economic activities, impact on forests, 229, 234
economic and financial analysis, 304–307
economic development, forest integration, 5
economic growth, role of natural resources, 31–32
economic impacts on forest stakeholders, 126
economic monitoring, 307b
economic reliance on wood, 93
economy, contribution of forests, 230
ecosystem services, 54, 72b, 141b
education reform, 231t
elite capture, 33b
employment, forest-related, 16
enabling environment, 65–66
energy sector reform, 206b, 213, 231t, 248b

Environmental and Social Management Framework (ESMF), 311b
Environmental Assessment (EA), 307–310, 321b
  consultations, 298, 326b
  identifying forests and habitats, 310–314
Environmental Assessment Policy (EAP), 8f, 9f, 288, 293
  Forests Strategy, 10–11
Environmental Assessment Sourcebook, 351
environmental classification of projects, 294–295
Environmental Control System on Rural Properties, 251b
environmental impact assessment (EIA), 240
environmental impacts, assessing and mitigating, 310b
Environmental Management Framework (EMF), 309, 309b
Environmental Management Plan (EMP), 310b, 321b
environmental protection, 178. *See also* protected areas
environmental services, 67, 86–87, 88
environmental services payments, 10, 23. *See also* Payments for Environmental Services approach
estimation costs, 260b
estimation methods, 259b
Europe, 255t
Europe and Central Asia (ECA), 7, 8f, 9f, 11
European Union (EU) Regulation and Action Plan on Forest Law Enforcement, Governance and Trade (FLEGT), 153
evaluation. *See* monitoring
exotics, 118
expert panel for analysis, 233t
exports, charges on, 187
extension programs, 120

F

FAO. *See* United Nations Food and Agriculture Organization
FCAG. *See* Forest Certification Assessment Guide
FCPF. *See* Forest Carbon Partnership Facility
feasibility studies, 37
fees, 188
FEMA/MT. *See* State Environment Foundation of Mato Grosso
FESP. *See* Forest & Environment Sector Program
Fiji, harvesting rights, 181b
financial access through partnerships, 75
financial capital, 140b
financial sector reform, impact on forests, 231t
financing, 4, 67
fines, 188
fiscal impact analysis, 306, 307b
fiscal incentives, 182–183
fiscal instruments, 180, 181, 185
  administration of, 183–184
fiscal policy, 183, 185, 203
fiscal reform, impact on forests, 229f
fiscal systems, 156, 181, 181b
  common problems, 180b, 182b
  summary of charges for forest sector, 187–188
Five Million Hectares Reforestation Project (5MHRP), 218b
FLEG. *See* Forest Law Enforcement and Governance
FLEGT. *See* Forest Law Enforcement, Governance and Trade
floating tranche, 227
FMIS. *See* Forest Monitoring and Information System

Indigenous Peoples, 44
  land administration, 19–20
protected areas, 4, 97f, 112n
  categories of, 316n
  conservation offsets, 314–315
  establishing new area, 315b
  existing and proposed, 296–297
  identification of, 104
  multiple uses of, 315–316
PRSC. *See* Poverty Reduction Support Credit
PRSLs. *See* Policy Reform Support Loans
PRSPs. *See* Poverty Reduction Strategy Papers
PSIA. *See* poverty and social impact analysis
public involvement, 328t
public voice, listening to, 327t
pulp and paper, 95b
pulp mills, 119
purchase agreements, 72b

Q

quantitative analysis, 308b
Quickbird, 279b, 280t

R

Rainforest Alliance, 56
Rainforest Expeditions, 72b
rapid CEAs (RCEAs), 209, 210b, 239
real exchange rate depreciation, 203
reduced emissions from deforestation and degradation (REDD),
  4, 157b, 247, 274
  baseline determination, 250–251, 252
reform, 49, 167, 174, 226
  agrarian, 208b
  entry points, 152f
  harmonization, 222
  macroeconomic, 207, 231–232, 231t
  tenure, 52, 53b
Regional Silvopastoral Project, 90b
regulator framework and crime prevention, 192
Remote Sensing (RS) technology, 251b, 254, 274
  cost and quality of, 279
  data availability, 274
  real time monitoring, 279b
  requirements, 276
rent capture, 180, 181b
reporting requirements, nationally and internationally, 252
research methods, improvement of, 234
resource rights, distribution and devolution of, 32
resource user associations, 19b
resources, wild, 15
results chains, 146b, 147, 147f, 148b
revenue sharing, 184–186
risk management, 331b
risk mitigation, 67, 74, 75
risks for development agencies, 196
roundwood, 1, 94b
royalties, 188, 189
royalty payments, 182

S

sales contracts, 66, 71t
Santa Catarina Natural Resource Management and Rural Poverty
    Reduction Project, 42b
SAR. *See* South Asia Region
satellites for forest monitoring, 279b, 280t
sawnwood, 94b
SEA. *See* Strategic Environmental Assessment
sector analysis for investment and lending, 41
service delivery, 171b
Sirleaf, Ellen Johnson, 168b
SIVAM-SIPAM, 251b
small and medium forest enterprises (SMFEs), 20, 66, 77, 78, 81
  attracting investment and negotiating deals, 79
  Brazil, 67b
  bureaucracy, 81b
  extension networks, 81b
  importance of understanding context, 80
  lack of information and market monopolies, 79
  lack of management capacity, 77, 80
  negotiating capacity, 79b
  program feasibility checklist, 84
  supporting local sovereignty, 78, 78b
smallholders, 115, 116, 298
  extension programs, 121
  incentives for, 100
  OP on Forests, 294
Smartwood, 111
Social Assessment (SA), 299, 301, 304
  for Indigenous Peoples, 348–349, 350b
social capital, 140b
social impact report, 302b
social inclusion, plantations, 119
social responsibility contracts, 66, 71t, 72b
social safeguards, 316
social welfare, SMFEs, 78
socioeconomic analysis, 299
South America, 255t
South Asia Region (SAR), 8, 8f, 9f, 11
Southeast Asia and the Pacific, forestry models, 31b
Southern African Natural Products Trade Association, 59b
spatial monitoring, 274, 275, 276
specialization, 79
SSA. *See* Sub-Saharan Africa
stakeholder analysis, 43, 299, 320–321
stakeholder consultation, 320–321
stakeholder participation, 97, 302b
  legal reform, 176–177
  OP on Forests, 298
  to support FLEG, 194–195
State Environment Foundation of Mato Grosso (FEMA/MT),
    251b
Stool of the Omanhene, Ghana, 72b
Strategic Environmental Assessment (SEA), 209, 240–242, 240b
  and development alternatives, 244
  Cameroon, 242b
  institution-centered, 243b, 245
    and impact-centered, 241–242